## Praise for *Women's Letters: America from the Revolutionary War to the Present*

"Here are heartwarming and heartbreaking stories, heartache suffered and inflicted, history told and repeated."　　　　　—Cokie Roberts, *Washington Post*

"Incredible breadth and depth."　　　　　　　—*Booklist* (starred review)

"Reading the personal, unfiltered words of so many women through the centuries spurs a much more intimate connection with the past—and a better understanding of it—than most college textbooks can."　—*Minneapolis Star Tribune*

"Whether as a rich primary source or simply an illuminating read, *Women's Letters* is . . . sure to be required reading not just for devotees of women's history or the fine art of letter writing but also for surveying the broad scope of American history itself."　　　　　　　　　　—*Library Journal*

## Praise for *Letters of the Century: America 1900–1999*

"Provides a sort of writerly syllabus to the entire century."　　　　　　　—Martin Arnold, *New York Times*

"Entertaining and informative . . . a social history made for browsing."　　　　　　　　　　—*USA Today*

"A riveting epistolary chronicle of the 20th century . . . one of the most original literary tributes to the closing century."　　　　　　　—*Publishers Weekly,* "Best Books of the Year"

"Hits every marker in what we consider the course of our national history: social, economic, political, cultural, and military. . . . A trip down Shared Memory Lane."　　　　　　　　　　—*Boston Sunday Globe*

*Also edited by Lisa Grunwald & Stephen J. Adler*

LETTERS OF THE CENTURY
America 1900–1999

# Women's Letters

America from the
Revolutionary War
to the Present

EDITED BY

## Lisa Grunwald & Stephen J. Adler

DIAL PRESS TRADE PAPERBACKS

WOMEN'S LETTERS
A Dial Press Trade Paperback Book

PUBLISHING HISTORY
Dial Press hardcover edition published October 2005
Dial Press Trade Paperback edition published May 2008

Published by
The Dial Press
A Division of Random House, Inc.
New York, New York

Cover based on a design by Robert de Vicq de Cumptich

Cover design by Belina Huey

Picture collages researched, edited, and designed by Vincent Virga

Library of Congress Catalog Card Number: 2005041446

ISBN 978-0-385-33556-0

Printed in the United States of America
Published simultaneously in Canada

www.dialpress.com

10  9  8  7  6  5  4  3  2  1

RRC

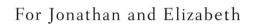

For Jonathan and Elizabeth

# Women's Letters

## America from the Revolutionary War to the Present

# Introduction

"Oh hell, I wanted to talk to you," Dorothy Parker wrote. "So here's this letter." Then she sat down and typed five single-spaced pages to Alexander Woollcott, five pages that make you feel as if you are sitting across a table from her, having smoke and memorable observations blown into your face. You hear her, and not just because she was such a vivid writer. You hear her because women's letters talk. They are monologues, dialogues, diatribes: They are voices fixed on paper. Like women talking over the back fence, the telephone, the breakfast plates, or the business lunch, women's letters rarely just exchange information. Instead, they tell stories; they tell secrets; they shout and scold, bitch and soothe, whisper and worry, console and advise, gossip and argue, compete and compare. And along the way, they—usually without meaning to—write history.

In these pages, you will hear the frontierswoman of 1852 and the feminist of 1974, the flirtatious teenager of 1777 and the runaway slave of 1862. You will hear the poet, the doctor, and the breast-cancer survivor, the devout Quaker and the president's mistress. You will hear the soldier's wife, the soldier's mother, and, even in the nineteenth century, the soldier. You will hear famous voices, like those of Abigail Adams, Jacqueline Kennedy, Amelia Earhart, and Katharine Graham. More often, you will hear voices of women whose names you never knew.

But for all the variations and intonations, you will hear something universal as well. In the course of our research, we rarely found a document that we thought had been written by a woman, only to get to the end and find that the signature was a man's. Apart from the fact that men tended to spell better and to have slightly less flowery handwriting, their letters naturally conducted more business, discussed and shaped more politics, in a public world where they were always more present and more powerful. Women's letters, by contrast, were often more casual, usually more intimate, and frequently more memorable.

Yet this is not really, or at least not only, a book about women. It is not limited to letters written *to* women or *about* women. It is really a book about America, as seen by women, which is why it is arranged chronologically rather than by theme. For most of America's history, women simply had no public forum in which to express the way they saw their own country. Letters (and diaries, but that's another book) were among their only outlets for recording what they saw of, how they felt about, and even how they helped to shape the world around them.

That world, of course, changed radically between the eve of the American Revolution, where this volume begins, and the war in Iraq, where it ends. The first letters here were written with quills, the last ones on computer laptops; the first ones were carried by horses, the last ones by ether. In 1775, American colonial women were living a largely rural existence, in constant proximity to death and disease, with God a palpable presence, invoked in nearly every letter. Where women lived, whether they were educated, what they worked at, and the number of children they bore were almost never choices they were able to make. Over time—but, as these letters suggest, by very small stages—the world of the American woman was radically altered—most powerfully by war, medicine, industrialization, electricity, birth control, and women's fight for equality. But luckily, through all the changes, the impulse women had to talk in writing never waned.

So what can you find in their letters? Most obviously, you can find historical events when they still sounded like the day's news. Dolley Madison told her sister about the burning of the White House. Cornelia Hancock described the Battle of Gettysburg, and a young immigrant widow wrote about the Triangle Shirtwaist fire. A day after the battle that began the American Revolution, Anne Hulton detailed what was not yet a legend:

> The People in the Country (who are all furnished with Arms & have what they call Minute Companys in every Town ready to march on any alarm), had a signal it's supposed by a light from one of the Steeples in Town.

And the day after Lincoln's assassination, Julia Shepherd, who had been in the audience at Ford's Theater, wrote:

The report of a pistol is heard. . . . Is it all in the play? A man leaps from the President's box, some ten feet, on to the stage. The truth flashes upon me. Brandishing a dagger he shrieks out "The South is avenged," and rushes through the scenery. No one stirs. "Did you hear what be said, Julia? I believe he has killed the President."

In these letters, you will also find events that are far less famous but were no less dramatic. On the home front, women faced such adversaries as illness, poverty, hunger, drought, rattlesnakes, and terrible loneliness, all of which you will hear and see them battling in these pages. In 1776, a Massachusetts woman named Christian Barnes described her encounter with a rebel soldier who forced his way into her house:

I went in and endeavored to pacify him by every method in my power, but I found it was to no purpose. He still continued to abuse me, and said when he had eat his dinner he should want a horse and if I did not let him have one he would blow my brains out.

After the fateful journey west with the Donner Party in 1847, Virginia Reed described the ordeal to her cousin:

we had to kill littel cash the dog & eat him   we ate his entrails and feet & hide & evry thing about him . . . there was 15 in the cabon we was in and half of us had to lay a bed all the time   thare was 10 starved to death then   we was hadly abel to walk . . .

And in 1855, still years before the use of anesthesia was common, Lucy Thurston had to undergo a mastectomy while fully conscious. Afterwards, she wrote to her daughter:

Dr. Ford looked me full in the face, and with great firmness asked: "Have you made up your mind to have it cut out?" "Yes, sir." "Are you ready now?" "Yes, sir . . . Have you your knife in that hand now?" He opened his hand that I might see it, saying, "I am going to begin now." Then came a gash long and deep, first on one side of my breast, then on the other.

While many women's letters boldly described such realities, others quietly confided dreams. Though particular to their times, they conveyed universal longings: for freedom, support, recognition, or love. In 1850, Hannah Whitall Smith told her sister:

> I think I would love to be a minister and make very noble sacrifices and have people to admire me and almost worship me....Oh! would it not be grand, and then I would travel all over the world, and do so much good. But I am only a woman, and women are so weak and dependent, and never do any good.

In 1862, a slave wrote to her husband, from whom she was forced to be separated:

> My love is just as great as it was the first night I married you, and I hope it will be so with you. My heart and love is pinned to your breast, and I hope yours is to mine. If I never see you again, I hope to meet you in Heaven.

A homesteader named Hilda Rose in 1919 confessed to a friend: "I want to go back, I don't care where, and have friends once more....I want to be elected president of a club, and go to socials, and I want to eat ice cream..." In 1965, a young Janis Joplin told her then boyfriend: "I wish I had fans that thought I was as good as I do."

When women dreamed of improving not just their own lives but the lives of those around them, their letters often expressed their commitment. Margaret Sanger wrote in favor of birth control, Jane Addams against war. Sojourner Truth championed the rights of ex-slaves and Rita Mae Brown the rights of lesbians. Lillian Hellman stood up for freedom of speech, and Katharine Graham for freedom of the press. And for the women who fought directly for equality—like Elizabeth Cady Stanton and Carrie Chapman Catt—the pen *was* the sword. This was never more true than for a suffragist named Febb Burn, who in 1920 sent a letter to her son that led him to break the deadlock in the vote for the Nineteenth Amendment. Wrote Mrs. Burn to the representative from Tennessee: "Don't forget to be a good boy and help Mrs. Catt put the 'rat' in ratification."

In these letters, too, you will find advice, which was offered in every decade, in most circumstances, and apparently whether solicited or not. In 1792, an aunt wrote to her niece, who had been scarred by smallpox: "You will find that there are other charms than those of beauty, and other joys than the praise of fools." A dying mother in 1823 told her son:

> You are likely to be left alone in a strange world. So have I been; and thus far the Lord hath led me on; so that I have never lacked any good thing. The way has been boisterous sometimes, But Judah's Lion guards the way, And guides the travellers Home. Make this friend yours.

The following year, a mother advised her daughter on marriage by saying: "Let the pleasing of that one person be a thought never absent from your conduct." Heartbreakingly, in 1969, a suicidal Anne Sexton told her daughter: "Live to the HILT! To the top . . . Be your own woman. Belong to those you love."

Of course women were not always stoic and committed and wise, and some of the most vivid letters in this volume are the ones that show them faltering. They could complain, like Mary Kincaid, pregnant and writing to a friend in 1896: "I stick out in the back as much as I do in front." They could be competitive, like Mary Todd Lincoln's cousin in a supposed note of congratulations: "You are an ambitious little woman and for many reasons I am delighted with your success." They could be self-pitying, like a spurned Aline Bernstein writing to Thomas Wolfe: "Your book will be so great that possibly the sum of my entire life will be nothing compared to it." They could despair, like Sarah Nichols, who during the Gold Rush begged her husband and son: "Save oh Save my life. . . . I cannot live if You go to California." And sometimes, they could nearly kill with contempt, like Abigail Grant, who in 1776 heard that her husband had been less than noble at Bunker Hill. Scorchingly, she wrote to him: "If you are afraid pray own the truth & come home & take care of our Children & I will be Glad to Come & take your place, & never will be Called a Coward."

This book has a happy parentage, and not just because it was edited by a husband and wife who are still speaking to each other. This book's real parent is our previous volume, *Letters of the Century*, which sought to tell the story of the twentieth century in America through letters. The women's letters we printed in that volume provided a hint of the riches we had in store for us, but the task of going back into the more distant past provided new challenges and new rewards.

Many of the challenges involved the oldest material. Half of all colonial women were illiterate at the time of the Revolution, so by necessity, the letters in this book usually represent only the most privileged citizens. Try as we might, we could not find a letter, petition, note, or written artifact of any kind (we would have bent our definition of *letter* happily) from a Native American in the eighteenth or early nineteenth century. We do have quite a few slave letters—some of them dictated—but there, too, we could only wonder about the women whose voices were never captured on paper.

As in our previous book, we did not alter texts either by additions or deletions, so some of the obscurities of the earliest letters remain. Whenever possible, we deciphered handwriting and tracked down references and expressions then familiar and now obscure. What were "linsey-woolsey," the *Otter,* a "repeater," an "air-tight," a "calash"? We did our best to find out. (Inevitably, some mysteries remained: the name of Cornelia Hancock's cousin, the outcome of Caroline O'Rourke's request, the definition of a "T.L. man.") We didn't alter spellings or punctuation. We did add spaces when sentences ran together, and we updated the old-fashioned *s,* the one that looks like an *f,* because it was slightly more annoying than quaint to try to read the *f.* We did not insert the word *sic,* because it would have had to be inserted too often. We added words in brackets only when we felt it was absolutely necessary. All ellipses represent omissions that were made by previous editors, and indicate that a complete version of the original manuscript was unavailable. We made the format of salutations and sign-offs uniform. Wherever possible, we supplied dates of birth and death for the authors and recipients of the letters.

Another challenge involved the sheer scope of this book and the hard choices that followed. Usually we limited ourselves to one letter per author and one letter per subject. Unavoidably, there are letters missing—both from great women and about great events. Political correctness was not a factor in our selection process, nor did we attempt at any time to fit into or steer clear of a particular academic school of thought. Historians, please note: We don't purport to be historians. Our choices were based on the simple standard that if we could imagine telling a friend about a letter in the normal course of a conversation, we would choose it. Sometimes that meant historic importance over literary merit, like the first letter in the book, which is just a note from Rachel Revere to Paul (but who knew that Rachel Revere sent a note to Paul?). And sometimes that meant literary merit over historic importance, like the letter from Sarah Orne Jewett to Willa Cather, which marks no particular milestone but offers beautiful, wise, and consoling advice.

Some letters we knew we would never find. Lizzie Borden apparently wrote several that are locked in a safe in Massachusetts. Betty Friedan gave her letters to Harvard with the proviso that they not be published until 2075. As far as we know, Betsy Ross never wrote any. Nor did Sacagawea. And Harry Houdini's mother's letters were buried in a black bag under the magician's head. Even the most dedicated researchers have to draw the line somewhere.

The rewards of trolling through more than two centuries of women's letters are, we hope, embodied in this book. Much of the research was done in the wake of 9/11 and in the shadow of terrorism and war. To hear the voices of women who had lived through other threats was not only comforting, but uplifting. Their fears—for their children, their husbands, their parents, their homes—were indistinguishable from the fears of the twenty-first century. And their resolves—to live and protect, create and build—were inspiring. The universality of their experience, the *us*-ness of them, was the great reward of this research. We hope you will feel it as we did. We hope that you will have half as much fun reading the letters as we had compiling them. And we hope that, as they did to us, these women's voices will speak to you.

—Lisa Grunwald and Stephen J. Adler

# REVOLUTION

# 1775

# ~

# 1799

I hear by Cap^tn Wm Riley news that makes me very Sorry
for he Says you proved a Grand Coward when the fight was
at Bunkers hill. . . . If you are afraid pray own the truth &
come home & take care of our Children & I will be Glad to
Come & take your place, & never will be Called a Coward,
neither will I throw away one Cartridge but exert myself
bravely in so good a Cause.

—*Abigail Grant to her husband*
*August 19, 1776*

# BETWEEN 1775 AND 1799...

**1775:** Patrick Henry attempts to persuade Virginia to arm its militia against the British, declaring: "I know not what course others may take, but as for me, give me liberty or give me death." ★ The first shots of the Revolutionary War are fired at Lexington and Concord. ★ In Salem, following the first news of the war, 13-year-old Susan Mason Smith chooses not to remove her shoes for several days, wanting to be prepared in case her family decides to flee. ★ Only about half the white women in the colonies are literate enough to sign their names. **1776:** With her husband, John, away at the Second Continental Congress in Philadelphia, Abigail Adams writes to him frequently and urges him to make sure that he and his colleagues "Remember the Ladies" while they are shaping the new nation; if they don't, she warns him, "we are determined to foment a Rebellion, and will not hold ourselves bound by any Laws in which we have no voice, or Representation." ★ Thomas Paine publishes *Common Sense,* a 50-page pamphlet that urges Americans to fight not only against taxation but also for independence; it sells more than half a million copies within its first few months. ★ Betsy Ross (according to the legend that's been neither proven nor refuted by evidence) is visited by George Washington

---

Clockwise from top left: Abigail Adams; Framers of the Constitution; Molly Pitcher; Phillis Wheatley; 1756 Philadelphia; "Boston's King Street Massacre (March 5, 1770)" by Paul Revere; Betsy Ross; the slave trade; the U.S. Constitution; a 1775 society of patriotic ladies in Edenton, North Carolina.

and asked to make a national flag; the stars on her design will have five points, rather than the six Washington suggests. ★ In his first draft of the Declaration of Independence, Thomas Jefferson writes: "We hold these truths to be sacred & undeniable; that all men are created equal & independant, that from that equal creation they derive rights inherent & inalienable, among which are the preservation of life, & liberty, & the pursuit of happiness." ★ For 67 days, the new country is called "The United Colonies of America"; in September, Congress gives the USA its official name. **1777:** Sybil Ludington, the 16-year-old daughter of a New York militia officer, rides almost 40 miles to muster troops against the British. ★ More than 100 women gather at the Boston store of Thomas Boylston to protest the merchant's high wartime prices. ★ General George Washington leads 11,000 militiamen to Valley Forge near British-occupied Philadelphia, where they are forced to spend a bitterly cold winter, plagued by widespread dysentery and typhus and a severe lack of food, clothes, and basic supplies. Washington writes in a letter that the soldiers' "marches might be tracked by the blood from their feet." **1778:** During the Battle of Monmouth Court House in New Jersey, Mary McCauly earns the name "Molly Pitcher" after making frequent trips with water to cool down both the men and the cannon in her husband's regiment. **1781:** Los Angeles is founded by Spanish settlers; its full name is El Pueblo de Nuestra Señora la Reina de los Angeles de Porciuncula. **1783:** The British evacuate New York. ★ The Paris Peace Treaty ends the Revolutionary War. ★ New Jersey, alone among the 13 states, enacts a statute giving women the vote; it will be put into sporadic use starting in 1787—and overturned in 1807. **1784:** Abel Buell engraves and publishes the first map of the United States, "layd down from the latest observations and best authority agreeable to the peace of 1783." ★ Judith Sergeant Murray publishes her essay "Desultory Thoughts upon the Utility of Encouraging a Degree of Self-Complacency, Especially in Female Bosoms," arguing that in the absence of sufficient confidence, women all too often marry impulsively to avoid the epithet *spinster*. **1786:** In his sermon "On Dress," John Wesley declares: "slovenliness is no part of religion.... 'Cleanliness is, indeed, next to godliness,'" but warns: "The wearing [of] gay or costly apparel naturally tends to breed and to increase vanity.... You know in your hearts, it is with a view to be admired that you thus adorn yourselves, and that you would not be at the pains were none to see you but God and his holy angels." **1787:** Despite Congress's plan merely to revise the 1777 Articles of Confederation, delegates draft a new constitution that gives increased power to a central government. **1788:** Nine states ratify the Constitution, and it goes into effect. **1789:** Though rich in land, George Washington must borrow £600 in cash to travel from Mount Vernon to New York City for his inauguration. **1790:** The total population of the United States is 3,893,874, of whom 694,207 are slaves. ★ Among white males, 791,901 are under the age of 16; 807,312 are 16 and over. **1791:** Vermont becomes the fourteenth state. ★ The national debt is $75,463,000, or roughly $18 a person. ★ The Bill of Rights is ratified. **1792:** George Washington signs an act providing for the creation of copper pennies and stipulating that "no copper coins or pieces whatsoever except the said cents and half-cents, shall pass current as money." ★ *The Old Farmer's Almanac* debuts, offering weather predictions, tide tables, and occasional advice; it costs sixpence and has a first-year circulation of 3,000 that will triple in a year and after two centuries pass four million. **1794:** Eli Whitney is granted a patent for the cotton gin, which combs and deseeds cotton 10 times faster than the nonmechanical process. **1796:** Amelia Simmons publishes the first American cookbook under the title *American Cookery, or the Art of Dressing Viands, Fish, Poultry and Vegetables, and the Best Modes of Making Puff-Pastries, Pies, Tarts, Puddings, Custards and Preserves, and All Kinds of Cakes, from the Imperial Plum to Plain Cake—Adapted to This Country and All Grades of Life.* **1798:** More than 2,000 people die in a yellow fever epidemic in New York City. **1799:** A Philadelphia Quaker named Elizabeth Drinker writes in her journal about the nearly novel experience of taking a bath: "I bore it better than I expected, not having been wett all over att once, for 28 years past."

**1775: CIRCA APRIL 18**

**RACHEL REVERE TO PAUL REVERE**

*On April 18, 1775, Paul Revere (1735–1818) made his famous midnight ride to Lexington, Massachusetts, warning his countrymen of the British troops' planned attack. Revere was captured later that night, but his actions marshaled colonial troops to the famous first battle on Lexington Green, where the American Revolution began the next day. Once released, Revere started back toward Boston, despite having neither money nor horse. With this note, his worried wife, Rachel Walker Revere (1745–1813), tried to send him help.*

Dr. Benjamin Church was trusted by Rachel as a fellow rebel but was in fact a British spy. Rachel's letter was promptly turned over to the British.

My dear by Doct$^r$ Church I send a hundred & twenty five pounds and beg you will take the best care of your self and not attempt coming in to this town again and if I have an opportunity of coming or sending out any thing or any of the Children I shall do it    pray keep up your spirits and trust your self and us in the hands of a good God who will take care of us    tis all my dependance for vain is the help of man    aduie    my

> Love from your
> affectionate R Revere

**1775: APRIL 22**

**ANNE HULTON TO ELIZABETH LIGHTBODY**

*Anne Hulton (?–1779) was the sister of Boston's commissioner of customs and, like some 15 to 35 percent of the white colonial population, a British Loyalist. In this letter to her friend Elizabeth Lightbody, in Liverpool, she described the beginning of the war as it would come to be seen on the other side of the Atlantic, right down to the outrage of having His Majesty's troops attacked from behind trees and fences.*

*By the end of the year, having endured months in a besieged city, Hulton would sail for England.*

"Inst" was a common abbreviation for instant, meaning "the month this was written." The Grenadiers were elite British troops who wore long red coats and tall bearskin hats. "Magazine," in this context, meant "warehouse." Hugh Percy was a British brigadier general. The *Otter* was a British sloop that would engage in battle in the first week of May.

I acknowledged the receipt of My Dear Friends kind favor of the 20th Sept^r the begin'ing of last Month, tho' did not fully Answer it, purposing as I intimated to write again soon, be assured as your favors are always very acceptable, so nothing you say, passes unnoticed, or appears unimportant to me. but at present my mind is too much agitated to attend to any subject but one, and it is that which you will be most desirous to hear particulars of, I doubt not in regard to your friends here, as to our Situation, as well as the Publick events. I will give you the best account I can, which you may rely on for truth.

On the 18th inst^t at 11 at Night, about 800 Grenadiers & light Infantry were ferry'd across the Bay to Cambridge, from whence they march^d to Concord, about 20 Miles. The Congress had been lately assembled at that place, & it was imagined that the General had intelligence of a Magazine being formed there & that they were going to destroy it.

The People in the Country (who are all furnished with Arms & have what they call Minute Companys in every Town ready to march on any alarm), had a signal it's supposed by a light from one of the Steeples in Town, Upon the Troops embark^g. The alarm spread thro' the Country, so that before daybreak the people in general were in Arms & on their March to Concord. About Daybreak a number of the People appeard before the Troops near Lexington. They were called to, to disperse. when they fired on the Troops & ran off, Upon which the Light Infantry pursued them & brought down about fifteen of them. The Troops went on to Concord & executed the business they were sent on, & on their return found two or three of their people Lying in the Agonies of Death, scalp'd & their Noses & ears cut off & Eyes bored out—Which exasperated the Soldiers exceedingly—a prodigious number of the People now occupying the Hills, woods, & Stone Walls along the road. The Light Troops drove some parties from the hills, but all the road being inclosed with Stone Walls Served as a cover to the Rebels, from whence they fired on the Troops still running off whenever they had fired, but still supplied by fresh Numbers who came from many parts of the Country. In this manner were the Troops harrased in thier return for Seven on eight Miles, they were almost exhausted & had expended near the whole of their Ammunition when to their great joy they were releived by a Brigade of Troops under the command of Lord Percy with two pieces of Artillery. The Troops now combated with fresh Ardour, & marched in their return with undaunted countenances, recieving Sheets of fire all the way for many Miles, yet having no visible Enemy to combat with, for they never woud face 'em in an open field, but always skulked & fired from behind Walls, & trees, & out of Windows of Houses, but this cost them dear for the Soldiers enterd those dwellings, & put all the Men to death. Lord Percy has gained great honor by his conduct thro' this day of severe Servise, he was exposed to the hottest of the fire & animated the Troops with great coolness & spirit. Several officers are wounded & about 100 Soldiers. The killed amount to near 50, as to the Enemy we can have no exact acc$^t$ but it is said there was about ten times the Number of them engaged, & that near 1000 of 'em have fallen

The Troops returned to Charlestown about Sunset after having some of 'em marched near fifty miles, & being engaged from Daybreak in Action, without respite, or refreshment, & about ten in the Evening they were brought back to Boston. The next day the Country pourd down its Thousands, and at this time from the entrance of Boston Neck at Roxbury round by Cambridge to Charlestown is surrounded by at least 20,000 Men, who are raising batteries on three or four different Hills. We are now cut off from all communication with the Country & many people must soon perish with famine in this place. Some families have laid in store of Provissions against a Siege. We are threatned that whilst the Out Lines are attacked w$^{th}$ a rising of the Inhabitants within, & fire & sword, a dreadful prospect before us, and you know how many & how dear are the objects of our care. The Lord preserve us all & grant us an happy Issue out of these troubles.

For several nights past, I have expected to be roused by the firing of Cannon. Tomorrow is Sunday, & we may hope for one day of rest, at present a Solemn dead silence reigns in the Streets, numbers have packed up their effects, & quited the Town, but the General has put a Stop to any more removing, & here remains in Town about 9000 Souls (besides the Servants of the Crown)   These are the greatest Security, the General declared that if a Gun is fired within the Town the inhabitants shall fall a Sacrifice. Amidst our distress & apprehension, I am rejoyced our British Hero was preserved, My Lord Percy had a great many & miraculous escapes in the late Action. This amiable Young Nobleman with the Graces which attracts Admiration, possesses the virtues of the heart, & all those qualities that form the great Soldier—Vigilent Active, temperate, humane, great Command of temper, fortitude in enduring hardships & fatigue, & Intrepidity in dangers. His Lordships behavior in the day of trial has done honor to the Percys. indeed all the Officers & Soldiers behaved with the greatest bravery it is said

I hope you and yours are all well & shall be happy to hear so. I woud beg of you whenever you write to mention the dates of my Letters which you have rec'd since you wrote specialy my last of March 2ᵈ

I am not able at present to write to our Dear friends at Chester    woud desire the favor of you to write as soon as you receive this, & present my respects to your & my friends there, and likewise the same to those who are near to you.

I wrote not long ago both to Miss Tylston & to my Aunt H:—have not heard yet from the Bahamas

Have never heard from Mʳ Gildart or Mʳ Earl yet

The Otter Man of War is just arrived Sunday Mornᵍ

What is marked with these Lines, you are at Liberty to make as publick as you please    Let the merits of Lord Percy be known as far as you can.


## 1775: APRIL 29
## CHRISTIAN BARNES TO ELIZABETH INMAN

*A known Loyalist, merchant Henry "Tory" Barnes was forced to leave his home in Marlborough, Massachusetts, to avoid capture. Terrified by the visit of a rebel soldier, Barnes's wife, Christian, described the incident to Elizabeth Inman (1726–1786), a Cambridge friend who shared her sympathies, if not her immediate peril.*
Along with hundreds of others who sympathized with the British, Henry Barnes would be officially banished from Boston in the fall.

It is now a week since I had a line from my dear Mrs. Inman, in which time I have had some severe trials, but the greatest terror I was ever thrown into was on Sunday last. A man came up to the gate and loaded his musket, and before I could determine which way to run he entered the house and demanded a dinner. I sent him the best I had upon the table. He was not contented, but insisted upon bringing in his gun and dining with me; this terrified the young folks, and they ran out of the house. I went in and endeavored to pacify him by every method in my power, but I found it was to no purpose. He still continued to abuse me, and said when he had eat his dinner he should want a horse and if I did not let him have one he would blow my brains out. He pretended to have an order from the General for one of my horses, but did not produce it. His language was so dreadful and his looks so frightful that I could not remain in the house, but fled to the store and locked myself in. He followed me and declared he would break the door open. Some people very luckily passing to meeting prevented his doing any mischief and staid by me until he was out of sight, but I did not recover from my fright for several days. The sound of drum or the sight of a gun put me into such a tremor that I could not command myself. I have met with but little molestation since this affair, which I attribute to the protection sent me by Col. Putnam and Col. Whitcomb. I returned them a card of thanks for their goodness tho' I knew it was thro' your interest I obtained this favor. . . . The people here are weary at [Mr. Barnes's] absence, but at the same time give it as their opinion that he could not pass the guards. . . . I do not doubt but upon a proper remonstrance I might procure a pass for him through the Camp from our two good Colonels. . . . I know he must be very unhappy in Boston. It was never his intention to quit his family. . . .

## 1775: CIRCA JUNE 15
## SARAH DEMING TO SALLY COVERLEY

*All we know about Sarah Winslow Deming (1722–1788) is that she was born in Massachusetts, the daughter of John and Sarah Winslow, and that, as this letter attests, she was a terrified witness to the very beginnings of the American Revolution. The troops she referred to were British, and this letter to her niece was a vivid reminder that the war would be fought not in far-off battlefields, but on the colonists' doorsteps.*

General Thomas Gage was Britain's military governor of Massachusetts. "Aceldama" refers to the land Judas purchased with the money he received for betraying Christ; the word means "field of blood." The "Sally" Sarah referred to in the letter was a different niece; Lucinda was a servant.

My Dear Niece

I engaged to give you & by you your papa and mamma some account of my peregrinations with the reasons thereof. The <u>cause</u> is too well known to need a word upon it.

I was very unquiet from the moment I was informed that <u>more troops</u> were coming to Boston. 'Tis true that those who had wintered there, had not given us <u>much molestation</u>, but an <u>additional strength</u> I dreaded and determined if possible to get out of their reach, and to take with me as much of my little interest as I could. Your uncle Deming was very far from being of my mind from which has proceeded those diflcutics which peculiarly related to myself—but I now say not a word of this to him; we are joint sufferers and no doubt it is God's will that it should be so.

Many a time have I thought that could I be out of Boston together with my family and my friends, I could be content with the meanest fare and slenderest accommodation. Out of Boston, out of Boston at almost any rate—away as far as possible from the infection of smallpox & the din of drums & martial musick as it is called and horrors of war—but my distress is not to be described—I attempt not to describe it.

On Saterday the 15th April p.m. I had a visit from Mr. Barrow. I never saw him with such a countenance.

The Monday following, April 17, I was told that all the boats belonging to the men of war were launched on Saterday night while the town inhabitants were sleeping except some faithful watchmen who gave the intelligence. In the evening Mr. Deming wrote to Mr Withington of Dorchester to come over with his carts the very first fair day (the evening of <u>this</u> day promising rain on the next, which accordingly fell in plenty) to carry off our best goods.

On Tuesday evening 18 April we were informed that the companies above mentioned were in motion, that the men of war boats were rowed round to Charlestown ferry, Barton's point and bottom of ye common, that the soldiers were run thro the streets on tip toe (the moon not having risen) in the dark of ye evening, that there were a number of handcuffs in one of the boats, which were taken at the long wharf, & that two days provision had been cooked for 'em on board one of the transport ships lying in ye harbor. That whatever other business they might have, the main was to take possession of the bodies of Mess. Adams & Hancock whom they & we knew where they were lodged. We had no doubt of the truth of all this, and that expresses were sent forth both over the neck & Charlestown ferry to give our friends timely notice that they might escape. N.B. I did not git to bed this night till after 12 oclock, nor to sleep till long after that, and then my sleep was much broken as it had been for many nights before.

Early on Wednesday the fatal 19th April before I had quited my chamber one after another came running to tell me that the kings troops had fired upon and killed 8 of our neighbors at Lexington in their way to Concord.

All the intelligence of this day was dreadful. Almost every countenance expressing anxiety and distress: but description fails here. I went to bed about 12 o. c. this night, having taken but little food thro the day, having resolved to quit the town before the next setting sun, should life and limbs be spared me. Towards morning I fell into a profound sleep, from which I was waked by Mr. Deming between 6 and 7 o. c. informing me that I was Gen. Gage's prisoner all egress & regress being cut off between the town and the country. Here again description fails. No words can paint my distress—I feel it at this instant (just eight weeks after) so sensibly that I must pause before I proceed.

This was Thursday 20th.; April. About 9 o. c. a.m. I was told that the way over the neck was opened for foot passengers but no carriage was permitted to cross the lines. I then determined to try if <u>my feet</u> would support me thro, tho I trembled to such a degree that I could scarce keep my feet in my own chamber, had taken no sustenance for the day & very sick at my stomach. I tyed up a few things in my handkerchief, put on my cloak & was just setting out upon my march with Sally & Lucinda when I was told that carriages were allowed to pass. By this time I was so faint that I was obliged to sit down. Mr. Scollay Mrs. Sweetser and who else I remember not, advised me to stay where I was, reconing Boston the safest place for me, but I had no faith in their opinion. I had been told that Boston would be an Alceldama as soon as the fresh troops arrived, which Mr. Barrow had told me were expected every minute. I therefore besought Mr. Deming to get a carriage for me. I had then heard that carriages were permitted to pass and carry me off with my frighted girls: and set me down anywhere out of Boston. He went out forth and over awhile & returned and told me there was not a carriage or another to be got for love or money: ah can any one that has not felt it know my sensation. Surely no. Mr. D. threw himself into the easy chair & said he had not strength enough to move another step. I expected to see Sally fall into hysterick fitts every minute. Lucinda holding herself up by anything she could grasp. I bid her however git us some elixer drops & when we had taken it in a little wine mixed with water which happened to be boiling I prayed Mr D. once more to let us try to get off on foot. He said he would presently & see me out but positively he would come back again. There is no describing my sensations. <u>This moment</u> I thot the <u>crisis</u> the <u>very crisis</u>—I had not walked out at the top of the Court since last October—I went down and out to the edge of the street where I saw and spoke with several friends near as unhappy as myself, in a few moments the light of a chaise, which I engaged to take me off when it returned from Roxbury where it was going with women and children, this somewhat lightened me. Before this chaise returned Mr Deming engaged another & while we were waiting I might have packed up many necessaries but nobody had any business that day—there was a constant coming and going; each hindered the other: some new piece of soldier barbarity that had been perpetrated the day before, was in quick succession brought in—I was very ill—but to cut short about 3 o'clock p.m. the chaises returned (for they both went to Jamaica Plain with Mr Waters wife children and maid he having first engaged them, one of 'em being his brother Thomson's which he Mr.

Thomson, offered to Mr. D while it was out & promised we should have it on its return.) We set off immediately Mr D & I in one Sally Lucinda with Jemmy Church to drive in the other. We were stopped and inquired of whether we had any arms &c by the first and second sentinels. but they treated us civilly and did not search us. The third & last sentinels did not chalenge us, so we got safe thro ye lines. We had not resolved where to go. In that respect we resembled Abraham & I ardently wished for a portion of his faith.

### 1775: JUNE 20
### LOIS PETERS TO NATHAN PETERS

---

*Lois Crary Peters (1750–1837) and her husband, Nathan (1747–1824), were living in Preston, Connecticut, and Lois was pregnant with the fourth of their nine children when Nathan joined the Continental army to fight the British. Their separation, which was to last several years, left Lois in charge of the household as well as of her husband's saddle business.*

The battle she mentioned was Bunker Hill, which had taken place (actually at nearby Breed's Hill) three days before.

Preston, June ye 20th at Night 1775

Dear husband

I this Moment Take Pen in Hand To Let you know that I am well and all our Friends here    have No news To write    wee have heard of the battle you have had Among you but wee hear So Many Storys wee no not what To believe    a report This Morning was very Current here that Genll Putnum was Missing but we had it contradicted befor knigh and Said he was only Sligtily wounded in the wrist    our fears are Many but wee all hope for the best    My heart akes for you and all our friends there but I Keep up as good Spirits as possibel    if you Could Spare your Mare Should bee very Glad you would Send her hom As Soon as possible for I Cant borrow at all and Should bee glad you would Send mee Some Money if you Can but Dont let that Troubel you for I am not Like To Suffer for any article To Support My family but Cannot Carry on The Trade without money    but that is the Least of my Troubels at Present    our Corn Looks well and our Woork goes on as well as I Could wish Pray write Every oppertunity    it being Late Must Coclude with wishing you the best of heavens blessing and hope that God in du Time will return you To your famely in Safty    am your Loving wife Til Death

Lois Peters

## 1775: SEPTEMBER 21

## MERCY OTIS WARREN TO JAMES WARREN

*A writer who was friends with many key figures of the Revolution, Mercy Otis Warren (1728–1814) was a poet, dramatist, propagandist, and historian whose volumes about the war (published in 1805) would be among the first written and the most widely read. She was married to James Warren (1726–1808), a member of the Massachusetts legislature, known as the General Court. Managing their Plymouth home and four sons while James became president of Massachusetts's provisional Congress, Mercy offered a vivid portrait of family life that, despite its archaic language, conjures thoroughly timeless behavior.*

The Warrens lived in Plymouth; the Congress usually met in Watertown, about forty miles away. The "sickly season" referred to the prevalent threat of smallpox. The Warrens' son Winslow was sixteen, Charles was thirteen, Henry was eleven, and George had just had his ninth birthday.

Just as I got up from dinner this day yours of the 15 & 18 came to hand; No desert was ever more welcome to a luxurious pallate, it was a regale to my longing mind: I had been eagerly looking for more than a week for a line from the best friend of my heart.

I had contemplated to spend a day or two with my good father, but as you talk of returning so soon I shall give up that and every other pleasure this world can give for the superior pleasure of your company. I thank you for the many expressions in yours which bespeak the most affectionate soul, or heart warmed with friendship & esteem which it shall ever be my assiduous care to merit.—but as I am under some apprehensions that you will be again disappointed and your return postponed, I will endeavor to give you some account of the reception I met from our little family on my arrival among them after an absence which they thought long: your requesting this as an agreeable amusement is a new proof that the Father is not lost in the occupations of the statesman.

I found Charles & Henry sitting on the steps of the front door when I arrived—they had just been expressing their ardent wishes to each other that mamah would come in before dinner when I turned the corner having our habitation. One of them had just finished an exclamation to the other "Oh what would I give if mamah was now in sight," you may easily judge what was their rapture when they saw their wishes instantly compleated.

The one leaped into the street to meet me—the other ran into the house in an extacy of joy to communicate the tidings, & finding my children well at this sickly season you will not wonder that with a joy at least equal to theirs I ran hastily into the entry; but before I had reached the stair top was met by all the lovely flock. Winslow half affronted that I had delayed coming home so long & more than half happy in the return of his fond Mother, turned up his smiling cheek to receive a kiss while he failed in the effort to command the grave muscles of his countenance.

George's solemn brow was covered with pleasure & his grave features not only danced in smiles but broke into a real laugh more expressive of his heartfelt happiness than all the powers of language could convey and before I could sit down and lay aside my riding attire all the choice gleanings of the Garden were offered each one pressing before the other to pour the yellow produce into their mamah's lap.

Not a complaint was uttered—not a tale was told through the day but what they thought would contribute to the happiness of their best friend; but how short lived is human happiness. The ensuing each one had his little grievance to repeat, as important to them as the laying an unconstitutional tax to the patriot or the piratical seazure of a ship & cargo, after much labour & the promising expectation of profitable returns when the voyage was compleat—but the umpire in your absence soon accommodated all matters to mutual satisfaction and the day was spent in much cheerfulness encircled by my sons. . . . My heart has just leaped in my bosom and I ran to the stairs imagining I heard both your voice & your footsteps in the entry. Though disappointed I have no doubt this pleasure will be realized as soon as possible by

Your affectionate<br>M. Warren

## 1775: OCTOBER 2
## DEBORAH CHAMPION TO PATIENCE

*Deborah Champion (1753–?) was the daughter of the Continental army's commissary general, Henry Champion. From Westchester, Connecticut, she rode to Boston carrying messages from her father to General George Washington. Her recounting of that adventure in this letter to a friend is filled with patriotism as well as a touching kind of wonder at her own courage.*

Linsey-woolsey was a blend of linen and wool often used for blankets and scarves. A close silk hood was one that fit tightly. A calash was an oversized bonnet that was apparently not a favorite fashion of the younger generation.

Westchester, Conn.
Oct. 2nd, 1775.

My dear Patience,

I know you are thinking it a very long time since I have written you, and indeed I would answered your last, sweet letter long before now, but I have been away from home. Think of it, and to Boston. I know you will hardly believe that such a stay-at-home as I should go, and without my parents too. Really and truly I have been.

It happened last month, and I have only been home ten days, hardly long enough to get over the excitement. Before you suffer too much with curiosity and amazement I will hasten to tell you about it. A few days after receiving your letter I had settled myself to spend a long day at my spinning being anxious to get the yarn ready for some small clothes for father. Just as I was busily engaged I noticed a horseman enter the yard, and knocking at the door with the handle of his whip, heard him ask for Colonel Champion, and after brief converse with my father, he entered the house.

Soon after my mother came to me and asked me to go to the store in town and get her sundry condiments, which I was very sure were already in the store-room. Knowing that I was to be sent out of the way, there was nothing left for me, but to go, which I accordingly did, not hurrying myself you may be sure. When I returned the visitor was gone but my father was walking up and down the long hall and with hasty steps and worried and perplexed aspect.

You know father has always been kind and good to me, but none know better than you the stern self repressment our New England character engenders, and he would have thought it unseemly for his child to question him, so I passed on into the family-room, to find mother and deliver my purchases. My father is troubled, is aright amiss, I asked. "I cannot say, Deborah," she replied, "You know he has many cares and the public business presses heavily just now. It may be he will tell us." Just then my father stood in the door way. "Wife, I would spake with you." Mother joined him in the keeping-room and they seemed to have long and anxious conversation. I had gone back to my spinning but could hear the sound of their voices. Finally I was called to attend them, to my astonishment.

Father laid his hand on my shoulder, (a most unusual caress with him) and said almost solemnly, "Deborah I have need of thee. Hast thee the courage to go out and ride, it may be even in the dark and as fast as may be, till thou comest to Boston town?" He continued, "I do not believe Deborah, that there will be actual danger to threaten thee, else I would not ask it of thee, but the way is long, and in part lonely. I shall send Aristarchus with thee and shall explain to him the urgency of the business. Though he is a slave, he understands the mighty matters at stake, and I shall instruct him yet further. There are reasons why it is better for you a woman to take the despatches I would send than for me to entrust them to a man; else I should send your brother Henry. Dare you go?"

"Dare, father, and I your daughter? A chance to do a service for my country and for General Washington;—I am glad to go."

So dear Patience it was settled we should start in the early morning of the next day, father needing some time to prepare the paper. You remember Uncle Aristarchus; he has been devoted to me since my childhood, and particularly since I made a huge cask to grace his second marriage, and found a name for the dusky baby, which we call Sophranieta. He has unusual wits for a slave and father trusts him. Well, to proceed,—early the next morning, before it was fairly light, mother called me, though I had seemed to have hardly slept at all. I found a nice hot breakfast ready and a pair of saddle bags packed with such things as mother thought might be needed. When the servants came in for prayer I noticed how solemn they looked and that Aunt Chloe, Uncle Aristarchus' wife, had been crying. Then I began to realize I was about to start on a solemn journey, you see it was a bright sunshiny morning and the prospect of a long ride, the excitement of what might happen had made me feel like singing as I dressed. I had put on my linsey-woolsey dress, as the roads might at times be dusty and the few articles I needed made only a small bundle.

Father read the 91st Psalm, and I noticed that his voice trembled as he read "He shall give His Angels charge over thee," and I knew into whose hands he committed me. Father seemed to have everything planned out and to have given full instructions to Uncle Aristarchus. We were to take the two carriage horses for the journey was too long for one horse to take us both, I riding on a pillion. John and Jerry are both good saddle horses as you and I know.

The papers that were the object of the journey I put under my bodice, and fastened my neckerchief securely down. Father gave me also a small package of money. You know our Continental bills are so small you can pack away a hundred dollars very compactly. Just as the tall clock in the hall was striking eight, the horses were at the door. I mounted putting on my camlet cloak for the air was yet a little cool. Mother insisted on my wearing my close silk hood and taking her calash. I demurred a little, but she tied the strings together and hung it on my arm, saying, "Yes daughter". Later I understood the precaution. Father again told me of the haste with which I must ride and the care to use for the safety of the despatches, and we set forth with his blessing. Uncle Aristarchus looked very pompous, as if he was Captain and felt the responsibility.

The British were at Providence in Rhode Island, so it was thought best for us to ride due north to the Massachusetts line and then east as best we could. The weather was perfect, but the roads were none too good as there had been recent rains, but we made fairly good time going through Norwich then up the Valley of the Quinnebaugh to Canterbury where we rested our horses for an hour, then pushed on hoping to reach Pomfret before dark. At father's desire I was to stay at Uncle Jerry's the night, and if needful get a change of horses. All went well as I could expect. We met few people on the road. Almost all the men are with the army, so we saw only old men, women and children on the road or in the villages.

Oh! War is a terrible and cruel thing. Uncle Jerry thought we had better take fresh horses in the morning and sun up found us on our way again. Aunt Faith had a good breakfast for us—by candle light. We got our meals after that at some farm house generally. I left that to Uncle Starkey. As it neared hungry time he would select a house, ride ahead, say something to the woman or old man and whatever it was he said seemed magical, for as I came up I would be met with smiles, kind words "God bless you" and looks of wonder. The best they had was pressed on us, and they were always unwilling to take pay which we offered. Everywhere we heard the same thing, love for the Mother Country, but stronger than that, that she must <u>must</u> give us our rights, that we were fighting not for independence, though that might come and would be the war-cry if the oppression of unjust taxation was not removed. Nowhere was a cup of imported tea offered us. It was a glass of milk, or a cup of "hyperion" the name they gave to a tea made of raspberry leaves. We heard that it would be almost impossible to avoid the British, unless by going so far out of the way that too much time would be lost, so plucked up what courage I could as darkness began to come on at the close of the second day. I secreted the papers in a small pocket in a saddle bag under some of the eatables that mother had put up. We decided to ride all night. Providentially the moon just past full, rose about 8 o'clock and it was not unpleasant, for the roads were better. I confess that I began to be weary. It was late at night or rather very early in the morning, that I heard a sentry call and knew that if at all the danger point was reached. I pulled my calash as far over my face as I could, thanking my wise mother's forethought, and went on with what boldness I could muster. I really believe I heard Aristarchus' teeth chatter as he rode to my side and whispered "De British missus for sure." Suddenly I was ordered to <u>halt</u>. As I could not help myself I did so. A soldier in a red coat appeared and suggested that I go to headquarters for examination. I told him "It was early to wake his Captain and to please let me pass for I had been sent in urgent haste to see a friend in need," which was true, if a little ambiguous. To my joy he let me go saying "Well, you are only an old woman any way." Evidently as glad to be rid of me as I of him. Would you believe me—that was the only exciting adventure in the whole ride.

Just as I finished that sentence father came into my room and said "My daughter if you are writing of your journey, do not say just how or where you saw General Washington, nor what you heard of the affairs of the Colony. A letter is a very dangerous thing these days and it might fall into strange hands and cause harm. I am just starting in the chaise for Hartford to see about some stores for the troops, I shall take the mare as the other horses need rest." What a wise man my father is. I must obey, but I can say I saw General Washington. I felt very humble as I crossed the threshold of the room where he sat in converse with other gentlemen, one evidently an officer. Womanlike I wished that I had on my Sunday gown. I had put on a clean kerchief. I gave him the paper, which from his manner I judged to be of great importance. He was pleased to compliment me most highly on what he called my courage and my patriotism.

Oh, Patience what a man he is, so grand, so kind, so noble. I am sure we shall not look to him in vain as our leader.

Well, here I am home again safe and sound and happy to have been of use. We took a longer way home as far as Uncle Jerry's, so met with no mishap.

I hope I have not tired you with this long letter. Mother desires to send her love.

> Yours in the bonds of love.
> Deborah.

P.S. I saw your brother Samuel in Boston. He sent his love if I should be writing you.

## 1775: NOVEMBER 27
## ABIGAIL ADAMS TO JOHN ADAMS

*Eloquent, feisty, intelligent, and politically informed, Abigail Smith Adams (1744–1818) would have been one of the great women of any era. She was the wife of one president, John Adams (1735–1826), and, though she didn't live to see him elected, the mother of another. At the time this letter was written, John was in Philadelphia at the Continental Congress, and Abigail was in Quincy at the family home. Her questions are a poignant reminder of the extent to which America's future remained an open question.*

James Warren was Mercy Warren's husband (see page 23).

27 November, 1775

Colonel Warren returned last week to Plymouth, so that I shall not hear any thing from you until he goes back again, which will not be till the last of this month. He damped my spirits greatly by telling me, that the Court had prolonged your stay another month. I was pleasing myself with the thought, that you would soon be upon your return. It is in vain to repine. I hope the public will reap what I sacrifice.

I wish I knew what mighty things were fabricating. If a form of government is to be established here, what one will be assumed? Will it be left to our Assemblies to choose one? And will not many men have many minds? And shall we not run into dissensions among ourselves?

I am more and more convinced, that man is a dangerous creature; and that power, whether vested in many or a few, is ever grasping, and, like the grave, cries "Give, give." The great fish swallow up the small; and he, who is most strenuous for the rights of the people, when vested with power is as eager after the prerogatives of government. You tell me of degrees of perfection to which human nature is capable of arriving, and I believe it, but, at the same time, lament that our admiration should arise from the scarcity of the instances.

The building up a great empire, which was only hinted at by my correspondent, may now, I suppose, be realized even by the unbelievers. Yet, will not ten thousand difficulties arise in the formation of it? The reins of government have been so long slackened, that I fear the people will not quietly submit to those restraints, which are necessary for the peace and security of the community. If we separate from Britain, what code of laws will be established? How shall we be governed, so as to retain our liberties? Can any government be free, which is not administered by general stated laws? Who shall frame these laws? Who will give them force and energy? It is true, your resolutions, as a body, have hitherto had the force of laws; but will they continue to have?

When I consider these things, and the prejudices of people in favor of ancient customs and regulations, I feel anxious for the fate of our monarchy or democracy, or whatever is to take place. I soon get lost in a labyrinth of perplexities; but, whatever occurs, may justice and righteousness be the stability of our times, and order arise out of confusion. Great difficulties may be surmounted by patience and perseverance.

I believe I have tired you with politics; as to news we have not any at all. I shudder at the approach of winter, when I think I am to remain desolate.

I must bid you good night; 'tis late for me, who am much of an invalid. I was disappointed last week in receiving a packet by the post, and, upon unsealing it, finding only four newspapers. I think you are more cautious than you need be. All letters, I believe, have come safe to hand. I have sixteen from you, and wish I had as many more.

Adieu, yours.

**1776: MARCH 31**

**ABIGAIL ADAMS TO JOHN ADAMS**

---

*Separated from John for long stretches of time while he worked with the Continental Congress, Abigail Adams honed her letter-writing skills, which were nowhere more evident than in this famous epistle, with its memorable admonition to "Remember the Ladies." Her relatively upbeat tone reflects the fact that the British had abandoned Boston just two weeks earlier. Several weeks later, John would respond: "We know better than to repeal our Masculine systems. . . . in Practice you know We are the subjects. We have only the Name of Masters, and rather than give up this, which would compleatly subject Us to the Despotism of the Peticoat, I hope General Washington, and all our brave Heroes would fight."*

John Murray, Lord Dunmore, was the royal governor of Virginia; weeks after Abigail wrote this letter, Dunmore would declare martial law in that colony and offer freedom to all slaves who would fight for the British. Mr. Crane, Mr. Trot, Becky Peck, Tertias Bass, and Mr. Reed were neighbors. "Your President" was John Hancock. Samuel Quincy was solicitor general. "Gaieti de Coar" was a misspelling of *gaieté de coeur,* meaning "happiness of the heart." Betsy Cranch was Abigail's niece. Saltpeter, also known as niter, was used for gunpowder and was also rumored to suppress sexual desire when taken orally.

Braintree March 31 1776

I wish you would ever write me a Letter half as long as I write you; and tell me if you may where your Fleet are gone? What sort of Defence Virginia can make against our common Enemy? Whether it is so situated as to make an able Defence? Are not the Gentery Lords and the common people vassals, are they not like the uncivilized Natives Brittain represents us to be? I hope their Riffel Men who have shewen themselves very savage and even Blood thirsty; are not a specimen of the Generality of the people.

I am willing to allow the Colony great merrit for having produced a Washington but they have been shamefully duped by a Dunmore.

I have sometimes been ready to think that the passion for Liberty cannot be Eaquelly Strong in the Breasts of those who have been accustomed to deprive their fellow Creatures of theirs. Of this I am certain that it is not founded upon that generous and christian principal of doing to others as we would that others should do unto us.

Do not you want to see Boston; I am fearfull of the small pox, or I should have been in before this time. I got Mr. Crane to go to our House and see what state it was in. I find it has been occupied by one of the Doctors of a Regiment, very dirty, but no other damage has been done to it. The few things which were left in it are all gone. Crane has the key which he never deliverd up. I have wrote to him for it and am determined to get it cleand as soon as possible and shut it up. I look upon it a new acquisition of property, a property which one month ago I did not value at a single Shilling, and could with pleasure have seen it in flames.

The Town in General is left in a better state than we expected, more oweing to a percipitate flight than any Regard to the inhabitants, tho some individuals discoverd a sense of honour and justice and have left the rent of the Houses in which they were, for the owners and the furniture unhurt, or if damaged sufficent to make it good.

Others have committed abominable Ravages. The Mansion House of your President is safe and the furniture unhurt whilst both the House and Furniture of the Solisiter General have fallen a prey to their own merciless party. Surely the very Fiends feel a Reverential awe for Virtue and patriotism, whilst they Detest the paricide and traitor.

I feel very differently at the approach of spring to what I did a month ago. We knew not then whether we could plant or sow with safety, whether when we had toild we could reap the fruits of our own industery, whether we could rest in our own Cottages, or whether we should not be driven from the sea coasts to seek shelter in the wilderness, but now we feel as if we might sit under our own vine and eat the good of the land.

I feel a gaieti de Coar to which before I was a stranger. I think the Sun looks brighter, the Birds sing more melodiously, and Nature puts on a more chearfull countanance. We feel a temporary peace, and the poor fugitives are returning to their deserted habitations.

Tho we felicitate ourselves, we sympathize with those who are trembling least the Lot of Boston should be theirs. But they cannot be in similar circumstances

unless pusilanimity and cowardise should take possession of them. They have
time and warning given them to see the Evil and shun it.—I long to hear that
you have declared an independancy—and by the way in the new Code of Laws
which I suppose it will be necessary for you to make I desire you would Remember the Ladies, and be more generous and favourable to them than your
ancestors. Do not put such unlimited power into the hands of the Husbands.
Remember all Men would be tyrants if they could. If perticuliar care and attention is not paid to the Laidies we are determined to foment a Rebelion, and will
not hold ourselves bound by any Laws in which we have no voice, or Representation.

That your Sex are Naturally Tyrannical is a Truth so thoroughly established
as to admit of no dispute, but such of you as wish to be happy willingly give up
the harsh title of Master for the more tender and endearing one of Friend. Why
then, not put it out of the power of the vicious and the Lawless to use us with
cruelty and indignity with impunity. Men of Sense in all Ages abhor those customs which treat us only as the vassals of your Sex. Regard us then as Beings
placed by providence under your protection and in immitation of the Supreem
Being make use of that power only for our happiness.

April 5

Not having an opportunity of sending this I shall add a few lines more; tho
not with a heart so gay. I have been attending the sick chamber of our Neighbour Trot whose affliction I most sensibly feel but cannot discribe, striped of
two lovely children in one week. Gorge the Eldest died on wednesday and Billy
the youngest on fryday, with the Canker fever, a terible disorder so much like
the thr[o]at distemper, that it differs but little from it. Betsy Cranch has been
very bad, but upon the recovery. Becky Peck they do not expect will live out the
day. Many grown person are now sick with it, in this [street?]. It rages much in
other Towns. The Mumps too are very frequent. Isaac is now confined with it.
Our own little flock are yet well. My Heart trembles with anxiety for them. God
preserve them.

I want to hear much oftener from you than I do. March 8 was the last date of
any that I have yet had.—You inquire of whether I am making Salt peter. I have
not yet attempted it, but after Soap making believe I shall make the experiment.
I find as much as I can do to manufacture cloathing for my family which would
else be Naked. I know of but one person in this part of the Town who has made
any, that is Mr. Tertias Bass as he is calld who has got very near an hundred
weight which has been found to be very good. I have heard of some others in the
other parishes. Mr. Reed of Weymouth has been applied to, to go to Andover to

the mills which are now at work, and has gone. I have lately seen a small Manu-scrip de[s]cribing the proportions for the various sorts of powder, fit for cannon, small arms and pistols. If it would be of any Service your way I will get it tran-scribed and send it to you.—Every one of your Friend[s] send their Regards, and all the little ones. Your Brothers youngest child lies bad with convulsion fitts. Adieu. I need not say how much I am Your ever faithfull Friend.

## 1776: JULY 21
## ABIGAIL ADAMS TO JOHN ADAMS

*The formal signing of the Declaration of Independence did not take place until Au-gust. In the meantime, the document was widely published, and Abigail duly recorded one of its many public readings in a short, joyous letter to John.*
Colonel Thomas Crafts headed several artillery regiments. James Bowdoin was a member of the Massachusetts executive council. Abigail's second paragraph was about a plot to assassi-nate George Washington that was rumored to have involved the mayor and governor of New York, as well as Washington's guard, Thomas Hickey, who on June 28 was hanged for treason. The "George" she mentioned was the king, and the line she quoted is from Alexander Pope's *Essay on Man:* "If plagues or earthquakes break not Heav'n's design, / Why then a Borgia, or a Catiline?"

Boston, 21 July, 1776

Last Thursday, after hearing a very good sermon, I went with the multitude into King Street to hear the Proclamation for Independence read and pro-claimed. Some field-pieces with the train were brought there. The troops ap-peared under arms, and all the inhabitants assembled there (the small-pox prevented many thousands from the country), when Colonel Crafts read from the balcony of the State House the proclamation. Great attention was given to every word. As soon as he ended, the cry from the balcony was, "God save our American States," and then three cheers which rent the air. The bells rang, the privateers fired, the forts and batteries, the cannon were discharged, the pla-toons followed, and every face appeared joyful. Mr. Bowdoin then gave a senti-ment, "Stability and perpetuity to American independence." After dinner, the King's Arms were taken down from the State House, and every vestige of him from every place in which it appeared, and burnt in King Street. Thus ends royal authority in this state. And all the people shall say Amen.

I have been a little surprised that we collect no better accounts with regard to the horrid conspiracy at New York; and that so little mention has been made of it here. It made a talk for a few days, but now seems all hushed in silence. The Tories say that it was not a conspiracy, but an association. And pretend that there was no plot to assassinate the General. Even their hardened hearts feel —— the discovery —— we have in George a match for "a Borgia or a Catiline"—a wretch callous to every humane feeling. Our worthy preacher told us that he believed one of our great sins, for which a righteous God has come out in judgment against us, was our bigoted attachment to so wicked a man. May our repentance be sincere.

### 1776: AUGUST 19
### ABIGAIL GRANT TO AZARIAH GRANT

*By the summer of 1776, the fighting between the British and the colonists had been going on for more than a year, and it would continue on land and at sea until the Treaty of Paris was signed in 1783. Anywhere from two hundred thousand to twice that number of American colonial men would fight at one point or another (estimates vary greatly, as many men enlisted more than once). But the fighting, as this letter from a wife to her husband suggests, was not always done in the most heroic fashion.* The original of this letter has not been found; the text below comes from a copy that was discovered among the papers of an old Connecticut family and reprinted in a nineteenth-century collection.

August ye 19th A.D. 1776

Loving Husband

   after Love to I would inform you that we are well through Gods mercy upon us and through the Same Mercy I hope these Lines will find you well also    I keep writing to you again & again & never can have only one Letter from you tho I hear by Cap^tn Wm Riley news that makes me very Sorry for he Says you proved a Grand Coward when the fight was at Bunkers hill & in your Surprise he reports that you threw away your Cartridges So as to escape going into the Battle    I am loath to believe it but yet I must unless you will write to me & inform me how it is, And if you are afraid pray own the truth & come home & take care of our Children & I will be Glad to Come & take your place, & never will be Called a Coward, neither will I throw away one Cartridge but exert myself bravely in so good a Cause. So hopeing you will let me know how it is, & how you do, So bidding you farewell, wishing you the best of heavens Blessings & a Safe & manlike return, subscribing myself your Loveing wife untill Death

Abigail Grant

### 1776: NOVEMBER 25
### MERCY OTIS WARREN TO JAMES WARREN

---

*Smallpox was the second great enemy of the Revolutionary era. Introduced to North America in the sixteenth century by Spanish conquistadors, it flourished with every war and by 1775 had become a full-scale epidemic. Estimates are that more than 130,000 North Americans, most of them Indians, were killed by smallpox during the Revolution. Being directly inoculated—an option available almost exclusively to wealthy white colonists—was only slightly less dangerous than catching smallpox naturally, and mothers like Mercy Warren (see page 23) who could actually afford the procedure for their children were terrified by it nonetheless.*

Plimouth 25 Nov 1776.

The letter my dear Mr. Warren will receive tomorrow I almost wish I had not wrote. I own I was a litle too Low spirited, but my mind was oppressed & I wanted to unbosom. it is this evening no less free from care though I feel a little Differently. I was ready to think the task of Governing & Regulating my Children alone almost too much—I now am forced to strive hard to keep out the Gloomy apprehension that the Burden may soon be lessened in some painful way. I have been this afternoon at the hospital where I left your three youngest sons. Poor Children—it was not possible to make them willing to give up the project. they thought it a mighty priviledge to be innoculated. I wish nor they nor we may have Reason to Regret it—but I cannot feel quite at Ease—I Want to Discourage Winslow from going in yet am afraid. Their accomodations are not altogether to my liking nor are their Nurses sufficient but they talk of getting more & better—but if my dear Children should be very ill I must go & take Charge of them myself Inconvenient as it is—48 persons were innoculated this afternoon & near as many will offer to-morrow. I think it is too many for one Class. But there they are—& it is as easy for the Great phisition of soul & Body to Lend Healing Mercy to the Multitude as to the Few, and if He Brings them Back in safty to their several Habitations I hope we shall Adore the Hand that Heals, and give Glory to the Rock of our salvation.

Wensday 24 of Nov. Your house Looks Lonely and Deserted in a manner you can hardly conceive—but three or four weeks will soon run away & if my family should then be Returned in safty to my own Roof I shall be thankful Indeed.

## 1777: JANUARY 4
## ELIZABETH INMAN TO JOHN INNES CLARK

*Born in Scotland, Elizabeth Murray Inman (see page 18) came to America with her two brothers when she was twelve. In Boston, she became a successful shop owner, embroidery instructor, and landlord. She was widowed twice; Ralph Inman, a retired businessman, was her third husband. She had no children herself, but she convinced her relatives in England to send her their children as apprentices in business. Like other British Loyalists, Inman experienced the War for Independence as a civil war. In this letter, she urged a friend, Providence merchant John Innes Clark, not to permit her nephew John Murray to join the American rebels.*

Whether John joined or not is unknown. Joseph Nightingale was Clark's business partner.

Boston, January 4th, 1777.

Dear Sir,—

Words are wanting to express my surprise and concern at reading J. Murrays letter by Mr. Sherry. I hope I never have nor never will give so much pain to an enemy as this does to me who has gloried in thinking I was his Aunt and friend. I have ever been proud of your Candor, generosity, Humanity, friendship and affection to me. I now rely on these good qualities and your promise. If your and Mr. Nightengale's authority is not sufficient to Check this youth I beg you'll make an errand for him to Boston. When I took him from his Fathers House I looked on myself as accountable to Him for the boy till he arrived at the age of 21. At that time I intended to advise him to visit his family and consult with them about settling. If he determins on taking up arms against them, farewell to his Fathers and Mothers happiness. They will bid adieu to their eldest darling Son and end their days in sorrow. Their fondness for him made them expect he would be the stay of the large family and the support of their old age. How blasted then their hopes. For God's sake let it not be. Assist me in Clearing him. Consider you have children, tho' young; you do not like disabedience in them, how would oposition like this affect you.

My respects to your Ladys. I expected to see them before Christenmas. Their company will give me pleasure.

Adieu.

\*    \*    \*

## 1777: MAY 22
## ANNE CHRISTIAN TO PATRICK HENRY

---

*Among revolutionary figures, Patrick Henry (1736–1799) distinguished himself as a lawyer, an orator ("give me liberty or give me death!"), a delegate to the Continental Congress, and by 1776, as Virginia's first governor. Perhaps slightly less attracted to sacrifice, his sister Anne Henry Christian (1740?–1790?) was miserable without her husband, William, then a representative in the Virginia legislature. In this letter, Anne asked her big brother to use his influence to have her husband sent home.* It is unlikely that Anne succeeded, as in June, William was still in Tennessee, helping to conclude a treaty with the Cherokee.

Haw Bottom, May 22ᵈ, 1777.

My Dear Brother:

Mʳ Christian has, I suppose, informed you of my intended Journey down being stopt, which deprives me of the pleasure of seeing you for a while; indeed our Family & cares increase so fast, that God knows when I shall be able to take another journey to see my dear friends below. Indeed Mʳ Christian is so much abroad that I am more confined on that account. I wish my dear brother could, by any means, be instrumental towards his quitting the public employment that he is engaged in, if it were only for a while, until he could get his affairs brought into some better way than at present. Cannot you assist in doing me this great favor? I am heartily sorry to trouble you on any domestic business, but I know you will excuse me. Some one certainly may be had that would answer as well to act in his place for the future, & at the same time save a whole family from ruin, as his stay at home might yet do; this is the case, & I am sorry to see that he is entering from one thing to another without considering his private affairs, which are almost desperate, & again I must entreat you to have some private conversation with him. . . . I hope you can find a few leisure moments to oblige a sister who is, & ever will be, Your ever affect.

A. Christian.

P.S. Shall I never be so happy as to see you up here. I have much to say but would not trouble you with a long letter, necessity urges me to say the above.

\*     \*     \*

## 1777: AUGUST 23
## LUCY KNOX TO HENRY KNOX

---

*Lucy Flucker Knox (1756–1824) had been married just three years when she sent this letter to her husband, Henry (1750–1806), one of George Washington's most trusted military leaders and the nation's first secretary of war. Writing from Boston, Lucy gave a lonely picture of her life, mourning particularly her "lost" family members, who, as British Loyalists, had been forced to flee the city.*

The couple would have thirteen children, only three of whom lived to be adults; "Little Lucy" was their first.

My dearest friend

I wrote you a line by the last post just to let you know I was alive, which . . . was all I could then say with propriety for I had serious thoughts that I never should see you again, so much was I reduced by only four days of illness but by help of a good constitution I am surprisingly better today. I am now to answer your three last letters in one of which you ask for a history of my life. It is my love barren of adventure and replete with repetition that I fear it will afford you little amusement. How such as it is I give to you. In the first place, I rise about eight in the morning so late an hour you will say but the day after that is full long for a person in my condition. I presently after sit down to my breakfast, where a page in my book and a dish of tea, employ me alternately for about an hour. When after seeing that family matters go on right, I repair to my work . . . for the rest of the forenoon. At two o'clock I usually take my solitary dinner where I reflect upon my past happiness. I used to sit at the window watching for my Harry, and when I saw him coming my heart would leap for joy when he was at my own side and never happy apart from me when the bare thought of six months absence would have shook him. To divert Alex's pleas I place my little Lucy by me at table, but the more engaging her little actions are so much the more do I regret the absence of her father who would take such delight in them. In the afternoon I commonly take my chaise and ride into the country or go to drink tea with one of my few friends . . . then with any. . . . I often spend the evening, but when I return home how [to] describe my feelings to find myself entirely alone, to reflect that the only friend I have in the world is such an immense distance from me to think that he may be sick and I cannot assist him. My poor heart is ready to burst, you who know what a trifle would make me unhappy can conceive what I suffer now. When I seriously reflect that I have lost my father, mother, brother, and sisters entirely lost them I am half distracted. . . . I have not seen him for almost six months, and he writes me without pointing at any method by which I may ever expect to see him again. Tis hard my Harry indeed it is I love you with the tenderest the purest affection. I would undergo any hardship to be near you and you will not let me.... The very little gold we have must be reserved for my love in case he should be taken.... [A person] if he understands business he might without capital make a fortune—people here without advancing a shilling frequently clear hundreds in a day, such chaps as Eben Oliver are all men of fortune while persons who have ever lived in affluence are in danger of want and that you had less of the military man about you, you might then after the war have lived at ease all the days of your life, but now, I don't know what you will do, you being long accustomed to command—will make you too haughty for mercantile matters—tho I hope you will not consider yourself as commander in chief of your own house—but be convinced tho not in the affair of Mr. Coudoe that there is such a thing as equal command.

I send this by Capt. Randal who says he expects to remain with you—pray how many of those lads have have you—I am sure they must be very expensive—I am in want of some square dollars—which I expect from you—to by me a peace of linen, an article I can do no longer without haveing had no recruit of that kind for almost five years. Girls in general when they marry, are wed stocked with those things but poor I had no such advantage.

Little Lucy who is without exception the sweetest child in the world—sends you a kiss—but where shall I take it from say you—from the paper I hope—but dare I say I sometimes fear that a long absence the force of bad example may lead you to forget me at sometimes. To know that it ever gave you pleasure to be in company with the finest woman in the world, would be worse than death to me—but it is not so, my Harry is too just, too delicate, too sincere—and too fond of his Lucy to admit the most remote thought of that distracting kind—away with it—don't be angry with me my Love—I am not jealous of your affection—I love you with a love as true and sacred as ever entered the human heart—but from a diffidence of my own merit I sometimes fear you will Love me less after being so long from me—if you should, may my life end before I know it, that I may die thinking you wholly mine.

Adieu my Love
LK

\*    \*    \*

## 1777: SEPTEMBER 22
## ALICE LEE SHIPPEN TO NANCY SHIPPEN

*Alice Lee Shippen (1736–1817) was evidently a woman on the edge when she sent this letter from Philadelphia to her fourteen-year-old daughter, Anne Hume Shippen (1763–1841), nicknamed Nancy. Though the war was clearly on Alice's mind, its threats did not stop her from urging her daughter to mind her manners, keep up with her sewing, and pursue all manner of self-improvements.*

Mrs. Rogers ran Nancy's boarding school, in Trenton, New Jersey, less than fifty miles from the recent landing of British troops at Elizabeth. Alice was married to William Shippen, head of the Continental army's hospital, and was the sister of Richard Henry Lee and Francis Lightfoot Lee, both signers of the Declaration. Dimity is a sheer cotton fabric.

My dear Nancy

I was extremely surprized when the waggon return'd the other evening without one line from you after I had been at the trouble & expence of sending for you as soon as I was inform'd 4000 troops were landed in Elizabeth-Town. Surely you should not omit any opportunity of writing to me, but to neglect such a one was inexcusable, but I shall say the less to you now, because you have been taught your duty & I take it for granted Mrs. Rogers has already reproved you for so great an omission, but do remember my dear how much of the beauty & usefulness of life depends on a proper conduct in the several relations in life, & the sweet peace that flows from the consideration of doing our duty to all with whom we are conected. I am sorry it is not in my power to get you the things I promised. It was late before I got to Philadelphia the afternoon I left you & the shops were shut the next day. I have looked all over this place but no muslin, satin or dimity can be got. However your Uncle Joe says he has a whole suit of dimity very fine & that you may have what you want. Get enough for two work bags one for me & the other for yourself.

Your Pappa thinks you had better work a pr. of ruffles for General Washington if you can get proper muslin. Write to me as soon as you receive this & send your letter to your Pappa. Tell me how you improve in your work. Needle work is a most important branch of a female education, & tell me how you have improved in holding your head & sholders, in making a curtsy, in going out or coming into a room, in giving & receiving, holding your knife & fork, walking & seting. These things contribute so much to a good appearance that they are of great consequence. Perhaps you will be at a loss how to judge wether you improve or not, take this rule therefore for your assistance. You may be sure you improve in proportion to the degree of ease with which you do any thing as you have been taught to do it, & as you may be partial to yourself as to your appearance of ease (for you must not only feel easy but appear so) ask M^rs. Rogers opinion as a friend who now acts for you in my place & you must look upon her as your parent as well as your Governess as you are at this time wholy in her care & you may depend upon it if you treat her with the duty & affection of a child she will have the feelings of a parent for you. Give my compliments to her & tell her I thank her for the care she takes of you. Give my compliments to the young Ladies. I am sorry Miss Stevens has left you. Dont offend Miss Jones by speaking against the Quakers. Tell Polly I shall remember her when I return. There is an alarm here the enemy are said to be coming this way, tis lucky you are not with me. Your Uncle F. Lee & his Lady & M^r & M^rs. Haywood are with me in the same house. They set out today for Lancaster & I for Maryland. I believe I will write to you as soon as I get settled. Farewell my dear. Be good & you will surely be happy which will contribute very much to the happiness of

Your Affect. Mother

## 1777: OCTOBER 19
## SALLY WISTER TO DEBORAH NORRIS

---

*Sally Wister (1761–1804) and Deborah Norris (1761–1839) grew up in Philadelphia and shared Quaker backgrounds, well-to-do upbringings, friends, school, and dozens of teenage intimacies. When Wister's family, fearing a direct attack, moved to a farmhouse fifteen miles from the city, the girls began putting their secrets on paper. At the time Wister wrote this gossipy account, the British had just roundly defeated the Continental army at the Battle of Brandywine. But the potential danger to her family and the frequent visits and occasional quartering of rebel officers only seemed to encourage Wister's sense of romance.*

"Second Day" was Tuesday in the Quaker week. Liddy, "Cousin P.," "Aunt F.," and Jesse were all members of the Foulke family, with whom the Wisters were staying. Sally's younger sister, Elizabeth, was called Betsy. "G. E." was George Emlen, husband of Sally's friend's sister. General William Smallwood commanded the Maryland troops. This letter was written as part of a journal addressed to Deborah Norris.

Second Day, October 19th

To Deborah Norris—

Now for new and uncommon scenes. As I was lying in bed, and ruminating on past and present events, and thinking how happy I should be if I could see you, Liddy came running into the room, and said there was the greatest drumming, fifing, and rattling of waggons that ever she had heard. What to make of this we were at a loss. We dress'd and down stairs in a hurry. Our wonder ceased. The British had left Germantown, and our army were marching to take possession. It was the general opinion they would evacuate the capital. Sister B. and myself, and G. E. went about half a mile from home, where we cou'd see the army pass. Thee will stare at my going, but no impropriety, in my opine, or I should not have gone. We made no great stay, but return'd with excellent appetites for our breakfast. Several officers call'd to get some refreshments, but none of consequence till the afternoon. Cousin P. and myself were sitting at the door; I in a green skirt, dark short gown, etc. Two genteel men of the military order rode up to the door: "Your servant, ladies," etc.; ask'd if they could have quarters for General Smallwood. Aunt F. thought she could accommodate them as well as most of her neighbors,—said they could. One of the officers dismounted, and wrote "Smallwood's Quarters" over the door, which secured us from straggling soldiers. After this he mounted his steed and rode away. When we were alone, our dress and lips were put in order for conquest, and the hopes of adventures gave brightness to each before passive countenance. . . . Dr. Gould usher'd the gentlemen into our parlour, and introduc'd them,—"General Smallwood, Captain Furnival, Major Stodard, Mr. Prig, Captain Finley, and Mr. Clagan, Colonel Wood, and Colonel Line." These last two did not come with the General. They are Virginians, and both indispos'd. The General and suite, are Marylanders. Be assur'd, I did not stay long with so many men, but secur'd a good retreat, heart-safe, so far. Some sup'd with us, others at Jesse's. They retir'd about ten, in good order. How new is our situation! I feel in good spirits, though surrounded by an army, the house full of officers, the yard alive with soldiers,— very peaceable sort of people, tho'. They eat like other folks, talk like them, and behave themselves with elegance; so I will not be afraid of them, that I won't. Adieu. I am going to my chamber to dream, I suppose, of bayonets and swords, sashes, guns, and epaulets.

# EXCHANGE

**1778**
**SARAH HODGKINS AND JOSEPH HODGKINS**

*Joseph Hodgkins (1743–1829) was a cobbler who lived in Ipswich, Massachusetts, and fought at Bunker Hill, Long Island, White Plains, and Princeton. By 1778, he had been made a captain and was suffering through the winter at Valley Forge. While he was gone, one of his three children died, and a fourth—a daughter conceived on a leave—was born. Joseph's wife, Sarah Perkins Hodgkins (1751?–1803), took his absence fairly stoically. But the four-year separation grew increasingly difficult. In the couple's letters to each other—more than a hundred survive—Joseph revealed the hardships and frustrations of life as a revolutionary soldier, and Sarah the hardships and frustrations of life as a revolutionary wife. Her fears for him notwithstanding, Joseph would not only survive the war but would live to see the fiftieth anniversary of the Battle of Bunker Hill.*

The "Defelties" (i.e., difficulties) that Joseph referred to were pregnancy and the birth of the daughter whom he would not see for months and whom he called "your child."

### JOSEPH TO SARAH

Valleyforge Camp   Jany ye 5 1778

My Dear   these fue Lines Bring my most affectionate Regards to you hoping they will find you & all friends in as good health as they Leave me at this time through the Goodness of god   I Received yours of the 15 of Decemr on Newyears Day and that of ye 7 Last Night and I am Rejoyced to hear that you have Been cumfortabley Carred through all the Defelties that you have Ben Called too in my absents   oh that we ware sencible of the goodness of god to us ward and ware more Devoted to his service   I wish I could have the sattisfaction of seeing you & our Children Esphaly my Little Darughters I am sorry to hear that the Babe is got that Distresing Coff But I hope god will appear for it & Rebuk its Disorder & Restore it to health again and give us an oppertunity of Rejoycing in his goodness

My Dear you say that you have not heard from me since the 17 of Octr   I Received your Letter of ye 17 Octor By the Post that minnet I left Albany & Could not Light of him afterwards to send By him   But I wrote about ye 16 Novemr from Kings farry & sent it By Capt Blasdon   But it seams you have not had that   But I have sent By Colol Colman a letter & some Cash wich I gudge you have Received By this time & have sent another By a Post since you say in your Letter of the 7 that you Depend on my Coming home if I am alive & well   But My Dear I thought when I wrote Last that I should not Try to get home this winter & wrote you some Reasons why I should not   But since I have Received your Letters & seeing you have made some Dependance upon my Coming home therefore out of Reguard to you I intend to Try to get a furlough in about a Month   But I am not sarting I shall Be sucksesfull in my attemptes therefore I would not have you Depend too much on it for if you should & I should fail of Coming the Disapointment would Be the Grater    But I will Tell you the Gratest incoredgement that I have of getting home that is I intend to Pertishion to the Genel for Liberty to go to New England to Tak the small Pox & if this Plan fails me I shall have But Little or no hope    I Believe I have as grate a Desire to Come home as you can Posibly have of having me for this winters Camppain Beats all for fatague & hardships that Ever I went through    But I have Ben Carred through it thus far & Desire to Be thankfull for it    we have got our hutts allmost Don for the men    But its Reported that Genl How intends to Come & See our new houses & give us a House warming    But if he should I hope we shall have all things Ready to Receive him & treet him in Every Respect according to his Desarts    you say you have Named your Child Martha & you Did not know weather I should Like the name    But I have nothing to say if it suts you I am content    I wish I could have the sattisfaction of seeing it    So I must conclude at this time By subscribing myself your most affectionate Companion Till Death

Joseph Hodgkins

### SARAH TO JOSEPH

Ipswich Februay ye 23 1778

My Dear after my tender regards to you I would inform you that I and my Children are in good health    I hope these lines will find you posest of the Same Blessing    I now set down to write between hope and fear hopeing you will come home before I get to the Bottom but fearing least you Should not come this winter    I heard of an oppertunity    Send a letter & I thoght I would not mis of it though you have of writing to me    Cousin Perkins told me he Saw you & you was well but he Says he don't think you will come home so he is but one of Jobs comforters    I was very glad to hear you was well but my Dear I must tell you a verbal Letter is what I Should hardly have expected from So near a freind at So greate a distance    it seems you are tired of writing    I am Sorry you count it troble to write to me Since that is all the way we can have of conversing together    I hope you will not be tired of receiveing letters    it is true you wrote a few days before but when you was nearer you wrote every day Sometimes    I was never tired of reading your Letters    I Long to See you    am looking for you every day    if you Should fail of comeing my troble will be grate surely it will be a troble indeed but I must hasten    I have a Sorryful piece of news to tell you    it is the Death of Cousin Ephraim Perkins   he died on his pasage from the west endies the fifth of January   he is much Lamented by all who know him

**JOSEPH TO SARAH**

                    Pennsylvania Head Quarters   April 17 1778
Loveing Wife these Lines Brings you my most afectionate Reguards hoping they will find you & our Children & all friends in as good health as they Leave me at this time through the goodness of god   I am Very well Now But since I wrote Last to you I have Ben a good Deal Trobled with the Rumetisen   But through mercy it is Left me & I feal harty   But I am Very uneasy in my mind about you for I am sarting that you have Long Looked for me home & I am affrade you will suffer for the Nesarys of Life for I am informed that these things are as Dear with you as they are hear & if that is the Case I wish you would Let me know it & if you Due suffer I am Determined to Come home and suffer with you   I Believe you think I Dont Care much about you as I Do not send any thing home   But my Dear You are always near my hart & in my thoughts   But I am sorry to inform you that I am obliged to spend grate Part of my wages or Ells I should suffer   But I should sent som money home Before now if I had not Expected to Come home myself Before this time   But I am all most out of Patience awaiting for things to Be settled so as I can get away on some terms or other which is my Determination to do as soon as Posibly I Can for the time seams as Long to me I Dare say as it does to you   there is a New arrangement of the army which is Likely to take Place sometime this Spring   we have Ben Expecting it to Come out Every Day for this month But the Reason it Dos not Come out is unknown to me   many officers were Very uneasey about the affair as many officers will Be obliged to Leave the sarvice   But for my Part Leaving the sarvice Dos not troble me for it will Be my Choice to Leave it   But to Be sent home without any Reason why is not agreable to me and if it should Be the Case I Believe I shall not troble the army much more   But when I think how I have spent three years in the war have Ben Exposed to Every hardship Venterd my Life & Limbs Broke my Constitution wore out all my Clothes & has got knothing for it & now not to be thanked for it seams two much for any man to Bare   no more of this for the Present   My Dear I Received your Letter By Mr Wescot the Post ye 21 of March & the 25 I wrote to you & sent it By a soldier that was gooing through Ipswich   But for fear it should Miscarry I would Just menchon that I have had the small Pox & all my men and they are all Pretty

well that Belong to Ipswich Except Josh Pettengill who has got the feavor    I
have sent By Mr Wescot the Post one hundred Dollars for which you may give
him your Recept & settle for the Postage which will Be one shilling on a pound
I have nothing more to write only I must Repeat my earnest Desire of seeing you
as soon as I Possibly Can & Beg you to make yourself as Contented as Possible
and now Commending you & my self & Children to the care of Kind Providence
hoping he will Presarve us while absent & in his good time give us an oppertunity of meeting to geather again which is the Harty Desire of him who is your
most affectionate & Loving Companion till Death

Joseph Hodgkins

Give my Duty to my Parence & Love to all friends    I Don't no But I must go
naked soon without I can get home But I would not have you send anything
without I send for it

### SARAH TO JOSEPH

Ipswich April ye 26 1778

My Dear
    these lines come with my afectionate regards to you hoping they will find you
in good health as they Leave me & the rest of my family at this time through the
goodness of God    but I am very full of trouble on account of your not comeing
home    I received your Letter of the 22 of febray by mr Horten    he told me you
was anoculated for the small pox a day a two before he came away    you wrote
me word you Should come home as soon as you could but did not set any time
when    I concluded you would come as Soon as you got well if you lived to get
well & I never heard a word from you Since till about ten days ago which you
must think gave me great uneasyness fearing how it was with you    Nat Treadwell
wrote a few lines home which they received about ten Days ago & he was So
kind as to Send word that you had had the Small pox & was got well which I was
rejoiced to hear and it gave me new corage to Look for you    but I have Looked
for you till I know not how to Look any longer    but I dont know how to give
over    your not writing to me gives me Some uneasyness for I am sure it is not
for want of oppertunitys to Send for I have heard of a number of oficers coming
home latly    I wrote to you by a post about two months ago & have had no returns Sence    I should be glad to know the reason of your not writing to me the
first oppertunity you have if it is not too much troble for you
    Monday afternoon    I am very Low in Spirits allmost despare of your coming

home   when I began I thought I would write but a few lines & begun upon a Small piece of paper but it is my old friend & I don't know how to leave off & Some is wrong end upwards & Some wright   if it was not that I have Some hope of your coming home yet I believe I Should write a vollum   I cant express what I feal but I forbear disapointments are alotted for me   So commiting you to the Care of kind providence I once more Subscribe myself your most afectionate Companion till Death

Sarah Hodgkins

PS Brother Perkins & sister Sends their love to you   Sister Chapman is got to bed with a fine Son   I have got a Sweet Babe almost Six months old but have got no father for it but Sally Stanwood

### 1778: JUNE
### ABIGAIL ADAMS TO JOHN QUINCY ADAMS

---

*Abigail and John Adams (see pages 28 and 30) had five children, of whom John Quincy Adams (1767–1848) was the second born and the eldest son. In 1778, he was accompanying his father for the first time on a diplomatic mission to Europe. It is hard to imagine that the recipient of Abigail's stern but expectant advice was just eleven years old.*

Abigail would die eight years before her son became president. The lines she quoted are again from Alexander Pope: "Vice is a monster of so frightful mien / As to be hated needs but to be seen; / Yet seen too oft, familiar with her face, / We first endure, then pity, then embrace." Despite what Abigail had heard, the Adamses' ship had landed safely, but not before encountering a violent storm, capturing a British ship, and losing one lieutenant to friendly fire.

June, 1778

My Dear Son,

    'Tis almost four months since you left your native land and embarked upon the mighty waters, in quest of a foreign country. Although I have not particularly written to you since, yet you may be assured you have constantly been upon my heart and mind.

    It is a very difficult task, my dear son, for a tender parent to bring her mind to part with a child of your years going to a distant land; nor could I have acquiesced in such a separation under any other care than that of the most excellent parent and guardian who accompanied you. You have arrived at years capable of improving under the advantages you will be likely to have, if you do but properly attend to them They are talents put into your hands, of which an account will be required of you hereafter; and being possessed of one, two, or four, see to it that you double your numbers.

The most amiable and most useful disposition in a young mind is diffidence of itself; and this should lead you to seek advice and instruction from him, who is your natural guardian, and will always counsel and direct you in the best manner, both for your present and future happiness. You are in possession of a natural good understanding, and of spirits unbroken by adversity and untamed with care. Improve your understanding by acquiring useful knowledge and virtue, such as will render you an ornament to society, an honor to your country, and a blessing to your parents. Great learning and superior abilities, should you ever possess them, will be of little value and small estimation, unless virtue, honor, truth, and integrity are added to them. Adhere to those religious sentiments and principles which were early instilled into your mind, and remember that you are accountable to your Maker for all your words and actions.

Let me enjoin it upon you to attend constantly and steadfastly to the precepts and instructions of your father, as you value the happiness of your mother and your own welfare. His care and attention to you render many things unnecessary for me to write, which I might otherwise do; but the inadvertency and heedlessness of youth require line upon line and precept upon precept, and, when enforced by the efforts of both parents, will, I hope, have a due influence upon your conduct; for, dear as you are to me, I would much rather you should have found your grave in the ocean you have crossed, or that any untimely death crop you in your infant years, than see you an immoral, profligate, or graceless child.

You have entered early in life upon the great theatre of the world, which is full of temptations and vice of every kind. You are not wholly unacquainted with history, in which you have read of crimes which your inexperienced mind could scarcely believe credible. You have been taught to think of them with horror, and to view vice as

> "a monster of so frightful mien
> That, to be hated, needs but to be seen."

Yet you must keep a strict guard upon yourself, or the odious monster will soon lose its terror by becoming familiar to you. The modern history of our own times, furnishes as black a list of crimes, as can be paralleled in ancient times, even if we go back to Nero, Caligula, or Caesar Borgia. Young as you are, the cruel war, into which we have been compelled by the haughty tyrant of Britain and the bloody emissaries of his vengeance, may stamp upon your mind this certain truth, that the welfare and prosperity of all countries, communities, and, I may add, individuals, depend upon their morals. That nation to which we were once united, as it has departed from justice, eluded and subverted the wise laws which formerly governed it, and suffered the worst of crimes to go unpunished, has lost its valor, wisdom and humanity, and, from being the dread and terror of Europe, has sunk into derision and infamy.

But, to quit political subjects, I have been greatly anxious for your safety, having never heard of the frigate since she sailed, till, about a week ago, a New York paper informed, that she was taken and carried into Plymouth. I did not fully credit this report, though it gave me much uneasiness. I yesterday heard that a French vessel was arrived at Portsmouth, which brought news of the safe arrival of the Boston; but this wants confirmation. I hope it will not be long before I shall be assured of your safety. You must write me an account of your voyage, of your situation, and of every thing entertaining you can recollect.

Be assured I am most affectionately yours,

### 1778: JUNE 3
### SALLY WISTER TO DEBORAH NORRIS

---

*The Quaker teenager (see page 41) continued her story—and her flirting. Somewhat surprisingly, according to an 1885 historical journal, Wister died unmarried. "Her manners," the editor wrote, "became quite serious after she grew to womanhood."*
Sally's quote was from "The Duel of Menelaus and Paris" by the ever-popular Alexander Pope: ". . . the beauteous Paris came: / In form a God! . . . His bended bow across his shoulders flung, / His sword beside him negligently hung." "Sister H." was Sally's ten-year-old sister, Hannah.

Fourth Day, Morn, 12 o'clock.

I was awaken'd this morn with a great racket of the Captain's servant calling him; but the lazy fellow never rose till about half an hour past eight. This his daylight ride. I imagin'd they would be gone before now, so I dressed in a green skirt and dark short gown. Provoking. So down I came, this Captain (wild wretch) standing at the back door. He bow'd and call'd me. I only look'd, and went to breakfast. About nine I took my work and seated myself in the parlour. Not long had I sat, when in came Dandridge,—the handsomest man in existence, at least that I had ever seen. But stop here, while I just say, the night before, chatting upon dress, he said he had no patience with those officers who, every morn, before they went on detachments, would wait to be dress'd and powder'd. "I am," said I, "excessively fond of powder, and think it very becoming." "Are you?" he reply'd. "I am very careless, as often wearing my cap thus" (turning the back part before) "as any way." I left off where he came in. He was powder'd very white, a (pretty colored) brown coat, lapell'd with green, and white waistcoat, etc., and his

> "Sword beside him negligently hung."

He made a truly elegant figure. "Good morning, Miss Sally. You are very well, I hope." "Very well. Pray sit down," which he did, close by me. "Oh, dear," said I, "I see thee is powder'd." "Yes, ma'am. I have dress'd myself off for you." Will I be excused, Debby, if I look upon his being powder'd in the light of a compliment to me? "Yes, Sally, as thee is a country maid, and don't often meet with compliments." Saucy Debby Norris!

'Tis impossible to write a regular account of our conversation. Be it sufficient to say that we had a multiplicity of chat.

About an hour since, sister H. came to me and said Captain Dandridge was in the parlour, and had ask'd for me. I went in. He met me, caught my hands. "Oh, Miss Sally, I have a beautiful sweetheart for you." "Poh! ridiculous! Loose my hands." "Well, but don't be so cross." "Who is he?" "Major Clough. I have seen him. Ain't he pretty, to be sure? I am going to headquarters. Have you any commands there?" "None at all; but" (recollecting), "yes, I have. Pray, who is your commanding officer?" "Colonel Bland, ma'am." "Please give my compliments to him, and I shou'd be glad if he would send thee back with a little more manners." He reply'd wickedly, and told me I had a little spiteful heart. But he was intolerably saucy; said he never met with such ladies. "You're very ill-natur'd, Sally." And, putting on the sauciest face, "Sally, if Tacy V*nd*r*n won't have me, will you?" "No, really; none of her discarded lovers." "But, provided I prefer you to her, will you consent?" "No, I won't." "Very well, madam." And after saying he would return to-morrow, among a hundred other things, he elegantly walk'd out of the room. Soon he came back, took up a volume of Homer's Iliad, and read to us. He reads very well, and with judgment. One remark he made, that I will relate, on these lines,—

> While Greece a heavy, thick retreat maintains,
> Wedg'd in one body, like a flight of cranes."

"G–d knows our army don't do so. I wish they did." He laugh'd and went away.

## 1778: JUNE 16
## BATHSHEBA SPOONER TO THE HONORABLE COUNCIL OF THE STATE OF MASSACHUSETTS BAY

*Bathsheba (also known as "Bathshua") Ruggles (1743–1778) married Joshua Spooner in 1766. Twelve years and four children later, with the help of three soldiers, she murdered him and stuffed him down a well. After the four of them—including Spooner's lover, a seventeen-year-old Continental soldier named Ezra Ross—were sentenced to death, Spooner wrote this plea from her Worcester jail on behalf of her unborn child. She was examined, apparently quite painfully, by two different panels of women, who concluded almost unanimously that she was lying about her pregnancy. The council rejected Spooner's petition, and on July 2, before a crowd of five thousand people, she was hanged. The autopsy that she had requested revealed a five-month-old male fetus, and her story became one of the most infamous in early American history.*

May it please Your Honors

With unfeigned gratitude I acknowledge the favor you lately granted me of a reprieve. I must beg leave, once more, humbly to lie at your feet, and to represent to you that, though the jury of matrons that were appointed to examine into my case have not brought in my favor, yet that I am absolutely certain of being in a pregnant state, and above four months advanced in it, and the infant I bear was lawfully begotten. I am earnestly desirous of being spared till I shall be delivered of it. I must humbly desire your honors, notwithstanding my great unworthiness, to take my deplorable case into your compassionate consideration. What I bear, and clearly perceive to be animated, is innocent of the faults of her who bears it, and has, I beg leave to say, a right to the existence which God has begun to give it. Your honors' humane Christian principles, I am very certain, must lead you to desire to preserve life, even in this its miniature state, rather than destroy it. Suffer me, therefore, with all earnestness, to beseech your honors to grant me such a further length of time, at least, as that there may be the fairest and fullest opportunity to have the matter fully ascertained; and as in duty bound, shall, during my short continuance, pray,

Bathshua Spooner,
Worcester Gaol
June 16, 1778

### 1778: CIRCA DECEMBER
### MARY BOON TO WILLIAM BOON

---

*William Boon was first mate on board the hundred-ton merchant ship* Rover, *which sailed back and forth between South Carolina and St. Thomas. When the* Rover *was captured by the British in 1778, several notes from William's apparently scorned wife, Mary, were found on board. In one of them, she wrote: "When I met you it was with a entent of making you hapy, and to see which of [us] cold make ech Eother the hapyest." In the note below, she gave up appeals to sentiment and— proving that emotions have no vintage—went for threats instead.*

Mrs. Suter was the wife of the ship's master.

My dear Husband

I have reseved your Kind faver and am mutch Ablidge to you for your Kind advise but you may Depend that I will take Such care that i will bee Defend^d to man Kind   for to Say Mrs. Boon has a son that is Rong   you will be sow Kind as to Send the pin that you Stoal from me the last Knight   if you do Knot gow out no more.

I remain your wife<br>Boon

I hope you dow Knot take it by turnes with mrs. Suter but if you let Me com aboard i will make the brig to hot for her and you both

### 1779: SUMMER
### MARY LUCIA BULL TO SUSANNA STOLL

---

*After almost four years of fighting, the British had managed to secure footholds only on Manhattan and in Newport, Rhode Island. Shifting their hopes and their operations to the south, they landed thirty-five hundred men in December of 1778 near Savannah, Georgia, prompting the surrender first of the city and then of the state. Britain's Augustine Prevost next crossed the Savannah River and marched toward Charleston, South Carolina, which was where Mary Lucia Bull (1723–1796) was living when she sent this letter to her friend Susanna Stoll.*

Prevost's campaign was stopped by General Benjamin Lincoln. But a year later, a renewed effort would succeed, and the capture of Charleston would be America's greatest single defeat in the war. "Sukey" was a nickname for Susanna. Prince William Parish was near the southern tip of South Carolina. "Pon-Pon" was the Indian name for the Edisto River. Ashley Ferry was a heavily fortified town on the Ashley River near Charleston.

Many thanks my Dr. Sukey, for your kind inquiry's about me & still more thanks for acquainting me of your situation. We left Prince Williams the day after you parted with us. My Brother attempted bringing his Negroes with him, but we were obliged to leave them in Pon pon River, from whence they returned home; thear was a few put on board Mr. River's Schooner—which arrived safe in Charles-Town; Nancy & self have six among them, they went about the Town for their victuals. We have our two maids with us; Mariah is with the rest of our negroes at Oakatees, (I believe,) under the care of Mr. Flower & Mr. M. Garvey. It is impossible for me to describe to you what I felt, while the British Army was on this side Ashley-Ferry, we never went in to our beds at night, had Candles constantly burning & were alarmed at every noise that we heard. Mrs. Bull was plundered of some of her clothes, my Aunt Bellinger's Chamber door was burst open & a great many of her things taken, in short everybody in the House lost something except Nancy & myself. As soon as we saw them taking things about the House we went into our Chamber, had the window shut & stood against the door, (for it could not lock.) One Man came & turned the Brass but did not push against it hard enough to find out it was not lock'd. But, good Heavens, my Sukey, think what we must have suffered when a parcel of Indians came bolting into the House, as for my part, I expected nothing but death, & indeed, at that moment it was indifferent to me whether I lived or died, yet I could not bear the thought of being murder'd by the Savages. One of the British Colonels came to the House, we told him we were very uneasy about the Indians & common Soldiers, he was sorry they disturbed us, (he said), but we had better fee him to stay with us, for he had good spirits, cou'd sing a good Song & had a deal of chitty-chatty, Whether he said that to divert us, (for we were very dull) or whether he felt as little for our distress as he appeared to do, I will not undertake to say. You ask me what we intend doing—that is a question that I know not how to answer. I am as yet quite undetermined what to do. I wait for my brother's advice, who is at the Indian-Land. Mrs. Kelsall (my brother informed me) has invited us to go to Georgia, but I see no possibility of our accepting his invitation. I am very glad to hear your Mamma has been so lucky, please remember us all kindly to her, if you have any opportunity of writing to her; I wish, my Sukey, I knew how to go & see you before you go to River-May, I would not mind your being at a Strangers, I believe I would jump up behind Isaac now, if Nancy would let me, but she wants to see you as much as I do, & she is so selfish she won't let me have the pleasure of seeing you alone.

And now, my Sukey, I must beg that you will not be uneasy about me, I am as happy as your absence and the times will permit me to be. Mrs. Bull, Nancy & Miss Polly Cameron desire to be remembered to you. I remain your unchangeable Friend,

> Mary Lucia Bull.

P.S.—Mrs Garvey & Miss Cameron stay'd at Prince William's.

## 1779: WINTER
## JULIANA SMITH TO BETSEY

---

*Thanksgiving as originally celebrated by the Puritans was not a single day, but, like other days of fasting or feasting, could be held anytime there was something to be grateful for. As a fixed national holiday that recalled the Pilgrims' famous harvest meal with the Indians, Thanksgiving would not come into its own until the nineteenth century (see page 303). In the meantime, thanksgiving days continued to be inspired by current events, and in October of 1779, Congress recommended that December 9 be set aside as "a day of public and solemn thanksgiving." Though the tradition held that the day should be spent, like a Sunday, in neither work nor play, it clearly involved both for eighteen-year-old Juliana Smith (1761–1823). Daughter of a minister, Juliana offered this spirited description to an absent cousin, ignoring the topic of war except insofar as it was responsible for the absence of some items from the holiday table.*

The Smiths lived in Sharon, Connecticut. "The five of us" referred to Juliana's siblings and herself. Most of the others at the table were orphans who were taught and cared for by her parents. Juliana would grow up to marry Jacob Radcliff, a future mayor of New York.

Dear Cousin Betsey,

When Thanksgiving Day was approaching, our dear Grandmother Smith, who is sometimes a little desponding of Spirit as you well know, did her best to persuade us that it would be better to make it a Day of Fasting & Prayer in view of the <u>Wickedness of our Friends & the Vileness of our Enemies</u>, I am sure you can hear Grandmother say that and see her shake her cap border. But indeed there was some occasion for her remarks, for our resistance to an <u>unjust Authority</u> has cost our beautiful Coast Towns very dear the last year & all of us have had much to suffer. But my dear Father brought her to a more proper frame of

Mind, so that by the time the Day came she was ready to enjoy it almost as well as Grandmother Worthington did, & she, you will remember, always sees the bright side. In the mean while we had all of us been working hard to get all things in readiness to do honour to the Day.

This year it was Uncle Simeon's turn to have the dinner at his house, but of course we all helped them as they help us when it is our turn, & there is always enough for us all to do. All the baking of pies & cakes was done at our house & we had the big oven heated & filled twice each day for three days before it was all done & <u>everything was</u> GOOD, though we did have to do without some things that ought to be used. Neither Love nor (paper) Money could buy Raisins, but our good red cherries dried without the pits, did almost as well & happily Uncle Simeon still had some spices in store. The tables were set in the Dining Hall and even that big room had no space to spare when we were all seated. The Servants had enough ado to get around the Tables & serve us all without over-setting things. There were our two Grandmothers side by side. They are always handsome old Ladies, but now, many thought, they were hand-somer than ever, & happy they were to look around upon so many of their de-scendants. Uncle & Aunt Simeon presided at one Table, & Father & Mother at the other. Besides us five boys & girls there were two of the Gales & three Elmers, besides James Browne & Ephraim Cowles. We had them at our table because they could be best <u>supervised</u> there. Most of the students had gone to their own homes for the week, but Mr. Skiff & Mr. ———— were too far away from their homes. They sat at Uncle Simeon's table & so did Uncle Paul & his family, five of them in all, & Cousins Phin & Poll. Then there were six of the Livingston family next door. They had never seen a Thanksgiving Dinner before, having been used to keep Christmas Day instead, as is the wont in New York Province. Then there were four Old Ladies who have no longer Homes or Chil-dren of their own & so came to us. They were invited by my Mother, but Uncle and Aunt Simeon wished it so.

Of course we could have no Roast Beef. None of us have tasted Beef these three years back as it must all go to the Army, & too little they get, poor fellows. But, Nayquittymaw's Hunters were able to get us a fine red Deer, so that we had a good haunch of Venisson on each Table. These were balanced by huge Chines of Roast Pork at the other ends of the tables. Then there was on one a big Roast Turkey & on the other a Goose, & two big Pigeon Pasties. Then there was an abundance of good Vegetables of all the old sorts & one which I do not believe you have yet seen. Uncle Simeon had imported the Seede from England just be-fore the War began & only this year was there enough for Table use. It is called

Sellery & you eat it without cooking. It is very good served with meats. Next year Uncle Simeon says he will be able to raise enough to give us all some. It has to be taken up roots & all & buried in earth in the cellar through the winter & only pulling up some when you want it to use.

Our Mince Pies were good although we had to use dried Cherries as I told you, & the meat was shoulder of Venisson, instead of beef. The Pumpkin Pies, Apple Tarts & big Indian Puddings lacked for nothing save <u>Appetite</u> by the time we got round to them.

Of course we had no Wine. Uncle Simeon has still a cask or two, but it must be saved for the sick, & indeed, for those who are well, good Cider is a sufficient Substitute. There is no Plumb Pudding, but a boiled Suet Pudding, stirred thick with dried Plumbs & Cherries, was called by the old Name & answered the purpose. All the other spice had been used in the Mince pies, so for this Pudding we used a jar of West India preserved Ginger which chanced to be left of the last shipment which Uncle Simeon had from there, we chopped up the Ginger small and stirred it through with the Plumbs & Cherries. It was <u>extraordinary</u> good. The Day was bitter cold & when we got home from Meeting, which Father did not keep over long by reason of the cold, we were glad eno' of the fire in Uncle's Dining Hall, but by the time the dinner was one half over those of us who were on the fire side of one Table was forced to get up & carry our plates with us around to the far side of the other Table, while those who had sat there were as glad to bring their plates around to the fire side to get warm. All but the Old Ladies who had a screen put behind their chairs.

Uncle Simeon was in his best mood, and you know how good that is! He kept both Tables in a roar of laughter with his droll stories of the days when he was studying medicine in Edinborough, & afterwards he & Father & Uncle Paul joined in singing Hymns & Ballads. You know how fine their voices go together. Then we all sang a Hymn and afterwards my dear Father led us in prayer, remembering all Absent Friends before the Throne of Grace, & much I wished that my dear Betsey was here as one of us, as she has been of yore.

We did not rise from the Table until it was quite dark, & then when the dishes had been cleared away we all got round the fire as close as we could, & cracked nuts, & sang songs & told stories. At least some told & others listened. <u>You know nobody</u> can exceed the two Grandmothers at telling tales of all the things they have seen themselves, & repeating those of the early years of New England, & even some in the Old England, which they had heard in their youth from their Elders. My Father says it is a goodly custom to hand down all worthy deeds & traditions from Father to Son, as the Israelites were commanded to do about the

Passover & as the Indians here have always done, because the Word that is spoken is remembered longer than the one that is written. . . . Brother Jack, who did
not reach here until late on Wednesday though he had left College very early on
Monday Morning & rode with all due diligence considering the snow, brought
an orange to each of the Grand-Mothers, but, Alas! they were frozen in his saddle bags. We soaked the frost out in cold water, but I guess they wasn't as good
as they should have been.

### 1780: JUNE 30
### ANNA RAWLE TO REBECCA SHOEMAKER

_____

*For most of the war, the only organized contributions by women were the signing of
petitions and the carrying out of boycotts. But after the fall of Charleston, Esther
Reed (see page 58) formed the Ladies Association of Philadelphia, the first major
volunteer group in America. Though the women in the group eventually raised
more than $300,000 in Continental money, they were a source of major derision for
Tory Quaker Anna Rawle (1757–1828), who described their fundraising efforts
in this rather catty letter to her mother, Rebecca Warner Rawle Shoemaker
(1725?–1819).*

The "genteel women" Rawle named were hardly alone; among the dozens who collected funds
were Benjamin Franklin's daughter and Benjamin Rush's wife.

June 30th 1780.

My dear Mother,—

   Tho' so little in the house belonged to us, packing them up furnished employ
for several mornings; one day, when thus engaged up stairs, Polly Birk, who was
the only person with me in the house, exclaimed, "Bless me if there is not a
whole company of soldiers at Mr. S——'s door!" I was frightened, and was going
down to my Aunt and Sister, when at the foot of the stairs I observed a man
placed, rattling the lock of his gun, as if trying to alarm—I ran up again, and in a
few minutes two men entered the room, and I soon found their business was to
search for arms. They looked in the closet, and desired me, not in the mildest
terms, to unlock my trunks. I told them they were already undone. They then
put their canes in, and by the greatest good luck in the world, the little plate
that belongs to me remained undisturbed at the bottom of the trunk; they would
have taken it, I am certain from their behaviour. Not finding arms they went
away—they treated my Aunt in the same manner, rummaging the closets and
draws, and placing a guard at the stairs. One of them said, when Peggy went up,

that it was to hide guns. There was but one or two houses where they treated people with so little ceremony; at other places they took there word.

But of all absurdities the Ladies going about for money exceeded everything; they were so extremely importunate that people were obliged to give them something to get rid of them. Mrs. Beech and the set with her, came up to our door the morning after thee went, and turned back again. The reason she gave to a person who told me was that she did not chuse to face Mrs. S. or her daughters.

H. Thompson, Mrs. Morris, Mrs. Wilson, and a number of very genteel women, paraded about the streets in this manner, some carrying ink stands, nor did they let the meanest ale house escape. The gentlemen also were honored with their visits. Bob Wharton declares he was never so teized in his life. They reminded him of the extreme rudeness of refusing anything to the fair, but he was inexorable and pleaded want of money, and the heavy taxes, so at length they left him, after threatening to hand his name down to posterity with infamy. I fancy they raised a considerable sum by this extorted contribution, some giving solely against their inclinations thro' fear of what might happen if they refused, and others to avoid importunities they could not otherwise satisfy— importunities carried to such an excess of meaness as the nobleness of no cause whatsoever could excuse.

A. R.

The freedom I have spoken with in this letter I know must not be used again— do not be uneasy we shall be cautious.

## 1780: JULY 31
## ESTHER REED TO GEORGE WASHINGTON

*Wife of George Washington's adjutant general and mother of five young children, Esther DeBerdt Reed (1746–1780) was determined that the money raised by her Ladies Association of Philadelphia not be spent on arms, food, or uniforms, but be given to the soldiers directly in cash. To her great dismay, General Washington (1732–1799) confessed he was afraid that the men would drink the money away; he asked that the women make shirts instead. The letter below records Reed's protest.*

Reed and the group ultimately did acquiesce and make more than two thousand shirts. She would die of dysentery at the age of thirty-four, before the project was complete.

Banks of Schuylkill, July 31st, 1780.

Sir,

Ever since I received your Excellency's favour of the 20th of this month, I have been endeavouring to procure the linen for the use of the soldiers, and it was not till Saturday last I have been able to meet with any fit for the purpose, it being unavoidably delayed so long. I have been informed of some circumstances, which I beg leave to mention, and from which perhaps the necessity for shirts may have ceased; one is the supply of 2000 sent from this State to their line, and the other, that a considerable number is arrived in the French fleet, for the use of the army in general. Together with these, an idea prevails among the ladies, that the soldiers will not be so much gratified, by bestowing an article to which they are entitled from the public, as in some other method which will convey more fully the idea of a reward for past services, and an incitement to future duty. Those who are of this opinion propose the whole of the money to be changed into hard dollars, and giving each soldier two, to be entirely at his own disposal. This method I hint only, but would not, by any means wish to adopt it or any other, without your full approbation. If it should meet with your concurrence, the State of Pennsylvania will take the linen I have purchased, and, as far as respects their own line, will make up any deficiency of shirts to them, which they suppose will not be many after the fresh supplies are received. If, after all, the necessity for shirts, which, though it may cease, as to the Pennsylvania Troops, may still continue to other parts of the army, the ladies will immediately make up the linen we have, which I think can soon be effected, and forward them to camp, and procure more as soon as possible, having kept in hand the hard money I have received, until I receive your reply. . . .

> I have the honour to be, dear Sir,
> With the highestest esteem,
> Your obedient servant,
> E. Reed.

## 1781: APRIL
## ABIGAIL DE HART TO PEGGY MARSHALL

*Elizabethtown, New Jersey, had been the site of two battles the previous year, but in this gossipy letter to a friend, twenty-year-old Abigail De Hart (1761–1842) seemed far less concerned with military than with romantic developments.*

Just a few years later, De Hart would marry Colonel John Mayo, who built a bridge over the

James River; their daughter Maria would in turn one day marry General Winfield Scott. The Shades was an isolated neighborhood in nearby Weehawken.

Elizabeth Town, April, 1781

Methinks there is an unusual coldness in your style, Peggy, you say you will visit us when <u>convenient</u>—how cool! I know very well that it is not in your temper to be ever making professions and I love you the better for it, but there was a <u>freeness</u> in your letters that was very pleasing. Let not distance lessen the affection I have been so long flattered with. You enquire who are the ladies that ask about you in this town—the answer is short—all, particularly Miss Chandler. She has been deeply distressed for the death of her brother, but the account is happily contradicted and cheerfulness has taken the place of melancholy. Nelly Noel is not one whit changed. She is very intimate with one Miss Bross, daughter-in-law to Major Adams that Billy Lawrence talks of. I saw her yesterday at Noel's for the first time—I only just saw her for she spoke not a word. Indeed I was glad that she did not open her mouth, for she so perfectly resembles the idea of a lioness that if I had seen her jaws move I should have given up my head for lost, and may be had died of Terror. You wonder how Jelf can live in the Shades as she does. I am surprised at it too. She can have no lover up there unless it is poor Sam Hackett, who I hear visits her often, but he is too enamored of the flowing bowl to admit a thought of even Miss Jelf's bright eyes. Susan Livingston has been fortunate, twice a bridesmaid in one season; when does she return to Jersey? Susan Livingston from Princeton is at Major Adams's, I called on her yesterday. She is a clever grave girl enough, vivacity does not tempt her to say indiscreet things—I say nothing of her beauty, you have seen it.

Not a single Beau in Town and what is worse no prospect of any. Now and then we see something that some of our ladies call gallants, but we have too little taste to honor 'em with that appelation, perhaps we have not sufficient discernment to see that they are <u>smart</u>—I console myself, I know you would join us. In pity, you who have so many, send us one to cheer us solitary girls.

### 1781: NOVEMBER
### ELIZABETH JACKSON TO ANDREW JACKSON

*Elizabeth Hutchinson Jackson (1740?–1781) arrived in America in 1765 and became a widow just two years later. During the war, she lost two of her three sons, the first in the aftermath of a skirmish with the British, the second to smallpox. In 1781, she managed to nurse her remaining child, fourteen-year-old Andrew Jackson*

*(1767–1845), through his own bout of smallpox. She then traveled to Charleston to nurse prisoners on board a ship, but contracted yellow fever and died. This letter was her last message to the man who would grow up to be the seventh president of the United States. He would quote these words to some military colleagues more than three decades after his mother's death.*

Andrew—

If I should not see you again I wish you to remember and treasure up some things I have already said to you: in this world you will have to make your own way. To do that you must have friends. You can make friends by being honest, and you can keep them by being steadfast. You must keep in mind that friends worth having will in the long run expect as much from you as they give to you.

To forget an obligation or be ungrateful for a kindness is a base crime—not merely a fault or a sin but an actual crime. Men guilty of it sooner or later must suffer the penalty.

In personal conduct always be polite, but never obsequious. No one will respect you more than you esteem yourself. Avoid quarrels as long as you can without yielding to imposition. But sustain your manhood always.

Never bring a suit in law for assault and battery or for defamation. The law affords no remedy for such outrages that can satisfy the feelings of a true man.

Never wound the feelings of others. If ever you have to vindicate your feelings or defend your honor, do it calmly. If angry at first, wait till your wrath cools before you proceed.

## 1782
## JULIANA SMITH TO JOHN SMITH

---

*In the enthusiasm of Juliana Smith (see page 54), the desire to keep up with the times may seem perfectly current. But the exotic object she requested from her younger brother, John Cotton Smith (1765–1845), would soon come to be known— without much fanfare—as the toothbrush.*
Until the toothbrush became popular in France in the eighteenth century, the accepted tool for cleaning teeth was a twig with one end mashed into a bristly surface.

Peggy Evertson has showed me a present her father brought her from Albany. It is a brush for the teeth made of fine, stiff, white bristles set in a back of mother of pearl. It is better than the sassafras twigs which Tite Caesar fringes out for us, because with the brush you can better cleanse the backs of the teeth.

You wanted to know what you should bring me from New Haven when you come back, so I write about this, if so be you might find me one. Only it need not have so fine a back, one of wood or horn would please me very well.

## 1782
## ELIZA WILKINSON TO MARY PORCHER

*Wed at seventeen, Eliza Yonge Wilkinson (1757–1813?) was widowed in her first year of marriage, then gave birth to a son who died in infancy. Returning to her father's plantation on Yonge's Island, thirty miles from Charleston, South Carolina, she found that her initial awe of the British soon changed to fear and disgust. Her letter reflects a distinctive feature of colonial warfare, whereby either army might descend upon people's homes.*

The end of the war would not come until September of 1783. Eventually Eliza remarried and had four children. The poetry was from Homer's *Iliad* (translator: Alexander Pope). Tory Daniel McGirth would be infamous for the path of destruction he cut through Georgia.

I seem to have an inexhaustible fund just now for letter writing; but it will amuse your leisure hours, and that hope encourages me to proceed. Without further preamble, I will present you with another scene, where my Father and Mother were spectators, and also sufferers. It was likewise on the 3d of June that my Father, with an old man who lived a few miles from him, and whose head was silvered o'er with age, (one Mr. Bryant,) was sitting in the Piazza, when they saw a party of men—some in red, others in green, coming up to the house furiously; the moment they arrived, they jumped from their horses, and ran into the house with drawn swords and pistols, and began to curse and abuse Father and the other man very much; indeed, took his buckles from his shoes, searched his pockets, and took all they found there; they then went to search Mr. Bryant's pockets; he threw his top jacket aside, and producing his under-one, "Here," said he, "I'm a poor old man," (he was so, sure enough.) They searched, but I believe found nothing, for by a lucky thought the "poor old man" saved several hundred pounds, by carelessly casting aside his top jacket, as if it had no pockets in it. They then went in the rooms up and down stairs, demolished two sets of drawers, and took all they could conveniently carry off. One came to search Mother's pockets too, (audacious fellow!) but she resolutely threw his hand aside. "If you must see what's in my pocket, I'll show you myself;" and she took out a thread-case, which had thread, needles, pins, tape, &c. &c. The mean wretch took it from her. They even took her two little children's caps, hats, &c. &c.; and when they took Mother's thread, &c. she asked them what they did with such things, which must be useless to them? "Why, Nancy would want them." They then began to insult Father again in the most abusive manner. "Aye," says one, "I told you yesterday how you'd be used if you did not take a protection! But you would not hear me; you would not do as I told you, now you see what you have got by it." "Why," said Mother, in a jeering way, "is going about plundering women and children, taking the State?" "I suppose you think you are doing your king a great piece of service by these actions, which are very noble, to be sure; but you are mistaken—'twill only enrage the people; I think you'd much better go and fight the men, than go about the country robbing helpless women and children; that would be doing something." "O! you are all, every one of you, rebels! and, old fellow," (to Father,) "I have a great mind to blow my pistol through your head." Another made a pass at him, (inhuman monsters—I have no patience to relate it,) with his sword, swearing he had "a great mind," too, to run him through the body.

What callous-hearted wretches must these be, thus to treat those who rather demanded their protection and support. Grey hairs have always commanded respect and reverence until now; but these vile creatures choose the aged and helpless for the objects of their insults and barbarity. But what, think you, must have been my Father's feelings at the time! used in such a manner, and not having it in his power to resent it; what a painful conflict must at that instant have filled his breast. He once or twice, (I heard him say afterwards,) was on the verge of attempting to defend himself and property; his breast was torn with the most violent agitations; but when he considered his helpless situation, and that certain death must ensue, he forbore, and silently submitted to their revilings and insults. It reminds me of poor old Priam, King of Troy, when he says,

> "As for my sons! I thank ye, Gods—'twas well—
> Well—they have perished, for in fight they fell.
> Who dies in youth and vigor, dies the best,
> Cover'd with wounds, all honest, on the breast,
> But when the Fates, in fury of their rage,
> Spurn the hoar head of <u>unresisting age</u>,
> This, this is misery, the last, the worst,
> That man can feel—man fated to be curst."

I think those are the lines; it is a great while since I read them.

But to proceed. After drinking all the wine, rum, &c. they could find, and inviting the negroes they had with them, who were very insolent, to do the same; they went to their horses, and would shake hands with Father and Mother before their departure. Did you ever hear the like? Fine amends, to be sure! a bitter pill covered with gold, and so a shake of the hand was to make them ample satisfaction for all their sufferings! But the "iron hand of Justice" will overtake them sooner or later. Though <u>slow</u>, it is <u>sure</u>.

After they were gone, poor old Bryant began to bless his stars for saving his money, and to applaud himself for his lucky invention; he was too loud with it; Father admonished him to speak lower, for, should any of the servants about the house hear him, and another party come, he might stand a chance to lose it after all; but still the old man kept chatting on, when lo! another company of horsemen appeared in view: the poor soul was panic-struck, he looked aghast, and became mute: these were M'Girth's men, who had just left <u>us</u>. They did not behave quite so civil to Mother as they did to us; for they took sugar, flour, butter, and such things from her; but not much. These particulars I had from Mother. And now, my dear, I'll conclude here; I expect company to spend the day, so will defer ending my long story till the next leisure hour, and will then have another epistolary chat with you. Adieu.

Eliza.

## 1782: MAY 6

## ELIZABETH FORBES TO THE NORTH CAROLINA ASSEMBLY

*Roughly six thousand American soldiers were wounded during the American Revolution, and another forty-five hundred were killed in battle. Like countless other war widows throughout the thirteen states, Elizabeth Forbes had no automatic legal right to her husband's funds, and thus was required to petition her local legislature to transfer his pension to herself and her six children.*

The Battle of Guilford Courthouse, in which Elizabeth's husband, Arthur, died, was the largest of the war in the South. Fought in Greensboro, North Carolina, it seriously weakened the British troops and led to their withdrawal from the Carolinas. Pension laws were constantly being revised throughout the Revolution to add incentive for enlistment. In Forbes's case, the legislature granted only "twenty-five barrels of Corn . . . for the year 1782, and the like Quantity . . . for 1783."

The Petition of Elizabeth Forbes humbly Sheweth

That your Petitioner formerly with the help of a Loving and Industrious Husband lived without being under the necessity of troubling your Honourable Body with either Petition or Remonstrance but my circumstances are so at present that I must trouble your Honourable Body with a small account of my distressed condition. It is well known by all the Friends of America in this County that your Petitioner's Husband from the commencement of this unnatural war has distinguished himself as a true friend to the American Cause, and that he was always ready and willing to go when called, in difence of his Country, and being in Service on the fifteenth of March in the year 1781 at the Battle of Guilford Court House where he received a mortal wound of which he afterward died. And your Petitioner being left with a helpless family of Small children is at this time in great distress. Your petitioner therefore humbly prays that your Honours would take her distressed condition into consideration and grant her such relief as your Hnour's think she stands in need of and your Petitioner as in duty bound shall ever pray &c.

## 1785: AUGUST 5
## MOLLY TILGHMAN TO POLLY PEARCE

*Mary ("Molly") Tilghman (1771?–?) and her cousin Mary ("Polly") Pearce (1762–1850) were both members of an extended and venerable Maryland family. Molly's father was an established lawyer; her brothers included a staunch British Loyalist and a general who was Washington's aide-de-camp. Polly's father was the presiding justice of the Cecil County court. The slight irreverence of Molly's tone, as she settles in for a good long gossip, suggests that none of this impressed her in the least.*

Molly's reference to an air balloon was timely: The first flight of one (it had carried a sheep, a duck, and a rooster) had occurred just two years before. Perry and Matt Tilghman and John Francis were all first cousins. "Old Gordon" was the Reverend John Gordon. "Henny" was Molly's sister Henrietta, who was pregnant at the time with her first child. "Hugh of Huntingdon" was Hugh Sherwood, who, despite Molly's appraisal, would eventually marry another Tilghman relative. Harry was Polly's brother. It is believed that Molly never married.

Bay Side August 5

I had begun to think my dear Polly, that I was entirely forgotten by all the World beyond twenty Miles of this place, when two Days ago I receiv'd a charming Packet of Letters among which was one from your Ladyship, for which you will accept my thanks in due form.

How unlucky was I in not being able to see Aunt Pearce. I maneuvred a thousand ways to bring it about but my evil genius prevail'd and as I was not happy enough (any more than yourself) to be mistress of an air Balloon, I was oblig'd to give the matter up.

I have lately spent ten days at Perry Tilghmans very agreeably. I return'd last Sunday. Never say I want resolution after the adventures of that day. In the first place I broil'd 6 Miles by Water, to the Bay Side Church in such a sun, it was enugh to coddle common flesh. I was then so stupified with old Gordons slow creaking, that I began to dream a dozen times before the Sermon was over, and finally I got into the Chariot with Aunt Tilghman, who met me by appointment, and encountered a perpetual Cloud of Dust, which prevented our seeing the Horses Heads or speaking a word lest we shou'd be choak'd. I came off alive it's true but suffer'd so much in the battle, that I have made a Vow to say my prayers at home till it rains, which I begin to think it never will again.

How often my dear Polly do I wish for you, particularly when the walking hour arrives, and I sally out by myself. O this Henny of ours is the saddest Creature you can conceive. If she drags her bloated self to the Wind Mill, she thinks so prodigious an exertion entitles her to groan and complain the whole Evening, till nine o'Clock, when she departs, and is seen no more till the next morning. Now is it not a melancholy thing to see a young person give themselves up to such horrid ways, because they are married? I declare it robs me of all patience. I again repeat, O that you were here What charming tete a tete walks shou'd I have. A fine Lady wou'd expire at the Idea of a female tete a tete, but you have been some what us'd to such sort of things, and will therefore bear it. it is a selfish wish in me too, for, what signifies lying—this place is cruelly lonesome. I am not averse to a decent portion of solitude, but it is possible to have too much of the best thing. I am sometimes worried to death with seeing nobody. I believe I have committed an Irishism, but no matter. Alas! My dear Poly the Country is no longer an Arcadia, where a gentle Shepherd is to be met with under every shady Tree. The sports of the green are no more, or at least I met with none of them.

The only Beau within my reach is the serene Hugh of Huntingdon, and I am sure he is what the Philosophers have so long been in search of, a perfect Vacuum. If you shou'd stumble on any of the learned tribe, pray send them to me, and I will conduct them to our neighbour. After these my complaints, you will not wonder at receiving no entertainment from my Letter. News, which is the life of Correspondence, is a Commodity not dealt in here. What on earth cou'd induce you to ask me about Mat Tilghman's Wedding. It was really sending from New Castle for Coals. Why Child, are you not in the high road of intelligence? Eight negotiating Letters in your hands at once, and yet ask information of me. You have certainly lost your wits, or know not how to make use of them which is much the same thing.

If you have receiv'd the threat'ned visit you were a fool for acting the speaking Trumpet for nothing. I'll engage I woul'd have cleft her ears with so many direct questions, that she wou'd have been glad to let me into the secret for Peace sake. Sister Betsy tells me that the tea Tables at Chester Town are oblig'd to Miss Piner for furnishing them with conversation, three Weeks have beheld M^r Bordley at the feet of the languishing fair, and it is fear'd she will at last banish him. She may now boast of subduing the extremes of Stupidity and brilliancy in her new and old admirer, for which we may conclude that a medium will at last be her choice. I wonder she does not like M^r B. they have both so large a portion of the attic Salt that they might be flint and steel to each other. So Harry is at last to be happy. I commend the Lady for not surrendering at the first summons—that wou'd have been cowardly indeed and I commend him as much for not being dishearten'd at one, two, or three repulses. So you are not for a long siege, very well Polly some day or other those words shall rise in judgment against you, depend on it. At present remember me to all yours, and M^r and M^rs Earle. My poor name is fairly distanc'd.

Johnny Francis is going to be married to a Miss Brown of Rhode Island. Peggy Chew says so, and that the Wedding is to be soon, these young Spriggs are all marrying.

Miss Pearce
At James Tilghman's Esq^r
Chester Town

## 1786: SEPTEMBER 17

## HANNAH THOMSON TO JOHN MIFFLIN

*Charles Thomson married Hannah Harrison (1728–1807) on September 4, 1774, and the next day was embarking on a Philadelphia honeymoon when a messenger came galloping up to ask whether he would agree to become secretary of the Continental Congress—immediately. Years later, Congress would present Hannah with a silver urn as thanks for forfeiting her wedding trip to the cause of the new government. Thomson would stay in the post as the first and only secretary of the Congress until the new government was installed in 1789. In 1786, still parked in a relatively quaint New York City, Hannah wrote to her Philadelphia friend John Mifflin—which of many John and Jonathan Mifflins in a large Quaker family it's hard to say—about some of the city's interesting folkways.*

A flesh brush—simply a large brush intended for the body—was prescribed in the eighteenth century as a cure for ailments like dropsy. "Cukies" (Thomson spelled it "Cookey" in another letter) were a relatively new discovery; culinary lore has it that a Dutch baker invented them accidentally while testing an oven for warmth and called the result a "little cake" or *koekje*. "Jack's Alive" was a game in which boys passed a stick with a burning cork around a campfire until no spark remained, whereupon a black mark was made on the face of the boy in whose hands "Jack" had died. "C. T." was Charles Thomson.

Sep 17—86

I have recd friend Johns letter after a very long silence. Am glad to hear of his Corpulancy. Fleshy Folks are apt to grow Indolent which I hope my Correspondent will guard against, and instead of the flesh Brush which Physicians advise in that case, take up the Pen and exert the Imagination and rather than miss a Post, miss a Dinner.

Many things as you observe in the course of a few months or weeks come to pass. Several Weddings have been here lately; The Gentlemen Citizens of the town a Mr. Rosewalt to a Miss Walton, a Mr. Tom Smith of Wall Street, to a near Neighbour of ours a Miss Taylor. I mention these two Gentlemen being citizens of the town gave us an opportunity of being Introduced to a Custom that you know nothing of. The Gentlemans Parents keep open house just in the same manner as the Brides Parents. The Gentlemen go from the Bridesgroom house to drink Punch with and to give joy to his Father. The Brides Visitors go In the same manner from the Brides to his Mothers to pay their compliments to her. There is so much driving about at such a time, that in our narrow streets, there is some danger. I am now at this Present writing a prisoner. Piles of Snow on each side of all our street only a narrow passage beaten in most all the streets. They visit Jaunt and go to Church in Sleighs. As I said before I am a Prisoner. I am afraid of meeting those flying machines in some of those narrow places. To keep out of danger I stay at home. A few days ago two Gentlemen were driving thro one of those narrow places with high banks of Snow on each side, they saw a Sleigh coming full tilt, the Horses had taken a fright and disputed the way with all they met. The Gentlemen thought it the wisest way to save themselves to jump out of their Sleigh & leave their Horses to contend with each other, which they did one droped down dead, and the other 3 almost dead. And so ended their frolick.

I wish cousin Isaac and you would come & eat yr Christmas dinner here I will give you as good mince pies & as fat a turkey as you can procure either from Molly Newport or Market Street. You wd be delighted with the Visiting parties a wishing happy New Year to each other and eating of <u>Cukies</u>, a little cake made for the occasion.

I want that paragraph in your last letter explained about the depredations you intend to make among my acquaintances. I hope you do not design to take any by surprize. Perhaps you have engaged Doctor Morgan's Balloon for yr Enterprize. But I can assure you we carry so much sail here that I doubt yr <u>Balloon Boat</u> wd soon overturn and then when too late you may wish you had consulted yr friends on the Island. Mrs. Osgood has lately Visited me and thinks Beulah is reserving herself for her Officer who is gone to the east Indies. When he returns he will find the Old Gentleman out of his Way, and nobody's leave to ask but her own.

Pray as thoughts jump one cant tell how, What is become of Jonathan. Does he remember that the Islanders were once his friends and friendship requires some communication to keep the flame alive—give him our compliments as the boys do the stick with fire at the end, and tell him that we say Jack alive & live like to <u>be</u> he shan't die in our hands & we send it to <u>thee</u>. I am much pleased to hear that Isaac Intends to build up the seat of his ancestors, when I write to Aunt Norris I shall say more upon the Occasion.

Remember me to all friends that remember me. C. T. Joins in compliments to you. I am &$^c$

> yr friend
> H. Thomson

## 1788: JULY

## ELIZABETH WHITMAN TO HER LOVER

*In 1788, a pregnant woman arrived alone at an inn in Danvers, Massachusetts. There, she sewed and read, rarely left her room, said she was waiting for her husband—and died some time later, after giving birth to a stillborn child. The news of her death inspired considerable gossip, numerous newspaper articles, and an early American potboiler, Hannah Foster's* The Coquette. *A resident of Hartford, Connecticut, Elizabeth Whitman (1752–1788) was said to have passed up several marriage offers. Her death was seen as a cautionary tale for women who didn't marry when they had the chance. This note was found among her possessions.*

Must I die alone? Shall I never see you more? I know that you will come, but you will come too late: This is, I fear, my last ability. Tears fall so, I know not how to write.—Why did you leave me in so much distress? But I will not reproach you: All that was dear I left for you: but do not regret it.—May God forgive in both what was amiss:—When I go from hence, I will leave you some way to find me;—if I die, will you come and drop a tear over my grave?

### 1788: OCTOBER 25
### ELIZABETH MURPHREY TO HER HEIRS

---

*Roughly half of colonial American women were still illiterate at the end of the eigh-
teenth century, and in many cases, the only written records they left were their wills.
Even among the literate, a woman's will was sometimes the most intimate document
she wrote, in effect a letter to her heirs. For Elizabeth Harrison Murphrey
(1705?–1788), a widow and the matriarch of a large North Carolina family, the
will created a vivid portrait, as drawn by the things she valued. It also reflected what
must have been her final effort to set a wayward son on the straight and narrow
path.*

By "deft ware," Murphrey must have meant delftware, a kind of Dutch pottery.

In the Name of the Most Holy Lord—Amen—

I, Elizabeth Murphrey of the parish of St Patricks, Dobbs County State of
North Carolina, being possessed of an ancient form but still retaining my right
mind do here by make & Ordain this to be my last will and Testament in the
manner following to wit:

It is my first desire that these old bones of mine be taken from the place of
my Demize to the graveyard hill on the Beare Garden planta. whereon I live &
there be layd to rest beside my late husband & children. It is also my desire that
my body be given a proper burial in the rights of the church of England which is
the Faith to which I still adhere despite the pursecution of that Faith brot about
by the late Unpleasant War. I ask that Revered Master Cuttin of Newbern be
brot to this place to preach over my Mortal remains and for my Soul as there has
not been a priest in this parish since the late war against the King.

I grant all my lands in Dobbs County including the plantation whereon I live
on Contentne river to my son John Murphrey only if he sell the place whereon
he now lives to one of his brothers and moves to this place. He is also to get all
my other property, both real and personal, save for some few items herein listed,
including all my slaves to the number of 20 (except the mulatter girl Phebe) and
is to sell what of them he deems necessary and the money arising from the sale
to be added to that receved from the sell of his plantation and both sums be
used to bring him & his family up out of the debts which he has occasioned of
late by his late run of bad investments. I pray most earnestly that from this point
on he learn to live a sober & industrious life in which frugality and good sence
play a major part.

It is my desire that my daughter in law, Polly Murphrey, for all the past favors she has showed me have my riding chair & Harness, my mare called Sugar Lumpe and 1 ladies saddle. Also all my deft ware and all my jewelry and plate not otherwise devised.

My son Jethro Murphrey is to have my picture which hangs in the dining room and the one of himself which is in the upper Hall and he is not to bother the pictures of myself and my late husband in the parlour or those of his grandparents in the lower hall, it being my desire that they go to my son John's children. He is also to have the Deerhall Track in Dobbs County on Louson Swamp adjoining Sugg and Howard. His wife Penny is to have the 3 Great enamaled Chargers and the bed and furniture which stands in the second best bedroom. Also the four silver bowls and the 12 dessart spoons marked EM & the diamond necklise & Drps.

My grandson Ben Murphrey is to get one half of my books and my grandson William Murphrey the other half.

My daughter Patsy Hill is to have her picture and the good Chinie tea sett plus what I have already given her.

My Sugg grandchildren are to have £ 50 each and their mother to have the pictures of herself & her husband and the Landskap that hangs in the back parlour with what I have already given her.

My daughter Nancy Caswell and her Heirs are to have the track of woodlands at Sandy Bottom adjoining Croom and the river & my mulatter girl Phebe, she to be extempt from those given to my son John.

All my other heirs are to have each a lock of my hair & £ 10.

The picture of my daughter Lany is to be sent to Mr. Frederic Dickson of Rainbow who was much enamored of her while she lived.

I hereby appoint my son John Murphrey and Mr. Murphrey Dickson the Executors to this my last will & Testament revoking all those I may have written. Signed sealed delivered & published by my own hand & in the presence of these wittnesses this 25 day of October in the Year of our Lord one Thousand seven hundred and eightyeight.

Elizabeth Murphrey


## 1789: SEPTEMBER 20

## MERCY OTIS WARREN TO CATHARINE MACAULAY

*A fully working government did not spring into existence overnight. At the start, there were debts, disagreements, threats of secession, and doubts about how long a republican government would last. George Washington was only half a year into his*

*first term as the nation's first president when Mercy Warren (see pages 23 and 35)*
*questioned in this letter whether too much power had been given to the new federal*
*government. The recipient of her letter, Catharine Macaulay (1731–1791), was a*
*well-known British historian.*

The Order of Cincinnatus was formed by a group of Revolutionary War veterans in honor of
George Washington; it was named for the Roman general who led his army to victory and then,
like Washington, returned to his farm.

Plimouth Sept 20 1789

My dear Madam

As I cannot excuse myself I will not attempt an apology for thus long neglecting to answer your favor dated October 29th 88. I feel really mortified at my own delay, as it has undoubtedly prevented me the pleasure of hearing from a very valuable & much esteemed friend whom nor time nor distance nor the accidents of life will ever lead me to view with an indifferent eye.

Yet we live in an age of revolution when not only the most extraordinary political events are exhibited, but the most sudden reverse of private friendship and a dissolution of all former attachments at once surprise & wound the heart disposed to cultivate the social affections to the last moment of existence. But from the instability of the human heart I have learned to expect every thing & to fear nothing (beneath the Supreme Being) so long as I feel a firmness of mind that will ever render us independent of popular opinion: of political change: of the versatility of individuals in high office: or the absurd enthusiasm that often spreads itself through the [illegible] of life.

I have often recollected an observation of yours on a very pleasant morning when you came to breakfast with me at Milton. So many caring, so many joyous faces, such an appearance of general happiness that you could scarcely forbear weeping that the people were trifling away their advantages & seemed almost ripe to relinquish the prize they had so recently purchased—if you were here now my dear madam perhaps you would indulge the tears—

But I forbear to draw a portrait of the moral & political situation of a country whose magnanimity, valour & virtue has made it an object of curiosity throughout the world.

It is time we have a government established & a Washington at its head. But we are too poor for Monarchy, too wise for despotism, and too dissipated selfish & extravagant for Republicanism. It ill becomes an infant government when the foreign & domestic arrearages are large & the resources small: to begin its career in all the splendor of Royalty. Should trade be blocked, manufacturing checked, the spirit of agriculture discouraged, & the people almost deprived of the means of subsistence to amass from for the payment of exorbitant salaries—in order to support the dignity of officers & keep up the ostentatious pomp for which the ambitious have sighed from the moment of the institution of the Order of Cincinnatus.

The <u>compensations</u> may appear small to current monarchic and powerful nations, but the exhausted Americans begin already to cry out that they are more than they can bear.

But I leave America to wait the success of her bold experiment, and wonder a moment with you at the intensifying revolution in France. Would it not be surprising if that nation should reap a greater advantage from the spirit of liberty lately diffused through the continent than the Americans may be able to boast after all their struggle and sacrifice, to become a free people.

But more of this subject in my next. I dare not yet prescience—I only retrospect the past & contemplate the probabilities of futurity, for so various are the practices, the interests & the principles among us that no human calculation can decide on the fate of America.

Shall I ask you madam if the treatise on education is finished, if the essay on truth is revised, & if you are . . . now writing the History of the American Revolution? If you are I shall be happy to see it. If you are not possibly you may see in two or three volumes the annals collected by your friend.

I am always gratified to hear of the welfare of your daughter or any with whom you are connected. My compliments with those of Mr. Warren & family to Mr. Graham & yourself.

And believe me to be as ever yours

Sincerely & affectionately
M. Warren

## 1789: DECEMBER 26
## MARTHA WASHINGTON TO MERCY OTIS WARREN

*Wife of the nation's first president, Martha Dandridge Custis Washington (1731–1802) was a gracious but reluctant first first lady. Having already shared her husband with the national interest since the beginnings of the war in which he had fought so famously, she once confided to a niece that she felt "more like a state prisoner than anything else." In this letter to Mercy Warren (see pages 23, 35, and 71), she longed to have a "privet life" once again. Washington, however, would stay in office for two terms.*

New York December the 26th 1789

My Dear Madam

Your very friendly letter of the 27th of last month has afforded me much more satisfaction than all the formal compliments and emty ceremonies of mear etiquette could possably have done.—I am not apt to forget the feelings that have been inspired by my former society with good acquaintances, nor to be insensible to thair expressions of gratitude to the President of the United States; for you know me well enough to do me the justice to beleive that I am only fond of what comes from the heart.—Under a conviction that the demonstrations of respect and affection which have been made to the President originate from that source I cannot deny that I have taken some interest and pleasure in them.—The difficulties which presented themselves to view upon his first entering upon the Presidency, seem thus to be in some measure surmounted: it is owing to this kindness of our numerous friends in all quarters that my new and unwished for situation is not indeed a burden to me. When I was much younger I should, probably, have enjoyed the inoscent gayeties of life as much as most my age;—but I had long since placed all the prospects of my future worldly happyness in the still enjoyments of the fireside at Mount Vernon—

I little thought when the war was finished, that any circumstances could possible have happened which would call the General into public life again. I had anticipated, that from this moment we should have been left to grow old in solitude and tranquility togather: that was, my Dear madam, the first and dearest wish of my heart;—but in <u>that</u> I have been disapointed; I will not, however, contemplate with too much regret disapointments that were enevitable, though the generals feelings and my own were perfectly in unison with respect to our predilictions for privet life, yet I cannot blame him for having acted according to his ideas of duty in obaying the voice of his country. The consciousness of having attempted to do all the good in his power, and the pleasure of finding his fellow citizens so well satisfied with the disintrestedness of his conduct, will, doubtless, be some compensation for the great sacrifices which I know he has made; indeed in his journeys from Mount Vernon—to this place; in his late Tour through the eastern states, by every public and by every privet information which has come to him, I am persuaded that he has experienced nothing to make him repent his having acted from what he concieved to be alone a sense of indespensable duty: on the contrary, all his sensibility has been awakened in receiving such repeated and unaquivocal proofs of sincear regards from all his country men. with respect to myself, I sometimes think the arrangement is not quite as it ought to have been, that I, who had much rather be at home should occupy a place with which a great many younger and gayer women would be prodigiously pleased.—As my grand children and domestic connections made a great portion of the felicity which I looked for in this world.—I shall hardly be able to find any substitute that would indemnify me for the Loss of a part of such endearing society. I do not say this because I feel dissatisfied with my present station—no, God forbid:—for everybody and everything conspire to make me as contented as possable in it; yet I have too much of the vanity of human affairs to expect felicity from the splendid scenes of public life.—I am still determined to be cheerful and to be happy in whatever situation I may be, for I have also learnt from experiance that the greater part of our happiness or misary depends upon our dispositions, and not upon our circumstances; we carry the seeds of the one, or the other about with us, in our minds, wherever we go.

I have two of my grand children with me who enjoy advantages in point of education, and who, I trust by the goodness of providence, will continue to be a great blessing to me, my other two grand children are with thair mother in virginia.—

The Presidents health is quite reestablished by his late journey—mine is much better than it used to be—I am sorry to hear that General Warren has been ill: hope before this time that he may be entirely recovered—we should rejoice to see you both, I wish the best of Heavens blessings, and am my dear madam with esteem and

> regard your friend and Hble
> Sert
> M Washington

## 1790: APRIL 2

## HARRIOT WASHINGTON TO GEORGE WASHINGTON

*In 1790, George Washington was concerned with (among other issues) war debts, the ratification of the Bill of Rights, and the future location of the nation's capital. None of which was apparently of the remotest interest to the president's fourteen-year-old niece, Harriot (1776–1822), who had only one object in mind.*

"Aunt Washington" was Martha; "Nelly" and the other "Washington" were Martha's grandchildren, Eleanor Parke Custis and George Washington Parke Custis. Their father (Martha's son from a previous marriage) had died in 1781, and they were adopted and raised by the president and the first lady.

Mt Vernon April 2d 1790

I now set down to write to my dear Uncle as I have not wrote to him since he left this place I should have done it but I thought you had so much business that I had better write to Aunt Washington yet I am sure you would be very glad to se me improveing myself by writeing letters to my friend's.

I am a going to ask you My Dear Uncle to do something for me which I hope you will not be against but I am sure if you are it will be for my good, as all the young Ladyes are a learning musick, I will be very much obleiged to you if you will send me a gettar, there is a man here by the name of Tracy that teaches to play on the harpsicord & gettar, a gettar is so simple an instrument that five or six lessons would be sufficient for any body to learn, If you think it proper to send me a gettar I will thank you if you will send it by the first opportunity I was informed the other day that you and Aunt Washington were certainly a comeing home this Summer which gave me a great deal of pleasure for I want to see you very much.

If you please to give my love to Aunt Washington Nelly & Washington. I am My Dear Uncle your Sincere Neice

Harriot Washington.

## 1792

## A. V. TO MARIA

---

*Whether hardships were caused by death, separation, or illness, submitting to God's will was a theme that pervaded eighteenth-century women's writings—and their lives. This note to the author's niece appeared in a Philadelphia magazine under the catchy title "A Letter from a Lady to her Niece, on her expressing great uneasiness at the Loss of her Beauty by the Small-pox."*

My Dear Maria,

We must distinguish those evils which are imposed by Providence, from those to which we ourselves give the power of hurting us. A small part of *your* calamity is the infliction of heaven; the rest is little more than the fretting of idle discontent. You have, indeed, lost that which may sometimes contribute to happiness, but to which happiness is by no means inseparably annexed. You have lost what the greater number of the human race never have possessed; what those on whom it is bestowed, for the most part, possessed in vain; and what you, while it was yours, knew not how to use. You have only lost early, what the laws of Nature forbid you to keep long; and have lost it while your mind is yet flexible, and while you have time to substitute more valuable and durable excellencies. Consider yourself, Maria, as a being born to know, to reason, and to act: rise at once from your dream of melancholy to wisdom, and to piety: you will find that there are other charms than those of beauty, and other joys than the praise of fools.

I am your affectionate aunt,<br>A. V.

## 1792: CIRCA FEBRUARY
## MARIA REYNOLDS TO ALEXANDER HAMILTON

---

*There is nothing new about political scandal, and nothing new about damage control. The letter below, written in desperation by a woman who was the mistress of Alexander Hamilton (1757–1804), would actually be published by Hamilton himself to disprove a charge of financial corruption—considered by many a worse crime than adultery. Maria Lewis Reynolds (1768–?) was the wife of a Treasury Department employee named James Reynolds, who first blackmailed Hamilton into payments, then spread the rumor that the treasury secretary was giving him privileged financial information. The publication of these letters by Hamilton was considered admirably honest by some, but the scandal is also thought to have ruined Hamilton's chances for the presidency.*

Monday Night Eight C, L

Sir,

I need not acquaint that I had Been Sick all moast Ever sence I saw you as I am sure you allready no It Nor would I solicit a favor wich Is so hard to obtain were It not for the Last time Yes Sir Rest assuirred I will never ask you to Call on me again I have kept my Bed those tow dayes and now rise from my pillow wich your Neglect has filled with the sharpest thorns I no Longer doubt what I have Dreaded to no but stop I do not wish to se you to to say any thing about my Late disappointments No I only do it to Ease a heart wich is ready Burst with Greef I can neither Eate or sleep I have Been on the point of doin the moast horrid acts at I shudder to think where I might been what will Become of me. In vain I try to Call reason to aide me but alas ther is no Comfort for me I feel as if I should not Contennue long and all the wish I have Is to se you once more that I may my doupts cleared up for God sake be not so voed of all humannity as to deni me this Last request but if you will not call some time this night I no its late but any tim between this and twelve A Clock I shall be up Let me Intreat you If you wont come to send me a Line oh my head I can rite no more do something to Ease My heart or Els I no not what I shall do for so I cannot live commit this to the care of my maid be not offended I beg

## 1792: DECEMBER 17
## MARTHA LAURENS RAMSAY TO DAVID RAMSAY

*Martha Laurens Ramsay (1759–1811) was the mother of eleven children (eight of whom lived), the wife of respected scholar and doctor David Ramsay (1749–1815), and the daughter of a wealthy rice- and slave-trader named Henry Laurens, who was president of the Continental Congress. She was also the accomplished author of a diary, numerous letters, and a series of religious exercises, and she taught her children—both daughters and sons—with energy and imagination. In this letter, she revealed her bereavement at her father's death, and her determination to bow to God's will.*

The "awful ceremony" was cremation, which Henry Laurens had requested.

Charleston, December 17, 1792.

My Very Dear Husband,

You have doubtless heard, by this time, that I am fatherless, and will feel for me in proportion to the great love you have always shown me, and your intimate knowledge of my frame, and the love I had for my dear departed parent. Never was stroke to an affectionate child more awful and unexpected than this has been to me. I had heard from my dear father, that he was somewhat indisposed, but not confined even to the house; however, last Tuesday and Wednesday week I was seized with so inexpressible a desire to see him, that nothing could exceed it, and nothing could satisfy it, but the going to see him. Accordingly, on Wednesday noon, very much against my family and personal convenience, I set out with faithful Tira and little Kitty, and slept that night at Mrs. Loocock's; the next morning it rained, but I could not be restrained. I proceeded to Mepkin, and arrived there at one o'clock, wet to the skin, I found my dear father indisposed, as I thought, but not ill. He conversed on indifferent matters; seemed very much delighted with my presence; told me I was a pleasant child to him; and God would bless me as long as I lived; and at twenty minutes before eight o'clock, retired to rest. The next morning, at seven o'clock, I went to his bedside; he again commended my tenderness to him, and told me he had passed a wakeful night; talked to me of Kitty and of you; had been up and given out the barn door key, as usual. At eight I went to breakfast. In about ten minutes I had despatched my meal, returned to him, and thought his speech thick, and that he wavered a little in his discourse. I asked him if I might send for Dr. M'Cormick; he told me if I desired a consultation, I might; but that he had all confidence in my skill, and was better. I asked him why his breathing was laborious; he said he did not know, and almost immediately fell into his last agony; and a bitter agony it was; though, perhaps, he did not feel it. At ten o'clock, next day, I closed his venerable eyes. Oh, my dear husband, you know how I have dreaded this stroke; how I have wished first to sleep in death, and therefore you can tell the sorrows of my spirit; indeed they have been, indeed they are very great. I have been, and I am in the depths of affliction; but I have never felt one murmuring thought; I have never uttered one murmuring word. Who am I, a poor vile wretch, that I should oppose my will to the will of God, who is all wise and all gracious; on the contrary I have been greatly supported; and if I may but be following Christ, am willing to take up every cross, which may be necessary or profitable for me. I left Mepkin at one o'clock on Saturday, as soon as the body of my dear parent was decently laid out, and I was sufficiently composed for travelling. I know, by information, that the awful ceremony was performed last Tuesday. I have never been able to write till this day. Our dear children are well. Eleanor comes to my bedside, reads the Bible for me, and tells me of a heavenly country, where there is no trouble. Feeling more than ever my dependance on you for countenance, for support and kindness, and in the midst of sorrow, not forgetting to thank God that I have so valuable, so kind, and so tender a friend; I remain, my dear husband, your obliged and grateful wife,

Martha Laurens Ramsay.

## 1795: MARCH 8
## JUDITH COCKS TO JAMES HILLHOUSE

*Slavery had existed in all thirteen colonies before the Revolution, and according to some estimates, roughly a fifth of all colonists were African American. During the war, an early emancipation proclamation had offered freedom to any slave who was willing to fight for the crown, and the newspapers teemed with notices describing— and requesting the return of—runaways, both male and female. By 1790, however, the census showed that just 8 percent of blacks were free, and women like the author of this letter remained at the mercy of their owners.*

Nothing is known about Judith Cocks. James Hillhouse (1754–1832) was a United States representative from Connecticut who, the following year, would be elected to the Senate for the first of four terms. By the turn of the century, he would be one of the leading anti-slavery advocates in Congress.

Marietta, 8th March 1795.

Sir

I have been so unhappy at Mrs. Woodbridges that I was obliged to leeve thare by the consent of Mrs. Woodbridge who gave up my Indentures and has offen said that had she known that I was so sickly and expencieve she would not have brought me to this Country   but all this is the least of my trouble and I can truly say sir had I nothing else or no one but myself I am sure I should not make any complaint to you   But my little son Jupiter who is now with Mrs. Woodbridge is my greatest care and from what she says and from the useage he meets with there is so trying to me that I am all most distracted   therefore if you will be so kind as to write me how Long Jupiter is to remain with them as she tells me he is to live with her untill he is twenty five years of age   this is something that I had no idea of   I all ways thought that he was to return with me to new England or at Longest only ten years   these are matters I must beg of you sir to let me know as quick as you can make it convenient   I hope you will excuse me of troub Ling you wich I think you will do when you think that I am here in A strange country without one Friend to advise me   Mrs. Woodbridge setts out for Connecticut and I make no doubt but she will apply to buy Jupiter's time which I beg you will be so good as not to sell to her   I had much reather he wold return and Live with you as she allows all her sons to thump and beat him the same as if he was a Dog   Mrs. Woodbridge may tell you that I have be-haved bad but I call on all the nabours to know wheather I have not behaved well and wheather I was so much to blame   She has called me A theif and I denie   I have don my duty as well as I could to her and all her family as well as my Strength wold allow of   I have not ronged her nor her family   the nabours advised me to rite you for the childs sake   I went to the Gentlemen of the town for these advise   thay told me I could get back without any dificulty   I entend to return   remember me to all your family if you please   I thank you for send-ing me word my dauter was well   this is my hand writing   I remain the great-est humility you Humble servant

Judith Cocks

please [don't?] show this to Mrs. Woodbridge

## 1797: FEBRUARY 24?
## HENRIETTA LISTON TO JAMES JACKSON

*Henrietta Marchant Liston (1752–1828) arrived in America in 1796, having just married the newly named British ambassador, Robert Liston. Over the next three years, in her role as diplomatic hostess, she came into contact with most of the powerful people of the day. Writing home to her uncle, James Jackson, she was able to provide a uniquely insightful outsider's perspective.*

Ricketts Amphitheater in Philadelphia was the site of America's first circus.

Philadelphia<br>Feby. 24 [?] 1797

My dear Uncle,

In my last I mentioned that Mr. Adams had carried his Ellection for President, it was only by three Votes. Washington is preparing for retirement with a very cheerful Countenance—Mrs. Washingtons heart seems a little melted, as she never expects to see Philadelphia again; she prest me to come to Mountvernon this Summer but I made my excuses, as our wishes bend to the North—on Wednesday last, the 22d of Feby. the Presidents Birth day was celebrated with all the splendour the Country could afford, Guns were fired and Bells rung—in the Morning the Gentlemen waited on the President, and the Ladies on Mrs. Washington, and were entertained with cake and wine—Ricketts Amphitheater was fitted up and in the Evening a Ball given to about a thousand Persons; the President appeared in the American Uniform, (blue and buff,) with the Cross of Cincinatus at his breast in diamonds, it is on this occasion only that the order is permitted to appear—you know, perhaps, that the fellow-soldiers of Washington had this order conferred upon them after the Revolution, the propriety of admitting any thing like hereditary honor which might be handed down to the Sons, was disputed in Congress, and it was, at last, agreed that on the Generals Birth day those who survived might show their cross, and to be remembered no more—this digression leads me from the Ball I went in about seven oClock to the Presidents Box, from which we had a very compleat view of the Company; the Country dances and cottillions were danced verging from the Centre, which admitted of ten, fifteen couple[s] in each, so that three hundred Persons moved at the same time. The American Ladies dance better than any set of People I ever saw, (I have several times been tempted to observe, in complimenting them, that it was the only advantage they seemed to have derived from their intercourse with the French: tho' Scotch dances are creeping-in.) the appearance was very beautiful, many pretty Women and all showing in their dress, cheerfull, happy, and gay; the Men did not make quite so good an Appearance, except the President himself, who moved a Monarch, and the foreign Ministers in Court-dresses of which My Husbands was rather the handsomest, cut velvet richly embroidered: at eleven oClock supper was announced, The President walked alone, his March playing, He was followed by Mrs. Washington handed by the Vice-President, I went next handed by the Portegueze Minister, then his Lady handed by Mr. Liston, the Wife of the first Senator handed by the Spanish Minister—the Company then followed as they pleased—the supper tables very splendid, the President and his Party sat at the centre one, the others going in straight lines from that, our repast was very short as many others were to be served, the only toast given was the day We celebrate— a trumpet sounded, and the Company huzzaed the President rose drank their health, and thanked them for the last honor done him—his Party then retired in the same order.—every thing was arranged and conducted by the set of Gentlemen who Manage the assemblys for the year, they waited at our backs, no Servants being admitted, the rest of the Gentlemen attended on their Partners—Mr. Liston and I stole away soon after our return to the Ball-room, He extremely entertained, and I tolerably tired, tho' pleased.

### 1797: APRIL
### SARAH McCLENDON TO HER FAMILY AND FRIENDS

*Drawn by the promise of deer and beaver, a number of hunters and land speculators had begun to populate Kentucky as early as the 1760s. By the eighties and nineties, settlement had begun in earnest. Among the pioneers were Sarah McClendon (1780?–1818?) and her husband, Benjamin, who left their native North Carolina to be among the earliest settlers of the northwest part of the state. Though clearly not well educated, McClendon wrote vividly of domestic life on the frontier.*
The McClendons would build a schoolhouse in Henderson County and have three sons. By "thisis," Sarah probably meant phthisis, a wasting disease.

Dear Mother, Daddie, Bruthurs, Susters, all our People, nebors and frunds—

We was surprised and thankful, when Preacher Hobson located yur little bilage and brought us yor leters and from Benjamin people. We red and rered and let all the pepople here red them. I was worred about Daddie sou glade the boys toke his worke over and had a good ductor. It is a lounge way hear to get a ductor. Preachur Hobson gave and renewed the word of salvation to us. He is pretching ever night here. Benjamin had bilt a circle for us to have church and covered it with timber, our new log church is almost done. The nebors and al are splitting logs, putting legs on for benches, all are getting animal skins dried to cover them with making animal oil lamps—Preacher Lambast left a bible, it is in alter of church on the pulpit, covered with skin.

Saturdaey

We are getting cloth spined to cover it. It is center of our litle vilage. Kiut worreng bout us not havin plenty to eat. We hade boiled wild geese, wild plum puddin, wild cherry perserves, corn bred, cracked hominy, wild greens, roaster deer, dandelions, beaten white bred, goseberry purserves made with honey, hog meat, milk, butter, kottage, cheze, gravy, mushrons. All this wild food is better than what you others have, popcorn, lots of other things we are healthier. We never go hungry. I never want for help. Benjamin is good to me, he still calls me Love, and I have a surprise now do not worry bout me. I am in the family way with my first baby, Benjamin say it makes him love me more, but I do not see how he could love me more. He said we will name him William that is a name in both our family. I never was in better health in all my life—my mid-wife Nancy is watching over me as all and they are happy for us. No women in our clan ever die when they have a baby and I have walked and lived with God, so has Benjamin and we want this baby.

Monday

We are well fixed for the cold weather and are well guarded from the wilds of our country. We like here. We live, love, pray, work together.

Friday

We have plenty warm clothes, We are progressing. Back home I know you have more in livirg than we do—but back there it started like we are here. Preacher Hobson is hear third time, he will stay here and marry Kanny Crampfell. She is getting her dress spined and will color it with berry and we will have a big weddin for them. The men and negroes are rushing to get there 2 room ready. Benjamin gave the land. We are nebors dividing our furniture.and everything. She is a pretty girl. We are giving her Fanny—14 years old and she can tran her to help. We want them to stay and preech hear and he will teech the youngins, soon our little William will be big to go. Mary is still with me. Benjamin is a good man, like my Daddie and Bruthers. I wood like to come back and we plan to some. You and Daddie ought to come here , they are making board boats now and could cume on them to Illinoisy. Benjamin has a fast, fat, fine steeds and will come and meat you. You wood like hear—not many sins here. I no all the youngins of you all are in school and hope all got nough money to pay for hime and live now alright. You all could help more people there like we do and feel better.

Each day I rite a little more and am trying to rite all I no so if some one get out this way I can sent it. Benjamin sends his love, not to worrie about us, when we get our family will bring back home to see you. If you here about the pirates coming round hear forget it. We love God and know he will be with us. Rok is here and sees after us. Poore Old Jim Smucker that come with us, got awful sick and died. Preech Hobson said the last rites. Mary has five of his children. Henry Upp is going to marry her, his wife Nancy died and he has her two boys. Both of them need each outher and he is a good working man. How did John little boy Billy get, does he still have the thisis or has he lost it. I pray for him as I do all of you. I love you all. I know you hated for us to leave but we never wish we had not. Sometime it was hard but we made it, all of us together and we wood not have it any other way. People tels it is worse than it is, They have not ben hear and don't know. We dry wild apples flavor better, crab apple purseves with honey—blackberry Jam, butter, hot bred, just like you have, wild rice all this wild flavor better than when you tame it. I hope you all will keep the negro to help you. You are getting older, we all want you and Daddie stay hear long time til God see fit to take you from us. I hope to do the same for mine, but what a loving sweet memory you will leave us. Tell Uncle Watch, Aunt Marry and everybody helo and I know they are still praying for us. Benjamin with his long bread and me still love you all. Will add to this—

Thursday

Yesterday the sun shined all are getting ready for spring work today a howling cold wind but the trees keep part of it away. The men all have a blacksmith shop, when cold cold they get in it swap tales of old, some make brew or wild peach brandy, some get too much but what can you do about it but Benjamin do not. We all like peach brandy seasoned with honey. I tell you this wild taste is a better taste—a beter for your health reason we are healthy here. We had lots of deep snow—we cut ice off creek and had wild grass piled up to covered the ice to make ice cream when it get hot. Nothing healthy more the creek runned all time with clear water. I wish you all could see this spring. It runs as far as you can see cutting the ditch wide and deep. Benjamin and the men are piling up big rocks and will put them inside the spring, make a wall, they will dig it deeper. It is pretty here, they take the pepperming put it in candy. Mary makes soap and puts wild roses in it, it makes you smell good. We have about what you have we eet it a different way. Preacher Lampkin brought us some champhor and fedita, we divide, Rok and the Indians showed us what weeds to make

medicine from with help of old Ductor Burdon that come with us, before he
died—Sam Crumbream it all from him so when we get sick and can not see
Ductor Rankin we get Ductor Sam. We buried Ductor Burdon and when
Preecher Hobson come he said the rites a lots of pretty things about him. Soem
time the hail and sleet gets so thick and heavy on the tree limbs they bend, bend
and creak, til they break off, it is kind of a music sound, when spring opens up
the mean chop them up, that is one way God helps us, sometime he send the
deer and buffalo by so we can have meet when the snow is awful deep, he send
the snow bird to chirp to us with the hail covered trees swaying crackling poping
with music, the bright sun coming up through the tree tops no place but heaven
could be prettyr than this, the eagle and birds flying or setting in the tree tops
with there music wabbles, just come and enjoy a while what we live with the
year rond in God Country where peach and sin is littler. Will ad to this.

We Was glad everbodie rote a little and sent in your letter, that tell us they
still love us.

## 1797: MAY 28
## RACHEL HUNTINGTON TO LUCY HUNTINGTON BROWN

*Rachel Huntington (1779–?) was visiting New York City from her home in Con-
necticut when she wrote to her sister Lucy Huntington Brown (1773–?). As this letter attests, New York City was, then as now, a place where fashion was both seen and
described with the utmost seriousness.*

George was one of Rachel and Lucy's three living brothers, and Hannah his wife. Dolls were
often used as a way of exhibiting the latest fashions. Rachel would marry a merchant named
William Tracy in 1800.

New York May 28th 1797

My dear sister
    The enclosed pacquet was intended to be sent by General Floyd, but he
went away before it was given to him—I have forgot what I wrote in it, but shall
send it along & perhaps there <u>may</u> be something entertaining in it—Lucy I believe most of the comissions from you & sister Hannah have been attended to
by Brother George or myself—I have bought two bands which are the most
fashionable trimings for beaver hats, a white one for the blue hat, & a yellow
one for the black one, they should be put twice around the crown & fastned forward in the form of a beau knot. Brother has got each of you a pink silk shawl
which are very fashionable also—Many Ladies wear them for turbans, made in

the manner that you used to make muslin ones last summer, George has given me one like them, The fine lace cost 10 shillings a yard, & I think it is very handsome. there is enough for two handkerchiefs & two double tuckers, the way to make handkerchief's is to set lace, or a ruffle on a strait piece of muslin, (only pieced on the back to make it set to your neck,) & put it on so as to show only the ruffle, & make it look as if it was set on the neck of your gown, many Ladies trim the neck of thier gowns with lace & go without handkerchiefs but I think it is a <u>neater</u> way to wear them—with fashionable gowns it will not be necessary to have much more than half a yard in the width of your tuckers—I send a doll, by Brother George which I intended to have dressd in a neater manner but really could not find time—it however has rather a fashionable appearance, the cap is made in a good form but you would make one much handsomer than I could, the beau to Miss <u>Dollys</u> poultice neck cloth is rather large but the thickness is very <u>moderate</u>—I think a cap crown & turban would become you—I have got a braid of hair which cost four dollars it should be fastned up with a comb, (without platting) under your turban if it has a crown & over it, if without a crown— Brother has got some very beautifull sattin muslin, & also some handsome "tartan plad" gingham for your gowns, there is a large pattern for two train gowns of the muslin, which should be made thre breadths wide two breadths to reach to the shoulder straps forward, & one breadth to be cut part of the way down before, to go over the shoulder & part of it to be pleated on to the shoulder straps, meeting the back breadths, & some of it to go around the neck, like the <u>doll's</u>— the pleats should be made pretty small, & not stitched to the lining, but you should wear binders over your shoulders—an inch & a half should be the width of your binders. (I must have done writing this pretty soon. the last sentence if you observe is quite <u>poetical</u>—but let me <u>stick to my text Fashion</u>) It is the fashion to have draw strings fastned on the corners of the shoulder straps by the sleves on the back, and have a tack large enough for them to run in, made to cross on the back, run under the arms an inch below the sleves & tie before—I should advise you to have your gingham one made in that way, with draw'd sleves for sister Hannah & I have seen as large Ladies as you with them, & I think they would look very well for you Sleves should be made half a yard wide & not drawd less than seven or eight times, I think they look best to have two or three drawings close together & a plain spot alternately—Some of the ladies have thier sleves coverd with drawing tacks, & have thier elbows uncover'd if you dont like short sleves, you should have long ones with short ones to come down allmost to your <u>elbows</u>, drawed four or five by the bottom—if yo want to walk with long gowns you must draw the train up thr'o one of the pocket holes, I have bought some callico for chints trimings for old gowns, if you have any that you wish to wear short they are very fashionable at present, & gowns that are trimed with them should be made only to touch the ground, there is enough of the dark stripe for one gown, & enough of the light for one there should be enough white left on the dark stripe to turn down to prevent its <u>ravelling</u>. I gave 10 shillings for the callico & have been laughed at for my "foolish bargain" but I am not convinced that it is foolish The William street merchants ask three shillings a yard for trimings like the wide stripe & two for the narrow—I guess you will like the narrow—the kid shoes are of the most fashionable kind, & the others, of the best quality Brother George keeps enquiring for my letter—& as I have fill'd up my paper I'll leave the <u>improvement</u> for you to make With love to sister Hannah & Benjamin I am my dear sister yours, most affectionately

R Huntington

## 1797: JUNE 15
## MARTHA WASHINGTON TO FRANCES WASHINGTON

*On the eve of retiring to Mount Vernon, Martha Washington (see page 73) turned her attention to matters of worms, spinets, shoes, and sleeping arrangements.*
Frances Washington (1763–1815) was Martha's niece, the daughter of George's brother Charles. William Pearce had been manager of Mount Vernon.

Philadelphia June the 15th 1797

My dear Fanny

I am sorry to hear by your Letter of the tenth that your little girl has been so ill—I hope she has got quite well before this—I have not a doubt but worms, is the principle cause of her complaints children that eat every thing as they like and feed as heartely as your does must be full of worms—indeed my dear Fanny I never saw children stuffed as yours was when I was down and reather wondered that they were able to be tolarable with such lodes as they used to put into their little stomachs—I am sure thare is nothing so pernisious as over charging the stomach of a child—with every kind of food that they will take—expearance will convince you of the impropriety if nothing else will—

I can with much truth say that I am realy sorry that I cannot come down to Mt Vernon this summer particularly on your account—the president says he cannot make a longer stay than a few days—which would make it very inconveniant to me, to be thare without him—besides I should not like to have any thing to do with Mr Pearces Family in the House    The President will bring two white men with him—one of them may sleep in Whitings room the other in the Garet—let thare be a bed put in the Garret-room—and one for the other man as they may be ready—The President talks of leving this on tuesday morn—and I suppose he will make all the dispach he can as he does not expect to be gon long from hear—

I sent to Mr Palmer as soon as your letter came to my hands—he is out of town and his work men knows nothing of your measure it will be as well for you to send one of your old shoes when the President returns and then you will be scertain that your shoes will fitt—and I will have them done as soon as I can it is difficult to get any thing done hear—the trades people suffered very much in the yellow fever—the shoe makers complain of the want of journeymen—I hope it will be better now the Congress is gon—every man must have some thing either to send or carry home—which constantly imployed the trades people in this city

My dear Fanny if M^rs Herberts spinnet is not sent home—I beg you will have it carefully [sent] up in the Boat when your things . . . with many thanks to her for the lone of it—I hope it has not got any injury staying in our house this winter—I charged Frank to have it sent up derectly but I fear there is not much dependance on him—my love and good wishes attend you and children and believe me my

> dear Fanny your
> most affectionate
> M. Washington

## 1799: DECEMBER 19
## HENRIETTA LISTON TO JAMES JACKSON

*The British diplomat's wife (see page 81) continued the narrative of her stay in America, which included the end of an era.*

> Philadelphia
> 19th Decr. 1799

My dear Uncle

I write a few lines hoping they will be in time to overtake the <u>Jane</u> from New york, to inform you of the <u>Death of George Washington</u>—an express arrived yesterday from Mount Vernon written to the President with the news; having but a few minnets to spare I enclose a news paper of this day, containing particulars. . . . Mr. Liston and I had experienced such uniform politeness and friendly attention from General Washington both while President and after his retirement as to have attached us warmly to him, and we feel extreme satisfaction from having visited him so lately, and parted from him so affectionately: It is difficult to say what may be the consequence of his Death to this Country, He stood the barrier betwixt the Northernmost and Southernmost States, He was the Unenvied Head of the Army, and such was the majic of his name that his opinion was a sanction equal to law.—General Washington was more the favourit of Fortune than any Man in the World, He lived to see accomplished every wish he had formed, and he died at a moment when his life was as critically necessary to his Country as at any preceding one—

# THE NEW NATION

## 1800

~

## 1844

I have this morning witnessed one of the most interesting scenes a free people can ever witness. The changes of administration, which in every government and in every age have most generally been epochs of confusion, villainy and bloodshed, in this our happy country take place without any species of distraction, or disorder.

*—Margaret Bayard Smith to her sister-in-law*
*March 4, 1801*

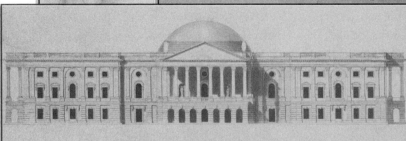

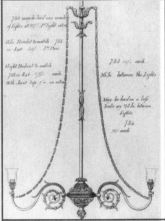

# BETWEEN 1800 AND 1844 . . .

**1800:** Washington, D.C., becomes the nation's new capital.  ★The U.S. population is 5.3 million, an increase of 35 percent in just 10 years.  **1803:** Ohio enters the Union as the seventeenth state.  ★ In one of his most influential acts as president, Thomas Jefferson arranges to have the United States buy the Louisiana Territory from France for $15 million.  **1804:** After years of political disagreements, and having heard rumors that Alexander Hamilton had insulted him at a political dinner, Aaron Burr kills Hamilton in a duel at Weehawken, New Jersey.  **1805:** Carrying her baby son on her back and serving as scout, interpreter, wildlife guide, nurse, and laundress, 17-year-old Sacagawea is the only woman to accompany Meriwether Lewis and William Clark on their expedition to the Pacific.  **1807:** Robert Fulton launches the first commercial steamboat service in the world when his boat, the *Clermont,* takes just 32 hours to travel 150 miles upstream on the Hudson River.  **1812:** Inflamed by Britain's attempts to bully American ships and impair trade, as well as by its apparent encouragement of Indian raids on frontier settlements, the United States embarks on the War of 1812, which is widely perceived as a second war of

---

Clockwise from top left: Ralph Waldo Emerson; "Pennsylvania Barroom Dancing" by John Lewis Krimmel; Dolley Madison; Gaslight; Angelina Grimké; Robert Fulton's self-portrait in his submarine; "The Star Spangled Banner" sheet music cover; "Woman's Holy War" by Currier & Ives; Lucretia Mott; Design for U.S. Capitol building, Washington, D.C., 1800.

independence.  **1814:** After watching the British attack Baltimore, Francis Scott Key writes the poem "Defence of Fort M'Henry"; set to the tune of an English drinking song, it will become popular as "The Star-Spangled Banner" and, still later, adopted as the national anthem; less well known than its first verse are its three others, which include the not quite memorable quatrain: "And where is that band who so vauntingly swore / That the havock of war and the battle's confusion / A home and a country should leave us no more? / Their blood has wash'd out their foul footsteps' pollution..."  **1813:** In Newport, Rhode Island, David Melville sets up a public demonstration of the gaslight he has invented, charging each onlooker 25 cents.  **1815:** Construction begins on the Cumberland Road, the first part of the first national highway, stretching from Cumberland, Maryland, to Wheeling, West Virginia; it is built of crushed stones.  **1820:** Congress passes the Missouri Compromise, allowing Maine to enter the union as a free state and Missouri to enter without slavery restrictions.  **1821:** Emma Hart Willard founds the first endowed school for girls, the Troy Female Seminary, in upstate New York.  **1822:** Lowell, Massachusetts, is established as the nation's first planned industrial town; by 1846, some 10,000 looms will be worked by mill girls, producing a million yards of cloth a week.  **1824:** The *Harrisburg Pennsylvanian* prints the results of the first public opinion poll, tallying readers' responses about how they intend to vote in the upcoming presidential election.  **1826:** Thomas Jefferson and John Adams die within hours of each other on July 4, exactly 50 years after Independence Day. Among Adams's last (though mistaken) words are: "Jefferson survives."  **1827:** At the Bowery Theater in New York, French dancer Francisquy Hutin performs the first ballet in the United States; some women in the audience leave because they are scandalized by Hutin's scanty attire.  **1828:** Sarah Josepha Hale, a 40-year-old widow and mother of five, begins editing the *Ladies' Magazine and Literary Gazette* (eventually *Godey's Lady's Book*), which is the first American magazine to offer original women's writing.  **1832:** President Andrew Jackson signs an executive order that substitutes coffee and sugar for the traditional soldiers' field ration of rum, whiskey, or brandy. **1835:** In the annual report of the newly formed Female Moral Reform Society of the City of New York, the board declares that some prostitutes have been "reclaimed," but, in keeping with the group's generally dire view of morality, the report adds: "While [members of the society] consider the reformation of abandoned females to be an important object, and while they hope that many will be reformed, they conceive that even the *reformation of thousands* would contribute but very little towards checking the tide of licentiousness that is rapidly increasing in our country." **1836:** After a 13-day siege during which they are outnumbered at least ten to one by Mexican troops, 183 Texans fighting for independence are slain at the Alamo, an 18th-century Franciscan mission in San Antonio. **1837:** Eighty-one delegates from 12 states attend the first convention of the National Female Anti-Slavery Society. ★ Embracing the reigning "cult of true womanhood," Eliza Farrar in *The Young Lady's Friend* offers women advice on how to avoid losing their virtue: "Sit not with another in a place that is too narrow; read not out of the same book; let not your eagerness to see anything induce you to place your head close to another person's." **1838:** Tennessee passes the first state temperance law, making it illegal to sell alcohol. **1839:** Mississippi passes the first Married Woman's Property Act, inspired by a court decision in favor of a Chickasaw woman whose tribal tradition gave married women property protection. **1840:** In an effort to make bathing more popular, Caroline Gilman writes a manual in which she reassures her readers: "You have nothing to do but to remove your clothing and apply the water to your whole body with your hands.... You may stand on a carpet or the floor to perform the operation, or ... you may have a shallow vessel like a large baking pan, if you choose, to stand in." **1844:** Demonstrating his new invention, Samuel F. B. Morse sends a telegraph message from Washington, D.C., to Baltimore; the message: "What hath God wrought?"

---

*By the turn of the century, despite the Revolutionary quest for independence and human rights, women's place in American society had changed little. Not until 1839 would the first state—Mississippi—overturn the laws of coverture; meanwhile, in keeping with that long-held convention, the legal status of married women remained essentially nonexistent. Before a woman married, she could make wills and contracts, and buy and sell property. But, as this petition from Elizabeth Whitworth suggests, once married, she had—barring an act of legislature—virtually no rights, no matter how badly her husband treated her.*

Stokes County is in North Carolina. Elizabeth Whitworth was granted a separate estate.

The Petition of Elizabeth Whitworth of Stokes County Humbly sheweth, that in the year 1786 She intermarried with a Certain John Whitworth, and that previous to her intermarriage with the said John, she was a Widdow with Two Children, and was in affluant circumstances, and immediately after the intermarriage, the said John betook himself to Gameing, Drinking & Contracting of Debts & thereby soon brought your Petitioner & family into indigent Circumstances, & in the year 1796 the said John deserted the said Elizabeth & has not yet returnd., and it is Currently reported that he is living in adultry with a woman in the State of' South Carolina, and your petitioner further Sheweth, that at the time of the desertion of the said John he was excessively indebted by Judgments, Bonds, Notes &c—and that she being anxious to Support herself & family by her & their Labour & cannot do it without being Subject to the payment of the extravagant Debts of the said John—Now your Petitioner prays that your Honorable body, would take her case under Consideration, & if they can pass an Act, that the property she may hereafter acquire shall not be Subject to the payment of the said Johns Debts which he has already or may hereafter

Contract, and that the said John shall have no more power or Authority to Sell or dispose of such acquired property, as your Petitioner may acquire, than any other Person Whatever.

and as in duty bound your Petitioner will ever Pray &c.

Elizabeth Whitworth

## 1801: MARCH 4
## MARGARET BAYARD SMITH TO SUSAN SMITH

*In 1801, the century was new, and so was the location of the nation's capital. The year before, Margaret Bayard (1778–1844) had married her second cousin, Na-*tional Intelligencer *editor Samuel Harrison Smith, and moved with him to Washington, D.C. An evocative and prolific letter writer, Margaret would prove to be a superb observer of political and social life, and in this letter to her sister-in-law Susan (1780–?), she expressed the optimism that so many Republicans felt at the prospect of having Thomas Jefferson become the third president.*

Partisan politics had evolved during the years of Washington's and Adams's administrations, with Republicans and Federalists emerging as the forerunners of today's Democrats and Republicans. Jefferson and Aaron Burr, both Republicans, had tied for the presidency in December of 1800, and the election had gone to the House of Representatives, which did not reach a deciding vote until February. William Charles Cole Claiborn was the new governor of Mississippi. Gouverneur Morris, Jonathan Dayton, and James Bayard (another cousin) were all Federalists. Mary Ann Smith was Susan's sister, Margaret's other sister-in-law.

March 4, 1801.

Let me write to you my dear Susan, e'er that glow of enthusiasm has fled, which now animates my feelings; let me congratulate not only you, but all my fellow citizens, on an event which will have so auspicious an influence on their political welfare. I have this morning witnessed one of the most interesting scenes, a free people can ever witness. The changes of administration, which in every government and in every age have most generally been epochs of confusion, villainy and bloodshed, in this our happy country take place without any species of distraction, or disorder. This day, has one of the most amiable and worthy men taken that seat to which he was called by the voice of his country. I cannot describe the agitation I felt, while I looked around on the various multitude and while I listened to an address, containing principles the most correct, sentiments the most liberal, and wishes the most benevolent conveyed in the most appropriate and elegant language and in a manner mild as it was firm. If doubts of the integrity and talents of Mr. Jefferson ever existed in the minds of any one, methinks this address must forever eradicate them. The Senate chamber was so crowded that I believe not another creature could enter. On one side of the house the Senate sat, the other was resigned by the representatives to the ladies. The roof is arched, the room half circle, every inch of ground was occupied. It has been conjectured by several gentlemen whom I've asked, that there were near a thousand persons within the walls. The speech was delivered in so low a tone that few heard it. Mr. Jefferson had given your Brother a copy early in the morning, so that on coming out of the house, the paper was distributed immediately. Since then there has been a constant succession of persons coming for the papers. I have been interrupted several times in this letter by the gentlemen of Congress, who have been to bid us their adieus; since three o'clock there has been a constant succession. Mr. Claibourn, a most amiable and agreeable man, called the moment before his departure and there is no one whose society I shall more regret the loss of. You will smile when I tell you that Gouveneur Morris, Mr. Dayton and Bayard drank tea here; they have just gone after sitting near two hours.

Mr. Foster will be the bearer of this letter; he is a widower, looking out for a wife; he is a man of respectable talents, and most amiable disposition and comfortable fortune. What think you my good sister Mary of setting your cap for him? As for you, Susan, you are rather too young, and I have another in my eye for you. One recommendation Mr. F. will have in your eyes, that he has been this winter on the most social and friendly terms with us, seen us very often and can tell you a great deal about us.

I trust my dear sisters we shall see you after you receive this letter. I have been so often interrupted while writing it, that I have felt inclined to throw it aside, but as I have a great many more letters to write by Mr. Foster, I must let you take it as it is. How is Mrs. Higginson? I wish to hear particularly something about her. If I had not so many correspondents already, I should ask communications from herself. I have written this in a hasty and desultory manner. Adieu.

## 1802: MARCH 1
## ELIZA SOUTHGATE TO MARY SOUTHGATE

*Born in Scarborough, Maine, Eliza Southgate (1783–1809) was the third of twelve children in a well-to-do, literate family. Having attended boarding school, an increasingly common option for girls whose parents could afford it, she turned her attention to a busy social life. In this vivid letter to her mother, Mary (1757–1824), about a snowy adventure, Eliza expressed the hopes and enthusiasms of a young woman at the start of a new era.*

"Assembly" was a common word for a dance or social function, whereas "meeting" referred to a church gathering. Southgate met Walter Bowne later the same year, married him in 1803, and had two children. After the birth of her second child, her health failed, and she died in 1809; she was only twenty-five.

Portland, March 1, 1802.

Such a frolic! Such a chain of adventures I never before met with, nay, the page of romance never presented its equal. 'Tis now Monday,—but a little more method, that I may be understood. I have just ended my Assembly's adventure, never got home till this morning. Thursday it snowed violently, indeed for two days before it had been storming so much that the snow drifts were very large; however, as it was the last Assembly I could not resist the temptation of going, as I knew all the world would be there. About 7 I went down-stairs and found young Charles Coffin, the minister, in the parlor. After the usual enquiries were over he stared awhile at my feathers and flowers, asked if I was going out,—I told him I was going to the Assembly. "Think, Miss Southgate," said he, after a long pause, "think you would go out to <u>meeting</u> in such a storm as this?" Then assuming a tone of reproof, he entreated me to examine well my feelings on such an occasion. I heard in silence, unwilling to begin an argument that I was unable to support. The stopping of the carriage roused me; I immediately slipt on my socks and coat, and met Horatio and Mr. Motley in the entry. The snow was deep, but Mr. Motley took me up in his arms and sat me in the carriage without difficulty. I found a full assembly, many married ladies, and every one disposed to end the winter in good spirits. At one we left dancing and went to the card-room to wait for a coach. It stormed dreadfully. The hacks were all employed as soon as they returned, and we could not get one till 3 o'clock, for about two they left the house, determined not to return again for the night. It was the most violent storm I ever knew. There were now 20 in waiting, the gentlemen scolding and fretting, the ladies murmuring and complaining. One hack returned; all flocked to the stairs to engage a seat. So many crowded down that 'twas impossible to get past; luckily I was one of the first, I stept in, found a young lady, almost a stranger in town, who keeps at Mrs. Jordan's, sitting in the back-seat. She immediately caught hold of me and beg'd if I possibly could accommodate her to take her home with me, as she had attempted to go to Mrs. Jordan's, but the drifts were so high, the horses could not get through; that they were compelled to return to the hall, where she had not a single acquaintance with whom she could go home. I was distres't, for I could not ask her home with me, for sister had so much company that I was obliged to go home with Sally Weeks and give my chamber to Parson Coffin. I told her this, and likewise that she should be provided for if my endeavors could be of any service. None but ladies were permitted to get into the carriage; it presently was stowed in so full that the horses could not move; the door was burst open, for such a clamor as the closing of it occasioned I never before heard. The universal cry was—"a gentleman in the coach, let him come out!" We all protested there was none, as it was too dark to distinguish; but the little man soon raised his voice and bid the coachman proceed; a dozen voices gave contrary orders. 'Twas a proper riot, I was really alarmed. My gentleman, with a vast deal of fashionable independence, swore no power on earth should make him quit his seat; but a gentleman at the door jump't into the carriage, caught hold of him, and would have dragged him out if we had not all entreated them to desist. He squeezed again into his seat, inwardly exulting to think he should get safe home from such rough creatures as the men, should pass for a lady, be secure under their protection, for none would insult him before them, mean creature!! The carriage at length started full of ladies, and not one gentleman to protect us, except our lady man who had crept to us for shelter. When we found ourselves in the street, the first thing was to find out who was in the carriage and where we were all going, who first must be left. Luckily two gentlemen had followed by the side of the carriage, and when it stopt took out the ladies as they got to their houses. Our sweet little, trembling, delicate, unprotected fellow sat immovable whilst the two gentlemen that were obliged to walk thro' all the snow and storm carried all the ladies from the carriage. What could be the motive of the little wretch for creeping in with us I know not: I should have thought 'twas his great wish to serve the ladies, if he had moved from the seat, but 'twas the most singular thing I ever heard of. We at length arrived at the place of our destination. Miss Weeks asked Miss Coffin (for that was the unlucky girl's name) to go home with her, which she readily did. The gentlemen then proceeded to take us out. My beau, unused to carrying such a weight of sin and folly, sank under its pressure, and I was obliged to carry my mighty self through the snow which almost buried me. Such a time, I never shall forget it! My great-grandmother never told any of her youthful adventures to equal it. The storm continued till Monday, and I was obliged to stay; but Monday I insisted if there was any possibility of getting to Sister's to set out. The horse and sleigh were soon at the door, and again I sallied forth to brave the tempestuous weather (for it still snowed) and surmount the many obstacles I had to meet with. We rode on a few rods, when coming directly upon a large drift, we stuck fast. We could neither get forward nor turn round. After waiting till I was most frozen we got out, and with the help of a truckman the sleigh was lifted up and turned towards a cross street that led to Federal Street. We again went on; at the corner we found it impossible to turn up or turn, but must go down and begin where we first started, and take a new course; but suddenly turning the corner we came full upon a pair of trucks, heavily laden; the drift on one side was so large that it left a very narrow passage between that and the corner house, indeed we were obliged to go so near that the post grazed my bonnet. What was to be done? Our horses' heads touched before we saw them. I jump't out, the sleigh was unfastened and lifted round, and we again measured back our old steps. At length we arrived at Sister Boyd's door, and the drift before it was the greatest we had met with; the horse was so exhausted that he sunk down, and we really thought him dead. 'Twas some distance from the gate and no path. The gentleman took me up in his arms and carried me till my weight pressed him so far into the snow that he had no power to move his feet. I rolled out of his arms and wallowed till I reached the gate; then rising to shake off the snow, I turned and beheld my beau fixed and immoveable; he could not get his feet out to take another step. At length, making a great exertion to spring his whole length forward, he made out to reach the poor horse, who lay in a worse condition than his master. By this time all the family had gathered to the window, indeed they saw the whole frolic; but 'twas not yet ended, for, unluckily, in pulling off Miss Weeks' bonnet to send to the sleigh to be carried back, I pulled off my wig and left my head bare. I was perfectly convulsed with laughter. Think what a ludicrous figure I must have been, still standing at the gate, my bonnet halfway to the sleigh and my wig in my hand. However, I hurried it on, for they were all laughing at the window, and made the best of my way into the house. The horse was unhitched and again set out, and left me to ponder on the incidents of the morning. I have since heard of several events that took place that Assembly night much more amusing than mine,—nay, Don Quixote's most ludicrous adventures compared with some of them will appear like the common events of the day.

### 1802: APRIL 16
### MARTHA JEFFERSON RANDOLPH TO THOMAS JEFFERSON

*By the time Thomas Jefferson (1743–1826) became president, he had been a widower for nineteen years and had been largely responsible for overseeing the education of his children. Now grown and married to Virginia congressman Thomas Mann Randolph, Jr., Martha Jefferson Randolph (1772–1836) remained a dutiful eldest daughter and, like her father, was both frank and watchful in regard to her own children's intellectual abilities.*

Edgehill was the Randolph family home in Virginia. The medal Martha referred to was a newly made Indian peace medal that bore a profile of Jefferson on one side and the words "peace and friendship" on the other. Jean-Antoine Houdon was considered the greatest portrait sculptor of the day. Eventually the Randolphs would have twelve children, including James Madison Randolph, the first child born in the White House. Those mentioned in this letter ranged in age from eleven-year-old Anne to one-year-old Virginia.

Edgehill April 16 1802

I recieved with gratitude and pleasure unexpressible, my dearest Father, the elegant medal you sent me. It arrived safely with out a scratch even, and is I think a good likeness; but as I found fault with Houdon for making you too old I shall have the same quarrel with the medal also. You have many years to live before the likeness can be a perfect one. Mr. R. desired me to tell you that as his trip to Georgia was but to take a view of the country, a few weeks sooner or later would make no material difference with him and his anxiety to conduct such a family of little children thro the difficulties of the journey would naturally induce him to pospone his as it will be attended by no inconvenience to himself. Ellen and Cornelia have had an erruption attended with fever which has been prevalent in the neighbourhood; certainly not the chicken pox but what else we cannot determine. Ellen is well and Cornelia much better. Virginia is certainly for size and health the finest child I ever had. Cutting her teeth with out fever, disordered bowels or other indication of her situation but the champing of her gums and the appearance of the teeth them selves. The others go on better than they did last winter. Jefferson is reading latin with his Papa but I am seriously uneasy at his not going to school. Mr. Murray with whom we proposed putting him has his number complete and will not I fear take another. Anne translates with tolerable facility, and Ellen reads, not very correctly it is true, but in a way speedily to do so I hope for which I really think we are indebted to your letter expressing your surprise at her having in so short a time learned to read and write; she began with it her self, and by continually spelling out lines and putting them together and then reading them to who ever would listen to her, she convinced me of the practicability of carrying on reading and spelling together before in the regular course of the business she had got into two syllables. The writing she attempted also but the trouble was so much greater than any end to be answered by teaching her at so early a period that very reluctantly I prevailed upon her to defer that part of her education to a more distant one. So much for my hopes and fears with regard to those objects in which they center. The former preponderate upon the whole, yet my anxiety about them frequently makes me unreasonably apprehensive. Unreasonably I think for surely if they turn out well with regard to morals I <u>ought</u> to be satisfied, tho I <u>feel</u> that I never can sit down quietly under the idea of their being blockheads. Adieu Dear adored Father. We look forward with transport to the time at which we shall all meet at Monticello tho not on my side unmixed with pain when I think it will be the precursor of a return to the world from which I have been so long been secluded and for which my habits render me every way unfit, tho the pleasure of seeing you every day is a good that will render every other evil light. Once more adieu. The children are clamorous to be remembered to you and believe your self <u>first</u> and unrivaled in the heart of your devoted child.

M. Randolph

## 1804: JULY 11
## ANGELICA SCHUYLER CHURCH TO PHILIP SCHUYLER

*Jefferson's vice president, Aaron Burr, and Alexander Hamilton had been political archenemies for decades, and in 1804, having heard rumors of a new insult from Hamilton, Burr challenged the former treasury secretary to a duel. The result would of course prove fatal to Hamilton, but when his sister-in-law, Angelica Schuyler Church (1756–1815), wrote this letter to her brother, Philip Schuyler (1768–1835), the news didn't yet seem that dire.*

William Bayard owned the house near Greenwich Street in New York City where Hamilton died. The sister Angelica referred to was Hamilton's wife, Elizabeth Schuyler.

At Mr. Bayard's, Greenwich.<br>Wednesday Morning.

My Dear Brother:

I have the painful task to inform you that Gen. Hamilton was this morning wounded by that wretch Burr, but we have every reason to hope that he will recover. May I advise that you repair immediately to my father, as perhaps he may wish to come down.

My dear sister bears with saintlike fortitude this affliction. The town is in consternation, and there exists only the expression of grief and indignation.

Adieu, my dear brother

Ever yours,
A. Church.

## 1806: JUNE 16
## SARAH CARY TO SAM CARY

*Sarah Cary (1783–?) was living in Massachusetts when she witnessed a total solar eclipse and described it in this letter to her brother Samuel (1773–1810). The eclipse would come to be known as "Tecumseh's Eclipse," because it was said to have been brought about by the Indian leader; his apparent power in controlling the heavens fortified his following.*

Cary would eventually marry Joseph Tuckerman, a Unitarian minister and pioneering social worker.

June 16, 1806.

My Dear Brother Sam,—

I have to day witnessed a total eclipse of the sun, the most grand and awful sight that I or perhaps any one ever beheld. I cannot tell if you could have been sensible of it or not, but at any rate I think you may feel some curiosity to know how it appeared here. In the first place, it was a most beautiful day; not one cloud to prevent the observation, or encourage terror in the imagination of any one. At ten o'clock we were first sensible of the moon's appearance, and observed her by degrees obscure the whole sun, which happened at half after eleven o'clock. And then, oh! I cannot find a word to express the grandeur and solemnity of the scene; the glorious sun was entirely covered by a black ball, which would indeed have been frightful but that from the whole circle of the <u>midnight</u> ball he gleamed forth his blessed rays of light as if to keep alive our hopes of his return. This lasted about four minutes and then, impatient of the gloom, he seemed to burst forth with greater splendor than ever, and in an hour entirely emerged from it. Our light at the time of greatest darkness was very like that the moon gives us when not at the brightest. We saw about six stars, and the air was cold and damp, like that of night. I wished that you were with us, and would have given anything to hear you say something about it.

We are all well, but have not heard from you for a great while. I am in a great hurry, as all the letters have gone already and the vessel sails to-morrow.

> Your very affectionate sister,
> S. C.

## 1812: AUGUST 12
## THEODOSIA BURR ALSTON TO AARON BURR

*Adored daughter of the former vice president, Theodosia Burr Alston (1783–1813) wrote to Aaron Burr (1756–1836) two months after the death of her ten-year-old son and only child. In December, Theodosia set sail from South Carolina on board the* Patriot *to see her father in New York, but her ship was lost at sea. Legend has it that her ghost still haunts the family plantation.*

Theodosia's husband, Joseph Alston, would be elected governor of South Carolina in December, but at the time of her writing he was awaiting a military court of inquiry about the legality of one of his own promotions. He was ultimately acquitted.

> Seashore, August 12, 1812.

Alas! my dear father, I do live, but how does it happen? Of what am I formed that I live, and why? Of what service can I be in this world, either to you or any one else, with a body reduced to premature old age, and a mind enfeebled and bewildered? Yet, since it is my lot to live, I will endeavour to fulfil my part, and exert myself to my utmost, though this life must henceforth be to me a bed of thorns. Whichever way I turn, the same anguish still assails me. You talk of consolation. Ah! you know not what you have lost. I think Omnipotence could give me no equivalent for my boy; no, none—none.

I wish to see you, and will leave this as soon as possible, though not so soon as you propose. I could not go alone by land, for our coachman is a great drunkard, and requires the presence of a master; and my husband is obliged to wait for a military court of inquiry, which he demanded, and is ordered on him. It will sit on the 10th of August. How long it will be in session I know not. After that we shall set off, though I do not perceive how it is possible to speak with certainty, because Mr. Alston has the command of a brigade here. When we do go, he thinks of going by water, but is not determined. It will probably be late in August before we go. God bless you, my beloved father. Write to me sometimes. What do you wish done with your papers if I should go by land?

I have been reading your letter over again. I am not insensible to your affection, nor quite unworthy of it, though I can offer nothing in return but the love of a broken, deadened heart, still desirous of promoting your happiness, if possible. God bless you.

Theodosia.

## 1814: AUGUST 23
## DOLLEY MADISON TO ANNA CUTTS

---

*Also known as the second war of American independence, the War of 1812 was provoked by trade and border disputes, and it represented Britain's last attempt to gain control of the United States. For two years, Americans struggled, enduring the failure of their own land campaign in Canada and the success of a British naval blockade in the East. At a particularly low moment, the British occupied Washington and set fire to the White House. Acting quickly, First Lady Dolley Payne Madison (1768–1849) became a national hero when she bravely saved state documents and the famous Gilbert Stuart portrait of George Washington.*

Dolley had three sisters. The one to whom she was closest, Anna Cutts (1779–1832), is believed to have been the recipient of this letter. The original document has been lost, and recent research suggests that what is considered the original is actually a copy that Dolley made—and perhaps emended—some twenty years after the fire. General William Winder was a Baltimore lawyer who commanded the forces around Washington; after being routed at nearby Bladensburg, he was generally blamed for the burning of the capital.

Tuesday Augt. 23d. 1814.

Dear Sister,—

My husband left me yesterday morng. to join Gen. Winder. He enquired anxiously whether I had courage, or firmness to remain in the President's house until his return, on the morrow, or succeeding day, and on my assurance that I had no fear but for him and the success of our army, he left me, beseeching me to take care of myself, and of the cabinet papers, public and private. I have since recd. two despatches from him, written with a pencil; the last is alarming, because he desires I should be ready at a moment's warning to enter my carriage and leave the city; that the enemy seemed stronger than had been reported, and that it might happen that they would reach the city, with intention to destroy it. . . . I am accordingly ready; I have pressed as many cabinet papers into trunks as to fill one carriage; our private property must be sacrificed, as it is impossible to procure wagons for its transportation. I am determined not to go myself until I see Mr Madison safe, and he can accompany me,—as I hear of much hostility towards him, . . . disaffection stalks around us. . . . My friends and acquaintances are all gone; Even Col. C with his hundred men, who were stationed as a guard in the enclosure. . . . French John (a faithful domestic,) with his usual activity and resolution, offers to spike the cannon at the gate, and to lay a train of powder which would blow up the British, should they enter the house. To the last proposition I positively object, without being able, however, to make him understand why all advantages in war may not be taken.

Wednesday morng., twelve o'clock.—Since sunrise I have been turning my spy glass in every direction and watching with unwearied anxiety, hoping to discern the approach of my dear husband and his friends, but, alas, I can descry only groups of military wandering in all directions, as if there was a lack of arms, or of spirit to fight for their own firesides!

Three O'clock.—Will you believe it, my Sister? We have had a battle or skirmish near Bladensburg, and I am still here within sound of the cannon! Mr. Madison comes not; may God protect him! Two messengers covered with dust, come to bid me fly; but I wait for him. . . . At this late hour a wagon has been procured; I have had it filled with the plate and most valuable portable articles belonging to the house; whether it will reach its destination; the Bank of Maryland, or fall into the hands of British soldiery, events must determine.

Our kind friend, Mr. Carroll, has come to hasten my departure, and is in a very bad humor with me because I insist on waiting until the large picture of Gen. Washington is secured, and it requires to be unscrewed from the wall. This process was found too tedious for these perilous moments; I have ordered the frame to be broken, and the canvass taken out;—it is done, and the precious portrait placed in the hands of two gentlemen of New York, for safe keeping. And now, dear sister, I must leave this house, or the retreating army will make me a prisoner in it, by filling up the road I am directed to take. When I shall again write you, or where I shall be tomorrow, I cannot tell!!

### 1814: AUGUST 25
### MARTHA SELDEN JONES TO MARTHA GIBSON

*The burning of Washington, including the Capitol, most government buildings, and several private homes, went on for two days. From a mansion called Chatham near Fredericksburg, Virginia, a frightened Martha Selden Jones (1762?–1837) wrote to her niece Martha Macmurdo Gibson (1792–1867), mingling details of the encroaching war with a far more mundane complaint.*

The war ended within months, and while the United States had hardly defeated Britain (at best the end was a stalemate), America's sovereignty would not be challenged again. The baby,

William Douglas Gibson, was the first of Gibson's four children. Martha Jones was herself childless. Cary Selden was a nearby relative. Chiloe was the home of Jones's sister in Cumberland County.

Chatham 25ᵗʰ August 1814

My dearest Child—

I have only a moment whilst the servants eat their breakfast—to tel you what heart felt pleasure your letter (without date) gave me—to hear that you & my dear Baby enjoy health—will be my comfort amidst all the horrors of War—We have every reason to fear that Washington were in flames last night from the appearance of fire, & redness in the Skies—& sound of Cannon—the British shipping lie in sight of Cary Seldens—which is only 7 miles from us—say six Ships—Tenders—& Barges—it is expected as soon as the main body of the troops compleats all the mischief they can do at Washington Alexandria—& else where, they will attack us—We have only about 600 raw melitia station at Cary Seldens, We have sent off 5 Waggon loads—& am still packing up—& shall leave this on the first alarm—Poor Chatham must stand it's ground, I expect it will be burnt certainly if Fredericks goes—Should their be the least alarm in Richmond pray sit off immediately for Chiloe—they have plenty of house roome, & you know would be happy to see you & all your family—you shall hear from me when ever I have leisure to write, which will not be very often—

I cannot comply with your request just now—as all the men belonging to the fulling mill are down with the melitia, as soon as quietness is again restored, I will attend to it, as you direct, with respect to the Bonnet you have ben so kind as to procure for me, I will thank you to keep for me, not wanting it just now in this state of confusion

I hope it is not made like the one I sent down as that was too Youth ful for me not having brim enough to shade the face—in hast—I bid adieu—my best my sincerest regards to you & yours—your affectionate

M. Jones

## 1815: JULY 30
## EMMA HART WILLARD TO ALMIRA HART

*A trailblazer in the field of women's education, Emma Hart Willard (1787–1870) would become famous in her later life for establishing the Troy Female Seminary, which was later renamed for her. She was still running her first school, in Middlebury, Vermont—and married to a physician named John Willard—when she sent this brutally pessimistic marital advice to her younger sister, Almira Hart (1793–1884).*

Almira ignored Emma's advice, married Simeon Lincoln, and stayed married until her husband's death. Years later, after herself being widowed, Emma would endure a brief and disastrous marriage to a gambler. "Little John" was Emma's only child, born in 1810.

Middlebury, *July* 30, 1815.

Dear Sister:

You think it strange that I should consider a period of happiness as more likely than any other to produce future misery. I know I did not sufficiently explain myself. Those tender and delicious sensations which accompany successful love, while they soothe and soften the mind, diminish its strength to bear or to conquer difficulties. It is the luxury of the soul; and luxury always enervates. A degree of cold that would but brace the nerves of the hardy peasant, would bring distress or death to him who had been pampered by ease and indulgence. This life is a life of vicissitude. A period of happiness, by softening and enervating the soul, by raising a thousand blissful images of the future, naturally prepares the mind for a greater or less degree of disappointment, and unfits us to bear it; while, on the contrary, a period of adversity often strengthens the mind, and, by destroying inordinate anticipation of the future, gives a relish to whatever pleasures may be thrown in our way. This, perhaps you may acknowledge, is generally true; but you cannot think it applies to your case—otherwise than that you acknowledge yourself liable to disappointment by death. But we will pass over that, and we will likewise pass over the possibility of your lover's seeing some object that he will consider more interesting than you, and likewise that you may hereafter discover some imperfection in his character. We will pass this over, and suppose that the sanction of the law has been passed upon your connection, and you are secured to each other for life. It will be natural that, at first, he should be much devoted to you; but, after a while, his business must occupy his attention. While absorbed in that he will perhaps neglect some of those little tokens of affection which have become necessary to your happiness. His affairs will sometimes go wrong, and perhaps he will not think proper to tell you the cause; he will appear to you reserved and gloomy, and it [will] be very natural in such a case for you to imagine that he is displeased with you, or is less attached than formerly. Possibly you may not in every instance manage a family as he has been accustomed to think was right, and he may sometimes hastily give you a harsh word or a frown. But where is the use, say you, of diminishing my present enjoyment by such gloomy apprehensions? Its use is this, that, if you enter the marriage state believing such things to be absolutely impossible, if you should meet them, they would come upon you with double force. We should endeavor to make a just estimate of our future prospects, and consider what evils, peculiar situations in which we may be placed, are most likely to beset us, and endeavor to avert them if we can; or, if we must suffer them, to do it with fortitude, and not magnify them by imagination, and think that, because we cannot enjoy all that a glowing fancy can paint, there is no enjoyment left. I hope I shall see Mr. L——. I shall be very glad to have you come and spend the winter with me, and, if he could with propriety accompany you, I should be glad to see him. I am involved in care. There [are] forty in our family and seventy in the school. I have, however, an excellent house-keeper and a very good assistant in my school. You seem to have some wise conjectures floating in your brain, but, unfortunately for your skill in guessing, they have no foundation in truth.

Little John says I must tell you he has learned a great deal. He goes to a little children's school, and is doing very well. Doctor has not yet gone to Pittsfield after mother, but expects to set out this week. We both feel very unpleasantly that he could not have gone before, but a succession of engagements made it impossible.

Yours affectionately,
Emma Willard.

### 1816: JULY 2
### SARAH ALLEN TO HER SISTER

*We have been able to learn nothing about the author or the recipient of this letter, which was first published in an 1816 book. Shipwrecks were not uncommon in the early part of the nineteenth century, but accounts as vivid as this one are rare in any age.*

A tun was a barrel or casket. A supercargo was the ship's officer who managed the business concerns.

New-York, July 2, 1816

Dear Sister,

You have undoubtedly suffered much anxiety about me of late—you complain that I have barely informed you of the shocking incident that attended me, on my late passage to New-Orleans, without acquainting you with any of the particulars of it; and having first had your mind rendered easy with regard to my life and health, you desire now a more circumstantial detail of my unhappy adventures. I can refuse you nothing; but it is a task that friendship alone could urge me to, as even the recollection of sufferings, like mine, must ever be attended with pain; I cannot reflect on the miseries I have passed through, without the severest shock: You will see to what an excess of despair my sufferings had reduced me; and will not be surprised, therefore, that they had exhausted my strength, weakened my constitution, and that a situation and circumstances so forlorn as mine, should have almost impaired my reason.

I shall now relate the circumstances of my misfortunes, just as they happened, without exaggeration. Having received a letter from my husband, requesting me to join him in the Louisiana country, where he had been the winter past, I took passage in May last in the ship Mary, bound to New-Orleans. We had pleasant weather for six or seven days after our departure, but on the 12th it became squally, while the clouds wore a threatening aspect. At twelve at night it was discovered that the ship had sprung a leak, which threw the crew into the utmost consternation—the captain ordered all the heavy articles to be thrown overboard, and the pumps to be worked continually to keep the ship from sinking. But all in vain. The water increased fast, and the strength of the hands at the pumps became less and less; so that, finding that it was impossible for the ship to float long, the captain ordered her steered for Pensacola—but in this he was disappointed, for the winds, which had now almost increased to a hurricane, continued still to oppose every endeavour that was made; so that we were left without resource, in the midst of an enraged ocean, against which we combated at unequal odds, deprived of all prospect of reaching any haven at all, expecting every moment the deep to open its waves, and swallow us up in its bosom.

As it was now found utterly impossible to save either ship or effects, the preservation even of our lives becoming every moment more difficult to us, the ship's crew began to employ every thought and deed to that single consideration, and unanimously agreed to run the vessel aground at the Apalaches, but were not able to achieve even this desperate adventure, and continued still the cruel sport of waves and wind, in a state between life and death, sighing over our misfortunes, certain of our destruction, and yet making indefatigable efforts to extricate ourselves from the perils that surrounded us.

At 8 o'clock the succeeding evening our ship struck with great violence upon a rock!—even the little hope that we had till then preserved, now failed us—on the instant the ship resounded with the lamentable exclamations of the mariners, who interchanged their last adieus, prepared for death, implored the mercy of their Creator, addressed their fervent prayers to Heaven, interrupted sometimes by vows, in the midst of a shocking certainty of never being in a capacity of accomplishing them.

What a spectacle, my dear sister, was here! One must have been a witness of it to form an adequate idea of our distress; and that which I am taking so much pains to trace out to you, falls infinitely short of the reality. Being the only female on board, my terror it cannot be expected was much less than that of the mariners—I submitted to the fate that attended me, when it was beyond my power to avoid it; I resigned my life to the Being who had lent it, and preserved an astonishing degree of fortitude.

The wind drove the ship over the rocks toward the land, but the agitation of the sea would not permit us to reach it—at midnight the gale having greatly increased, our ship was once more thrown upon the rocks by the force of the waves. The moon which till this moment, had lent us a feeble light, interrupted only now and then by the intervention of the clouds, now left us suddenly in the dark, and in such circumstances, we found it impossible to reach the land. What an age of night it was! Alas! Sister, it would be vain for me to attempt to paint to your imagination a true description of my deplorable situation! While the rain fell in torrents, the waves rising every instant covered our bark, and rolled their mountains over our heads; the heavy peals of thunder roared through the air, and the quick intervals of lightning only served to open to us the horizon, and a devouring sea, ready to swallow us up, every moment, which was as quick succeeded by the most dismal darkness.

In such a situation, the ship thrown nearly upon her beam ends, and we drenched with rain and exhausted with the constant efforts we were obliged to exert against the fury of the waves, we at length perceived the morning's dawn, only to afford us a clearer view of the dangers we had passed, and those we had yet to encounter.

As the storm had somewhat abated, we perceived the main land at about a mile's distance—but the sentiment of joy, with which the first sight of it inspired us, was much abated upon a more distinct view of the enormous rocks which appeared to rise perpendicularly along the coast. The ship's boat was too small to contain the whole of the crew, and the raging of the sea would have daunted the stoutest and most expert swimmers; for the waves rolled with such fury, that whoever had delivered himself over to them, must have run the risk of being launched back into the main ocean, or dashed to pieces against the rocks—indeed it appeared as if we had made this fatal land only to render it a witness of our loss.

The day was again near closing, we reflected with terror on the last night, and trembled beforehand at that which was to come. We had a wretched boat, indeed, but in no sort of condition to weather even the short passage that appeared to lie between us and the land. The situation in which the ship lay upon her beam ends rendered it difficult to get at the inside of her, we remained, consequently, all this while, without meat or drink to recruit our strength or support our spirits; and without sleep, also, to forget our miseries, for the shortest moment. Fate seemed to have emptied its quiver of the sharpest arrows against us, and never could death appear with more horrid aspect to wretches before.

As night approached, the horizon was again obscured by black and angry looking clouds, and the wind which during the whole day had been moderate, by nine in the evening blew a tremendous gale—the sea, agitated by the wind, dashed against the stranded ship in every direction, and indeed with so much force, that at midnight, contrary to all expectation we found her once more afloat, and that having nearly righted, she was driving toward the main land—it was so very dark that only when assisted by the light of the sharp flashes of lightning, we could not perceive an object the shortest distance from us—our ship was driven once more stern foremost upon the rocks, while one of a perpendicular descent and of a great height before us, prevented our discovering during the night that these rocks communicated with the main land; when the discovery was made by day-light, how is it possible to describe the transport of all on board? It was expressed by shrieks, by most delicious tears, and mutual embraces, felicitating one another.

Having with some difficulty reached the summit of the huge rock before us, our first emotion was upon our bended knees to offer up our thanksgivings to Heaven, for having still preserved us alive even in such a deplorable situation, to raise up our suppliant hands in petition to Providence to complete its miracle, by affording us some unforeseen means of reaching some hospitable dwelling. There never was sure, a more fervent prayer.

The joy to find ourselves, at length, secure from those dangers which had so long kept us in the most cruel alarms, caused us to forget, for a moment, that we had only escaped one kind of death, probably to endure another more terrible and painful. As the rain continued to fall in torrents, attended with a tremendous wind, frightful peals of thunder and the sharpest lightning that I ever before witnessed, it was thought by all the most prudent step to erect a tent upon the spot where we were, as a shelter until the storm should abate; when the ship's crew calculated that they should be enabled to obtain provision, fireworks, and many other articles from the ship which we stood greatly in need of.—But, alas, how sadly were we disappointed—during the night the storm rather increased than abated, and the wind and sea which had combined to compel us to quit the wreck, now apparently redoubled their efforts to destroy her—we were apprized of our fate by the noise of her breaking up, which the morning's dawn comfirmed, as there was not a vestige of ship or cargo any where to be discovered.

Thus, my dear sister, were we once more plunged into a state of unutterable dispair!—nineteen souls of us on a wild and probably an uninhabited coast, without food or a prospect of obtaining any to satisfy the cravings of nature, and without the means to obtain a fire, by which to dry our cloaths and warm our limbs, now quite benumbed with cold and wet. This last distress being now our most pressing evil, made the crew apply their whole thoughts and diligence to remedy it. They tried the method said to be used by the savages, of kindling a fire, by rubbing two sticks quick and hard against each other; but, whether through aukwardness, or some other impediment, the experiment failed them, and they gave over all further projects of this kind. The oysters that we happily found on the coast furnished us with a truly delicious repast; the total privation of food we had sustained for so long a period, gave them a peculiar relish.

As the storm had now somewhat abated we began to think more seriously of our deplorable situation. We had esteemed ourselves happy when we looked back upon our miraculous escape: but ceased to be so when we looked forward to our future safety. We were cast upon a desert coast—we perceived no beaten path to conduct us to any inhabited spot: we had great forests to pass through where we must run the hazard of losing our way every step. Wild beasts were to be apprehended, and the meeting of savages, perhaps not less dangerous than they.

As there prevailed among the ship's crew a difference of opinion, with regard to what course it would be most advisable to pursue, they now divided into two seperate parties, the sailors (thirteen in number) with the second mate, composed one, and the supercargo, captain, mate and myself the other. The seperation being decided upon, and the object of each party being to reach St. Marks, that headed by the second mate chose to pursue a rout bordering upon the sea, while the captain, with those attached to his party, preferred a more inland course. This indeed proved an unfortunate circumstance, for us, for had we acquiesced in the opinion of the sailors, and accompanied them, our sufferings would have been much less, as they reached their place of destination three days before us.

Behold us now, dear sister, about to penetrate a wild and pathless forest, without resource, without food, and without arms to procure subsistence, and without an article of cloathing except what we wore on our backs! What a shocking situation! What hope, what possibility, even was left us now! And what could avail the noblest fortitude in such circumstances of despair?

It was now the 16th of May, when at about 10 o'clock in the morning we set forward—so little progress did our company make in penetrating a thick forest, that by the setting of the sun, it was thought that we had not travelled more than eight or nine miles—the extreme weariness we sunk under, and the fear of travelling in the night, made my miserable companions early seek a place of safety for the night—they made choice of a piece of rising ground, where several large trees, whose branches now furnished with leaves, sheltered us from the wind and dews. Here we hoped to have passed the night in peace, as our fatigue had inclined our eyes to sleep, and our limbs to rest, which, indeed, we much wanted; but no sooner had we reposed ourselves, than we were awakened with such dreadful howlings, as struck our hearts with terror and dismay; they seemed to answer each other, and encompass us on all sides. 'Tis impossible to conceive the horror with which we were seized, expecting every moment to become a prey to these ferocious animals, that seemed to approach us nearer and nearer, as the din grew louder at every howl. Happily, as the morning approached, the howlings which had so much terrified us, grew less and less, and seemed every moment to retire to a greater distance as day light appeared. The welcome morn at length arrived, and by driving the beasts back to their dens, relieved our alarms, which had hitherto suspended the cruel sensations of hunger: but, as soon as our fears were abated, these began to operate to a severe degree.

We early set out in hopes of meeting with some vegetable or other, fit to eat, and tried every plant in the desert, but in vain—they were either dry heath or leafless brambles, whose stems were only a hard wood, which we could scarcely set our teeth in, and which we could not prevail on ourselves to swallow the juice of, after we had chewed them.

Every experiment we made failed equally of success, forced tears from our eyes, and sunk us to the utmost depth of despair. Toward evening, we arrested our course, oppressed with the agonies of grief, and without the least ability to proceed one step further: we laid ourselves down on the ground, doubtful whether we should ever be able to raise our limbs from it again. O! my dear sister, it is impossible for you to conceive what were my sensations at this moment! The horrid din of the wild beasts, with which we had been used to the preceding nights, began now to strike our ears at a distance! However, none of them approached us so near as to injure us, and before the morning's dawn we fell into a slumber, and so received relief from our very weakness.

We early arose to pursue our uncertain journey; and directed our steps towards the forest, in further quest of Providence: its thickness and gloom made me tremble; the trees stood so close together, that there were but few opens left for us to pass through. We journeyed, for two days, with great difficulty and fatigue, sometimes labouring through strong high bulrushes, at other times through brambles, thorns, and various kinds of prickly plants, that tore our legs, and cut our feet in such a manner as occasioned great loss of blood, to weaken us still further.

This distress, though less miserable than hunger, retarded us considerably, and the stings of the musketoes, of sandflies, and an armed host of other winged insects, peculiar to that climate, had disfigured us so much, that it was difficult for either of us to distinguish a feature in the other; our faces, our hands, and legs being so swelled, with the venom of their bite.

In order to rid ourselves of such troublesome enemies, it was proposed by my unhappy companions, that we should again retire from the trees that harboured them, and travel along the sea-side, as we might there more probably meet with something that might serve to appease our hunger. We accordingly, at the first opening that pointed towards the right, directed our course that way, and happily reached the shore. We were not quite disappointed in our expectation; for, when the weather was fair and the tide out, we met with some small flounders, which the mate hooked up out of the water, with a sort of harpoon which he made of a branch of a tree, crooked and pointed at the end. But of such food, we never could procure sufficient, at any one time, for a meal; and but seldom had the good fortune to meet with them. It was, however, some little relief to us, and for which we most gratefully returned our thanks to Providence.

I cannot, my dear sister, give you, day by day, an account of our difficult and fatiguing journey, the end of which seemed to be still farther off, the longer we travelled. The sea-reeds, which spread all along the coast, gave us as much labour to pass through, as the thorns and brambles of the forest.

The wild beasts kept us in terror, every night; to which was added the horror of our very meals, as we never eat till we had finished our journey for the day. One evening, when we came to our usual halt, I felt myself so extremely feeble, that I had not strength to stand on my feet—my suffering companions, I could perceive, all viewed me with an eye of pity—the captain, mate, &c. gave me all the assistance that their miserable situation would enable them to do, always imparting to me a great portion of such food as they were enabled to obtain. On our next day's journey we met with a new sort of provision, that was extremely palatable, and nourishing to us—it was a wild Turkey, which the mate was so fortunate as to kill with a stone—it was very large, and supplied us with food for two days.

The succeeding day our journey was interrupted by a river that ran across our path into the sea. It was not broad, but its current was extremely rapid. The captain went in to sound it, to see if it possibly could be forded, but found the passage impracticable; the depth of water, prevented his wading through it, and had he or any one attempted to swim over, the violence of the stream, which no strength could stem, would have hurried him along with it into the ocean. There was then no other measure to take than to travel along by the side of the river, towards its source, and seek where we might find the current more gentle, or some shallow that might render the fording of it practicable.

We then proceeded in this direction, and continued it for two intire days, without perceiving any place that afforded us the least probability of compassing our end, for the further we went the more dangerous the attempt still appeared to be. Our inquietude and despondency increased with our difficulties, and we even began to despair of ever being able to get out of this desert.

We had not the good fortune to meet with any manner of aliment, during these two days progress, and we were consequently obliged to feed upon the leaves and roots of trees! Terrified at the past, distressed with the present, diffident of the future, and impatient at the obstinate continuance of our misfortunes, we passed the dismal hours in faint hopes, heavy sighs, and then closing our reflections in absolute despair. The continual view of a river always rapid, added to the weariness of our minds; the impossibility of passing it, with the necessity, however, of still marching forward, quite out of our purposed course, without the least prospect of meeting with a fordable passage, now finally damped all the spirit and courage we had yet been able to preserve through all our unexampled miseries.

Toward the latter end of the second day, while we were tracing the source of this river, the mate happened to turn up a tortoise, of an uncommon size. This precious gift of Providence suspended the murmurs which used to escape us every minute before, and changed them into exclamations of gratitude—and what added to our good fortune, we about sun-set succeeded in crossing the river.—Upon the banks of the river we passed the night, with the usual precautions; and, the next morning, being a little recruited by food and sleep, we set forward for St. Mark, in the Apalachian mountains, bearing our course eastward, as much as we could, and trembling every step of the way, for fear of mistaking our road.

A wood that we met with in our course, we found it almost impracticable to pass through, on account of the strong reeds and briars it was choaked up with, so that our feet and legs suffered severely from the thorns and brambles, while our hands and faces were exposed to the musketoes, sandflies, and wasps as before, whose poisonous bites and stings soon swelled our bodies to an enormous size! We struggled, for many days, through all these difficulties, which were augmented still by repeated sufferings, both of mind and body. No longer did fond hope sustain our drooping spirits, with expectations flattering, though vain; all distinction of our limbs and features was lost, and we resembled moving tuns, rather than human creatures. We marched heavily along, hardly able to set one foot before the other; and when we sat down to rest; it required our utmost efforts to raise ourselves from the ground again. In fine, we were now sunk to the lowest abyss of misery and despair.

I had until now been enabled to display an equal degree of fortitude, and to keep pace with my companions in misery, but the weight of our misfortunes became, at last, too heavy for my strength, or rather weakness to support.

One morning, not being able to stir one step farther, totally debilitated, and almost deprived of sight by the blisters which the venom of the insects had raised about my eyes, I laid myself down on the shore, which we had reached, about an hundred yards from the sea; and, after reposing my limbs for an hour, beneath a spreading tree, I attempted to rise again, with a purpose of continuing our march; but in vain. I felt as if the earth I pressed had been heaped upon me.

"It is over with me now, (said I, to my companions) hear must I remain forever; my grave encompasses me; this spot is, at length, the final end of my journey, of my misfortunes and my life. Avail yourselves of what powers you have yet remaining, to hasten forward to some inhabited part of the country, and do not idly spend them in waiting longer here with me; you see that fate has opposed my farther progress, and that my dissolution is beginning, from this moment; the ability which still remains to you shews that it is more favourably inclined towards you: take then the advantage of its kindness, and reflect sometimes with tenderness on the unfortunate associate of your miseries—should any of you survive to reach once more your native homes, do acquaint my husband and friends of my wretched fate!"

My unhappy companions could only answer me with tears and moans; their sensibility affected me; it is a consolation to the unhappy to see themselves the objects of compassion. The captain took my hands between his, and pressed them with the utmost tenderness, while I continued to persuade him to our seperation, urging the absolute necessity of it, in vain. "No, my dear friend (said he) I will not abandon you; exert your spirits, and your strength may return again—we will now go in search on the borders of the sea, for some fresh nourishment, which may possibly recruit your strength once more."—With saying this my companions left me, but in a short time again returned with a small tortoise, of which the first use I made was to wash my stings and blisters in its warm blood, as I imagined it allayed the heat and swelling—having made a refreshing meal of the flesh, we composed ourselves to rest, for some time, but my weakness was not relieved; and I found myself growing so much worse, after I awoke, that I had reason to conclude I had not many hours to survive.

While thus meditating on my wretched condition, we were all suddenly aroused by the accents of a human voice—and soon after discovered two Indians, armed with muskets, who did not appear to have yet perceived us. This sudden appearance reviving our courage, gave us strength to rise and advance towards them with all the dispatch we were able.

As soon as they saw us they stopped, as if their feet had been nailed to the ground. They looked stedfastly at us, motionless with surprize and horror. Besides the astonishment that must naturally have been excited in them at the unexpected meeting with four strangers in a desert, our appearance alone must have been sufficient to shock the most intrepid. Our clothes hanging in rags, our eyes concealed by the bloated prominence of our lived cheeks, the monstrous bulk to which all our limbs were swelled, our hair flowing in disorder down our shoulders, must, altogether, have given us a frightful appearance. However, as we advanced, a thousand agreeable sensations were displayed in our countenances: some shed tears, and others laughed for joy. Though these peaceable signs were calculated, in some degree, to remove the fears of the Indians, they did not yet manifest the least inclination to approach us, and certainly the disgust which our whole figure must have produced, sufficiently justified their coldness. The captain now advanced toward them, holding out his hand in a supplicating attitude, which they seized and gave it a hearty shake, which is the mode of salutation usual among these savages.

They then began to manifest some marks of compassion. One of them, who could speak English, begged of the captain to inform them from whence we came, and what accident had conducted us to that spot. As he seemed to be deeply affected with our narrative, he was asked if he could furnish us with any provisions. He replied in the affirmative, and taking up his musket, without saying a word, went away with his companion.

Notwithstanding the distress in which we were for food, hunger was not, at least with me, the most pressing want. The good fire, which by our request the Indians had made, added much to my relief having passed so many days of suffering from damp chills.

Three hours had elapsed since the departure of the Indians, and my afflicted companions began to lose all hope of seeing them again, when we perceived them turning a projecting point of land, and rowing towards us in a canoe of bark. They soon came on shore, bringing a large piece of smoked venison, and a bladder filled with fish oil. They boiled the meat in an iron pot, and when it was dressed they took care to distribute it among us in a very small quantity, with a little oil, to prevent the dangerous consequences which might have resulted from our voracity in the debilitated state to which our stomachs were reduced.

This light repast being over, they offered to conduct us to their habitations, which they represented as situated upon an island but a short distance—we accordingly all embarked, and soon reached the island, where upon landing we were received by three Indians and a dozen women or children, and by whom we were conducted to their huts or wigwams, four in number. We were treated by these good people with the kindest hospitality; they made us swallow a kind of broth, but would not permit us, notwithstanding our intreaties, to eat meat, or to take any other too substantial nourishment.

Upon finding ourselves at length thus safe among these savages, after enduring so much, caused sensations which it is impossible for me to express.—The hut appeared to us the abode of bliss. The savages, by the description which we gave them, appeared to be well acquainted with the place where our ship was wrecked, observing that had we proceeded in a proper course from thence, we might have reached St. Marks in six days, whereas we had been fifteen days travelling, and then some distance from our place of destination.

The savages offered to conduct us to St. Marks for a small compensation, which they represented about fifty miles distant by water, which offer we gladly accepted of.—Our good fortune had delivered us into the hands of a generous and benevolent people, whose kindness we experienced in every instance. What would have been our condition if we had met with persons of less sensibility, those who more deserving of the name savages, might have unfeelingly stripped us and left us to perish. But by providence it appeared to be ordained, that there should now be an end to our sufferings; they had commenced in a shocking manner, the 12th of May, and continued till the 31st. What a centery did it appear to us! Through how many miseries had we passed during that unhappy interval!—What persons in the world were ever so wretched for the time?

Could it therefore, my dear sister, be extraordinary that my constitution should be broken; the surprize must certainly be much greater that I was able to support myself at all under such severe trials, and that I should ever have recovered my mind and health again. My situation indeed was critical for several days, but rest and proper nourishment, taken in small portions, at a time, restored me by degrees, and repaired those ails which hunger and unwholesome diet had afflicted me with.

After we had recovered sufficient strength, we embarked with the Indians for St. Marks, where we safely arrived after a pleasant passage of 12 hours. Here we had the pleasure to meet with the remainder of the ship's crew (who arrived three days before us) except two, one of whom in the course of their journey, died in consequence of a bite received from a poisonous reptile, and the other was drowned in attempting to cross a river. In a few days after our arrival we were so fortunate as to obtain a passage to St. Augustin, and from thence to New York, where I arrived on the 25th June.

Thus, dear sister, have I, as you requested, furnished you with some of the particulars of my unparalleled sufferings—I doubt not but that the sad relation will affect you much, and cause you to tremble at the very thoughts of my wretched fate. But, as it was the will of Him, whose pleasure it finally was to resque me from my perilous situation, that I should thus suffer, I ought not to murmur. If you please, oblige my friends in Boston with the perusal of this letter, and should they think the whole or any part of it worth publishing, they have the consent of your

> Affectionate sister,
> Sarah Allen

## 1817: JANUARY
## TABITHA BROWN TO NOYES AND POLLY BROWN

*Married at nineteen to the Reverend Clark Brown, Tabitha Moffatt Brown (1780–1858) was in her mid-thirties when she endured, in close succession, the deaths of her six-year-old son and her husband. It is hard to imagine that the bereft widow who wrote this letter would rally to become a teacher, support her three remaining children, and eventually create a legend by making a treacherous journey to Oregon at the age of sixty-six. But Brown had more inner strength than she knew, or at least expressed to her brother-in-law Noyes (1775–1845?) and his wife, Polly (1780–1861), who were living in Stonington, Connecticut.*

William and Mary's Parish, Maryland
January, 1817

Dear Brother and Sister:

Consider how uncertain is human life with all its enjoyments and alluring prospects. For weeks and even months Death had been standing at the door, but was not permitted to enter until the twelfth of January at half-past ten in the morning to give the fatal blow. Oh, how excruciating the thought! The bitter cup would not pass. I am bereft of my dear, beloved husband; my children, of an earthly father; and you, of a loving brother.

His body sleeps undisturbed beside the altar, beneath the flooring of William and Mary's Church, while I have reason to believe his soul is partaking of celestial enjoyments with the ransomed in Heaven. The tenor of his life corresponded with his profession.

He was happy in his connection with the Episcopal churches. He never regretted leaving New England on any account but the dread of a sickly climate and the distance from his friends.

Not only his life, but his dying words, are consoling to his friends. For a number of years previous to his death he was strictly orthodox in that he continued unshaken to the day of his death. His faith was a sweet cordial in his dying hours. When asked by a gentleman if he was willing to leave this world, his answer was: "Yes, I do not know that I shall ever be better prepared, but I am sorry to part with my wife and children who are dear to my soul; am sorry to leave them in this unhealthful climate, and with but little property, but God is a Father to the widow and He will hear the orphans when they cry."

But a few minutes previous to his departure, he wished me to read prayers. My little family knelt beside his bed, and with one heart and voice put forth our petitions to our Heavenly Father in behalf of your dear brother, at the close of which, he gave the "Amen" for the last time on earth.

My friends, reflect for a moment on what must be the anguish of my heart at this and at the closing scene. In a moment, as it were, deprived of all my earthly dependence, in a strange land, at a distance from all my former friends and acquaintances, and with but little property for my support.

All involves upon a poor woman—I have not only to clothe and feed my children, but I must endeavor, into their young and tender minds, all principles of religion to instill, or great will be my responsibility.

When I parted with my sweet little boy, I thought nothing could exceed the anguish of my heart; but that was only a choice blossom. The destroyer has

taken away the tree. I have nothing left but a few tender sprouts that need nursing and care.

Never were your brother's prospects so inviting as since his connection with
this people; he was delighted with them and they with him. They manifested
much concern for him and his family during our sickness, which was of six
months' continuance. They were constantly sending their servants with presents and to make inquiries if they could help us to anything. We had many gal-
lons of wine given us, money, preserves of various sorts, and everything
necessary for the family. Three of the best physicians in this vicinity attended
us, but all in vain....

Man appoints, but God disappoints—all is vanity, but all is just and right,
and without doubt for the best. Amidst all my disappointments and trials, even
in the most heartrending I ever experienced, when my children were crying,
"Oh, Mama, oh Mama, poor Pappa is dying!"... I was sedate and tranquil. I was
wonderfully supported.

### 1817: SEPTEMBER 5
### MARY DODD TO FRONTIER WIDOWS

*Though westward expansion would not begin in earnest until the 1840s, frontier
living already had its trademark flavor when an angry woman sent this letter via the
Kentucky Reporter.*

#### TAKE NOTICE

And beware of the swindler JESSE DOUGHERTY, who married me in November
last, and some time after marriage informed me that he had another wife alive
and before I recovered, the villain left me, and took one of my best horses—one
of my neighbors was so good as to follow him and take the horse from him, and
bring him back. The said Dougherty is about forty years of age, five feet ten
inches high, round-shouldered, thick lips, complexion and hair dark, grey eyes,
remarkably ugly and good-natured, and very fond of ardent spirits, and by profession a notorious liar. This is therefore to warn all widows to beware of the
swindler, as all he wants is their property, and they may go to the devil for him
after he gets that. Also, all persons are forewarned from trading with the said
Dougherty, with the expectation of receiving pay from my property, as I consider
the marriage contract <u>null</u> and <u>void</u> agreeably to law: you will therefore pay no
attention to any lies he may tell you of his property in this county. The said

Dougherty has a number of wives living, perhaps eight or ten, (the number not positively known,) and will no doubt, if he can get them, have eight or ten more. I believe that is the way he makes his living.

Mary Dodd.

Livingston county, Ky. Sept. 5, 1817.

### 1818: JANUARY 15

### A CHEROKEE WOMAN TO A GOVERNMENT OFFICIAL

---

*By some estimates, the Cherokee ceded more than 90 percent of their land to white settlers between the years 1721 and 1819, and despite assimilation of white customs, farming practices, and, at times, the Christian religion, the tribe members were relentlessly pushed from their homelands. Having been educated near Georgia by the missionary John Gambold, the Cherokee author of this letter tried to appeal to the government in the name of the religious values that she had been taught.*
*The author's uncle, Chief Charles Renatus Hicks, was considered the most influential Chero-kee in the nation and was known as the tribe's first convert to Christianity. The president at the time, James Monroe, would prove little help, using his administration to champion expansion both internally and abroad.*

Mountjoy, Jan. 15, 1818.

Honored Sir,—

You often write to my dear brother Gambold, and hear that you are a true friend to the poor despised Indians. God bless and reward you for it and grant you long life and happiness.

Now, as my uncle, Ch. Hicks, is gone to Washington, to plead our cause before our dear father, the President, and make our distresses known, I take the liberty to write this to you. I wish you to be on my uncle's side, if I dare ask this favor: for we poor Indians, feel very much humbled.

I really know if our friends there with you knew our situation, they would sincerely pity us. Oh for the sake of God's love and mercy pity us! If we do not get help from that quarter, we are undone.

Our neighbouring white people seem to aim at our destruction. They have not the fear of God before their eyes; they seem not to believe in a Saviour ; they set wicked examples before the poor ignorant Indians; they insult our poor people who bear it patiently. I cannot cease from weeping to our merciful Saviour.

to shew mercy to us, and help from the hand of our oppressors. We are persuaded if our honored father the President could see our great distress into which we are brought, he would weep over us, he would pity us, he would help us. Yet we live far off from him and he cannot see us. Yet we constantly look from a distance to him for help, as poor helpless children look up to their Father, crying to have pity on them.

Since I have experienced grace and mercy from my dear Saviour, and have become truly happy in him and with his children, it is my constant prayer that my whole dear nation might enjoy the same blessings that I enjoy.

This grieves me more than I can tell, that at a time when there is a good prospect that many more will join the few who have embraced christianity, we shall be driven away from the land of our fathers, which is as dear to us as our lives; from our improved farms, from our beloved teachers, into a land strange to us; yea into savage life again. Dear Sir, I declare I would prefer death to such a life again.

I am in hopes, and many more with me, that our beloved father the President will certainly help his poor children, when he hears from my uncle our distressed situation. Yes, God the Father of all mankind, will incline his heart to consider our case and help us. Oh sir, I implore you, for the sake of the dear crucified Saviour, who shed his blood for the poor red, as well as the white people, continue to be our friend. Pray for us; plead for us, and the blessings of those, who are ready to perish will come upon you, and the great judge of all flesh will at the great day of retribution, remember your kindness to our poor people. I take the liberty to subscribe myself your humble friend.

### 1820: FEBRUARY 21
### RUTH PATTEN TO WILLIAM PATTEN

*William Patten (1763–1839) was pastor of the 2nd Congregational church at Newport, Rhode Island, when his mother, Ruth Wheelock Patten (1739–1831), sent him this letter of advice. Though great strides would be made in medical research in the nineteenth century, most popular cures were still based on the theory that disease resulted from extra fluids that needed to be removed by bleeding or purging. It is not clear from this letter what exactly was ailing Patten, but despite Ruth's timelessly maternal intentions, it is difficult to imagine that her proposed cure was any better than his sickness.*

Ruth Patten was the daughter of the Reverend Eleazar Wheelock, founder of Dartmouth College.

February 21st.

My very Dear Son,—

Mr. Tenney called and gave some account of your situation. I am persuaded your disorder is bilious, and that to a great degree—a disease very destructive to the system and often proves fatal. There is a remedy, which has cured in almost all instances where it has been tried. Flake off some hard soot from the chimney back, blow of the dust, put it in a vessel, pour on boiling water, let it stand a short time, pour it off, beat a new egg and a little sugar—take a large wine glass two or three times in a day, if it sets well on the stomach. Sometimes it proves physical—so much the better if it does. I advise you to make hop beer your constant drink. Cider I think detrimental. May God graciously bless the means that may be used for your recovery, or prepare us all for the event. If we may but enjoy the light of our dear Redeemer's countenance, having the oil of gladness shed into our souls, we shall be happy, hardly contented to wait our appointed time. Then how would our hearts leap for joy, at the prospect of exchanging worlds. But O, these unbelieving, cold, deceitful hearts. May God enable us to understand His loving kindness, and put our whole trust in His divine perfections, that whether we live or die, we may do honor to the religion we profess—commit our families, people, friends and the dear church to the care and keeping of our glorious Redeemer.

My family unites in best love to yourself and yours, with

Your affectionate mother,
Ruth Patten.


Rev. Wm. Patten.


**1823: SEPTEMBER 19**

**SUSAN MANSFIELD HUNTINGTON TO JOSEPH HUNTINGTON**

*A poet, journal writer, and author of a book about children's morals, Susan Mansfield Huntington (1791–1823) was the daughter of a minister and the wife of a pastor. Her husband had died in 1819 at the age of thirty-three, and two of her six children died two years later. She was in Boston, on her own deathbed, when she wrote this hauntingly beautiful letter to her eleven-year-old son, Joseph (1812–1900).*

"Mr. C." was Joseph's guardian at Andover.

September 19, 1823.

My beloved child.

Though I am very feeble, I feel a great desire to write you a few lines. My love and anxiety for you, are greater than any but a parent can know; and yet I tell you your faults. I want you to settle this truth in your mind for life, my J., that <u>he is your best friend who takes the most pains to correct your errors</u>. Beware of the person who tries to make you think well of yourself especially when your own conscience is not quite satisfied.

Always love your sisters. Consider yourself as, in a sense, their protector and guardian. Write to them often: pray for them. You are likely to be left alone in a strange world. So have I been; and thus far the Lord hath led me on; so that I have never lacked any good thing. The way has been boisterous sometimes, But Judah's Lion guards the way, And guides the travellers Home. Make this friend yours.—But I must close. Love Mr. C., always love him. He is one of your best friends; and <u>faithful</u> friends are not very plenty in this treacherous world, my J. But, oh! that I could see you securing the friendship of your God. Remember, his vows are upon you, and you cannot, must not, go back. Farewell, beloved child. The Lord be with you continually.

## 1824: MAY
## Z.D.R. TO HER DAUGHTER

*Nineteenth-century women's magazines played an important role in reinforcing what came to be known as the "cult of true womanhood." In article after article, the ideal woman was depicted as pious, pure, submissive, and cheerfully domestic. This vision reflected the widely shared belief that men and women were fundamentally different: Men were born to act and to build, women to preserve the moral order by raising children, caring for men, and suffering in silence. Eventually, the kind of mother-daughter lesson below, which appeared in the pages of* The Ladies' Magazine, *would be challenged by social-reform movements, the westward push, and industrialization. In the meantime, the anonymous author of this letter seemed to personify the magazine's subtitle: "Intended to Aid the Causes of Piety, Religion, and Morality."*

Before this can reach you the hand that writes it, and the heart that dictates, shall be mouldering in the grave. I mean it to supply some cautions which I should think it my duty to deliver to you should I live to see you a wife.

The precepts it contains you have often heard me inculcate, but I know that general observations on a possible event have less force than those which apply to our immediate condition. In the fate of a woman, Marriage is the most important crisis. It fixes her in a state of all others the most happy, or the most wretched, and though mere precept can do but little in any case, yet there is a natural propensity to try its efficacy in all. She who writes this paper has been a wife and a mother. The experience of the one, and the anxiety of the other, prompts her instruction; and she has been too happy in both characters to have much doubt of their truth, or fear of their reception. Sweetness of temper, affection to a husband, and attention to his interest, constitute the duties of a wife, and form the basis of matrimonial felicity; these are indeed the texts from which every rule for attaining this felicity is drawn.

The charms of beauty and the brilliancy of wit, though they may captivate in the friend, will not long delight in the wife. They will shorten their own transitory reign; if, as I have seen in many wives, they shine more for the attraction of every body else, than of their husbands. Let the pleasing of that one person be a thought never absent from your conduct. If he loves you as you would wish, he will bleed at heart if he should suppose it for a moment withdrawn. If he does not, his pride will supply the place of love, and his resentment that of suffering. Never consider as a trifle what may tend to please him—the great articles of duty he will set down as his own, but the lesser attentions he will mark as favours, and trust me, for I have experienced it, there is no feeling more delightful to one's self than that of turning those little things to so precious a use.

If you marry a man of a certain sort, such as the romance of young minds generally paints for a husband, you will deride the supposition of any possible decrease in the ardour of your affections; but wedlock, in its happiest state, is not exempted from the common fate of all sublunary blessings. There is ever a delusion in hope, which cannot abide with possession. The rapture of extravagant love will evaporate and waste; the conduct of the wife must substitute other regards as delicate, and more lasting; I say the conduct of the wife; for marriage, be a husband what he may, reverses the prerogative of sex; his, will expect to be pleased, and ours must be seduluos to please. This privilege a good man may wave—he will feel it however due, and third persons will have penetration enough to see, and may have malice to remark, the want of it in his wife. He must be a husband unworthy of you who could bear the degradation of suffering this in silence: the idea of power, on either side, must be totally banished from the system; it is not sufficient that the husband should never have occasion to regret the want of it, the wife should so behave that he may never be conscious of possessing it. But, my daughter, if a mother's fondness deceives me not, stands not much in need of cautions like these. I cannot allow myself the idea of her wedding a man on whom she would not be dependent, or whose inclinations a temper like hers would desire to control; she will be more in danger from that softness, and sensibility of soul, which will yield perhaps too much for the happiness of both. The office of a wife includes the exertions of a friend; a good one must strengthen and support that weakness which a bad one would endeavour to overcome. There are situations where it would not be enough to love, cherish and obey; she must teach her husband to be at peace with himself, to be reconciled to the world, to resist misfortune, to conquer adversity.

Alas, my child, I am here an instructress but too well skilled; the tears with which this paper is soiled fell not in the presence of your father, though now they but trace the remembrance of what then it was my lot to feel.

Think it not impossible to restrain your feelings, because they are strong. The enthusiasm of feeling will sometimes overcome distresses, which the cold heart of prudence had been unable to endure. But misfortune is not always misery; I have known this truth, I am proud to believe that I have sometimes taught it to R. Thanks to that power whose decrees I reverence. We always tempered the anguish of our sufferings 'till there was a sort of luxury in feeling them.—Then is the triumph of wedded love.

The tie which binds the happy may be dear, but that which links the unfortunate is tenderness unutterable.

Z. D. R.

## 1825: MAY 3

## PEGGY AND SUSANNA McINTOSH TO DUNCAN CAMPBELL AND JAMES MERIWETHER

*Along with the Cherokee (see page 125), the Creek nation had been pushed relentlessly west, and by the early nineteenth century, they were being pressured by the government to give up what little remained of their land. In February of 1825, Chief William McIntosh signed the Treaty of Indian Springs, ceding the remaining Creek lands to the United States in exchange for a promise of territory west of the Mississippi. Before the move could take place, he was murdered by members of his tribe who bitterly opposed the arrangement. In this letter, two of McIntosh's three widows pleaded for help from Colonel Duncan Campbell (1787–1828) and Major James Meriwether (1789–1854), the commissioners who had negotiated the treaty. It is unclear which of the two women was the "I" in the letter, but according to one story,*

Susanna McIntosh covered her husband's body with her own for three days, until help came to bury him.

May 3, 1825

Gentlemen

When you see this letter stained with the blood (the last drop of which is now spilt—for friendship he has shown for your people) I know you will remember your pledge to us in behalf of your Nation, that in the worst events you would assist & protect us; And when I tell you that at day light on Saturday morning last hundreds of the hostiles surrounded our house and instantly murdered Gen'l McIntosh and Thomas Tustunnuggee by shooting near one hundred balls into them (Chilly and Moody Kinnard making their escape through a window) they then commenced burning and plundering in the most unprincipalled way—so that here I am driven from the ashes of my smoking dwelling, left with nothing but my poor naked hungry children who need some immediate ade from our White Friends, and we lean upon you, while you lean upon your government: About the same time of the morning that they continued the horrid act on Gen'l another party caught Col. Sam'l Hawkins and kept him tied until about 3 o'clock, when the Chief returned from our house and gave order for his execution in the same way, and refused to leave his wife any impliments to cover his body up with; so that it was left exposed to the fowls of the air and the beasts of the forrest and Jenny and her child are here in the same condition as we are   this party consisted of Oakfuskies, Talledgas and Muckfaws tho there were others with them; the Chiefs that appeared to head the party were Intock chungo (of Mockfaw) and Minnowaway, but I know not where he was from, who said they were ordered to do it by the Little Prince and Hopthle Yoholo, and that they were supported and encouraged in it by the Agent and Chiefs that were left after the Big Wariors death, in a council at Broken Arrow, where they decreed that they would murder all the Chiefs, who had any hand in selling the land and burn and destroy and take away all that they had, and then send on to the President that he should not have the land. I have not heard of the murders of any others, but expect all are dead that could be catcht, but by reason of a great Freshett on the Chattahooche, they could not get Col. Miller or Hagy McIntosh, nor the Darisaus, and they and Chilly are gon to the Govornor, our country is in a most ruined state, so far as I have heard (tho by reason of the high waters—word has not circulated fast) all have fled from their homes in our parts and taken refuge among their White Friends & I learn they are now at

Gen'l Wares (near his place) from 150 to 200 of them are afraid to go to their homes to get a grain of what little corn they have to eat, and if you and your people do not assist us, God help us, we must die, either by the sword or by the famine—This moment Gen'l Ware has come in & will in a few minutes start with a few men and a few Friendly Indians to try to get a little something for us to eat—I hope so soon as you read this you will lay it before the Govornor and the President—, that they may know our miserable condition and afford us relief as soon as possible. I followed them to their camp about 1 1/12 miles, to try to by of them something to cover the dead with but it was denied me; I tried also to get a horse to take my little children, and some provisions to last us to the White settlement, which was given up to me and then taken back, and had it not been for some White men, who assisted in burrying the dead and getting us to the settlement, we should have been worse off than we were, if possible. Before I close I must remark that the whole party so far as I know them were hostile during the late ware

Peggy and Susanna McIntosh

## 1828: SPRING
## PHILIPPINE DUCHESNE TO WILLIAM CARR LANE

*Born in France and educated as a sister of the Sacred Heart, Philippine Duchesne (1769–1852) came to America in 1818 and, leading a group of four other nuns, founded the first free school west of the Mississippi. During the next thirty-eight years, Duchesne opened schools in Missouri and Louisiana and eventually did mission work among Indians in what is now Kansas. Her standards as well as her spirit were clearly evident in this letter of complaint to William Carr Lane (1789–1863), who was mayor of St. Louis at the time. His response is unknown.*
Saint Rose Philippine Duchesne was canonized by Pope John Paul II in 1988. Lane would eventually become governor of the New Mexico Territory.

Sir,

I have recourse to your authority for the redress of an abuse which I look upon as very much against the welfare of our establishment. You know, Sir, that our young ladies, day schollars, in order to reach our house have to pass the creek that runs all around our house. The warm weather invites a number of men and boys to swimming in the creek, and every day our young ladies meet with that disagreeable sight, both coming and leaving the house; and as I understand that some regulation of court forbids swimming in public places, I suppose that it is merely by some negligence of the sheriffs in discharge of their duty that it takes place.

As you are, Sir, the father of an amiable family I need not say how much that rudeness is against the delicacy of sentiments we strive to endow our young ladies with, and I am convinced that you will be so good as to use your power to remove that obstacle. I offer you beforehand my thanks and beg you to believe me with deep respect,

> Sir,
> Your most obed. servt.
> Philippine Duchesne
> Supr.

## 1830: JUNE
## SARAH HODGDON TO MARY HODGDON

*Sarah Hodgdon (1814–?) was sixteen when she left her home in Rochester, New Hampshire, for the mills of Lowell, Massachusetts, where huge factories and a female workforce were both relatively new innovations of the just-dawning industrial revolution. By the end of the decade, financial pressures would drive mill owners to cut wages and increase hours. But at the time Hodgdon wrote this letter to her mother, Mary (1788?–?), conditions were still relatively comfortable, affording many young women their first taste of independence.*

The seat that Sarah mentioned was in a church pew; many city churches charged a fee at the time. Eventually, Hodgdon moved to Great Falls (now Somersworth), New Hampshire, and worked for a mill just a few miles from her home. She married a shoemaker named William Jenness in 1845.

Dear mother

I take this opertunity to write to you to informe you that I have gone into the mill and like very well. I was here one week and three days before I went into the mill to work for my board. We boord tgether. I like my boording place very well. I enjoy my health very well. I do not enjoy my mind so well as it is my desire to. I cant go to any meetings except I hire a seat therefore I have to stay home on that acount. I desire you pay that it may not be said of me when I come home that I have sold my soul for the gay vanitys of this world. Give my love to my farther tell him not to forget me and to my dear sister and to my brothers and to my grammother tell her I do not forget her and to my Aunts and to all my enquiring friends. I want that you should write to me as soon as you can and when you write to me I want that you should write to me the particulars about sister and Aunt Betsy. Dont fail writing. I bege you not to let this scrabling be seen.

Sarah Hodgdon

## 1830: AUGUST
## ELIZABETH TO HER MOTHER

---

*The author of this letter remains obscure. What is clear is that she was on hand at the dawn of railroad history, when railroad cars were drawn by horses, not powered by locomotives. The car Elizabeth described, the first long-distance horse-drawn railroad car in America, had been opened to the public earlier in the year, and the structure she wrote about—the Carrollton Viaduct outside Baltimore—is still in use and is the oldest railroad bridge in the world.*

The revolutionary change to steam power would take place within the month, as would a legendary (and possibly mythical) race between the little steam locomotive "Tom Thumb" and a victorious horse-drawn car. The Washington monument that Elizabeth mentioned is located in Baltimore; it was completed in 1829, and was designed by Robert Mills, who would later design the Washington Monument in the nation's capital. A repeater was a watch with a timer mechanism. The *Rocket* and the *Novelty* were early locomotives.

Baltimore, Aug. 1830

My dear Mother,—

I am so delighted with every thing I see, that I cannot find in my heart to be homesick, if I would. I often think of my dear good Boston friends, notwithstanding, and wish I could see you and them; but then, I am so happy, and every body is so kind, that I almost wish you were here, and that this was our home.

You recollect that article in the "American Monthly Magazine" last spring, where the writer said, "I should like to sketch Baltimore gay and wicked." I assure you it was a mistake; much as I respect the writer's judgment on other subjects; and I strongly suspect, that, either he has never been here to judge for himself, or else they must have reformed amazingly since that time. And you know Mr Stedman said, that "the Baltimore ladies were not readers." Now my dear mother, it is not so. They do read. I saw a lady yesterday reading the life of Bishop Heller; and I assure you, that Mrs Bascom has read more or less every day since I have been here. They have an immense deal of foreign literature; annuals and periodicals, which the young ladies read. They do not make so many books here, perhaps, as they do in Boston, but I am told they are beginning to think on the subject. At any rate, they discover good taste in those which they have made.

I told you in my last, of our visit to the Washington monument, and some of the beautiful country-seats, and that delightful garden. I thought they exceeded every thing. But yesterday my uncle took me to ride on the Rail Road. Our party consisted of Mr and Mrs Bascom, my uncle and myself. O, I would have given anything if you had been with us! As you have seen the Quincy rail road, I will not attempt a description of the road itself, except that it has a double track, and is completed as far as Ellicott's Mills, 13 miles from Baltimore. We started precisely at 3 o'clock in the afternoon. The weather was extremely warm, and you cannot imagine how cool and comfortable we were, seated on what I call the upper deck, of a new and most splendid car. There were twelve persons in the upper tier, and the same number in the lower tier, and then the driver in front, with one on each side of him. A merry load certainly for one horse to draw. There were seven other cars following in rapid succession, all crowded with passengers.

A large gentleman sat very near my uncle, who seemed quite disturbed about something; I could not imagine what, as every one else appeared so cheerful and happy. He held an elegant gold repeater in one hand, and a gold headed cane in the other. He kept one eye on the watch, and the other was employed in viewing, sometimes the company and sometimes the scenery. With his cane he seemed to express the different degrees of uneasiness which afflicted him.

"We move at the rate of thirteen miles an hour," said my uncle, looking at his watch. Thump went the gold-headed cane, on the floor of the car.

"Yes," said Mr Bascom, "this would soon take us to Wheeling." Thump went the cane again; and such fidgeting about, that I thought to be sure the large gentleman was crowded for room, and I tried to move along. Just then we came to the bridge, (or Viaduct, as it is called,) over Gwynn's Falls. I thought I had seen bridges before, but this outdoes them all. It is 312 feet in length, and 40 feet or more in height; and is built of the most beautiful granite. While Mr Bascom and my uncle were eulogising the workmanship, and commenting on the vast expense, etc. the large gentleman brought his cane down with such emphasis, and writhed himself about with such apparent agony, that I was quite distressed, for fear he had a fit of the gout on him. And really, as my uncle was a physician, if I had not been sadly afraid, before so many people, I should have begged him to prescript something for his relief. But soon we came to the half-way house, where we changed horses, and to my astonishment, the whole was explained. The car no sooner stopped, than the large gentleman began to dismount with all possible dispatch, muttering all the way something about <u>Hing-land</u>, and the fatigue of such a <u>snail's pace</u>; and when he had fairly gotten his feet on <u>terra firma</u>, he turned round to the company, and giving his cane a most dexterous flourish, "How," said he, "would ye like to take a trip in the <u>Novelty</u> or the <u>Rocket</u>, that makes nothing of cutting through the <u>hair</u> at the rate of forty miles an hour?—Ye'd soon tire of dragging along with a paltry <u>orse</u>." So saying, he walked himself into the house, and that was the last I saw of the large gentleman.

The scenery on the Petapsco is beautiful. I wish I could describe it to you. It resembles very much that delightful hill and dale scenery in Dutchess county, New York, which you used to admire so much. We reached <u>Ellicott's</u> about four, and took a ramble through the romantic grounds. The fields as far as the eye could reach, were dressed in full green; and from an eminence which commanded an extensive view, we feasted our eyes on the most beautiful landscape I ever beheld. I know what you would have said, if you had been there—that such scenes ought to raise our admiration and our best affections to the Great Author. Surely no one could witness so much beauty and elegance without worshipping, like a christian, not the creature, but the <u>Creator</u>. I am certain this neighborhood must be favorable to the muses; and I earnestly hope, that next summer you, and all our northern and eastern poets and poetesses, will visit Baltimore, and take <u>a trip to Ellicott's Mills</u>.

I am, dear mother, your most affectionate daughter,

Elizabeth.

### 1831: DECEMBER
### MARY AUSTIN HOLLEY TO CHARLES AUSTIN

*In 1831, Texas was still part of Mexico, which had been independent of Spain for just a decade. Texas's Anglo-American population had grown to nearly twenty thousand, thanks in part to settlements organized by Stephen Austin. Stephen's cousin Mary Austin Holley (1784–1846) was a widow when she made her first visit to the new colony. Her letters to her brother Charles (1793?–1849) about that trip were published in 1833 and proved to be excellent publicity for the growing community. Three years later, Holley published the first history of Texas in English.*

Bolivar, Texas, December, 1831

One's feelings in Texas are unique and original, and very like a dream or youthful vision realized. Here, as in Eden, man feels alone with the God of nature, and seems, in a peculiar manner, to enjoy the rich bounties of heaven, in common with all created things. The animals, which do not fly from him; the profound stillness; the genial sun and soft air,—all are impressive, and are calculated, both to delight the imagination, and to fill the heart, with religious emotions.

With regard to the state of society here, as is natural to expect, there are many incongruities. It will take some time for people gathered from the north, and from the south, from the east, and from the west, to assimilate, and adapt themselves to new situations. The people are universally kind and hospitable, which are redeeming qualities. Every body's house is open, and table spread, to accommodate the traveller. There are no poor people here, and none rich; that is, none who have much money. The poor and the rich, to use the correlatives, where distinction, there is none, get the same quantity of land on arrival, and if they do not continue equal, it is for want of good management on the one part, or superior industry and sagacity on the other. All are happy, because busy; and none meddle with the affairs of their neighbours, because they have enough to do to take care of their own. They are bound together by a common interest, by sameness of purpose, and hopes. As far as I could learn, they have no envyings, no jealousies, no bickerings, through politics or fanaticism. There is neither masonry, anti-masonry, nullification nor court intrigues.

The common concerns of life are sufficiently exciting to keep the spirits buoyant, and prevent everything like ennui. Artificial wants are entirely forgotten, in view of real ones, and self, eternal self, does not alone, fill up the round of life. Delicate ladies find they can be useful, and need not be vain. Even privations become pleasures: people grow ingenious in overcoming difficulties. Many latent faculties are developed. They discover in themselves, powers, they did not suspect themselves of possessing. Equally surprised and delighted at the discovery, they apply to their labours with all that energy and spirit, which new hope and conscious strength, inspire.

You wish to know my opinion, if it will do for all sorts of people to emigrate to Texas, and if I would advise J—— and S—— to sell out and remove. On this point, I should say, industrious farmers will certainly do well, and cannot fail of success; that is to say, if abundant crops, and a ready market with high prices, will satisfy them. Substantial planters, with capital and hands, may enlarge their operations here to any extent, and with enormous profits. One gentleman, for instance, whom I visited, has ninety-three acres under cultivation, by seven hands. His crop, this year, consists of eighty bales of cotton, two thousands bushels of corn, five hundred bushels of sweet potatoes, besides other articles of minor importance.

Those persons, however, who are established in comfort and competency, with an ordinary portion of domestic happiness; who have never been far from home, and are excessively attached to personal ease; who shrink from hardship and danger, and those who, being accustomed to a regular routine of prescribed employment in a city, know not how to act on emergencies, or adapt themselves to all sorts of circumstances, had better stay where they are. There is no better advice, than, "to let well enough alone." All changes may be for the worse as well as better, and what we are used to, though not so good as might be, may suit us best. New shoes, though handsomer and better than old ones, may pinch and fret the wearer. Happiness is relative. A high standard for one person, is a low one for another, and what one prizes, another may think worthless. So that even conceding all the advantages I have claimed for Texas, it does not follow that the happiness of all would be promoted, by emigrating to this country. It depends much upon the spirit of the man.

He whose hopes of rising to independence in life, by honourable exertion, have been blasted by disappointment, whose ambition has been thwarted by untoward circumstances; whose spirit, though depressed, is not discouraged; who longs only for some ample field on which to lay out his strength; who does not hanker after society, nor sigh for the vanished illusions of life; who has a fund of resources within himself, and a heart to trust in God and his own exertions; who is not peculiarly sensitive to petty inconveniences, but can bear privations and make sacrifices, of personal comfort—such a person will do well to settle accounts at home, and begin life anew in Texas. He will find, here, abundant exercise for all his faculties, both of body and mind, a new stimulus to his exertions, and a new current for his affections. He may be obliged to labour hard, but riches are a very certain reward for his exertions. He may be generous, without fear of ruin. He will learn to find society in nature, and repose in solitude, health in exertion, and happiness in occupation. If he have a just ambition, he will glow with generous pride, while he is marking out an untrodden path, acting in an unhackneyed sphere, and founding for himself, and his children after him, a permanent and noble independence.

Affectionately, yours, &c.

**1832: JANUARY 19**

**WOMEN OF AUGUSTA COUNTY TO THE VIRGINIA GENERAL ASSEMBLY**

---

*Beginning in August of 1831, Nat Turner organized the country's first sustained uprising against the entrenched institution of slavery. Planning to capture an arsenal in Jerusalem, Virginia, Turner led a group of fellow slaves on a campaign that caused the deaths of more than fifty white people and ultimately brought retribution in the form of hundreds of murders by white mobs, as well as even more repressive slave laws. Turner himself was hanged, then skinned. But the rebellion— immortalized in William Styron's novel* The Confessions of Nat Turner—*also inspired some Southern women to speak out against slavery in an organized way, even if mainly out of fear.*

Memorial of the Ladies of Augusta to the General Assembly of Virginia
Praying the Adoption of Some Measure for the Speedy Extirpation of
Slavery from the Commonwealth
Signed by 215 Ladies

To the Hon. the General Assembly of the State of Virginia,
memorial of the subscribing females of the county of Augusta humbly represents that although it be unexampled in our beloved State, that females should interfere in its political concerns, and although we feel all the timidity incident to our sex in taking this step, yet we hold our right to do so to be unquestionable, and feel ourselves irresistably impelled to the exercise of that right by the most potent considerations and the perilous circumstances which surround us. We pretend not to conceal from you, our fathers and brothers, our protectors by your investment with the political power of the land, the fears which agitate our bosoms, and the dangers which await us as revealed by recent tragical deeds. Our fears, we admit, are great, but we do not concede that they are the effects of blind & unreflecting cowardice; we do not concede that they spring from the superstitious timidity of our sex. Alas! we are indeed timid, but we appeal to your manly reason, to your more mature wisdom to attest the justice & propriety of our fears, when we call to your recollection the late slaughter of our sisters & their little ones, in certain parts of our land, & the strong probability that that slaughter was but a partial execution of a widely projected scheme of carnage. We know not, we cannot know the night, nor the unguarded moment, by day or by night, which is pregnant with our destruction, & that of our husbands,

& brothers, & sisters, & children; but we do know that we are, at every moment, exposed to the means of our own excision, & of all that is dear to us in life. The bloody monster which threatens us is warmed & cherished in our own hearths. O hear our prayer, & remove it, yes protectors of our persons, ye guardians of our peace!

Tell us not of the labors & hardships which we shall endure when our bond-servants shall be removed from us. They have no terrors for us. Those labors & hardships cannot be greater, or so great as those we now endure in providing for & ruling the faithless beings who are subjected to us. Or were they greater, still they are, in our esteem, less than the small dust in the balance, compared with the burden of our fears and our dangers. But what have we to fear, from these causes, more than females of other countries? Are they of the east, & of the West, of England, of France, more "cumbered with much serving" than we are? Are they less enlightened, or less accomplished? However we may be flattered, we will not be argued out of our senses, & persuaded into a belief which is contradicted by experience, & the testimony of sober facts. Many, very many of our sisters & brothers have fled to other lands, from the evils which we experience: and they send us back the evidences of their contentment & prosperity. They lament not their labors & hardships, but exult in their deliverance from servitude to their quondam slaves: And we, too, fly—we, too, would exult in similar deliverance, were our destiny not otherwise ordered than it is. That destiny is in your hands, & we implore your high agency in ordering it for the best. We would enjoy such exultation on our native soil. Do not slight our importunities. Do not disregard our fears. Our destiny is identified with yours. If we perish, alas! what will become of you & your offspring?

We are not political economists, but our domestic employments, our engagements in rearing up the children of our husbands & brothers, our intimate concern with the interests & prosperity of society, we presume, cannot but inform us of the great & elementary principles of that important science. Indeed it is impossible that that science can have any other basis than the principles which are constantly developing themselves to us in our domestic relations. What is a nation but a family on a large scale? Our fears teach us to reflect & reason. And our reflections & reasonings have taught us that the peace of our homes, the welfare of society, the prosperity of future generations call aloud & imperiously for some decisive & efficient measure—and that measure cannot, we believe, be efficient, or of much benefit, if it have not for its ultimate object, the extinction of slavery, from amongst us. Without, therefore, entering upon a detail of facts & arguments, we implore you by the urgency of our fears, by the love we bear you as our fathers & brothers, by our anxieties for the little ones around us, by our estimate of domestic & public weal, by present danger, by the prospects of the future, by our female virtues, by the patriotism which flows in & animates our bosoms, by our prayers to Almighty GOD, not to let the power with which you are invested lie dormant, but that you exert it for the deliverance of your-selves, of us, of the children of the land, of future ages, from the direst curse which can befal a people. Signalize your legislation by this mighty deed. This we pray: and in duty will ever pray.

## 1833: DECEMBER 20
## MRS. JAMES HINE TO HER MOTHER

*All we know of Mrs. Hine is that she was twenty years old and visiting Georgia from New York. But she was vivid in her descriptions of the wretched accommodations that a traveler of her time might encounter along the stage road. The frontier was still extremely rough-and-tumble, and the rusticity of the residents clearly as-tounded her.*

Dublin, Laurens County
December 20, 1833

My dear Mother:

I scarcely know where to begin—so much that is new to me meets me at every step. We left Savannah on the 8th. When we got to Norwood's, where we were to spend the first night, evening was closing in around us. The house was of logs, a single story in height, presenting but one window and one door, the window unglazed and a ponderous wooden shutter used to close it. I supposed the building to be the barn, and in my own mind pronounced upon the un-thriftiness of the man who had no better outhouses. What was my astonishment upon finding that it was the dwelling—the house of the family with whom we were to stay! This stage road passes through a very barren and desolate section of country, as poor perhaps, if not poorer, than any land in the state.

This house where we stayed contained three rooms—one large one, into which the door opened, with a huge chimney at the end almost the width of the room, constructed of sticks piled upon each other. It was built outside of the house. The side where the chimney joined on to the house was left open, and the logs sawed out to make the fireplace. The interstices between the sticks were filled with clay, with which also the whole thing was daubed outside and in. This room was used as hall, parlor, dining room and bedroom. On the side of

this was a bedroom of a fair size and behind it a piazza, on one end of which another very small bedroom was partitioned off. The furniture of the room into
which we were shown was a large pine table and a half-dozen chairs of country
make—turned legs and splint bottoms.

The family had retired for the night when we got there, but the man and his
wife got up and "made a light," as he expressed it. He set fire to some pieces of
resinous pine and put them in the chimney, which I found was their substitute
for a lamp, and when we sat down to the supper, which was bountiful and well
cooked, Mr. Norwood took two of the burning sticks from the fireplace and held
the blazing, smoking torch above our heads to give us light to eat by. He was a
coarse, rough-looking man with no clothes on but shirt and trousers of the
coarsest kind of homespun, not even a shoe or stocking and with his bloused
head of long and bushy hair and unshorn beard. His wife, who came in from the
kitchen (which was a small log building back of the house) to preside at the
table, was almost equally repulsive in dress and appearance. She had on her
head all the evening—not only as she was going back and forth to the kitchen to
attend to supper arrangements, but as she sat at the head of the table pouring
the coffee—one of those long cracker bonnets, projecting far over the face, made
of coarse homespun.

After the supper was finished I sought quarters for the night, and they
showed me into the little room on the end of the piazza. It was barely large
enough to hold a small bedstead and have a space of about two feet on one side
of it. There was no space for the door to open; it had to open outside. There was
no article of furniture in the room but the bedstead and one chair, not even a
table to hold a light; but that, of course, was quite unnecessary, as I had no light
to put on it and was expected to go to bed by such light as came in through the
open door, for there was no window to the room, or else satisfy myself with such
light as came in through the cracks between the planks which formed the walls.
The bedstead was a rough specimen of home manufacture, and the bed, pro-
fessedly of feathers, though there were not enough feathers in it to have made a
decent pair of pillows, while the dimensions of the pillows given me were about
twelve by eighteen inches in size, with barely feathers enough in them to show
the purpose they were intended to serve. There was no mattress, but a dried
cowhide laid upon the cords to prevent what feathers there were in the bed
from sinking down between them. The door to my room simply closed with a
wooden latch which was lifted with a string. I felt very much as if I had got on
the extreme border of civilization but one remove from savage life. I have read
much of frontier life, but I never pictured to myself anything so wild as this. I

was greatly relieved when the streaks of daylight found their way through the chinks in the walls. Throwing open the door of my room, I went out on the piazza, where I found a pail of water and gourd and a wash pan placed there for family use and a towel for everybody's use.

Our wayside accommodations were very simple all the way. The features of life in these squatters' cabins were so different from any which had ever before come under my notice—though we had no second experience as rough as the first night developed. On two occasions when night overtook us we found ourselves at stage stands where the drivers of public stages changed their horses and drivers and passengers took supper or breakfast. These houses were more spacious and had a sprinkling of city comforts, procured probably through the drivers as they passed back and forth from Savannah to Macon.

The buildings, though, are almost universally made of logs, that is the body of them. The larger houses here are what they term "double pen" log houses, that is two separate cabins made of logs and notched and fitted into each other at the corners and sometimes hewn on all four sides. These are placed some little distance from each other, perhaps ten or fifteen feet apart, and connected by rafters overhead and one long roof stretched from end to end of the two buildings, covering the open space as well, which is floored and serves as a hall or passageway to the house and is the main entrance, a door opening into each of these two log rooms on the right and left hand. Then there are piazzas built back and front, extending the whole length of the cabins and the passageway, which sometimes embraces forty or fifty feet. At either end of these piazzas small bedrooms are boarded in, called shed rooms, and as they are small they have a long stretch of piazza between them. The front piazza is general sitting room about nine months of the year, and the back one (overlooking the kitchen, which is always a separate building, though generally in close proximity to the houses) is used as a dining room.

One of the stage stands at which we stopped was kept by an old lady called "Auntie Collins." She always has her head tied up with a handkerchief and over that wears a man's broad-brimmed straw hat out of doors and in, at the table and everywhere. She is utterly bald-headed, having been scalped by the Indians when a child. Her house goes by the name of the "Pewter Platter House." She has an immense pewter platter which extends almost from side to side of her table, and when she has many to feed she puts her fish, flesh and fowl all on that one dish. A gentleman told me yesterday that he had eaten there when she had fried fish, ham and eggs, venison, chicken, partridges, sausages and roast pork all on that huge pewter dish.

This stage road passes through as poor a section of country as there is in the state. Those who are too poor to buy productive land can get a home here for almost nothing. They come here perhaps with one horse and a cart and their all of earthly possessions in it. This propitious climate is everything to a farmer who is poor. He can keep his family warm in an open house, can clear new ground, split rails for fencing and get his grounds in good shape for culture 'ere the season comes to plant. It is a matter of unceasing surprise to me how many home comforts these people who are so remote from any market or mart of trade can make for themselves.

One house particularly, which was a marvel of neatness, too—occupied by a young couple—had scarcely anything about it which was not the work of their two pairs of hands. The house was simply one large room. He had got the logs out himself and hewed them square to make it more sightly. His neighbors had helped him to raise it. He rived out the shingles to cover it and put them on himself, and built his own chimney of sticks, plastered with mud. There were two bedsteads in the room of his own make, the mattresses made of straw from their own wheat, while the beds had evidently been supplied with feathers from a large flock of geese which were ranging about the premises, and the ticks and the sheets and the spreads were all manifestly the work of the wife. He had made his own table also. There was not a chair in the house, but a number of three-legged stools—some with legs long enough to use at the table in eating and others made with shorter legs—a long, low settle, which would seat four or five, which was most comfortable, made evidently from the half of a hollow log, friction applied to it until it was very smooth. This was mounted on four legs. The doors to the house were upright planks nailed together by battens and their fastenings wooden latches whittled out by hand, which worked with a string. The window shutters were made the same as the doors and closed with a string, which was tied to a nail driven in the shutter and wound around a nail driven in the house.

Their household vessels for holding milk, lard, salt and various other things were gourds. The clothing of both the man and his wife and their little baby was evidently spun and woven by the woman herself. Her spinning wheel stood there in the corner of the room, and the loom just outside of the house with a shelter built over it. The man said he had dug his own well. The bucket he used in it was a cypress knob, hollowed out. A string of plaited grass served as a handle. The only thing we saw on the whole premises which had been bought at a store were some simple tableware and a few cooking utensils. Against one side of the room were long shelves, resting on huge wooden pegs driven into the logs, which were piled with bedding and clothing. These shelves served the purpose of wardrobe and bureau and closet. The family, consisting of Mr. Fleming, his wife and their little one, looked the picture of contentment and happiness. Everything about them was neat and in sparkling order. So many times I have thought of them and their simple life, which rivals that of Robinson Crusoe.

## 1835: EARLY AUGUST
## HELEN JEWETT TO RICHARD ROBINSON

*There has been a "crime of the century" proclaimed in every century and in most decades as well, but the murder of Helen Jewett (1813–1836) is a strong contender for the nineteenth-century title. A twenty-three-year-old prostitute who in April of 1836 was found axed to death in a burned bed, Jewett (née Dorcas Doyen) had a history of seducing her clients by word and letter as well as by deed, and Richard Robinson (1817?–1855), known at the brothel as Frank Rivers, was not the only man with whom she'd had an ongoing arrangement. But Robinson clearly meant something different to her than the others had. She wrote this letter to him when she discovered that he was involved with another woman.*
What Jewett meant to Robinson will doubtless never be known. After his cloak and an axe from the store where he worked were found near her room, he was arrested for her murder, but he was eventually acquitted.

I resume my pen to you with much pleasure as I have now half an hour which I hope I shall be able to call my own, if I am not called upon to do something to oblige the ladies. You must pardon me for the <u>ungenerous</u> remarks I might have made the last night you remained with me, but really I could not help it. It is indeed a misfortune that <u>jealousy</u> should have been so lavishly used among the ingredients of my composition. It has often made me unhappy and I have vainly tried to cover it. There are very few men who <u>understand</u> the feelings of poor women. We are often obliged to smile and hide with a cold exterior, the feelings which sometimes nearly cause our hearts to break. Women only can understand woman's heart. We cannot, dare not complain, for sympathy is denied us if we do.

With man it is otherwise. He can with impunity express all, nay, more than he feels; court sympathy and obtain it, while at the same time poor neglected woman cannot be allowed to share in the many pursuits and pleasures which man has to occupy his time; of course he does not need to be pitied, unless it be for his vices and excesses.

You will recollect I spoke to you relative to visiting me oftener than twice a week. It is now the only pleasure I receive, when every one else is unkind to me, to have my dear Frank to tell all my feelings, who will listen patiently and then pity me. And it is indeed a pleasure to sit for hours and work for you and think of you: not as I think of the rest of the world, but to really feel grateful. These to me are enviable feelings, aye, ones which I could not be induced to relinquish for anything which I can now recollect. You must reply to me soon at length.

Your devoted,<br>Helen

## 1835: AUGUST 30
## ANGELINA GRIMKÉ TO WILLIAM LLOYD GARRISON

*Angelina Grimké (1805–1879) and her older sister, Sarah, were two of the most outspoken and effective abolitionists of their day. Growing up in South Carolina, the daughters of a slave owner, they developed a lifelong antipathy toward slavery that, combined with a search for education, led them north, to Philadelphia, where they became Quakers. In 1835, a riot broke out in Boston when a mob stopped an antislavery meeting and dragged abolitionist William Lloyd Garrison (also 1805–1879) through the streets at the end of a rope. In the aftermath of the riot, Angelina sent this letter to Garrison, who published it in his newspaper,* The Liberator. *It was effectively the beginning of Angelina's career in public life.*

Philadelphia, 8th month, 30th, 1835.

Respected Friend:

It seems as if I was compelled at this time to address thee, notwithstanding all my reasonings against intruding on thy valuable time, and the uselessness of so insignificant a person as myself offering thee the sentiments of sympathy at this alarming crisis.

I can hardly express to thee the deep and solemn interest with which I have viewed the violent proceedings of the last few weeks. Although I expected opposition, yet I was not prepared for it so soon—it took me by surprise, and I greatly feared Abolitionists would be driven back in the first onset, and thrown into confusion. So fearful was I, that though I clung with unflinching firmness to our principles, yet I was afraid of even opening one of thy papers, lest I should see some indications of compromise, some surrender, some palliation. Under these feelings, I was urged to read thy Appeal to the citizens of Boston. Judge, then, what were my feelings, on finding that my fears were utterly groundless, and that thou stoodest firm in the midst of the storm, determined to suffer and to die, rather than yield one inch. My heart was filled with thanksgiving and praise to the Preserver of men; I thanked God, and took courage, earnestly desiring that thousands may adopt thy language, and be prepared to meet the Martyr's doom, rather than give up the principles you (i.e. Abolitionists) have adopted. The ground upon which you stand is holy ground: never—never surrender it. If you surrender it, the hope of the slave is extinguished, and the chains of his servitude will be strengthened a hundred fold. But let no man take your crown, and success is as certain as the rising of to-morrow's sun. But remember you must be willing to suffer the loss of all things—willing to be the scorn and re-proach of professor and profane. You must obey our great Master's injunction: "Fear not them that kill the body, and after that, have nothing more that they can do." You must, like Apostles, "count not your lives dear unto yourselves, so that you may finish your course with joy."

Religious persecution always begins with mobs: it is always unprecedented in the age or country in which it commences, and therefore there are no laws, by which Reformers can be punished; consequently, a lawless band of unprinci-pled men determine to take the matter into their hands, and act out in mobs, what they know are the principles of a large majority of those who are too high in Church and State to condescend to mingle with them, though they secretly ap-prove and rejoice over their violent measures. The first martyr who ever died, was stoned by a lawless mob; and if we look at the rise of various sects—Methodists, Friends, &c.—we shall find that mobs began the persecution against them, and that it was not until after the people had thus spoken out their wishes, that laws were framed to fine, imprison, or destroy them. Let us, then, be prepared for the enactment of laws even in our Free States, against Abolition-ists. And how ardently has the prayer been breathed, that God would prepare us for all he is preparing for us; that he would strengthen us in the hour of conflict, and cover our heads (if consistent with his holy will) in the day of battle! But O! how earnestly have I desired, not that we may escape suffering, but that we may be willing to endure unto the end. If we call upon the slave-holder to suffer the loss of what he calls property, then let us show him we make this demand from a deep sense of duty, by being ourselves willing to suffer the loss of character, property—yea, and life itself, in what we believe to be the cause of bleeding hu-manity.

My mind has been especially turned towards those, who are standing in the fore front of the battle; and the prayer has gone up for their preservation—not the preservation of their lives, but the preservation of their minds in humility and patience, faith, hope, and <u>charity</u>—that charity which is the bond of perfectness. If persecution is the means which God has ordained for the accomplishment of this great end, <u>Emancipation</u>; then, in dependence <u>upon Him</u> for strength to bear it, I feel as if I could say, let it come; for it is my deep, solemn, deliberate conviction, that <u>this is a cause worth dying for</u>. I say so, from what I have seen, and heard, and known, in a land of slavery, where rests the darkness of Egypt, and where is found the sin of Sodom. Yes! let it come—let <u>us</u> suffer, rather than insurrections should arise.

At one time, I thought this system would be overthrown in blood, with the confused noise of the warrior; but a hope gleams across my mind, that <u>our</u> blood will be spilt, instead of the slave-holders'; <u>our</u> lives will be taken, and theirs spared—I say a <u>hope</u>, for all things I desire to be spared the anguish of seeing our beloved country desolated with the horrors of a servile war. If persecution can abolish slavery, it will also purify the Church; and who that stands between the porch and altar, weeping over the sins of the people, will not be willing to suffer, if such immense good will be accomplished. Let us endeavor, then, to put on the <u>whole</u> armor of God, and, having done all, to stand ready for whatever is before us.

I have just heard of Dresser's being flogged: it is no surprise it all; but the language of our Lord has been sweetly revived—"Blessed are ye when men shall revile you, and persecute you, and say all manner of evil against you <u>falsely</u>, for my sake. Rejoice, and be exceeding glad, for great is your reward in heaven." O! for a willingness and strength to suffer! But we shall have false brethren now, just as the Apostles had, and this will be one of our greatest griefs.

A. E. GRIMKE.

### 1837: FEBRUARY 17
### MRS. A. M. SMYTHE TO HER COUSIN

---

*In Virginia, as elsewhere in the South, some slave owners saw the humanity in their slaves, even as they seemed to ignore the inhumanity of slavery.*

Smythe's background and the outcome of her request are unknown. Saint Vitus' dance (a popular name for Sydenham's chorea) is a neurological disease that causes involuntary motions.

My Dear Cousin

I must beg a favor of you which I trust you will grant. at March court our little all will be sold for debt. You know how much I am attached to Sally and her children. attached to them because they are the best of slaves. I never knew so faithful and valuable a family of negroes. you have it in your power to purchase them. if you do so I can leave the country with peace of mind. the first of April we will set out for the North Western territory, a howling Wilderness.

My Husband will be in Abingdon this week, he told me, he would visit you, his spirits are so low I fear he will not. if you see him, say every thing to cheer him.

My Mother is unable to raise the money at present to buy the family I speak of—Harry would I suppose but his Wife will sell a negro upon the most trivial offence. none can please her.

Martha the oldest of the children is 16 she has been afflicted with St. Vitus's dance 8 winters. in the Spring Summer, and Fall she is perfectly well, Doct. Floyd told me in the commencement of the disease that lime was the only cure, for several winters it has been gradually leaving her, this winter she has been confined only one day of course she will go lower in consequence of it. she does all kinds of work, that is usual about a house. and knits all the Woolen socks and stockings that are worn in the family—Mary is 13 she can sew very well—Madison is 10, a very capable and likely boy. there are three younger ones. Sally will have another in June.

I wish My Dear Cousin you would write as soon as you can—

My love to yourself and family

I am My Dear Cousin Yours truly and sincerely

AMS

## 1837: DECEMBER

## SARAH MAPPS DOUGLASS TO WILLIAM BASSET

*Despite the fact that Philadelphia's Quakers had decided to admit blacks to their meetings, the reality that resulted was at best a segregated one. Among those who tried to change the situation was Sarah Mapps Douglass (1806–1882), a member of a free black Philadelphia family and a co-founder of the Philadelphia Female Anti-Slavery Society. In the letter below, she detailed her early meeting-house experiences to William Basset, a Quaker abolitionist in Lynn, Massachusetts.*

Abolitionists Sarah and Angelina Grimké (see pages 146 and 152) were among Douglass's friends for some four decades; "A.E.G." referred to Angelina. Douglass's quote comes from Shakespeare's *Othello:* "Speak of me as I am; nothing extenuate, / Nor set down aught in malice."

Phila
December, 1837.

Esteemed Friend.

Your favor of the 7th came safe to hand. It needed no apology. The fact of your being an abolitionist; the friend of my beloved sisters Sarah and Angelina Grimké, the friend of my poor and oppressed bretheren and sisters enti[t]les you to my warmest gratitude and esteem. I thank God that he has enabled you to renounce error and strengthened you to come up to the help of the Lord against the mighty. I pray that you may run the race set before you without halting, keeping your eye stedfastly fixed on the great Captain of our salvation.

The questions you ask me, make me feel my weakness, and in view of the great responsibility that rests upon me in answering them, my flesh trembles; yet will I cast my burden on Him, who is strength in weakness and resolve to do my duty; to tell the truth and leave the consequences to God. I thank you for the "Letter to a member of the Society of Friends". I can set my seal to the truth of the following paragraph, extracted from it. "It will be allowed that the Negro Pew or its equivalent may be found in some of our meeting houses where men and women bretheren and sisters by creat[i]on and heirs of the same glorious immortality are seated by themselves on a back bench for no other reason but because it has pleased God to give them a complexion darker than our own." And as you request to know particularly about Arch Street Meeting, I may say that the experience of years has made me wise in this fact, that there is a bench set apart at that meeting for our people, whether <u>officially</u> appointed or not I cannot say; but this I am free to say that my mother and myself were told to sit there, and that 2 friends sat at each end of the bench to prevent white persons from sitting there. And even when a child my soul was made sad with hearing five or six times during the course of one meeting this language of remonstrance addressed to those who were willing to sit by us. "This bench is for the black people." "This bench is for the people of color." And oftentimes I wept, at other times I felt indignant and queried in my own mind are these people Christians. Now it seems clear to me that had not this bench been set apart for oppressed Americans, there would have been no necessity for the oft-repeated and galling remonstrance, galling indeed, because <u>I believe they despise us for our color</u>. I have not been in Arch Street meeting for four years; but my mother goes once a week and frequently she has a <u>whole long bench</u> to herself. The assertion that our people who attend their meetings prefer sitting by themselves, is not true. A very near friend of ours, that fears God and who has been a constant attender of Friends meeting from his childhood, says "Thou mayest tell William Basset, that I know that 'Friends' appointed a seat for our people at the meeting which I attend. Several years ago a friend came to me and told me that 'Friends' had appointed a back bench for us. I told him with some warmth that I had just as lief sit on the floor as sit there. I do not care about it, Friends do not do the thing that is right." Judge now, I pray you, whether this man preferred sitting by himself. Two sons of the person I have just mentioned, have left attending Friends meetings within the last few months, because they could no longer endure the "scorning of those that are at ease, and the contempt of the proud." Conversing with one of them today, I asked, why did you leave Friends. "Because they do not know how to treat me, I do not like to sit on a back bench and be treated with contempt, so I go where I am better treated." Do you not like their principles and their mode of worship? "Yes, I like their principles, but not their practice. They make the highest profession of any sect of Christians, and are the most deficient in practice." In reply to your question "whether there appears to be a diminution of prejudice towards you among Friends," I unhesitatingly answer, no. I have heard it frequently remarked and have observed it myself, that in proportion as we become intellectual and respectable, so in proportion does their disgust and prejudice increase.

Yet while I speak this of Friends as a body, I am happy to say that there is in this city a "noble few", who have cleansed their garments from the foul stain of prejudice, and are doing all their hands find to do in promoting the moral and mental elevation of oppressed Americans.

Some of these are members of Anti-Slavery Societies and others belong to the old abolition School.

While I have been penning this letter living desires have sprung up in my soul that I might "nothing extenuate nor set down ought in malice". Doubtless you know that our beloved A. E. G. is convalescent. Did all the members of Friends society feel for us, as the sisters Grimké do, how soon, how very soon would the fetters be stricken from the captive and cruel prejudice be driven from the bosoms of the professed followers of Christ. We were lying wounded and bleeding, trampled to the very dust by the heel of our bretheren and our sisters, when Sarah and Angelina Grimké passed by; they saw our low estate and their hearts melted within them; with the tenderness of ministering angels they lifted us from the dust and poured the oil of consolation, the balm of sympathy into our lacerated bosoms; they identified themselves with us, took our wrongs upon them, and made our oppression and woe theirs. Is it any marvel then that we call them blessed among women? We value them not because they belong to the great and the mighty of our land, but because they love Christ and our afflicted bretheren. Most cordially do we approve every step they have taken since they left us, believing that the unerring spirit of truth is their leader [and] friend. I hope this letter may be satisfactory to you; use it, and the account of my brother in any way you may think proper, but do not give my name unless it is absolutely necessary. Please tell our beloved A. E. G. that her friends entreat her not to exert herself until she is quite strong. May the Lord bless you, and may you anchor your little bark on the rock, Christ Jesus; that so, when the storm of persecution arises, You may suffer no loss.

Prays fervently

Sarah M. Douglass

## 1838: FEBRUARY 17
## ANGELINA GRIMKÉ TO THEODORE WELD

---

*Eventually the Grimkés spoke not just for abolition, but—especially after a group of Massachusetts ministers denounced female reformers and preachers—for women's rights as well. The fact that neither sister was married gave their enemies something to use against them, but in 1836 Angelina met fellow abolitionist Theodore Weld (1803–1895). After several years of earnest correspondence about the cause, Weld professed his love in a letter, and Angelina delved into the matter in a series of questioning responses. They married later in the year.*

Jane Smith was one of Grimké's closest friends. The passage quoted was a slight misquote from Weld's first love letter.

One thing I want to ask you, My Dear Brother. Ought God to be <u>all in all</u> to us <u>on earth</u>? I tho't so, and am frightened to find <u>He is not</u>, that is, I feel something else is necessary to my happiness. I laid awake thinking why it was that my heart longed and panted and reached after you as it does. Why my Savior and my God is not enough to <u>satisfy</u> me. Am I sinning, am I ungrateful, <u>am I an</u> IDOL-ATOR? I trust <u>I am not</u>, and yet—but I cannot tell how I feel. I am a mystery to myself. Then again, why does not the love of my own dear sister and of my faithful Jane satisfy, if as a human being I must have <u>human love</u>? <u>Why</u> do I <u>feel</u> in my inmost soul that you, <u>you only</u>, can fill up the deep void that is there? Am I sinning against <u>them</u> too, am I ungrateful for <u>all</u> they have done for me? God forbid. Then again I think I can say with you "it is the <u>spirit</u>, the <u>spirit</u>, not a brother spirit, or a sister spirit but a disimbodied spirit, with none of the associations or incidents of the physical nature, which moves upon me with overcoming power." But <u>if</u> this <u>is so</u>, <u>why</u> do I so anxiously desire to hear from you, to see you? O! I am distressed that I should feel as I do. <u>Am I sinning</u>, is the solemn, earnest enquiry which I am continually making at our Father's throne. The conflict is great, <u>for I want to know where</u> I am, I want to be <u>purified</u>. I want my will to be swallowed up in <u>His will</u>, and I charge you before Him <u>not</u> to take a single step without Divine guidance. I think I see it will be best for you <u>not</u> to be at our Meetings, best for the <u>cause</u>, the holy cause which we both love and desire to serve. The Lord Jesus has promised to stand at our right hand. I know He will help us, and I know He will bless and lead you in the right way. <u>Why should I desire anything more?</u> if my love is pure and void of selfishness. Farewell in the love of the Lord and the bonds of the poor broken hearted slave. <u>Pray</u>—PRAY for me.

### 1838: APRIL 4
### MARY GRIMKÉ TO ANGELINA GRIMKÉ

*The Grimkés' mother (who had given birth to twelve other children) had not been happy that Sarah and Angelina were unmarried. In this letter, written soon after Angelina had sent word that she planned to wed Weld, Mary Smith Grimké (1764–1839) revealed a maternal love that could triumph over anything—even a daughter's success.*

Charleston, S.C. April 4th, 1838

My dearest Angelina

I have just received your last affectionate and interesting letter; the importance of the contents demand an immediate answer, which I will endeavour to give as well as the circumstances of the case will admit. I feel assured that my dear daughter will marry no one who is not equal to her in every sense of the word; and from the description given of your lover by Sarah and yourself, he seems to be suitable to you in all respects. . . . You will now have a protector, and therefore whatever you do will be in future <u>sanctioned</u> by him; I shall myself [be] relieved from the same anxiety that has <u>hitherto</u> rested on me; for if he approves, I have no right to interfere: I have always believed you acted from <u>conscientious</u> motives, and have often prayed for your success, (altho' differing so widely from you,) if it were indeed doing the work of the Lord: After you become a <u>Matron</u>, I hope you will feel that retirement is best suited to your station; and you will desire to retire from the busy scenes of publicity, and to enjoy that happiness which I hope your home will yield you: you have been always moderate in your wishes and I have no doubt will be satisfied with the comforts of life; this I trust, you will secure; for it would be prudent so to do; the struggle for a support destroys happiness, and is <u>injurious</u> to the temper; this I trust you will provide against, for you have never known what it is to want the necessaries of life while single, and would feel it much more in a married state; as many things would be requisite then that you can now do without: these considerations I would bring to your view, for the' I have never prayed for riches or honours for my Children, I would crave for them a <u>competency</u>. . . . You have not mentioned the time fixed; and whether you shall go to housekeeping immediately, and what are your prospects: neither have you said what sort of a looking person he was. Now I should like to know everything concerning him. . . . I do indeed most freely grant you my blessing, and can assure you, <u>Notwithstanding</u> our difference of opinion, my love for you has in <u>nowise</u> diminished.

—your affectionate Mother and Sincere Friend<br>Mary S. Grimké.

## 1838: APRIL 18
### LETHE JACKSON TO VIRGINIA CAMPBELL

*When David Campbell became governor of Virginia in 1837, he and his wife moved to Richmond, and the care of Montcalm, his home in Abingdon, was entrusted to two house slaves named Hannah Valentine and Lethe Jackson (1771–1843). In this letter to the Campbells' niece Virginia (1821?–1866), Jackson gave ample evidence that, as she put it, "my heart is large enough to hold you all."*

Jackson's letter was apparently dictated.

Montcalm April 18th 1838

My dear and much respected Miss Virginia

I was much pleased at receiving your letter and was very highly flattered to think that you in the gay metropolis so much admired and caressed should still condescend to remember old Aunt Lethe on the retired hill of Montcalm and be assured my sweet young mistress that old Aunt Lethe still remembers you with feelings of the utmost respect and esteem—And my Mistress too I am glad to hear she is getting better and that she has not forgotten lowly <u>me</u>—I hope she will still live to be a blessing to all of us—

Everything is going on finely and prospers in my hands—The flowers in the garden are putting out and it begins to look like a little paradise and the Calves and the Chickens and the children are all fine and lively—just waiting your return to complete their happiness—

I am sorry that Masters cow has so little manners as to eat Onions—in the City of Richmond too—well what a disgrace! I wish you to tell her that our Mountain Cows are better trained than that—and that if she will come up here we will learn her to be more genteel and not spoil the Governers milk—Tell My Master I think all the world of him and long once more to see his dignified steps up our hill—Tell Mistress I hope I shall soon hear of her recovery and that we long for the time when she will be again here to give her directions and have every thing as it ought to be and as she wants it—We have all done the best we could since she went away but still there is nothing like having a person of sense to dictate—and then if we are obedient every thing goes on smoothly and happy—I try Miss Virginia to be contented at all times and am determined not to let anything make me unhappy, we are taught to resemble our Maker and He is always happy, therefore it is our duty to be happy too—knowing that his divine Providence is over all our changes and that the very hairs of our head are numbered—I feel very happy and my mind is continually aspiring to that heavenly place where all our sorrows will terminate—You say in your letter "that we have a very good lot if we will improve it" I think so too and when we know that our good Lord is Divine Love & Wisdom in its utmost perfection and that, that Love & Wisdom is continually exerted for our welfare how grateful, how active, and how obedient, ought we to be and how confident, in all his mercies—Miss Virginia I feel extremely happy when I think what a good Lord & Savior we have and I feel determined to serve him to the best of my knowledge. You say that "the spring is a bright season and that the hours flit so lightly away we scarcely notice them" And so it is with the spring time of Life—When one is young the days and weeks pass rapidly by and we are surprised when we find them gone. and how pat we are in the buoyant days of youth to forget—that the Autumn of age, and Winter of death, is coming. But I am persuaded it is not so with you— I know that you do reflect on these things—I know there are a few young persons who are pious as you are and I have a well grounded hope that in all the relations of life you will sustain yourself like a Christian I wish I could hear some of the good preaching you speak of but the good being is every where. he is at Montcalm in the still breath of evening as much as in the "City full" yes he is evry where present—and even condescends to visit old Aunt Lethe's heart—Oh Miss Virginia my heart is so full I know not what to say—Tell Eliza I thank her for her letter and she must take part of this to herself as I think one letter is enough for such a poor creature as me for I can tell you all I am setting very frail—to what I used to be. Oh Master! Oh Mistress! Oh Miss Virginia I want to see you al and Michael and Eliza and Richard and David and all; my heart is large enough to hold you all—I pray that the Lord till take care of you and keep you from all evil—I hope I have not made to free in any think I said—I wanted to write as if I was talking to you—With every sentiment of veneration and esteem I remain You faithful servant

Lethe Jackson

I have a keg of butter which will be too old to use when you come—if you are willing Mr Lathem thinks it best to sell it—please to write by the next mail and say if you wish us to sell it or not. I think it would be best to sell it—L J

### 1838: APRIL 21

### E. E. PORTER TO THE <u>ADVOCATE OF MORAL REFORM</u>

---

*As cities became more populated, troubles became more visible, and the 1830s and 1840s saw a huge increase in the number of women's societies dedicated to one reform or another. Many of these involved abolition; others involved women's rights; and still others were ardently committed to "moral reform," an attempt to check the behavior of "fallen women," as well as the men accused of preying upon them. E. E. Porter lived in Windham, Ohio, and was moved to send this report to the Advocate of Moral Reform, a New York journal that had begun publishing in 1835 and soon had more than twenty thousand readers.*

At our annual meeting in 1837, the Society numbered 32. Since then it has gained 23. Two have been called at a distance from us, but we trust they are laborers with us still in this important cause.

It will hardly be worth while to inform you, that it is our lot to share with others in the usual opposition which the espousel of the cause of Moral Reform has called forth. We have many friends, and also may foes. The young gentlemen of this place have very decidedly come out against us. They say, "You have raised your sacrilegious hands against a custom both ancient and honorable." I will state an article in our Constitution. It is called by them "The 9 o'clock Article."

"Believing that the prolonging of visits with any gentleman after the usual hour of retirement, is one of the first steps towards licentiousness, we pledge ourselves to discountenance such practices by precepts and example."

Had not this article become binding upon us, they say, "We would not notice you." As it is, they have formed a society, and pledged themselves not to associate with us, because we are bringing into disrepute an innocent practice, handed down to them by their venerable forefathers, and which has been to them a source of great pleasure and enjoyment. There are quite a number of ladies with whom they associate, who do not belong to a Moral Reform Society. They are told to "remain firm," and in so doing they are assured of receiving "the respect and attentions of all" "gentlemen of honor," which is the title they have taken to themselves, and those who countenance them are called "ladies of respectability." We are sorry to have offended the gentlemen, but our Master said, "This is the way, walk ye in it;" and if they do not like our Society and principles, we will cherish a spirit of kindness, and pray that their minds may be enlightened from on high.

> On behalf of the Society,
> Affectionately yours,
> E. E. Porter.

### 1838: APRIL 23
### LIDIAN JACKSON EMERSON TO LUCY JACKSON BROWN

*Second wife of the poet and philosopher Ralph Waldo Emerson, Lidian (née Lydia) Jackson Emerson (1802–1892) was a force in her own right, religiously devoted, bright and literate, and no less committed to correcting society's wrongs than many of the better-known reformers of her day. In this letter to her older sister, Lucy Jackson Brown (1798–1868), Lidian displayed a talent for argument as well as for outrage. Between 1838 and 1839, approximately sixteen thousand Cherokee were rounded up by the U.S. army in Alabama, Georgia, North Carolina, and Tennessee and forcibly marched to Indian territory in what is now Oklahoma. Some four thousand died along the route, which would become known as the Trail of Tears. In May, Washington's* Daily National Intelligencer *printed an open letter to President Martin Van Buren from Ralph Waldo Emerson.*

"Harpy" in this context meant "predatory." Ebenezer Rockwood Hoar was a well-known judge and abolitionist. Mary Russell was a young woman who lived with the Emersons for a time and later had a romance with Henry David Thoreau. "G.P.B." was George P. Bradford, another member of the Concord circle. Ichabod Morton owned a local store.

Concord April 23d 1838

Dear Lucy—

Doing good you know is all out of fashion but there happens just now to occur a case so urgent that one must lay aside for awhile all new-fangled notions—and attempt in the good old way to do a little good—by speaking our word, and doing what deeds we may in behalf of the poor Cherokee nation. If you see no papers and few people, you do not know I suppose, that in one month from to-day the Cherokees old & young—sick and well—are to be forcibly dragged from their homes by <u>harpy</u> government-contractors;—and conveyed without regard to their comfort health or even life during the journey—into the wilderness beyond the Mississippi This is done by Congress on the strength of a treaty obtained by fraud of a few individual Cherokees—although a solemn and pathetic protest has been formally entered against its validity signed by 15,000 of the nation which consists of but 18000. I would write more particulars but probably you can borrow the "Liberator" or some other paper which contains the "Appeal." Yesterday after church, a meeting of the Concord people was held to consider whether any thing could be done by them to arrest this terrible deed—and in any case to wash their hands of it by a Memorial to Congress protesting against it as an act of awful iniquity. Mr Emerson made the first address; stating the case. and reading to the assembly the "Appeal of the Cherokees"—He also expressed his sentiments on the subject very decidedly. Mr Hoar spoke next and told the whole story of the Cherokee nation after which he denounced the behaviour of the government towards them in the strongest terms calling it precisely the same crime as highway robbery. Mr Wilder spoke next; and then Rockwood Hoar after a short but most beautiful speech asked leave to read a "Memorial to Congress" which he had drawn up in the hope it might be signed by all the citizens of the town. It was approved by the assembly and I believe is to be sent to Washington directly. Other things were done and said; but this will be enough to give you an idea of what Plymouth may and should do to bear her testimony against this wickedness in high places. Every town and every individual that does not at least raise a <u>voice</u> in condemnation of such an outrage on humanity—must share the disgrace and the blame of its perpetration. So I pray you do your share in calling the attention of some of the friends of goodness to this evil that Plymouth may speedily follow Concord in cleansing its hands of it wholly. Speak to Mary Russell—Jane Goodwin—& Mrs Briggs that they may mention it to the gentlemen most likely to care that something be done. But do not let this letter be spoken of—it may seem an impertinence. I should not suppose it needful for me to take it upon myself to remind my Plymouth friends of a duty—only that most of the newspapers have been silent on this subject—and people are not generally informed that such a case exists. Besides this the case is so desperate that those who do know of it are prevented by despondency from doing the little that is possible in any event. I will send you the Liberator if I can and then you will feel when you have read the story that you <u>must</u> do what you can. The "Atlas" is the paper which has said most about it. It can I suppose be found at the Reading-room. Mr. Emerson very unwillingly takes part in public movements like that of yesterday preferring individual action. But this occasion seemed to require <u>all</u> modes of action—so he gave his aid—But he intends still to do what as an individual he may—I will wr again—on common matters—and hope to have a letter from you to answer—But now I must leave off or lose the mail.

Your affte sister,<br>Lydia

Ask Mary and Jane G. directly from me—to speak to the gentlemen if they think it worth while—and speak yourself to G.P.B. if you should see him—which you can any day that you sit at the <u>window</u>. Ichabod Morton I suspect is already in motion—as he probably takes the "Liberator." I repeat that I hope you will not let my name be spoken if you can help it. Tell M. & J. not to speak of this letter.

## 1839
## KEZIAH KENDALL TO SIMON GREENLEAF

*The name of this letter writer is almost certainly fictitious, as no records of this Kendall family in Cambridge have been found, and as "Keziah" and her sisters all-too-fittingly share the names of the three daughters in Job. But the issue Kendall raised—the legal rights of women—continued to be extremely real, and, as she wrote to Harvard Law School co-founder Simon Greenleaf (1783–1853), she was none too thrilled with his academic and accepting view of the situation.*

The Lyceum lecture movement had been organized in the 1820s as a way to offer local communities exposure to ideas, current events, and, eventually, well-known authors. By the 1840s, there was a regular circuit that paid for visits from such speakers as Emerson, Thoreau, and Susan B. Anthony. Wives whose husbands died without leaving wills were granted a minimum of a third of their husband's estates, popularly known as "widow's thirds." A mantua was a loose-fitting gown. "Antimasonry" referred to the Anti-Masonic Party, which came into existence in the 1820s in an attempt to eliminate the secret society of Freemasonry.

I take the liberty to write to you on the subject of the Lyceum lecture you delivered last Feb. but as you are not acquainted with me I think I will introduce myself. My name is Kezia Kendall. I live not many miles from Cambridge, on a farm with two sisters, one older, one younger than myself. I am thirty two. Our parents and only brother are dead—we have a good estate—comfortable house—nice barn, garden, orchard &c and money in the bank besides. Jemima is a very good manager in the house, keeps everything comfortable—sees that the milk is nicely prepared for market—looks after everything herself, and rises before day, winter and summer—but she never had any head for figures, and always expects me to keep all accounts, and attend to all business concerns. Keranhappuck, (who is called Kerry) is quite young, only nineteen, and as she was a little girl when mother died, we've always petted her, and let her do as she pleased, and now she's courted. Under these circumstances the whole responsibility of our property, not less than twenty five thousand dollars rests upon me. I am not over fond of money, but I have worked hard ever since I was a little girl, and tried to do all in my power to help earn, and help save, and it would be strange if I did not think more of it than those who never earned anything, and never saved anything they could get to spend, and you know Sir, there are many such girls nowadays. Well—our milkman brought word when he came from market that you were a going to lecture on the legal rights of women, and so I thought I would go and learn. Now I hope you wont think me bold when I say, I did not like that lecture much. I dont speak of the manner, it was pretty spoken enough, but there was nothing in it but what every body knows. We all know about a widow's thirds, and we all know that a man must maintain his wife, and we all know that he must pay her debts, if she has any—but I never heard of a yankee woman marrying in debt. What I wanted to know, was good reasons for some of those laws that I cant account for. I do hope if you are ever to lecture at the Lyceum again, that you will give us some. I must tell my story to make you understand what I mean. One Lyceum lecture that I heard in C. stated that the Americans went to war with the British, because they were taxed without being represented in Parliament. Now we are taxed every year to the full amount of every dollar we possess—town, county, state taxes—taxes for land, for movables, for money and all. Now I dont want to go representative or any thing else, any more than I do to be a "constable or a sheriff," but I have no voice about public improvements, and I dont see the justice of being taxed any more than the "revolutionary heroes" did. You mention that women here, are not treated like heathen and Indian women—we know that—nor do I think we are treated as Christian women ought to be, according to the Bible rule of doing to others as you would others should do unto you. I am told (not by you) that if a woman dies a week after she's married that her husband takes all her personal property and the use of the real estate as long as he lives—if a man dies his wife can have her thirds—<u>this</u> does not come up to the Gospel rule. Now the young fellow that is engaged to our Kerry, is a pleasant clever fellow, but he is not quite one and twenty, and I dont s'pose he ever earned a coat in his life. Uncle told me there was a way for a woman to have her property trustee'd, and I told it to Kerry—but she, poor girl has romantic notions owing to reading too many novels, and when I told her of it, she would not hear of such a thing—"What take the law to keep my property away from James before I marry him—if it was a million of dollars he should have it all." So you see I think the law is in fault here—to tell you the truth I do not think young men are near so careful about getting in debt as girls, and I have known more than one that used their wife's money to pay off old scores. I had a young friend who was without parents, married when she was twenty years old. She had sixteen thousand dollars all in Bank stock. She has lived in a good house, and dressed well since, but I have never known her to have a five dollar bill to give away, and I know she had an own Aunt sent to the poor-house last year. She is a generous woman and this would not have been if she had her own money. I had rather go to my mantua maker to borrow twenty dollars if I needed it, than to the richest married woman I know. Another thing I have to tell you—when I was young I had a lover, Jos. Thompson, he went into business in a neighboring town, and after a year or two while I was getting the wedding things—Joe failed, he met with misfortunes that he did not expect,—he could have concealed it from me and married, but he did not—he was honorable, and so we delayed. He lived along here two or three years, and tried all he could to settle with his creditors, but some were stiff and held out, and thought by the by we would marry, and they should get my property. Uncle said he knew if we were married, there were those who would take my cattle and the improvement of my land. Joseph used to visit me often those years, but he lost his spirits and he could not get into business again, and he thought he must go to sea. I begged him not to, and told him we should be able to manage things in time, but he said no—he must try his luck, and at least get enough to settle off old scores, and then he would come here and live and we would make the best of what I had. We parted—but it pleased God he should be lost at sea. What I have suffered, I cannot tell you. Now Joe was no sailor when I engaged with him, and if it had been a thing known that I should always have a right to keep possession of my own, he need never have gone to sea, and we might have lived happily together, and in time with industry and economy, he might have paid off all. I am one that cant be convinced without better reasons that I have heard of, that women are dealt with by the "gospel rule." There is more might than right in such laws as far as I can see—if you see differently, do tell us next time you lecture. Another thing—you made some reflections upon women following the Anti's. When the fuss was about Antimasonry, the women did nothing about it, because there were no female masons, and it was none of their business. Women have joined the Antislavery societies, and why? women are kept for slaves as well as men—it is a common cause, deny the justice of it, who can! To be sure I do not wish to go about lecturing like the Misses Grimkie, but I have not the knowledge they have, and I verily believe that if I had been brought up among slaves as they were, and knew all that they know, and felt a call from humanity to speak, I should run the venture of your displeasure, and that of a good many others like you. I told Uncle that I thought your lecture was a onesided thing—and he said, "why Keziah, Squire Greenleaf is an advocate, not a judge, you must get him to take t'other side next time." Now I have taken this opportunity to ask you to give us a remedy for the "legal wrongs" of women, whenever you have a chance. The fathers of the land should look to these things—who knows but your daughter may be placed in the sad situation I am in, or the dangerous one Kerry is in. I hear you are a good man, to make it certain—do all the good you can, and justify no wrong thing.

Yours with regard
Keziah Kendall.

### 1839: SEPTEMBER
### MARGARET FULLER TO SAMUEL WARD

*Margaret Fuller (1810–1850) was a charter member of America's Transcendental circle, a leading figure in the growing literary and philosophical movement at a time when it was still surprising to find women stepping out of their accustomed home sphere. Extraordinarily accomplished as a critic, poet, lecturer, journalist, and editor, Fuller was somewhat less successful in her romantic life. She fell in love with Samuel G. Ward (1817–1907), another member of the circle; he eventually became a banker, and left Fuller for another woman. In this letter, with the eloquence she had so often used for public statements, she expressed her private pain.*

The following year, Ward would marry, and Fuller would become founding editor of *The Dial*. Some years later, she fell in love with Giovanni Ossoli, had his child out of wedlock, and then married him. All three drowned when their ship sank off Fire Island. *Isola* is Italian for "island."

I believe,
in the first days of
Septr 1839

To ———

You love me no more—How did you pray me to draw near to you! What words were spoken in impatience of separation! How did you promise to me, aye, and doubtless to yourself, too, of all we might be to one another.

We are near and with Spring's fairest flower I poured out my heart to you.— At an earlier period I would fain have broke the tie that bound us, for I knew myself incapable of feeling or being content to inspire an ordinary attachment. As soon as I saw a flaw I would have broke the tie. You would not—You resented, yet with what pathetic grace, any distrust on my part. <u>Forever,</u> <u>ever</u> are words of which you have never been, are not now afraid.

—You call me your best of friends, your dearest friend, you say that you always find yourself with me. I doubt not the depth of your attachment, doubt not that you feel my worth. But the confiding sweetness, the natural and prompt expression of attachment are gone—are they gone forever?

You do not wish to be with me; why try to hide it from me, from yourself? You are not interested in any of my interests. My friends, my pursuits are not yours. If you tell me of yours, it is like a matter of duty, not because you cannot help it, and must write or speak to relieve the full heart and mind.

The sympathizing contemplation of the beautiful in Nature, in Art is over for us. That for which I loved you first, and which made that love a shrine at which I could rest upon my weary pilgrimage.—Now—moons wax and wane, suns rise and set, the summer segment of the beautiful circle is filled, and since the first flush on the cheek of June we have not once seen, felt, admired together. You come here—to go away again, and make a call upon me in the parlor while you stay! You write to me—to say you could not write before and ask me why I do not write.—You invite me to go and see Michel's work—by myself! You send me your books and pictures—to ask me what I think of them! Thus far at least we have walked no step together and my heart deceives me widely if this be love, or if we live as friends should live:

Yet, spite of all this, sometimes I believe when I am with you, and, come what may, I will be faithful myself. I will not again draw back: it shall be all your fault if we break off again. I will wait—I will not complain—I will exact nothing—I will make every allowance for the restlessness of a heart checked in its love, a mind dissatisfied with its pursuits. I will bear in mind that my presence is like to recal all you have need to forget and will try to believe that you would not be with me lest I "spoil you for your part on life's dull scene," or as you have said "call up the woman in you"

You say you love me as ever, forever. I will, if I can, rely upon your word, believing you must deem me entitled to unshrinking frankness.

You have given me the sacred name of Mother, and I will be so indulgent, as tender, as delicate (if possible) in my vigilance, as if' I had borne you beneath my heart instead of in it. But Oh, it is waiting like the Mother beside the sepulchre for the resurrection, for all I loved in you is at present dead and buried, only a light from the tomb shines now and then in your eyes. But I will wait, to me the hardest of all tasks, will wait for thee whom I have loved so well. I will never wound thy faith, nor repel thy heart, never, never! Only thyself shall have power to divorce my love from its office of ministry,—not even mine own pride shall do it. So help me God, as I keep this vow, prays

Isola

### 1840: OCTOBER 27
### SARGRY BROWN TO HER HUSBAND

*Because slaves were property, they could not be parties to contracts. Marriage thus did not exist as a legal state among slaves, nor did it provide any obstacle to a change in status, location, or master.*

We could learn nothing of Sargry Brown or her husband.

Richmond Va. october 27 1840

Dear Husband—

This is the third letter that I have written to you, and have not received any from you; and don't no the reason that I have not received any from you. I think very hard of it. the trader has been here three times to Look at me. I wish that you would try to see if you can get any one to buy me up there. if you don't come down here this Sunday, perhaps you wont see me any more. give my love to them all, and tell them all that perhaps I shan't see you any more. give my love to your mother in particular, and to mamy wines, and to aunt betsy, and all the children; tell Jane and Mother they must come down a fortnight before christmas. I wish to see you all, but I expect I never shall see you all—never no more.

I remain your Dear and affectionate Wife,

Sargry Brown.

## CIRCA 1841: NOVEMBER 19
## MARTHA COFFIN WRIGHT TO LUCRETIA MOTT

*When Martha Coffin Wright (1806–1875) wrote this letter to her sister, Lucretia Coffin Mott (1793–1880), she was in her second marriage (to attorney David Wright) and trying to run a household while caring for four children. Seven years later, Martha and Lucretia would both join Elizabeth Cady Stanton (see page 195) in organizing the groundbreaking women's rights convention at Seneca Falls. Meanwhile, Martha chronicled a day in the life of a household at a time when the only real labor-saving devices were other people.*

Maria was a maid and Sarah presumably a predecessor. Wright's children were Marianna, Eliza, Tallman, and Ellen. She would have three more in later years. By "Paphaan," Wright must have meant Paphian, meaning "wanton."

Auburn, Nov. 19th.

12 o'clock & I have not had time since breakfast to rest, having the dining room to sweep, my bed room &c &c—before which I left Ellen in Eliza's care, & made some gingerbread which was very good with the slight omission of ginger—so I went to work & made another batch remembering that important ingredient. . . . 17 years yesterday since I was first married & 12 since the last, Ellen is 15 ms old to-day, & the snip is just waking when she has only slept while I wrote the above.

26th . . . I am not at all disposed to dispute the truth of Mother's remark that hateful as Maria was, it was better to have her & be mad than to have to work hard,—and be mad—but I bore with her as long as I could, and when she sneaked out, vehemently dressed in a very light dress in a driving snow storm, just when she ought to have been making her fire to get tea, I felt so mad that I could not resist the temptation to tell her that if she did not come back at tea time, she should not at all—for I had told her in the morning that as David was away, we would have early tea, and she could then have a long evening if she wished to go out—to which she made no reply. You are too good, all of you, have your feelings too well disciplined ever to feel so angry as I did when I opened the window as she was sneaking off, and spoke to her. I know I never found it so difficult to speak the few words that I did & when I closed the window—my heart beat so that I could hardly breathe, from the effort I had made to appear pacific. I wanted to look in the glass to see if I did not look like Byron, but the children being present I read the newspaper. Byron said that when he felt himself paling with anger, he was dangerous or something like it. Mother knows just how mad we used to feel with Maria. David said I ought to have dismissed her long ago & he did not know how I had done to keep her so long as I did. When she came to pack up her things late the next morning I told her I would give her one more trial if she wd promise to do better but she wd make no such promise—she had always gone out when she pleased to spend the afternoon & night, and always would. I went down in the afternoon to see Aunt Clara. She was not surprised and expressed much regret that I had had so much trouble, wd try & get another girl for me, if her Irish girl knew of any. I shall keep Eliza at home this quarter. She assists in the care of Ellen & washes most of the dishes—gets tea & toasts bread—sets the table &c. David had to leave in the cars at 10 o'clock Sunday night for Waterloo—he only returned the day before from Seneca Falls. I never felt more lonely than when I locked the door after him—only myself & the children in the house & I did not rest much that night, as every noise woke me, & the wind being high there were plenty of all sorts of noises. It was delightful to see him with his valise on his way home at 2 o'clock yesterday—3 days & a half and as I had been teaching Eliza how to roast chickens while Ellen slept, there were three that I had just set away on the hanging shelf—fearing they would not keep I had them all roasted & set away to warm over—the other three I cut up and stewed. Day before yesterday I was engaged some time in the <u>laundry</u>, having selected from the basket of clothes that await a washer 2 dozen that would be needed before one came. I dried them in the kitchen, and ironed them the next day & thought I was a bug, as I never washed so much before. . . . Sarah having taken the chief care of all such things for 12 years, I have not fairly got my hand in yet. My bread has been excellent—we got a new barrel of flour to-day. . . .

To-day I was sweeping the porch when a spare young woman presented herself, to know if I wanted a girl. After seating her & settling a few preliminaries I ventured to suggest a hope that she was steady, as I had just dismissed a girl very capable & satisfactory in other respects. She sd she should think she was old enough to be steady—she was 27. So much the better thought I perhaps she has sowed her wild oats. Mrs. Dennis recommended her, she had formerly lived with her. . . . So it was settled that she wd come tomorrow afternoon, so as to be here ready to go to washing. My first business after she left was to run in & inquire of Eunice why she didn't take her herself. She told me she was a most excellent girl to work & neat BUT her chracter was not good when she lived with her. She begged her to take her & assured her she was not as she used to be, & Eunice said she told Caroline perhaps she had reformed & she was almost sorry she had not taken her, but as she had a young girl in the kitchen she thought it would not answer, tho' if she had been able to be about herself she should not have hesitated. Thinks I, are there none good in Auburn? no, not one? However perhaps she told the truth & had reformed, & if so it wd be cruel not to give her a trial—and my hands were so shock'n rough, so to short & long I feel pretty well satisfied. Eunice sd she was one that wd take good care of things & be good with the children—that she had a good disposition. From there I went over to see Miss Townsend & let her know why Eliza had not been. As soon as [Eliza] heard of the girl she sd "now I can go to school this yr." I told Miss T that I had thought before [when] I was without a girl of keeping Eliza out. . . .

29th   Yesterday I rose a little earlier than usual so as to have every thing in the order I wished my Magdalen to find it, & kept the kitchen warm all day but she ne-er came—this morning David put on the boiler for me & I hoped to see her after breakfast, but when D. came up to dinner he found me busy, & wanted to know if he was not a prophet when he sd she wd not come—but toward night she appeared & I have been showing her how we manage about washing &c—a doleful task. Tallman is a pretty good auxiliary as he knows the places of things pretty well. . . . She tells the children she can't read, her sight not being good, for which I am sorry as I was going to lend her "Live & Let Live" and "some novels." The first evening Henrietta came to live with me two yrs ago, she sent one of the children to me to know if I wd please to lend her some novels. Esther wished to know if I wd please to lend her a sharp pen knife to cut her corns—Sylvia wanted a comb—Lucinda a shawl—Mercy a pair of gloves—Maria, a thimble—Nancy Anna wanted a trunk to journey to the Eastward &c &c. My present Magdalen, like her prototype, rejoices in the name of Polly—Polly Magdalen! . . . Ellen does not seem so much afraid of Polly Mag as she did of Maria. I have entirely done feeding her thickened milk. She eats a great deal of bread & three or four times a day, drinks a little cup of milk, unboiled—since the cold weather I found it necessary to make that change in her diet. N.B. Polly smokes a pipe. . . .

Polly seems disposed to do her best—and is a very good cook, & saving but her health is not good & she is pretty slow—she says "jest" let her keep steady on & she can do a great deal of work but she "aint as swift as some" & that is a fact—but I don't care, as long as she does as well as she has, & is contented. She spent one evening out "to a party" promising to be back by 10 & was as good as her word. I was going out this morning and she wished to know if I was going "up street," "cause if ye are I will be very much obliged to ye if ye'll just stop at the milliners if ye go by there, and see if my hat's done." Imagine sister Lucretia stopping at the milliners to inquire for a "hat" for one of the Paphaan damsels next door to Ann Frosh's. I rather think I didn't stop. . . . I have finished all Ellen's little green aprons, four in all. I made Eliza a quilted hat to race about with, out of one breadth—myself a nice apron out of one & a half, & made Ellen two cunning little Machester frocks out of the one Marianne wore on her journey to Kimberton, afterward her blackberrying dress. Last winter, it was Eliza's everyday dress & now it looks as neat on Ellen as Lydia Davis' three-breadths-of-muslin-de-laine ones. Moreover I have knit a pr of gloves for Thomas to wear at the factory & finished a pr of long stockings for Ellen as her little legs were quite rough. My mending, in addition to the above, has kept me as busy as I could be, for most of the afternoon I have to give up everything & amuse Ellen as she gets lonesome. . . .

## 1843: FEBRUARY 17
## LIDIAN JACKSON EMERSON TO RALPH WALDO EMERSON

---

*On his deathbed, remembering his firstborn son, Ralph Waldo Emerson (1803–1882) would one day exclaim: "Oh that beautiful boy!" The child, Waldo, died of scarlet fever at the age of five, just a few months after Lidian Jackson (see page 157) had given birth to the couple's second daughter, Emily (their first, Ellen, had been born in 1839). With this letter, written to Ralph in New York just about a year after Waldo's death, Lidian confided her own grief to her husband, yet described the simple joys of celebrating Ellen's birthday. The Emersons would go on to have another son, Edward, in July of 1844.*

Lucy Jackson Brown was Lidian's sister; Mary Brown was Lucy's daughter. Emeline Barrett ran a boardinghouse. Charles Spear was a Universalist minister. A "curtain lecture," after a line in a poem by Dryden, was a wife's nagging bedtime speech. Bradbury & Soden were publishers; "Henry" was Henry David Thoreau, the writing in question his essay "A Walk to Wachusett." Louisa Dunbar was Thoreau's aunt. William and Susan were Lidian's brother- and sister-in-law.

Concord Feb 17th 1843—

Here is a fine little omen for us—for me certainly for it comes to me and I accept it; and if for me, for thee, dear Husband. In some dry, dry, earth with which I was filling a flower pot—I found a little root of Heart's-ease which had been torn up, with heedless hand, when the earth was taken, months ago from the garden; and laid till then deeply buried in the neglected box of earth. But it was found as fresh and green as when first uprooted and was hailed by its discoverer—or uncoverer—as the remembrances of summer days.—And now being set anew in growing position, with plenty of light air & water—smiles upon its benefactress and tells her of other Hearts-ease which lying buried is not dead but shall re-appear and flourish in light.

...I will send you a page I wrote yesterday for Ellen, that I may save myself the trouble of telling you the story it will tell. Will you return it when you send a pacquet that I may send it to Mary. Ellen has come forward fast in reading. She yesterday took up a book of nursery Rhymes she had not before seen, and read with great interest, almost without spelling, one of the stories. She is a year in advance of Waldo in reading. Torn is my heart as I write that cherished name. The wound of separation is as fresh as it was a year ago—at least it seems so to me. I am bruised in heart—and cannot be healed by Time. Only a new spiritual experience can bring balm to that wound. "Time heals not the heart-stricken." "They think that I forget"—but I never forget. Flowers grow over the grave—Yet is it a grave no less. I know there is healing but it has not yet come to me. I trust it will—though probably not in this life....

I am happy in telling you that Lucy is to board at Emeline B's—and with fair prospect of being kindly treated and made comfortable. "We shall see"—I will say to you if you doubt that Lucy will be contented. I have a confession to make concerning the buying of a book. Mr. Spear the peace-man (who makes a practice of carrying his book about for sale, instead of dealing with the disappointing race of Booksellers), brought me the book and earnestly requested that I would take it and give him one dollar in exchange. I knew we had more books than I could read and that my Husband had no particular taste for books on the "Names & Titles of Jesus"—but the man said he had laboured hard—had searched through many many books—had seriously injured his health by hard study & late hours—and had spent much money to make the book—& make it as perfect as he could.—and also that he had a family dependent on his exertions. So though I at first was only seeking the best mode of saying "no," I presently remembered it was not human or humane to turn away when a brother pathetically besought a dollar—and even offered me for it the price of his life or health. I also remembered a saying of Jesus "Give to him &c" and gave the dollar with a good grace—not fearing you would disapprove. I took the book also—and think I should like to read it—only that its author did not seem quite dignified in the manner & tone of his application. What nonsense to take up time & space with all this! I could have told you as well after your return. It would have done for one of the Curtain Lectures under which you so surely & so sweetly fall asleep. Did I tell you that Bradbury & Soden have refused to pay

Henry more than two thirds of the money they promised for his "Walk to W," and that they postpone the payment even of that? Will it not do for you to call on your return through Boston and demand it for him? . . .

Feb. 22th I think I will send you this sheet, poor as are its contents. I rather hope it will be better than none. Your pacquet has been here some days—and we are eagerly looking now to hear from you again by mail. Ellen is entirely delighted with your letter to her; she reads & re-reads—but is not particular to look exactly where she is reading, to-day I observe, for she knows much or all of it by heart. It is beautiful to see her earnest innocent look as she reads. No present, nor new dress, even—ever made her so happy—She said to me yesterday, "Mama we shall all go to heaven and when I am in heaven I shall not go to sleep (go to bed, she meant, I suppose), but rest on the soft clouds." She says things once in a while that I wish much to retain but cannot. Once as she was reading your letter she said something much better than I can recollect—it was about the letter being "written with such beautiful words" &c. I did not think at the time she alluded to the <u>printing</u>. She asked to have a party on her birth-day, which I at first refused on account of the coldness of the weather. But on Friday afternoon I went out to walk, and finding the weather mild, I called at the houses where Ellen's playmates were to be found, and engaged them for Saturday afternoon. Then I went to Mrs How's and bought some figs & oranges; and coming home told Mrs Stevens, our cook, she must add some currant cakes to her baking the next day. So our preparations were speedily & easily made. All the children came, excepting two of the little Hosmers who were sick; and <u>we all</u> had a fine time. Abby Gourgas was especially remembered in deciding upon who should be asked. There were 24 in all, who came. Mr Potter's shop furnished a great bundle of sugar plums which were tastefully inserted—with due regard to their colour—in the crust of the round cakes. I set a long table, with a big vase of Ever greens in the centre and the sugar-plum—& currant cakes, ginger-bread-cakes, soda-biscuit, figs, sliced apple & oranges made a show that pleased the babies well.

We greatly regretted that Elizabeth could not come to the party—She was confined to the house with a bad cold—But to-day we were happily surprised by a visit from her. She was not <u>quite</u> well, but came she most kindly said, because she had heard I was sick and was afraid there might be nothing left of me when she came if she did not come speedily. She made me feel as if I was worthy to live—for the moment. I had felt only fit to go hence—and be <u>absolutely</u> no more. I was taken on Saturday with one of my slow-feverish attacks. It did not interfere however with the social duties of that festive day—and I am still able to write & work—sometimes in bed, sometimes out of bed. I've had the Dr. today.

. . . I think I will send you two of Louisa's notes which will bring Edith before your eyes, and pay papa well the cost of conveyance; for it is partly to send them that I make a pacquet.—I've invited Henry to write, & shall apply to Elizabeth. . . .

Your wife Lidian—

Love to William Susan & the boys from us all

Thinking it not amiss to try New York varieties of seeds in our next summer's garden—I send you a list which you can get if you please. I send for the asparagus shoots because our asparagus bed is still poorly supplied—and they have a better sort in N.Y. than in Boston and also will not, I hope, send such mean little roots as came from B. I have sent also a few flower seeds which you shall do as you like about buying.

Ellen will not tell you about her party as I have invited her to. She says "I can tell him when he comes home."

This letter would have gone to-day but I kept it that it might contain the answer to a letter that I hope to have from you tomorrow. I have felt sadly disappointed—when I found the mail came in vain for us—ever since last Saturday; it is now Tuesday.—Why have you been silent so long?

Wednesday eveg.

I dreamed last night that no letter came from you came to-day and I was very sorry. But the letter did nevertheless come with the morning. I hope we shall receive yet another and that it will tell us whether we may look for you on Thursday and in which stage.

## 1844: APRIL

## MARY ANN WATERMAN TO LUCRETIA SIBLEY

---

*As abolitionists gained influence in New England in the 1830s and 1840s, many Southerners contended for the moral high ground by offering religious justifications for slavery. Both the Old and New Testaments condoned slavery, Southern preachers and politicians maintained, and a slaveholder's duty was not to free his servants but to give them humane treatment and the Christian religion. Mary Ann Cutler Waterman (1800–1863) was living in Virginia when she wrote this letter to her Rhode Island cousin, Lucretia Sibley (1798–1876?). Until the Civil War, the cousins would continue to argue the issue in their correspondence; Waterman died before the end of the war decided the question.*

Lucretia Carter had married Royal Sibley in 1819; he died three years later. The couple had two children.

I have just returned from Mr. Beidleman's. It made my heart ache to see those little motherless children. In some respects they look deserted. True they have enough to eat but their clothes were ragged. Mr. B. does all he can for them and neglects his important business to stay with them. He needs a house-keeper bad enough. What say you my dear cousin, to taking that place! I do not know another person in the world I should like to see as a mother to my dear sister's children so well as yourself. You will be asking by this time, what business I have to make such a proposition! Why, I will tell you. I have found out that it would be very agreeable to the party concerned, if you would agree to it, but he thinks that you have remained a widow so long that you could not be prevailed to change your situation, or manner of living. Is it so! I know you would not be willing to worst yourself, but you know the situation of things here—a house full of everything necessary for the comfort, and convenience of life, an excellent and liberal provider of everything wanted, and help enough if well managed, to shield you from any hard work what ever. There are girls there that with a few months training could take nearly all the sewing and knitting off [your] hands, and two women to do housework. I do not see anything to prevent you from living quite at your ease. I could if I were there. I suppose this thing of slavery will rise up as a mighty bugbear, to fright you from a comfortable home. But it need not. . . . I do believe that thousands will praise God through vast eternity that they were ever brought under the sounds of the gospel, though it was by the chains of slavery. Now I believe you can act with an eye single to the glory of God, and have a conscience <u>void of offence</u> and yet own slaves. You had no hand in bringing them into a state of bondage and if you consent to place yourself in a situation to make their lives more comfortable and pleasant I cannot see that you will be doing wrong. They are a good conditioned set of servants, and having a <u>predilection</u> for you, would I believe give you less trouble than anyone else. Think about it my dear cousin and try to think favorably and let me know your thoughts as soon as possible.

If I knew of anything more to say that thought would have any influence I should certainly say it; for I feel a great repugnance to having an entire stranger take the place there, when I know it would be so pleasing to all to have you there.

Mary Ann Waterman

## 1844: SEPTEMBER 18
## MARIANNE DWIGHT TO FRANK DWIGHT

---

*Utopian communities were part of the Transcendental movement of the nineteenth century. Probably best known of them was Brook Farm in Roxbury, Massachusetts. There, communal living, shared labor, and modern educational methods were all employed in the pursuit of a better life. Among Brook Farm's original shareholders were Nathaniel Hawthorne and Charles Dana, and among its interested visitors were Margaret Fuller, Ralph Waldo Emerson, and Horace Greeley. Marianne Dwight (1816–1901) had joined Brook Farm in the spring of 1844, and over several autumn days she wrote to her brother, Benjamin Franklin Dwight, about a few flaws in the utopia.*

George Ripley, a former Unitarian minister, had founded the community in 1841. The Phalanstery was to be a large central building, but it burned down just after it was built. Charles Fourier was a French socialist, many of whose theories were embraced by the Brook Farmers. The "fancy group" sewed clothes with the goal of selling them and enabling women to be financially independent. Elizabeth Palmer Peabody was a well-known educator of the day. Anna Parsons was a close friend who lived in Boston. Dora Hannah Ripley was a niece of the founder.

Wed. eve Sept 18 '44

Dear Frank,

This eve & all evenings find me busy as ever.—I have about 10 minutes before going to teacher's meeting, and will <u>commence</u> a letter;—I have new cares now, & you must not be surprised, if when you see me again, you shd find me looking several years older.—for I stand now in the relation of protectress or mother to Caspar & Wm. H. Goldermann.—They came yesterday noon,—seem like very good, orderly little boys.—I have just been into their room to see that they are safe in bed & bid them good-night &c.—I have not yet discovered many of their propensities.—have seen some slight indication that the older one likes to "<u>lord it</u>" over the younger. They understand very well the art of washing, dressing & taking some tolerable care of themselves wh. will make my lack all the lighter. Mrs. Ripley has been too ill to leave her room these two days, but will probably go to Boston tomorrow. I have not found out yet whether we can get up a party of ladies (partly) to go in to the Fourier meeting friday eve.—I hope to—but fear we shall not. <u>You</u> must go. You will see Fred probably, & other Brook-farmers— now off for teacher's meeting.

Thursday a.m. Came home from the meeting last eve too late to finish this letter:—now the consistory work is just finished & Mrs. Ripley & Mrs. White-house are desiring my immediate presence in the fancy group—but they will not have it just yet, for I'm determined to write.—Wish I cd do so at my leisure <u>for yr sake</u>. You are having a great day in Boston to day, are you not? Several of our people have gone in, perhaps you will fall in with some of them.—Mr New-comb, Mr. List, Clarke, Flosman? &c. I have very little idea of what the show will be.—Yesterday Mr. List & Mr. Reynolds were unanimously expelled from the carpenter's group in consequence of their being discordant elements,—so they went to the <u>general direction</u> requesting to be furnished with work, and that body have set them to work upon the frame of the Phalanstery,—so they are working right in the midst of the group, but not of the group, doing just what they are told to do,—a sort of <u>solitary labor & imprisonment</u>. It is quite an amus-ing state of things. The group who thought to get rid of their company are foiled in that.

It is a most magnificent day—the perfection of autumn, except that we have needed rain for a long time—And what are you about? The same old round of labor I suppose, only you may be anxiously laying new plans.—Oh! that we could prepare ourselves to meet all changes & disappointments without any vexation of spirit, and with a cheerful trust that all will work out right.—Nay, better, if we could feel that all is <u>right now</u>! But there <u>is a sense</u> in wh. all is not right.—& perhaps it is this that disturbs us. I wish you were here, Frank,—tho' I don't feel inclined to hurry you.—For myself, I would not exchange this life for any I have ever led.—I cd not feel contented again with the life of <u>iso-lated houses</u>, & the conventions of civilization.—I enjoy here more than I ever enjoyed—& it is true likewise that I have had some very keen suffering.—In the present state of association & with my sensibilities I feel that I must be continu-ally exposed to suffering;—but constant activity is a good counterpoise,—& life is so full and rich here, that I feel as if my experience were valuable, & I were <u>growing</u> somewhat faster than when I lived in Boston. We have thought much of yr circumstances & long to have you settled here with us, & shall rejoice when you are <u>ready</u> to come,—but I repeat we wd not hurry you.—I do hope you will find yourself comfortably situated in Boston ere long.—wish I cd help or cheer you in any way. But you <u>will</u> be of good cheer, I trust. Too all, we never know what a day may bring forth, the very next leaf that is turned over may be full of goodness & light. I think you will prosper in life, if you don't let any foolish pride stand in yr way.—for you have energy & activity, not to mention some other pleasing & valuable qualities.—

Our Fourier class went off finely—some people from the street came over.—

Hope to go to Boston tomorrow evening, but don't know. If we do, shall stop at E. P. Peabody's I suppose.

Hearing a great <u>hurrah</u>, I have just been to the window, and lo! Martin & a group of boys returning from their work,—little <u>Fourierites</u> with <u>banners</u> flying. I believe if they have been idle, the banners are not permitted to wave. The boys are really getting to enjoy their work, & these <u>banners</u> are a grand excitement. Probably the fancy group will have to work them a very handsome one.

I long for a walk to day the weather is so fine, but feel I cannot take it. Anna wrote to me that she & Dora & Hannah Ripley had planned it to pass last Sunday here. I will probably come next Sunday.—I guess Anna's <u>visit</u> will be in October.—You will come out next Saturday will you not. I should not wonder if Mary L. shd come with Fred, who is going in on Friday.—He found the error in his balance the next morning & now it is all right.

Fanny sends her love.

Yours ever affectionately
Mary Ann

.

# EXPANSION

# 1845

# ~

# 1860

Our journey, so far, has been pleasant. The roads have been good, and food plentiful. . . . We feel no fear of Indians. Our cattle graze quietly around our encampment unmolested. . . . Indeed if I do not experience something far worse than I have yet done, I shall say the trouble is all in getting started.

*—Tamsen Donner to her sister*
*June 16, 1846*

# BETWEEN 1845 AND 1860 . . .

**1845:** Author, editor, and teacher Margaret Fuller publishes *Woman in the Nineteenth Century,* an early and articulate study of women's rights; its exceptional author has been described by Edgar Allan Poe in the statement: "Humanity is divided into three classes: men, women, and Margaret Fuller." **1846:** Massachusetts inventor Elias Howe patents the sewing machine; by 1860, more than 100,000 will be produced in the United States alone. ★ Paulina Wright Davis tours the East Coast, giving lectures to women on anatomy; for demonstration purposes, she uses a mannequin that she has imported from Paris and encounters reactions ranging from curiosity to fainting. **1847:** The first U.S. postage stamps are issued, with images of Benjamin Franklin (five cents) and George Washington (ten cents); printed in sheets, they are not perforated and need to be cut apart with scissors. **1848:** Sixty-five years after the Continental Congress first proposed that an equestrian statue be erected in honor of George Washington, a 24,500-pound white marble cornerstone is dragged through the streets of Washington, D.C., to the site where the Washington Monument will be constructed. ★ In California, a shiny nugget is accidentally discovered by James Marshall as he helps build a sawmill for John Sutter;

---

Clockwise from top left: Harriet Beecher Stowe; *Uncle Tom's Cabin* theatrical poster; Sojourner Truth; Margaret Fuller; Abraham Lincoln's 1860 campaign banner; Lucy Stone; New York City Crystal Palace; 1855 *Godey's Lady's Book* fashion plate; John Brown; '49-er gold miner and pack mule.

Jennie Wimmer, the wife of Marshall's construction assistant, tests the nugget by boiling it along with the soap she is making; it withstands the lye intact, is declared authentic gold, and sets off the Gold Rush. ★ In Seneca Falls, New York, the first women's rights convention is held, under the leadership of Elizabeth Cady Stanton and Lucretia Mott; participants sign a "Declaration of Sentiments and Resolutions" that is in effect a battle cry for the women's rights movement. ★ Bookkeeper and aspiring songwriter Stephen Foster sells "Oh, Susanna!" to a music publisher for $100. **1849:** The *Illinois State Journal* prints "The Gold Hunter's Farewell to His Wife," featuring the lyrics "So you must do the best you can! / Fix my old pants for Johnny; / The children, too, will help you plan, / While I am in California." ★ After withstanding months of harassment at the Geneva Medical College in New York State, Elizabeth Blackwell graduates at the head of her class, becoming the first modern female medical doctor. ★ New York mechanic Walter Hunt patents the safety pin. **1850:** The population of the United States is 23,191,876, of whom just 9.7 percent are foreign-born. **1851:** In her speech before the Women's Convention in Akron, Ohio, former slave Sojourner Truth famously declares: "That man over there says that women need to be helped into carriages, and lifted over ditches, and to have the best place everywhere. Nobody ever helps me into carriages, or over mud-puddles, or gives me any best place! And ain't I a woman? Look at me! Look at my arm! I have ploughed and planted, and gathered into barns, and no man could head me! And ain't I a woman? I could work as much and eat as much as a man—when I could get it—and bear the lash as well! And ain't I a woman? I have borne thirteen children, and seen most all sold off to slavery, and when I cried out with my mother's grief, none but Jesus heard me! And ain't I a woman?" **1852:** Harriet Beecher Stowe publishes *Uncle Tom's Cabin; or, Life Among the Lowly,* which sells 300,000 copies in its first year; about the novel, its author will say: "I did not write it. God wrote it. I merely did his dictation." **1853:** An article in *Godey's Lady's Book* tells young female travelers how to use proper manners when eating in a hotel: "In the first place, the lady awaits her escort, father, brother, or friend, in the ladies' parlor, and either takes his arm or follows his guidance into the dining-room, at the sound of the gong or bell. It is his place to find her a comfortable seat, and to summon the waiter. If at breakfast or tea, his first inquiry will be 'Tea or coffee?' and it will be brought on a tray without milk or sugar, both of which will be found within reach, and our novice need have no scruple in helping herself as freely as she chooses." ★ In front of a large crowd at New York's Crystal Palace Exposition, Elisha Otis gives a dramatic demonstration of his new "safety elevator": after a car raises him in an open-sided shaft, an assistant cuts the cable, and the car is caught by the teeth in the shaft. **1855:** Abolitionist and women's rights activist Lucy Stone marries Henry Blackwell (brother of Elizabeth) and, in a gesture of independence, keeps her maiden name; women who do the same will thereafter be called "Lucy Stoners." ★ At the urging of Secretary of War Jefferson Davis, Congress appropriates $30,000 for "the purchase of camels and the importation of dromedaries, to be employed for military purposes." **1857:** After a survey expedition using the Egyptian camels whose purchase has been authorized by Congress, an enthusiastic Colonel Edward Beale declares: "I look forward to the day when every mail route across the continent will be conducted...with this economical and noble brute." ★ The Supreme Court rules in its Dred Scott decision that, despite the fact that Scott has lived parts of his life in a free state and a free territory, he has, as a black man, "no rights which the white man was bound to respect"; the case—which also declares the Missouri Compromise unconstitutional—galvanizes support for abolition and inspires Abraham Lincoln's famous speech before the Illinois Republican Convention, in which he declares, "A house divided against itself cannot stand." **1859:** Abolitionists led by John Brown raid the arsenal at Harpers Ferry in an unsuccessful attempt to ignite a widespread slave insurrection. **1860:** Abraham Lincoln is elected the sixteenth president of the United States. ★ South Carolina secedes from the Union.

## 1845: FEBRUARY 6
## LYDIA MARIA CHILD TO ANNA LORING

---

*Between 1820 and 1860, the population of America's cities increased by 800 per-cent, and New York led the expansion, with more than half a million residents in 1850. Yet even the most cosmopolitan U.S. city still had its rustic side. In 1845, as author Lydia Maria Child (1802–1880) discovered in her visit to Margaret Fuller (see page 162), Manhattan's East Forty-ninth Street was still a very exotic destination.*

Anna Loring (1830–1896) was a young Boston friend. Though Child wrote more than a dozen books, and was truly famous in her time, her best-known writing today comes from her poem "A Boy's Thanksgiving Day": "Over the river and through the wood / To grandfather's house we go." Blackwell's (now Roosevelt) Island was the site of hospitals and a prison. Rossini's opera *Semiramide* had opened the season at Castle Garden at the southern tip of Manhattan. The ac-tual lines of poetry that Child quoted—both indeed from William Wordsworth—are "every gift of noble origin / Is breathed upon by Hope's perpetual breath" and "A cheerful life is what the Muses love, / A soaring spirit is their prime delight."

New York Feb. 6th, 1845.

Dear Anna,

You always say you like to receive letters from me, and so it makes me happy to write, because I think I may give you some pleasure. A little while ago, I set forth to make our friend Margaret Fuller a visit. It was an undertaking for <u>me</u>, I assure you; for we live three miles apart, and the roads were one mass of mud. I went out in the Harlem omnibus to <u>forty ninth street</u>, where she told me she lived. But instead of a street, I found a winding zigzag cart-track. It was as rural as you can imagine, with moss-covered rocks, scraggly bushes, and a brook that came tumbling over a little dam, and ran under the lane. After passing through three great swing-gates, I came to the house, which stands all alone by itself, and is as inaccessible, as if <u>I</u> had chosen it, to keep people off. It is a very old house, with a very old porch, and very old vines, and a very old garden, and very old summer-houses dropping to pieces, and a very old piazza at the back, over-grown with very old rose-bushes, which at that season were covered with red berries. The piazza is almost <u>on</u> the East river, with Blackwell's Island in full view before it. Margaret's chamber looks out upon a little woody knoll, that runs down into the water, and boats and ships are passing her window all the time. How anything so old and picturesque has been allowed to remain standing near New York so long, I cannot imagine. I spent three or four delightful hours with Margaret, and then trudged home in the mud, afoot and alone. I carried out your likeness, and she seemed so extremely pleased with it, and so glad to see it, that I left it with her. It was so plain that she grudged it to me, that I should have given it to her, if I could have brought my mind to part with your dear father and mother's present. I like Margaret <u>very</u> much. We had many pleasant little anec-dotes to tell each other about you.

I hope you will go to the opera to hear Pico and Sanquirico. I was charmed, carried away with Pico, when I heard her in the opera of Semiramide. They told me Borghese was the Prima donna, that musicians all gave her the palm. "Let them give it," said I, "to their heart's content. The <u>soul</u> the <u>genius</u> is with Pico." I felt the electric spark from her soul into mine; and that I did not with Borghese. All the reasoning in the world never convinces me, like the thrill from the afore-said spark. Semiramide is a charming opera, too; as full of beautiful melodies as it can hold. And I was <u>so</u> pleased to find my increasing perception and enjoy-ment of the <u>harmonies</u>; and

Some of them were
So rich and grand!
Sanquirico is a jewel,
Too, in his way—the very genius of fun.

My good John is lying here beside my lightstand, on three chairs and a pillow, reading a novel. Mr. Child is in the next room writing a letter, but sings out that I must give his love to all your household, and Nonny especially. The good old gentleman is well and cheerful, and we all jog on comfortably, with the usual proportion of sunshine and shadow. All of us think of you all with heartfelt, un-abating love. What <u>has</u> become of Augusta? Is she dead, or married? Give my best love to her. Please ask dear father whether it is Wordsworth who says, "All gifts of noblest origin are breathed upon by Hope's perpetual breath." "A cheer-ful heart is what the Muses love, a soaring spirit is their prime delight."

Farewell, dear child. Don't forget to love

Aunt Maria.

1846: JUNE 16

TAMSEN DONNER TO ELIZA POOR

---

*Of the nearly three thousand people who made the arduous trip west in the year
1846, the most famous would be the members of the ill-fated Donner Party. Led by
an Illinois farmer named George Donner, the eighty-seven emigrants would find
themselves snowbound in the Sierra Nevada mountains for five months. Nearly half
the group would die, and survivors would resort to cannibalism. Five months before
being snowbound, the leader's wife, Tamsen Eustis Donner (1801–1847), sent this
cheerful letter back home to a friend. Not wanting to leave her dying husband,
Tamsen would ultimately refuse rescue by three relief parties. When the fourth
party came, they found a sole survivor, who confessed to having eaten Tamsen's
remains.*

Linsey, short for linsey-woolsey, was a blend of linen and wool. John Denton, Hiram Miller,
and Noah James were all teamsters. Denton, twenty-eight, died. Miller and James survived.

Near the Junction of the North and South Platte
June 16, 1846

My Old Friend:—

We are now on the Platte, 200 miles from Fort Laramie. Our journey, so far,
has been pleasant. The roads have been good, and food plentiful. The water for
a part of the way has been indifferent—but at no time have our cattle suffered
for it. Wood is now very scarce, but "Buffalo chips" are excellent—they kindle
quick and retain heat surprisingly. We had this evening Buffalo steaks broiled
upon them that had the same flavor they would have had upon hickory coals.

We feel no fear of Indians. Our cattle graze quietly around our encampment
unmolested. Two or three men will go hunting twenty miles from camp;—and
last night two of our men lay out in the wilderness rather than ride their horses
after a hard chase. Indeed if I do not experience something far worse than I
have yet done, I shall say the trouble is all in getting started.

Our waggons have not needed much repair, but I cannot yet tell in what respects they may be improved. Certain it is they cannot be too strong. Our preparations for the journey, in some respects, might have been bettered. Bread has
been the principal article of food in our camp. We laid in 150 lbs. of flour and
75 lbs. of meat for each individual, and I fear bread will be scarce. Meat is
abundant. Rice and beans are good articles on the road—cornmeal, too, is very
acceptable. Linsey dresses are the most suitable for children. Indeed if I had

one it would be comfortable. There is so cool a breeze at all times in the prairie that the sun does not feel so hot as one would suppose.

We are now 450 miles from Independence. Our route at first was rough and through a timbered country which appeared to be fertile. After striking the prairie we found a first rate road, and the only difficulty we had has been crossing creeks. In that, however, there has been no danger. I never could have believed we could have travelled so far with so little difficulty. The prairie between the Blue and Platte rivers is beautiful beyond description. Never have I seen so varied a country—so suitable for cultivation. Every thing was new and pleasing. The Indians frequently come to see us, and the chiefs of a tribe breakfasted at our tent this morning. All are so friendly that I cannot help feeling sympathy and friendship for them. But on one sheet, what can I say?

Since we have been on the Platte we have had the river on one side, and the ever varying mounds on the other—and have traveled through the Bottom lands from one to ten miles wide with little or no timber. The soil is sandy, and last year, on account of the dry season, the emigrants found grass here scarce. Our cattle are in good order, and where proper care has been taken none has been lost. Our milch cows have been of great service—indeed, they have been of more advantage than our meat. We have plenty of butter and milk.

We are commanded by Capt. Russel—an amiable man. George Donner is himself yet. He crows in the morning, and shouts out "Chain up, boys!—chain up!" with as much authority as though he was "something in particular." John Denton is still with us—we find him a useful man in camp. Hiram Miller and Noah James are in good health and doing well. We have of the best of people in our company, and some, too, that are not so good.

Buffalo show themselves frequently. We have found the wild tulip, the primrose, the lupine, the ear-drop, the larkspur, and creeping hollyhock, and a beautiful flower resembling the bloom of the beech tree, but in bunches large as a small sugar-loaf, and of every variety of shade, to red and green. I botanize and read some, but cook a "heap" more.

There are 420 waggons, as far as we have heard, on the road between here and Oregon and California.

Give our love to all enquiring friends—God bless them.

Yours truly<br>
Mrs. George Donner

*    *    *

## CIRCA 1846: WINTER

## BETSY STRONG TO SARAH AND NATHAN STRONG

*Sarah ("Sally") Strong (1790–1852) and her husband, Nathan (1783–1862), were among the early settlers of a utopian community in Wisconsin called Ceresco, arriving there in the winter of 1844. Their daughter Betsy (1807–1887), and son Nathan, Jr., would join them the following February, but in the meantime, still home in Vermont, Betsy described a litany of New England woe so dreadful that it may help explain why some pioneers were willing to risk the hazards of the trip.*

Dear and Much esteemed Parents.

I sit down to inform you of my health which is very poor this winter. I have not been able to do but a little work this winter   I have been to Doren Stevens to finish a job I commenced in the fall but was not able to finish it yet but hope. This week your stack of hay was burnt up   Last week I bought Mother shers   the price was nine shillings. Mr. Bulen had no shoes would fit her tremens he was deranged through his sickness declaring he was in Hell   Eld. Lothrop preach the funeral sermon   Mary Ann Stone washed last monday and took cold and settled on her lungs and she died on Friday and was buried today   She was Shelie Ann school mate. Yesterday was our covenant meeting and it was a good one   today we had a communion season   it was truly a pleasant time to me. Mrs. Dolitle has been sickly to the south

I often dream of you that you are a keeping house and I am living with you but I am mistaken   I waked a few nights ago calling Mother but she did not hear me but I find it a comfort to dream of those I love   I may never see you again as death is on every side but I want to be prepared for the change that I may meet my Judge with joy and not with grief. I should like to know how you prosper in religion at the domain   Be assured that I should like to have a letter from my father although I am unworthy of it

Jan 6   I have been to Blodgets to day and they are all well   Issac has got judgement against Mr. Stevens the old man put his property out of his hands has secured him for the judgement but he is afraid of damages.

Jan 12   I have been to meeting to day and we had preaching would have done you good to hear it. Elder Lothrop he preaches better and better he is very much engaged this winter   there will be a donation held for Eld. L a week from next thursday night   Nathan and myself are on the committee and we meet to-morow night to make arrangements for the part it is to be held at the temperence house. It is sickly in town this winter   Mr. Pulcifer is not expected to live   he has the consumption   there is a good many sick here   there are needy and they beg all to do clothing they can and make it . . . for children and knit stockings and bed quilts and make comforters   they bought a piece of coton and made sheets and pilow cases of it   I joined last Friday   we meet every week at Mrs. Fisks there is a great many that are destitute   Sarah is not much better but she is very anxious to go to the domain and Nathan has made up his mind to go if he can be excepted there.

Betsy Strong

**1847: APRIL 25**
**HANNAH WHITALL TO ANNIE WHITALL**

*Back in the eighteenth century, Bishop George Berkeley famously posed a question that rocked the hard, clear world of empiricism: If a tree falls in a forest, and there's no one around to hear it, does it make a sound? By the nineteenth century, when American Transcendentalists themselves started questioning the nature of reality, the idea had trickled into the popular mind. One result: the following note, written to her cousin by a fifteen-year-old Quaker girl who, as Hannah Whitall Smith (1832–1911), would eventually become famous as a Christian writer and evangelist.*

Philadelphia, April 25, 1847

Now dear Annie, I am going to tell thee something, though I have not the least idea thee will believe it. I was out to tea the other night when someone said, that it is said that unless there is somebody within hearing thunder even would make no noise, that is, that there is no noise of any kind unless there is an ear to hear it; I think it is the most ridiculous idea ever heard of, but they say that it is gradually gaining ground among scientific men.

Ask thy father what he thinks, I don't see how it can be possible, just suppose a house was to fall down and nobody near to hear it, according to that it would make no noise, but if someone came by in the midst it would begin to make a noise, oh! it cannot be.

**1847: MAY 16**
**VIRGINIA REED TO MARY KEYES**

*Only two families survived the Donner Party calamity (see page 185) without loss of life. Thirteen-year-old Virginia Elizabeth Reed (1833–1921) was a member of one of them. A month after the last survivor was rescued from the east side of the Sierra Nevada, Reed described her family's ordeal in this letter to her cousin Mary Keyes (1833–?).*

Sutter's Fort, in California, was the party's original destination. The decision to take the relatively untried "Hastings Cutoff," which was supposed to go south of the Great Salt Lake, was what led to the disaster. In addition to Virginia, there were three Reed children along: Thomas, four; James, Jr., six; and Martha ("Patty"), eight. Patrick Breen, William Eddy, and Eliza Williams survived; Franklin Graves and Milt Elliott did not. The man Virginia Reed describes meeting was Charles Stanton, who would also perish. Eventually Virginia married a man named John Murphy, who had come west in 1844. By "cashing," Virginia meant caching, or hiding.

Napa Vallie
California
May the 16th 1847

My Dear Cousin

I take this oppertunity to write to you to let you now that we are all Well at present and hope this letter may find you all well to   My Dear Cousin I am going to write to you about our trubels geting to Callifornia. We had good luck til we come to big Sandy   thare we lost our best yoak of oxens   we come to Brigers Fort & we lost another ox   we sold some of our provisions & baut a yoak of Cows & oxen and thay pursuaded us to take Hastings cutof over the salt plain   thay said it save 3 Hundred miles. we went that road & we had to go through a long drive of 40 miles With out water   Hastings said it was 40 but i think 80 miles   We traveld a day and night & a nother day and at noon pa went on to see if he coud find Water. he had not bin gone long till some of the oxen give out and we had to leve the wagons and take the oxen on to water   one of the men staid with us and the others went on with the cattel to water   pa was a coming back to us with water and met the men & thay was about 10 miles from water   pa said thay get to water that nite and the next day to bring the cattel back for the wagons and bring some water   pa got to us about noon   the man that was with us took the horse and went on to water   We wated thare [hoping] he [would] come   we wated till night and We thought we [would] start and walk to Mr Donners wagons that night   we took what little water we had and some bread and started   pa caried Thomos and all the rest of us walk   we got to Donner and thay were all a sleep so we laid down on the ground   we spred one shawl down   we laid down on it and spred another over us and then put the dogs on top   it was the couldes night you most ever saw   the wind blew

and if it haden bin for the dogs we would have Frosen    as soon as it was day we
went to Mrs Donners    she said we could not walk to the Water and if we staid
we could ride in thare wagons to the spring    so pa went on to the water to see
why thay did not bring the cattel    when he got thare thare was but one ox and
cow thare    none of the rest had got to water    Mr. Donner come out that night
with his cattel and brought his wagons and all of us in    we staid thare a week
and Hunted for our cattel and could not find them    so some of the compania
took thare oxens and went out and brout in one wagon and cashed the other tow
[two] and a grate many things all but What we could put in one wagon    we
Had to devied our provisions out to them to get them to carie it    We got three
yoak with our ox & cow    so we went on that way a while and we got out of provisions and pa had to go on to Callifornia for provisions    we could not get along
that way.    in 2 or 3 days after pa left we had to cash our wagon and take Mr
graves wagon and cash some more of our things. well we went on that way a
while and then we had to get Mr eddies wagon    we went on that way a while
and then we had to cash all our close except a change or 2 and put them in Mr
Bri [Breen's] Wagon and Thomos & James rode the other 2 horses and the rest
of us had to walk. we went on that way a While and we come to a nother long
drive of 40 miles and then we went with Mr Donner    We had to walk all the
time we was a travling up the truckee river    we met a man and to Indians that
we had sent on for provisions to Suter Fort    thay had met pa not fur from
Suters Fort    he looked very bad he had not ate but 3 times in 7 days and the
three last days without any thing    his horse was not abel to carrie him    thay
give him a horse and he went on    so we cashed some more of our things all but
what we could pack on one mule and we started    Martha and James road behind the two Indians    it was a raing then in the Vallies and snowing on the
montains so we went on that way 3 or 4 days till we come to the big mountain or
the Callifornia. Mountain    the snow then was about 3 feet deep    thare was
some wagons thare    thay said thay had atempted to croos and could not. well
we thought we would try it so we started and thay started again with those wagons    the snow was then up to the mules side    the farther we went up the
deeper the snow got    so the wagons could not go    so thay pack thare oxens
and started with us carring a child a piece and driving the oxens in snow up
to thare wast    the mule Martha and the Indian was on was the best one    so
thay went and broak the road and that indian was the Pilet    so we wint on that
way 2 miles and the mules kept faling down in the snow head formost and the
Indian said he could not find the road    we stoped and let the Indian and
man go on to hunt the road    thay went on and found the road to the top of the

mountain and come back and said thay thought we could git over if it did not
snow any more    well the Weman were all so tirder caring there Children that
thay could not go over that night    so we made a fire and got something to eat &
ma spred down a bufalo robe & we all laid down on it & spred somthing over us
& ma sit up by the fire & it snowed one foot on top of the bed    so we got up in
the morning & the snow was so deep we could not go over & we had to go back
to the cabin & build more cabins & stay thar all winter without Pa    we had not
the first thing to eat    Ma maid arrangements for some cattel giving 2 for 1 in
callifornia    we seldom thot of bread for we had not any since I [could remem-
ber] & the cattel was so poor thay could not git up when thay laid down    we
stoped thare the 4th of November & staid till March and what we had to eat i
cant hardley tell you & we had that man [Stanton] & Indians to feed to    well
thay started over a foot and had to come back    so thay made snowshoes and
started again & it come on a storm & thay had to come back    it would snow
10 days before it would stop    thay wated till it stoped and started again    I was
a going with them & I took sick & could not go. thare was 15 started & thare,
was 7 got throw    5 weman & 2 men    it come a storme and thay lost the road &
got out of provisions & the ones that got throwe had to eat them that Died    not
long after thay started we got out of provisions & had to put matha at one cabin
James at another Thomas at another & Ma and Elizia & Milt Eliot & I dricd up
what little meat we had and started to see if we could get across & had to leve
the childrin    o Mary you may think that hard to leve theme with strangers &
did not now whether we would see them again or not    we couldnt hardle get a
way from them but we told theme we would bring them Bread & then thay was
willing to stay    we went & was out 5 days in the mountains    Eliza giv out &
had to go back    we went on a day longer    we had to lay by a day & make snow-
shows & we went on a while and coud not find the road so we had to turn back    I
could go on verry well while i thout we were giting along but as soone as we had
to turn back i could hadley get along but we got to the cabins that night & I froze
one of my feet verry bad    that same night thare was the worst storme we had
that winter & if we had not come back that night we would never got back    we
had nothing to eat but ox hides    o Mary I would cry and wish I had what you all
wasted    Eliza had to go to Mr. Graves cabin & we staid at Mr Breen    thay had
meat all the time. & we had to kill littel cash the dog & eat him    we ate his entrails and feet & hide & evry thing about him    o my Dear Cousin you dont now
what trubel is yet. Many a time we had on the last thing a cooking and did not
now wher the next would come from but there was awl weis some way provided
there was 15 in the cabon we was in and half of us had to lay a bed all the time

thare was 10 starved to death then    we was hadly abel to walk    we lived on little cash a week and after Mr. Breen would cook his meat we would take the
bones and boil them 3 or 4 days at a time    ma went down to the other cabin
and got half a hide carried it in snow up to her wast    it snowed and would cover
the cabin all over so we could not git out for 2 or 3 days    we would have to cut
pieces of the logs in sied to make the fire with    I could hardly eat the hides and
had not eat anything 3 days    Pa stated out to us with provisions and then come
a storm and he could not go    he cash his provision and went back on the other
side of the bay to get a compana of men and the San Wakien [Joaquin] got so
hye he could not cross    well thay Made up a Compana at Suters Fort and sent
out    we had not ate anything for 3 days & we had onely half a hide and we was
out on top of the cabin and we seen them a coming

O my Dear Cousin you dont now how glad i was    we run and met them
one of them we knew    we had traveled with him on the road    thay staid there
3 days to recruit us a little so we could go    thare was 21 started    all of us
started and went a piece and Martha and Thomas give out and the men had to
take them back    Ma and Eliza & James and I come on and o Mary that was the
ha[r]des[t] thing yet to come on and leiv them thar    did not now but what thay
would starve to Death    Martha said well Ma if you never see me again do the
best you can    the men said they could hadly stand it    it maid them all cry but
they said it was better for all of us to go on for if we was to go back we would
eat that much more from them    thay give them a little meat and flore and took
them back and we come on    we went over great hye mountain as strait as stair
steps in snow up to our knees    litle James walk the hole way over all the mountain in snow up to his waist. he said every step he took he was a gitting nigher Pa
and somthing to eat    the Bears took the provision the men had cashed and we
had but very little to eat    when we had traveld 5 days travel we me[t] Pa with
13 men going to the cabins    o Mary you do not now how glad we was to see
him    we had not seen him for 6 months    we thought we woul never see him
again    he heard we was coming and he made some seet cakes to give us    he
said he would see Martha and Thomas the naxt day    he went in tow days what
took us 5 days    some of the compana was eating them that Died but Thomas &
Martha had not ate any    Pa and the men started with 17 peaple    Hiram G.
Miller carried Thomas and Pa caried Martha and thay wer caught in [storms]
and thay had to stop two days    it stormed so they could not go and the Bears
took their provisions and thay were 4 days without any thing    Pa and Hiram
and all the men started    one Donner boy [sentence unfinished] Pa a carring
Martha    Hiram caring Thomas and the snow was up to thare wast and it a

snowing so thay could hadly see the way. thay [w]ra[p]ped the children up and never took them out for 4 days   thay had nothing to eat   in all that time Thomas asked for somthing to eat once   them that thay brought from the cabins some of them was not able to come and som would not come   that was 3 died and the rest eat them   thay was 11 days without any thing to eat but the Dead   Pa braught Tom and pady on to where we was   none of the men was abel to go   there feet was froze very bad so thay was a nother Compana went and brought then all in   thay are all in from the mauntains now but four   thay was men went out after them and was caught in a storm and had to come back thare was a nother compana gone thare was half got through that was stoped thare   thare was but [two] families that all of them got [through]   we was one   O Mary I have not rote you half of the truble we have had but I have rote you anuf to let you now that you dont now what truble is   but thank god we have all got throw and the onely family that did not eat human flesh   we have left everything but i dont cair for that   we have got throw with our lives   but Dont let this letter dishaten [dishearten] anybody   never take no cutofs and hury along as fast as you can.

### 1847: NOVEMBER 9
### ELIZABETH BLACKWELL TO AN UNKNOWN RECIPIENT

*Born in England, Elizabeth Blackwell (1821–1910) was the daughter of liberal parents who believed in women's rights, abolition, and education for women. They emigrated to America in 1832. After the death of her father in 1838, Blackwell helped her mother and sisters run a private school, but medicine was her true ambition. Rejected by the major schools, she was accepted by the Geneva Medical College in New York. She described the trials of her opening days there in the letter below. Two years later, Blackwell graduated first in her class and thus became the country's first female medical-school graduate and the country's first modern female doctor.*

An air-tight was a stove. Charles Lee was dean of the college. Joseph Warrington was a Quaker physician who initially advised Blackwell to try Paris instead. Lee's prediction about the percentage of female medical students would prove to be hugely optimistic: by 1905, women still represented only 4 percent of medical students in the United States.

Geneva: November 9, 1847.

I've just finished copying the notes of my last lecture. Business is over for today; I throw a fresh stick into my "air-tight," and now for refreshment by a talk with my own dear sister. Your letter containing E.'s was the first to welcome me in my new residence; right welcome, I assure you, it was, for I was gloomy— very. It was on Monday evening your letter came—my first work-day in Geneva. It had rained incessantly; I was in an upper room of a large boarding-house without a soul to speak to. I had attended five lectures, but nevertheless I did not know whether I could do what I ought to, for the Professor of Anatomy was absent, and had been spoken of as a queer man. The demonstrator hesitated as to my dissecting; I had no books, and didn't know where to get any; and my head was bewildered with running about the great college building—never going out of the same door I went in at.

This evening, however, I have finished my second day's lectures; the weather is still gloomy, but I feel sunshiny and happy, strongly encouraged, with a grand future before me, and all owing to a fat little fairy in the shape of the Professor of Anatomy! This morning, on repairing to the college, I was introduced to Dr. Webster, the Professor of Anatomy, a little plump man, blunt in manner and very voluble. He shook me warmly by the hand, said my plan was capital; he had some fun too about a lady pupil, for he never lost a joke; the class had acted manfully; their resolutions were as good as a political meeting, &c.

He asked me what branches I had studied. I told him all but surgery. "Well," said Dr. Lee, "do you mean to practise surgery?" "Why, of course she does," broke in Dr. Webster. "Think of the cases of femoral hernia; only think what a well-educated woman would do in a city like New York. Why, my dear sir, she'd have her hands full in no time; her success would be immense. Yes, yes, you'll go through the course, and get your diploma with great éclat too; we'll give you the opportunities. You'll make a stir, I can tell you."

I handed him a note of introduction from Dr. Warrington, and then he told me to wait in the ante-room while he read it to the medical class, who were assembled in the amphitheatre for his lecture, which was to be preparatory to one of the most delicate operations in surgery, and I suppose he wanted to remind them of their promise of good behaviour. I could hear him reading it. When his age and experience were spoken of there was a shout of laughter, for he can't be more than forty-five and not much of dignity about him; but at the conclusion there was a round of applause, after which I quietly entered, and certainly have no reason to complain of medical students, for though they eye me curiously, it is also in a very friendly manner. After the lecture was over, the demonstrator, who now shows the utmost friendliness, explained to me at the Doctor's request a very important subject which I had lost. It was admirably done, illustrated on the subject, and if to-day's lessons were a fair specimen, I certainly shall have no cause to complain of my anatomical instructors. The plan pursued here is admirable, and New York and Philadelphia may learn more than one lesson from Geneva. Dr. Webster came to me laughing after the first lecture, saying: "You attract too much attention, Miss Blackwell; there was a very large number of strangers present this afternoon—I shall guard against this in future." "Yes," said Dr. Lee; "we were saying to-day that this step might prove quite a good advertisement for the college; if there were no other advantage to be gained, it will attract so much notice. I shall bring the matter into the medical journals; why, I'll venture to say in ten years' time one-third the classes in our colleges will consist of women. After the precedent you will have established, people's eyes will be opened."

Now, all this kind feeling encourages me greatly, and I need it; for though my purpose has never wavered, a flat, heavy feeling was growing upon me from constant disappointment. I was fast losing that spring of hope that is so pleasant; consequently praise cannot make me vain, and the notice I attract is a matter of perfect indifference. I sit quietly in this large assemblage of young men, and they might be women or mummies for aught I care. I sometimes think I'm too much disciplined, but it is certainly necessary for the position I occupy. I believe the professors don't exactly know in what species of the human family to place me, and the students are a little bewildered. The other people at first regarded me with suspicion, but I am so quiet and gentle that suspicion turns to astonishment, and even the little boys in the street stand still and stare as I pass. 'Tis droll; sometimes I laugh, sometimes I feel a little sad, but in Geneva the nine days' wonder soon will cease, and I cannot but congratulate myself on having found at last the right place for my beginning.

## 1848: JULY 16
## LUCRETIA MOTT TO ELIZABETH CADY STANTON

*In 1840, the World's Anti-Slavery Convention in London refused to recognize Lucretia Mott (see page 165) and Elizabeth Cady Stanton (1815–1902) as delegates because they were women. Walking back to their lodging house arm in arm, they began to plan what would become, eight years later, the first women's rights convention in the United States. Its location—Seneca Falls—was a quiet town in west-central New York State, also Stanton's home. Three days before the historic gathering of several hundred men and women, Mott wrote to Stanton from nearby Auburn, New York, to firm up plans for what she imagined would at best be "a beginning." When the meeting was convened, it was actually chaired by Mott's husband, James, because it was still considered improper for women to speak in public.*

Auburn 7 Mo. 16th. 48

Dear Elizabeth

I ought to have answered thy first kind letter of information & invitation, other than by verbal message sent by our mutual friend Mary Ann McClintock, who hoped to see thee a few minutes on her return from Derington—. I requested her to tell thee how poorly my husband was, and that it was not likely I should be able to go to Seneca Falls, before the morning of the Convention. James continues quite unwell—I hope however that he will be able to be present the 2nd day.

My sister Martha will accompany me on 4th day morning & we will with pleasure accept thy kind invite to your house that night if you should not be too much crowded with company. My daughter Martha thinks she is not quite enough of a reformer to attend such a Convention. The true reason however, I presume is, that she is more interested just now, with her cousins here, & her time being short she dont incline to leave them.

James says thy <u>great</u> speech thou must reserve for the second day, so that he and others may be able to hear it. I was right glad to hear of thy resolve, and hope thou wilt not give out.

The convention will not be so large as it otherwise might be, owing to the busy time with the [illegible] &.—But it will be a beginning & we may hope it will be followed in due time by one of a more general character.

I have just returned from a meeting with the [illegible] & many others—have another appointment this evening @ 6 at the Universalist Church—

Are you going to have any reform or other Meeting during the sittings of the Convention?

We shall go from the cars directly to the Meeting on 4th day.

Give thyself no trouble about meeting us. There will be enough to conduct us thither.

Lovingly thine,
Lucretia Mott

### CIRCA 1849
### CATHARINE BEECHER TO ZILPAH GRANT BANISTER

*Daughter of the illustrious minister Lyman Beecher, sister of preacher Henry Ward Beecher and author Harriet Beecher Stowe, Catharine Esther Beecher (1800–1878) was the eldest sibling in her famous family and in some ways the most conventional. She was author of the influential household handbook* A Treatise on Domestic Economy *and founder of several private girls' schools. But even as an outspoken proponent of women's education, she insisted that educational reform was necessary mainly so that it could make women better mothers and wives. In this letter to her fellow educator Zilpah Grant Banister (1794–1874), Catharine also revealed her faith in a new water cure for the kind of "nervous complaints" that were typically diagnosed at midcentury and, in an ever more activist era, seen as a cause for action.*

David Ruggles was an African American abolitionist, bookseller, and editor. At his Northampton, Massachusetts, clinic he promoted hydropathy—using water to bathe in or drink to cure ailments ranging from lame limbs to piles and "Erysipalis Humors," a serious infectious disease of the skin. The Round Hill Establishment, also offering a water cure, had recently opened in Northampton as well.


My dear Friend

I want you to come here & spend a day or two—& for two reasons—the first is—that I am satisfied that Dr. Ruggles has a power in <u>the ends of his fingers</u> in detecting the <u>seat of diseased action</u>—which no physicians can approach & that he has a method of applying water <u>safer</u>, <u>surer</u> & <u>more delicate</u> than any I have yet known—You would be greatly interested in the mode & results of his examination of my case.

My other reason involves a longer story—& I tell it to you because I know you would wish me to do it—& would do it for me in similar circumstances, and I shall only "do as I would be done by."—

Every time I have visited you I have wondered how you could live in such perpetual care & excitement & not <u>die</u>.—& I have always felt <u>tired</u> by the mere action of sympathy with you when I visit you. And I never think of you without that sense of <u>hurried feeling</u> that I seemed to feel from mere sympathy with you. It seemed to me your mind was under constant unceasing responsibility—But I always consoled myself with hoping that the times when I saw you were rather <u>exceptions</u> than the general rule.

This fall I met Mrs. Misner & was startled by an enquiry from her as to whether I had noticed any mental failure in you—I, in reply, stated the above & found that her experiences were like mine & that she & other friends who have had the best chance to observe have noticed what they regard as a preternatural mental excitement which if not remedied they fear will become irretrievable. She mentioned Mrs. Spalding as one—& she can tell you exactly what the case is—if she has not done it already.

Now what I urge is that you simply come here & let Dᴿ R. give you his views of your case & then that you consult Dᴿ Wood & <u>then</u> decide whether or no you will come & spend a month here with me or if you prefer at the Round Hill

Estab. where I will go if you wish. I can keep on D^r Ruggles treatment there as well as here. I have a nice little pony chaise & pony to drive you about—this is just the best season of the whole year for water cures & I want you to come here as soon as you can—so as not to lose the fine weather. I believe you have erysipelas—& that another winter, with your exciting cares & that weather, will end your life or affect your reason most disastrously.

D^r Ruggles is a most remarkably sagacious common sense man & is careful & cautious—I told him your case as well as I could. He says he cannot tell whether it is best for you to try a water cure till he has investigated to see whether you have vital energy sufficient—and he is very cautious, for his own reputation not to take any but those he feels confident he can cure—He has turned away multitudes this summer & yet has been thronged—his cures have many of them been remarkable.

Let me hear from you soon & believe me as ever sincerely your friend

C. E. Beecher

## 1849: NOVEMBER 11
## MARY JANE MEGQUIER TO MILTON BENJAMIN

*James Marshall found gold at John Sutter's mill near the Sacramento River in January of 1848. By the next year, some eighty thousand forty-niners—almost all of them men—were heading to California. Life there was harsh and sometimes lawless, and the conditions were fierce. But for the women who made it to California, the financial possibilities were extraordinary. To wash clothes, bake bread, cook meals, run a boardinghouse, or offer any traditional domestic skill was to have a vital—and potentially lucrative—place in the new mining towns. In the case of Mary Jane ("Jennie") Cole Megquier (1813–1899), who had left her children back in Maine, the lure was not gold itself, but an income from housing the seekers. After crossing the Isthmus of Panama (according to family lore, she was the first woman to do so), she settled in San Francisco, running a boardinghouse while her husband, a physician, practiced medicine and ran a drugstore.*

"W" was Winthrop, the Megquiers' hometown. J. Milton Benjamin (1823–1909) lived there and helped take care of the Megquier children.

San Francisco, Nov. 11.

Very dear Friend, Milton,

Your kind letter was received last week, there can be no estimate made of the pleasure it gave us to hear from you and others of our kind friends in W. it being the first since we left the states. I suppose you have heard one thousand and one stories of this land of gold and wonders, they may differ widely but still all be true. Every one writes in some degree as he feels, some will get into business the moment they put foot on land, in three months will find themselves worth fifty thousand, while others whose prospects are much brighter, will in the same short space of time be breathing their last in some miserable tent without one friend, or a single dime to pay their funeral charges, they are tumbled into a rough box with their clothes on, in which they died, this has been the fate of thousands since I have been here, yet there never was a place where money is spent so lavishly as here, it is said that one million changes hands, every day at the gambling tables. When we arrived the first of June there was but very few storehouses, all kinds of provisions were lying in every direction in the streets, carts running over bags of flour, and rice, and hard bread, pork selling at six dollars per barrel, now flour is selling at forty dollars per barrel, pork at sixty five. sugar we paid three cents a pound, when we came, is now fifty, and other things at the same rates, a pair of thick boots sold on Saturday for ninety six dollars. gold is so very plenty it makes but very little difference what they have to pay, There are but few arrivals now, some days in September, and October, there were twenty vessels arrived a day every one with more or less passengers.

The mines are yeilding about the same as when first discovered but it is mighty hard work to get it, but they are bound to get it if they work, many, very many go there who never done a days work in their life, dig for a day or two without much success, get discouraged and return in disgust, say it is all a humbug, many are sick, and die there but it is not considered very unhealthy, This town is so situated when the thermometer is one hundred and fifteen in the mines there is a tremendous cold wind blowing here, I have had a fire every day for comfort, since I have been here, excepting a few days in the months of Sept. Oct which were delightful, now it is beginning to rain which makes the street nearly impassable, the mud is about a foot deep, the draymen have four dollars for a load of one hundred if they do not take it ten rods.

We have a fine store which is now nearly completed, the upper part will rent for one thousand per month a pretty little fortune of itself if rents continue as they now are, but it is doubtful, Our motto is to make hay while the sun shines, we intend to sell the first good offer and return forthwith, although there are many things here that are better than in the states yet I cannot think of staying from my chickens a long time, and it is not just the place for them at present, no schools, churches in abundance but you can do as you please about attending, it is all the same whether you go to church or play monte, that is why I like, you very well know that I am a worshipper at the shrine of liberty. The land is very rich would yield an abundance if it was cultivated, but no one can wait for vegetables to grow to realize a fortune, potatoes are twenty cents a pound, beets one dollar and seventy five cents a piece, tomatoes, dollar a pound but we have them for dinner notwithstanding, we have made more money since we have been here than we should make in Winthrop in twenty years, the Dr often makes his fifty dollars, a day in his practice then we have boarders to pay our house rent, they make great profits on their drugs, to show you some of the profits on retail, the Dr bought a half barrel of pickle in salt, after soaking them, I put up fourteen quart bottles, sold them for six dollars more than we gave for the whole, which still left me the same bulk I had at first. They are getting quite interested in politics, the locos take the lead, they pretend they are no party men, but you will find they are very sure not to have a whig nominated to fill any office. The seat of government is established at San Hosea, about 60. miles from this, in a most delightful spot where they have plenty of fruit and vegetables, articles which cannot be found here. I shall ever feel grateful to you and others for the interest you took in our boy, As for wages I care nothing about them, I only want him to have some employment to keep him out of mischief, if anything occurs to prevent my coming home within a year we shall send for him to come here, in the spring, but I want him treated as one of the family wherever he is. If there is no other way we will hire his board and have him go to school. We have sent some money and there is enough more where this came from you. You must give an abundance of love to all of our friends especially Sam, and Judy, if all stories are true you are getting in the same box. The Dr wants a little spot left for him. Be sure to answer this the first mail for it is the greatest pleasure we have in this country to hear from our friends. You see I am working up hill by my writing. Be sure and write and accept this from your Sincere friend

Jennie

### 1850: JANUARY 19
### FRANCES GATES WILLIS TO ANDREW WILLIS

---

*Married in 1845, Frances Gates Willis (1825–1867) had two young sons and a very lonely life in Missouri when she urged her gold-seeking husband, Andrew (1817–1852), to reconsider his priorities and return home.*

Andrew was heading west on the Santa Fe Trail. He would be gone for nearly two and a half years and would die soon after his return.

January 19, 1850

Dear Husband

It is with pleasure I take my pen in hand to try to write, my self and children are well at present. hoping when this comes to hand to find you enjoying the same blessing. I received yours of the 10th of Nov which gave me more pleasure than I am able to express to hear from you, although I was truly sorry to hear of your illness. I fear that you suffered for want of attention & nourishment while sick. I had allmost give up all hopes of ever seeing or hearing from you a gain as being a live for I could not hear anything direct from those that came in. all the information that I could get was that you had gone to the mines. You stated that Benjamin Embree had left for home. he has not arrived that I have heard of yet. Solon Shepard & one of the Furnishes landed a few days ago. Joel Furnish died on his return below St. Louis. I hear of a great many of our acquaintances who have died that went out last spring which has caused a great deal of trouble & distress among their Families & friends who are left behind. I am at Pa's at this time and have been for the last four weeks. they are all well at this time. I [expect] to go back to aunt Betsys as soon as the weather will admit, Oscar says tell Pa I want to see him mighty bad, they both speak of you very often. Fount says he is a going to eat a heap of meat and grow to be a big man. he makes large calculations him self. you would not [know] them. they have grown so much. Fount can talk as plain if not plainer than Oscar. he will try to say anything we tell him. he is not afraid nor ashamed of nobody. he loves to talk about the ladies. Oscar is rather on the timid order. I often look at them and wish for you here as I know its a pleasure you delighted in before you went a way. I was sadly disappointed your not returning last fall. I made sure calculations on haveing you here to spend the Christmas with us. I therefore earnestly entreat you not to delay comeing home this spring. I want you to come Gold or no Gold. if [you] can get enough to get home with I will be satisfied. hearing of so many deaths & so much suffering I am always miserable. I have pleasnt dreams of being with you all most every night which I hope [I] realize before a great while if kind providence smiles. as I have but little hopes of your getting this before you start home I will not add a great deal at present. I hope that you will write oftener as I am allways anxious to hear from you. I will add nomore but remain yours truly u[n]til death

Frances G. Willis
to A. J. Willis

### 1850: FEBRUARY 17
### HANNAH WHITALL TO ANNIE WHITALL

---

*Despite the nearly hopeless view of women she expressed in this letter to her cousin,
eighteen-year-old Hannah Whitall (see page 188) would indeed become a minister.
She also became a founder of the Woman's Christian Temperance Union, and the
author of the popular 1875 devotional classic* The Christian's Secret of a Happy
Life. *In her youth, Hannah once prayed for a ghost or angel to appear, and she put
out a chair for the visitor.*

Samuel Bettle and Thomas Evans were both well-known Quaker ministers.

Philadelphia, Feb. 17, 1850

Did thee have a good meeting? Sarah and I had very; we thought Sammy
Balderston was preaching to us when he said that silence was not worship, and
that many came to meeting and sat down in silence without any thought of worship; I verily believe that was us, for really Cousin Anne, Meeting is such a
grand place to lay out plans and build air castles. Does thee ever think good? I
do sometimes positively; I think I would love to be a minister and make very
noble sacrifices and have people to admire me and almost worship me, as I do
Samuel Bettle and Thomas Evans. Oh! would it not be grand, and then I would
travel all over the world, and do <u>so much</u> good. But I am only a woman, and
women are so weak and dependent, and never do <u>any good</u>. There is no chance
is there? I shall have to be content to plod on in the same humdrum path, making pies and cooking and scrubbing, and mending stockings and making shirts,
and feel proud if I may claim relationship with great and noble men.

Here it is nearly eleven, and I am sitting up in our study all alone, waiting for
the thieves to come and steal my watch—a perfect martyr to my poor journals. I
can't help thinking what a rich treat the editor of "Memorials of Hannah
Whitall" will have one day.

### 1850: SEPTEMBER 22
### MARGARET McCARTHY TO HER FAMILY

---

*Between 1845 and 1849, more than a million Irish people starved to death or died
of typhus because of their native potato famine, and perhaps another million and a
half were forced to emigrate. Among them was Margaret McCarthy, who, like many
young Irish women, tried to pave the way for the rest of her family.*

It is not known what happened to McCarthy's family.

New York September 22nd, 1850.

My Dr. Father and Mother Brothers and Sisters,

I write these few lines to you hopeing That these few lines may find you all in as good State of health as I am at present thank God    I received your welcome letter To me Dated 22nd. of May which was A Credit to me for the Stile and Elligence of its Fluent Language but I must Say Rather Flattering    My Dr. Father I must only say that this is a good place and A good Country for if one place does not Suit A man he can go to Another and can very easy please himself    But there is one thing thats Ruining this place Especially the Frontirs towns and Cities where the Flow of Emmigration is most    the Emmigrants has not money enough to Take them to the Interior of the Country which oblidges them to Remain here in New York and the like places for which Reason Causes the less demand for Labour and also the great Reduction in wages    for this Reason I would advise no one to Come to America that would not have Some Money after landing here that [would] Enable them to go west in case they would get no work to do here    but any man or woman without a family are fools that would not venture and Come to this plentyful Country where no man or woman ever Hungerd or ever will and where you will not be Seen Naked, but I can asure you there are Dangers upon Dangers Attending Comeing here    but my Friends nothing Venture nothing have    Fortune will favour the brave    have Courage and prepare yourself for the next time that, that worthy man Mr. Boyen is Sending out the next lot, and Come you all Together Couragiously and bid adieu to that lovely place the land of our Birth. that place where the young and old joined Together in one Common Union, both night and day Engaged in Innocent Amusement, But alas. I am now Told its the Gulf of Misersry oppression Degradetion and Ruin of evry Discription which I am Sorry to hear of so Doleful a History to Be told of our Dr. Country    This my Dr. Father induces me to Remit to you in this Letter 20 Dollars that is four Pounds thinking it might be Some Acquisition to you untill you might Be Clearing away from that place all together and the Sooner the Better for Beleive me I could not Express how great would be my joy at seeing you all here Together where you would never want or be at a loss for a good Breakfast and Dinner. So prepare as soon as possible for this will be my last Remittince untill I see you all here. Bring with you as much Tools as you can as it will cost you nothing to Bring them    And as for your Clothing you need not care much    But that I would like that yourself would Bring one good Shoot of Cloth that you would spare until you come here    And as for Mary She need not mind much as I will have for her A Silk Dress A Bonnet and Viel according    and Ellen I need not mention what I will have for her   I can fit her well   you are to Bring Enough Flannels and do not form it at home as the weay Flannel at home and here is quite different for which reason I would Rather that you would not form any of it untill you Come, with the Exception of whatever Quantity of Drawers you have you can make them at ahome   But make them Roomly Enough   But Make No jackets.

My Dr. Father I am Still in the Same place but do not Intend to Stop here for the winter. I mean to come into New York and there Spend the winter   Thade Houlehan wrote to me Saying that if I wished to go up the Country that he would send me money but I declined so doing untill you Come and then after you Coming if you think it may be Better for us to Remain here or go west it will be for you to judge but untill then I will Remain here. Dan Keliher Tells me that you Knew more of the House Carpentery than he did himself and he can earn from twelve to fourteen Shilling a day that is seven Shilling British and he also Tells me that Florence will do very well and that Michl can get a place Right off as you will not be In the Second day when you can Bind him to any Trade you wish And as for John he will Be Very Shortly Able to Be Bound two So that I have Every Reason to Believe that we will all do will Together   So as that I am sure its not for Slavery I want you to Come here no its for affording My Brothers and Sisters And I an oppertunity of Showing our Kindness and Gratitude and Comeing on your Seniour days that we would be placed in that possision that you my Dr. Father and Mother could walk about Lesuirly and Indepenly without Requireing your Labour an object which I am Sure will not fail even by Myself if I was oblidged to do it without the assistance of Brother or Sister for my Dr. Father and Mother.

I am proud and happy to Be away from where the County Charges man or the poor Rates man or any other Rates man would have the Satisfaction of once Inpounding my cow or any other article of mine   Oh how happy I feel and am sure to have look as The Lord had not it destined for me to get married to Some Loammun or another at home that after a few months he and I may be an Incumberance upon you or perhaps in the poor house by this, So my Dr. Father according as I had Stated to you I hope that whilst you are at home I hope that you will give my Sister Mary that privelage of Injoying herself Innocently on any occation that She pleases so far as I have said Innocently and as for my Dr. Ellen I am in Raptures of joy when I think of one day Seeing her and you all at the dock in New York and if I do not have a good Bottle of Brandy for you Awaiting your arrival its a Causion.

Well I have only to tell my Dr. Mother to Bring all her bed Close and also to bring the Kittle and an oven and have handles to them and do not forget the

Smoothing Irons and Beware when you are on board to Bring some good flo[u]r and Ingage with the Captain Cook and he will do it Better for you for very little and also Bring some whiskey and give them the Cook and some Sailors that you may think would do you any good to give them a Glass once in a time and it may be no harm.

And Dr. Father when you are Comeing here if you Possiblely can Bring My Uncle Con I would Be glad that you would and I am sure he would be of the greatest acquisision to you on board and also Tell Mary Keeffe that if her Child died that I will pay her passage very Shortly and when you are Comeing do not be frightened    Take Courage and be Determined and bold in your Undertaking as the first two or three days will be the worst to you and mind whatever happens on board    Keep your own temper and do not speak angry to any or hasty    the Mildest Man has the best chance on board    So you make your way with evey one and further you are to speak to Mr Boyan and he I am sure will get one Request for you    Mr Boyan will do it for me, when you are to Come ask Mr Boyan to give you a few lines to the Agent or Berth Master of the Ship that will Secure to you the Second Cabin which I am sure Mr Boyan will do    and as soon as you Receive this letter write to me and let me know about every thing when you are to come and what time and state Particulars of evry thing to me and Direct as before. And if you are to come Shortly when you come to Liberpool wright to me also and let me know when you are to sail and the name of the Ship you sail in as I will be uneasy untill I get an answer.

No more at present But that you will give Mr and Mrs Boyan my best love and respect    And let me know how they and family are as they would or will not Be ever Better than I would wish them to be    also Mrs Milton and Charles Mr and Mrs Roche and family Mr and Mrs day and family Mr Walsh and as for his family I am sure are all well    Mr and Mrs Sullivan and family Mrs O Brien Con Sheehan wife and family all the Hearlihys and familys Tim Leahy and family own Sullivan of Cariganes and family Darby Guinee and family John Calleghan and family Timoth Calleghan and family Timothy Sheehan and Mother    So no more at present form your Ever Dear and Loveing Child.

Margaret MCarthy.

## CIRCA 1850
## ANTOINETTE BLACKWELL TO LUCY STONE

*Emboldened by the response to the women's rights convention at Seneca Falls (see page 195), American women found more and more ways to voice their concerns and organize their efforts. One of the earliest platforms was a reform and temperance magazine called* The Lily, *begun in 1849 by Amelia Bloomer. Though she was not the first to wear "the new costume" (billowing pantaloons, known as "Turkish trousers," under a shorter skirt), Bloomer became known for it in the pages of* The Lily, *and the trousers in turn became known as "bloomers." Among those who followed Bloomer's dress-reform efforts were suffragists Antoinette Brown Blackwell (1825–1921) and Lucy Stone (1818–1893).*

Blackwell and Stone had been friends since childhood; Blackwell was married to one brother of Dr. Elizabeth Blackwell (see page 193), and Stone to another. Henrietta, New York, was Blackwell's home.

Dear Lucy

A lady told me half an hour ago about Mrs. Bloomer's putting on the new costume. She said she sent for a mutual friend of theirs, a gentleman, to call on her; but when he went into the house and saw her in such a dress, he just put up both hands, turned away his head and backed out of her presence making grimaces; and when called back by Mrs. Bloomer and her husband, his only reply was "Don't speak to me! Oh, don't speak to me!" I suppose this was of course in joke, partly at least; but I fancy "Don't speak to me!" would be the heart language of a great many of our friends if we were to adopt this costume. I find, though, much more prejudice against it among the ladies than the gentlemen. Some of our Henrietta men are anxious to have it adopted, and some of the Misses also, if their mammas will allow them, are willing to try the "new fashion" because it is new, I suppose. My mother seems perfectly willing to have the girls wear those dresses, and if they were not already fitted for the summer I think they would put them on immediately.

Nettie

## 1851: FEBRUARY 12
## MARIA TRENHOLM HAYDEN

*Modern spiritualism—the belief that the dead could and would communicate with the living through the help of a medium—was essentially born in 1848 when two sisters named Kate and Maggie Fox reported hearing unexplained raps in their Hydesville, New York, home and eventually decoded them as messages from beyond. A few years later, the practice of holding séances had taken off, and Maria B. Trenholm Hayden (1826–1883) had become a popular medium in Boston. In this letter,*

*she recorded the conversation—in the voice of her client, Dexter Pierce—that had*
*supposedly taken place with his dead daughter, Jane.*

In the coming years, with the enormous death toll of the Civil War, spiritualism would attain even greater popularity.

Boston feb 12th 1851 At 3 to 4 P.M.

The following is a coppy of a communication with my Spirit Daughter Jane Elizabeth through the mediumship of Mrs W, R, Hayden In 5 Hayward Place.

After being seated at the table with the Medium & hearing the raps of several Spirits I asked

Ques 1st What was the name of the Spirit that would like to communicate with me

Ans 1st The alphabet being there called for And <u>Jane</u> was spelled out I then stated the <u>Jane</u> had another name that of Elizabeth. When it was requested by raps that the same or Elizabeth be written   Thus <u>Jane</u> Elizabeth   I then asked

Ques 2d Who was it that influenced me the 15th of last month

Ans 2d It was I dear Father hence

And I have influenced you many times since and shall many times more for you have a great mission to do on this earth and we shall all work through you for the benefit of the diseased portion of the human family—So dear Father hold yourself in readiness for we may come to you at any time whenever ocasione requires

Ques 3d Have you any communication to make to your Mother & Sisters

Ans 3d Tell my dear Mother that I am allways hovering near and arround her soothing her earthly cares and trying to elevate her Soule to look up to the right sourse for true pure happiness as it is poured down from Heaven through Gods ministers for the direct benefits of the human family

And to you dear sisters I come and pour into your Souls the purest sentiments and most Holy aspirations that can be imparted by or through an angel of light

How little you ken or realize the pleasure that this affords me to come and make myself manifest and be able to give words of advise and comfort—I thought when I left the form that my eyes were closed and my tongue sealed forever

But what must have been my surprise when I found I was not dead and that I could come and hover around you and ken your thoughts and many times when your hearts were Sad pour into your Souls peace and love that could not be given by the cold world or its people

And I have been near to you when your hearts were joyous and happy and mingled in with you unseen by your natural eyes   But the soul would vibrate upon its thousand cords with new and untold melodies and you would say within your selfs "how happy I am, I wonder if dear Jane sees or can hear mee speak" and like things that my ear has not been deaf to—And now dear ones just think of her who has left your fireside with Joy—Do not let one feeling of sorrow escape you for her who you have thought dead lives and is happy beyond anything that she can express

I am going to do much through dear Father and you will have an opportunity to see some of my power

May God bless you all is the Prayer of <u>Jane</u>

At the close of the above I felt verry thankfull and spoke of leaving when the spirit or <u>Jane</u> raped and the mediums hand became influenced and wrote the following

Well you know my dear Father that I am always near to you and will stand near and help you sew the seeds that shall ripen for you not only in this life but will bloom in the happy life that is beyond what has been better known as the dark portals of the grave—But dear Father it is not dark it is all bright and glorious   <u>All</u> joy and love friend meets friend and is happy—They have none of the perplexities that overshadow their lifes on earth—All that is left behind with the clay while the spirit sours aloft to the mansions of love to worship the true God in sincerity and truth

Dear Father Jane loves you verry much and will be a guardian angel to guide you through life

From <u>Jane</u>

After the close of the last I said that I must leave the medium But I hoped that Jane would not leave me

It was answered That <u>Jane</u> would not leave me

Which She did not as I was under jentle Spirit Influence until near bed time & After retiring to bed I saw a vision

## 1851: MAY 16
## ELIZABETH CADY STANTON TO THE AKRON FALLS WOMEN'S CONVENTION

*The 1850s saw large numbers of activists gathering all around the country for women's suffrage conventions. In Akron, Ohio, on May 28 and 29, reports were*

*made about education, labor, and law; some clergymen tried to argue against women's equality, and in response, the former slave Sojourner Truth gave her famous "Ain't I a Woman?" speech, with the memorable conclusion: "If the first woman God ever made was strong enough to turn the world upside down all alone, these women together ought to be able to turn it back, and get it right side up again!" Some notable women who could not be present sent their letters, including this stirring call to action from Elizabeth Cady Stanton (see page 195).*

Begun in 1830, *Godey's Lady's Book* was the great-great-grandmother of all fashion magazines. "Father Gregory's pattern daughters" probably refers to potential followers of an eighteenth-century instructional book on manners, John Gregory's *A Father's Legacy to His Daughters*.

Seneca Falls, May 16th, 1851.

Dear Friends:—

It is often said to us tauntingly, "well, you have held Conventions, you have written letters and theorized, you have speechified and resolved, protested and appealed, declared and petitioned, and now what next? why do you not do something? I have as often heard the reply, "we know not what to do." Having for some years rehearsed to the unjust judge our grievances, our legal and political disabilities and social wrongs, let us at this time just glance at what we may do—at the various rights of which we may even now quietly take possession. True, our right to vote we cannot exercise until our State Constitutions are re-modeled; but we can petition our legislators every session, and plead our cause before them. We can make a manifestation by going in procession to the polls at each returning election, bearing banners, with inscription thereon of glorious sentiments handed down to us by our fathers, such as "no taxation without Representation," "no just government can be formed without the consent of the governed," c., c. We can refuse to pay taxes, and like the English dissenters suffer our good to be seized and sold, if must be. Such manifestations would arouse a class of minds that take no note for our Conventions, or their proceedings—who never dream even, that woman thinks herself defrauded of a single right. The trades and professions are all open to us; let us quietly enter and make ourselves, if not rich and famous, at least independent and respectable. Many of them, are quite proper to woman, and some peculiarly so. As merchants, postmasters, silversmiths, teachers, preachers and physicians, woman has already proved herself fully competent. Who so well fitted to fill the pulpits of our day as woman; for all admit her superior to man in the affections, high moral sentiments, and religious enthusiasm; and so long as our popular theology and reason are at loggerheads, we have no need of acute metaphysicians or skillful logicians; those who can make the most effective appeals to our imagination, our hopes and fears, are most desirable for the duties of this high office.

Again, as Physicians; how necessary to have educated women in this profession. Give woman knowledge commensurate, with her natural qualifications, and there is no position she could assume that would be so permanently useful to her race at large and her own sex in particular, as that of ministering angel to the sick and afflicted,—not an angel capable of sympathizing with suffering merely, but with the power to relieve it. The science of obstetrics is a branch of the profession which should be wholly monopolized by women. It is an outrage on common decency which nothing but the tyrant custom can excuse, for man to practice in this branch of the professions. "It is now in this country and in England almost exclusively in the hands of the male practitioner, though from the earliest history down to 1663, it was practiced by women. The distinguished individual first to make the innovation on the ancient, time-sanctified custom, was no less a personage than a court prostitute, the Duchess of Villiers, a favorite mistress of Louis XIV, of France." This is a formidable evil, and productive of much immorality, misery and crime. Now that some medical colleges are open to women, and one has been established in Philadelphia exclusively for our sex, I hope this custom may be abolished as speedily as possible. It seems to me its existence argues a much greater want of delicacy and refinement in woman, than would the practice of the profession by her, in all its various branches.

But the great work before us is the proper education of those just coming on the stage. Begin with girls of this day, and in twenty years we can revolutionize this nation. The childhood of woman must be free and untrammeled; the girl must be allowed to romp and play, climb, skate and swim,—her clothing must be more like that of the boy; strong, loose-fitting garments, thick boots c., that she may be out in all seasons, and enter freely into all kinds of sports. Teach the girls to go alone, by night and, day—if need be on the lonely highway or through the busy streets of the metropolis. The manner in which all courage and self-reliance is early educated out of the girl—her path portrayed with danger and difficulties that never exist, is melancholy indeed. Better, far, suffer occasional insults, or die outright, than live the life of a coward, or never more without a protector. The best protection that any woman can have, one that will serve her at all times and in all places, is <u>courage</u>, and this she must get by experience, and experience comes by exposure. Let the girl be thoroughly developed in body and soul,—not moulded like a pieces of clay after some artificial specimen of humanity, with a body after some plate in Godey's book of fashion, and a mind after the type of Father Gregory's pattern daughters, loaded down with the traditions, proprieties and sentimentalities of generations of silly mothers and grandmothers, but left free to be, to grow, to feel, to think and to act. Development in one thing—that system of cramping, restraining, torturing, perverting and mystifying, called education, is quite another. We have had women enough befouled under the one system; pray let us try the other. The girl must early be impressed with the idea that she is to be a "hand and not a mouth"—a worker and not a drone, in the great hive of human action. She must be taught to look forward to a life of self-dependence, and like the boy, prepare herself for some lucrative trade or profession.

Woman has relied, heretofore, too entirely on her needle for support; that one-eyed demon of destruction, that evil genius of our sex which slays its thousands annually, and in spite of all our devotion, will never make us healthy or wise. The girl must be taught that it is no part of her life to cater to the prejudices of those around her; make her independent of public sentiment, by showing her how worthless and rotten a thing it is. It is a settled axiom with me that public sentiment is utterly false on every subject. I know not one in which it is not in direct violation of all the holiest, and noblest aspirations of our nature, and yet what a tyrant it is over us all, over woman especially, who is so educated that it is her very life to please, her highest ambition to be approved. But one outrage this tyrant, place yourself beyond his jurisdiction, taste the joy of free thought and action, and how powerless is his rule over you!—his sceptre lies broken at your feet—his very bubblings of condemnation are sweet music in your ears!—his darkening frown is sunshine to your heart! for they tell of your triumph and his discomfit. Think you, women thus educated, would be the frail, dependent beings we now find them? By no means. Depend upon it, they would soon settle this whole question of woman's rights. As educated capitalists and skillful laborers, they would not be long in finding their true level in political and social life.

Yours sincerely,
E. C. Stanton.

## 1851: SEPTEMBER 30
## LOUISE CLAPPE TO MOLLY SMITH

*Author of what became known (for their pseudonymous signature) as the "Shirley Letters," Louise Amelia Knapp Smith Clappe (1819–1906) accompanied her husband, Fayette, to California in 1849 and lived with him for several years in mining*

*camps near the Feather River. Rich Bar was a mining community, and, as "Dame*
*Shirley" explained so vividly in this letter to her sister, Mary Jane ("Molly") Smith,*
*what life lacked there in comforts it definitely did not make up for in refinements.*
*In one letter, Clappe described the best log cabin in the area as having a window*
*made of a line of glass jars set between the logs.*

Fayette was a doctor. Eventually the Clappes divorced, and Louise remained in San Francisco, teaching public school for the next two decades. "On the tapis" meant "under consideration." John Horne Tooke was a British politician who wrote an early study of the English language.


Rich Bar,
East Branch of the North Fork of Feather River,
September 30, 1851


I think that I have never spoken to you of the mournful extent to which profanity prevails in California. You know that at home it is considered <u>vulgar</u> for a gentleman to swear; but I am told that here, it is absolutely the fashion, and that people who never uttered an oath in their lives while in the "States," now "clothe themselves with curses as with a garment." Some try to excuse themselves by saying that it is a careless habit, into which they have glided imperceptibly, from having been compelled to associate so long with the vulgar and the profane; that it is a mere slip of the tongue, which means absolutely nothing, etc. I am willing to believe this, and to think as charitably as possible of many persons here, who have unconsciously adopted a custom which I know they abhor. Whether there is more profanity in the mines than elsewhere, I know not; but during the short time that I have been at Rich Bar, I have <u>heard</u> more of it than in all my life before. Of course, the, most vulgar blackguard will abstain from swearing in the <u>presence</u> of a lady, but in this rag and card-board house, one is <u>compelled</u> to hear the most sacred of names constantly profaned by the drinkers and gamblers who haunt the bar-room at all hours. And this is a custom which the gentlemanly and quiet proprietor, much as he evidently dislikes it., cannot possibly prevent.

Some of these expressions, were they not so fearfully blasphemous, would be grotesquely sublime. For instance; not five minutes ago, I heard two men quarrelling in the street, and one said to the other, "only let me get hold of your beggarly carcase once, and I will use you up so small that God Almighty himself cannot see your <u>ghost</u>!"

To live thus in constant danger of being hushed to one's rosy rest by a ghastly lullaby of oaths, is revolting in the extreme. For that reason, and because it is infinitely more comfortable during the winter season, than a plank-house, F. has concluded to build a log-cabin, where, at least, I shall not be <u>obliged</u> to hear the solemn names of the Father and the dear Master so mockingly profaned.

But it is not the swearing alone which disturbs my slumber. There is a dreadful flume, the machinery of which, keeps up the most dismal moaning and shrieking all the livelong night—painfully suggestive of a suffering child. But, oh dear! you don't know what that is, do you? Now, if I was scientific, I would give you such a vivid description of it, that you would see a pen and ink flume staring at you from this very letter. But alas! my own ideas on the subject, are in a state of melancholy vagueness. I will do my possible, however, in the way of explanation. A flume, then, is an immense trough. which takes up a portion of the river, and, with the aid of a dam, compels it to run in another channel, leaving the vacated bed of the stream ready for mining purposes.

There is a gigantic project now on the <u>tapis</u> of fluming the entire river for many miles, commencing a little above Rich Bar. Sometimes these fluming companies are eminently successful; at others, their operations are a dead failure.

But in truth, the whole mining system in California is one great gambling, or better perhaps—lottery transaction. It is impossible to tell whether a "claim" will prove valuable or not. F. has invariably sunk money on every one that he has bought. Of course, a man who works a "claim" himself, is more likely—even should it turn out poor—"to get his money back," as they say—than one who, like F., hires it done.

A few weeks since, F. paid a thousand dollars for a "claim," which has proved utterly worthless. He might better have thrown his money into the river than to have bought it; and yet some of the most experienced miners on the Bar, thought that it would "pay."

But I began to tell you about the different noises which disturb my peace of mind by day, and my repose of body by night, and have gone instead, into a financial disquisition upon mining prospects. Pray forgive me, even though I confess that I intend some day, when I feel <u>statistically</u> inclined, to bore you with some profound remarks upon the claiming, drifting, sluicing, ditching, fluming and coyoting politics of the "diggins."

But to return to my sleep murderers. The rolling on the bowling alley never leaves off for ten consecutive minutes at any time during the entire twenty-four hours. It is a favorite amusement at the mines; and the only difference that Sunday makes, is, that then it never leaves off for <u>one</u> minute.

Besides the flume and the bowling alley, there is an inconsiderate dog, which <u>will</u> bark from starry eve till dewy morn. I fancy that he has a wager on the subject as all the other <u>puppies</u> seem bitten by the betting mania.

<u>A propos</u> of dogs; I found dear old Dake—the noble New Foundland which H. gave us—looking as intensely black, and as grandly aristrocratical as ever. He is the only high-bred dog on the river. There is another animal, by the plebeian name of John (what a name for a <u>dog</u>!) really a handsome creature, which looks as if he might have a faint sprinkling of good blood in his veins. Indeed, I have thought it possible that his great-grandfather was a bull-dog. But he always barks at <u>me</u>—which I consider as proof positive that he is nothing but a low-born mongrel. To be sure, his master says, to excuse him, that he never saw a woman before; but a dog of any chivalry would have recognized the gentler sex, even if it <u>was</u> the first time that he had been blessed with the sight.

In the first part of my letter, I alluded to the swearing propensities of the Rich Barians. Those of course would shock you; but though you hate slang, I know that you could not help smiling at some of their <u>bizarre</u> cant phrases.

For instance, if you tell a Rich Barian anything which he doubts, instead of simply asking you if it is true, he will <u>invariably</u> cock his head interrogatively, and almost pathetically address you with the solemn adjuration, "Honest Indian?" Whether this phrase is a slur or a compliment to the aboriginees of this country, I do not know.

Again; they will agree to a proposal, with the appropriate words, "Talk enough when horses fight!" which sentence they will sometimes slightly vary to "Talk enough between gentlemen."

If they wish to borrow anything of you, they will mildly inquire if you have it "about your clothes." As an illustration; a man asked F. the other day, "If he had a spare pick-axe about his clothes." And F. himself gravely inquired of me this evening at the dinner-table, if I had "a <u>pickle</u> about my clothes."

If they ask a man an embarrassing question, or in any way have placed him in an equivocal position, they will triumphantly declare that they have "got the dead-wood on him." And they are everlastingly "going narry cent" on those of whose credit they are doubtful. There are many others which may be common enough every where, but as I never happened to hear them before, they have for me all the freshness of originality. You know that it has always been one of my pet rages, to trace cant phrases to their origin; but most of those in vogue here, would, I verily believe, puzzle Horne Tooke himself.

**1851: NOVEMBER 25**

**LOUISE CLAPPE TO MOLLY SMITH**

---

*There were twenty-three "Shirley Letters" to Molly in all, and in 1854 they were published in* The Pioneer *magazine. The author Bret Harte was said to have based several of his stories on them.*

"Xantippean," meaning "shrewish," referred to Socrates' wife Xanthippe. To have a "soul above buttons" meant to be suited for better things. The quote is from James Russell Lowell's poem "The Vision of Sir Launfal."

> From our Log Cabin, Indian Bar,
> November 25, 1851

Nothing of importance has happened since I last wrote you, except that I have become a <u>mineress</u>; that is, if the having washed a pan of dirt with my own hands, and procured therefrom three dollars and twenty-five cents in gold dust, (which I shall inclose in this letter), will entitle me to the name. I can truly say, with the blacksmith's apprentice at the close of his first day's work at the anvil, that "I am sorry I learned the trade;" for I wet my feet, tore my dress, spoilt a pair of new gloves, nearly froze my fingers, got an awful headache, took cold and lost a valuable breastpin, in this my labor of love. After such melancholy self-sacrifice on my part, I trust you will duly prize my gift. I can assure you that it is the last golden handiwork you will ever receive from "Dame Shirley."

<u>Apropos</u>, of lady gold-washers in general,—it is a common habit with people residing in towns in the vicinity of the "Diggings," to make up pleasure parties to those places. Each woman of the company will exhibit on her return, at least twenty dollars of the <u>oro</u>, which she will gravely inform you she has just "panned out" from a single basinful of the soil. This, of course, gives strangers a very erroneous idea of the average richness of auriferous dirt. I myself thought, (now don't laugh,) that one had but to saunter gracefully along romantic streamlets on sunny afternoons, with a parasol and white kid gloves, perhaps, and to stop now and then to admire the scenery, and carelessly rinse out a small panful of yellow sand, (without detriment to the white kids, however, so easy did I fancy the whole process to be), in order to fill one's workbag with the most beautiful and rare specimens of the precious mineral. Since I have been here, I have discovered my mistake, and also the secret of the brilliant success of former gold-washeresses.

The miners are in the habit of flattering the vanity of their fair visitors, by scattering a handful of "salt" (which, strange to say, is <u>exactly</u> the color of gold dust, and has the remarkable property of often bringing to light very curious lumps of the ore) through the dirt before the dainty fingers touch it; and the dear creatures go home with their treasures, firmly believing that mining is the prettiest pastime in the world.

I had no idea of permiting such a costly joke to be played upon me; so I said but little of my desire to "go through the motions" of gold washing, until one day, when, as I passed a deep hole in which several men were at work, my companion requested the owner to fill a small pan, which I had in my hand, with dirt from the bedrock. This request was, of course, granted, and, the treasure having been conveyed to the edge of the river, I succeeded, after much awkward maneuvering on my own part, and considerable assistance from friend H., an experienced miner, in gathering together the above specified sum, All the diggers of our acquaintance say that it is an excellent "prospect," even to come from the bedrock, where, naturally, the richest dirt is found. To be sure, there are now and then "lucky strikes"; such, for instance, as that mentioned in a former letter, where a person took out of a single basinful of soil, two hundred and fifty-six dollars. But such luck is as rare as the winning of a hundred thousand dollar prize in a lottery. We are acquainted with many here whose gains have <u>never</u> amounted to much more than "wages": that is, from six to eight dollars a day. And a "claim" which yields a man a steady income of ten dollars <u>per diem</u>, is considered as very valuable.

I received an immense fright the other morning. I was sitting by the fire, quietly reading "Lewis Arundal," which had just fallen into my hands, when a great shout and trampling of feet outside attracted my attention. Naturally enough my first impulse was to run to the door; but scarcely had I risen to my feet for that purpose, when a mighty crash against the side of the cabin, shaking it to the foundation, threw me suddenly upon my knees. So violent was the shock, that for a moment I thought the staunch old logs, mossed with the pale verdure of ages, were falling in confusion around me. As soon as I could collect my scattered senses, I looked about to see what had happened. Several stones had fallen from the back of the chimney, mortar from the latter covered the hearth, the cloth overhead was twisted into the funniest possible wrinkles, the couch had jumped two feet from the side of the house, the little table lay on its back holding up <u>four</u> legs instead of <u>one</u>, the chessmen were roiling merrily about in every direction, the dishes had all left their usual places, the door, which ever since has obstinately refused to let itself be shut, was thrown violently open, while an odd looking pile of articles lay in the middle of the room, which, upon investigation, was found to consist of a pail, a broom, a bell, some candlesticks, a pack of cards, a loaf of bread, a pair of boots, a bunch of cigars, and some clay pipes—the only things, by the way, rendered utterly <u>hors de combat</u> in the assault. But one piece of furniture retained its attitude, and that was the elephantine bedstead, which nothing short of an earthquake could move. Almost at the same moment several acquaintances rushed in, begging me not to be alarmed, as the danger was past.

"But what has happened?" I eagerly inquired.

"Oh, a large tree which was felled this morning, has rolled down from the brow of the hill," and its having struck a rock a few feet from the house, losing thereby the most of its force, had alone saved us from utter destruction.

I grew sick with terror when I understood the awful fate from which Providence had preserved me; and even now my heart leaps painfully with mingled fear and gratitude, when I think how closely that pale death shadow glided by me, and of the loving care which forbade it to linger upon our threshold.

Every one who saw the forest giant descending the hill with the force of a mighty torrent, expected to see the cabin instantly prostrated to the earth. As it was, they all say that it swayed from the perpendicular more than six inches.

Poor W.—whom you may remember my having mentioned in a former letter as having had a leg amputated, a few weeks ago, and who was visiting us at the time, (he had been brought from the Empire in a rocking chair), looked like a marble statue of resignation. He possesses a face of uncommon beauty, and his large, dark eyes have always, I fancy, a sorrowful expression. Although he knew from the first shout what was about to happen, and was sitting on the couch which stood at the side of the cabin where the log must necessarily strike, and in his mutilated condition, had, as he has since said. not the faintest hope of escape, yet the rich color, for which he is remarkable, paled not a shade during the whole affair.

The woodman, who came so near causing a catastrophe, was, I believe, infinitely more frightened than his might-have-been victims. He is a good natured, stupid creature, and did not dare to descend the hill until some time after the excitement had subsided. The ludicrous expression of terror which his countenance wore, when he came in to see what damage had been done, and to ask pardon for his carelessness, made us all laugh heartily.

W. related the almost miraculous escape of two persons from a similar danger last winter. The cabin, which was on Smith's Bar, was crushed into a mass of ruins almost in all instant; while an old man and his daughter, who were at dinner within its walls, remained sitting in the midst of the fallen logs, entirely unhurt. The father immediately seized a gun and ran after the careless woodman, swearing that he would shoot him. Fortunately for the latter (for there is no doubt that in the first moments of his rage the old man would have slain him) his younger legs enabled him to make his escape, and he did not dare to return to the settlement for some days.

It has heretofore been a source of great interest to me to listen to the ringing sound of the axe, and the solemn crash of those majestic sentinels of the hills, as they bow their green foreheads to the dust; but now I fear that I shall always hear them with a feeling of apprehension, mingling with my former awe, although every one tells us that there is no danger of a repetition of the accident.

Last week there was a post mortem examination of two men who died very suddenly in the neighborhood. Perhaps it will sound rather barbarous, when I tell you that, as there was no building upon the Bar which admitted light enough for the purpose, it was found necessary to conduct the examination in the open air, to the intense interest of the Kanakas, Indians, French, Spanish, English, Irish and Yankees, who had gathered eagerly about the spot. Paganini Ned, with an anxious desire that Mrs. —— should be amused as much as possible in her mountain home, rustled up from the kitchen, his dusky face radiant with excitement, to inform me "that I could see both the bodies by just looking out of the window!" I really frightened the poor fellow by the abrupt and vehement manner in which I declined taking advantage of his kindly hint.

One of the deceased, was the husband of an American lady-lecturess of the most intense description, and a strong-minded "Bloomer" on the broadest principles.

Apropos, how can women,—many of whom, I am told, are really interesting and intelligent, how can they spoil their pretty mouths and ruin their beautiful complexions, by demanding with Xantippean fervor, in the presence, often, of a vulgar, irreverent mob, what the gentle creatures, are pleased to call their "rights?" How can they wish to soil the delicate texture of their airy fancies, by pondering over the wearying stupidities of Presidential elections, or the bewildering mystifications of rabid metaphysicians? And, above all, how can they so far forget the sweet, shy coquetries of shrinking womanhood, as to don those horrid "Bloomers?" As for me, although a wife, I never wear the ——, well you know what they call them, when they wish to quiz henpecked husbands,—even in the strictest privacy of life. I confess to an almost religious veneration for trailing drapery, and I pin my vestural faith with unflinching obstinacy to sweeping petticoats.

I knew a "strong-minded Bloomer," at home, of some talent, and who was possessed, in a certain sense, of an excellent education. One day, after having flatteringly informed me, that I really <u>had</u> a "soul above buttons" and the nursery, she gravely proposed that I should improve my <u>mind</u>, by poring six hours a day over the metaphysical subtleties of Kant, Cousin, &c; and I remember, that she called me a "piece of fashionable insipidity," and taunted me with not daring to go out of the beaten track, because I <u>truly</u> thought, (for in those days I was a humble little thing enough, and sincerely desirous of walking in the right path as straightly as my feeble judgment would permit,) that there were other authors, more congenial to the flower-like delicacy of the feminine intellect than her pet writers.

When will our sex appreciate the exquisite philosophy and truth of Lowell's remark upon the habits of Lady Red-Breast and her <u>sposa</u> Robin, as illustrating the beautifully varied spheres of man and woman:—

"He sings to the wide world, she to her nest;
In the nice ear of Nature, which song is the best?"

Speaking of birds, reminds me of a misfortune that I have lately experienced, which, in a life where there is so little to amuse and interest one, has been to me a subject of real grief. About three weeks ago, F. saw on the hill, a California pheasant, which he chased into a coyote hole and captured. Knowing how fond I am of pets, he brought it home and proposed that I should try to tame it. Now from earliest childhood, I have resolutely refused to keep <u>wild</u> birds, and when I have had them given to me—which has happened several times in this country—young blue-birds, etc.—I have invariably set them free; and I proposed doing the same with the pretty pheasant; but as they are the most delicately exquisite in flavor of all game, F. said "that if I did not wish to keep it, he would wring its neck and have it served up for dinner." With the cruelty of kindness, often more disastrous than that of real malice, I shrank from having it killed, and consented to let it run about the cabin.

It was a beautiful bird, a little larger than the domestic hen. Its slender neck, which it curved with haughty elegance, was tinted with various shades of a shining steel color. The large, bright eye glanced with the prettiest shyness at its captors, and the cluster of feathers forming its tail, drooped with the rare grace of an ostrich-plume. The colors of the body were of a subdued brilliancy, reminding one of a rich but somber mosaic.

As it seemed very quiet, I really believed that in time we should be able to

tame it—still it <u>would</u> remain constantly under the sofa or bedstead; so F. concluded to place it in a cage, for a few hours of each day, in order that it might become gradually accustomed to our presence. This was done, the bird appearing
as well as ever; and after closing the door of its temporary prison one day, I left it
and returned to my seat by the fire. In less than two minutes afterwards, a light
struggle in the cage, attracted my attention. I ran hastily back, and you may
imagine my distress, when I found the beautiful pheasant lying lifeless upon the
ground. It never breathed or showed the faintest sign of life afterward.

You may laugh at me, if you please, but I firmly believe that it died of homesickness. What wonder that the free, beautiful, happy creature of God, torn
from the sight of the broad. blue sky, the smiling river and the fresh, fragrant fir
trees of its mountain home, and shut up in a dark, gloomy cabin, should have
broken in twain its haughty, little heart? Yes, you may laugh, call me sentimen-
tal, etc., but I shall never forgive myself, for having killed, by inches, in my selfish and cruel kindness, that pretty creature.

Many people here call this bird a grouse; and those who have crossed the
plains say that it is very much like a prairie hen. The Spanish name is <u>gallina del
campo</u>, literally, "hen of the field." Since the death of my poor, little victim, I
have been told that it is utterly impossible to tame one of these birds; and it is
said, that if you put their eggs under a domestic fowl, the young, almost as soon
as hatched, will instinctively run away to the beloved solitudes of their congenial homes; so passionately beats for liberty, each pulse of their free and wild na-
tures.

Among the noteworthy events which have occurred since my last, I don't
know how I came to forget, until the close of my letter, two smart shocks of an
earthquake, to which we were treated a week ago. They were awe-inspiring, but
after all were nothing in comparison to the timber-quake, an account of which I
have given you above. But as F. is about to leave for the top of the Butte Mountains with a party of Rich Barians, and as I have much to do to prepare him for
the journey, I must close.

## 1852
## HARRIET BEECHER STOWE TO CALVIN STOWE

*Uncle Tom's Cabin was published in March of 1852 and sold an astonishing three
hundred thousand copies in its first year. The novel of slavery—embraced by abolitionists, reviled by slave owners—was considered so influential in shaping public
opinion that when Abraham Lincoln met its author a decade later, he is said to have*

*asked: "So this is the little lady who made this big war?" Harriet Beecher Stowe (1811–1896) was the daughter of Lyman Beecher and the sister of Catharine Beecher (see page 196). In this letter to her husband, Calvin (1802–1886), she revealed the sincerity of the sentiments she had expressed in her famous book. Mary and Emily Edmondson were two slaves whom Stowe and her father were raising the money to buy and then free.*

The famous Swedish singer Jenny Lind had been touring America for two years and met Stowe on the eve of giving a farewell concert in New York. She was particularly moved by the cause of abolition.

The mother of the Edmondson girls, now aged and feeble, is in the city. I did not actually know when I wrote "Uncle Tom" of a living example in which Christianity had reached its fullest development under the crushing wrongs of slavery, but in this woman I see it. I never knew before what I could feel till, with her sorrowful, patient eyes upon me, she told me her history and begged my aid. The expression of her face as she spoke, and the depth of patient sorrow in her eyes, was beyond anything I ever saw.

"Well," said I, when she had finished, "set your heart at rest; you and your children shall be redeemed. If I can't raise the money otherwise, I will pay it myself." You should have seen the wonderfully sweet, solemn look she gave me as she said, "The Lord bless you, my child!"

I have received a sweet note from Jenny Lind, with her name and her husband's with which to head my subscription list. They give a hundred dollars. Another hundred is subscribed by Mr. Bowen in his wife's name, and I have put my own name down for an equal amount. A lady has given me twenty-five dollars, and Mr. Storrs has pledged me fifty dollars. Milly and I are to meet the ladies of Henry's and Dr. Cox's churches to-morrow, and she is to tell them her story. I have written to Drs. Bacon and Dutton in New Haven to secure a similar meeting of ladies there. I mean to have one in Boston, and another in Portland. It will do good to the givers as well as to the receivers.

But all this time I have been so longing to get your letter from New Haven, for I heard it was there. It is not fame nor praise that contents me. I seem never to have needed love so much as now. I long to hear you say how much you love me. Dear one, if this effort impedes my journey home, and wastes some of my strength, you will not murmur. When I see this Christlike soul standing so patiently bleeding, yet forgiving, I feel a sacred call to be the helper of the helpless, and it is better that my own family do without me for a while longer than that this mother lose all. <u>I must redeem her.</u>

### 1852: OCTOBER 9
### LOUISA McCORD TO MARY DULLES

*Sticklers as we are for consistency, we must print this letter in its entirety, but we respectfully direct you to the postscript, which is the passage of real interest. Louisa Susanna Cheves McCord (1810–1879) was a conservative thinker and author who was incensed by the portrayal of Southerners in* Uncle Tom's Cabin. *Writing from Columbia, South Carolina, to her cousin Mary Cheves Dulles (1830–1905), McCord used the last part of her letter to express her outraged belief that Stowe's novel was flagrantly exaggerated fiction. (In some Southern states, it quickly became illegal to own a copy of the book.) The following year, Stowe would publish* A Key to Uncle Tom's Cabin, *a collection of documents and facts gathered to prove the accuracy of her portrayals.*

In Stowe's novel, Mrs. Shelby is the very religious wife of the plantation owner; Mr. St. Clare, Uncle Tom's subsequent owner, is the father of the angelic and doomed Little Eva.

Columbia, Oct 9th, 1852

Dear Mary

I will not write you a letter, but one line to thank you for the little box sent by Mrs. Lieber. The girls would have answered your kind epistle to them, but I have been too busy to rule paper etc. for the poor little things who have been rather neglected by me, owing to my having my hands full with Mr. McCord who has been seriously sick ever since I wrote to you. I do not know what has been the matter with him. He has been bothered and plagued by numbers of things and people of late and all sorts of disagreeable affairs (I don't mean anything of our own at home) and in truth I believe it just broke him down. He is doing better now; indeed has improved very much in the last 36 hours and I believe is going to get pretty well again. He is a regular spoiled one though and wants a deal of nursing.

If Hayney comes to Philadelphia, do give my love to him. Tell him he ought to have written to me. I have not known his direction all the Summer. I guess he is glad to escape the persecution of my epistles.

I think I may as well stop; my head is splitting with pain. I have slept very irregularly for the last fortnight, and to cap the climax of unrest, last night when every thing else got quiet, one of my carriage horses began to kick in the stable. Ben goes off every night and there was nobody to quiet it, and so it kicked away to its heart's content and I lay awake to listen to it, and this morning I feel pretty much as if I had got all the kicks on my head instead of only in my ears.

Please any time, if not too troublesome, get me some gloves a size larger for the girls. Those sent are very pretty but rather tight. 2 pair each will do, and 2 or 3 pair more for <u>me</u> will last for six months. I am a terrible glove-consumer.

Goodbye—Love to all—Write to me soon.

Your's affectionately
Louisa S. McCord—

Oh! Mrs. Stowe! One word of that abominable woman's abominable book,—I have read it lately and am quite shocked at <u>you</u>, my dear Cousin, Miss Mary C. Dulles, for thinking it as if I remember right, you said you did, a strong exposition against slavery. It is one mass of fanatical bitterness and foul misrepresentation wrapped in the garb of Christian Charity. She quotes the Scriptures only to curse by them. Why! Have not you been at the South enough to know, that our gentlemen dont keep mulatto wives, nor whip negroes to death nor commit all the various other enormities that she describes? She does not know what a gentleman or a lady is, at least according to our Southern notions any more than I do a Laplander. Just look at her real benevolent gentleman (as she means him to be) her Mr. St. Clare, or her sensible woman Mrs. Shelby and two more distressing fools and hypocrites I never met with. The woman (Mrs. Stowe I mean) has certainly never been in any Southern State further than across the Kentucky line at most, and there in very doubtful society. All her Southern ladies and gentleman talk coarse Yankee. But I must stop. The thought of Mrs. Stowe doubles my infliction of horses heels. Read the book over again my dear child and you will wonder that you ever took it for anything but what it is, i.e. as malicious and gross an abolitionist production (though I confess a cunning one) as ever dis-graced the press. Encore adieu—

Yours always
L. S. Mc——

## 1852: OCTOBER 26
## ELLEN CRAFT TO THE <u>BRITISH ANTI-SLAVERY ADVOCATE</u>

*America's first fugitive slave law, which allowed slave owners to track and reclaim runaways without benefit of jury trial, had been passed by Congress in 1793. Resistance from the North, in the form of personal-liberty laws and an early underground railroad, had been in evidence since 1810. But by 1850, Congress passed the Fugitive Slave Act, imposing harsher penalties on people who helped slaves and on marshals who didn't arrest them. Ellen Craft (1826–1891) and her husband, William, had escaped Georgia in 1848, with Ellen posing as William's white male owner. In*

*Boston, they found work and spoke at antislavery meetings. Word got back to their former owners in Georgia, who tried to have them captured. By the time the Crafts reached safety in England, Ellen was disturbed to read what some Americans were saying about her. She wrote this letter to set the record straight.*

Ockham School, near Ripley, Surrey,
Oct. 26th, 1852.

Dear Sir,—

I feel very much obliged to you for informing me of the erroneous report which has been so extensively circulated in the American newspapers: "That I had placed myself in the hands of an American gentleman in London, on condition that he would take me back to the family who held me as a slave in Georgia." So I write these few lines merely to say that the statement is entirely unfounded, for I have never had the slightest inclination whatever of returning to bondage; and God forbid that I should ever be so false to liberty as to prefer slavery in its stead. In fact, since my escape from slavery, I have got on much better in every respect than I could have possibly anticipated. Though, had it been to the contrary, my feelings in regard to this would have been just the same, for I had much rather starve in England, a free woman, than be a slave for the best man that ever breathed upon the American continent.

Yours very truly,
Ellen Craft

**1853: JANUARY 23**
**JANE PIERCE TO BENNY PIERCE**

*The story is that during the presidential campaign of 1852, Jane Appleton Pierce (1806–1863) fainted in horror when she heard that her husband had been chosen on the forty-ninth ballot to break a deadlock among four Democratic contenders. As it turned out, Franklin Pierce won the party nomination and also the election, but Jane would face much greater hardship than life in Washington. Two months before the inauguration, the Pierces were in a train wreck, and their eleven-year-old son, Benjamin, was killed. In her grief, Jane Pierce wrote this letter to her dead child.*
The Pierces had no other surviving children; two older sons had died earlier.

My precious child—

I <u>must</u> write to you, altho' you are never to see it or know it—How I long to see you and say something to you as if you were as you always have been (until these last three dreadful weeks) near me. Oh! How precious do those days now seem, my darling boy—and how I should have praised the days passed with you had I <u>suspected</u> they might be so short—Dear, dear child—I cannot bear to think of that agonizing time, when I had just seen you all alive to what was passing around and near me, but not <u>near enough</u>—oh had you but been within reach of your dear father—in a moment changed my dear boy bright form into a lifeless one insensible to your parents' agony—But you <u>spirit yourself</u>, my dear one—was not your redeeming savior ready to receive you? Your sweet little brother? Your dear Uncle Lawrence?—but you are beyond my knowledge at once—Ah, I trust in <u>joy</u>, but I would fain have kept you here—I know not how to go on without you—you were my comfort dear—far more than you thought. I was thinking how pleasantly we should go on together when we found ourselves at home again—and I would do everything to make you love me and have confidence in me and bring you along gently and sweetly—Oh! You were indeed "a part of mine and of your father's heart". When I have told you dear boy how much you depended on me, and felt that you could not do without me—I did not say too how much I depended on you and oh! My precious boy how gladly would I recall all that was unreasonable—or hasty—or mistaken in my conduct toward you. I see surely and I did frequently see afterward that I had wronged you—and would have gladly acknowledged it only that I feared it might weaken your confidence in me and perhaps on that account not be as well for you—and now I am at home again dear boy. Oh what anguish was mine on returning without you, and feeling that it must still be so, while I live—to see your little bed that you loved so much—and which I look at many times in the day, and at night feel as if I must see it shake out again and the clothes turned down for you— and unconsciously look in the morning for it and you—and listen for your bright cheerful voice your blithe "good morrow"—and oh! to look around and see your books and everything so connected with you—your dear self—and now on this Sabbath which you loved so much as you said often how I have marked for you each hour with its wonted occupation—and oh to think of you kneeling by me at our evening prayer tonight, dear child—has not the Savior made you His as we so often asked. But now I must kneel <u>alone</u> and beg for strength and support under this crushing sorrow, that the blessed Savior would comfort the heart of your pain stricken Mother—and help me better to bear the burden of your loss which has brought desolation such as I have <u>never</u> (with all my former griefs) known.

Dear precious boy! I have passed through the bitter time of leaving our home, and without my child, my own dear Benny. How did I think of you—dear—in every moment—of all your little parting notes and the many good-byes—and again the ride in those rail cars agonizing to my soul—we went in to the same little saloon as when we went down to Andover the last time—we three then, now only two—but we seemed to see you as when there before—and now we are in Boston, still without <u>you</u>, but I fancying what I should do and what I should say to you—continually, and now we must "journey on e'en when grief is sorest" with the whole head sick and the whole heart faint. I will "look to Jesus" (how often I have directed <u>you</u> to him my precious one) and sought his blessing for you and myself—but my son, my dear son, how much I feel my own faults in regard to you—I know that I did not take the right way and should have dealt with you very gently often when I judged hastily and spoke harshly. I can see that I was "unreasonable" and sometimes almost wonder that you loved me at all. God help me now to correct in bitterness my errors when oh! It is too late for you to have the sweet benefit of it—and now this Sabbath evening you will come in fancy before me and I sit close by you, with your hand in mine perhaps, or you will lean against me on the sofa, or as sometimes you did on Sunday evening sit on my lap a little while and we talk together and say hymns and then play and then by and by you go to bed first putting your arms around me and laying your dear head on my shoulder and then you get in your bed and we have our Sabbath night kiss—but to think I can never have another—Oh Benny, I have not valued such a sweet blessing as I ought.

## 1853: MAY 6
## VIRGINIA BOYD TO RICE CARTER BALLARD

*Virginia Boyd was a pregnant slave who apparently had had sex with her master, Judge Samuel Boyd. In this letter, she begged one of Boyd's business partners, a planter and slave trader named Rice Carter Ballard (1800?–1860), to keep her from being sold. The plea apparently was futile.*

I am at present in the city of Houston in a Negro traders yard, for sale, by your orders. I was present at the Post Office when Doctor Ewing took your letter out through mistake and red it a loud, not knowing I was the person the letter alluded to. I hope that if I have ever done or said any thing that has offended you that you will for give me, for I have suffered enough Cince in mind to repay all that I have ever done, to anyone, you wrote for them to sell me in thrity days, do you think after all that has transpired between me & the old man, (I don't call names) that its treating me well to send me off among strangers in my situation to be sold without even my having an opportunity of choosing for my self; its hard indeed and what is still harder for the father of my children to sell his own offspring Yes his own flesh & blood. My God is it possible that any free born American would brand his character with such a stigma as that, but I hope before this he will relent & see his error for I still beleave that he is possest of more honer than that. I no too that you have influence and can assist me in some measure from out of this dilemma and if you will God will be sure to reward you, you have a family of children & no how to sympathize with others in distress. . . .

Is it possible that such a change could ever come over the spirit of any living man as to sell his child that is his image. I dont wish to return to harras or protest his peace of mind & shall never try [to] get back if I am dealt with fairly. . . .

I have written to the Old Man in such a way that the letter cant fail to fall in his hands and none others I use every precaution to prevent others from knowing or suspecting any thing I have my letters written & folded put into envelope & get it directed by those that dont know the Contents of it for I shall not seek ever to let any thing be exposed, unless I am forced from bad treatment &c

Virginia Boyd

## 1853: OCTOBER 10

## SARAH HICKS WILLIAMS TO SARAH AND SAMUEL HICKS

*A native of New Hartford, New York, Sarah Hicks (1827–1917) spent eight years of her life refusing to marry a North Carolina planter and physician named Benjamin Franklin Williams—mainly because she couldn't imagine living in the South. When she finally relented, and moved with her new husband to his North Carolina plantation, she sent this letter home to her somewhat doubtful parents, Sarah (1794–1880) and Samuel Hicks (1785–1876). Its descriptions suggest the extent to which the North and South, on the eve of the Civil War, were already in some respects foreign countries.*

Williams would live in the South until her death. Mary and Harriett were, respectively, Benjamin's younger sister and niece.

Clifton Grove, Oct. 10, 1853
Monday

My dear Parents:

I arrived safely at my new home on Friday last, but have had no time to write until now. . . . You may imagine I have seen many strange things. As for my opinions, in so short a time, it would not be fair to give them. I have seen no unkind treatment of servants. Indeed, I think they are treated with more familiarity than many Northern servants. They are in the parlor, in your room and all over. The first of the nights we spent in the Slave Holding States, we slept in a room without a lock. Twice before we were up a waiting girl came into the room, and while I was dressing, in she came to look at me. She seemed perfectly at home, took up the locket with your miniatures in it and wanted to know if it was a Watch. I showed it to her. "Well," she said, "I should think your mother and father are mighty old folks." Just before we arrived home, one old Negro caught a glimpse of us and came tearing out of the pine woods to touch his hat to us. All along the road we met them and their salutation of "Howdy (meaning How do you) Massa Ben," and they seemed so glad to see him, that I felt assured that they were well treated. As we came to the house, I found Mother Williams ready to extend a mother's welcome. Mary and Harriett were both here and delighted to see me. I felt at home. At dinner we had everything very nice. It is customary when the waiting girl is not passing things at table, to keep a large broom of peacock feathers in motion over our heads to keep off flies, etc. I feel confused. Everything is so different that I do not know which way to stir for fear of making a blunder. I have determined to keep still and look on for a while, at any rate. Yesterday I went to Church in a very handsome carriage, servants before and behind. I began to realize yesterday how much I had lost in the way of religious privileges. We went six miles to church, as they have preaching at Snow Hill only every one or two Sabbaths. On arriving I found a rough framed building in the midst of woods, with a large congregation, consisting of about equal numbers of white and black. These meetings are held about one a month and then addressed by two or three exhorters, who are uneducated, and each speaks long enough for any common sermon. The singing is horrible. Prize your religious privileges. They are great and you would realize it by attending Church here once. I shall miss these much. Things that Northerners consider essential, are of no importance here. The house and furniture is of little consequence. To all these differences I expect to become accustomed in time. My husband is all kindness and loves me more than I am worthy. With him I could be happy anywhere. I have seen enough to convince me that the ill-treatment of the Slaves is exaggerated at the North but I have not seen enough to make me like the institution. I am quite the talk of the day, not only in the whole County, but on the plantation. Yesterday I was out in the yard and an old Negro woman came up to me, "Howdy, Miss Sara, are you the Lady that won my young Master. Well, I raised him." Her name was Chaney and she was the family nurse. Between you and me, my husband is better off than I ever dreamed of. I am glad I didn't know it before we were married. He owns 2000 acres of land in this vicinity, but you must bear in mind that land here is not as valuable as with you. But I'll leave these things to talk of when I see you, which I hope may be before many months. I will write you more fully when I have the time. Some of our friends leave this morning and I must go and see them. Write soon, very soon. Ben sends love. Love to all. Ever your

Sara

I wish you could see the cotton fields. The bolls are just opening. I cannot compare their appearance to anything but fields of white roses. As to the cotton picking, I should think it very light and pleasant work. Our house is very unassuming. Not larger than Mary's. I shall feel unsettled until my furniture comes and after our return from Charleston next month. Then I hope to settle down and be quiet for a while. The house has been full of relatives ever since we came and more friends are expected tomorrow. Direct to Clifton Grove, near Snow Hill, Green Co., N.C.

## 1854: APRIL 3
## ELIZABETH CHACE TO SAMUEL CHACE

*A native of Rhode Island and a staunch Quaker, Elizabeth Buffum Chace (1806–1899) was a suffragist, an abolitionist, a temperance leader, and the mother of ten children, only three of whom would live to adulthood. Chace herself lived to be ninety-three, and in the course of her long life, she offered her home as a stop on the Underground Railroad, tried to improve conditions for mill workers, and, for twenty-seven years, served as president of the Rhode Island Woman's Suffrage Association. As a forty-eight-year-old mother, however, she described somewhat less global goals—such as disciplining her children—to her husband, cotton manufacturer Samuel Chace (?–1870).*

Valley Falls, 4th mo., 3rd, 1854.

Yesterday I promised Eddie that I would buy a stick of molasses candy for him, but I forgot it until after supper tonight and then gave Lillie three cents to go and buy some. She wished Arnold to go with her. When they returned, she brought four sticks and, according to my promise, I gave Eddie one. I then broke one in two and gave it to Arnold, bidding him give one half to Sammy. He said he wanted a whole stick, and kept on fretting and scolding. Finally he threw the half stick in my lap and said he would not have it. I said he should not and arose with it. He screamed and endeavored to force it from me and finding he could not, he commenced striking me. I seized his hands and held them and bade Mary help me to undress him, but he kicked so we could not and I sent out after Michael; I holding his hands the meanwhile and he kicking and pulling in the most violent anger. Michael came and all three of us with the utmost difficulty divested him of his clothing, put on his nightgown, and then Michael laid him in bed. All this time I felt perfectly calm, without the slightest irritation. Something whispered encouragement in my spirit, saying, "Do it thoroughly; it will be the last time." At first I told Michael to sit down by the bedside, for I feared he would attempt to get out the window; but I soon saw he had no idea of doing that, and so I sent Michael out. Arnold opened the door into the bathroom and I let it remain so. He took all his bedclothes and strewed them on the floor; pulled off the mattresses, pulled out the bed cord and then went to the bookcase, which stood in the room and took out every book and paper and threw it on the floor. The other children had gone to bed and nobody interfered with him. Then his angry passion seemed to have spent itself. He lay down and wept. It grew pretty dark and he was alone. After a while he came out sobbing and said, "Mother, will thee get me a little stick to put the strings into my bedstead?" (meaning the bed cord. The bedstead has holes for the cord to go through). I gave him a fork and he went back. Sammy volunteered his assistance and by the dim twilight they put in the cord and put on the beds and then Sammy left him and he made up the bed. Then he went to the bookcase and commenced putting up the books and papers, in the dark. I let him work a while and then set a light in the room and he returned them all nicely to their places. Then he brought out the light, bade me farewell, and went to bed. I hoped he would come and acknowledge his fault, but did not think it best to draw this from him but to leave him entirely to his own thoughts. It was a crisis to which he had been for some time tending and I think it will do him good.

Should this record meet his eye in the future years, I doubt not that he will gratefully acknowledge that his mother did him no injustice and that her firmness helped him to overcome his obstinacy.

## 1854: SEPTEMBER
## G. TO PAULINA WRIGHT DAVIS

*Another active reformer, Paulina Wright Davis (1813–1876) was probably best known for founding* The Una, *the first publication dedicated to women's rights and owned and edited by a woman. Though it was in business for only two and a half years, the newspaper attracted contributions from Elizabeth Cady Stanton (see page 195), Lucy Stone (see page 205), and this anonymous author, who offered some remarkably modern advice about the need for women to take risks.*

Mrs. Davis—

It seems to me that one great obstacle to woman's success in the unaccustomed walks of life, and particularly in the professions, is her pride or vanity. She must be sure she will succeed creditably, or she will undertake nothing. This is a feeling we all share, and too frequently express. We are unwilling to see a woman do anything unusual unless she can do it a good deal better than men ordinarily do. This is partially right perhaps, because the greater difficulties in their way make a peculiar adaptation to the chosen calling more necessary, but I think we generally are too sensitive on this point. It should be remembered that all things are to be <u>learned</u>, that we can learn only by trying—that our brothers fail in fifty cases, where one succeeds—that we must enter on the various occupations of life prepared to struggle and overcome: to persevere amid the sneers and jeers of those who always knew women were unfit for anything but the needle or house-work: and if failing in one pursuit go bravely to another.

If it were only the gifted and superior women who need remunerative labor or social freedom, this might do: but we all need to find our right place, and must therefore be willing to try and to learn, to make many mistakes and many failures, for the sake of the ultimate good. Let us not wait to be assured of our talents or ability to shine in some peculiar vocation before we will venture out of the beaten path of helplessness and dependence. Let us wait for nothing but a right good will, and let us welcome as helpers all who have this one qualification.

G.

# EXCHANGE

## 1855
## SALLY McDOWELL AND JOHN MILLER

---

*Daughter of Virginia Governor James McDowell, Sally Campbell Preston McDowell (1821–1895) was thirty-three years old and running the family plantation when John Miller (1819–1895), a thirty-five-year-old Presbyterian minister visiting from Philadelphia, fell in love with her. Miller, a widower with two children, promptly*

*proposed. But McDowell, who had been granted a divorce after a disastrous mar-*
*riage to Maryland Governor Francis Thomas, was hesitant. For two years, the cou-*
*ple wrote to each other nearly daily. The letters below follow their decision to*
*postpone their wedding and enter into a long-term engagement. They were finally*
*married in 1856 and would remain married for nearly forty years, until their deaths*
*a week apart.*

## SALLY TO JOHN

Colalto was the family plantation, which Sally managed. *Jehovah-Jireh* means "The Lord will provide."

Colalto
Saturday Nov 24. 1855

My dear John,

The morning is a bad time for me to write to you. I get up in uncontrollable agony after a night of restlessness and anxiety, and am scarcely fit for any effort of any kind. Yet I find it a momentary relief to come and pour out my heart to you. I am beset with a thousand fears, yet the greatest of all, and the most terrible of all is that of your affection. And I want you to tell me John with the utmost solemnity & truth <u>just</u> how much you love me, & what sort of love it is. Do re-assure me on this point, for every thing future hinges upon it. However much I love you, under our threatened embarrassment & difficulties, I could not, I think, with any hope of happiness to myself or you, venture to marry you if I doubted the fervency and respect & tenderness of your love. So tell me about it: and tell me truly. I wont bind you by any refined notion of honor to any engagement between us, if your affection wanes. It is <u>that</u> that I want & want it as I have described it to you a hundred times. When the world grows cold & the storm beats, if I cannot wrap myself up warmly in it, then nothing human can avail me.

I have always wanted to stand by you as a helper in your work. I dont sympathize in your Studies because I dont understand them, but feeling to you as to my husband I should I hope soon learn to concentrate all my pleasures in you and yours.

I find my present trouble—brings me back stronger & stronger, to the true source of comfort—and I am more willing to submit all to the disposal of the great Disposer of all: and I pray for Guidance, and have the words Jehovah-jireh strongly sounding in my ears.

Do write to me every day & as fully as you can. And May God bless & protect you

My darling John
S. C. P. McDowell

## JOHN TO SALLY

Alonzo Potter ("Bp Potter") was Episcopal bishop of Pennsylvania and married to Sarah Potter, the sister of Miller's first wife; Margaret Hunter ("Mrs. H.") was her aunt. Courtland Van Rensselaer was secretary of the Presbyterian board of education and helped Miller draft an early version of a "minute" (i.e., an official motion) to the church.

Church Study
Nov: 27th 55.

My Darling,

You cant conceive what pleasure these new expressions of love give me. You never <u>wrote</u>—"Darling" before. If you could feel the gush of tenderness that such an endearment awakens you would not bind me so solemnly to tell you of my love.

Now, Sally, listen! If I <u>knew</u> that I must wait twenty years to marry you & that all that time you would love me & that occasionally I might see you, I would rather be in that relation to <u>you</u> than have all the past steeped in the waters of oblivion & have the warmest love of any other woman I have ever seen. As to the tinges of bitterness that my wild love for you has occasioned I say with the most honest certainty, Darling, that I <u>never</u> loved you with so much respectful tenderness as the morning I looked back at you as you stood in the front door bidding me good bye as I left you. Indeed, Sally, I love you still so much better than you love me that the anxiety ought to be all the other way. I was describing my feelings towards you this morning to Mrs Potter & I was quite ashamed of the warmth & glow of my expressions.

But, Sally, my heart <u>bleeds</u> when I hear of such a thing as your "uncontrollable agony". <u>Think</u> of it: you <u>possess</u> me entirely. I am yours beyond the hope or wish of recall. I shall live for you alone (if you will allow me) the rest of my life. I am <u>sure</u> of this. And in <u>my</u> feelings of love this is the <u>great</u> thing. If you were not <u>mine</u> I should be plunged in the deepest depression. As you <u>are</u> mine I look upon this <u>arrest</u> of our marriage only as a painful self-denial.

You ask me <u>how</u> I love you. I will tell you. If I could live in the same house with you. If you would sit by my fire while I studied. If you would ramble with me thro' the woods in the Summer afternoons. If you would talk with me about my peculiar passions & ambitions. If you would lean as you did at Colalto upon my side & let me kiss you, & our relations, therefore, were like the relations of sisters nine tenths of the yearnings of my heart would be fully satisfied—so much of my love consists of that very tenderness & respect, & let me say, congeniality, about which you raise the question. My whole passion for you is built upon a substratum of respect & could not exist without it. So behave, Child, & keep quiet.

Now about my mornings work I feel sad. I write most shrinkingly, but I will tell you all. Dr Van R. is still sick. I saw Bp. Potter. As I feared when Mrs H. spoke as she did he has changed very much. He speaks with the utmost kindness, but began by advising our settling in Va a thing which for this reason I cant abide. He says he has been near Frederick & there is a difference of opinion there about the <u>expediency</u> of the marriage (well, that is not a very serious thing). But then he implies that he has scruples about the step itself because the divorce was not on the right ground. He says public opinion here is strongly against us. He hears it on every side. He says he is grieved that he gave me a wrong impression. He could not have conceived that he could have changed so, & yet he said he was not <u>sure</u> that excitement might not blow over in time. I saw Mrs P. She was under the same influence said that it would not influence <u>her</u> conduct in the heart but on the contrary she would insist on all we had promised as to her house but still she seemed to say as Mrs H. did, if you <u>love</u> the lady dont marry. One of Bp Potters emphatic speeches was, If I were Mrs M D with such a position as she has I wouldnt marry you. And they told me what seemed to have surprised them both, that the public seemed to make no distinction between the different cases of divorce.

Now, to-morrow, I shall probably hear something just as strong on the other side. I am determined no <u>light</u> thing shall shake me in my own convictions. I am determined to marry no one <u>else</u> than you. And I beg you, Darling, not to desert me as you threatened to do if sheer <u>certainty</u> that you will lose your position should raise an outcry against the marriage & force you to decide that you will postpone it further.

It seems cruel that with all the pain I feel I should have this additional that I give you so much. But, Sally, if I love you so tenderly that in the sight of God I still prize your affection to me in spite of all its pains as my greatest treasure, is that no support to you? I will write daily without exception. Keep up your spirits & I shall still hope to send you good news. I wish we had taken the Potters in their first mood & yet perhaps they would have turned then more unpleasantly. I may get a <u>minute</u> in our favour. I have some hopes.

Tell me if my love seems of any value to you if we have to postpone our marriage.

> Yours fondly
> Jno Miller

I am convinced we ought to marry <u>soon</u> if we venture upon it under existing circumstances. And but <u>the certain loss of your position socially</u> will deter me for a moment. Dare we incur that with our eyes open?

### SALLY TO JOHN

Both McDowell and Miller were evangelical Christians who believed in the primacy of God's will. Though McDowell had been legally divorced, the Presbyterian Confession of Faith declared adultery the only acceptable grounds for it, and she had not made that charge. As she wrestled with the question of whether she was morally free to remarry, she also worried about the effect the marriage would have on Miller's career. Ultimately, he would resign his Philadelphia pastorate, though he resumed the ministry once the couple married and settled in Virginia.

> Colalto,
> Thursday, Nov 27. 1855.

Dear John,

I cannot express to you all the pain and anguish of the last three or four days. Some day, if God ever throws us together again, I shall tell you about it. Mean time I write off in a hurry the things that fill my mind in regard to our present circumstances.

First of all, I want to impress upon my own mind and yours, the Truth, that we are not blindly to seek our own happiness either in this, or in any other act in life. The question with us <u>now</u> sh be, not "May I seek my happiness in this marriage if it be in accordance with God's will"?, but, happiness aside, "How shall I act so as most to glorify God?" This is, the highest standard of Christian action, & the most difficult; yet it is the one I want to reach myself, and the one I want you to attain too. Weak as I am in this sort of piety and strong as I am in the degree of my love to you, I find it excessively difficult,—as yet impossible, to decide by which feeling, in looking to further action, I am biassed. But I pray for guidance for us both, and am hoping that it may be given clearly and decidedly.

If your plans of study stretched over a lifetime—there might be little or no hesitation; but as they have to be tested, and may be exploded, and then you wd like to return to the pulpit, the case becomes very different. This marriage, will <u>probably</u>, Cousin John thinks <u>certainly</u>, cast you off always from the Ministry. He says, you could not find a Church in Virginia even, tho' he thinks, the more closely he considers it, that the marriage is in full accordance with Scripture & with both points made in the Confession of Faith. Now, the question is Have you a right to give up the Ministry for the selfish promotion of your own happiness? Years hence, should your Studies, prove delusive dreams, wouldn't your conscience upbraid you with wicked disloyalty to your high Office? This is for you to settle. My motives of action, & range of inquiry must be somewhat different, tho' at some points meeting these questions of yours. I need not press them upon you now. I haven't time, nor ability at present to do it.

If these questions, on your part, are settled clearly & conscientiously in favor of a marriage, then, if the strongest love on my part, and the most earnest desire to promote your personal, & public (as much of it as you have) usefulness, can be, in any sort a guarantee of happiness, you shall have it just whenever you choose to claim it. But I hope never to love you in a way to be the occasion of injury to you. I mourn now, that heretofore, I have loved you so much as a Man, & so little as Minister. I hope it will be different hereafter; I pray you help me to make it so.

And now, my darling John, we need to be watchful and prayerful—do let us become so.

I hear no news, & see nobody, but men on business & Cousin John & Benton. I have been totally unfit for any business arrangements, and don't know what kind to make even if I were able.

God bless & guide you.

Affectionately<br>S. C. P. McDowell

## 1855

## LUCY THURSTON TO MARY THURSTON

*A harrowing and unforgettable account, the letter below was written by Lucy Goodale Thurston (1795–1876), a missionary who lived in Hawaii for more than fifty years. She was sixty at the time of the operation she describes—a mastectomy performed without anesthesia—and astonishingly enough, she lived another twenty-one years after it.*

The first successful use of anesthesia had been in 1842; a decade later, it was still extraordinarily rare. Lucy's doctor had considered using chloroform, but decided it would be too dangerous because she had had an incident of paralysis following the birth of one of her children. Mary Thurston (1831–1889) was the fourth of Lucy's five children. Asa, Persis, and Lucy were Mary's older siblings, Thomas her younger brother; Sarah was Asa's wife. Mr. Taylor was Persis's husband. "Capital" operations were potentially fatal ones. The first quote is from Deuteronomy: "As thy days, so shall thy strength be"; the second quote is from an eighteenth-century hymn.

My Dear Daughter Mary:

I have hitherto forborne to write respecting the surgical operation I experienced in September, from an expectation that you would be with us so soon. That is now given up; so I proceed to give a circumstantial account of those days of peculiar discipline. At the end of the General Meeting in June your father returned to Kailua, leaving me at Honolulu, in Mr. Taylor's family, under Dr. Ford's care. Dr. Hillebrand was called in counsel. During the latter part of August they decided on the use of the knife. Mr. Thurston was sent for to come down according to agreement should such be the result. I requested him to bring certain things which I wished, in case I no more returned to Kailua. Tremendous gales of wind were now experienced. One vessel was wrecked within sight of Kailua. Another, on her way there, nearly foundered, and returned only to be condemned. In vain we looked for another conveyance. Meantime, the tumor was rapidly altering. It had nearly approached the surface, exhibiting a dark spot. Should it become an open ulcer, the whole system would become vitiated with its malignity. Asa said he should take no responsibility of waiting the arrival of his father. Persis felt the same. Saturday p.m., the doctors met in consultation, and advised an immediate operation. The next Tuesday (12th of September), ten o'clock a.m., was the hour fixed upon. In classifying, the Dr. placed this among "capital operations." Both doctors advised not to take chloroform because of my having had the paralysis. I was glad they allowed me the use of my senses. Persis offered me her parlor, and Asa his own new bridal room for the occasion. But I preferred the retirement and quietude of the grass-thatched cottage. Thomas, with all his effects moved out of it into a room a few steps off. The house was thoroughly cleaned and prettily fitted up. One lady said it seemed as though it had been got up by magic. Monday, just at night, Dr. Ford called to see that all was in readiness. There were two lounges trimmed, one with white, the other with rose-colored mosquito netting. There was a reclining Chinese chair, a table for the instruments, a wash-stand with wash bowls, sponges, and pails of water. There was a frame with two dozen towels, and a table of choice stimulants and restoratives. One more table with the Bible and hymn book.

That night I spent in the house alone for the first time. The family had all retired for the night. In the still hour of darkness, I long walked back and forth in the capacious door-yard. Depraved, diseased, helpless, I yielded myself up entirely to the will, the wisdom, and the strength of the Holy One. At peace with myself, with earth, and with heaven, I calmly laid my head upon my pillow and slept refreshingly. A bright day opened upon us. My feelings were natural, cheerful, elevated. I took the Lord at his own word: "As the day is, so shall thy strength be." There with an unwavering heart, I leaned for strength and support. Before dressing for the occasion, I took care to call on Ellen, who had then an infant a week old by her side. It was a cheerful call, made in a common manner, she not being acquainted with the movements of the day. I then prepared myself for the professional call. Dr. Judd was early on the ground. I went with him to Asa's room, where with Asa and Sarah we sat and conversed till other medical men rode up. Dr. Judd rose to go out. I did the same. Asa said: "You had better not go, you are not wanted yet." I replied: "I wish to be among the first on the ground, to prevent its coming butt end first." On reaching my room, Dr. Ford was there. He introduced me to Dr. Hoffman of Honolulu, and to Dr. Brayton of an American Naval ship, then in port. The instruments were then laid out upon the table. Strings were prepared for tying arteries. Needles threaded for sewing up the wound. Adhesive plasters were cut into strips, bandages produced, and the Chinese chair placed by them in the front double door. Everything was now in readiness, save the arrival of one physician. All stood around the house or in the piazza. Dr. Ford, on whom devolved the responsibility, paced the door-yard. I stood in the house with others, making remarks on passing occurrences. At length I was invited to sit. I replied: "As I shall be called to lie a good while, I had rather now stand." Dr. Brayton, as he afterwards said, to his <u>utter astonishment</u> found that the lady to be operated on was standing in their midst.

Dr. Hillebrand arrived. It was a signal for action. Persis and I stepped behind a curtain. I threw off my cap and dressing gown, and appeared with a white flowing skirt, with the white bordered shawl purchased in 1818, thrown over my shoulders. I took my seat in the chair. Persis and Asa stood at my right side; Persis to hand me restoratives; Asa to use his strength, if self-control were wanting. Dr. Judd stood at my left elbow for the same reason; my shawl was thrown off, exhibiting my left arm, breast and side, perfectly bare. Dr. Ford showed me how I must hold back my left arm to the greatest possible extent, with my hand taking a firm hold of the arm of my chair: with my right hand, I took hold of the right arm, with my feet I pressed against the foot of the chair. Thus instructed, and everything in readiness, Dr. Ford looked me full in the face, and with great firmness asked: "Have you made up your mind to have it cut out?" "Yes, sir." "Are you ready now?" "Yes, sir; but let me know when you begin, that I may be able to bear it. Have you your knife in that hand now?" He opened his hand that I might see it, saying, "I am going to begin now." Then came a gash long and deep, first on one side of my breast, then on the other. Deep sickness seized me, and deprived me of my breakfast. This was followed by extreme faintness. My sufferings were no longer local. There was a general feeling of agony throughout the whole system. I felt, every inch of me, as though flesh was failing. During the whole operation, I was enabled to have entire self control over my person, and over my voice. Persis and Asa were devotedly employed in sustaining me with the use of cordials, ammonia, bathing my temples, &c. I myself fully intended to have seen the thing done. But on recollection, every glimpse I happened to have, was the doctor's right hand completely covered with blood, up to the very wrist. He afterwards told me, that at one time the blood from an artery flew into his eyes, so that he could not see. It was nearly an hour and a half that I was beneath his hand, in cutting out the entire breast, in cutting out the glands beneath the arm, in tying the arteries, in absorbing the blood, in sewing up the wound, in putting on the adhesive plasters, and in applying the bandage.

The views and feelings of that hour are now vivid to my recollection. It was during the cutting process that I began to talk. The feeling that I had reached a different point from those by whom I was surrounded, inspired me with freedom. It was thus that I expressed myself. "It has been a great trial to my feelings that Mr. Thurston is not here. But it is not necessary. So many friends, and Jesus Christ besides. His left hand is underneath my head, His right hand sustains and embraces me. I am willing to suffer. I am willing to die. I am not afraid of death. I am not afraid of hell. I anticipate a blessed immortality. Tell Mr. Thurston my peace flows like a river.

> "Upward I lift mine eyes.
>   From God is all my aid:
> The God that built the skies,
>   And earth and nature made.
> God is the tower
>   To which I fly;
> His grace is nigh
>   In every hour."

God disciplines me, but He does it with a gentle hand. At one time I said, "I know you will bear with me." Asa replied, "I think it is you that have to bear from us."

The doctor, after removing the entire breast, said to me, "I want to cut yet more, round under your arm." I replied, "Do just what you want to do, only tell me when, so that I can bear it." One said the wound had the appearance of being more than a foot long. Eleven arteries were taken up. After a beginning had been made in sewing it up, Persis said: "Mother, the doctor makes as nice a seam as you ever made in your life." "Tell me, Persis, when he is going to put in the needle, so that I can bear it." "Now-now-now," &c. "Yes, tell me. That is a good girl." Ten stitches were taken, two punctures at every stitch, one on either side. When the whole work was done, Dr. Ford and Asa removed my chair to the back side of the room, and laid me on the lounge. Dr. Brayton came to my side, and taking me by the hand said: "There is not one in a thousand who would have borne it as you have done."

Up to this time, everything is fresh to my recollection. Of that afternoon and night, I only remember that the pain in the wound was intense and unremitting, and that I felt willing to be just in the circumstances in which I was placed. I am told that Dr. Ford visited me once in the afternoon, and once in the night, that Persis and Asa took care of me, that it seemed as if I suffered nearly as much as during the operation, and that my wound was constantly wet with cold water. I have since told Persis that "I thought they kept me well drugged with paregoric." He replied, "We did not give you a drop." "Why then do I not remember what took place?" "Because you had so little life about you." By morning light the pain had ceased. Surgeons would understand the expression, that the wound healed by a "union of the first intention."

The morning again brought to my mind a recollection of events. I was lying on my lounge, feeble and helpless. I opened my eyes and saw the light of day. Asa was crossing the room bearing a Bible before him. He sat down near my couch, read a portion, and then prayed.

For several days, I had long sinking turns of several hours. Thursday night, the third of suffering, Thomas rode nearly two miles to the village for the Dr., once in the fore part of the evening, again at eleven. At both times he came. At two o'clock he unexpectedly made his third call that night. It was at his second call that he said to Persis: "In the morning make your mother some chicken soup. She has starved long enough." (They had been afraid of fever.) Persis immediately aroused Thomas, had a chicken caught, a fire made, and a soup under way that same midnight hour. The next day, Friday, I was somewhat revived by the use of wine and soup. In the afternoon, your father arrived. It was the first time since the operation, that I felt as if I had life enough to endure the emotion of seeing him. He left Kailua the same day the operation was performed. A vessel was passing in sight of Kailua. He rowed out in a canoe and was received on board. Hitherto, Persis, Asa and Thomas, had been my only nurses both by day and by night. The doctor gave directions that no one enter the room, but those that took care of me.

For weeks my debility was so great, that I was fed with a teaspoon, like an infant. Many dangers were apprehended. During one day, I saw a duplicate of every person and every thing that my eye beheld. Thus it was, sixteen years before, when I had the paralysis. Three weeks after the operation, your father for the first time, very slowly raised me to the angle of 45 degrees. It seemed as if it would have taken away my sense. It was about this time that I perceptibly improved from day to day, so much so, that in four weeks from my confinement, I was lifted into a carriage. Then I rode with your father almost every day. As he was away from his field of labor, and without any family responsibilities, he was entirely devoted to me. It was of great importance to me, that he was at liberty and in readiness ever to read simple interesting matter to me, to enliven and to cheer, so that time never passed heavily. After remaining with me six weeks, he returned to Kailua, leaving me with the physician and with our children.

In a few weeks, Mother, Mr. Taylor, Persis, Thomas, Lucy, Mary, and George bade farewell to Asa and Sarah, and to little Robert, their black-eyed baby boy. Together we passed over the rough channels up to the old homestead. Then, your father instead of eating his solitary meals, had his family board enlarged for the accommodation of three generations.

And here is again your mother, engaged in life's duties, and life's warfare. Fare thee well. Be one with us in knowledge, sympathy, and love, though we see thee not, and when sickness prostrates, we feel not thy hand upon our brow.

Your Loving Mother.

## 1855: DECEMBER 2
## HANNAH ANDERSON ROPES TO ELIZA CHANDLER

---

*Before there was a vast Civil War, there was a small civil war. Like the large one, it lasted years and was conjoined with the issue of slavery. Unlike the large one, it took place in only one location, which gave it its name: "Bleeding Kansas." The immediate cause of the fighting was the 1854 Kansas–Nebraska Act, which called for the two newly organized territories to decide the issue of slavery themselves. Nebraska was far enough north to be clearly free, but Kansas quickly became a battleground, with Northerners and Southerners rushing in to claim a majority. Hannah Anderson Ropes (1809–1863) spent six months homesteading in the Kansas Territory, having traveled west from Massachusetts with her two children. Her letters home, including this one to her sister-in-law, gave a vivid description of life on the edge. Eventually Ropes served as a nurse during the Civil War (see page 291).*

Missouri, a slave state, was directly east of the Kansas Territory. Large-scale fighting broke out in the town of Lawrence five months after this letter was written. Fifty-five people were killed, and the violence was responsible for hundreds of thousands of dollars in damage. Ultimately, Kansas would be admitted to the Union as a free state in January of 1861.

Lawrence, Dec. 2, 1855

My dear Sister,

We have suffered a very great deal from pain, sickness, and from want of comfortable things to make us warm, but not for food. The sick moan for good water—for lemons, oranges, and, as they get better, for oysters, and a thousand things a weakened mind remembers as among the luxuries of other times. But then came in quails, prairie chickens, and venison such as your epicures would smack their lips over, and when I am on my feet my head is as good as ever. Now I must tell you, we are in the midst of most serious preparations for <u>defensive war</u>. It is a week today since the rumor first reached Lawrence, that it is to be destroyed. Everybody is armed and everybody sleeps with their arms about them and clothes on. My sick Mr. Conry has been sent off, up into the territory, his brother is here: a drilled soldier from Baltimore, and when he is not on <u>watch</u>, which is two nights out of four, he rolls himself in his buffalo over my head. Edward and Lowrie, who is Adjutant General, sleeps in the tent made of the piano cloth in the corner of my room. I am getting quite used to fire arms. They all give me charge whenever they get in, at whatever hour, to be sure and call them if I hear the <u>call drum</u>—Our cabin is on the outskirts of the town, and quite in view of the prairie over which the Missourians must come. You can imagine how many times I listen while the weary men sleep, and how often I take a peep off to see if they are coming in upon us in the night time. Several tribes of Indians have sent in word that they will stand by us, and over two hundred soldiers have marched in from different settlements. Mr. Lowrie came in Wednesday and said, laughing, "What do you think that young varmint son of yours has been after? Why, he came up into our meeting, and demanded a sharp rifle! Of course we gave him one." Of course I am no judge of what is to be. I am most happy to bear witness, that in all things this Yankee town has shown the greatest forbearance and firmly resolved <u>not</u> to strike the first blow. Conservative Boston <u>might</u>, if she deigned to look so far off, be <u>proud</u> of the sturdy spirit of her sorely tried sons in Kanzas. I do not feel much like writing. I shall send my journal to <u>you</u> to be taken by <u>you</u> to my mother. I wish it preserved with the greatest care, as I shall sell it to some publisher if possible.

I have found Gov. Reeder a most agreeable acquaintance. There is also a Mr. Coats a lawyer from Philadelphia who has been most devotedly kind to us all through our sickness. He watched here many nights. I refused all others for myself. I hope you write often, tell me all about the family.

H. A. R.

## 1856: FEBRUARY 15
## ANNA PALFREY TO JOHN GORHAM PALFREY

*This letter was written by Anna Palfrey (1825–1900) to her father, future congressman John Gorham Palfrey (1796–1881). We offer it to refute the claim—or at least give evidence to the contrary—that Americans eat less healthily now than they did in decades past.*

Boston, Feb. 15th, 1856

Sarah joined us in soup and a chop at ½ past 2, and we then proceeded to the important business of the day, dressing for Emily's beautiful dinner. The guests were eighteen and went into the dining room after this fashion. Mrs. Parker and Nat. Emily and Gardiner. Lissy and Frank. Slade and I. Mr. and Mrs. Wm. Rodgers, Major Bowditch an Sam. Miss Deconimak (from Baltimore) and Willy Mason. Miss Lilly Mason and Charley Appleton. Miss Isabella Mason and Charles Gibson. Mrs. P. wore the rich black moire antique dress which Emily brought her. The younger ladies all wore evening dresses—blue, pink and yellow— low in the neck and short-sleeved—with coiffures of flowers or ribbons. The table was set with fruit, candy ornaments, bon-bons, bouquets, silver, china, and glass; but no dishes of meat or vegetables. All those things were handed from side-tables by 4 waiters. We began with white soup, and black. Then cusk à la creme, and smelts. Turkey with truffles. A fancy dish of chicken, which looked like Charlotte Russe. Venison, with mushrooms. Oyster patties. Sweet-breads. Grouse. Canvass-backs. Jelly. Tomatoes. Peas. Potatoes. Asparagus. Corn. Roman punch. Chocolate Blanc Mange. Wine Jelly. Apple Meringue. Cheesecakes. Tutti-frutti. Ice-cream. Frozen pudding. And several other dishes of this kind. Oranges. Grapes. Fine pears. Candied fruits of several kinds. Wines, etc. After dinner, tea and coffee in the drawing-room. And then almost all the guests adjourned to Mrs. Richard Fay's, to see beautiful Tableaux Vivants. Emily's dinner, even to uninitiated eyes, appeared superb, and the amateurs pronounce it very recherché and exquisite. It seems to have been considerably talked over, about town. I have been so completely out of the current of city life this winter, that I regard it with the primitive feelings of a rustic, and it surprises me to see the strength, and time, and still more the amount of interest, which the Boston girls bestow upon their daily and nightly plans of pleasure—flying so eagerly from one amusement to another, while to me it seems so hollow, and artificial, and unsatisfactory; indeed so wholly unattractive. I feel more seriously than ever that I am no longer young, and there seems to be a wall of separation arising between me and society, and shutting me out from the gay and laughter-loving. From the <u>happy</u>, I cannot say, because I have so much to make me happy, and I am so happy; but I sometimes fear it may be in rather a narrow and selfish way. . . .

### 1857: FEBRUARY 4
### MARY MICHIE TO JAMES MINOR

*As early as 1815, a black Quaker named Paul Cuffee had advocated the return of African-American immigrants to Africa, where they could "rise to be a people." It was a proposition that provided common ground for the slaveholders and abolitionists who shared the belief that blacks could never live comfortably in America. In 1820, the first expedition of the American Colonization Society, financed partly by a congressional grant, took eighty-eight black settlers to West Africa. By 1847, when Liberia declared itself an independent nation, some six thousand black Americans were living there. Ten years later, Mary Michie wrote this letter to James Minor, the nephew of her former owner.*

Monrovia, the capital of Liberia, was named for James Monroe, who was the United States president during the country's founding.

Monrovia Feby 4th 1857

My dear Sir

It affords me great pleasure to have this opportunity to address a letter to you. In the midst of danger & death, while we could discern nothing above, & around us but the blue canopy of heaven, & under ous the deep, deep blue sea, we we were Providentially cared for, and bless to reach this our destined port, Monrovia. I am much pleased with this place inded, Monrovia is nearly as large as Charlotsville and has some fine houses in it. The people here are very genteel. I thought to find things different, and that we would have to enlighten tha people, but I find that we need teaching ourselves. There was not a death during the passage out, and up to this date all our folks are well, and very well satisfied indeed. For myself, I would not go back to America no how. I leave to day for to go up the St Pauls river and see how it looks up there: and when I have got a better knowledge of the Country, I want to write you all about: so as you may be informed and others through you how & what the country is.

I expect to live in Monrovia, and would be pleased if would send me out some means to assist me in building me a place to live in, whatever you may be pleased to send me will be acceptable.

I beg to assure you that I have not experienced as warm a day yet in Liberia as I have generally experienced in the Summer in America, and this is the Summer season in Liberia. Just as soon as I can, I want to send you some Coffee from this country.

Since I have been here, I came across one member of the Paxton family who came to Liberia some years ago, you may know something about them. they came from the Carr family, Mr James O. Carr I think will have some knowledge of this family if you will mention it to him. The young man's name is John Henry Paxton, was but an infant when brought to this country, and is anxious to hear from his friends; he had an Aunt he says as his mother Huldah Paxton told him, that lived in Boucher Carr's family. Please direct our letters to his care as Post Master General.

Give my love to Mrs Minor, and the children and also receive a great portion for yourself, as well as the fulness of a greatful heart for the kindness of [your] dear unkle in emmancipating us, and your kindness in endeavoring to carry out his wishes & providing for us. My family all join in love to you. Give our love to all the colored folks, tell them how well we are and how pleased we are with the country. Fowls of the same kind as you have among you are here, hogs, sheep, goats, Cows &c Potatoes Yams, plantains, bananas, cassada, Rice, eddoes, tomatoes & vegetables of all kinds suited to tropical climates grow here. Our love to your dear children

I am your obedent servant

Mary Michey

*    *    *

### 1857: AUGUST 29
### VILET LESTER TO PATSEY PATTERSON

*Unlike Mary Michie (see previous letter), Vilet Lester was still living in slavery when she expressed loving feelings for a former mistress, to whom she described her succession of more recent owners.*

Georgia Bullock Co August 29th 1857

My Loving Miss Patsy

 I hav long bin wishing to imbrace this presant and pleasant opertunity of unfolding my Seans and fealings Since I was constrained to leav my Long Loved home and friends which I cannot never gave my Self the Least promis of returning to. I am well and this is Injoying good hlth and has ever Since I Left Randolph. Whend I left Randolf I went to Rockingham and Stad there five weaks and then I left there and went to Richmon virgina to be Sold and I Stade there three days and was bought by a man by the name of Groover and braught to Georgia and he kept me about Nine months and he being a trader Sold me to a man by the name of Rimes and he Sold me to a man by the name of Lester and he has owned me four years and Says that he will keep me til death Siperates us without Some of my old north Caroliner friends wants to buy me again. my Dear Mistress I cannot tell my fealings nor how bad I wish to See you and old Boss and Mss Rahol and Mother. I do not now which I want to See the worst Miss Rahol or mother I have thaugh that I wanted to See mother but never befour did I no what it was to want to See a parent and could not. I wish you to gave my love to old Boss Miss Rahol and bailum and gave my manafold love to mother brothers and sister and pleas to tell them to Right to me So I may here from them if I cannot See them and also I wish you to right to me and Right me all the nuse. I do want to now whether old Boss is Still Living or now and all the rest of them and I want to now whether balium is maried or no. I wish to now what has Ever become of my Presus little girl. I left her in goldsborough with Mr. Walker and I have not herd from her Since and Walker Said that he was going to Carry her to Rockingham and gave her to his Sister and I want to no whether he did or no as I do wish to See her very mutch and Boss Says he wishes to now whether he will Sell her or now and the least that can buy her and that he wishes a answer as Soon as he can get one as I wis him to buy her an my Boss being a man of Reason and fealing wishes to grant my trubled breast that mutch gratification and wishes to now whether he will Sell her now. So I must come to a close by Escribing my Self you long loved and well wishing play mate as a Servant until death

> Vilet Lester
> of Georgia
> to Miss Patsey Padison
> of North Caroliner

My Bosses Name is James B Lester and if you Should think a nuff of me to right me which I do beg the faver of you as a Sevant direct your letter to Millray Bullock County Georgia. Pleas to right me So fare you well in love.

### 1857: SEPTEMBER 21
### JULIA LOUISA LOVEJOY TO THE <u>INDEPENDENT DEMOCRAT</u>

---

*A native of Lebanon, New Hampshire, Julia Louisa Hardy Lovejoy (1812–1882) moved to Kansas with her minister husband, Charles, and their children two years before writing this letter. While they were on their way west with an antislavery group called the New England Emigrant Aid Company, the Lovejoys' youngest child contracted measles and died. Julia persevered. Apart from the perils of the still-fractious "Bleeding Kansas" (see page 241), she found herself facing heat, illness, and—as she made particularly clear in this letter home to her local newspaper—the ever present threat of snakes.*

To "look someone out of countenance" meant to make them ashamed. "Miss Bidd" may have referred to a biddy, a nineteenth-century word for chick.

> Palmyra, K.T.
> Sept. 21, 1857

Messrs. Editors:—

We will here give our experience in getting acclimated to Kansas, as we have spent three summers here. The first summer, we suffered but little sickness, as a family, and began to congratulate ourselves, that whatever else we might suffer here, we should enjoy as good health as in New Hampshire. The following summer our entire family had the "fever and ague," and some of us for months. Last spring, Mr. L. had the ague again for weeks, severely, and the present dry summer the most of our family have been sick, and I have not seen a day when I felt well and able to work as formerly. Others we meet with, who have not suffered with sickness at all.

As our letter is not full, and we write but little at a time, in detached sentences, we would like to tell your lady readers what has been, and is still, the bane of our life, in this beautiful country—we refer to <u>snakes</u>! We can face a wild cat, and endeavor to "look him out of countenance," when he became too tame to be endured, as we have stood in our cabin door, at the "Mouth of the Big Blue," and done more than once, and with uplifted axe, drove the intruder to the woods, after he had throttled and devoured the last of the race of Miss Bidd's, in our possession, save one, and that, through our powers of locomotion and self-possession, was rescued from a fearful ride, of perhaps twenty rods, on his back, with her head in his teeth, tho' the poor creature was so dreadfully lacerated in the encounter, she suffered decapitation immediately after the rescue!

We will tell some of the little boys, in New Hampshire, if ever we go there, how, day after day, when he would come into the dooryard, and up under our little window, we would get Charlie's big double-barrelled gun, and rest it on the window-sill, so near that ten feet would have reached him, yet we never had courage to go through the experiment, notwithstanding Charlie's systematic lessons and training, we never could come to the practical part of it, and he was sure to come when we were alone, or in the night.

Let a copper-head or a rattlesnake make their appearance, and our courage is all gone. We have never enjoyed a walk in the garden, or gathering plums, or, indeed, sleeping in our unfinished cabin in warm weather, on account of these intruders. I will tell three stories, if not more, about our neighbors' being bitten by snakes. Mrs. Sanders, wife of Capt. Sanders, formerly of Massachusetts, one extremely warm night, spread her bed on the ground inside of their cabin, as they had no floor, took her babe and one or two other children, and lay herself down to sleep. In the night she turned herself over to nurse her babe, and felt something sting her under lip severely; the pain increasing, she called on her husband, who slept elsewhere, who got a light and went to a trunk to get some "pain-killer," and there coiled behind the trunk was a rattlesnake; her lip continuing to swell shockingly, he ran for some neighbors, and when he returned found two more rattlesnakes in his cabin, and his poor wife in awful agony—her lip turned black, and one who saw it informed me that it looked as large as her arm—her head and neck swelled to her shoulders—her eyes assumed the peculiar look of a snake's eyes, and as long as she could speak, in piteous tones, she begged "them to keep the snakes from biting her children." It was with great difficulty the physician could keep her from choking to death; he scar[r]ed her neck all around in places that had turned black, and by a miracle almost, though great suffering, she was saved!

Now taking all the attendant circumstances into the account, is not this an unparalleled kiss? Another:—A young lady living about a mile from us, felt something crawling up her side, as she lay reclining on the other in bed, and supposing it to be her little "pet kitten," and not wishing to be disturbed in her slumbers, rudely pushed it away with her hand, when lo! the ominous sound! she shrieked to her mother, "a rattlesnake!" and sprung for a light, and there lay his snakeship, who was soon captured by mother and daughter, and expiated his detestable propensities, by being mauled to death with "sundry billets of wood."

Mrs. Anderson, a lady 50 or more years of age, who lived on the opposite side of the Big Blue from us, threw her arms over her head in the night, as was her wont, when she felt a peculiar stinging sensation on her hand; she called for a light, and to her horror, saw a large copper-head over the head of her bed; she set up a terrific scream, supposing, probably, she had received her "death wound"—a messenger was dispatched for Dr. W., our son-in-law, who has had a number of such cases, and though her arm swelled dreadfully, to her shoulder, she was soon entirely cured.

Our only daughter was bitten on the side of her foot, through a kid bootee, as she was walking in the grove near our dwelling; and her husband being from home, it devolved on us, ignorant as we were in such cases, to try and save her life; and for the benefit of those in a similar dilemma, we will tell the process, which was afterwards pronounced "right." We first tied a strong ligature tightly above the ankle, applied our lips to extract the poison as far as possible, and gave her as much whiskey as we could get her to take, to keep it from her stomach— (by the way, the first "ardent spirits," under any circumstances, placed to the lips of a child by the writer.) The Doctor soon returned, and, though somewhat alarmed, the patient recovered, after suffering the pain of a swollen foot and some lameness. A timber rattlesnake, and prairie, are very different, the former being far worse than the latter.

Julia Louisa Lovejoy.

## 1859: FEBRUARY 20
## LUCY STONE TO ANTOINETTE BLACKWELL

*With a wistfulness that would be felt by generations of working mothers, suffragist Lucy Stone (see page 205), whose daughter, Alice, was not yet two, confided her new priorities to her sister-in-law Antoinette Blackwell. Eventually, Stone resumed her hectic lecture schedule as well as her broader societal goals. In 1893, her dying words to Alice would be: "Make the world better."*

Thomas Wentworth Higginson was an abolitionist, women's rights crusader, and Unitarian minister who had officiated at the marriage of Stone and Henry Blackwell. Frederick Douglass was the famous black abolitionist. E. P. Whipple was a well-known critic and lecturer.

Sunday, Feb. 20, 1859

Dear Nettie:

Today you are preaching for Mr. Higginson. It is the day you were to have been here. I felt a little chagrined at the result of our plan. Now if you will come I do think we can get you up some meetings that will pay you even better than $100, & your expenses.

Fred Douglass had a very large audience paying twenty-five cents, & you would draw as well as he did. I wish I felt the old impulse & power to lecture, both for the sake of cherished principles & to help Harry with the heavy burden he has to bear,—but I am afraid, & dare not trust Lucy Stone. I went to hear E. P. Whipple lecture on Joan d'Arc. It was very inspiring, & for the hour I felt as though all things were possible to me. But when I came home & looked in Alice's sleeping face & thought of the possible evil that might befall her if my guardian eye was turned away, I shrank like a snail into its shell, & saw that for these years I can be only a mother—no trivial thing either. I hope you gave a good sermon today.

Yours truly,<br>Lucy

### 1859: AUGUST 30
### ADDIE BROWN TO REBECCA PRIMUS

---

*It is not known when or how Addie Brown (1841–1870) met Rebecca Primus (1836–1932). Brown was a relatively uneducated black servant who worked in a variety of New England homes, and Primus was a black educator from a prominent Hartford, Connecticut, family. Somehow, despite the differences in their backgrounds, they forged a friendship that was extraordinarily intimate, and, as the letter below suggests, almost certainly sexual.*
Primus moved to the South after the Civil War to teach freed slaves. Both women eventually married.

Waterbury Aug. 30 1859

My ever Dear Friend

I no doubt you will be surprise to received a letter so soon I think it will be received with just as much pleasure this week as you will nexe my <u>Dearest Dearest</u>

<u>Rebecca</u> my heart is allmost broke   I dont know that I ever spent such hours as I have my loving friend   it goes harder with me now then it ever did   I am more acquainted with you   it seem to me this very moments if I only had the wings of a <u>dove</u> I would not remain long in Waterbury   although we cant allway be together O it tis hard

O Dear I am so lonesome I barely know how to contain myself   if I was only near you and having one of those <u>sweet</u> kisses. Man appoint and God disappoints. There is not much news here worthy to attention   there is going to be a picnic tomorry the Childrens temperance Jubilee. The hand of hope will be celebrated to   it will be a grand affair. Mr. Pete Sinclair the well known apostle of temperance will address the Gathering   I supose it tis quit gay in Hartford

O my <u>Dear</u> Friend how I did miss you   last night I did not have any one to hug me and to kiss. Rebecca dont you think I am very foolish   I dont want anyone to kiss me now   I turn Mr Games away this morning no <u>kisses</u> is like yours

You are the first Girl that I ever <u>love</u> so it you are the <u>last</u> one   Dear Rebecca do not say anything against me <u>loving</u> you so for I mean just what I say   O Rebecca it seem I can see you now casting those loving eyes at me   if you was a man what would things come to   they would after come to something very quick   what do you think the matter   dont laugh at me   I must say I dont know that I every injoyed myself any better than I did when I was at your parents house. I was treated so rich by all the Family I hope I may have the extreme pleasure returning the same pleasure to you all   each will remember the visit   as for your self Dear H there is no one like her if you was to travel all over united states

Affectionate Friend<br>Addie

PS give my love to all the Family and kiss also to your Mo.

Addie

please to write soon

## 1859: OCTOBER 17
## MARY MAUZY TO EUGENIA BURTON

---

*Harpers Ferry, a town then in Virginia (now in West Virginia), was the site of a federal arsenal and the target of the famous raid that would galvanize both sides in the Civil War. Abolitionist John Brown, along with sixteen fellow white men and five black men, seized the armory and sixty hostages on the night of October 16. Their goal: to set up a separate area for freed slaves in the mountains of Virginia and Maryland. Local and federal troops were called in, seventeen people were killed (including two of Brown's sons), and two days later, the remaining raiders were arrested. Before it was over, Mary Mauzy, mother-in-law of the former head of the armory, described the events in this frightened letter to her daughter, Eugenia Burton.*

October 17, 1859
Monday afternoon
4 o'clock

Oh my dear friend such a day as this. Heaven forbid that I should ever witness such another.

Last night a band of ruffians took possession of the town, took the keys of the armory and made Captive a great many of our Citizens. I cannot write the particulars for I am too Nervous. For such a sight as I have just beheld. Our men chased them in the river just below here and I saw them shot down like dogs. I saw one poor wrech rise above the water and some one strike him with a club   he sank again and in a moment they dragged him out a Corpse. I do not know yet how many are shot but I shall never forget the sight. They just marched two wreches their Arms bound fast up to the jail. My dear husband shouldered his rifle and went to join our men May god protect him. Even while I write I hear the guns in the distance   I heard they were fighting down the street.

I cannot write any more   I must wait and see what the end will be.

M. E. Mauzy

## 1859: OCTOBER 26
## LYDIA MARIA CHILD TO HENRY WISE

*John Brown's raid proved to be a powerful catalyst; in his poem "The Portent," Herman Melville would call Brown "the meteor of the war." For Lydia Maria Child (see page 183), as for many Northern abolitionists, Brown's violence was abhorrent, but his cause was never in question. When, in this letter, Child asked Governor Henry Wise (1806–1876) to let her visit and nurse the wounded Brown, she gave a glimpse of the martyrdom he would eventually attain. Wise, in his reply, said there was no legal reason why Child should not visit, but added: "We have no sympathy with your sentiments of sympathy."*

Ultimately Child did not visit; in a letter, Brown asked her instead to help raise money for his remaining children, daughters-in-law, and wife.

Wayland, Mass., Oct. 26th, 1859.

Governor Wise:

I have heard that you were a man of chivalrous sentiments, and I know you were opposed to the iniquitous attempt to force upon Kansas a Constitution abhorrent to the moral sense of her people. Relying upon these indications of honor and justice in your character, I venture to ask a favor of you. Enclosed is a letter to Capt. John Brown. Will you have the kindness, after reading it yourself, to transmit it to the prisoner?

I and all my large circle of abolition acquaintances were taken by surprise when news came of Capt. Brown's recent attempt; nor do I know of a single person who would have approved of it, had they been apprised of his intention. But I and thousands of others feel a natural impulse of sympathy for the brave and suffering man. Perhaps God, who sees the inmost of our souls, perceives some such sentiment in your heart also. He needs a mother or sister to dress his wounds, and speak soothingly to him. Will you allow me to perform that mission of humanity? If you will, may God bless you for the generous deed!

I have been for years an uncompromising Abolitionist, and I should scorn to deny it or apologize for it as much as John Brown himself would do. Believing in peace principles, I deeply regret the step that the old veteran has taken, while I honor his humanity towards those who became his prisoners. But because it is my habit to be as open as the daylight, I will also say, that if I believed our religion justified men in fighting for freedom, I should consider the enslaved every where as best entitled to that right. Such an avowal is a simple, frank expression of my sense of natural justice.

But I should despise myself utterly if any circumstances could tempt me to seek to advance these opinions in any way, directly or indirectly, after your permission to visit Virginia has been obtained on the plea of sisterly sympathy with a brave and suffering man. I give you my word of honor, which was never broken, that I would use such permission solely and singly for the purpose of nursing your prisoner, and for no other purpose whatsoever.

Yours, respectfully,<br>L. Maria Child

*    *    *

1859: NOVEMBER 20
MAHALA DOYLE TO JOHN BROWN

*Although best known for his Harpers Ferry action, John Brown (1800–1859) had also been active in the "Bleeding Kansas" war (see page 241). In 1856 he had led a brutal uprising against a group of proslavery settlers at Pottawatomie Creek. Mahala Doyle, the widow of one of the victims there, made her feelings about Brown clear in this letter.* By all accounts, Brown received this type of hate mail, as well as hundreds of visitors from both sides, with profound grace. To his wife he wrote: "I have been *whiped* as the saying *is,* but am sure I can recover all the lost capital occasioned by that disaster; by only hanging a few moments by the neck." Brown was found guilty of murder, treason, and slave insurrection; he was hanged on December 2.

Chattanooga, Tennessee Nov. 20th, 1859

John Brown:—Sir,—

Altho' vengence is not mine, I confess that I do feel gratified to hear that you were stopped in your fiendish career at Harper's Ferry, with the loss of your two sons, you can now appreciate my distress in Kansas, when you then & there entered my house at midnight and arrested my Husband and two boys, and took them out of the yard and in cold blood shot them dead in my hearing, you can't say you done it to free slaves, we had none and never expected to own one, but has only made me a poor disconsolate widow, with helpless children, while I feel for your folly I do hope & trust that you will meet your just reward. O how it pained my heart to hear the dying groans of my Husband & children, if this scrawl gives you any consolation you are welcome to it

Mahala Doyle

N.B. My son John Doyle whose life I beged of you is now grown up and is very desirous to be at Charlestown on the day of your execution, would certainly be there if his means would permit it that he might adjust the rope around your neck if Gov. Wise would permit it.

M. Doyle

1859(?): DECEMBER 15
FRANCES ELLEN WATKINS HARPER TO WILLIAM STILL

*Hard statistics are difficult to come by, and estimates of the number of slaves helped to freedom by the Underground Railroad vary from forty thousand to one hundred thousand. What is clear is that before the Civil War, an organized network of secret destinations, known as "stations," provided support for runaways, known as "packages," on routes, known as "lines," that moved from southern to northern states. Born in the free state of Maryland, Frances Ellen Watkins Harper (1825–1911) was orphaned at the age of three and raised by an uncle who was a teacher and abolitionist. She became a poet, a novelist, and, by the 1850s, an antislavery speaker. William Still (1821–1902), a free black Philadelphian, was part of the Railroad network.*

I send you to-day two dollars for the Underground Rail Road. It is only a part of what I subscribed at your meeting. May God speed the flight of the slave as he speeds through our Republic to gain his liberty in a monarchical land. I am still in the lecturing field, though not very strong physically. . . . Send me word what I can do for the fugitive.

## 1860: FEBRUARY 20
## SARAH LOGUE TO J. W. LOGUEN

*The mounting frustration of a Tennessee slave owner is bizarrely evident in the letter she wrote to a former slave, whose new status she was as unwilling to accept as she was powerless to change. Jermain Wesley Loguen (1814–1872) was a station-master on the Underground Railroad and had already published his autobiography the year before receiving this letter. He went on to become a bishop of the African Methodist Episcopal Zion Church. To this letter from his former owner, he responded: "You say 'You know we raised you as we did our own children.' Woman, did you raise your own children for the market? Did you raise them for the whipping post?"*

Maury County, State of Tennessee,
Feb. 20, 1860.

To Jarm:—

I now take my pen to write you a few lines, to let you know how we all are. I am a cripple, but I am still able to get about. The rest of the family are all well. Cherry is as well as common. I write you these lines to let you know the situation we are in,—partly in consequence of your running away and stealing Old Rock, our fine mare. Though we got the mare back, she never was worth much after you took her;—and, as I now stand in need of some funds, I have determined to sell you, and I have had an offer for you, but did not see fit to take it. If you will send me one thousand dollars, and pay for the old mare, I will give up all claim I have to you. Write to me as soon as you get these lines, and let me know if you will accept my proposition. In consequence of your running away, we had to sell Abe and Ann and twelve acres of land; and I want you to send me the money, that I may be able to redeem the land that you was the cause of our selling, and on receipt of the above-named sum of money, I will send you your bill of sale. If you do not comply with my request, I will sell you to some one else, and you may rest assured that the time is not far distant when things will be changed with you. Write to me as soon as you get these lines. Direct your letter to Bigbyville, Maury County, Tennessee. You had better comply with my request.

I understand that you are a preacher. As the Southern people are so bad, you had better come and preach to your old acquaintances. I would like to know if you read your Bible. If so, can you tell what will become of the thief if he does not repent? and, if the blind lead the blind, what will the consequence be? I deem it unnecessary to say much more at present. A word to the wise is sufficient. You know where the liar has his part. You know that we reared you as we reared our own children; that you was never abused, and that shortly before you ran away, when your master asked you if you would like to be sold, you said you would not leave him to go with any body.

Sarah Logue

## 1860: MAY 21

## ANNIE DICKSON TO MARY TODD LINCOLN

*Three days after the Chicago convention at which Abraham Lincoln received the Republican Party's nomination for president, Annie Parker Dickson, a cousin of Mary Todd Lincoln (1818–1882), wrote her a letter of congratulations that is remarkable only for its pettiness.*

Annie's husband, William Martin Dickson, was a Republican lawyer and activist who would eventually help frame the Emancipation Proclamation. Salmon Chase was governor of Ohio and a candidate for the nomination. The Dicksons lived in Cincinnati.

Dear Cousin Mary,

Let me congratulate you upon the success of your husband, whom I have always loved so much. You are an ambitious little woman and for many reasons I am delighted with your success. I have a little ambition myself in a <u>quiet way</u>

My husband has as much as your self, <u>his day is to come</u>. Yours has come and I do wish Mr Lincoln success I was delighted that the <u>Judge</u> was defeated for delegate to the convention, for his hands would have been tied by Chase while his heart was with Lincoln. Hurrah for old Abe!!! We will do what we can to make him <u>President</u>!

I have just come from Mr. White's (Mag Wooley of Lexington)   Cousin Lydia Wilson is there, they will take tea with me to morrow evening. I take particular pleasure in expressing my delight—knowing that not a Wickliffe will give a vote to Lincoln. I am on this side of the line & what I please for my heart is with old Abe on the slavery question   Keep cool cousin Mary for you might be disappointed

as ever your cousin
Annie Dickson

## 1860: OCTOBER 18
## GRACE BEDELL TO ABRAHAM LINCOLN

*As the presidential election neared, an eleven-year-old New York girl felt moved to send this bold suggestion to Abraham Lincoln (1809–1865). The coming war would soon make it almost unimaginable for Lincoln to take time to answer such a letter. But he did reply, asking: "As to the whiskers, having never worn any, do you think people would call it a piece of silly affection if I were to begin it now?"*
By the following year, when, as president-elect, he met Bedell, Lincoln had grown his famous beard. Hannibal Hamlin was Lincoln's running mate and first vice president.

Westfield, Chatauque Co NY
Oct 18—1860

Dear Sir

My father has just home from the fair and brought home your picture and Mr. Hamlin's. I am a little girl only eleven years old, but want you should be President of the United States very much so I hope you wont think me very bold to write to such a great man as you are. Have you any little girls about as large as I am if so give them my love and tell her to write to me if you cannot answer this letter. I have got 4 brother's and part of them will vote for you any way and if you will let your whiskers grow I will try and get the rest of them to vote for you   you would look a great deal better for your face is so thin. All the ladies like whiskers and they would tease their husband's to vote for you and then you would be President. My father is a going to vote for you and if I was a man I would vote for

you to but I will try and get every one to vote for you that I can    I think that rail
fence around your picture makes it look very pretty    I have got a little baby sister she is nine weeks old and is just as cunning as can be. When you direct your
letter dirct to Grace Bedell Westfield Chatauque County New York

    I must not write any more    answer this letter right off

                Good bye

                Grace Bedell

# CIVIL WAR

# 1861

~

# 1865

Forgive your dying daughter. I have but a few moments to live. My native soil drinks my blood. I expected to deliver my country but the fates would not have it so. I am content to die. Pray, Pa, forgive me.

*—A soldier to her father*
*November 24, 1863*

THE UNION VOLUNTEER.

# BETWEEN 1861 AND 1865 . . .

**1861**: Mississippi, Florida, Alabama, Georgia, Louisiana, and Texas secede from the Union and, along with South Carolina, establish the Confederate States of America, with Jefferson Davis as provisional president. ★ Confederates capture Fort Sumter in South Carolina; several days later, a *New York Times* reporter writes: "The excessive excitement which followed the first announcement of the bombardment and reduction of Sumter is succeeded by a more calm and settled appreciation of the great fact that civil war is upon us." ★ Congress abolishes the practice of flogging in the army. ★ Under a new law pertaining to real estate tax collection, being a married woman is described as a "disability" equivalent to being an infant or an insane person. ★ To help finance the war, the U.S. government introduces paper money; popularly called greenbacks (because of the color of their reverse sides), the notes must be hand-signed by representatives of the Treasurer and the Register of the Treasury. **1862**: The U.S. issues greenbacks engraved with the signatures of the Register of the Treasury and the Treasurer rather than hand-signed. ★ Julia Ward Howe publishes "Battle Hymn of the Republic"

---

Clockwise from top left: Julia Ward Howe; "The Lincoln Assassination at Ford's Theatre" by Currier & Ives; Richmond defeated; Charleston *Mercury* "Extra" announcing South Carolina's secession from the Union; Clara Barton; Dead Civil War soldier; "The Union Volunteer" sheet music cover; Emancipation Proclamation commemorative broadside; Belle Boyd; New York City Draft Riots.

anonymously in *The Atlantic Monthly*. ★ Richard Gatling patents the machine gun, but it will not be accepted by the U.S. ordnance department until after the war. ★ In Massachusetts, an editorial writer for the *Adams Transcript* rails about the first White House ball ever given: "The ladies were dressed in the highest style of fashion and extravagance, especially Mrs. Lincoln. . . . About 12 the supper room was thrown open, and exhibited . . . a temple of Liberty, a fort and a war steamer, admirably moulded in candy, and a ton of turkeys, ducks, venison, pheasants, partridges, &c., all exquisitely prepared by Maillard, of New York. . . . While the country is shaken as by an earthquake by the mightiest and most unnatural civil war recorded in history . . . such an extravagant and foolish display is shocking." ★ Some 23,000 Americans are wounded or killed in two days of fighting at Shiloh in Tennessee—more than in all previous American wars combined. ★ During the Battle of Antietam, a bullet passes through nurse Clara Barton's sleeve and kills the man she is tending. ★ Abraham Lincoln signs the Homestead Act into law, making roughly 10 percent of United States land available to private citizens who are willing to put up an $18 filing fee, live on their claim, farm it for five years, and build a home. ★ Having provided information to General Stonewall Jackson about Union plans, Confederate spy Belle Boyd is informed on by her lover and arrested; she will later be released in a prisoner exchange. **1863:** Lincoln issues the Emancipation Proclamation, abolishing slavery. ★ Dr. James Caleb Jackson introduces the first breakfast cereal; called Granula, it is so thick with bran that it has to be soaked overnight to be chewable. ★ In New York City, 11 black men are lynched and $1.5 million of property damage is done during four days of riots protesting the draft and the federal provision that allows wealthier draftees to buy their way out of the army. ★ James Plimpton of Medford, Massachusetts, invents the four-wheeled roller skate; unlike the in-line wheels of earlier versions, the "quad" allows more control and initiates an international roller-skating fad. ★ The *Confederate Receipt Book* recommends that for a sore throat, diphtheria, or scarlet fever, one should, "Mix in a common size cup of fresh milk two teaspoonfuls of pulverized charcoal and ten drops of spirits of turpentine. Soften the charcoal with a few drops of milk before putting into the cup. Gargle frequently, according to the violence of the symptoms." ★ At the dedication of the National Cemetery, Lincoln delivers the Gettysburg Address before a crowd of thousands; the next day, the ceremony's main speaker, Edward Everett, writes to Lincoln: "I wish that I could flatter myself that I had come as near to the central idea of the occasion in two hours as you did in two minutes." **1864:** Following new currency legislation, the words "In God we trust" appear for the first time, on a two-cent coin; the previous law pertaining to mottoes on currency had called only for the word "Liberty." ★ Within this year, according to her diary, author Lydia Maria Child corrects the proofs for a forthcoming book, writes 53 new articles, tends sick friends and family members, sews 83 items of clothing and linen (in addition to mending others), and "Cooked 360 dinners; Cooked 362 breakfasts; Swept & dusted sitting-room & kitchen 350 times; Filled lamps 362 times." ★ Union General William Tecumseh Sherman begins his march across Georgia to the sea. **1865:** John B. Stetson opens his first factory in Philadelphia, making the "ten-gallon hat," so called because its waterproof lining allows it to be used as a bucket; in fact, its capacity is a half gallon. ★ Robert E. Lee says: "It would be useless and therefore cruel to provoke the further effusion of blood, and I have arranged to meet with General Grant with a view to surrender"; on the afternoon of April 9, Lee surrenders to Grant at Appomattox Courthouse in Virginia. ★ On the evening of April 14, Lincoln is fatally shot by John Wilkes Booth; in Lincoln's pockets are newspaper clippings, two pairs of glasses, a lens polisher, a watch fob, a penknife, a handkerchief, and a small wallet holding a $5 Confederate bill.

*Abraham Lincoln was elected on November 6, 1860, and was sworn in on March 4, 1861, as the sixteenth president of the United States. In the interim, tensions soared, six states seceded from the Union, and, as this virulent letter from a militant prosecessionist Virginian attests, the dialogue between North and South grew ever more shrill.*

We were unable to locate any information about the author of this letter; its recipient, almost as obscure, was apparently married to someone who worked in the Richmond auditor's office. She was also the sister of an Alexandria innkeeper named James Jackson, who became famous for shooting Elmer Ellsworth, the man many consider to have been the first casualty of the war (Jackson promptly became the second). Major Robert Anderson commanded the Federal troops stationed at Fort Sumter. Henry Wise was governor of Virginia and had been in office during John Brown's capture and execution. Peter Schlemihl (not Schymel) was the title character in a novel by Adelbert Chamisso. A kirtle was a long dress worn with a coronation gown.

Capitol Hill
Jany. 8th 1861

My dear Mrs. T.

I waded over to Geo Town the other day in the mud, cold, slush, snow & Geo Town nastiness generally, to try & hear some account of you & your politic. You may believe I was some what "rampant" when Mrs Stewart told me that you had been to W. City & was actually living in Alexandria yes living in town—and I all the time thinking of you as the innocent charming spirit of the woods and mistress of the darling romantic cottage.... it was provoking in you not to say a word or send me a line as to the moving crisis—& of your Secession from <u>dear</u> Fairfax to woe begone Alexandria. How do you know but that I might have gotten up some Military display for upon my word your perseverence & energy in carrying the point of "going to town to live" in spite of all obsticles equals Major Andersons removal to Fort Sumpter—I suppose tho' that you no longer care for

us unhappy doomed Washingtonians, & that already you look upon our beautiful city as the future Pigstye of Black republicanism—My Dear is'nt it awful to
think what we are coming to—no wonder respectable Virginians feel a contempt for a people who say Lincoln must be peaceably inaugurated in our midst
to live in the "White House" surrounded by his black faced & hearted followers
that he is to dictate, usurp & ride rough shode generally over Southern blood—
I declare it is frightful—if Virginia dont rally to the rescue—there is no knowing
what will become of us—if she dont—& in the future you see us all leaning on
the arms & acknowledging great fat niggers for our "Lords & Masters"—dont
blame us or think it is our own taste or judgement but remember one has to suc-
comb to circumstances. When I think over the times & fall into a train of
thought I exclaim to myself is it possible, I have lived an old maid up to this time
to end in becoming a niggers wife—Would to heaven I had married old Pete
Cash years ago—but patience & a hope & trust in Virginias aid—maybe we can
"Keep 'em" out 4th March—I heard of your brothers company—& I said all hail
& honor be to your good & patriotic son of your country—if we had a few such
as you no fear of the great spindle shank flat footed villians of the "Linkum"
order, casting an anchor this ground—I go my death for Jims company, & have a
mind to give them a Flag—with the inscription, Lincoln the elect of traitors to
the South—away with him, we own him not & never shall his presence pollute
the roof that once sheltered the immortal Washington—"Ain't that splendid sister Milly"    I was surprised to find Mrs. Stewart & your brother Charles Union
& compromise, & calling Jim cracked on the subject—I felt chocked full of
fight—& would have pitched into them—but for fear of raising the convent
alarm bells—of course you think as I do everlasting ruin & confusion to Lincoln
& company. If it was'nt for Sue, I don the pantaloons & musket join Gov. Wise
& be one of the first to put the halter on old Abe's neck—I expect you will be
worried to death reading this letter for I am not half done yet but my dear friend
politic is my existance now I eat politic—drink politic (Tea is no wheres with
me) only think of that—I sleep on politic, dress up in politic, & when I say my
prayers say I Believe in God, the South & Governor Wise, unconditional secession the utter destruction, hanging up and shooting down of Abe Linkums party
& followers, the resurrection of the South with Virginia as its head leader &
Washington City its Capitol I tell you I feel equal to becoming a second Joan
d'Arc—Now I want Mr Thomas to come out—now is his time—<u>now he has the
oppertunity</u> to bring out the elements of success in his character that have hitherto slept now is the time for a man to leave his name to fame, when his ashes
shall have mingled with earth & consecrated the soil upon which they repose—

Now is Mr Thomas for himself & his country—now if he leaves the quibbling talking scarey distrustful of the future party, and onward in faith with a voice that shall ring forth over the country. Virginia foremost in freeing herself from English despotism, is also ready to repel the vile traitorous Republican invaders of her fireside & of her sister states. Great & stirring times bring forth the contingent points in mens character & how often a decided action, turns the wheel of fortune when all seems against us & places us upon a stand of immortality. For a man of talent to belong to a party—that preaches us "let us wait a while" in such times as these, it is a moral suicide—and he undeserving of christian burial—You see I am on the "rampage" about Mr. Thomas. Dont you think I had better write him & may be he would show the letter to "Lundy" & so I'd have the consolation of rescuing two standerd bearers to my countrys glory—If you want to become a great mans wife, now is your time—If Virginia takes her stand, & does the fair thing all will come out glorious & prosperous in end—if she dont why we are the meanest dirtiest set on earth we are no better than Easeau who sold his birth right for mess of potage & a great deal worse than Peter Schymel, who sold his shadow to the devil—When I look over at the Capitol, & down our broad avenue—then at the clear blue sky resting as it were up the unfinished top of Washingtons Monument in an embrace of love & protection, at the bright waters of the old Potomac worshiping at is base—I think is this all to pass into the hands of traitors—who are trying to pull down the institutions he built up with his blood, that men whose wifes breakfast at candle light—scour tins & mop up the floors of their houses—are to ride rampant over us, I say Good Lord! Shade of Washington! & Mrs Martha's velvet Kirtle preserve us from such a vulgar calamity—As soon as you can come up—it is only ten cents now, between us, and who would'nt pay ten cents to hear me on Politic. How are you & the children—If I can I will run down & see you but my dear for the truth you know, outside politic I have a deal of writing to do—& have to be punctual but I will run over if I can—but for heaven sake keep Mr Thomas on the right side— & dont you notic any one, that dont preach everlasting smash, fire & sword to a union under Lincoln—Love to all the children & as ever

Your friend<br>Julia Matie

P.S. my best respects & three cheers for Jim & his soldiers

*   *   *

### 1861: FEBRUARY
### A LADY TO ABRAHAM LINCOLN

---

*Between his election and his inauguration, Abraham Lincoln received nearly eighty written death threats, as well as letters reporting dreams, prophecies, premonitions, and, as in the case below, assassination plots.*

February 1861

Dear Sir

I think it my duty to inform you that I was assured last night by a gentleman that there existed in Baltimore, a league of ten persons, who had sworn that you should never pass through that city alive—This may be but one of the thousand threats against you that have amanated from some paltry Southerners, but you should know it that your friends may be watchful while you are in the place, as it was asserted positively to be the fact. God defend and bless you—The prayers of many go with you!

A Lady

Friday Morning
11 1/2 A. M.

### 1861: FEBRUARY 9
### MARY CUSTIS LEE TO ELIZABETH STILES

---

*Choosing sides in the war would not always be clear-cut. As a U.S. Army general, Robert E. Lee was ordered out of Texas when it seceded from the Union on February 1. Back home in Arlington, Virginia, he awaited his own state's decision, writing to a friend: "I can anticipate no greater calamity for the country than the dissolution of the Union." In this letter, Lee's wife, Mary Custis Lee (1808–1873), expressed similar sentiments to Elizabeth Mackay Stiles (1809–1867), the wife of William Henry Stiles, a Georgia planter and politician.*

In April, Lee would be offered the command of the Union army, but despite his objections to secession, he would decline the offer, declaring, "I cannot raise my hand against my birthplace, my home, my children." In due time he became general in chief of the Confederate army—and the man who surrendered at Appomattox. Custis, Rooney, Mildred, Rob, Mary, Annie, and Agnes were the nicknames of the Lees' children. Haman, the fifth-century B.C. Persian minister, was hanged on the gallows he had prepared for the Jewish hero Mordecai.

Arlington February 9th 1861

I only this evening my dear friend received your letter written on the 5th of January. Where could it have been all this time? Not intercepted I hope by the Secessionists. You directed it to Alex[andri]a whereas we have changed our Post Office now to Arlington near <u>Washington</u> DC. I am so much obliged to you for thinking of me in these troubled times, tho I have thought much of you & yours & a few days since had determined to write to you to know if you <u>could approve</u> of all these riotous proceedings. Has all love & pride in their Country died at the South? That they are willing to tear her in pieces & some even to exult to see her glorious flag trailing in the dust. It should rather have drawn tears from their eyes. We have lived & fought & prospered under this flag for so many years & tho the South has <u>suffered</u> much from the <u>meddling</u> of Northern fanatics, yet do they expect to fare better now; are there no rights & privileges but those of negro slavery? You by your situation are removed from any <u>active</u> interference, whereas *we* in the border states are so much annoyed that our slaves have become almost useless. In our own family we have lost numbers who have been decoyed off, & after my Father's death we were preserved from an outbreak excited by two abolitionists who were constantly over here (as we learned afterwards, one of whom I am happy to say is now in the penitentiary for 14 years) we were preserved I say by the <u>special</u> mercy of God. The Tribune & New York Times published the most <u>villainous</u> attacks upon my husband by <u>name</u> & upon my Father's memory in language I would not pollute my lips by repeating, & yet after all these wrongs—I would lay down my life could I save our "Union." What is the use of a government combined as ours is of so many parts the <u>Union</u> of which forms its strength & power if any <u>one part</u> has the right for any wrong real or imaginary of withdrawing its aid & throwing the whole into confusion as Carolina who refuses all overtures for peace & imagines the world will admire her independence, whereas they laugh at her folly, which is perfectly suicidal—you know my feelings are all linked with the South & you will bear with me in the expression of my opinion, but while there are many of the Northern politicians who deserve no better fate than to be <u>hung</u> as high as Haman, believe me that those who have been <u>foremost</u> in this Revolution will deserve & meet with the reprobation of the world either North or South, for having destroyed the most glorious Confederacy that ever existed. You have lived abroad, you have known many excellent people at the North & all your sympathies & feelings cannot be confined to your <u>state</u> to the exclusion of your <u>Country</u>—The Almighty may intend to punish us for our National Pride. I pray now that He will preserve us from Civil War. We can never boast again as a Nation unless all could be restored—Believe me my dear friend whatever may happen you & yours will be always dear to my heart & at least our love & association will be unbroken. I only wish the other Southern States had left Carolina <u>alone</u> & the government had let her alone & she would now have been tired of her <u>sovereignty</u>. She has been restless & anxious to show her independence for many years & it would have been well for her to try the experiment <u>alone</u>—Mr. Lee is in Texas deeply grieved at the state of things. Custis is here with us in his absence & goes over daily to his office. He denies to be most kindly remembered to you & all his friends in Savannah. You have got the advantage of me. I have only one grandson Rooney's boy called Robert Edward & I haven't seen him since he was 3 weeks old. Rooney is such a busy farmer he thinks he cannot leave home. Mildred is at boarding school in Winchester & Rob at the University. I do not know if I have written to you since they both became communicants a subject of great joy to me. Mary Annie & Agnes have been with me all the winter tho Mary is now making a little visit in Washington to her Aunt Mrs. S S Lee.

### 1861: APRIL 15
### ELLEN EMERSON TO LIDIAN JACKSON EMERSON

*On April 12, at 4:30 in the morning, Confederate General Pierre Beauregard opened fire on the Federal garrison at Fort Sumter in Charleston, South Carolina. More than three thousand shells were fired at the fort over two days. There were no direct casualties (one man died when a cannon exploded), but even as far north as Dorchester, Massachusetts, there was no question about the meaning of the attack. Ellen Tucker Emerson (1839–1909), the twenty-two-year-old daughter of the famous author, wrote to her mother, Lidian (see pages 157 and 168), on the same day that Lincoln issued a proclamation calling for seventy-five thousand militiamen.*
"Aunt Lizzy" was Lidian's sister Elizabeth Jackson; Haven, William, and Charley were Ellen's cousins, the children of Ralph's brother William and his wife, Susan. Edward was Ellen's brother.

Dorchester. April 15th. 1861

Dear Mamma

   The Doctor has just gone after his usual declaration that my cure progresses uninterruptedly, and fast. He says I may go to the steamer on Wednesday to see Aunt Lizzy off. I hope that I may be dismissed when the 6 weeks are over. Alas! that Fort Sumter should be lost so easily. We were told yesterday morning just before church. Mr Smith and I went to meeting at "Meeting-house-hill." Mr Morrison of Milton was the minister and I was sorry, but on the contrary it was grand. In the first place it was an April day and the church was alternately dark and bright. Then he read almost all the 24th chapter of Matthew—about wars and rumours of wars which sounded so different on such a day. Then the text "If thou hadst known, even thou, in this thy day, the things which belong to thy peace", and the sermon which was so good so exactly the right thing. Sometimes I wanted to stand up, and sometimes I could see the men around feel the fire. Mr Smith who likes very different things from what I do, of course, was equally satisfied with myself. But he liked the way it was put together and "there are some things infinitely worse than war", and I did too, but I preferred "there are some things better than peace," and what I liked most was what he said about our dear grandfathers, how they fought, themselves and for every one of them it was a real sacrifice "but what are we doing now? We have hired foreigners to fight for us, and are to tax our posterity to pay them. Woe to the land whose battles are not fought by her own sons!" And then he said that was the best safeguard against unjust wars, we had no right to fight for anything for which we wouldn't give our very best. All that went to my heart. I had just read in the Tribune that ⅓ of our soldiers were Germans, and ⅓ Irishmen. And there at the South they are almost all, the real people. As we came out of church I looked to see if there were any young men who might have cared, and behold in the whole crowd of boys and middle-aged men I could only see 3 young men, and one of those was a scholar-looking fellow, but then I only saw one aisle-ful. Then I considered all my relations, Edward won't be old enough for three years, Haven wasn't made to fight. William was, but I suppose he isn't strong enough, and really the last of all, which I wonder at, Charley marched proudly into my head, old enough, the right shape, great strong "the fighting-man of the Family" as Haven told us sometime ago, and I was so elated at the thought of him that I forgot that Mr Smith wasn't the person to speak to and cried out all of a sudden "Oh, one boy I have!" and had to explain, and he was very much amused. I suppose Uncle William and Aunt Susan wouldn't entirely agree with my plans for Charley, but I can't help feeling rejoiced at the thought of his being a soldier, especially when I remember how much he would probably like it himself. And the idea of Edward's coming to it, if this lasts long enough, is equally charming. I try in vain to consider that probably youth and inexperience have run away with me, if I am run away with, I am, whether it is inexperience or not, and I can't help it. I preach non-resistant principles to myself, but they don't go to the right spot, and whenever they get to talking about the times at the table, Mrs Smith will say "How you do like War!" They gave me a note from my poor dear papa with three more dollars for his cormorant. I often try to contrive a way of doing without an outfit this summer but I don't see any possibility, I must have at least a bonnet and two new gowns, and 20 yards of cotton. Last night Mr Smith came in and sat in the parlour, and Mrs Smith said "Come, Mr Smith, let's sing." So I supposed it was their Sunday night custom and they did all sing, some hymns, and Mr Smith sang a solo from the Messiah. And I was quite contented, but the trouble was, that the room was too small for so much voice; if I had been in the entry, I should have enjoyed it very much.

After dinner. I have got another note from Father. How good he is to write so often! In great expectation of seeing you day after tomorrow!

E.T.E.

### 1861: APRIL 16
### MRS. EDWIN FITCH TO JOSEPH BROWN

*Hundreds of thousands of Southerners enlisted in the Confederate army. Not every-one, however, did so with unmixed emotions.*

Joseph Brown (1821–1894) was governor of Georgia. Fitch's background and the outcome of her request are unknown.

Atlanta
April 16, 1861

Dear Sir:

I must necessarily address you, although I feel a delicacy in doing so. I write to ask you to release my husband from his place in the army. He has enlisted in the Georgia army and is now in Savannah. He was under the influence of liquor when he did enlist, and now he regrets it very much. After it was done, he could not help himself but had to go.

### 1861: JULY 22
### CLARA BARTON TO STEPHEN BARTON

*The first battle of the Civil War was fought in Virginia, near a railroad center called Manassas Junction, at a field beside the creek called Bull Run. It was there that the Confederate soldiers first showed their mettle, defying the North's early claims of victory and rallying behind General Thomas J. Jackson, who gained the nickname "Stonewall" that day because of his unwillingness to yield. Though the casualty*

*numbers were fairly even (in all, forty-five hundred men were killed, wounded,
or captured), the day ended in a Union retreat. In Washington, Clara Barton
(1821–1912) wrote this two-part letter to her father, Stephen Barton (1774–1862).
She would go on to organize clothing and medicine for the wounded and, though
she had no formal training, to serve as a nurse on the battlefield (see page 292).*

(see page 292).

Washington, D. C., July 22nd, 1861
Monday evening, 6 o'clock, P. M.

My dear Father:

It becomes my painful duty to write you of the disaster of yesterday. Our
army has been unfortunate. That the results amount to a <u>defeat</u> we are not willing to admit, but we have been severely repulsed, and our troops returned in
part to their former quarters in and around the city. This has been a hard day to
witness, sad, painful, and mortifying, but whether in the aggregate it shall sum
up a defeat, or a victory, depends (in my poor judgment) entirely upon circumstances; viz. the tone and spirit in which it leaves our men; if sad and disheartened, we are defeated, the worst and sorest of defeats; <u>if roused to madness,
and revenge</u>, it will yet prove VICTORY. But <u>no mortal</u> could look in upon this
scene to-night and judge of effects. How gladly would I close my eyes to it if I
could. I am not fit to write you now, I shall do you more harm than good.

July 26th, Friday noon

You will think it strange that I <u>commenced</u> so timely a letter to you and
stopped so suddenly. But I did so upon more mature reflection. You could not
fail to know all that I could have told you so soon as I could have got letters
through to you, and everything was <u>so</u> unreliable, vague, uncertain, and I confidently hoped exaggerated, that I deemed it the part of prudence to wait, and
even now, after all this interval of time, I cannot tell you with certainty and accuracy the things I would like to. It is certain that we have at length had the
"<u>Forward Movement</u>" which has been so loudly clamored for, and I am a living
witness of a corresponding <u>Backward</u> one. I know that our troops continued to
go over into Virginia from Wednesday until Saturday, noble, gallant, handsome
fellows, armed to the teeth, apparently lacking nothing. Waving banners and
plumes and bristling bayonets, gallant steeds and stately riders, the roll of the
drum, and the notes of the bugle, the farewell shout and martial tread of armed
men, filled our streets, and saluted our ears through all those days. These were
all noble sights, but to <u>me</u> never pleasant; where I fain would have given them a
smile and cheer, <u>the bitter tears would come</u>; for well I knew that, though the

proudest of victories perch upon our banner, many a brave boy marched down to die; that, reach it when, and as they would, the Valley of Manassas was the Valley of Death.

Friday brought the particulars of Thursday's encounter. We deplored it, but hoped for more care, and shrewder judgment next time. Saturday brought rumors of <u>intended</u> battle, and most conflicting accounts of the enemy's strength; the evening and Sunday morning papers told us reliably that he had eighty thousand men, and constantly reënforced. My blood ran cold as I read it, lest our army be deceived; but then they <u>knew</u> it, the news came from them; surely they would never have the madness to attack, from open field, an enemy of three times their number behind entrenchments fortified by batteries, and masked at that. No, this <u>could not be</u>; then we breathed freer, and thought of all the humane consideration and wisdom of our time-honored, brave commanding general, that he had never needlessly sacrificed a man.

## 1861: JULY 23
## ELIZABETH BLAIR LEE TO SAMUEL PHILLIPS LEE

*For many Americans, the first Battle of Bull Run (or Manassas, as it was called in the South) meant the first harsh realities of war. Elizabeth Blair Lee (1818–1906) heard the sounds of battle from her family's country home in Silver Spring, Maryland. She sought safety in Philadelphia, and then went on to Atlantic City, New Jersey; and Bethlehem, Pennsylvania. She returned to Maryland in October.*
Elizabeth's husband, Samuel Phillips Lee (1812–1897), would command both the North Atlantic and Mississippi navy squadrons for the Union. He was away at sea often enough that the couple never owned their own house. When she wasn't in Maryland, Elizabeth stayed at her family's other home, across the street from the White House, still famous today as Blair House. Dr. Hugh Hodge was Elizabeth's physician. *Rhode Island* was a supply ship for the North. Betty was Elizabeth's niece, and "Apo" was Appoline Blair, one of Elizabeth's sisters-in-law.

Philadelphia   July 23, 1861

Dear Phil

The most comfortable sensation I have about this move from my home is that it will be a relief to you & that after this you will never have an anxious thought about us—feeling we have the most cautious care taken of us—

News from Washington indicates a revival of energy in Washn They are sad & the secessionist too are equally busy over their dead & wounded   Mr. Pryor a brother of the M.C. says their loss was awful even before he was taken prisoner early in the day—It must have been or they would have follwed up their Victory more vigorously which they had not done at 2 olk today   Patterson's men are ready to mob him so one of them told me today   They say he is as more of an ally to the South than even Genl Jo Johnston   The rumors about our loss is all uncertain for the rolls were not called at midday to day & I saw many of the soldiers straggling in late last night & early the morning—One of them sat in the rain on the stone foundation of brother's front fence—I asked if he was hungry? No! Thirsty? no, sick? no,—wounded no no only mad—we are beat & badly because we have no generals—no competent officers   He was almost heart broken from his tone & manner—a very respectable looking man—The Citizens treated them well—fed & sheltered them from the storm—Maryland seems *steady*—All was quiet in Balt—as we came thro it—& I saw 50 flags when I saw ten in June—

I shall still stay here a few days & then go to Bethlehem for Mary Blairs party without Dr Hodge advises me to go to the Sea shore for these headaches which I think comes from the same cause that makes specs comfortable—& if he advises me to go to the sea—Ill go with Mira & Mr. Dick to the Atlantic City—across New Jersey & just 2 hours from here & until this is settled I'll home here under Aunt Becky's care—Blair & Becky are my best protection in my wanderings—& our dear child is certainly a great comfort—He was joyous today in the Cars with hope of going to see Papa   I do hope you will soon come into port—tho this Rhode Island provision looks like keeping you all out but the rest have had their turn & you ought to have yours—

Ever yr devoted
Lizzie

Betty & Apo go to New York tomorrow—Betty to martins & Apo to Connecticut

## 1861: SEPTEMBER 23
## MRS. E. A. SPAULDING TO ABRAHAM LINCOLN

*The Connecticut-based author of this letter, clearly not particularly impressed by her own gender, was nonetheless unwavering in her condemnation of slavery and in her willingness to criticize the president.*

Lincoln had appointed the explorer John Frémont to be commander of the Western Department, hoping to capitalize on Frémont's popularity in a difficult area of the country. But on August 30, without permission, Frémont issued his own emancipation proclamation, freeing all slaves in Missouri. On September 11, a vexed Lincoln ordered Frémont to conform to the

Confiscation Act, which allowed only slaves on the Confererate side to be freed. In 1861, the Civil War was still less about abolishing slavery and more about preserving the Union.

Central Village Sept 23d

Dear Sir,

When it becomes necessary for a female, a <u>weak insignificant</u> female in view of the times to lift up her voice in defence of right, it most conclusively proves that there is an existing wrong. Feeling that in the prosperity or adversity of the country woman is as much concerned as man; that in the continuation or declination of our republic she has as much at stake. I am emboldened you on a subject which did I omit, I might feel responsible for the "<u>one talent</u>" committed to my care. It is with the <u>deepest</u> sorrow that I find you <u>disapprobated</u> the measures taken by Gen Fremont relative to the rebel Missourians. And it is said that, that gallant officer disheartened, that acts which he conceived to be an imperative duty and a policy for the good, should be thought at all reprehensible is likely to resign—more than that, rumors are afloat that he is likely to be superseded. God grant that he may not forsake the cause voluntarily, or be supplanted in his command by another! And are you, our Chief Magistrate quite sure, that you have not already weakened the Union cause by thus disproving his course? From every direction do I hear the mutterings of the populace—It is said moreover, that it is in <u>your</u> power to abolish Slavery—that by so doing, the war will be ended. If this be so, why not push the advantage and lay the axe at the root of our trouble? Very certain I am, that were I a soldier I would lay my arms down in disgust if after the present contest was ended, <u>Slavery</u> was to exist. Female though I am I am learned enough to <u>know</u> Slavery is the cause of the war; Female though I am, I am intelligent enough to <u>see</u> in the perpetuity of Slavery a never ending bone of contention; Female though I am, I have reason enough to <u>judge</u> that it is abhorrent to God and to every well-balanced mind   Never, no never, will [division?] and anarchy cease in our beloved country, till these great truths are recognized—viz. that "all men are created free and equal"—that all born on American soil, of whatever shade of complexion, are entitled to "life, liberty and the pursuit of happiness." No, until the Peculiar Institution is abolished, Civilization is impeded, Humanity languishes and our boasted land of Freedom is a Practical Lie.

Yours very respectfully
Mrs E A Spaulding

\*     \*     \*

## 1861: NOVEMBER 17

## ROSE GREENHOW TO WILLIAM SEWARD

---

*Unlike the author of the previous letter, Rose O'Neal Greenhow (1817–1864) saw herself as neither "weak" nor "insignificant." A Confederate spy, Greenhow had successfully warned General Beauregard in July that Union troops were advancing toward Manassas. Arrested in August, Greenhow was initially confined to her house, from which she sent the following letter to Secretary of State William H. Seward (1801–1872). When the letter was published, she was moved to jail. Tried in the spring of 1862, she was deported back to Richmond, where she was greeted as a hero. In 1862, Greenhow was sent to Europe to tout the Confederate cause and make diplomatic contacts. Upon her return by boat in 1864, she drowned, reportedly weighed down by the gold she had received from the sales of her memoir.*

Greenhow's daughter, Rose, was eight years old at the time of her mother's arrest. The words Greenhow quoted here, from the French Revolutionary heroine Charlotte Corday, can be translated "It's the crime that brings the shame, not the scaffold."

Washington, Nov. 17th, 1861,
398 Sixteenth Street.

To the Hon. Wm. H. Seward,
    Secretary of State:

Sir—For nearly three months I have been confined, a close prisoner, shut out from air and exercise, and denied all communication with family and friends.

"Patience is said to be a great virtue," and I have practised it to my utmost capacity of endurance.

I am told, sir, that upon your <u>ipse dixit</u>, the fate of citizens depends, and that the sign-manual of the ministers of Louis the Fourteenth and Fifteenth was not more potential in their day, than that of the Secretary of State in 1861.

I therefore most respectfully submit, that on Friday, August 23d, without warrant or other show of authority, I was arrested by the Detective Police, and my house taken in charge by them; that all my private letters, and my papers of a life time, were read and examined by them; that every law of decency was violated in the search of my house and person, and the surveilance over me.

We read in history, that the poor Maria Antoinette had a paper torn from her bosom by lawless hands, and that even a change of linen had to be effected in sight of her brutal captors. It is my sad <u>experience</u> to record even more revolting outrages than that, for during the first days of my imprisonment, whatever <u>necessity</u> forced me to seek my chamber, a detective stood sentinel at the open door. And thus for a period of seven days, I, with my little child, was placed absolutely at the mercy of men without character or responsibility; that during the first evening, a portion of these men became brutally drunk, and boasted in my hearing of the "<u>nice times</u>" they expected to have with the female prisoners; and that rude violence was used towards a colored servant girl during that evening, the extent of which I have not been able to learn. For any show of decorum afterwards was practiced toward me, I was indebted to the detective called Capt. Dennis.

In the careful analysis of my papers I deny the existence of a line I had not a perfect right to have written, or to have received. Freedom of speech and of opinion is the birthright of Americans, guaranteed to us by our Charter of Liberty, the Constitution of the United States. I have exercised my prerogative, and have openly avowed my sentiments. During the political struggle, I opposed your Republican party with every instinct of self-preservation. I believed your success a virtual nullification of the Constitution, and that it would entail upon us the direful consequences which have ensued. These sentiments have doubtless been found recorded among my papers, and I hold them as rather a proud record of my sagacity.

I must be permitted to quote from a letter of yours, in regard to Russell of the London Times, which you conclude with these admirable words: "Individual errors of opinion may be tolerated, as long as good sense is left to combat them." By way of illustrating <u>theory</u> and <u>practice</u>, here am I, a prisoner in sight of the Executive Mansion, in sight of the Capitol where the proud statesmen of our land have sung their paeans to the blessings of our free institutions. Comment is idle. Freedom of thought, every right pertaining to the citizen has been suspended by what, I suppose, the President calls a "<u>military necessity</u>." A blow has been struck, by this total disregard of all civil rights, against the present system of Government, far greater in its effects than the severance of the Southern States. Our people have been taught to contemn the supremacy of the law, to which all have hitherto bowed, and to look to the military power for protection against its decrees. A military spirit has been developed, which will only be subordinate to a <u>Military Dictatorship</u>. Read history, and you will find, that the causes which bring about a revolution rarely predominate at its close, and no people have ever returned to the point from which they started. Even should the Southern State be subdued and forced back into the Union (which I regard as impossible, with a full knowledge of their resources,) a different form of Government will be found needful to meet the new developments of national character. There is no class of society, no branch of industry, which this change has not reached, and the dull, plodding, methodical habits of the poor can never be resumed.

You have held me, sir, to man's accountability, and I therefore claim the right to speak on subjects usually considered beyond a woman's ken, and which you may class as "errors of opinion." I offer no excuse for this long digression, as a three months' imprisonment, without formula of law, gives me authority for occupying even the precious moments of a Secretary of State.

My object is to call your attention to the fact: that during this long imprisonment, I am yet ignorant of the causes of my arrest; that my house has been seized and converted into a prison by the Government; that the valuable furniture it contained has been abused and destroyed; that during some periods of my imprisonment I have suffered greatly for want of proper and sufficient food. Also, I have to complain that, more recently, a woman of bad character, recognized as having been seen on the streets of Chicago as such, by several of the guard, calling herself Mrs. Onderdonk, was placed here in my house, in a room adjoining mine.

In making this exposition, I have no object of appeal to your sympathies, if the justice of my complaint, and a decent regard for the world's opinion, do not move you, I should but waste your time to claim your attention on any other score.

I may, however, recall to your mind, that but a little while since you were quite as much proscribed by public sentiment here, for the opinions and principles you held, as I am now for mine.

I could easily have escaped arrest, having had timely warning. I thought it impossible that your statesmanship might present such a proclamation of weakness to the world, as even the fragment of a once great Government turning its arms against the breasts of women and children. You have the power, sir, and may still further abuse it. You may prostrate the physical strength, by confinement in close rooms and insufficient food—you may subject me to harsher, ruder treatment than I have already received, but you cannot imprison the soul. Every cause worthy of success has had its martyrs. The words of the heroine Corday are applicable here: "C'est la crime qui fait la honte, et non pas l'echafaud." My sufferings will afford a significant lesson to the women of the South, that sex or condition is no bulwark against the surging billows of the "irrepressible conflict."

The "iron heel of power" may keep down, but it cannot crush out, the spirit of resistance in a people armed for the defence of their rights; and I tell you now, sir, that you are standing over a crater, whose smothered fires in a moment may burst forth.

It is your boast, that thirty-three bristling fortifications now surround Washington. The fortifications of Paris did not protect Louis Phillippe when his hour had come.

In conclusion, I respectfully ask your attention to this protest, and have the honor to be, &c.,

Rose O. N. Greenhow

## 1861: DECEMBER
## JULIA WARD HOWE TO JAMES FIELDS

*With this flippant note to the editor of* The Atlantic Monthly, *Julia Ward Howe (1819–1910) submitted her "Battle Hymn of the Republic," the poem that would make her famous. James T. Fields (1817–1881) paid Howe five dollars for it and published it in February of 1862. It became, in effect, the anthem of the North.*
Howe had conceived the poem to be set to an old folk melody that had also been the tune for "John Brown's Body."

Fields!

Do you want this, and do you like it, and have you any room for it in January number? I am sad and spleeny, and begin to have fears that I may not be after all, the greatest woman alive.

## 1862: FEBRUARY 3
## ELLEN EMERSON TO RALPH WALDO EMERSON

*The second year of the war began with apparent stalling on the part of Union general George McClellan. In January, Lincoln issued an order for a Union offensive to take place by Washington's birthday, on February 22. Meanwhile, in sheltered Concord, Massachusetts, women continued with their war work, and Ellen Emerson (see page 270) wrote to her father about some good old-fashioned (and by today's standards unbelievably impressive) amusements.*
Ellen was probably referring to Union general John Frémont (see page 275), who had been removed from command. Edward Pierce was superintendent in charge of the so-called Port Royal Experiment, an effort on the part of the War Department to teach former slaves in Port Royal, South Carolina. Haven was Ellen's cousin.

Concord    February 3rd 1862.

Dear Father,

We are regretting that I forgot in my last letter to tell you to see Fremont. I suppose you will laugh at that, but after a consultation on the subject we think you will not think of it. Mr. Conway inflamed our minds by his stories of him—he seems to consider him the best man there is. I am to spend next Sunday with Ida. But that letter of Edward Pierce's, which you heard mentioned, having been widely read, there is to be a mass-meeting of sewers here on Thursday to make clothes for the negroes at Port Royal. It seems probable that I shall be wanted at home to take care of this society, so perhaps I shan't go till Saturday. On Friday night last we had a capital dramatic evening at the school-house. I wish you could have seen Wilkie act—and Lily Nelson. And on Saturday night we had a game party where we played various new games, and had a new form of writing poetry. Miss Bartlett invited us to write a sonnet, and took one of Wordsworth's sonnets in her hand. "The end of the first line is boat", she said. So we all wrote a line ending in boat. "The end of the 2nd line is satisfied." So we all wrote a line ending with satisfied, and so on. The reading was very entertaining. Edward's was—

> A boy took a pretty girl out in a boat.
> And she with the compliment seemed satisfied,
> And he was delighted to sit by her side.
> He'd invited the lady by means of a note
> To join him in taking this jolly good float,
> Not to tell her old grandam for fear she should chide,
> And to the bottom she's bet they would glide.
> She had met him that morn in a valley remote,
> Though their voices were drowned in a tabby-cat's mew
> Who went through with the vowels a, e, i, o, u,
> He asked her however with him for a crew
> To sail on the river and gaze at the hues
> Of the trees, and his eyes, and blue sky above.
> He outwitted the grandam and cut with his love.

I can't remember enough of the others to write, but here is mine to compare it with.

> A sled is better than the finest boat,
> And with a sled my mind is satisfied.

But with a sled one wants a steep hillside
And every bird around sounding his note.
Better it is to coast than 'tis to float,
Though not that pastime either would I chide.
But gay it is down the steep slope to glide
And gayest when the valley is remote.
The boat may be a proper place to muse
And may be most attractive, friend, to you
If ever you were in the Harvard Crew.
But if you love of snow and sky the hues
You'll find the sled is much the boat above
And that the coasting will engage your love.

There, you see how different they can be, and some of them were most characteristic. If you have time while you are in N.Y. you had better get Haven to take you to Central Park which you haven't seen, I believe, and Haven is a great Conductor.

Your affectionate daughter
Ellen T. Emerson

## 1862: FEBRUARY 18
## LAURA WILLIAMS TO GREEN BERRY WILLIAMS, JR.

*Fort Henry and Fort Donelson, both near the Kentucky-Tennessee border, were crucial to the Confederate protection of the Tennessee River and to the South's strongholds of Nashville, Tennessee; and Columbus, Kentucky. With the Union troops led by a determined Ulysses S. Grant, both forts fell within ten days. At Donelson, three thousand men escaped, but fifteen thousand surrendered. News and rumors of the defeat flooded nearby Gallatin, Tennessee, where Laura Williams (1844?–1906) wrote this vivid letter to her brother Green (1841?–1863), offering an up-close glimpse of a town in the midst of terror. Despite Laura's fears that her brother was still in battle, he had already left Fort Donelson. He died a year later in an Atlanta hospital.*

Liquor was often destroyed to keep it from enemy hands. The trains were stopped by Confederate forces. Though it was rumored that Confederate president Jefferson Davis had called for the defense of Nashville, the report proved wrong: the Union troops ("Lincolnites") did not reach Nashville until February 23. Rufus Reese was a corporal in Green's regiment; Robert Sindle was a private. Elkanah ("Cana") Turner Bush had been taken prisoner. The Wyleys were neighbors. Julius Trousdale was son of the governor. Leodocia was Laura's ten-year-old sister, and Zachary Taylor her twelve-year-old brother.

Gallatin, Tenn. Feb. 18, 1862

My Dearest Brother,

I am still spared to write to you once more though I must acknowledge that yesterday I thought that happy privilege would never again be permitted me. Such a day I never spent and I trust that I may never see such another in Gallatin. The men all looked like their last moments had come. Women and children were flying in every direction. Some left their homes and everything else to fly to some place of safety. Many of the families have left town to go around in the country thinking they would there be more safe. We heard the Lincolnites were about 40 miles from here and yesterday everybody was huddled around the streets looking every minute for them to come to Gallatin. They had a meeting in town and emptied and buried together every drop of whiskey in town. After our defeat at Fort Donelson everybody seems deranged. We did not expect yesterday but what the Lincolnites would have possession of Gallatin and Nashville by this time. We heard that our forces were going to surrender Nashville without a fight, and we knew if they took that place we were gone too, but we heard that Davis had sent word for them to hold it at any hazards and he would send them as many troops as they wanted, so I am every day expecting to hear of your being at Nashville. All the cars have stopped on the Nashville and Louisville railroad so we have no way to send you a letter only by hand and as Rufus sent us word this morning that he was going to leave tomorrow for Bate's Regiment so I thought it the best opportunity of sending you a letter that I would have. I just wish you could be here just to see how scared the people are. I do believe the men are worse scared than the women. Some of the men (Be it said to their shame) did raise several white flags in town but somebody tore them down this morning. I wish you all had of been here to of shot it down. We commenced packing and hiding our clothes. I was determined they should never have my clothes. Tell Bob me and Ma put his and your clothes in a trunk and packed them away in a safe place. Your absence caused our greatest distress. If we could still get letters to you but all the communications will be cut off if we are whipped at Nashville. Everybody is in Sack Cloth and Ashes. I cannot half describe it to you. I wish you could be here to see and know for yourself. We have not heard any particulars from the fight at Fort Donelson. We do not know who is killed yet. I heard today that Cana Bush was killed though I cannot say whether or not it is reliable. I heard also today that our people had attacked Fort

Donelson again though I do not believe it. They say Nashville presented the most awful appearance yesterday that was ever seen, that the Lincolnites were there last night and the women and children were running and screaming all over the place. Again this morning we hear no Lincolnites there so we never know when to believe anything we hear. Some say Bate's Regiment is at Knoxville, others say you were in the fight at Donelson, and somebody else says you all are coming home. So if you please when you get this write, if you can, possibly get us a letter here and let us know where you are and what you are going to do. I rather think you will come to Nashville. I can't hear a word from Cousin John. He was at Donelson, I don't know whether he is dead or not. A portion of Floyd's Brigade got away and are at Nashville. He may be there. If you come there look for him. He is in the 14th Mississippi Regiment—Capt. Crumpton's Company. A great many think that we had better give up at once for the South is whipped, but I am not going to think so yet. I believe I have written you all about our scare that I can now think of. I have nothing else to write about. Jule and Mrs. Wyley moved over to Wilson Co yesterday. You asked me about Duch Turner. Him and Julius Trousdale, Charley Wiley, and several others started for Bate's Regiment yesterday. We have had two soldiers staying with us for several days, one of them was sick and the other came to wait on him, but yesterday when we expected the Lincolnites, he became so uneasy that he would go home anyhow. He thought that as he was sick they would kill him as he wasn't able to defend himself. We had the house full of soldiers the other day. You ought to have been here. The cars broke down here at the gate and they all came in to warm and get something to eat. I got acquainted with a very nice Lieutenant named Ewing. He is in the First Arkansas Regiment so if you ever see him you just make yourself known. We are all as well as usual. Pa, you know, is nearly deranged about our country. Ma says she is going to write to you herself. Docia and Taylor send their love. Docia says she will write to you herself. When you come home, I reckon the Lincolnites will have all your chickens eat up if they ever get here which I hope they may never do. We heard just now that Johnston is throwing shells into Washington City today. Is it so or not? Do write if you can when you get this. Be a good boy, don't rush into danger. I will write a short letter to Bob,

> Love to all.
> Laura

\*     \*     \*

1862: APRIL 5

## SALLY BAXTER HAMPTON TO WILLIAM MAKEPEACE THACKERAY

*Sally Baxter Hampton (1833–1862) was one of uncountable American women whose loyalties during the war were divided by birth and marriage. In her case, a Northern upbringing and a Southern husband meant both a geographic and emotional isolation. As a nineteen-year-old New Yorker, Hampton had met the British novelist William Makepeace Thackeray (1811–1863) when he was on his first American lecture tour in 1852. Their mutual flirtation (he was more than twenty years older than she) produced the character of Ethel Newcome in his novel* The Newcomes, *as well as a correspondence and friendship that culminated in this touching letter, written just months before Hampton's death from tuberculosis.*
Carolina Jessamine is a yellow flower that blooms in the South. "Soger" was dialect for "soldier."

You will see that my sympathies are not, cannot be heartily with either side, yet there are many, both men and women, in this broad land with hearts equally divided. While I write, the Fort Sumter band is serenading in the street below some military chief returned freshly from some battlefield, or wending his way to another. As I listen to the Adelaide, Strauss waltzes, the Schoensten Augen, memory carries me back ten, perhaps twenty years, who knows? to the days of my ball room belle-dom. I feel the hot breath of the glaring gas, the choking fragrance of the flowers, the quiver of the dancer's steps. I see you, head and shoulders above the crowd, looking through those [a drawing of spectacles], as you were wont to do in certain moods, (not over them as in certain others) with a smile, half cynical, half pitying, at the Ethel of the evening, with her little court about her. Where are they all now?—would you like to know, kind friend?

That slender youth, with the close cut black mustache and big melancholy eyes, that gave such emphasis to his social nothings, he, the petted darling of society for all these years, is dead on a sandbar, of a fever, in sight of the country he had come to devastate, if he could. The mother who weeps for him at home was born on that very shore, her home in youth might have been perhaps his first prize,—her brother is in waiting behind that distant earthwork to welcome the invaders, "with bloody hands, etc." among his sister's sons. Another—"the little gentleman" you called him—he has married since, and carried to the snows of New York a girl nurtured on Carolina Jessamine and sunshine. He has left her now among the icicles, to bring fire and sword to the house where she was born, and where their first born lies buried. C'est assez, n'est-ce pas? This shows you the sorrows among which we live, and against which we must struggle—none are exempt, for to those who have no divided hearts, comes the dread division of Death, the widow and orphan mourn their dead, and the destitute the happy homes now in ruins, or the camp-ground of the enemy. Upon the fertile smiling islands are marauding bands of runaways who have spurned the old masters, and, in turn, refuse the new. In every swamp and thicket are fugitives, fleeing from they know not what,—dreading like death the "Yankee soger," yet seeking to leave the master they love, and the home they have adored, in a vague and nameless terror. The more simple, and guileless and mild, the greater the fear and dread and apprehension,—this is what philanthropy does for the negro, and abolition for the slave, and civil war for the white man.

And what does it do for me? Do you care to know? Apart from home and friends, alone amongst strangers, the husband for whom I left all, in arms against the country where are still all I love,—dying slowly of a disease which baffles all physic and all care, I am far different from the gay girl you perhaps remember, years and years ago. I have been at death's door for many months now with one hemorrage after another wasting my little remaining strength. My poor Father and Mother, my only sister, do not even know that I live, or if they do, only that,—for a year we have had little intercourse,—for six months, none. I hear from then now and again to say they live and are well. If you get this, write and tell them of me, or send the letter. If you care to write to me, and you will care, I am sure, when you think how doubly dear the letter will be to me now, send it enclosed to the house of Fraser, Trenholm and Co., Liverpool, directed inside to me, Charleston. It will run the blockade, and come to me safely and secretly, or go to the bottom of the fathomless ocean, that tells no tales.

## 1862: APRIL 16
## EMILY DICKINSON TO THOMAS WENTWORTH HIGGINSON

*Though none of her earliest verses remain, Emily Dickinson (1830–1886) is believed to have begun writing in the 1850s. By 1862, she had summoned enough courage to ask the reformer and author Thomas Wentworth Higginson (1823–1911) for his opinion. She sent this letter from her Amherst, Massachusetts, home.*
Higginson had published an article in *The Atlantic Monthly* encouraging young writers.

April 16, 1862

Mr Higginson,—

Are you too deeply occupied to say if my verse is alive?

The mind is so near itself it cannot see distinctly, and I have none to ask.

Should you think it breathed, and had you the leisure to tell me, I should feel quick gratitude.

If I make the mistake, that you dared to tell me would give me sincerer honor toward you.

I enclose my name, asking you, if you please, sir, to tell me what is true?

That you will not betray me it is needless to ask, since honor is its own pawn.

## 1862: APRIL 23
## A LADY OF LOUISIANA TO PIERRE BEAUREGARD

*The bloodiest battle to this point had been fought at Shiloh in Tennessee in early April. In just two days, more than twenty thousand soldiers—nearly one in four— were killed, wounded, or lost. A Southern woman, moved by the plight of the injured, offered her help to Confederate general Pierre Beauregard (1818–1893). Despite the fact that the Confederates would be immobilized for weeks by their casualties, the general courteously replied: "Your friends are right when they inform you that this is no place for a Young Lady."*

Sir

I hope you will pardon the liberty I take in addressing you as the subject on which I write is interesting to all.

I have long been anxious to offer myself as a nurse for the poor wounded soldiers, but as I am a young lady my friends object, and tell me that I can be of no service, that young ladies are not wanted &c. Now I think differently. I think I could go in company with an elderly lady, and be of great service. My heart is in the work and I do not consider any sacrifices I would be called upon to make for our brave soldiers; my heart bleeds for them, and could I not alleviate their sufferings I would deem myself happy. My country is dearer to me than life itself and they are its defenders. I know General that you are the best judge whether I can be of any assistance, and if your opinion coincides with my own you will confer a great favor by informing me of it through the columns of the "Picayune" I am General

Yours respectfully

A Lady of Louisiana

## 1862: APRIL 26
## EMILY DICKINSON TO THOMAS WENTWORTH HIGGINSON

*Emily Dickinson (see page 286) wrote this letter as a follow-up to the poems she had sent Thomas Higginson. While he encouraged her to correspond with him and was clearly taken by what he called her "sparks of light," only seven poems of hers would be published in her lifetime. During the Civil War alone, she wrote approximately eight hundred.*

"Circumstance" was a recently published Gothic story by Harriet Prescott Spofford.

Mr Higginson,—

Your kindness claimed earlier gratitude, but I was ill, and write to-day from my pillow.

Thank you for the surgery; it was not so painful as I supposed. I bring you others, as you ask, though they might not differ. While my thought is undressed, I can make the distinction; but when I put them in the gown, they look alike and numb.

You asked how old I was? I made no verse, but one or two, until this winter, sir.

I had a terror since September, I could tell to none; and so I sing, as the boy does of the burying ground, because I am afraid.

You inquire my books. For poets, I have Keats, and Mr and Mrs Browning. For prose, Mr Ruskin, Sir Thomas Browne, and the <u>Revelations</u>. I went to school, but in your manner of the phrase had no education. When a little girl, I had a friend who taught me Immortality; but venturing too near, himself, he never returned. Soon after my tutor died, and for several years my lexicon was my only companion. Then I found one more, but he was not contented I be his scholar, so he left the land.

You ask of my companions. Hills, sir, and the sundown, and a dog large as myself, that my father bought me. They are better than beings because they know, but do not tell; and the noise in the pool at noon excels my piano.

I have a brother and sister; my mother does not care for thought, and father, too busy with his briefs to notice what we do. He buys me many books, but begs me not to read them, because he fears they joggle the mind. They are religious, except me, and address an eclipse, every morning, whom they call their "Father."

But I fear my story fatigues you. I would like to learn. Could you tell me how to grow, or is it unconveyed, like melody or witchcraft?

You speak of Mr Whitman. I never read his book, but was told that it was disgraceful.

I read Miss Prescott's <u>Circumstance</u>, but it followed me in the dark, so I avoided her.

Two editors of journals came to my father's house this winter, and asked me for my mind, and when I asked them "why" they said I was penurious, and they would use it for the world.

I could not weigh myself, myself. My size felt small to me. I read your chapters in <u>The Atlantic</u>, and experienced honor for you. I was sure you would not reject a confiding question.

Is this, sir, what you asked me to tell you?

> Your friend,
> E. Dickinson.

## 1862: MAY 11
## MARY CUSTIS LEE TO UNION SOLDIERS

*Having been military adviser to Confederate president Jefferson Davis, General Robert E. Lee in May assumed command of the Army of Northern Virginia, just as Union troops approached the capital at Richmond. Reluctantly, the general's wife, Mary Custis Lee (see page 268), abandoned her family home at White House Landing, the place where George Washington had once courted Martha Custis, her great-grandmother. Before leaving, Mary tacked this note to the door.*

In deference to Lee—and perhaps to history—Union general McClellan camped on the lawn instead of in the house. But after he moved on the next day, a Federal soldier set fire to the building.

Northern soldiers who profess to reverence Washington, forbear to desecrate the home of his first married life, the property of his wife, now owned by her descendants.

> A Grand-daughter of Mrs. Washington

## 1862: SEPTEMBER 21
## MARY BULLOCK TO THE CONFEDERATE WAR OFFICE

*When their husbands, fathers, and brothers went to war, Confederate women were left with fear and uncertainty, and also with farms to run, bills to pay, children to raise, and slaves to manage. For some women, such as a Mississippi wife named*

*Mary Bullock, the threat of economic disaster seemed inseparable from the terror of personal harm.*

The law Bullock referred to, passed by the Confederate Congress in October, was known as the Twenty-Slave Law; it allowed all men managing twenty or more slaves to be exempted from military service. While the law returned some Southern men to their plantations (whether Bullock's husband was one of them is unknown), it also led some Confederate soldiers to believe that they were, as the saying went, poor men fighting a rich man's war.

Dear Sir

I have the boldness to address you; but the peculiarly trying circumstances by which I am surrounded must excuse me for calling your attention to a matter so insignificant when compared to matters of a great nation struggling for independence. When the stars & bars of our beloved South were almost hurled to the dust by the hirelings of the North, and the hope of separate nationality was almost blasted by our many disasters in the early part of the present year, my husband left home with a heart fired with patriotism and entered the ranks as a private soldier, not with blind enthusiasm as many have done, but from the conscientous conviction of the faithful discharge of christian duty in so doing.

He left me and our little boy (four years old), servants, place &c. in charge of a nephew, who has since he left, arrived at the age of eighteen (18) years, which compels him to now leave me alone on the place at the mercy of the servants. The conscripts and militia laws have almost taken the entire male population from the neighborhood and I find it impossible to get any one to take charge of the place, and plainly see my own inability to perform the duties incumbent on me. I live only twelve (12) miles from the Yazoo river where the gunboats of Yankees have once landed, and destroyed some private property and taken some negroes, which seems to have had the effect of impregnating the minds of the negro population of their speedy deliverance from bondages which renders them very obstinate to female authority. If I understand the last law of Congress relative to the matter, it renders it unlawful for a place worked by slaves to be left with a woman alone on it.

—Mr Bullock is besides a government officer having had charge of the post office at Borina Miss as a deputy for five (5) years and for the last three years post Master by appointment which you can see by referring to the Post office book of appointments. I hope this plain simple statement of facts—together with the brightening aspect of our countrys affairs will lead you to a favorable consideration of my appeal for my husbands return home, and excuse me for my boldness in addressing you. I would be very thankful for a reply if you will condescend to answer a lone woman who has the assurance to address you in behalf of her only protector. My husbands name is William W. Bullock is in Jackson's command, Longstreets division, Featherstons brigade, and a member of Capt Moores company of Vicksburg Volunteers. It has been more than a month since I last heard from him. If you consider my appeal favorably please let him know as his presence at home is greatly needed.

My address is Mrs. Mary E. Bullock, Borina, Warren Co Miss

## 1862: NOVEMBER
## HANNAH ANDERSON ROPES TO ALICE ROPES

*Estimates vary greatly about the number of women who worked as nurses during the Civil War. Some sources say two thousand; others say eight thousand. The question is bound to remain open, as so few nurses left records of their service. One magnificent exception was Hannah Anderson Ropes (see page 241), who, in this and other letters to her daughter, Alice Shephard Ropes (1841–?), seemed very much aware that she was writing history. With her essential combination of tenderness and strength, Ropes continued her nursing duties at a Union hospital in Washington until her own death, from pneumonia, just two months after she wrote this letter.*

November, 1862

My dear little girl,

However much I may desire to go and see you all on Thanksgiving Day it is out of the question. I can't leave "my boys." More than you imagine they need me, at all hours. If they are getting better the star of their hope is to be able to walk into my room, a mysterious place of comfort from which springs all their little luxuries and which I amuse them by telling about what part of the building it is in, how many steps they will have to go down to reach it, and they shall have two spoonsful of wine in a little tumbler and a Boston cracker if they will be good and try to get well. That last you will think strange of. Yet it is even so. The poor fellows are weary of life; a week ago one sent for me to come to him, the nurse telling me he could not live till night. I talked with him awhile, and found he had made up his mind to die. I told him he had no right to any mind about it, no man could know the bounds of his life, and he must consider his, worn and emaciated as it was, the gift of God, for him to use as long as the gift was placed at his command. I came down and sent up a half tumbler of best port wine by the needle woman, telling her to give it <u>all</u> to him. He said, never anything tasted so good as that. In two hours I sent up a cup of arrowroot seasoned with wine; that, with Mrs. Warren's declaration to him that she should dance at his wedding, brought almost a smile upon his lips. Last night I went again to see him. He certainly is better. Who knows but this Virginian may live to tell of the war to his grandchildren?

Mrs. Boyce calls on Sunday with her carriage and takes me home to dine with her—that is my only pastime and it is great.

She is to help me about pies for Thanksgiving, for the whole house, 250 people! Give my love to Grandma, Mrs. Sumner, and Mrs. Barnard <u>particularly</u>, and everybody else. <u>Keep all my letters</u>, gather them up everywhere you can. We live so much that I forget, and my discussions in letters are always the most graphic. Keep the ms. <u>carefully</u>. . . .

Your mother

H.A.R.

## 1862: DECEMBER 12
## CLARA BARTON TO VIRA STONE

*Ensconced at the headquarters of the Union's Army of the Potomac, Clara Barton (see page 272) wrote this haunting letter to her cousin Elvira Stone.*

The next day's battle, at Fredericksburg, would lead to 12,653 Union casualties, as fourteen successive but futile assaults were attempted on the rebel line. Barton would go on to found the American Red Cross.

Head Quarters 2nd Div.

9th Army Corps—Army of the Potomac

Camp near Falmouth, Va.

December 12th, 1862—2 o'clock A. M.

My dear Cousin Vira:

Five minutes time with you; and God only knows what those five minutes might be worth to the—may be—doomed thousands sleeping around me.

It is the night before a battle. The enemy, Fredericksburg, and its mighty entrenchments lie before us, the river between—at tomorrow's dawn our troops will assay to cross, and the guns of the enemy will sweep those frail bridges at every breath.

The moon is shining through the soft haze with a brightness almost prophetic. For the last half hour I have stood alone in the awful stillness of its glimmering light gazing upon the strange sad scene around me striving to say, "Thy will Oh God be done."

The camp fires blaze with unwanted brightness, the sentry's tread is still but quick—the acres of little shelter tents are dark and still as death, no wonder for us as I gazed sorrowfully upon them. I thought I could almost hear the slow flap of the grim messenger's wings, as one by one he sought and selected his victims for the morning. Sleep weary ones, sleep and rest for tomorrow toil. Oh!

Sleep and visit in dreams once more the loved ones nestling at home. They may yet live to dream of you, cold lifeless and bloody, but this dream soldier is thy last, paint it brightly, dream it well. Oh northern mothers wives and sisters, all unconscious of the peril of the hour, would to Heaven that I could bear for you the concentrated woe which is so soon to follow, would that Christ would teach my soul a prayer that would plead to the Father for grace sufficient for you, God pity and strengthen you every one.

Mine are not the only waking hours, the light yet burns brightly in our kind hearted General's tent where he pens what may be a last farewell to his wife and children and thinks sadly of his fated men.

Already the roll of the moving artillery is sounded in my ears. The battle draws near and I must catch one hour's sleep for tomorrow's labor.

Good night dear cousin and Heaven grant you strength for your more peaceful and less terrible, but not less weary days than mine.

Yours in love,<br>Clara

## 1862: DECEMBER 28
## FANNIE TO NORFLEET

---

*The love letter is one thing that flourishes in wartime. This one was written by a slave to her husband, most probably with the help of their owner's seventeen-year-old daughter. Fannie was at the Levin Perry plantation in Texas. Norfleet was with the Perrys' son Theophilus, who was stationed in Arkansas. Whether the letter ever reached its destination is unknown.*

Octavia Perry, known as "Miss Ock," was the wife of Levin Perry's brother. A candy stew was a party for making pulled molasses candy. The line Fannie quotes was part of a traditional Valentine greeting.

Spring Hill. Dec. 28th 1862.

My Dear Husband,

I would be mighty glad to see you and I wish you would write back here and let me know how you are getting on. I am doing tolerable well and have enjoyed very good health since you left. I haven't forgot you nor I never will forget you as long as the world stands, even if you forget me. My love is just as great as it was the first night I married you, and I hope it will be so with you. My heart and love is pinned to your breast, and I hope yours is to mine. If I never see you again, I hope to meet you in Heaven. There is no time night or day but what I am studying about you. I haven't had a letter from you in some time. I am very anxious to hear from you. I heard once that you were sick but I heard afterwards that you had got well. I hope your health will be good hereafter. Master gave us three days Christmas. I wish you could have been here to enjoy it with me for I did not enjoy myself much because you were not here. I went up to Miss Ock's to a candy stew last Friday night, I wish you could have been here to have gone with me. I know I would have enjoyed myself so much better. Mother, Father, Grandmama, Brothers & Sisters say Howdy and they hope you will do well. Be sure to answer this soon for I am always glad to hear from you. I hope it will not be long before you can come home.

> Your Loving Wife
> Fannie

"If you love me like I love you no knife can cut our love into"

### 1863: JANUARY 2
### ELIZA QUINCY TO MARY TODD LINCOLN

*After the Battle of Antietam in September of 1862, Abraham Lincoln called on the rebel states to return to the Union before the next year or face the emancipation of their slaves. True to his word, the president issued the official edict on January 1 of 1863, and it was read publicly in a number of places around the country, including Boston. It was intended to free only those slaves held in secessionist states, leaving slavery intact in border states still loyal to the Union, and it depended on a Union victory to be put into effect. Nonetheless, as this letter from Bostonian Eliza Quincy (1793–1884) to the first lady suggests, the proclamation was a cause for Northern celebration.*
Quincy was the wife of Josiah Quincy, a former congressman, Boston mayor, and Harvard president.

My dear Madam

I enclose the Programme of the celebration of the President's Proclamation at the Boston Music Hall,—yesterday,—with M.S. notes of the incidents which occurred, during the performance.—

In full confidence of the steadiness of the President's purpose,—the arrangements were all made several weeks ago.—But it was not until the vast audience had assembled and the performances had commenced that the news arrived that the Proclamation was actually on the wires of the telegraph.—

The reception of this intelligence was worthy of "the Declaration of Emancipation",!—which must rank in future with that of Independence,—& the 1st of January 1863,—with the 4th of July 1776.—

It was a sublime moment,—the thought of the millions upon millions of human beings whose happiness was to be affected & freedom secured by the words of President Lincoln, was almost overwhelming.

To us also the remembrance of many friends who had worked & labored in this cause, for many years, but who had departed without the accomplishing of those hopes, which we had lived to witness was very affecting.

It was a day & an occasion never to be forgotten.—I wish you & the President could have enjoyed it with us, here.—

On our return home we found my father with your welcome packet in his hand.—For that it his privilege to thank you.—With our best respects to the President & our best wishes for 1863,—for him & for yourself

I am very sincerely

Yrs

Eliza S. Quincy

## 1863: APRIL

## MARY ANNA JACKSON TO STONEWALL JACKSON

*Mary Anna Morrison (1831–1915) married Thomas "Stonewall" Jackson (1824–1863) in 1857. They had two daughters, the first of whom died soon after birth, the second of whom was just five months old when Mary Anna sent this letter. A few weeks later, Jackson was wounded by friendly fire and had his arm amputated. General Robert E. Lee wrote: "He has lost his left arm; but I have lost my right arm." On May 10, Jackson died of pneumonia. Mary Anna never remarried and became known as "The Widow of the Confederacy."*

My precious husband—

I will go to Hanover and wait there until I hear from you again, and I do trust I may be permitted to come back to you again in a few days. I am much disappointed at not seeing you again, but I commend you, my precious darling, to the merciful keeping of the God of battles, and do pray most earnestly for the success of our army this day. Oh! that our Heavenly Father may <u>preserve and guide and bless you</u>, is my most earnest prayer.

I leave the shirt and socks for you with Mrs. Neale, fearing I may not see you again, but I do hope it may be my privilege to be with you in a few days. Our little darling will miss dearest Papa. She is so good and sweet this morning.

God bless and keep you, my darling

Your devoted little wife.

## 1863: JUNE 1
## REBECCA McDOWELL TO FRANCIS SMITH

*Rebecca Brevard McDowell (1823–1904) was a cousin of Mary Anna Jackson's (see previous letter) and very mindful of Stonewall Jackson's recent death when she sent this remarkably frank note about her son to Francis Smith (1812–1890), head of the Virginia Military Institute.*

William McDowell was just sixteen when his mother wrote this letter.

June 1st, 1863

Col. Smith

I write for information concerning the time when the exercises at Lexington commence; as you promised Mrs. Jackson last winter that you would take him in July but did not state what time in July. Please let me know the time, the regulations, and terms.

I might obtain the necessary information from my cousin but her grief is too recent, too great, & sacred to obtrude upon with my concerns. Virginia had reason to be proud of & thankful for such a chieftain as <u>Jackson</u>. A great & good man, a pure & unselfish patriot, and it is a pleasure to us to think that we can do something by kind offices & soothing attentions, to cheer his widow on her lonely way. We all <u>mourn him</u>, through the length & breadth of this Confederacy.

You will find our child careless & thoughtless, but high principled, & too firm to be led astray. I hope his conduct & deportment may be unexceptionable as it has been hitherto. And let me beg of you to take an interest in him. I can scarce hope to have him with me much more after he goes to you—as when he leaves you twill be to enter the army. He has been a good obedient child to me and I would feel relieved to know that far from home and among strangers he has found one friend and protector.

Please direct you[r] letter to Mrs. R. R. McDowell, Mt. Mourne, P. O. Iredell
Cty, N.C.

Very respectfully,
R. R. McDowell

## 1863: JUNE 5
### ROSETTA WAKEMAN TO EMILY AND HARVEY WAKEMAN

*Like the estimates of the number of women nurses, figures vary for women who ac-
tually served as soldiers during the Civil War. Most sources agree that there were
hundreds—perhaps even four hundred—though there may well have been more. To
be a female soldier meant to dress as a man, enlist as a man, live and fight and sometimes die as a man. One who did all of these was a five-foot-tall New York farm girl
named Sarah Rosetta Wakeman (1843–1864). Calling herself Private Lyons Wakeman, she served in the Union army for two years before dying of dysentery at a marine hospital in New Orleans. In this letter, she tried to explain to her parents,
Emily (1823–1884) and Harvey (1821–1865), why she had left home.*
Alfonzo Stewart was forty-five years old and living with the Wakeman family; census reports
listed his occupation as "none." In addition to the forts Wakeman names, there were more than
a hundred forts and batteries defending Washington, D.C., in 1863.

Alexandria Va.
June the 5, 1863

Dear Parents,

It is with Affectionate love that I Write to you and let you know that I am well
at Present and enjoying myself the best I can. I am glad that you did not let Rolf
have any of that money I sent to you. When I send you money I want you to lay
it out for the family.

I can tell you what made me leave home. It was because I had got tired of
stay in that neighborhood. I knew that I Could help you more to leave home
than to stay there with you. So I left. I am not sorry that I left you. I believe that
it will be all for the best yet. I believe that God will spare my life to come home
once more. When I get out of this war I will come home and see you but I Shall
not stay long before I shall be off to take care of my Self. I will help you all I can
as long as I live.

If I ever own a farm It will be in Wisconsin. On the Prairie. I enjoying my Self
better this summer than I ever did before in this world. I have good Clothing

and enough to eat and nothing to do, only to handle my gun and that I can do as well as the rest of them.

I don't want you to mourn about me for I can take care of my Self and I know my business as well as other folks know them for me. I will Dress as I am a mind to for all anyone else, and if they don't let me Alone they will be sorry for it.

Write to me all about Alfonzo. Tell him that I can make the best soldier than he would. I can't think of anything more to Write, so good-by for this time.

Rosetta Wakeman

As I set here a Write I can hear the Cannon Roar from Fort Lyon. Fort Lyon is on one side of us and Fort Ellsworth on the other side.

### 1863: JULY 7
### CORNELIA HANCOCK TO HER COUSIN

*The Battle of Gettysburg was fought from July 1 to July 3, three brutal days that led to a Confederate defeat and some of the war's heaviest casualties: twenty-three thousand Northern and twenty thousand Southern troops. Four days after the end of the fighting, a brave young Union nurse named Cornelia Hancock (1840–1927) attempted to describe to a cousin what she had seen.*

Will was Cornelia's brother. "Butternut" was slang for a Confederate soldier. A gill was about a half a cup. Edwin Stanton was secretary of war. Henry Halleck was a Union officer often at odds with Stanton. Robert Schenk, a former Ohio congressman, had led a division of the Army of Virginia at Second Manassas. Dorothea Dix was superintendent of army nurses.

Gettysburg, Pa. July 7th, 1863.

My dear cousin

I am very tired tonight; have been on the field all day—went to the 3rd Division 2nd Army Corps. I suppose there are about five hundred wounded belonging to it. They have one patch of woods devoted to each army corps for a hospital. I being interested in the 2nd because Will had been in it, got into one of its ambulances, and went out at eight this morning and came back at six this evening. There are no words in the English language to express the sufferings I witnessed today. The men lie on the ground; their clothes have been cut off them to dress their wounds; they are half naked, have nothing but hard-tack to eat only as Sanitary Commissions, Christian Associations, and so forth give them. I was the first woman who reached the 2nd Corps after the three days fight at Gettysburg. I was in that Corps all day, not another woman within a half mile. Mrs. Harris was in first division of 2nd Corps. I was introduced to the surgeon of the post, went anywhere through the Corps, and received nothing but the greatest politeness from even the lowest private. You can tell Aunt that there is every opportunity for "secesh" sympathizers to do a good work among the butternuts; we have lots of them here suffering fearfully. To give you some idea of the extent and numbers of the wounds, four surgeons, none of whom were idle fifteen minutes at a time, were busy all day amputating legs and arms. I gave to every man that had a leg or arm off a gill of wine, to every wounded in Third Division, one glass of lemonade, some bread and preserves and tobacco—as much as I am opposed to the latter, for they need it very much, they are so exhausted.

I feel very thankful that this was a successful battle; the spirit of the men is so high that many of the poor fellows said today, "What is an arm or leg to whipping Lee out of Penn." I would get on first rate if they would not ask me to write to their wives; that I cannot do without crying, which is not pleasant to either party. I do not mind the sight of blood, have seen limbs taken off and was not sick at all.

It is a very beautiful, rolling country here; under favorable circumstances I should think healthy, but now for five miles around, there is an awful smell of putrefaction. Women are needed here very badly, anyone who is willing to go to field hospitals, but nothing short of an order from Secretary Stanton or General Halleck will let you through the lines. Major General Schenk's order for us was not regarded as anything; if we had not met Miss Dix at Baltimore Depot, we should not have gotten through. It seems a strange taste but I am glad we did. We stay at Doctor Horner's house at night—direct letters care of Dr. Horner, Gettysburg, Pa. If you could mail me a newspaper, it would be a great satisfaction, as we do not get the news here and the soldiers are so anxious to hear; things will be different here in a short time.

Cornelia

## 1863: JULY 31
## HANNAH JOHNSON TO ABRAHAM LINCOLN

*In the South, captured black Union soldiers were considered not just prisoners but spoils of war. Even if they had never been slaves to begin with, they were often sold into slavery, or killed. In this letter to the president, one Union mother expressed a hope shared by many: that if the Confederates continued with their prisoner-of-war abuses, Lincoln should be prepared to retaliate with force.*

Buffalo July 31 1863

Excellent Sir

My good friend says I must write to you and she will send it    My son went in the 54th regiment. I am a colored woman and my son was strong and able as any to fight for his country and the colored people have as much to fight for as any. My father was a Slave and escaped from Louisiana before I was born morn forty years agone    I have but poor edication but I never went to schol, but I know just as well as any what is right between man and man. Now I know it is right that a colored man should go and fight for his country, and so ought to a white man. I know that a colored man ought to run no greater risques than a white, his pay is no greater his obligation to fight is the same. So why should not our enemies be compelled to treat him the same, Made to do it.

My son fought at Fort Wagoner but thank God he was not taken prisoner, as many were    I thought of this thing before I let my boy go but then they said Mr. Lincoln will never let them sell our colored soldiers for slaves, if they do he will get them back quck he will rettallyate and stop it. Now Mr Lincoln don't you think you oght to stop this thing and make them do the same by the colored men they have lived in idleness all their lives on stolen labor and made savages of the colored people, but they now are so furious because they are proving themselves to be men, such as have come away and got some edication. It must not be so. You must put the rebels to work in State prisons to making shoes and things, if they sell our colored soldiers, till they let them all go. And give their wounded the same treatment. it would seem cruel, but their no other way, and a just man must do hard things sometimes, that shew him to be a great man. They tell me some do you will take back the Proclamation, don't do it. When you are dead and in Heaven, in a thousand years that action of yours will make the Angels sing your praises I know it. Ought one man to own another, law for or not, who made the law, surely the poor slave did not. so it is wicked, and a horrible Outrage, there is no sense in it, because a man has lived by robbing all his life and his father before him, should he complain because the stolen things found on him are taken. Robbing the colored people of their labor is but a small part of the robbery    their souls are almost taken, they are made bruits of often. You know all about this.

Will you see that the colored men fighting now, are fairly treated. You ought to do this, and do it at once, Not let the thing run along    meet it quickly and manfully, and stop this, mean cowardly cruelty. We poor oppressed ones, appeal to you, and ask fair play.

Yours for Christs sake
Hannah Johnson

## 1863: AUGUST 13

## ELIZABETH GAY TO ABIGAIL HOPPER GIBBONS

---

*Gettysburg was a fresh and devastating reality when Lincoln called for the drafting of three hundred thousand more Union soldiers. Names were drawn in New York City starting on July 11, and for four days, mobs of more than fifty thousand burned buildings, looted stores, attacked citizens, and caused $1.5 million worth of damage. Of the many angry groups, Irish immigrants were probably the most virulent. Already impoverished, they resented the fact that Lincoln's draft law allowed the rich to pay $300 to avoid service; moreover, the Irish competed for jobs with Northern blacks and found the prospect of fighting a war for them completely unacceptable. The draft riots, as they were called, in turn provoked anger from the more comfortable classes: Elizabeth Neall Gay (1819–1907), wife of newspaper editor Sydney Howard Gay, confessed her rage to Abigail Hopper Gibbons (1801–1893), whose New York house had been looted.*

Elizabeth's father was likely the abolitionist Daniel Neall, who was tarred and feathered after being dragged from a friend's house in Delaware.

Staten Island, Aug. 13, 1863

If thinking of you all daily and hourly could do you any good, you would have been wonderfully blessed as far as I am concerned, since your late misfortune. But the truth is, I have been in too great a rage to meddle much with pen and paper. Nothing would satisfy me but pistols. Non-resistance to Irish savages howling for one's life-blood, seemed the feeblest subterfuge of cowardice. All my early peace principles were swept away. I, who had meekly borne the brunt of half a dozen mobs, who had gone out from my father's roof expecting to see it again only a heap of ashes,—who had suffered in his person the grossest indignities—tar and feathers and rail—without a thought of defection from traditional views as well as those of mature conviction, at this crisis found myself ready for war. I cried for arms. I fired pistols, who had never held a loaded firearm before, I was ready to kill anybody who came in my way with riotous intentions.

When the news came of the sacking of your house, that seemed a drop too much. I was in nightly expectation of being fired myself, and, that night, sat up till four o'clock watching. The sight of an Irish man or woman became so odious to me, that I <u>could not</u> treat them with external decency.

\*　　\*　　\*

## 1863: AUGUST 24
## ELEANOR GRISWOLD TO ARVINE WALES

*Just over a month after the New York draft riots, William Quantrill and a group of Confederate raiders staged one of the most brutal attacks of the war, burning much of Lawrence, Kansas, which was an abolitionist stronghold, and killing some 150 men in fierce guerrilla raids. In neighboring Leavenworth, a woman named Eleanor Griswold wrote to Ohio civic leader Arvine C. Wales (1827–1882) about the devastation.*

Canton and Massillon, Ohio, are neighboring towns. The "Morgens scene" referred to July raids in Ohio led by John Hunt Morgan.

Monday

The most horrid transaction! Lawrence our next town is consum^d and the most prominent citizens butcher^d. It is horrid the papers do not tell half. We are all excitement. The whole town in arms. Little boys were shot and pounded to a jelly and roasted, for a while every men who look^d—but to see what was going on was shot—few of the inhabitants were out of bed—one man was shot whose wife in her frenzy endeavour^d to save by stepping over him and hiding him with her skirts, they jam^d the pistol under and blew out his brains. They went to a clothing store and a lad to save life fitted them with the best & made nice packages of whatever else they fancied. They then said, "We are through with you", and shot him through the heart. One of Quantrill's men return^d and was caught. He was given to Indians who took him to the woods & shot him dead with arrows!—Next day another was found wounded in the bush, he was drag^d through town at the horses heals—half our town is out after them, Jim Lane, whose house was burn^d, heading. The excitement is so great they will [show] no quarter. Lawrence was to Leavenworth what Canton & Massillon are to each other, a great rivalry but private friendships. It was a beautiful place, far handsomer than this but not as large.

The Copperheads here dare not peep from their doors. Our landlord has just turn^d-out two, my next room mates.

I'll send you papers. What I now most dread is the retaliation.

Your Morgens scene was nothing to this—he did not murder.

\*    \*    \*

**1863: SEPTEMBER 28**

**SARAH JOSEPHA HALE TO ABRAHAM LINCOLN**

---

*Sarah Josepha Buell Hale (1788–1879) didn't begin her career as writer and editor until after her husband's death left her with five young children to support. As a poet, she was best known for "Mary Had a Little Lamb." As a nonfiction writer, she was best known for the* Woman's Record, *a thirty-six-volume collection of women's biographies. As an editor, she was best known for taking over* Godey's Lady's Book, *which under her leadership grew to have a circulation of some 150,000. From Hale's position at the magazine, she agitated for improvements in women's education and children's welfare, and, in this letter to the president, for the designation of Thanksgiving as a national holiday.*

On October 3, Lincoln issued a proclamation declaring that "In the midst of a civil war of unequaled magnitude and severity," Americans should nonetheless "observe the last Thursday of November . . . as a day of Thanksgiving and Praise to our beneficent Father who dwelleth in the Heavens." Nathaniel Banks and Edwin Morgan were the governors of Massachusetts and New York, respectively. William Seward was secretary of state.

*Private*

Philadelphia, Sept. 28th 1863.

Sir.—

Permit me, as Editress of the "Lady's Book", to request a few minutes of your precious time, while laying before you a subject of deep interest to myself and—as I trust—even to the President of our Republic, of some importance. This subject is to have the <u>day of our annual Thanksgiving made a National and fixed Union Festival</u>.

You may have observed that, for some years past, there has been an increasing interest felt in our land to have the Thanksgiving held on the same day, in all the States; it now needs National recognition and authoritive <u>fixation</u>, only, to become permanently, an American custom and institution.

Enclosed are three papers (being printed these are easily read) which will make the idea and its progress clear and show also the popularity of the plan.

For the last fifteen years I have set forth this idea in the "Lady's Book", and placed the papers before the Governors of all the States and Territories—also I have sent these to our Ministers abroad, and our Missionaries to the heathen—and commanders in the Navy. From the recipients I have received, uniformly the most kind approval. Two of these letters, one from Governor (now General) Banks and one from Governor Morgan are enclosed; both gentlemen as you will see, have nobly aided to bring about the desired Thanksgiving Union.

But I find there are obstacles not possible to be overcome without legislative aid—that each State should, by statute, make it obligatory on the Governor to appoint the last Thursday of November, annually, as Thanksgiving Day;—or, as this way would require years to be realized, it has ocurred to me that a proclamation from the President of the United States would be the best, surest and most fitting method of National appointment.

I have written to my friend, Hon. Wm. H. Seward, and requested him to confer with President Lincoln on this subject. As the President of the United States has the power of appointments for the District of Columbia and the Territories; also for the Army and Navy and all American citizens abroad who claim protection from the U. S. Flag—could he not, with right as well as duty, issue his proclamation for a Day of National Thanksgiving for all the above classes of persons? And would it not be fitting and patriotic for him to appeal to the Governors of all the States, inviting and commending these to unite in issuing proclamations for the last Thursday in November as the Day of Thanksgiving for the people of each State? Thus the great Union Festival of America would be established.

Now the purpose of this letter is to entreat President Lincoln to put forth his Proclamation, appointing the last Thursday in November (which falls this year on the 26th) as the National Thanksgiving for all those classes of people who are under the National Government particularly, and commending this Union Thanksgiving to each State Executive: thus, by the noble example and action of the President of the United States, the permanency and unity of our Great American Festival of Thanksgiving would be forever secured.

An immediate proclamation would be necessary, so as to reach all the States in season for State appointments, also to anticipate the early appointments by Governors.

Excuse the liberty I have taken
With profound respect

> Yrs truly
> Sarah Josepha Hale,
> Editress of the "Ladys Book"

## 1863: OCTOBER 3
## REBECCA McDOWELL TO FRANCIS SMITH

*With her son, William, now enrolled at the Virginia Military Institute (see page 296), Rebecca McDowell sent this request to the head of the school. It would prove to be sadly prescient. William died in battle seven months later. About his death, one observer wrote: "That little boy was lying there asleep, more fit, indeed, for the cradle than the grave. He was barely sixteen, I judge, and by no means robust for his age. . . . He had torn open his jacket and shirt, and, even in death, lay clutching them back, exposing a fair breast with its red wound."*

The daguerreotype was made, and was found among McDowell's belongings after his death (see page 309).

Oct 3d 1863

Genrl Smith

I enclose you $10 for the use of my son William H. McDowell, with which I beg that you will have a good Daguerreotype, or photograph of him taken. He is my eldest child, and is far from me. And should any misfortune befall him, I would wish some likeness of him preserved. I have no idea of the cost of such a thing at the present time, and should this be insufficient for the purpose I will remit more. Should it be more than enough, tis subject to your discretion. Willie can retain the daguerreotype until there is an opportunity of sending it to us. By attending to this request, you will confer a favor on

R. R. McDowell

## 1863: NOVEMBER 15
## CORNELIA HANCOCK TO AN UNKNOWN RECIPIENT

*Having left Gettysburg for Washington, D.C., Cornelia Hancock (see page 298) described the plight of the "contrabands"—former slaves who had come north and were seen as the enemy's confiscated property—now gathered in hospitals and camps, with little if any means of support.*

Contraband Hospital, Washington. Nov. 15th, 1863.

I shall depict our wants in true but ardent words, hoping to affect you to some action. Here are gathered the sick from the contraband camps in the northern part of Washington. If I were to describe this hospital it would not be believed. North of Washington, in an open, muddy mire, are gathered all the colored people who have been made free by the progress of our Army. Sickness is inevitable, and to meet it these rude hospitals, only rough wooden barracks, are in use—a place where there is so much to be done you need not remain idle. We average here one birth per day, and have no baby clothes except as we wrap them up in an old piece of muslin, that even being scarce. Now the Army is advancing it is not uncommon to see from 40 to 50 arrivals in one day. They go at first to the Camp but many of them being <u>sick</u> from exhaustion soon come to us. They have nothing that any one in the North would call clothing. I always see them as soon as they arrive, as they come here to be vaccinated; about 25 a day are vaccinated. This hospital is the reservoir for all cripples, diseased, aged, wounded, infirm, from whatsoever cause; all accidents happening to colored people in all employs around Washington are brought here. It is not uncommon for a colored driver to be pounded nearly to death by some of the white soldiers. We had a dreadful case of Hernia brought in today. A woman was brought here with three children by her side; said she had been on the road for some time; a more forlorn, wornout looking creature I never beheld. Her four eldest children are still in Slavery, her husband is dead. When I first saw her she laid on the floor, leaning against a bed, her children crying around her. One child died almost immediately, the other two are still sick. She seemed to need most, food and rest, and those two comforts we gave her, but clothes she still wants. I think the women are more trouble than the men. One of the white guards called to me today and asked me if I got any pay. I told him no. He said he was going to be paid soon and he would give me 5 dollars. I do not know what was running through his mind as he made no other remark. I ask for clothing for women and children, both boys and girls. Two little boys, one 3 years old, had his leg amputated above the knee the cause being his mother not being allowed to ride inside, became dizzy and dropped him. The other had his leg broken from the same cause. This hospital consists of all the lame, halt, and blind escaped from slavery. We have a man & woman here without any feet theirs being frozen so they had to be amputated. Almost all have scars of some description and many have very weak eyes. There were two very fine looking slaves arrived here from Louisiana, one of them had his master's name branded on his forehead, and with him he brought all the instruments of torture that he wore at different times during 39 years of hard slavery. I will try to send you a Photograph of him he wore an iron collar with 3 prongs standing up so he could not lay down his head; then a contrivance to render one leg entirely stiff and a chain clanking behind him with a bar weighing 50 lbs. This he wore and worked all the time hard. At night they hung a little bell upon the prongs above his head so that if he hid in any bushes it would tinkle and tell his whereabouts. The baton that was used to whip them he also had. It is so constructed that a little child could whip them till the blood streamed down their backs. This system of proceeding has been stopped in New Orleans and may God grant that it may cease all over this boasted free land, but you may readily imagine what development such a system of treatment would bring them to. With <u>this</u> class of beings, those who wish to do good to the contrabands must labor. Their standard of morality is very low.

## 1863: NOVEMBER 24
## EMILY TO HER FATHER

---

*Like Rosetta Wakeman (see page 297), Emily (her last name is unknown) left her home to enlist in the Union army as a man. She was seventeen when she was mortally wounded in the Battle of Lookout Mountain in Chattanooga, Tennessee. Before she died, she dictated this telegram to her father.*

Eph was Emily's little brother.

Forgive your dying daughter. I have but a few moments to live. My native soil drinks my blood. I expected to deliver my country but the fates would not have it so. I am content to die. Pray, Pa, forgive me. Tell ma to kiss my daguerreotype.

Emily.

P. S.—Give my gold watch to little Eph.

## CIRCA 1863
## CHARLOTTE ANN JACKSON TO AN UNKNOWN RECIPIENT

---

*Nothing is known about the author of this letter, except that she was a former slave living in a contraband camp when she wrote it.*

When i was liveing whith White People i was tide down hand and foot and they tide me to the Post and whip me till i Could not stand up and they tide my Close over my head and whip me much as they want and they took my Brother and sent him to Richmond to stay one year   And sent my Aunt my Sister my farther away too and said if he did not go away they would kill him   they said they was Goin to Put me in Prisens   But the light has come   the Rebles is put down and Slavry is dead   God Bless the union Forever more   and they was puting people in tubs and they stead me to Death and i hope slavly shall be no more   and they said that the yankees had horns and said that the yankees was Goin to kill us and somthing told me not to Believe them and somthing told me not to Be afraid   and when they Come here they would not let me Come out to see them and when i was out in the Street they was Stead i would go away from them and they said I Better stay whith them for the yankees would kill me I would Better stay

Charlotte Ann Jackson

## 1864: JULY 25
## REBECCA McDOWELL TO HER AUNT

*Having received the news of her son's death in May, Rebecca McDowell (see pages 296 and 304) shared her grief with her aunt.*

John Thomas Lewis Preston was founder of the Virginia Military Institute. William S. White was a Presbyterian minister.

July 25th, 1864

My Dear Aunt,

I have been intending to write to you but have felt so badly that I put it off from day to day, hoping that my heavy sorrow would grow lighter. But it does seem to me that it only deepens as I reflect on it and realize my loss as days pass away.

At first, I could think of every blessing that had been vouchsafed me in connection with it. But now, altho' I do not murmur or complain and can from the heart say "Thy will be done," yet I recall the mercies remaining, but can't feel the <u>same gratitude</u>.

I felt so thankful that the poor, dear child was not wounded & taken prisoner by our cruel foes—that he did not linger in agony and that as he <u>had</u> to die, that he died in the discharge of his duty to his God & his country, and not a craven coward, [illegible] away his life. I realized that there are some things, harder to bear than <u>death</u>, the disgrace of those we love. I felt <u>so</u> thankful that I had full assurance of happiness & that he passed from earth to Heaven with but one sigh.

But <u>now</u> I only feel my loss. I can't think of him in Heaven with that bright angelic host mingling his praises with the Redeemed. I only feel that his loss <u>to me</u> is [irreparable]. That I shall no more see his form—so erect—no more gaze at his beautiful eyes—lit up with mirth or enthusiasm—no more see those dimples in his cheeks as he would break out into his merry peal of laughter or look at the long dark lashes when he was in thought. <u>This</u> was the <u>month</u> in which he was to have been at home, and when I had expected to send him into the army with my prayers & blessings. I had made up my mind to give him to his God & country, but O not so soon! Could I weep, it would bring relief, but I cannot.

Before these Union people, some of whom I have heard of exulting him his death, I talk of my noble hero boy. I am calm—cheerful. I tell how thankful I am that he fell at the post of honor & duty & c. But my heart—O how it aches! Afterwards—but if I died, they should not know if was with grief. My child died in defence of the South. To that cause my life is devoted and my God in his mercy take all that are dear to me & myself before we ever bend to yankee rule.

We had a kind & sympathizing letter from a gentleman in Lex whose son was a room mate of Willie's on last Saturday. He says that his son Edward Tutwiler & Willie were "fast friends" & that his son was much attached to him—that a short time before the Yankees took possession of Lexington he visited the room the boys occupied for the purpose of getting away the clothes & other things left by his son & on examination he found several articles belonging to our son, among them his <u>daguerreotype</u>. He says that he looked for his trunk but it could not be found & Col Preston writes that it is believed to have been burnt in the Inst or carried off by free negroes before.

His watch (his father's gold one, bought while he was in college) cannot be heard of, neither his Bible. Col Preston's son, who was Capt of the Company, said that he assisted in burying him, that there was no mutilation, no bruise on the body except where the fatal ball entered but neither his watch nor Bible were on his person. Mr. Tutwiler says that his son in writing to him from New Market said "my roommate McDowell was killed, in the front rank. I know he has gone to heaven for he was a sincere Christian" & the Father adds in his letter— "This should cheer you, in your sad affliction, for you loss has been His gain."

Revd Dr. White of Lexington, whom I've met with at the Gen'l [illegible], has sent us part of his hair, retaining the other half for fear it might be lost, and writes that he hears Willie spoken of by every body who knew him in the most flattering terms—by Profs. & c. Dr. White & Col. Preston have both lost most promising sons in battle, & seem to sympathise much with us. We have been treated with much kindness by all our friends & had very many kind letters.

Willie had not been social until grace sanctified his heart. But on his last visit home his health was better & he was so bright & merry and his associates always spoke of him as being so intelligent, & well read, so truthful & reliable, despising everything low & mean. He had the qualities that would have ensured success—integrity, perseverance & energy with great [illegible]

We had such a kind letter from dear James about Willie. May God spare him

to you, dear Aunt & bless you all. With much love to Lizzie & Carrie, yr attached
niece,

R A McD

## 1864: JULY 26
## JULIA UNDERHILL TO LEEMON UNDERHILL

*With her husband, Leemon, serving in the Union army, Julia Underhill (1842?–1864)
left her home in Wisconsin, moved to Boston, entrusted the care of her children to
two aunts, and tried to earn a decent income. Her strategy, as she explained it in
this letter, was simple: Disguise herself as a teenage boy, make a boy's wages, and,
while doing so, avoid all unwanted advances and the inevitable charges of impropriety that would have resulted. The plan worked fine until Underhill came down with
a fever. She died in a boardinghouse near the Lanesboro Iron Works in Massachusetts, where she had worked. Leemon received the news of her death while he himself was waiting to be discharged from an army hospital.*

Lainsborough July 26th 1864

My Dear Leemon,

I have not recieved a letter from you for two weeks. I am still away from home
at work. I hear from the babys every week and my aunt Hannah puts all of my
letters that come to their P Office in a large envelope and send them to me. the
babys are well and getting along first rate. in my last letter I sent you my likeness
I hope you will get it. don't I make quite a good looking boy. I have got a good
place to work and am my employer's pet boy. I get the easiest jobs allways. rainy
days and Sundays I am learning a trade to run a stationary engine. it generally
take 3 years to learn the trade. my employer says he thinks I will be a good engineer in three months, then I can get 75 dollars per month and board. I am verry
lonesome but I must beer it; times are so hard that I must work in this way to
support the babys. there is a verry severe drouth most all over northern states.
there will be about ⅔ the usual grain raised it will be verry hard times. I hope
the war will end this fall so you can come home. try and get your discharge. in
one of your last letters you say I write as though I was doing something unpleasant. I love you as much as I ever did. but of course my stile of living would make
some difference in my letters. I wonder what you will say to me after you get
these letters. I hope you will not be angry with me. it is the easiest way to support myself and now I am free from insult. my employer says I am the smartest
best boy he ever saw. there is 10 or 12 men works here. last Saturday a man was

turned off for ill treating me. I think my position working as I do a thousand times more honorable than to sell my honor and if I get found out it will be an honor to me.

I left the place where I worked when I wrote to you last. I had to work to many hours and I found a better man to work for and easier work, better board. if you do not object, I think I shall work here until you come back from the war. I can go home once a month. I wish you was here. it is an iron factory where I work where they make pig iron. they don't put me into any dangerous places or give me disagreeable work. A colledge student works here who will teaches me evenings this winter. sunday my employer told me that he thought I would make a <u>mark in the world</u>, and that <u>boys like me</u> were scarce. he is a verry particular man and I am steady, use <u>no rough language</u>, am <u>strictly temperate</u> and this suits him. I <u>appear happy</u> and contented, <u>but Leemon</u> I am <u>so lonesome</u>. I can tell now how you feel away from all, but I must. 'tis necessary, times are so hard cotton sheeting is $1.00 per yard. everything according—Gold $2.55.

Don't think any more that I don't <u>Love you</u> or doubt me again. <u>I could not forget you or cease to love you as long as you were true to me.</u> I shall feel verry impatient untill I get an answer to these letters. I wonder what you will say to me. I shall write every sunday. I am verry buissy.

Write often and <u>don't forget me</u>,

Ever your own

J——

## 1864: NOVEMBER 17
## SOJOURNER TRUTH TO ROWLAND JOHNSON

*Sojourner Truth (1797?–1883) was in her late sixties when she went to visit President Lincoln and, afterwards, being illiterate, dictated this letter about their conversation. A former slave (born Isabella Baumfree) who had been mistreated by several masters, she had escaped to freedom in 1827 and by the early 1840s had become an itinerant preacher and reformer. She was a stirring speaker who campaigned actively throughout the Civil War to raise funds in Washington for black soldiers.*
Rowland Johnson (1816–1886) was a New Jersey Quaker who had supported Lincoln. Jane Grey Cannon Swisshelm was an editor, lecturer, abolitionist, and feminist. Henry Highland Garnet was an antislavery leader. George Carse was superintendent of Freedman's Village, which, while initially set up to help freed slaves, lasted for more than three decades. The "shadows" Truth mentioned were small photographs that were used as visiting cards. Oliver Johnson was an associate editor of the *National Anti-Slavery Standard*.

Freedman's Village, Va., Nov. 17, 1864.

Dear Friend:—

I am at Freedman's Village. After visiting the President, I spent three weeks at Mrs. Swisshelm's, and held two meetings in Washington, at Rev. Mr. Garnet's Presbyterian Church, for the benefit of the Colored Soldiers' Aid Society. These meetings were successful in raising funds. One week after that I went to Mason's Island, and saw the Freedman there, and held several meetings, remained a week and was present at the celebration of the Emancipation of the slaves of Maryland, and spoke on that occasion.

It was about 8 o'clock, a.m., when I called on the President. Upon entering his reception room we found about a dozen persons in waiting, among them two colored women. I had quite a pleasant time waiting until he was disengaged, and enjoyed his conversation with others; he showed as much kindness and consideration to the colored persons as to the whites—if there was any difference, more. One case was that of a colored woman, who was sick and likely to be turned out of her house on account of her inability to pay her rent. The President listened to her with much attention, and spoke to her with kindness and tenderness. He said he had given so much he could give no more, but told her where to go and get the money, and asked Mrs. C——n to assist her, which she did.

The President was seated at his desk. Mrs. C. said to him, "This is Sojourner Truth, who has come all the way from Michigan to see you." He then arose, gave me his hand, made a bow, and said, "I am pleased to see you."

I said to him, "Mr. President, when you first took your seat I feared you would be torn to pieces, for I likened you unto Daniel, who was thrown into the lions' den; and if the lions did not tear you into pieces, I knew that it would be God that had saved you; and I said if He spared me I would see you before the four years expired, and he has done so, and now I am here to see you for myself."

He then congratulated me on my having been spared. Then I said: "I appreciate you, for you are the best President who has ever taken the seat." He replied thus: "I expect you have reference to my having emancipated the slaves in my proclamation. But," said he, mentioning the names of several of his predecessors (and among them emphatically that of Washington), "they were all just as good, and would have done just as I have done if the time had come. If the people over the river (pointing across the Potomac) had behaved themselves, I could not have done what I have; but they did not, which gave me the opportunity to do these things." I then said: "I thank God that you were the instrument selected by him and the people to do it." I told him that I had never heard of him before he was talked of for President. He smilingly replied, "I had heard of you many times before that."

He then showed me the Bible presented to him by the colored people of Baltimore, of which you have no doubt seen a description. I have seen it for myself, and it is beautiful beyond description. After I had looked it over, I said to him: "This is beautiful indeed; the colored people have given this to the Head of the government, and that government once sanctioned laws that would not permit its people to learn enough to enable them to read this Book. And for what? Let them answer who can."

I must say, and I am proud to say, that I never was treated by any one with more kindness and cordiality than were shown to me by that great and good man, Abraham Lincoln, by the grace of God President of the United States for four years more. He took my little book, and with the same hand that signed the death-warrant of slavery, he wrote as follows:

"For Aunty Sojourner Truth,

"Oct. 29, 1864.

A. Lincoln."

As I was taking my leave, he arose and took my hand, and said he would be pleased to have me call again. I felt that I was in the presence of a friend, and I now thank God from the bottom of my heart that I always have advocated his cause, and have done it openly and boldly. I shall feel still more in duty bound to do so in time to come. May God assist me.

Now I must tell you something of this place. I found things quite as well as I expected. I think I can be useful and will stay. The Captain in command of the guard has given me his assistance, and by his aid I have obtained a little house, and will move into it to-morrow. Will you please ask Mrs. P., or any of my friends, to send me a couple of sheets and a pillow? I find many of the women very ignorant in relation to house-keeping, as most of them were instructed in field labor, but not in household duties. They all seem to think a great deal of me, and want to learn the way we live in the North. I am listened to with attention and respect, and from all things I judge it is the will of both God and the people that I should remain.

Now when you come to Washington, don't forget to call and see me. You may publish my whereabouts, and anything in this letter you think would interest the friends of Freedom, Justice and Truth, in the Standard and Anglo-African, and any other paper you may see fit.

Enclosed please find four shadows (carte de visites). The two dollars came safely. Anything in the way of nourishment you may feel like sending, send it along. The captain sends to Washington every day. Give my love to all who inquire for me, and tell my friends to direct all things for me to the care of Capt. George B. Carse, Freedman's Village, Va. Ask Mr. Oliver Johnson to please send me the <u>Standard</u> while I am here, as many of the colored people like to hear what is going on, and to know what is being done for them. Sammy, my grandson, reads for them. We are both well, and happy, and feel that we are in good employment. I find plenty of friends.

Your friend,
Sojourner Truth

## 1865
## ANNIE TO MARK TWAIN

*Offering a bit of comic relief, even in the midst of war, Mark Twain (Samuel Clemens, 1835–1910) complained bitterly in print about the caliber of most of the letters he was receiving. To illustrate his point, he quoted one letter from an aunt who had been foolish enough to include war news. "I could never drive it into those numskulls," Twain wrote, "that the overland telegraph enabled me to know here in San Francisco every day all that transpired in the United States the day before." As a model of contrast, he offered this letter from an eight-year-old girl, saying it "contains more matter of interest and more real information than any letter I ever received from the East."*

St. Louis, 1865.

Uncle Mark,

if you was here I could tell you about Moses in the bulrushes again, I know it better now. Mr. Sowberry has got his leg broke off a horse. He was riding it on Sunday. Margaret, that's the Maid, Margaret has taken all the spittoons and slop buckets and old jugs out of your room, because she says she don't think you are coming back any more, you have been gone too long. Sissy McElroy's mother has got another little baby. She has them all the time. I have got a new doll, but Johnny Anderson pulled one of the legs out. Miss Dusenbury was here yesterday; I gave her your picture, but she didn't want it. My cat has got more kittens—Oh! you can't think—twice as many as Lottie Belden's. And there's one, such a sweet little buff one with a short tail, and I named it for you. All of them's got names now—General Grant, and Halleck, and Moses, and Margaret, and Deuteronomy, and Capt. Semmes, and Exodus, and Leviticus, and Horace

Greeley—all named but one, and I am saving it because the one I named for you's been sick all the time since, and i reckon it'll die. Uncle Mark, I do believe Hattie Caldwell likes you, and I know she thinks you are pretty, because I heard her say nothing could hurt your good looks—nothing at all—she said, even if you were to have the small-pox ever so bad, you would be just as good looking as you were before. And ma says she is ever so smart. So no more this time, because General Grant and Moses are fighting.

Annie

## 1865: JANUARY
## ROSE FORBES TO EDITH PERKINS

*Like other wars, the Civil War could not completely halt the business of life. Children continued to grow up, and even to marry, and mothers continued to dispense maternal advice. From Boston, Rose Smith Forbes (1802–1885) wrote to her daughter, Edith Forbes Perkins (1843–1925), on the occasion of her four-month wedding anniversary.*

Edith's husband, Charles Elliott Perkins, was a second cousin. A railroad manager, he had entered the army in 1863 but had been forced to resign because of eye trouble. The month this letter was written, he became general superintendent of the B&M railroad. James Murray Forbes was Edith's younger brother.

Four months you say since your wedding day! It seems to me as many years. I think the first year of married life is almost always the hardest in many respects, for let a man and woman love each other ever so well, it is a great change, and it takes a good while to <u>understand each other</u> and to <u>settle down</u>. Father and I have been married thirty-two years this 20th of January! I can hardly realize it. We have had all sorts of reverses, all sorts of sorrows, but never a doubt of our mutual love and faith. I know this will be so with you and Charley—and it is <u>everything</u>. Then I never knew Father to do anything that was not honorable and chivalrous. I think he would have been a noble paladin—and I think so of Charley, too—but I don't know how I came to say all this—I am sure I did not intend to. I suppose it was that I was thinking of you a great deal and feeling how much you must miss us all, and that you were having rather a hard time . . . and that I reason on to the conclusion that true love is the first best thing—that you had that, and that the rest would be added in due time.

We have had capital letters from Murray, and Father has had a letter from

Mr. Tyson, saying how much he was satisfied with Murray—that he is faithful, intelligent, and that he thinks he is sure to succeed.

## 1865: FEBRUARY 24
## MARY MAXCY LEVERETT TO MILTON LEVERETT

*Union General William T. Sherman had begun his famous march to the sea in November of 1864. By the time he arrived in Savannah in December, he had left a wake of destruction sixty miles wide and three hundred miles long. Peace talks between Lincoln and Confederate vice president Alexander Stephens followed in February but proved fruitless. Sherman marched on to South Carolina and on February 17 reached Columbia. A horrified Mary Maxcy Leverett (1808?–1897) described the burning of the capital city to her son Milton Leverett (1838–1908), who was a Confederate soldier.*

With her husband, a planter and Episcopal minister named Charles Leverett, Mary had six daughters (Annie, Mame, Julie, Carrie, Kate, and Tilly) and four sons (Edward and Milton, as well as Frederic and Charles, adopted). Lou was Annie's daughter. Jacob, Billy, Hercules, Sary, Quash, and Lewis were slaves. John Parker was a physician and head of the South Carolina Lunatic Asylum. Wade Hampton III would eventually be a U.S. senator. Cornelia Raoul and Dr. Henry Fuller were neighbors. Lieutenant General William Hardee led General Beauregard's troops in the South Carolina low country. Nickerson's was a hotel. The campus was South Carolina College. Colonel Henry Rutledge commanded a North Carolina unit. John Wallace Fuller was a brigadier general in the Union army.

Farm, Columbia, Feb, 24, 186[5]

My beloved son—

The long week of agony is over. We are safe. Being uneasy about you I send Jacob to find you, if he can, and remain with you the rest of the war. We are entirely in the dark as to the situation of affairs at Charleston—some say it is evacuated others that it is to be defended—Hardee is abhorred and condemned by all. If Billy is still in statu quo, perhaps he had better have leave to go to see his wife at Robertville (where Dr H F. left all of his negroes) and then come here. The fair city of Columbia is now a heap of ruins, little more than the outskirts remaining. We sent Annie & Lou, Mame & Julie, bedding, clothes & provisions, to the Asylum, where Dr Parker & his family were, who welcomed them heartily, & there they remained until all was over. If our men never fought before, tell them I say they must do it now: if they give up, or their knees shake, I won't count them as men, but as dogs who deserve to, deserve to die. When the fight first commenced it was near Granby where the enemy endeavored to throw across a pontoon bridge, Hampton stopt it, & the fight was kept up following the course of the river gradually until some got across on a bridge above Columbia & some just at the street which runs to the river, the fine bridge across was destroyed by Col. B Rutledge <u>without orders</u> (which ought to be a lesson to military men) and so spoilt a fine scheme of Beauregard's & he was very angry. We had but eight thousand men & they forty thousand in reality, I believe, but they told me boastfully <u>60,000</u> another said <u>80,000</u> and a common soldier was fool enough to try and convince me they were 125,000. Beauregard holds them at 35,000, anyhow they were four to one, but <u>no negro</u> soldiers, only a pioneer set. The Mayor surrendered the Town at 8 o'clock next morning. The girls saw the two flags of truce meet in old Geiger's field & in no time they rushed in. Terms were, private property respected, women & children unmolested. Now hear how they were kept. I forgot to say however they <u>bombarded</u> the Town, your sister (who stayed with us to take care of Kate & Carrie who had measles) stood in the piazza and saw several as they burst over town, one fell on Nickersons, fragments fell one in the Coffins yard & Mrs. Keating's kitchen, two men were killed, but it did not last over a day. The Asylum was untouched (yellow flag) & the Hospital at Campus also, but when the burning was commenced the Ladies Hospital was burnt. I must be brief if possible for there is too much to say. In the shortest time you could suppose after the main body of their army entered (12 o'clock) & immediately after our men filed out of town by our road, in rushed the wretches into our house to pillage, smashed open desks (all of the Greggs & ours) broke open drawers with axes, asked for keys to corn house & smoke house, & I laughed to myself to think how nicely we had tricked they by, a few hours before, ripping open Cornelia's pillows, empting the feathers & packing nearly all our meat & rice & flour, sent to Asylum with the girls,—they found therefore but little to eat, but drank the few bottles Champagne & eat Cornelias sweetmeats, drank my milk & took the bit of butter. They went thro' every room and took every thing except our beds & bed clothes & for the honour of human nature I will add, whenever they opened the room where Tilly & the children were, she told them they were sick, & begged them to go back, & they did. In my room they even crept under the bed & hunted in every hole & corner & have not left me a second suit of underclothes, all your shirts are gone, even the comb with which I comb my hair & your fathers hair brush & his razor were taken, broke open my work box & stole my scissors, emptied my writing desk & carried that, as well as the little writing case of yours out of my drawer. About one o'clock two officers came, looked around, said it was contrary to orders & a shame and left promising to send a guard to protect us; in the buggy they came in, they showed me the old State House flag with a look of exultation & one of them argued hotly with me to prove it all our own fault &c &c. The rest of the day passed in the same riotous scenes, I was everywhere endeavouring to control the thieves, parry questions, lead them astray about everything when I could & gleaning information in my turn. I kept your father out of the way as much as possible, for I was more uneasy about him than myself, finding I could manage them better, but he <u>would</u> come occasionally & show himself thinking to help me. I was on my feet all day, a tremor all over me (but I determined they should not see I was afraid) & often in the room with a crowd of armed men, &c &c about night time a polite & curteous young man Lieut. Farnhame came and let me know that Gen. Fuller would make it his Headquarters, which relieved me, for it made us safe for the night. The Gen. was very polite, so that your father absolutely conversed with him as if he was a friend & told him all he thought of them & that he was writing a History against them! What madness! I carried a cup of milk & putting it on the table told him I was sorry I had nothing better to offer, as his soldiers had taken everything. He politely asked me to take coffee, which I politely declined, telling him I had just taken a cup of tea Sweetened with <u>syrup</u> & was quite accustomed to Confederate diet. In the meantime a horrible scene was going on in Town. They were robbing & setting on fire, drinking whiskey and acting like demons. As the houses burnt down one after another the terrified women & children rushed into the Asylum for safety surrounded by these yelling devils, who tore open their trunks & gave to negroes or tore to atoms. Poor Lizzie Logan as she ran in, threw herself into Annie's arms and cried "O Mrs. DeSaussure, *is* there a God in Heaven!" The fiends raged curseing, screaming up and down in front of the Asylum swearing they were going to blow up the Asylum that night. The poor ladies believed it and thought their last hour had come. One (old Mrs Henry) died of fright others were very ill & children the same, in all 500 ladies & children were there, and the scene was indescribable. Your Aunt Tils house is burnt down & she is at Mrs Pringle's, Mary H. & Annie H. at the Seminary, they brought out their things themselves, Til saved very little. I invited all here, but as Mrs. P. has a plenty of provisions Til said she'd stay there & the others saved provisions too. The Coffins spent the whole night in the woods amid scenes of horror, and the wretches would say to them "Ladies, it is a very cold night, why don't you go into your city to warm yourselves?" Cold blooded wretches to taunt defenseless women & bid them warm by the flames of their burning homes! The Yankees intend to try and prove the fire was set by Negroes <u>but it was not</u>. The ladies saw the Yankees set different houses on fire. One lady saw a Yankee who seemed to be provided systematically with the means of doing so, he daubed grease all round the window frames, walls &c. then did the same with turpentine or terebene, then strewed matches on the floor & set fire. One lady had a baby only a <u>few minutes</u> old she was very ill & Dr Trezevant who was with her, saw the Yankee soldiers take matches & deliberately set fire to the house she was in, <u>three</u> times & each time some more humane, put it out, and even prepared a litter to carry her out in case the others succeeded. I can't tell you half. If you are still in Sumter let all this be told in the papers, our men <u>must know</u> how we have been treated. There is not a cock to crow within miles—all our poultry killed, put in our wagon & carried off, mule gone, Quash & family except Lewis, gone. Sary & Hercules stuck to us & that & Jake together made Daphne's family stay. I can't tell you how kindly Sary behaved to us. One Yankee put a bayonet to your father threatening, one put a pistol to Mrs D. Hamilton's head & one shot at Mad. Sowsnowski, who jumped aside. I conversed with a large number of officers of all grades, they regretted the burning of Columbia & said <u>we</u> caused it by giving the soldiers whiskey. I asked why didn't Sherman destroy the whiskey if he didn't wish them to get it? They seemed to think me a very notable rebel, and officers were all day coming to converse with me. I wish all I said could have been set down, for I felt as if inspired & repeatedly put them to silence. They are dreadfully afraid of our putting negro soldiers in the field & say, if we do they can't say <u>when</u> the war will end, but if we do not they will end it very soon, that our men do not fight with half the enthusiasm they once did. They all long for peace and anxiously inquired my opinion and one after the other asked, & whether we had not been beaten enough to want peace, see their force how immense, see how they had destroyed our resources, railroads &c. I told them "we did want peace, but would agree to none but an honorable peace." Their countenances fell. They pointed to Columbia & referred to the wholesale destruction going on over the State, & asked if we were not ready to give up. I said "No! It would make us more determined & drive every man into the field with feelings more embittered & intense than ever. It was a <u>good thing</u> for us." Again they were disconcerted. Then said "the men would have to come home to take care of their families." I said "No, we would take care of ourselves, that I had suffered (pointing to our sacked house) but was willing to suffer. I could bear calamity. They referred to Georgia, how they had ruined her! "I said Georgia was recovering already, like an India rubber ball, and so would we." This is not half that passed. The ladies wish our men to know all about it & you had better let <u>some</u> Editor extract what they please.

God bless my dear Son<br>Mary Leverett

## 1865: APRIL 9
## SARAH ANDREWS TO JAMES ANDREWS

---

*By March, the Confederate army was beset by a shortage of supplies, men, and morale. In a last assault on Southern soil, Ulysses S. Grant took Richmond, Virginia, on April 3. Six days later, at nearby Appomattox Courthouse, Robert E. Lee surrendered. The news traveled the country immediately, and out west in Wisconsin, a Baptist teacher named Sarah Andrews (1835–1898) wrote to her brother James (1845–1930) with glee.*

Charles Andrews was another brother. Both survived the war.

Hudson, Wis. April 9th, 1865

Dear Brother Jimmie;

Our hearts were very much rejoiced last night by receiving a letter from both our soldier boys. It had been over a week since we had heard from Charlie. You can imagine we were feeling very solicitous about him. He wrote a short letter, he did not say anything about his journey to St. Louis. I think some of his letters must have been lost.

Jimmie we have glorious, glorious news today. Lee and his whole army is captured.

There is more noise in our quiet little town than was ever known before on Sunday. I hear the booming of the anvil. The band just passed drawn by a four horse team. There were other wagons which were filled [with] exultant people besides the usual number of small boys to bring up the rear.

They stopped in front of Mr. Keley's and played a National air after which Mr. Keley made a few remarks. I suppose they are excusable to celebrate today when we have such good news.

I think if this news is really so, you and Charley will soon be discharged. I can hardly wait for the time to come, but I think it is coming much quicker than I had thought it would.

Little Charlie sings "the boys will shout, the girls will all turn out, when Jimmie and Charlie come marching home."

We had a little snow storm this morning; it is somewhat warmer now. I think we will have pleasant weather again in a few days. Mother has been up to Aunt Lydia's all the afternoon, and just come back. She thinks Aunt a little better today. She was not as well this morning.

Your last letter, the one we received last night, was written two weeks ago today. Some time on the route.

> Goodbye for this time. Write soon to,
> Sarah

## 1865: APRIL 16
## HELEN DuBARRY TO HER MOTHER

*An actor and one-time Confederate spy who had been involved in an unsuccessful attempt to kidnap Lincoln, John Wilkes Booth was apparently unwilling to accept the North's victory. There were approximately a thousand people in the audience to see* Our American Cousin *at Ford's Theatre on the night of April 14, the night Booth shot Lincoln. Helen DuBarry was one of them. In this letter, written the day after Lincoln's death, she described the historic event to her mother.*

Young friends of the Lincolns, Clara Harris and her fiancé, Major Henry Rathbone, were sharing the presidential box. Booth was said to have shouted *"Sic semper tyrannis,"* meaning "Thus always to tyrants." Laura Keene was the star of *Our American Cousin.*

April 16, 1865

My Dear Mother

Beck has not come from the Office yet and I have not received your letter but as I have a good deal to write I will begin now. I suppose by tomorrow the mail will go out from Washin. No trains left yesterday. What I have to write is with reference to the great Tragedy which has caused a Nation to mourn. I had the misfortune to be at Ford's Theatre on Friday evening and to hear the shot which deprived us of a President.

It was given out during the day that Mrs. Lincoln had engaged a "Box" for the President and Genl. Grant and having a desire not only to see them but to see the "American cousin" performed, we determined to go. Before we went Beck knew that the Genl. would not be there as he was to leave for his home in the evening. We went a few moments before the time and waited some time for the President to arrive and as he did not come until late the performances commenced and we thought we were to be disappointed in not seeing him. In the midst of the 2nd scene there was a great applause and cheering and our attention was directed from the stage to the Dress circle—close to the wall walked

Miss Harris—Mrs. Lincoln—Major Rathbun—a gentleman the President & another gentleman behind him. These two gentlemen were watchmen in citizens dress who have always accompanied the President since the War commenced. We followed him with our eyes until he entered the Box little thinking we were looking for the last time at him. He sat looking on the stage his back to us and out of our sight behind the flags except occasionally when he would lean forward. Mrs. Lincoln was in front of him and we only saw her occasionally. We saw her smile & turn towards him several times. It was while every one's attention was fastened upon the stage that a pistol shot was heard causing every one to jump (as an unexpected shot will) & look up at the President's Box merely because that was the direction of the sound and supposing it to be part of the performance we all looked again on the stage—when a man suddenly vaulted over the railing—turned back & then leaped to the stage—striking on his heels & falling backward but recovered himself in an instant and started across the stage to behind the scenes flourishing a knife—the blade of which appeared in the reflection of the bright lights to be half as long as man's arm—and making use of the expressions you have seen in the Papers. He had nearly disappeared before we could understand what it was or what had happened. We first thought it was a crazy man—when he jumped on to the stage we jumped to our feet & stood spell bound—as he crossed the stage some few started towards the stage crying—our President! our President is shot! catch him—hang him! Miss Harris was seen to lean over the railing for water & that was all that broke the stillness in that box. If those watch had called out soon as the man jumped to give us an idea of what had happened he could have been caught—& said "take out the ladies & hang him here on the spot." Beck fearing a mob hurried me out—leaving the audience still standing awed & speechless. We waited outside until a young man came out and said "He is dead—no doubt about it!"

Before we got out of the door some one said "It was J. Wilkes Booth" and before I got out, the idea that our Chief was gone—almost our sole dependence—overcome me & I could not control myself & sobbed aloud We met several outside the door just coming in asking "For God's sake tell me is it true?" as if they had heard already rumors of the great tragedy. The reason that we could not suddenly realize what had occurred was because we could not anticipate that an assassin could be in the Box with the President. His only danger seemed to be from a shot fired by one of the audience.

Booth entered the front door and asked some one there if Genl. Grant was there that night—then went along to the door of the Box—just where we had seen the President enter knocked at the door & to the watch who opened it, said he wished to speak to the President, that he had a communication for him showing an Official envelope & giving him a card with the name of a Senator written on it. The watch stepped aside & the assassin entered & fired immediately while Mr. Lincoln was looking on the stage.

The excitement that night was intense & a mob of about 2000 went to the Old Capitol Prison to burn it & they called upon the people to come out & see the rebels burn. The Police & troops were out & put a stop to it or it would have been done. The assassin at Sewards first stabbed the nurse through the lungs & killed him I believe—knocked the skull of Fred Seward with a butt of a pistol & stabbed another son—all had opposed his entrance and the old man hearing the scuffle at the door & thinking it was some one after him, rolled out of bed to stab him so he only had two cuts—on his neck & face—which will not prove serious if he has strength after his former sickness. There is no doubt that it was Booth who killed the President. Laura Keene says she can testify that it was him.

The secessionists here have all draped their houses in crape—and acknowledge that it was the worst thing for the South that ever happened—their best friend is gone & Andy J.—will be more severe than ever Lincoln was—Andy Johnson joined the Temperance Society after the Inauguration and every one who saw him at his own Inauguration were much pleased with his manner as he seemed impressed with the responsibility before him.

There are rumored changes to be made in the Cabinet already. There was a strange coincidence at the Theatre Friday evening. In the play the American Cousin won the prize at Archery and on receiving the medal was congratulated. He said he hadn't done nothing—all it required was a steady hand a clear eye—to pull the trigger & the mark was hit as he said it he looked right up at the President.

That was in the play & he looked there merely because he was the principal person present but afterwards it struck every one as a strange coincidence.

On Friday Beck received a letter from Duane who is a prisoner at Point Lookout begging him to forget the Past & to find out for him if he would be allowed to take the oath of allegiance to the U. S. that he was sick enough of the Confederacy and very sorry he had ever had any thing to do with it. That afternoon Beck went to the Comm. Genl. of prisoners but he was out—and of course after the awful tragedy Beck did not feel like interceding for a rebel I do not know what he will do now—he may go to Genl. Grant—if Hoffman won't do anything. Don't say anything about it.

I suppose you have read all I have told you, in the Papers but being there myself I supposed you would like to hear it over just as I saw it. The Authorities think that there is no chance for the assassins to escape but I think it is like hunting for a needle in a haystack. . . .

>                                    your aff dau
>                                    Helen DuB

## 1865: APRIL 16
## JULIA ADELINE SHEPHERD TO HER FATHER

*Also at Ford's Theatre (see previous letter) was Julia Adeline Shepherd, who wrote this account of the assassination to her father.*
Booth's plot targeted Vice President Andrew Johnson and Secretary of State William Seward as well, and co-conspirator Lewis Thornton Powell managed to wound Seward and three others at his house. Calcium lights were spotlights.

Dear Father:—

It is Friday night and we are at the theatre. Cousin Julia has just told me that the President is in yonder upper right private box so handsomely decked with silken flags festooned over a picture of Washington. The young and lovely daughter of Senator Harris is the only one of the party we can see, as the flags hide the rest. But we know that "Father Abraham" is there; like a father watching what interests his children, for their pleasure rather than his own. It has been announced in the papers he would be there. How sociable it seems, like one family sitting around their parlor fire. How different this from the pomp and show of monarchial Europe. Every one has been so jubilant for days, since the surrender of Lee, that they laugh and shout at every clowning witticism. One of the actresses, whose part is that of a very delicate young lady talks of wishing to avoid the draft, when her lover tells her, "not to be alarmed for there is no more draft," at which the applause is long and loud. The American cousin has just been making love to a young lady, who says she will never marry but for love, yet when her mother and herself find he has lost his property they retreat in disgust at the left of the stage, while the American cousin goes out at the right. We are waiting for the next scene.

The report of a pistol is heard. . . . Is it all in the play? A man leaps from the President's box, some ten feet, on to the stage. The truth flashes upon me. Brandishing a dagger he shrieks out "The South is avenged," and rushes through the scenery. No one stirs. "Did you hear what be said, Julia? I believe he has killed the President." Miss Harris is wringing her hands and calling for water. Another instant and the stage is crowded—officers, policemen, actors, and citizens. "Is there a surgeon in the house?" they say. Several rush forward and with super-human efforts climb up to the box. Minutes are hours, but see! they are bring-ing him out. A score of strong arms bear Lincoln's loved form along. . . . Major Rathbone, who was of their party, springs forward to support [Mrs. Lincoln], but cannot. What is it? Yes, he too has been stabbed. Somebody says "Clear the house," so every one else repeats "Yes, clear the house." So slowly one party after another steals out. There is no need to hurry. On the stairs we stop aghast and with shuddering lips—"Yes, see, it is our President's blood" all down the stairs and out upon the pavement. It seemed sacrilege to step near. We are in the street now. They have taken the President into the house opposite. He is alive, but mortally wounded. What are those people saying. "Secretary Seward and his son have had their throats cut in their own house." Is it so? Yes, and the mur-derer of our President has escaped through a back alley where a swift horse stood awaiting him. Cavalry come dashing up the street and stand with drawn swords before yon house. Too late! too late! What mockery armed men are now. Weary with the weight of woe the moments drag along and for hours delicate women stand clinging to the arms of their protectors, and strong men throw their arms around each other's necks and cry like children, and passing up and down enquire in low agonized voices "Can he live? Is there no hope?" They are putting out the street lamps now. "What a shame! not now! not to-night!" There they are lit again, Now the guard with drawn swords forces the crowd backward. Great, strong Cousin Ed says "This unnerves me; let's go up to Cousin Joe's." We leave Julia and her escort there and at brother Joe's gather together in an upper room and talk and talk with Dr. Webb and his wife who were at the the-atre. Dr. W. was one of the surgeons who answered the call. He says "I asked Dr. ——— when I went in what it was, and putting his hand on mine he said, 'There!' I looked and it was 'brains'. . . .

Last Thursday evening we drove to the city, and all along our route the city was one blaze of glorious light. From the humble cabin of the contraband to the brilliant White House light answered light down the broad avenue. The sky was ablaze with bursting rockets. Calcium lights shone from afar on the public buildings. Bonfires blazed in the streets and every device that human Yankee in-genuity could suggest in the way of mottoes and decoration made noon of mid-night. Then as the candles burned low and the rockets ceased, we drove home through the balmy air and it seemed as though Heaven smiled upon the rejoic-ings, and Nature took up the illumination with a glory of moonlight that tran-scended all art.

To-day I have been to church through the same streets and the suburbs with the humble cottages that were so bright that night shone through the murky morning, heavy with black hangings, and on and on, down the streets only the blackness of darkness. The show of mourning was as universal as the glorying had been, and when we were surrounded by the solemn and awe-stricken congregation in the church, it seemed as though my heart had stopped beating. I feel like a frightened child. I wish I could go home and have good cry. I can't bear to be alone. You will hear all this from the papers, but I can't help writing it for things seen hard to write now. I dare not speak of our great loss. Sleeping or waking, that terrible scene is before me. . . .

## 1865: APRIL 18
## EMMA YARNELL TO L. R.

*The mourning for Lincoln was widespread and deep. On Friday, April 21, a funeral train bearing his body left Washington for stops in Baltimore, Harrisburg, and Philadelphia, where an estimated three hundred thousand people viewed his open coffin. Emma Yarnell was among them.*

Lincoln's train continued on for the next two weeks, making numerous stops along a sixteen-hundred-mile route, before ending in Springfield, Illinois, where the president was buried.

Philadelphia, 18-4-65.

I am sure, my dear friend, that thou wilt feel with me that words are entirely insufficient to give an adequate idea of the effects of the shock we have received, of the thrill of anguish and horror which penetrated our hearts, when the awful news reached us:—of the almost overwhelming grief which the loss of our honoured and beloved President has caused. The sudden revulsion of feeling gave a deeper shade to the gloom; since the fall of Richmond, so quickly followed by the surrender of Lee, our city, and indeed the whole country, had been in a state of joyful excitement, the streets crowded with all classes, showing their exhilaration in a variety of ways—music, bells, whistles, day and night, hundreds of flags flying proudly in the breeze, and every one of us rejoicing that our terrible war seemed nearly ended; when, just at the moment of our highest triumph, the dreadful blow fell upon us, and sorrow seized every heart, the tokens of mourning have replaced those of joy, and the countenances of all show their participation in this great calamity, which we almost thought would be irreparable to our country. Indeed, we feel we have each lost a dear friend, a father, one in whom we relied most confidingly, whom we trusted with the certainty he would never betray our confidence, on whose uprightness, purity, and conscientiousness we might safely depend. His character grows on us wonderfully, his entire simplicity in some sort hid his greatness, but now his excellencies stand out boldly—his utter unselfishness, his true kindness of heart, the total absence of all malice, revenge, evil thoughts, of all party feeling, of onesided motives—the great sagacity which enabled him to see the right moment to act, the caution which held him back from too hasty a step, the firmness which resisted every attack or persuasion, and the evident deep religious feeling which influenced him, the settled conviction that he was but an instrument in the Divine hand to work out purposes which he hardly saw or understood—all now impress forcibly, and, while they enhance the value of our loss, make us feel that for him death has but brought the peace and rest and perfect happiness of Heaven.

It is an inexpressible comfort that he did not suffer—that no consciousness of pain disturbed his last hours. There are, too, other causes for consolation— such awful fiendish crime brings its own punishment—if there were any influences which might induce a difference of sentiment in the North they are now forgotten, and all are more than ever <u>united</u> in one common effort to sustain our country—our rulers—to for ever crush the sin which has been the sole cause of all our suffering, the only fear being lest indignation should carry us too far in visiting upon the whole South the crime of a few. They have lost their <u>best friend</u>. Our estimation of our new President is constantly increasing, though as yet but little has transpired to require much exposition of his views: yet, as there is no change of Cabinet, and our late beloved President had, in a very important meeting the day of his death, given his plans for future action, we trust they will be regarded, and on the whole, not varied. There is the strongest feeling to uphold Johnson, and not the least depression about our entire triumph and final reconstruction, as a Union, not again to be easily broken. It is impossible to think of anything else—the horror has not passed away from our minds—the deep feeling of sorrow is yet too strong. I cannot speak of our Y.M. which is now in session, nor dwell on other topics, which at another time would occur to me. . . . I wish I could spend an hour or two with thee—there are so many things I want to tell thee, so many details I could give of the great event which still fills our minds and hearts.

To-morrow evening the remains are to arrive here, and lie in Independence Hall on First-day—the public having the privilege of passing in to see them. I should not wish to view them in such a crowd; but if it had been possible to have the privilege, as my friend S. F. Smiley had, of looking at him in the quiet of his home, greatly should I have valued it. I had a letter from her describing her visit in Washington, and thinking thou wouldst like to see it, I have copied all relating to our dear President. I wish thou could see our city with the signs of mourning—there is such <u>universal</u>, true, <u>heartfelt</u> sorrow. On fourth day, all stores were shut, all houses barred—even Friends, who so seldom give public demonstrations of either joy or sorrow, were participants in this, so far as closed shutters, though we of course showed no draped flags. The churches were open and the streets, during the noon hours, almost deserted—in the afternoon the great thorough-fares were crowded with the lower classes looking at the various mourning draperies, &c., but all moving in a quiet subdued manner— no boisterous talking, no confusion—it was very impressive—such a different scene from the joyous one we had anticipated in the great illumination we were to have had for Lee's surrender. A friend of mine had a most touching account from Bishop Simpson (Methodist), of the last day of our lamented President's life, which he had from Mrs. Lincoln herself, when he visited her in her sick room, where she has been ever since the sad tragedy. It was a remarkably happy day, beautifully clear, bright and lovely externally, and wonderfully full of <u>events</u>. His son, the captain, breakfasted with them, and gave many narrations of recent affairs in Richmond, which greatly pleased his father—then a most satisfactory interview with Grant, and afterwards with the whole Cabinet except Seward—a most important meeting, in which he spoke of his future policy.

After dinner he took a drive with his wife, who said he was so <u>happy</u>—he spoke of his delight at the near approach of peace—his great satisfaction in the unanimity of his Cabinet, and on the whole prospect before him as regarded the country—she scarcely thought she had seen him so buoyant with pleasure since he came to Washington. Was not his work done, and has he not passed away at the moment of his greatest triumph, when his fame was at its zenith, and can never now be dimmed! . . .

Three hours after the death of President Lincoln, his successor was inaugurated without commotion—without any unnecessary ceremony—no confusion anywhere; and all the people in the length and breadth of our land, move quietly on with an increased confidence in their strength, and a firmer determination to uphold their chief. I think every one, even the rebels themselves, feel that the awful tragedy strengthens <u>our</u> cause. <u>They</u> regret it sincerely, knowing the injury it must do them. <u>His</u> voice, who always pleaded for mercy and pardon, being silenced, they can but dread that justice and judgment will take their places—we trust, <u>not</u> with any feelings of <u>revenge</u>, though some fears are felt that our new Head may prove in some cases too severe. But public confidence in him has increased, and we hope for good out of all this terrible evil.

23rd

The body of our beloved President is lying in Independence Hall, and from a <u>very</u> early hour this morning, Chestnut Street has been crowded with people passing in to see him—no confusion—no loud words—but with hushed, yet impatient feeling, each awaits his turn. Canst thou not picture the scene in that old room where thou lingered one morning? His head rests at the foot of the great bell whose motto is so appropriate "Proclaim liberty throughout the land to all the inhabitants thereof." F. Y. tells me that the carrying in of the bier through the long avenue by night, was most solemn and imposing: while the wide walk was lighted with intense brilliancy, all the rest was in darkness, and the hushed tread of the bearers, amid a voiceless multitude, while he whom they so loved was borne past, was something never to be forgotten. We can neither think nor speak of much else. S. Bettle's sermon was upon the same subject, and touched us much. Oh! my dear friend, how much we have lost! Yet we do try not to lose sight of the mercy which has been mingled with this awful stroke, and prevented the consummation of the horrible crime at an earlier period: for certainly there was no time since he first was chosen President, when his death would not have been <u>far more</u> disastrous—and many crises when it might have been <u>fatal</u> to our cause. We tremble when we think of the consequences which would probably have ensued if it had happened before his <u>last</u> election! And we strive to still trust the protecting hand of our Almighty Father, who has so marvellously helped us so far. Though I have written so much, I have only showed the truth of my first sentence that words are utterly inadequate to give a <u>just</u> idea of all we feel—but thou wilt supply what the poor words do not give, for I know thou wilt feel with us.

## 1865: JUNE 6
## VARINA DAVIS TO MONTGOMERY BLAIR

*Even as the nation variously mourned Lincoln's death and celebrated or rued the North's victory, Confederate president Jefferson Davis and his cabinet were pursued in their flight south from Richmond. When he was captured by Union soldiers in Georgia in early May, Davis was wearing his wife's cloak, and the Northern newspapers, getting wind of this, had a field day crowing over his supposed cowardice in*

*disguising himself as a woman. Not in a particularly forgiving mood, Confederate*
*first lady Varina Davis (1826–1906) sent this account (only this section of the letter*
*has survived) to an old friend, postmaster Montgomery Blair (1813–1883).*

Davis was eventually jailed in Virginia and released on bail in 1867. He neither received nor

sought any pardon. The "infamous accusation" to which Varina referred was Andrew Johnson's

contention that Jefferson Davis had been involved in Lincoln's assassination plot; a $100,000

reward had been issued for his capture. Lieutenant Colonel Benjamin D. Pritchard led the

capture.

... therefore handed them to one of his aides—he did not intend to camp with us that night, but to ride forward and meet the marauders if possible before they reached us. He therefore left his pistols in their holsters on the saddle, in the possession of his servant. As night drew on he seemed so exhausted that he decided to stay all night with us.

Before I left Richmond, in order to pay all the outstanding debts and to procure money enough to go away from there, I sent my silver, china, glass, and little ornaments, not excluding the little gifts received from dear friends, years ago—also as much of my clothing and of Mr. Davis as was not absolutely in use—to be exposed for public sale—some at auction, some at different stores. I also sold the debris of our magnificent library, several hundred volumes, which had been sent us after the Federals robbed us of all they considered it worth their while to steal or sell. As these things were sold for Confederate money, I left it in Richmond to be converted into gold and sent to me by some convenient opportunity. Judge Reagan brought it to me in a pair of saddlebags upon a pack mule and told me it amounted to a little over $8,000 in gold, this was left in the ambulance in which we travelled. This money, and a pair of fine carriage horses, which poverty had compelled me to sell and which the citizens of Richmond bought and returned to me, constituted all my worldly wealth. Just before day the enemy charged our camp yelling like demons. Mr. Davis received timely warning of their approach but believing them to be our own people, deliberately made his toilette and was only disabused of the delusion when he saw them deploying a few yards off. He started down to the little stream hoping to meet his servant with his horse and arms—but knowing he would be recognised, I plead with him to let me throw over him a large water-proof which had often served him in sickness during the summer season for a dressing gown, and which I hoped might so cover his person, that in the grey of the morning he would not be recognised. As he strode off I threw over his head a little black shawl which was around my own shoulders, seeing that he could not find his hat and after he started sent my colored woman after him with a bucket for water, hoping that he would pass unobserved. He attempted no disguise, consented to no subterfuge, but if he had, in failure is found the only matter of cavil. Had he assumed an elaborate female attire as a sacrifice to save a country, the heart of which trusted in him, it had been well. When he had proceeded a few yards, the guards around our tents with a shocking oath called out to know who that was. I said it was my mother and he halted Mr Davis, who threw off the cloak with a defiance and when called upon to surrender did not do so—and but for the interposition of my person between his and the guns would have been shot. I told the man to shoot me if he pleased, to which he answered he "would not mind it a bit" which I readily believed.

While this was transpiring a scene of robbery was going on in camp, which beggars description—trunks were broken open, letters and clothing scattered on the ground, all the gold taken, even our prayer books and bibles taken from the ambulances—these latter articles were easily recovered, as being of no use to the robbers. My baby's little wardrobe was stolen almost entirely, the other children shared the same fate—When we reached Savannah, the city contributed a part of their children's clothes to clothe them until I could have more made. The negroes were robbed of their wardrobe and the Federal soldiers wore their clothing before them, though reminded of the fact by the negroes. Our faithful slave Robert owned his horse, which was taken from him and turned over to one of the officers, as were my horses. Capt. Hudson (so said his men) received my gold, took the lion's share and secreted the rest for the soldiers, consequently Col. Pritchard's search for it among the valuables of the men was unsuccessful. Col. Pritchard did what he could to protect us from insult, but against robbery he was powerless to give us protection, though I feel sure he tried to prevent it. We were robbed not once nor twice, but every time the wagons stopped. When we had progressed about ten miles on our dreary return from the scene of our capture, a man met us waving a paper, containing the first copy the cavalry had seen, of Mr. Johnson's infamous accusation against Mr. Davis, and the reward offered for his apprehension. It gave him no uneasiness and was evidently not believed by the men to be founded in truth. In conversation with some of the officers, Mr. Davis' staff were told that it was fortunate that no resistance was made—for they were ordered, if any was offered to fire into the tents (there being only two, and those two containing women and children) and "make a general massacre." Another said "bloody work" should have been made of the whole party—Col. Pritchard told me he did not expect to find Mr. Davis with me but came out to take my train and carry it back to Macon. . . .

*If any of the losses the North had suffered were softened by victory, defeat in the South was simply defeat. Eva Berrien Jones (1841–1890) was an educated Georgia woman and the wife of Charles Colcock Jones, Jr., a lawyer, military officer, and former Savannah mayor. For her, the end of the Civil War brought what she described to her mother-in-law, Mary (1808–1869), as an inescapable sense of sadness.*
Ruthie was Charles's daughter from a previous marriage. "D. V." stands for *Deo volente,* meaning "God willing."

Augusta, Tuesday, June 13, 1865

Dear Mother,

It is with sad and heavy hearts we mark the dark, crowding events of this most disastrous year. We have seen hope after hope fall blighted and withering about us, until our country is no more—merely a heap of ruins and ashes. A joyless future of probable ignominy, poverty, and want is all that spreads before us, and God alone knowing where any of us will end a life robbed of every blessing and already becoming intolerable. You see, it is with no resigned spirit that I yield to the iron yoke our conqueror forges for his fallen and powerless foe. The degradation of a whole country and a proud people is indeed a mighty, an all-enveloping sorrow.

I have uninterruptedly sought forgetfulness, or rather temporary relief, from these present griefs in a most earnest application to study. Some fourteen volumes of history have claimed my recent attention. And yet the study of human nature from the earliest epochs affords one little comfort. How vice and wickedness, injustice and every human passion runs riot, flourishes, oftentimes going unpunished to the tomb! And how the little feeble sickly attempts of virtue struggle, and after a brief while fade away, unappreciated and unextolled! The depravity of the human heart is truly wonderful, and the moiety of virtue contained on the historic page truly deplorable. How often have these same sorrows and unmerited punishments that we are now undergoing been visited upon the brave, the deserving, the heroic, and the patient of all ages and in all climes! . . . Virtue, like the violet, modest and unnoted, blossoms in silence and fades softly away; the fragrance it threw on the morning breeze was very sweet and very rare; but the breeze died away, and the memory of the virtuous dies too. I fear you will think I am growing very allegorical, but really "the common course of events" is so out-of-date that it needs a few extra flourishes on everything we do at present to mark this most unnatural era. Had it not been for my dear books, the one comfort as yet unmolested (I do not refer to those we left in Savannah), I am inclined to believe I should have been constrained to apply for a suite of apartments in some lunatic asylum—if they too have not vanished with other national comforts!

Charles, thank Heaven, is very well and just the same immaculate darling he always was, but just now so deeply and exclusively busy at the plantation, earning his daily bread "by the sweat of his brow," that I only am occasionally enchanted with a flying visit. He received a week or two ago a letter from you which we were both rejoiced to receive, and which, by the way, he immediately answered, I enclosing a note. But after having written, some farther developments of Yankee policy being foreshadowed, he waited to see the results, and as he was suddenly called away, left me with directions "not to send the letter." I do not feel at liberty to do so until I hear more from him.

I suppose you have learned even in the more secluded portions of the country that slavery is entirely abolished—a most unprecedented robbery, and most unwise policy. So it must appear even to the ignorant. I know it is only intended for a greater humiliation and loss to us, but I should think that even the powerful and unconscientious conqueror would reap the ill effects of so unguarded a movement. However it is done; and we, the chained witnesses, can only look on and draw inferences and note occurrences—"only this and nothing more." There has been a great rush of the freedmen from all families in the city and from neighboring plantations. Adeline, Grace, and Polly have all departed in search of freedom, without bidding any of us an affectionate adieu. All of Dr. Joe's servants have left save Titus and Agrippa and children, I think he told me. . . . We have lost many of our servants, but a sufficient number have remained to serve us, and as yet these appear faithful and anxious to please. On our plantation everything is "at sixes and sevens." One day they work, and the next they come to town. Of course no management of them is allowed. Our Yankee masters think that their term of slavery having expired, that the shackles they have abandoned, more firmly riveted, will do for us their former owners. And we meekly bow the head, receive chains and insults, and observe a mute and most submissive demeanor. Veritably like lambs we are led to the slaughter, and like sheep before the shearers we are dumb. And they shear ahead—in a manner most wonderful to behold.

Very shortly I will, D. V., leave "these scenes so charming" to forget in a summer sojourning among my best-loved friends some of these present miseries. After the annual delight of a Sparta trip I hope to visit some friends in Athens;

and from thence I spend the remainder of the summer in the mountain breezes of Clarkesville with my dear aunt. I trust I'll find both health and flesh in the delightful summer retreat of my aunt, for I need both sorely—although I am a little stronger for the past few days, or rather <u>two days</u>.

I fear I am quite wearying you with my unusual volubility. My dearest mother unites with me in warm love to yourself and Ruthie. I suppose the little lady is grown entirely beyond one's recollection. Kiss her for me. I know her papa would send a very affectionate one for her were he here. Dismayed at the divers accumulations of great poverty, hopeless and in the depths of an abyss of despair, faintly I reiterate:

> Affectionately yours,
> Eva.

# RECONSTRUCTION AND THE GILDED AGE

## 1866

~

## 1899

It is hard to write, or speak, or think of anything else, and the one subject that Southerners discuss whenever they meet is, "What is to become of us?"

—*Frances Butler*
*April 12, 1866*

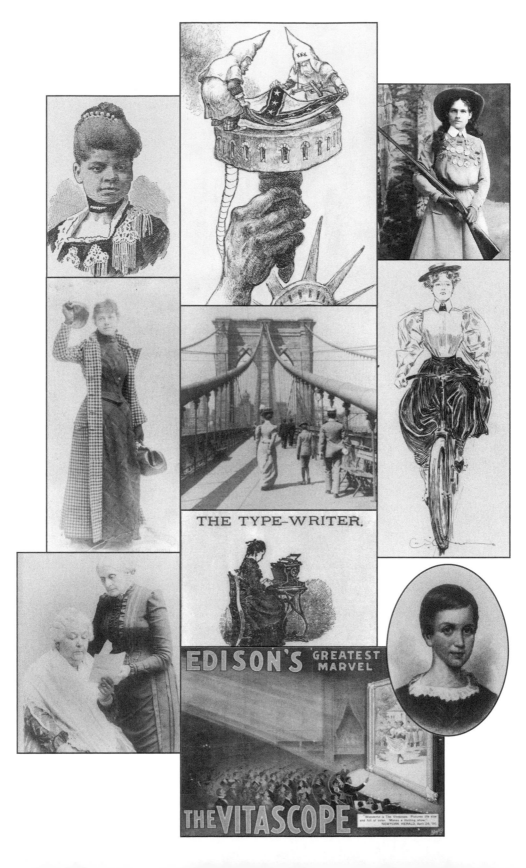

THE TYPE-WRITER.

EDISON'S GREATEST MARVEL

THE VITASCOPE

# BETWEEN 1866 AND 1899...

**1866:** The Freedmen's Bureau, established by Congress, sets out to offer medical, educational, and economic aid to the roughly four million freed slaves. ★ Susan B. Anthony and Elizabeth Cady Stanton found the American Equal Rights Association, with the goal of achieving universal suffrage. ★ The Ku Klux Klan is organized by Confederate veterans. ★ Congress authorizes a five-cent coin to be made of nickel. **1867:** The United States buys Alaska from Russia for $7.2 million. **1868:** The Fourteenth Amendment, granting citizenship and equal protection under the law to blacks, is ratified, despite the objections of Southern states. ★ Louisa May Alcott publishes the best-selling *Little Women*. **1869:** Louisa May Alcott writes in her journal: "Paid up all the debts...thank the Lord!" ★ Hoping to attract women to its motley population of gamblers, transients, and miners, Wyoming Territory gives women the vote. **1870:** The population of the United States is 38,558,371. ★ Only 3 percent of the total female population is 65 or older. ★ New York is the largest U.S. city, with nearly a million inhabitants, followed by Philadelphia, Brooklyn, and St. Louis. ★ Despite the

---

Clockwise from top left: Ida B. Wells; Ku Klux Klan by Oliver Harrington; Annie Oakley; Gibson girl on bike by Charles Dana, from *Scribners* June 1895; Emily Dickinson; Vitascope poster; Elizabeth Cady Stanton (seated) and Susan B. Anthony; Typewriter advertisement from *Illustrated Photographic World,* March 1896; Nellie Bly; Brooklyn Bridge.

resistance of women hoping for a universal suffrage amendment, the Fifteenth Amendment is ratified, granting the vote to black men. 1871: Tony Pastor establishes a free "Ladies Night" at his New York theater, offering valentines, dress patterns, and flour as incentives to gain family audiences. ★ P. T. Barnum introduces the "Greatest Show on Earth" in Brooklyn. ★ The Chicago fire leaves 98,000 people homeless and is responsible for 250 deaths and the destruction of more than 17,000 buildings. 1873: William "Boss" Tweed is accused of defrauding New York City of some $200 million. ★ Thirteen women are enrolled in classes at Yale University. ★ Mark Twain and Charles Dudley Warner publish *The Gilded Age,* a novel whose title comes to stand for a period of greed, ostentation, and political corruption. ★ The first typewriters are mass-produced. ★ The Woman's Christian Temperance Union is founded in upstate New York. 1876: Dr. Mary Jacobi wins Harvard's prestigious Boylston Prize for "The Question of Rest for Women during Menstruation," an essay in which she offers statistical and medical evidence that women's strength and health—contrary to popular assumptions—are not lessened during their monthly cycles. 1879: Thomas Edison perfects the incandescent lightbulb. 1881: President Garfield is assassinated. ★ Atlanta Baptist Female Seminary, later Spelman College, is established in Georgia for the education of black women. 1882: In *The Sexual System and Its Derangements,* Dr. E. C. Abbey explains that during pregnancy, a growing child "can inherit traits of character from both parents, or physical peculiarity or deformity, or it can resemble the person who has made the first agreeable sexual impression upon the mother." 1883: The Brooklyn Bridge is opened. ★ L. A. Thompson introduces the roller coaster at Coney Island's Luna Park; it costs five cents to ride, earns $600 a day, and pays for itself within three weeks. 1885: The Home Insurance Company Building, the first "skyscraper," is completed, at a height of ten stories, in Chicago. 1888: George Eastman introduces the Kodak camera and, with it, popular photography; unlike other cameras, which require users to develop their own film, the Kodak is sent back to the manufacturer, where the film is developed and the camera reloaded. **1889**: Carrying currency, a watch, underwear, veils, caps, slippers, a dressing gown, writing equipment, sewing equipment, a cup, a flask, and a jar of cold cream, journalist Nellie Bly sets out around the world with the goal of breaking the 80-day record of Jules Verne's fictional Phileas Fogg. **1890**: After 72 days, 6 hours, 11 minutes, and 14 seconds, Nellie Bly returns to Jersey City, triumphant. ★ Women make up 17 percent of the labor force. ★ Three percent of white married women work. **1893**: During its six months of operation, the Chicago world's fair, known as the World's Columbian Exposition, draws more than 27 million visitors and offers exhibits featuring everything from electricity and the dynamo to a map of the United States made entirely of pickles. **1894**: *The Ladies' Standard Magazine* proposes bicycling costumes—some featuring buckles for keeping skirts at the ankle—that are designed to preserve a woman's modesty while preventing her skirts from becoming entangled. One woman is quoted as saying, "I climb hills impossible before.... With my bloomers and heavy undergarments, leggins to my knees, a corset waist, and in cool weather a double-breasted box coat, which amply protects me from chilling, I enjoy my riding." **1895**: Elizabeth Cady Stanton publishes *The Woman's Bible,* in which she questions how "divinely" women's "Divinely ordained sphere" has been ordained. **1896**: In the *Youth's Educator for Home and Society,* readers are instructed: "The children in a household should be encouraged to talk, but not permitted to show off, and say smart things." **1898**: Victory in the Spanish-American War turns the United States into a true world power. **1899**: Scott Joplin writes "Maple Leaf Rag." ★ In *The Education of Mr. Pipp,* Charles Dana Gibson highlights the hourglass-shaped "Gibson Girl," whose tiny waist and confident gaze will become an ideal for early-twentieth-century women.

*For five years, Southern women had dreamed of having their lives return to normal after the war. The reality was vastly different. One of every four Confederate soldiers had died. Homes were in shambles, and many plantations lacked livestock or seed— not to mention the slaves who had worked the land. In Georgia, Frances Butler (1838–1910) accompanied her father, Pierce, when he reclaimed their three plantations and, with the initially willing help of their former slaves, began to try to piece things back together. It was not unusual for freed slaves who were unable to find jobs or buy land to return to their former owners with the hope of being paid to do the same work they had done in bondage.*

The island Frances mentions was named Butler's Island and was the site of the family's plantations. Frances was the daughter also of the well-known actress Fanny Kemble, who, unlike her husband, disapproved of slavery; they had divorced in 1849.

April 12, 1866

Dearest S——,

I have relapsed into barbarism total! How I do wish you could see me; you would be so disgusted. Well, I know now what the necessaries of life mean, and am surprised to find how few they are, and how many things we consider absolutely necessary which are really luxuries.

When I wrote last I was waiting in Savannah for the arrival of some things the overseer had taken from the Island, which I wished to look over before I made any further purchases for the house. When they came, however, they looked more like the possessions of an Irish emigrant than anything else; the house linen fortunately was in pretty good order, but the rest I fancy had furnished the overseer's house in the country ever since the war; the silver never reappeared. So I began my purchases with twelve common wooden chairs, four washstands, four bedsteads, four large tubs, two bureaux, two large tables and four smaller ones, some china, and one common lounge, my one luxury—and this finished the list.

Thus supplied, my maid and I started last Saturday morning for the Island; halfway down we stuck fast on a sand-bar in the river, where we remained six hours, very hot and devoured by sand-flies, till the tide came in again and floated us off, which pleasant little episode brought us to Darien at 1 A.M. My father was there, however, to meet us with our own boat, and as it was bright moonlight we got off with all our things, and were rowed across to the island by four of our old negroes.

I wish I could give you any idea of the house. The floors were bare, of course, many of the panes were out of the windows, and the plaster in many places was off the walls, while one table and two old chairs constituted the furniture. It was pretty desolate, and my father looked at me in some anxiety to see how it would affect me, and seemed greatly relieved when I burst out laughing. My bed was soon unpacked and made, my tub filled, my basin and pitcher mounted on a barrel, and I settled for the rest of the night.

The next morning I and my little German maid, who fortunately takes everything very cheerily, went to work, and together we made things quite comfortable; unpacked our tables and chairs, put up some curtains (made out of some white muslin I had brought down for petticoats) edged with pink calico, covered the tables with two bright-coloured covers I found in the trunk of house linen, had the windows mended, hung up my picture of General Lee (which had been sent to me the day before I left Philadelphia) over the mantelpiece, and put my writing things and nicknacks on the table, so that when my father and Mr. J—— came in they looked round in perfect astonishment, and quite rewarded me by their praise.

Our kitchen arrangements would amuse you. I have one large pot, one frying-pan, one tin saucepan, and this is all; and yet you would be astonished to see how much our cook accomplishes with these three utensils, and the things don't taste <u>very</u> much alike.

Yesterday one of the negroes shot and gave me a magnificent wild turkey, which we roasted on one stick set up between two others before the fire, and capital it was. The broiling is done on two old pieces of iron laid over the ashes. Our food consists of corn and rice bread, rice, and fish caught fresh every morning out of the river, oysters, turtle soup, and occasionally a wild turkey or duck. Other meat, as yet, it is impossible to get.

Is it not all strange and funny? I feel like Robinson Crusoe with three hundred men Fridays. Then my desert really blooms like the rose. On the acre of ground enclosed about the house are a superb magnolia tree, covered with its queenly flowers, roses running wild in every direction; orange, fig, and peach trees now in blossom, give promise of fruit later on, while every tree and bush is alive with red-birds, mocking-birds, blackbirds, and jays, so as I sit on the piazza the air comes to me laden with sweet smells and sweet sounds of all descriptions.

There are some drawbacks; fleas, sandflies, and mosquitoes remind us that we are not quite in Heaven, and I agree with my laundry woman, Phillis, who upon my maid's remonstrating with her for taking all day to wash a few towels, replied, "Dat's true, Miss Louisa, but de fleas jist have no principle, and day bites me so all de time, I jist have to stop to scratch."

The negroes seem perfectly happy at getting back to the old place and having us there, and I have been deeply touched by many instances of devotion on their part. On Sunday morning, after their church, having nothing to do, they all came to see me, and I must have shaken hands with nearly four hundred. They were full of their troubles and sufferings up the country during the war, and the invariable winding up was, "Tank the Lord, missus, we's back, and sees you and massa again." I said to about twenty strong men, "Well, you know you are free and your own masters now," when they broke out with, "No, missus, we belong to you; we be yours as long as we lib."

Nearly all who have lived through the terrible suffering of these past four years have come back, as well as many of those who were sold seven years ago. Their good character was so well known throughout the State that people were very anxious to hire them and induce them to remain in the "up country," and told them all sorts of stories to keep them, among others that my father was dead, but all in vain. One old man said, "If massa be dead den, I'll go back to the old place and mourn for him." So they not only refused good wages, but in many cases spent all they had to get back, a fact that speaks louder than words as to their feeling for their old master and former treatment.

Our overseer, who was responsible for all our property, has little or nothing to give us back, while everything that was left in charge of the negroes has been taken care of and given back to us without the hope or wish of reward. One old man has guarded the stock so well from both Southern and Northern marauders, that he has now ninety odd sheep and thirty cows under his care. Unfortunately they are on a pine tract some twelve miles away up the river, and as we have no means of transporting them we cannot get them until next year.

One old couple came up yesterday from St. Simon's, Uncle John and Mum Peggy, with five dollars in silver half-dollars tied up in a bag, which they said a Yankee captain had given them the second year of the war for some chickens, and this money these two old people had kept through all their want and suffering for three years because it had been paid for fowls belonging to us. I wonder whether white servants would be so faithful or honest! My father was much moved at this act of faithfulness, and intends to have something made out of the silver to commemorate the event, having returned them the same amount in other money.

One of the great difficulties of this new state of things is, what is to be done with the old people who are too old, and the children who are too young, to work? One Northern General said to a planter, in answer to this question, "Well, I suppose they must die," which, indeed, seems the only thing for them to do. To-day Mr. J—— tells me my father has agreed to support the children for three years, and the old people till they die, that is, feed and clothe them. Fortunately, as we have some property at the North we are able to do this, but most of the planters are utterly ruined and have no money to buy food for their own families, so on their plantations I do not see what else is to become of the negroes who cannot work except to die.

Yours affectionately,

F.

### 1867: APRIL 25
### HARRIET JACOBS TO EDNAH DOW CHENEY

*Born into slavery, Harriet Jacobs (1813–1897) had escaped her owner, James Norcom, at the age of twenty-two, but spent the next seven years hiding in the attic crawlspace of her grandmother's house so that she could be near her children. By 1853, having successfully come north, Jacobs wrote an article for the* New York Tribune *that led to her autobiography,* Incidents in the Life of a Slave Girl, *published in 1861. During the war, she brought supplies, medical care, and information to freed slaves, and when Reconstruction began, she returned to her first home, in Edenton, North Carolina, to help her former neighbors make the most of their freedom. She wrote this letter to Boston abolitionist Ednah Dow Cheney (1824–1904) from her grandmother's old house.*

Daisy was Cheney's daughter.

Edenton, April 25th

Dear Mrs Cheney

I felt I would like to write you a line from my old home. I am sitting under the old roof twelve feet from the spot where I suffered all the crushing weight of slavery. thank God the bitter cup is drained of its last dreg. there is no more need of hiding places to conceal slave Mothers. yet it was little to purchase the blessings of freedom. I could have worn this poor life out there to save my Children from the misery and degradation of Slavery.

I had long thought I had no attachment to my old home. as I often sit here and think of those I loved of their hard struggle in life—their unfaltering love and devotion toward myself and Children. I love to sit here and think of them. they have made the few sunny spots in that dark life sacred to me.

I cannot tell you how I feel in this place. the change is so great I can hardly take it all in   I was born here, and amid all these new born blessings, the old dark cloud comes over me, and I find it hard to have faith in rebels.

the past winter was very severe for this region of Country   it caused much suffering, and the freedmen with but few exceptions were cheated out of their crop of cotton. their contract masters shiped it for them, and when they ask for a settlement, they are answered I am daily expecting the returns. these men have gone to work cheerfully, planted another crop without the returns to live on until their present crop is made. many of the large plantations of the once wealthy Planter, is worked under the control of Colored Men. the Owners let their Plantations to the freedmen in prefference to the poor Whites. they believe the Negro determined to make money, and they will get the largest portion of it. last years experience I think will be a proffitable lesson   many will learn to act for themselves. Negro suffrage is making a stir in this place. the rebels are striving to make these people feel they are their true friends, and they must not be led astray by the Yankees. the freedmen ask if Abraham Lincoln led them astray, that his friends is their friends his enemies their enemies.

I have spent much of my time on the Plantations distrubuting seed and trying to teach the women to make Yankee gardens. they plant everything to mature in the summer, like their corn and cotton fields. I have hunted up all the old people, done what I could for them. I love to work for these old people. many of them I have known from Childhood

there is one School in Edenton well attended. on some of the Plantations there is from 15 to 25 Chrildren that cannot attend School, the distance is so far. some of the freedmen are very anxious to establish Plantation schools, as soon as the more advanced Schools, can send out teachers. many of the freedmen are willing and will sustain their teachers. at present there is a great revival in the colored Churches. the Whites say the Niggers sung and prayed until they got their freedom, and they are not satisfied. now they are singing and praying for judgment. the white members of the Baptist Church invited the colored members to their Church, to help them sing and pray. I assure you they have done it with a will. I never saw such a state of excitement   the Churches have been open night and day. these people have time to think of their souls, now they are not compelled to think for the Negro.

my love to Miss Daisy. I send her some Jassmine blossoms   tell her they bear the fragrance of freedom.

Yours Truly<br>
H Jacobs

## 1867: JUNE 23
## FRANCES BUTLER TO AN UNKNOWN RECIPIENT

*A year and some months after her father had reclaimed his Georgia plantations, Frances Butler (see page 341) painted a much less optimistic picture of their future, and a much less sanguine view of the freed slaves. The sectioning of the South into five districts, the coming to power of blacks and Northern carpetbaggers, and the imposition of Republican rule, were features of the decade-long era known as Reconstruction. In this letter, Butler expressed the profound resentment shared by many conservative Southerners.*

Gesler was the legendary fourteenth-century ruler who demanded that all his subjects, including the renowned William Tell, bow down before the ducal hat of Austria. Samuel White Baker and Paul Belloni DuChaillu were both well-known African explorers. Butler's father died later in the summer, and she would run the plantations off and on for nine more years. In 1871, she married James Wentworth Leigh, a British clergyman, and moved with him to London in 1877.

June 23, 1867

Dearest S——,

We are, I am afraid, going to have terrible trouble by-and-by with the negroes, and I see nothing but gloomy prospects for us ahead. The unlimited power that the war has put into the hands of the present Government at Washington seems to have turned the heads of the party now in office, and they don't know where to stop. The whole South is settled and quiet, and the people too ruined and crushed to do anything against the Government, even if they felt so inclined, and all are returning to their former peaceful pursuits, trying to rebuild their fortunes, and thinking of nothing else. Yet the treatment we receive from the Government becomes more and more severe every day, the last act being to divide the whole South into five military districts, putting each under the command of a United States General, doing away with all civil courts and law. Even

D—— who you know is a Northern republican, says it is most unjustifiable, not being in any way authorised by the existing state of things, which he confesses he finds very different from what he expected before he came. If they would frankly say they intend to keep us down, it would be fairer than making a pretence of readmitting us to equal rights, and then trumping up stories of violence to give a show of justice to treating us as the conquered foes of the most despotic Government on earth, and by exciting the negroes to every kind of insolent lawlessness, to goad the people into acts of rebellion and resistance.

The other day in Charleston, which is under the command of that respectable creature General S——, they had a firemen's parade, and took the occasion to hoist a United States flag, to which this modern Gesler insisted on everyone raising his cap as he passed underneath. And by a hundred other such petty tyrannies are the people, bruised and sore, being roused to desperation; and had this been done directly after the war it would have been bad enough, but it was done the other day, three years after the close of the war.

The true reason is the desire and intention of the Government to control the elections of the South, which under the constitution of the country they could not legally do. So they have determined to make an excuse for setting aside the laws, and in order to accomplish this more fully, each commander in his separate district has issued an order declaring that unless a man can take an oath that he had not voluntarily borne arms against the United States Government, nor in any way aided or abetted the rebellion, he cannot vote. This simply disqualifies every white man at the South from voting, disfranchising the whole white population, while the negroes are allowed to vote en masse.

This is particularly unjust, as the question of negro voting was introduced and passed in Congress as an amendment to the constitution, but in order to become a law a majority of two-thirds of the State Legislatures must ratify it, and so to them it was submitted, and rejected by all the Northern States with two exceptions, where the number of negro voters would be so small as to be harmless. Our Legislatures are not allowed to meet, but this law, which the North has rejected, is to be forced upon us, whose very heart it pierces and prosperity it kills. Meanwhile, in order to prepare the negroes to vote properly, stump speakers from the North are going all through the South, holding political meetings for the negroes saying things like this to them: "My friends, you will have your rights, won't you?" ("Yes," from the negroes.) "Shall I not go back to Massachusetts and tell your brothers there that you are going to ride in the street cars with white ladies if you please?" ("Yes, yes," from the crowd.) "That if you pay your money to go to the theatre you will sit where you please, in the best boxes if you like?" ("Yes," and applause.) This I copy verbatim from a speech made at Richmond the other day, since which there have been two serious negro riots there, and the General commanding had to call out the military to suppress them.

These men are making a tour through the South, speaking in the same way to the negroes everywhere. Do you wonder we are frightened? I have been so forcibly struck lately while reading Baker's "Travels in Africa," and some of Du Chaillu's lectures, at finding how exactly the same characteristics show themselves among the negroes there, in their own native country, where no outside influences have ever affected them, as with ours here. Forced to work, they improve and are useful; left to themselves they become idle and useless, and never improve. Hard ethnological facts for the abolitionists to swallow, but facts nevertheless.

It seems foolish to fill my letter to you with such matters, but all this comes home to us with such vital force that it is hard to write, or speak, or think of anything else, and the one subject that Southerners discuss whenever they meet is, "What is to become of us?"

Affectionately yours,

F

### 1867: AUGUST 1
### CARRIE HALL TO CHRISTIAN RAUSHENBERG

---

*Marriage between the black and white races was hardly a new thing in 1867, but in the midst of the movement toward greater rights for freedmen, it loomed as a threat to white Southerners already questioning whether their supremacy would last. All too aware of this reaction, a white Georgia woman named Carrie Hall wrote to a local official named Christian Raushenberg about her marriage to a black man. Raushenberg worked for the Freedmen's Bureau, which had been created by the federal government two years earlier in anticipation of the troubles that four million slaves would encounter after the war.*

Many miscegenation laws would be repealed during Reconstruction, then reformulated at the end of the nineteenth century. If not the concept, the word "miscegenation" was relatively recent. It had been coined in an 1863 pamphlet by two Democratic newspapermen who were trying to scare voters into thinking that the North advocated widespread intermarriage. The fate of the Halls remains unclear, although there is no record that they were either prosecuted or physically harmed.

Georgetown, ga. Augt. the 1, 1867

Dr Rosinburg
Dear sir

as you are the Beaurau Aigent of this County I have some advise to Ask of you, if you please, conserning myselef and Husband. I am A white Woman and my Husband is A Colord Gentleman. Some two or three yeares ago I Became verry much Atached to this colord gentleman for whom my dissier grew stronger and stronger everry day of my life and my whole dissier was to choose him for my Companion and Husband through life and he was the only one on this earth that I dissierd for A Husband and I never would have Bin happy without him. But of Course we had to keep all of this A secreit to our selfes fiering the white people would trouble him About me and I would not have him hurt on my accout no way in this world for my respect and love was too grate fur towards him for eney thing of that kind to trouble his mind. and I would stand up in eney croud to save him frome eney trouble if I had it to do or if I have it to for it is me that has Bin the cause of this Being carried on as far as it is so By me carging him to Marry me. we came to the conclusion some two or three monthes ago that we would get Married and see what would Be the trouble with us eney way. So he got his licenes and paid for them and we ware Married By an ordaind Minster of the Gospil. though our Marrieg was somewhat secrietly we arc lawuly and honestly and truley Husband and wife Before god and man and would Be one of the happest Copple in the world if it was not for this: some of the white people have learnt some way or other that we are married or at least that I have married this Colord gentleman and I hear they are making grate talk of what they are going to do and my mind is in grate trouble fearing they may try to carry out some of theare planes. and I have no relationes near me to interfear with us and Besides I am an orphan and have Bin working for my selfe everry since I was Eleven yeares of age and now I am twenty six yeares of age and no one has eney right to interfeare with me or my Husband or at least I don't think they have under the circumstantes as he was my choice. and now my Dear Sir the advise I Ask of you is this: if you please to let me know has eney one eney rightes or law or Authority to interfeare with us and if not will you Be kind Enough <u>to give each of us frome your hand A writing that will save us frome eney trouble, that is, if it is in your power to do so, and if not and you can not Atend to it for us will you please informe me who to Apply to</u> and if you can please give us two notes one for my Husband and one for me. my Husband is liveing in Ala. and I am living in ga. the reason we are not living togetha: he is in

A contract on A plantation and cannot leave till the end of the year and I left that Neihberhood knowing that the white people would Be against me for marring this colord gentleman and I am living with my Husbands Uncle in georgetown ga. and if you can understand my trouble By this letter and can help me out please do so as soon as you can and I never can thank you Enough as long as I live. I will now give you my Husbands name: Sandy Alexander Hall lives near Eufaula, Barbour Co., Ala. and my name is carrie Hall living in Georgetown, Ga. I write you Confidentianly please answer this as soon as you can and excuse my Bad writing and spelling and all so the letter. I wrote it in the Best of my knowledg and hope you my understand it.

> yours
> verry respectfully,
> Carrie Hall

Direct your letter Back to Mr. Seaborn Hall, georgetown, ga.

### 1867: AUGUST 27
### MATILDA FRIX TO THE FREEDMEN'S BUREAU

*Though the specific goals of the Freedmen's Bureau were to help with labor contracts; open schools and hospitals; and supply food, clothes, and land to former slaves, its overarching purpose was to protect civil rights. In a time when those rights were frequently resented, that was rarely easy. Local branches of the bureau were besieged with letters like those of Carrie Hall (previous letter) and Matilda Frix, a former slave who lived in Calhoun, Georgia.*

Calhoun, August 27, 1867

On Tuesday night, on or about the 20th of August, 1867, late in the night, don't know what time, three men came into the house where myself and Cheany Ransom, colored, are living in the town of Calhoun, about fifty yards west of the railroad depot. We had the door fastened by putting a shovel under it. These three men forced the door open, came in, cursed and swore, tore around generally, came and pulled the cover from me, said they would get into bed. I complained of being sick. One of the party stood in the middle of room, fired off his pistol, don't know at what he fired. Think he fired out the door. The moon was shining bright, could see them quite plain. Could not tell which one of them fired the pistol. I know that Matt Thompson and a Mr. Finchen was there. Am not positive who the third man was, think it was Mr. Pinson.

On Friday night, the 23rd of August, 1867, three men came into my house away late in the night. Had a chair behind the door. They forced the door open, came in, struck a light, walked around the room, pulled the covering from my face, went over to Cheany Ransom's bed, pulled the covering from her face. She started to holler and shout. Pulled out a pistol, rubbed it over her face, said they would blow her brains out if she made any noise. Jim Printen, a colored man, and my brother from the country, was sleeping in the house. Jim Printen started out of the door. Those men fired at him two shots in the house. Started out after him, could not catch him. Some of the party said, "Let us burn them out!" Had a light and was trying to catch Cheany's dress on fire. Think their intention was to burn us out and drive us away from town. In fact, they told Cheany Ransom to get out of here or they would kill her.

On the evening of the 24th, we got some men to come and put a fastening on our door, so that no person could come in. Went to bed. Some time in the night was awakened by some party throwing large rocks in through the windows, smashing in the windows, firing pistol shots through the house, just above our bed. Do not know who they were but think it was the same party. The reason for their doing so was, I think, because Cheany Ransom had complained to the Bureau Agent about Mrs. Hunt owing her for services and could not get anything from her. They had a trial over it before Mr. Blacker, the Agent, and he ordered Mrs. Hunt to pay Cheany $20. Mrs. Hunt said that same night if she had to pay her that Cheany should not live here to enjoy it.

### 1868: JUNE
### LOUISA MAY ALCOTT TO THOMAS NILES

*Louisa May Alcott (1832–1888) had volunteered as a nurse during the Civil War, and though she was soon sent home with typhoid, her* Hospital Sketches, *published in 1863, brought her considerable recognition as a writer. Up until then, in addition to working as a maid and a teacher, she had published gothic thrillers under the name A. M. Barnard. She was thirty-five and in need of financial security when she wrote the novel that would make her truly famous. It was her publisher, Thomas Niles (1825–1894), who had suggested a "girls' story," and Alcott wrote* Little Women *in two and a half months, though she complained: "Never liked girls or knew many, except my sisters; but our queer plays and experiences may prove interesting, though I doubt it." The novel would be a terrific success, but Alcott, in this letter to Niles, showed a typical practicality about what she had wrought.*

There would indeed be a "No 2." In subsequent years, Alcott would publish *An Old-Fashioned*

*Girl, Little Men,* and *Jo's Boys,* among others. *The Earthly Paradise* was an epic poem by William Morris. Charles-Augustin Sainte-Beuve was a French literary critic. British author Jean Ingelow was far better known than Alcott at the time.

Mr Niles

I think "Little Women," had better be the title for No 1. "Young Women," or something of that sort, for No 2, <u>if</u> there is a No 2.

Twenty chapters are all that I planned to have & there are but eight more. I dont see how it can be spun out to make twenty four chapters & give you your 400 pages. I will do my best however. I liked the looks of the page which you sent.

We are enjoying the books which accompanied the blocks. "The Earthly Paradise" I particularly like. Saint Beuve also is very interesting, but I can see how people who know little of the personal history of his celebrated women might feel disappointed at finding portraits & not lives. Jean Ingelow's stories have begun to circulate among my young friends, & the "Black Polyanthus" is the favorite of them all.

With many thanks I am

yours respectfully
L. M. Alcott

## 1869: MARCH 22
## MARY TODD LINCOLN TO MARY HARLAN LINCOLN

*The assassination of Abraham Lincoln left his wife, Mary Todd Lincoln (1818–1882), shattered, and her mental health had not always been rock-solid before. Even as first lady, she had been accused of reckless extravagance in her purchases of clothing and other material goods. Now, with her fifteen-year-old son, Thomas ("Tad") Lincoln, she traveled Europe, buying fabric, jewelry, and furniture, and sending much of it—along with insistent instructions and the occasional diatribe—to her older son, Robert, and his wife, Mary Harlan Lincoln (1846–1937). Two years later, the death of Tad further unhinged Mary Todd Lincoln, and she became terrified of solitude, convinced that someone was trying to poison her, and certain that an Indian spirit was menacing her. In 1875, positive that her only remaining child was dying, she came back to the States, where Robert asked the court to commit her. As it happened, the letter below—and others, similar in their evidence of how erratic she was—was never needed in court: A jury took just three hours to find her insane.*

Mary's hostility to Julia Dent Grant predated Ulysses S. Grant's 1869 inauguration, and Julia's dislike of Mary is said to have been one of the reasons the Grants declined the Lincolns' invitation to join them at *An American Cousin*. Strangely, despite Mary's talk of beauty, Julia was not known for being particularly pretty. The Chicago house that Mary bought was at 375 West Washington Street. It is not clear who "E. H." was. Bettie Stuart and Lizzie Brown were both relatives.

Frankfort.
March 22<sup>d</sup>

My very dear Mary:

After a most tedious journey from Nice, of constant travelling for 3 days—I arrived here this morning. Of course, I sent immediately for my Taddie, & he has just left me for an hour, I feel that I cannot refrain from writing you—for your most welcome letter of March 1<sup>st</sup> has just been read. It pains me beyond expression, to learn of your recent illness & I deeply deplore—that I was not with you, to wait upon you. Let me urge upon you, my dear child, to take good care of your precious health—<u>even</u> the <u>thought</u> of you, at this great distance, is a great alleviation, to the sorrow, I am enduring. When "Mrs Grants' sudden! "beauty & attractiveness," shall have ceased to BEWILDER the vacillating & <u>time serving</u>, American people, and they will have ceased to remember—"<u>the great contrast</u>," then perhaps I may quietly return to you, as it is, nothing can please me, in what is beyond doubt—most necessary at the present time—to me—both to my peace of mind & health—<u>this</u> change of scene—My thoughts have been constantly with you, for months past—and oh how I have wished day by day, that you could be with me & enjoy the air and the sunshine, of the lovely climate I have just left. It would have been utterly impossible for me, with my present health & sad state of mind, to have taken the least interest, in <u>Italian</u> cities, this winter. I return to find my dear boy, much grown, in even so short a time & I am pained to see his face thinner, although he retains his usual bright complexion. He is doubtless greatly improving in his studies, yet I am very sure—the food he gets at his school—does not agree with him. <u>This</u>, you may be sure, is a most painful belief to me—When I am here—I can always give him, his dinner—as he has their permission to be absent. His presence has become so necessary, even to my life. In two days time, he will have his Easter vacation for ten days, & he is urging me to take him <u>somewhere</u> at that time—and if I was not so fatigued, I would gladly consent to do so, but I suppose, it will end, in my acquiescence, with his wishes.

I wish my dear Mary, you would gratify me, by taking any lace or muslin waists you may see—as of course, I shall never need them again—Also take any lace of any description—for it is all yours—or any thing you see—Every thing is only getting soiled, by being laid aside—There are also needle worked kchfs with "M L"—worked in them, which are pretty—do oblige me by considering me as a mother—for you are very dear to me, as a daughter. <u>Any thing & every thing</u> is yours—if you will consider them worth an acceptance. One lace waist, which I never wore was particularly pretty—composed entirely of lace—do make use of it & other things, as they are entirely yours—There is a white crape shawl—very rich & new—which I hope you will accept, it will be pretty, in the evening air there is a needle worked white flounced muslin dress with narrow flounces—it was never done up—<u>do</u> have this made over for yourself—in Europe—those dresses are so much worn—you will find the cape of it—<u>near by</u>—perhaps. My mind was so distracted with my grief, in that house, 375—I cannot remember, where any thing was put. It will be such a relief to me to know, that articles, that were costly, can be used & enjoyed by you—There are some spring silks—to be made up—which I think would be pretty for you. Remember, every thing is yours and feeling so fully assured as you must be—of my love—will you not, my dear girl, consider them as such? I have scarcely the least recollection of any of the articles—I know you have all you wish, but remember <u>everything</u>, in that upper room, will never be worn by me & is yours—to do with—as you please, Oh! that I could be with you! for with the lonely life, I impose upon myself, separation from those I love so much, at this trying, heart rending time, is excruciating pain—if when we meet, I find you restored to health, I will feel in a measure compensated for the dreary absence. I am glad you enjoyed your visit to Springfield—They are all so pleasantly situated—so hospitable—& so fully prepared to receive you with the greatest affection—Do make the promised visit to Mrs. E—in the summer—and go to the sea side—and <u>rest quietly for a month</u>—no less time. Let me beseech you, dear Mary, to take care of your health—My headache now aches for the tears I have shed, this morning, in thinking of you, & you sickness. And our loving boy Taddie, with his <u>great</u>, <u>good</u> heart—loves you so devotedly. I shall try & think of you, as with your dear Mother, <u>at present</u>—whilst it is, so cold in Chicago I know they will be careful of you I have the loveliest white Paris hat to send you—with the Sweetest white & green wreath—Flowers are altogether worn on these hats—a lovely apple green & white silk—for a costume a green malachite set of Jewellry & one or two other things, I found in Italy—all simple and not very expensive—but very pretty. If I only could meet with an opportunity, <u>now</u> of <u>sending</u> them—I never see, any thing, that is <u>particularly</u> pretty—that I do not wish, it was yours. My spirit is very willing, but my purse, not very extensive. I think it is time, the generous American people, would let me alone—I am sure, they, do not disturb my thoughts. I can fancy entre—nous—that the present inflated dynasty, will not be very much enjoyed by your Mother in W—Perhaps E. H.—will now add, Mrs Grant—to her group of "loveliest ladies." When I think of the wickedness, of that woman, my breath is almost taken away. It is, just such characters, who stem the tide. I am pained to hear of Bettie Stuart's death—She was a most amiable woman. And her father—is a very dearly loved Cousin. A most affectionate relation Did you see Mrs. Lizzie Brown in Springfield a very sweet woman—I am wearying you, with a very long letter. I shall, dear Mary, await most anxiously, news from you—If I do not hear soon, I shall imagine every trouble. If you will write to dear Taddie—you will gratify both him & myself very much— Tell Bob, I draw on the 17th of this month, $1,000—francs—at Nice. Do write immediately—with much love to all.

Always, most affectionately yours
M. L.

## 1870: SEPTEMBER 19
## LUCRETIA GARFIELD TO JAMES GARFIELD

*Lucretia ("Crete") Rudolph Garfield (1832–1918) spent most of her early marriage apart from her husband, James Garfield (1831–1881), who served first in the Union army and then in the House of Representatives. Despite their many separations—as well as several apparent infidelities on his part—she sounded very much in love with the future president when she wrote him this exceptionally beautiful letter.*
The Garfields had seven children together, five of whom survived to adulthood. In 1881, Garfield would become the second American president to be assassinated (see page 385).

Hiram, September 19, 1870

My Own Darling:

After the children were all quietly asleep this evening, I sat in our room by the stove, just warmed enough to make one dreamy, a long time musing over the years so long gone and the friends and loved ones who belonged to them. Then the thread of our lines grew tangled in the web, and ran wandering through it disturbed and disturbing until I stopped amazed to find myself sitting by our fireside, the loved and loving wife, and the conviction came anew, strengthened and deepened that the All-loving Father had done all for us. That his arm of strength alone had lifted us up from the confusions and out from the entanglements and had set us down alone with souls to each other transfigured by the light and glory of love. I felt that we are not living on the same plain as heretofore, that we are scarcely the same beings, but like conquering sovereigns we live in high isolation, wedded in heart and soul and life.

I am sitting now at your desk to tell you this although it may not go to you before you come to me, but however it fulfill its mission whether by going to meet you or staying here to greet you, I want it to reveal the abiding joy that reigns in my heart, and the trust which no more forsakes it. With kisses and love my spirit and my pen say to you good night.

Your own forever.
Crete.

### 1870: SEPTEMBER 22
### TOPSY TURVY TO THE WOMAN'S JOURNAL

*For nearly a decade, the priorities of women's rights reformers had been overshadowed by the war. But women had by necessity gained independence and experience during those years. In 1866, Elizabeth Cady Stanton and Susan B. Anthony had created the American Equal Rights Association to pursue both female and black suffrage. In 1868, however, the Fourteenth Amendment specifically defined citizens and voters as male, and the women's movement largely broke off from the black suffrage movement. By 1870, when a Kansas writer who called herself "Topsy Turvy" wrote to* The Woman's Journal, *the task of attaining women's enfranchisement may have seemed all but impossible.*

"General T." was presumably General Turvy. "Pusley," also called purslane, is an herb that can grow as a weed. "Bantling" meant infant. "Grum" meant glum.

Lofty Level, Kansas, Sept. 22, 1870

Dear Journal:—

The shirts are done! And now I write you because the General wants me to. You know all the "Woman's Rights" women like to please good men, the anti-Woman's Rights people to the contrary notwithstanding.

The other day General T. says, "Topsy, why don't you write for the Woman's Journal? I don't see a single Kansas woman's name in it."

Now the General knows I'm a wife, mother and housekeeper—have painted my house outside and in, this summer—make the bread and pastry for a family of six and seven—make butter to sell, and pack every week, besides supplying the family—cultivate the flowers and raise the vegetables—do all the cutting, fitting and sewing for my own family, and some for my neighbors—give music lessons to two pupils—and that amid the multiplicity of cares I've written but very few articles this summer for my favorite temperance paper; so said I, "General, when shall I write?"

"O, when you get my shirts done!"

Well, the shirts are done. Now for my article, which may find a lodgment in your waste paper basket. In that case, I might better spend my time pulling "pusley," (properly purslain), or digging potatoes for market, than scribbling. But do what you deem best with my bantling. If it is doomed to the basket, I'll rejoice that our Journal is amply filled by abler pens.

To give you some idea of the condition of the female mind in this particular locality, permit me to relate a portion of a canvasser's experience while soliciting subscribers for the Woman's Journal last spring. We'll begin with young, blue-eyed Mrs. D.

Canvasser.—"And how do you like the Journal?"

Mrs. D.—"O, very much!"

Canvasser.—"Then, I shall have the pleasure of adding your name to the list of subscribers?"

Mrs. D.—"Well, it will have to be as Mr. D. says—he carries the purse; if he'll foot the bill I'll take the paper."

Mr. D.—(in grum voice) "I've no money to pay for her papers; if she wants to read, she can read mine. There's the Ledger and the New York Tribune; got plenty good reading; enough in 'em for anybody."

So she left Mrs. D., with no help or comforter save her liege lord and husband, to rock her two babies and read his good papers, comforting herself with the thought, that in the eyes of some divines she was filling woman's highest mission—"having her desire (for reading matter and intellectual improvement—ungratified) unto her husband," while she tarried at home and "brought from her own peculiar domain the living." (Pres. Fairchild.)

Next called on Mrs. M.

Canvasser.—"What say you to subscribing for the Woman's Journal this year?"

Mrs. M.—"O, I like it. I believe in Woman's Rights some—but then, I'm afraid they are carrying it too far. You know the gentlemen grant us privileges and show us favors now, that they would not if they knew we believed in Woman's Rights. You've heard of the lady on the cars. A gentleman asked her if she believed in Woman's Rights; she said she did. He told her she could stand and enjoy her rights, then, like a man. I wouldn't like to be treated in that way. I won't subscribe for it now; perhaps I will some time."

Canvasser.—"Mrs. G., wouldn't you like to take the Woman's Journal?"

Mrs. G.—"What! a Woman's Rights paper! Oh we don't any of us believe in it at our house—we've no use for it."

Canvasser.—"Better take it, and find out what the learned men and women of the land are doing; then some of you may be converted."

Mrs. G.—"Oh, we don't want to be converted to that doctrine—we don't believe in it. No, we don't want the paper at all."

Canvasser.—"Mrs. C., have you decided to take the Journal?"

Mrs. C.—"I hardly know. It treats of subjects I don't say much about, but I think all the more—especially since Mr. C.'s death for I'm left alone and must learn to do business for myself. I think I'll take it; let me see—$2.50 per year—high for the size of the paper. I've recently subscribed for other periodicals—have some money to pay out soon—I really can't pay so much for a paper just now. I'll try and get some one else to take it with me."

Canvasser grows anxious. She has made many calls beside those recorded, on persons like Mrs. E., who "has all the rights and all the papers she wants"— happy souls!—and Mrs. S., who "hopes never to live to see the day when women vote." This is the nearest a subscription she has come yet, so she closes the bargain with Mrs. C. by agreeing to pay the balance of the subscription, and thus secures one subscriber after several days trial.

Rejoining in hope, she calls on her friend, Mrs. W.

Canvasser.—"Mrs. W., of course you are going to subscribe for the Journal?"

Mrs. W.—"Oh, it would never do for me to take it!"

Canvasser.—"Why! Why not? I've counted strong on you, knowing you are in full sympathy with its sentiments." (She knew, too, that she "carried the purse," being a widow.)

Mrs. W.—"O yes, I'm in sympathy with it—would like the paper very much—read everything of the kind I come across—but then, it would never do for me to take a paper of that kind; I'm so rabid now on Woman's Rights the community can scarcely tolerate me."

Mrs. K.—"Oh I don't want anything to do with Woman's Rights
    papers—the leaders are of such a character."
Canvasser.—"Ah! and what have they done?"
Mrs. K.—"Well I don't know much about them, only what I've heard,
    but they say they go for free love."

This bugbear is removed, and then Mrs. K.—thinks she won't take the paper
now—but will wait a little.

We might enumerate other cases, but forbear. The leaven of one subscriber is
working, and will continue to work until the third and fourth generation of the
liberty-loving—when, if not before, we firmly believe there will be a strong
Woman Suffrage Association in Lofty Level and throughout the State.

We have many noble women in Kansas whose practice is versus theory on
the woman question. I may write you of some, and their worthy deeds, at another time. Yours, for the right.

Topsy Turvy

## 1870: NOVEMBER 15
## MARY CUSTIS LEE TO LETTIE

_In the aftermath of the Civil War, Robert E. Lee gained stature as a hero, if not a
martyr, but the Custis home in Arlington was taken over by the federal government.
With seven children, only moderately good health, and no source of income, Lee accepted a job as president of Washington College (now Washington and Lee University) in Lexington, Virginia. After galvanizing his students there to rebuild the state
of Virginia and the nation, he died of a heart attack in October of 1870. A month
later, his widow, Mary Custis Lee (see page 268), described the end to a friend
named Lettie._

Eleanor Agnes Lee was the fifth of the Lees' seven children. Custis was the eldest.

Lexington 15 Nov 1870

I have long intended to write to you my dear Lettie ever since I heard of the
death of Rosa's dear little boy but was prevented by many things. What a sorrow
it must have been to them & to you all & you never saw him. I know what a joy a
baby is in a house & it was her first. You must give my affectionate love to her &
tell her I have often thought of her. Will she not come & see you all this winter
or some of you go to her? The sympathy of friends is very grateful to us when we
know it is sincere & in my trouble dear Lettie I feel that it is all heartfelt that

there is no feigned grief for him who all mourn who could appreciate true excellence & though it is very sad for me to lose the strong arm & caring heart on which I have leaned for so many eventful years, yet I mourn not for him but for myself. It never crossed my mind for one moment that I would outlive him, that a life so valueless as mine could be spared & his taken, so important to his family & country, but God knows what is best for us all & I am content. I would not recall him if I could. The toils of his crowded and eventful life are ended & had he succeeded in gaining the cause which cost him so much labor & sacrifice, he could not have been more beloved & lamented than he is now. Only the Hero of a lost cause yet as the blood of the Martyrs built up the Church so may the sacrifice of this Martyr yet produce fruit for his country that we know not of. "God moves in a mysterious way, His wonders to perform."

My husband's last day on earth was crowded with cares & labors for others & when late in the evening he reached home and sank back in his chair unable to articulate a word I saw in the look of resignation on his face as he sat perfectly calm & upright waiting the arrival of the physicians that he knew the summons had come & though from the nature of his disease he did not express his feelings, never smiled & rarely spoke, yet he never expressed a single thought or anxiety for aught but lay calmly & quietly awaiting his end. Once when Agnes urged him to take some medicine, which he always seemed to take with great repugnance, he said quite plainly "tis no use" but took it as it was ordered. When he came so much better that they were very hopeful of his recovery, the Dr said "you must soon mount your favorite grey." He shook his head very emphatically & looked upward. He knew us all, welcomed us with a warm pressure of the hand & seem to like us around him, especially Custis who was a most efficient nurse. He slept a great deal & the last 48 hours the Dr. assured us was insensible to all pain & after a long night of breathing heavily awoke to rest with one deep long sigh. I cannot even now realise that he has gone. I listen for his step at the usual time & when he does not enter feel my sad disappointment. We had determined to remain here this winter & if Custis accepts the Presidency of the College may continue to make it our home for more years. I have been quite sick for more than 3 weeks first with a bilious attack & then a violent inflammation of my leg ankle & foot which was so painful that I could scarcely turn in bed & had to be lifted in & out of it, & still though it is much better, I spend part of every day in bed & out with my limbs spread out before me in such an uncomfortable position that I write with difficulty which must be my apology for this letter. The girls all desire to be particularly remembered to you

& all your family & to Rosa to express their deep sympathy—also remember us to Mrs. Meredith & other kind friends. Do you ever hear anything of the Bufords now? Or of from Nat Burwell. Did he ever get the little dress? We have had the most beautiful weather ever known since that dreadful storm which commenced just about the hour when my husband was taken as if the very elements were in convulsive thrusts weeping with us, & since the skies have been radiant with beauty as rejoicing over the freed spirit in his glorified mansion. I would I had been able my dear Lettie to detail to you all the circumstances attend his last moments but I cannot now & will only subscribe myself your faithful friend,

M. C. Lee

## 1870: DECEMBER
## FRANCES ELLEN WATKINS HARPER TO AN UNKNOWN
## RECIPIENT

---

*During the Civil War, Frances Ellen Watkins Harper (see page 254) continued to lecture and write and give proceeds from her books to the Underground Railroad. During Reconstruction, she traveled the South. In Alabama, as she described in the letter below, she saw, firsthand, the efforts of freed slaves to find a better life.*
The "emigration question" probably concerned Liberia (see page 244). Santo Domingo, now known as the Dominican Republic, was the site of the 1791 slave uprising that led to Haitian independence, often cited as a cautionary tale by those who believed that blacks and whites could never coexist peacefully.

Last evening I visited one of the plantations, and had an interesting time. Oh, how warm was the welcome! I went out near dark, and between that time and attending my lecture, I was out to supper in two homes. The people are living in the old cabins of slavery; some of them have no windows, at all, that I see; in fact, I don't remember of having seen a pane of window-glass in the settlement. But, humble as their homes were, I was kindly treated, and well received; and what a chance one has for observation among these people, if one takes with her a manner that unlocks other hearts. I had quite a little gathering, after less, perhaps, than a day's notice; the minister did not know that I was coming, till he met me in the afternoon. There was no fire in the church, and so they lit fires outside, and we gathered, or at least a number of us, around the fire. To-night I am going over to Georgia to lecture. In consequence of the low price of cotton, the people may not be able to pay much, and I am giving all my lectures free. You speak of things looking dark in the South; there is no trouble here that I know of—cotton is low, but the people do not seem to be particularly depressed about it; this emigration question has been on the carpet, and I do not wonder if some of them, with their limited knowledge, lose hope in seeing full justice done to them, among their life-long oppressors; Congress has been agitating the St. Domingo question; a legitimate theme for discussion, and one that comes nearer home, is how they can give more security and strength to the government which we have established in the South—for there has been a miserable weakness in the security to human life. The man with whom I stopped, had a son who married a white woman, or girl, and was shot down, and there was, as I understand, no investigation by the jury; and a number of cases have occurred of murders, for which the punishment has been very lax, or not at all, and, it may be, never will be; however, I rather think things are somewhat quieter. A few days ago a shameful outrage occurred at this place—some men had been out fox hunting, and came to the door of a colored woman and demanded entrance, making out they wanted fire; she replied that she had none, and refused to open the door; the miserable cowards broke open the door, and shamefully beat her. I am going to see her this afternoon. It is remarkable, however, in spite of circumstances, how some of these people are getting along. Here is a woman who, with her husband, at the surrender, had a single dollar; and now they have a home of their own, and several acres attached—five altogether; but, as that was rather small, her, husband has contracted for two hundred and forty acres more, and has now gone out and commenced operations.

### 1871: NOVEMBER 10
### ANNA HIGGINSON TO MRS. MARK SKINNER

*Catherine O'Leary spent years trying to refute the rumor that it was her cow that had kicked over a lantern and started the infamous Chicago Fire of 1871. Historians and history buffs have since suggested other causes, ranging from shifty neighbors to asteroids, but whatever the source of the fire, the result was devastation. Chicago, like other Northern cities, had grown a great deal during the Civil War years, but in three days, four square miles and roughly $192 million in property were destroyed. Anna Tyng Higginson was the wife of a real estate man named George Higginson. The month after the fire, she wrote this eyewitness account to a Mrs. Mark Skinner, probably the wife of a prominent local judge and philanthropist.*

I little thought when I received your kind & most welcome letter that so long a time would pass before I acknowledged it, or that so many sorrows & anxieties would crowd the space which lay between your letter & my reply.

I need not tell you of the greatness of the calamity which has fallen upon us. We can all feel that and most of us, I imagine, will feel it more & more as time advances. Men are full of excitement now & hope, the smoke of the battle has as yet not fairly cleared away—the realization, to be followed in many cases by depression & despair, will come soon enough. Nothing can describe the desolation which reigns over the whole North Side & nothing can be more depressing, unless it be the efforts at restoration upon the South. To see the lines of rough sheds which are taking the places of all the magnificent buildings destroyed is simply heart-breaking. Chicago is thrown back now to where it was twenty-five years ago, & I for one do not expect to see it restored to where it was a few short weeks ago. The men of Chicago are heroes, their energy, cheerfulness & determination are something almost sublime; but I fear many a brave heart will sink under difficulties utterly unsurmountable.

You have heard, I have no doubt, account after account of the progress of the fire, so I will not fill my paper with that; indeed it would be a waste of time—no words can give an idea of the horrors of that night. The wind, blowing a hurricane, howling like myriads of evil spirits drove the flames before it with a force & fierceness which could never be described or imagined; it was not flame but a solid wall of fire which was hurled against the buildings & the houses did not burn, they were simply destroyed. The flames would dash themselves against the sides of a solid block, in one instant passing out through the other side & the whole just melted away & disappeared. The courthouse burned in twenty minutes, while that long block of forty houses on LaSalle St. opposite Lincoln Park burned in just seven. The air was full of cinders; pieces of blazing shingles & boards & great strips of tarred felt fell in every direction, now on the roofs of houses yet unburned & then on the loads of furniture & bedding which people were trying to save & which they were continually obliged to abandon in the street in order to save themselves.

The course of the main body of fire was rather below us, so that the water works & all beyond burned before our house caught & many people thought we would be spared; but the fire worked up gradually along the North Branch & the instant the wind caught it the fire was hurled the whole length of the city; in that way our house was burned at last. As I went out of it & saw the vine-covered walls & the windows filled with flowers all shining so peacefully in the moonlight, it seemed impossible to realize that in a few moments the smoke &

flame I saw all around me would seize that too & that I was looking upon my home for the last time. We had time to save most of our furniture if there had been any way of carrying it off or any apparent place of safety for it, the only means of conveyance being a wheelbarrow & our own hands. We saved some clothing, most of our silver & a few pictures, though part of what we rescued from the house was afterwards burned. We succeeded finally in procuring a sand wagon on which we placed ourselves & the few worldly goods which remained to us & rode to the West Side in company with thousands of other refugees like ourselves—dusty, smoky, forlorn in every way, the wind blowing a hurricane, the air full of blinding dust & smoke & behind us our ruined homes, with all their years of accumulated treasures & associations of every kind. It is for those I grieve, not over the loss of money—my Mother's Bible, the clothing & toys of my dead children, all the keepsakes & mementos of a lifetime.

People sometimes check me for being too despondent when I say I shall never have a home again; a house somewhere, undoubtedly I shall have—I must live out my appointed time—but a house which simply bears the mark of the builder & upholsterer could never be home to me if it were ever so elegant.

We came directly out here to the Bryan's & have been here ever since, most kindly cared for. Indeed, if it be true "that it is more blessed to give than to receive," there must be a great many happy people in the world now, for the outpoured sympathy & kindness of the world is ours & we need it. Hardly a family on the North Side saved a change of clothing, & every shop in the city & every office & bank being burned, no one had any money to purchase anything or anything to purchase if they were able. You may imagine how I felt on meeting Mrs. Arnold coming from the Relief Society with a bundle of clothing for Mr. Arnold, though I think she felt rather uplifted by the necessity, appearing somewhat in the character of a martyr, & when Dr. Rylance went to see her & seizing her hands with one of his characteristic gushes exclaimed: "You noble woman," I am sure she felt abundantly repaid for all she had undergone. We have come to the literal fulfillment of the injunction: "Let him that hath two coats, give to him that hath none," for we all share & share around in a way that partakes very strongly of the ludicrous. I found when I examined the sheet which contained my wardrobe that I had one nightgown & six white skirts. Mrs. LeMoyne had fifty homeless ones in her house the night after the fire, not one of whom had a change of clothing. Mrs. Ryerson had on a wrapper & man's hat tied down with a handkerchief. Tille D'Wolf had a calico wrapper with a bed blanket by way of shawl, & in that state appeared at Judge Drummond's. Mrs. Winston saved a pink silk dress trimmed with lace, but very little else; one lady had a carriage full of party dresses & another a half dozen bonnets. One man was seen running from the fire with two immense turnips & another with a piece of broken furniture of some kind. The Rumseys just succeeded in getting out with all their children, leaving all else behind. Old Mrs. McCagg was taken out at the last moment & forced to run, delicate as she is, to Chicago Ave. where she fell exhausted & would have burned in the street if her friends had not seized an express wagon & placed her in it. Ezra McCagg has lost every dollar of income & all his fine library, though his pictures were saved; his greenhouses look strangely enough in the midst of all the surrounding desolation. Washington Park is full of the barracks built by the city for the houseless poor—they are the only neighbors Mr. Ogden has within a mile. One of the men whom we employed for a day told Charlie "that they had not many neighbors, but they were very select!" meaning the Ogdens. I think Mrs. O. feels worse, living in her elegant, untouched house, than we do who are altogether homeless, & I do not wonder at it, as they live in fear of their lives, with their house watched day & night by policemen.

The Arnolds have taken a small furnished house on the South Side & one servant. The Scudders are with them; poor Mary lost all her wedding presents; what were not burned in the house were melted in Mr. Magie's lot where they buried them. The Magies had a very narrow escape, as they waited in the house loth to give it up till the fence took fire & were both severely burned; indeed, they gave up all hopes of life & went & stood under one of the trees in their yard to wait for the end, when they saw a place where the fence had burned away & rushed through.

Albert Munger has lost about four hundred thousand dollars, Mr. Ogden about three millions. The losses of that whole family are tremendous as they were insured almost entirely in home companies. Mr. Ryerson, too, seems to be very much injured by the fire (financially I mean). Mrs. King is out here at their little country place. Mr. King lost heavily, but his credit is unimpaired, so he feels in very good spirits, as he stands with Field, Leiter & Co. & a few others among those who mean to pay dollar for dollar. It must be a great mortification for J. V. Farwell to be obliged to ask for time. I understand that Mr. Bross has lost almost everything but his picture, which he was seen during the fire carrying off on horseback—the only thing he saved. Jessie has behaved nobly, as of course she would; it is said she looking for a situation of some kind. Clarence Dyer had just got nicely settled in his own house & has lost that & his coal yard which must be very hard for him. They were with Mrs. Turnley immediately after the fire; I have not heard since.

All in that part of the town were driven by the flames toward the lake & most of them suffered terribly. Mary Howe & her baby took refuge on the pier with the Arnolds & many others & were there for hours. Some went into the lake itself; some got off in small boats & were out all night before they could get back again. Thousands were out on the prairie & in Lincoln Park all night exposed to the heavy rain which came just twenty-four hours too late. Essie Stockton was married the Thursday after the fire in a white petticoat with a morning dress looped over it & departed on her wedding trip with her "trousseau" tied up in a pillow case! Louise Goodwin & her devoted went off on theirs with passes furnished by the Relief Society! The sick had a terrible time—one lady with a baby a few days old got up from her bed & walked a mile; one with a baby a few minutes old was laid on a mattress & driven off in a wagon; hundreds of children were born on the prairies the next few days—but all those things you can imagine.

I fear I have written a very incoherent letter, for I seem to have lost my faculties since the fire. I hardly remember from hour to hour what I am doing, though the last few nights I have begun to sleep more & hope soon to feel better. I long to hear of you all.

Yours most affectionately,
Anna E. Higginson

## 1871: DECEMBER 20
## ALICE KIRK GRIERSON TO BENJAMIN HENRY GRIERSON

*Alice Kirk Grierson (1828–1888) was at her parents' home in Chicago, recuperating after the loss of her three-month-old daughter, when she wrote this anguished letter to her husband, Colonel Benjamin Henry Grierson (1826–1911), who remained at his Oklahoma frontier post. In confiding to him her feelings about her other pregnancies, she offered a reminder of the extent to which pregnancy was viewed as the inevitable outcome of sexual relations, and physical separation its only reliable means of prevention.*

The Griersons had seven children: Charles Henry; John Kirk (who died in infancy); Robert Kirk; Edith Clare; Benjamin Henry, Jr.; George Theodore; and, lastly, Mary Louisa, the baby who had just died when this letter was written. Both Charles and Robert would suffer from mental illness in the coming years, and Edith would die of typhoid fever at the age of thirteen.

Chicago Dec. 1871

My dear Ben

There is no use in planning for another trip for me, in all probability after I have been with you a few months I shall be in no condition for travelling, if it can possibly be avoided. There is no use in "going it blind," when we both have eyes to see, and commonsense to comprehend the facts of the case. Both of us will know one thing, which will inevitably occur, if the good Lord permits us to meet again, and are both well aware of the <u>possible</u> consequences which may follow.

<u>We are</u> the temples of "the living god," and these temples must never again be desecrated by an incomplete act of worship, (union). I think it is desirable that the parents of every unborn human being, should, from the first hour of their knowledge, that by their own voluntary act such being exists, accept the fact with at least quiet joy, and thankfulness.

Charlie's existence I accepted as a matter of course, without either joy or sorrow. Kirkie's with regret, for so soon succeeding him. Robert came nearer being welcomed with joy, than any other. Edie was gladly welcomed so soon as I knew her sex, but I was exceedingly thankful she did not come until the close of the war. Harry succeeded her too soon to give me as much rest, as I would have liked, and it was so hard for me, to learn to harmonize public life, with nursery duties, and other family cares, that I used to feel as if I had scarcely natural affection for Harry, and told you before he was a year old, that I would rather die, than have another child, yet no sooner was he weaned, than Georgie came into life, but I was neither tempted to commit suicide, nor the fearfully frequent National crime of abortion.

I was so greatly debilitated in the spring, before he was a year old, that Dr. Kilburn did not think I could nurse him through the summer nor did I think I could have done so except for the constant stimulant of Sherry wine, which I used by his consent, and your approval. I believe if I had not been nursing him, he would have died, when he was so ill in August, and came so near doing, although the wine may have saved his life. I firmly believe it injured me, as so soon as I weaned him, and was again immediately pregnant, my nerves became irritable to such a degree, that life has ever since, been nearer a burden to me, than is at all desirable.

When our precious baby died, you said to me, "bear up, darling, she was with us for some purpose." How often I think of your words, and what is the purpose, for which she was with us? I can think of many purposes which her brief life may have been intended to accomplish but one thing I shall always believe, and

that is, if it had been possible for us only to have had our own family last summer, that she might have lived. Or had I been possessed of a great deal more
philosophy, and religion, than I was, so that I could have taken life as it came,
without any fretting, she might have lived, but you well know, I was neither
saint, nor angel, and I did the very best I knew how, both for her and myself, and
the results you are well aware of.

Now if I remain here until the 1st of March and return to Ft. Sill by, or before
the 10th, I will endeavor to be in such a state of body, and mind, as to accept
whatever the Lord has in store for us, joyfully, thankfully. But whether I am
again a Mother or not, I hope you will agree with me, both in theory, and practice, that quiet home joys entirely within our reach, are just the best, and most
to be sought after, of all earth's good gifts. Mr. Helmer said in his excellent sermon last Sunday, that in good and loving homes, paradise was trying to retain a
foothold on earth.

I hope you can believe me when I say, I do not wish to take advantage of
being "mistress of the situation" but really desire to do what is for the very best
good, of all parties concerned. When I first wrote you that I might stay all winter, I could see from the tone of your reply how annoyed you were, but after
thinking of the matter over night you wrote a manly generous letter, like your
better self. So now, you must think over all sides of the question, and see if we
can't come to a decision.

good bye, dearest.

### 1873: AUGUST 6
### EMMA SPAULDING BRYANT TO JOHN BRYANT

*Emma Spaulding (1844–1901) met John Emory Bryant (1836–1900) in 1860,
when she was a student of his in Maine. By 1864, when they married, she had become a math teacher and he a Union soldier. They stayed married for thirty-six years
and died within a year of each other. But that longevity was not without its challenges. John was apparently a difficult man, fiercely committed to abolitionism and
Republican politics, and frequently leaving his wife alone through miscarriages and
poverty. Much of their surviving correspondence suggests great tolerance, even deference, on Emma's part. The exception can be found in the letters below, Emma's
riveting replies to John's accusation that she had committed adultery with an Ohio
gynecologist. Extraordinary for the self-possession they showed, the letters are also
unusual in their frankness about medical matters that were rarely discussed in the
late nineteenth century on paper, if at all.*

Emma was staying with her sister in Wakeman, Illinois, and John was at their home in Georgia when this and the following letter were written.

In all my life I have never been grossly insulted until now—and that <u>by my husband</u>

Do not dare to write me again, or expect ever to receive another line from me until you can assure me of your <u>unlimited confidence</u> in me and feel <u>sincerely repentant</u> for the terrible things you have said to me. I have never lived with you on other terms than those of the most perfect <u>love</u> and <u>trust</u> and <u>equality</u>.

I <u>never intend to live with you on other terms</u>. I love you and I hope to be your true wife for time and eternity but I cannot (God helping me) <u>will not</u> cast my womanhood from me. I trust you fully in spite of circumstances if need be—I will receive nothing less in return.

Emma

### 1873: AUGUST 7
### EMMA SPAULDING BRYANT TO JOHN BRYANT

*It becomes clear in Emma's succeeding letters that John must also have suggested—without apparent sympathy—that if she hadn't willingly caused her own "ruin," then perhaps she had been raped.*

Lucy was Emma's sister. Augusta, Georgia, had been the Bryants' home when John worked for the Freedmen's Bureau. Mrs. Sherman was a landlady. The baby was named Emma Alice. Earl, Emma's brother, was living in Toledo.

Wakeman, Aug. 7, 1873

My Darling Husband,

I wish to add something to what I sent in Lucy's letter yesterday (I retract nothing of it) First of all, I want to tell you that from the very depths of my heart I grieve that you have been and are so distressed. Even my woman's indignation at the unspeakably dreadful things that you have written to me is overborne by my sorrow for you, and my desire to help you out of your distress.

Have you forgotten the old saying that "Whom the Gods wish to destroy they first make mad."? You <u>are</u> mad, both angry and insane. And <u>beware</u> that you do not thereby destroy the happiness of both of us!

Do you imagine that I could ever lay my head upon your breast again without the <u>fullest recall</u> of every sentiment and insinuation of your letters of the past week? without the assurance of your <u>full</u>, <u>unmeasured</u> confidence in me?

If you think that I could or would you have not learned to know me in these nine years of our wedded life.

Now, my darling, in true honest love let me remind you of the confidence I have had in you, and the confidence (or <u>lack</u> of it) that you have returned me for it. In all your social relations with ladies I have always trusted you fully—have never allowed circumstances which even seemed suspicious to make me doubt your honor—have been ready to believe that I was mistaken, that circumstance lied—anything but to believe you false.

If I even had doubts of any lady the fact that she was a trusted friend of yours has been sufficient for me to battle against those doubts and refuse to entertain them. Whenever you venture to visit any lady—to be with her alone at night— or under any circumstances without first "<u>consulting me</u>" I do not reproach you with lack of <u>obedience</u> or falsity to your duties as a husband. There should be no chains in love (those pertain to slavery instead).

I expect and wish you to exercise your own judgement when away from me: I grant you "the same right—to do as you please" not as a "single person" has, but as a married woman has.

I never wrote you in more sincere honest love than I write this letter!

Now look at the other side. Since I married you I have never felt other than repulsion at the thought of a kiss or caress of any kind from any man but you unless it be my immediate family or yours.

Have never had that feeling toward any man but yourself that would make his kiss pleasant to me. From the present time till now not only my acts but the thoughts of my heart have been open to your inspection.

Now for the medical question.

When I was sick in Augusta you did not scruple to send old Dr. Em in to see me with the expectation that he would treat me for uterine difficulties which of course presupposed the "examination" (of which you have such a distorted idea) you were in the house at the time and I really wished you with me and yet you did not come in you left me in my room alone—"abed" in the room—expecting an examination—and Dr. Em I would quite as soon suspect of licentiousness as Dr. Saunders, of <u>indelicacy</u> with his patients <u>much sooner</u>. I have been informed by a woman who has employed Dr. Em and who has been with him in other cases that he is sometimes a very vulgar old fellow with his patients. The only cases in which <u>my person was ever exposed in the least degree</u> to the gaze of any man but you were <u>slightly</u> in Portland when Dr. Fitch examined me with the speculum (which Dr. Saunders does not use), and at the birth of our first baby when a Dr. of <u>your selection</u> raised the clothes in applying the cloths to me after birth (as Mrs. Sherman tells me), I was in that condition that I did not realize it and was not able to defend myself, as, Thank God! I now am—

Still again when I went with you and baby to consult a strange physician in Savannah, after we received direction regarding baby you took baby out for a walk and left me alone with a strange physician in his office (in a much more retired spot than Dr. Saunders office is) to consult him about uterine difficulties, when the natural expectation always is that a physician will wish to make an examination when there are such difficulties, or otherwise he cannot tell what treatment the case requires.

After all these things do you wonder that I supposed you had lost your old objection to my being <u>alone</u> with a physician for consultation on treatment of uterine difficulties? It had so far made me forget your former scruples that the thought of them never even entered my mind.

Now we come to going to Dr. Saunders—

For ten years or more I have suffered from this weakness, to your distress as well as mine—Lucy has been under Dr. Saunders treatment for the same difficulties, only much more serious ones, for three years—she recommends him to me—I have found no physician in the South to whose skill I could trust. Mr. Sherman has treated me, helping but not curing me and not able to tell me why I do not fully recover. I go to Dr. Saunders and by making an examination by inserting the finger in the vagina (which is what I meant by saying that his treatment is like Mr. Sherman, i.e. that neither of them use the speculum, which is attended with something of pain and exposure) he tells me that there is ulceration of long standing, that it is gradually weakening me (as I have so long realized) that it will be comparatively easy of cure and that by a weeks treatment he can alleviate it and give me remedies with which to heal myself.

Lucy had not the funds to enable her to remain with me, but she would take baby home and take care of her.

On thinking over my funds I concluded I had barely enough to take me through the weeks treatment—If I waited I should not incur the expense of going again—If I went to Earl I could not have treatment short of Chicago then it would be alone with a <u>strange</u> physician, for my sister could not leave her family to go with me and would consider it the greatest absurdity if she could. I remained supposing that my husband would be delighted to hear that there was so good a prospect of my being restored to sound health. The Dr. gave no more indication of sensual feeling or of thinking that he was doing <u>anything</u> indelicate than he would if he had been treating my face or my hand.

If he had shown passion, do you think so <u>meanly</u> of me as to believe that I could not and would not <u>instantly</u> have repulsed him and left for home? Why have you sought to humiliate your wife, and injure yourself by such dreadful suspicions as you have cast upon me. I was safe both because I could have detected the designs of a passionate man in the very beginning and defended myself, and because no physician of the character and standing of Dr. Saunders or indeed of any standing in the medical fraternity would compromise himself by offering insult to his patients, much less by overcoming them by brute force.

I am not safer walking the crowded street than I was in the Dr's office. Do you think I have no love of my <u>own</u> virtue, no <u>pride</u>, no <u>temper</u> or <u>will</u> of my own that you fancied me so helpless in his hands? The matter of going at bet. 7 & 8 o'clock in the evening is a mere bugaboo—I asked him if it would be as well for me to go in the afternoon and when he gave me the reasons why it would not I readily see the reasonableness of it—It was precisely this—he inserted a small piece of medicated sponge between the lip of the uterus and the rectum, the sponge to keep the uterus in position and the medicine upon it to cure the ulceration. He inserted one in the morning which I was to retain through the day till after tea when I withdrew it using my syringe and went to the office between 7 & 8 PM and had a fresh one put in which was to remain till the next morning—he had no office hour later than four, 4 PM until evening and that would have permitted the morning sponge to remain too short a time and the evening too long a time.

He treated me twice a day simply because I could remain so short a time. His manner of treatment was perfectly delicate and such as all women afflicted with such disease and wishing to recover must receive at the hands of some male physician until there are sufficient educated female physicians to supersede the males.

I consider treatment at a physician's office if it is situated like Dr. Saunders as safer and therefore better than at a lady's home.

It is not customary among ladies to have anyone with them when treated—I know that Clarinda told me years ago when she was under Dr. Getcher's care that she would not have any one but the Dr. present (that it added to her mortification). These ladies have told me the same thing. My character <u>has been</u> and <u>is</u> above suspicion and you would pity me if you knew <u>how</u> humiliated I feel to <u>even explain</u> to you. I resolved that I would not but hoping to restore you from your present state of insanity I have done it and I have written very fully meaning it to be the only and final vindication of my character on my part.

In regard to going out to church on Sunday night the Dr. had left the office when we returned and after waiting some little time for him Charlie took me home and I missed treatment altogether for that night. To sum up—I have applied to a physician of skill and standing well known to sister Lucy for more than three years—and have received medical treatment precisely the same as thousands of pure women have done and are doing and my husband repays my full trust in him by torturing himself with the vilest suspicions of me—even inclining to the opinion that I am "ruined" or at the very least, <u>injured</u>—<u>panic</u>!

Taunts me with leaving my baby for a few days in care of her Grandma and aunty! Morally raises the lash over me and says "now will you obey? will you be my inferior, my obedient child?" To him I answer <u>Never</u>—I will be your true loving wife, your companion and equal in every and the fullest sense—the mother of your children—nothing <u>less</u> and nothing <u>else</u> With a true love kiss for my <u>husband</u>—the man whom I married and have been happy with all these years—not the diseased imagination which has addresses these terrible letters to me, I am

> Your loving wife,
> Emma

August 7—At night

I have just received yours of last Saturday and Sunday and am more and more deeply wounded. What am I to suppose—that you believe me ruined by my own voluntary act, or that if I had been in any manner insulted by brute force you would lose your love for me and put me from you—which of the two terrible meanings must I put upon your words? Are you my husband, or are you some false spirit entered into him?

Have you never thought that if my ruin had been compassed or attempted, I was as utterly wretched as you could possibly be? and yet you have not one word of love for me—of pity for me—your arms stretch out toward me, not in love, but in reproach and anger—To the wife who has never in all her married life received from any other man than you the lightest token of love or passion you can address these <u>selfish unloving insulting</u> words that you have written me. I cannot realize it—I am <u>stupified</u> by it. You do not even call our baby by my name, and yet you profess at the worst to fear that I have only been a helpless victim in the hands of a bad man. This utter lack of love for me—this perfection of selfishness is harder for me to bear than your insulting suspicions have been. Did you ever <u>really love</u> me, or did you only hold me as a possession tributary to your pleasure to be cast aside if you became displeased with it? If it were <u>possible</u> for you to do so I should <u>entreat you to come to me</u> immediately. Do you realize how <u>cruelly</u> you have <u>stabbed</u> me? Through all these terrible suspicions which you have entertained of me I have never been so heartbroken as I am to-night to think that if I had been in any way injured my husband would push me from him, reproaching me for the misery to himself without one single thought of my wretchedness—Through all these terrible things that you have written me I have never lost my love, never ceased to be sorry that you were in distress, but I have watched in vain for a <u>single unselfish loving</u> thought toward me. It <u>is not you</u>, <u>it is not like you</u>—write and tell me that some raving madness has possessed you and that you in your own proper self never wrote such things. If it were in my power I think I should start for Savannah to-morrow leaving baby here. I want to see you face to face.

Aug. 8 A.M. I have sent to Earlville for my letter. If I receive that on Monday or Tuesday I shall probably go to Earl on Wednesday—or rather leave him on Wed. morning—reach Swanton beyond Toledo after noon stop the night with my cousins there and go on to Chicago by the next forenoon train—I shall expect sister to meet me in Chicago.

In my present state of mind I would much prefer to go without stopping but I had before this terrible occurrence written to my cousin that I would visit her: and she writes me that she has lost her only sister and her brother (an only one) is lying with consumption—her mother is already dead, too, and she feels very lonely and depends much upon seeing her. If my own heart is heavy I will not refuse to comfort another if in my power.

<u>Our</u> baby is well—has improved much since she came here in size, strength and talking. Mother has received yours of 4th. I probably shall wait a week or two longer instead of going to Earl on Wed.

**1873: SEPTEMBER 7**
**ISABELLA BIRD TO HENRIETTA BIRD**

---

*In 1869, workers on the transcontinental railroad drove a golden spike into the tracks that united the nation geographically. In 1872, Yellowstone was made the first national park in the world. By 1873, when an adventurous British visitor named Isabella Lucy Bird (1831–1904) wrote this letter to her sister, Henrietta (1835?–1880), the West was about to become a destination not just for settlement but for tourism. Bird had originally started traveling on the advice of a doctor, and though she would venture alone to Australia, Kurdistan, China, and many other places, the trip she described in her book* A Lady's Life in the Rocky Mountains *would have the greatest influence. At the age of forty-one, with only a borrowed pony named Birdie and a one-eyed guide named Mountain Jim, Bird explored—and memorably captured—the untamed and extraordinary landscape of the far western part of the country.*

Truckee, California, and Donner Lake (named for the ill-fated Donner Party) are in the Sierra Nevada. The story Isabella told here presumably referred to Tamsen Donner and was considerably embellished (see page 185). In 1881, a year after Henrietta's death, Isabella would marry a British doctor named John Bishop.

Cheyenne, Wyoming
September 7

As night came on the cold intensified, and the stove in the parlor attracted every one. A San Francisco lady, much "got up" in paint, emerald green velvet, Brussels lace, and diamonds, rattled continuously for the amusement of the company, giving descriptions of persons and scenes in a racy Western twang, without the slightest scruple as to what she said. In a few years Tahoe will be inundated in summer with similar vulgarity, owing to its easiness of access. I sustained the reputation which our countrywomen bear in America by looking a "perfect guy"; and feeling that I was a salient point for the speaker's next sally, I was relieved when the landlady, a ladylike Englishwoman, asked me to join herself and her family in the bar-room, where we had much talk about the neighborhood and its wild beasts, especially bears. The forest is full of them, but they seem never to attack people unless when wounded, or much aggravated by dogs, or a shebear thinks you are going to molest her young.

I dreamt of bears so vividly that I woke with a furry death hug at my throat, but feeling quite refreshed. When I mounted my horse after breakfast the sun was high and the air so keen and intoxicating that, giving the animal his head, I galloped up and down hill, feeling completely tireless. Truly, that air is the elixir of life. I had a glorious ride back to Truckee. The road was not as solitary as the day before. In a deep part of the forest the horse snorted and reared, and I saw a cinnamon-colored bear with two cubs cross the track ahead of me. I tried to keep the horse quiet that the mother might acquit me of any designs upon her lolloping children, but I was glad when the ungainly, longhaired party crossed the river. Then I met a team, the driver of which stopped and said he was glad that I had not gone to Cornelian Bay, it was such a bad trail, and hoped I had enjoyed Tahoe. The driver of another team stopped and asked if I had seen any bears. Then a man heavily armed, a hunter probably, asked me if I were the English tourist who had "happened on" a "Grizzly" yesterday. Then I saw a lumberer taking his dinner on a rock in the river, who "touched his hat" and brought

me a draught of ice-cold water, which I could hardly drink owing to the frac-
tiousness of the horse, and gathered me some mountain pinks, which I admired. I mention these little incidents to indicate the habit of respectful
courtesy to women which prevails in that region. These men might have been
excused for speaking in a somewhat free-and-easy tone to a lady riding alone,
and in an unwonted fashion. Womanly dignity and manly respect for women are
the salt of society in this wild West.

My horse was so excitable that I avoided the center of Truckee, and skulked
through a collection of Chinamen's shanties to the stable, where a prodigious
roan horse, standing seventeen hands high, was produced for my ride to the
Donner Lake. I asked the owner, who was as interested in my enjoying myself as
a West Highlander might have been, if there were not ruffians about who might
make an evening ride dangerous. A story was current of a man having ridden
through Truckee two evenings before with a chopped-up human body in a sack
behind the saddle, and hosts of stories of ruffianism are located there, rightly or
wrongly. This man said, "There's a bad breed of ruffians but the ugliest among
them all won't touch you. There's nothing Western folk admire so much as
pluck in a woman." I had to get on a barrel before I could reach the stirrup, and
when I was mounted my feet only came half-way down the horse's sides. I felt
like a fly on him. The road at first lay through a valley without a river, but some
swampishness nourished some rank swamp grass, the first <u>green</u> grass I have
seen in America; and the pines, with their red stems, looked beautiful rising out
of it. I hurried along, and came upon the Donner Lake quite suddenly, to be
completely smitten by its beauty. It is only about three miles long by one and a
half broad, and lies hidden away among mountains, with no dwellings on its
shores but some deserted lumberers' cabins. Its loneliness pleased me well. I
did not see man, beast, or bird from the time I left Truckee till I returned. The
mountains, which rise abruptly from the margin, are covered with dense pine
forests, through which, here and there, strange forms of bare grey rock, castel-
lated, or needle-like, protrude themselves. On the opposite side, at a height of
about 6,000 feet, a grey, ascending line, from which rumbling, incoherent
sounds occasionally proceeded, is seen through the pines. This is one of the
snow-sheds of the Pacific Railroad, which shuts out from travelers all that I was
seeing.

The lake is called after Mr. Donner, who, with his family, arrived at the Truckee River in the fall of the year, in company with a party of emigrants bound for
California. Being encumbered with many cattle, he let the company pass
on, and, with his own party of sixteen souls, which included his wife and four

children, encamped by the lake. In the morning they found themselves surrounded by an expanse of snow, and after some consultation it was agreed that the whole party except Mr. Donner who was unwell, his wife, and a German friend, should take the horses and attempt to cross the mountain, which, after much peril, they succeeded in doing; but, as the storm continued for several weeks, it was impossible for any rescue party to succor the three who had been left behind. In the early spring, when the snow was hard enough for traveling, a party started in quest, expecting to find the snow-bound alive and well, as they had cattle enough for their support, and, after weeks of toil and exposure, they scaled the Sierras and reached the Donner Lake. On arriving at the camp they opened the rude door, and there, sitting before the fire, they found the German, holding a roasted human arm and hand, which he was greedily eating. The rescue party overpowered him, and with difficulty tore the arm from him. A short search discovered the body of the lady, minus the arm, frozen in the snow, round, plump, and fair, showing that she was in perfect health when she met her fate. The rescuers returned to California, taking the German with them, whose story was that Mr. Donner died in the fall, and that the cattle escaped, leaving them but little food, and that when this was exhausted Mrs. Donner died. The story never gained any credence, and the truth oozed out that the German had murdered the husband, then brutally murdered the wife, and had seized upon Donner's money. There were, however, no witnesses, and the murderer escaped with the enforced surrender of the money to the Donner orphans.

This tragic story filled my mind as I rode towards the head of the lake, which became every moment grander and more unutterably lovely. The sun was setting fast, and against his golden light green promontories, wooded with stately pines, stood out one beyond another in a medium of dark rich blue, while grey bleached summits, peaked, turreted, and snow slashed, were piled above them, gleaming with amber light. Darker grew the blue gloom, the dew fell heavily, aromatic odors floated on the air, and still the lofty peaks glowed with living light, till in one second it died off from them, leaving them with the ashy paleness of a dead face. It was dark and cold under the mountain shadows, the frosty chill of the high altitude wrapped me round, the solitude was overwhelming, and I reluctantly turned my horse's head towards Truckee, often looking back to the ashy summits in their unearthly fascination. Eastwards the look of the scenery was changing every moment, while the lake for long remained "one burnished sheet of living gold," and Truckee lay utterly out of sight in a hollow filled with lake and cobalt. Before long a carnival of color began which I can only describe as delirious, intoxicating, a hardly bearable joy, a tender anguish, an indescribable yearning, an unearthly music, rich in love and worship. It lasted considerably more than an hour, and though the road was growing very dark, and the train which was to take me thence was fast climbing the Sierras, I could not ride faster than a walk.

The eastward mountains, which had been grey, blushed pale pink, the pink deepened into rose, and the rose into crimson, and then all solidity etherealized away and became clear and pure as an amethyst, while all the waving ranges and the broken pine-clothed ridges below etherealized too, but into a dark rich blue, and a strange effect of atmosphere blended the whole into one perfect picture. It changed, deepened, reddened, melted, growing more and more wonderful, while under the pines it was night, till, having displayed itself for an hour, the jewelled peaks suddenly became like those of the Sierras, wan as the face of death. Far later the cold golden light lingered in the west, with pines in relief against its purity, and where the rose light had glowed in the east, a huge moon unheaved itself, and the red flicker of forest fires luridly streaked the mountain sides near and far off. I realized that night had come with its <u>eeriness</u>, and putting my great horse into a gallop I clung on to him till I pulled him up in Truckee, which was at the height of its evening revelries—fires blazing out of doors, bar-rooms and saloons crammed, lights glaring, gaming tables thronged, fiddle and banjo in frightful discord, and the air ringing with ribaldry and profanity.

I. L. B.

## 1875: FEBRUARY 19
## EMILY FITZGERALD TO HER MOTHER

*Wife of an army surgeon, twenty-five-year-old Emily McCorkle FitzGerald (1850–1912) had been living in remote Sitka, Alaska, for barely six months when she wrote this letter to her mother back home in Pennsylvania. The U.S. had purchased Alaska from Russia in 1867 and was relying on the army to govern a land populated mostly by Indians and Russians. While grappling with life on the farthest frontier of her nation's expansionist drive, FitzGerald focused here on the universal wonder of being both mother and daughter.*

The mail steamer, eagerly anticipated by FitzGerald, arrived in Sitka about once a month. The FitzGeralds' children, Bess and Bert, were both under two years at the time of this letter. A devilfish is a kind of ray.

Friday
February 19, 1875

How I wish I could show you my babies. I believe I love you a great deal more than I ever did before since I have had these babies of my own. When I think how much these little people are to me and then know you have felt to me just as I feel about them, it seems to me I have never loved you half enough and I just want you right away to show you what a good daughter I am going to be to you for the rest of your life and mine. When I think how far you are from me and how short life is even at best, I get frightened. I am afraid I am very wicked, Mamma. I know I could not say, "It is all for the best," if you should die, or the Doctor, or one of my babies. When I think sometimes of the changes a day may make in my life, I get sick and cold all over. I am not going to write in this horrible style any more. I don't know what has gotten over me.

We are looking for the steamer daily now. I hope she will come tomorrow. Doctor came in this morning to get some money and told me to wait a moment and he would show me a sight. Pretty soon he came to my room and held up the most horrible things—three arms of a devilfish, each about a yard and a half long. They tapered, were large at the top, small below, and were covered with enormous suckers as big as a big morning glory. They are very different from the arms and suckers of the other fish I told you about, which Doctor says was a huge cuttlefish. Doctor bought these arms from an Indian and he is going to alcohol them. The Indian said the body of the fish was as big as Doctor and that there were many of them about the rocks on the shores of their islands. Horrors! I hope none of my family will fall into the water.

## 1876: JULY 16

## EMILY FITZGERALD TO HER MOTHER

*In 1876, the FitzGeralds (see previous letter) were transferred to Fort Lapwai in Idaho Territory, where Emily promptly heard of General George Armstrong Custer's attack at the Little Bighorn River in Montana Territory and his crushing defeat at the hands of the Northern Plains Indians. In this letter to her mother, FitzGerald affirmed the conviction that the enemy was irremediably—and incomprehensibly— violent.*

Fort Lapwai was surrounded by the Nez Perce Indians, with whom the U.S. would battle in 1877. The Centennial Exposition had opened in May in Philadelphia.

Fort Lapwai
July 16, 1876

Dear Mamma,

I heard from you this week and got the Centennial pictures from Aunt Annie. Thank her very much. The little book particularly is such a nice thing to keep to remember the event.

Did I write you from Sitka and speak of Bert being vaccinated? He had two awfully sore arms and has two good marks. We thought one arm was not going to take and had the other vaccinated. And both took!

We are all well. My brown babies are the picture of health, but such solid, round, little brown toads you never saw.

Did you ever hear anything more terrible than the massacre of poor Custer and his command? This whole part of the country is excited about it, as indeed, judging from the papers, is the entire country. We wait for the news here most anxiously and hope the Indians will be shown no quarter. War is dreadful anyway, but an Indian war is worst of all. They respect no code of warfare, flags of truce, wounded—nothing is respected! It is like fighting to exterminate wild animals, horrible beasts. I hope and pray this is the last Indian war. Don't let anybody talk of peace until the Indians are taught a lessen and, if not exterminated, so weakened they will never molest and butcher again. These Sioux Indians will give trouble as long as they exist, no matter how we treat them, "for 'tis their nature to." They will never stay on their reservations and the lives of settlers in this entire western country are not safe as long as the Indian question is unsettled. This is all we talk about out here, but I won't write any more. Love to all from all of us.

Your loving daughter,
Emily F.

## 1879: SPRING
## LUCRETIA GARFIELD TO SARA SPENCER

*In any age, political gossip is a powerful force. For Lucretia Garfield (see page 355), rumors about her husband, allegedly repeated by a friend, were too much to take in silence. The year before James Garfield's election to the Senate, "Crete" made this point rather sharply in a letter to Sara Spencer (1837–1909), a Republican who three years before had been the first woman to address a committee at a Republican presidential convention.*

Some days later, Garfield told Crete that Spencer had visited him "in great grief" and had denied playing any role in spreading the gossip. Garfield wrote: "I think we are bound to accept her statement of the case until we have other evidence."

My Dear Mrs. Spencer

I don't know how else to address you although my heart is full of bitterness toward you. A story has come to me so straight that I cannot doubt it, namely that while you were in Cleveland attending some convention, you said to a Miss Keller that General Garfield was a bad, licentious man and gave as proof that on a certain occasion he went to New York with a notorious woman, having told his wife that he was going on business. That a friend of Mrs. G's in New York met them on the street and telegraphed to her, and that she went on and confronted them. Now that whole story is nothing more nor less than an infamous lie. You may have heard it. The General has malignant enemies who not only turn to his disadvantage every act which they can torture into wrong, but who willfully say what they must know to be false.

But when you who have professed friendship for so many years could have given credence and currency to such a report and branded with licentiousness the reputation of a man whom you have been able to know so much about, I am utterly unable to explain to my own mind how it could have been unless in your infatuation over the Rights of Woman you allowed spite to triumph over reason and all friendship in your opinion of a man whose councils led him to disagree with you, and I must say to you that you could have given me no better proof of your unfitness to be in public life, no better illustration of the methods you would employ to gain your ends than you have given in coming with compliment and praise and with friendly kiss to ask favors of a man whom, if what you have said of him you believe to be true, you should have felt it contamination to approach, except to rebuke.

Pardon me if I am unjust. I can pass an avowed enemy by with silent disdain when they can gratify their hate only with calumny. But when one whom we have called friend strikes such a wicked blow I cannot let the bitterness in my heart be silent and keep up the appearance of friendship.

With sorrow and regret that I must say these things to you, I am as ever,

Lucretia R. Garfield

## 1879: NOVEMBER 18
## HELEN HUNT JACKSON TO CHARLES DUDLEY WARNER

*A native of Amherst, Massachusetts, Helen Maria Fiske (1830–1885) was a class-mate and longtime friend of Emily Dickinson's, and an early success as the poet, essayist, and novelist "H.H.H." Eventually, she would take the names of her two husbands: U.S. Army Captain Edward Hunt, who died in an accident during the Civil War; and William Jackson, a railroad executive and banker. After outliving two sons, Helen Hunt Jackson was sent west by a doctor for her health. Overwhelmed by the plight of the Indians, she began to write, lecture, and raise money on their behalf. Two years after sending this plea to editor and author Charles Dudley Warner (1829–1900), she would publish* A Century of Dishonor, *a landmark work on the subject that attracted enormous attention.*

The Ponca Indians, having been driven repeatedly from their land, had been arrested for trying to return to their home in Nebraska; led by Chief Standing Bear, and with the help of sympathetic whites, they successfully petitioned the court. Warner had written about deer hunting in his book *In the Wilderness*. Carl Schurz was secretary of the interior. Gail Hamilton and Lucia Isabella Gilbert Runkle were both contemporary writers.

New York

Nov. 18,1879

Brevoort House

Dear Mr. Warner—

To prove to you that I am the most imprudent woman alive, I shall ask you to do something for me—no less a thing than to reprint in your paper an article in this weeks Independent about the Ponca Indians. It is only one whole side of the Independent & a little more—and it is thrillingly interesting. Will you do it?—Do help, and don't be funny about the Indians. They are right & we are wrong—and the one chance the race has for freedom and right—and our one chance for decency as a nation in our treatment of them, is just now, in this movement toward the courts, by the Poncas.—

I wish you would write something about them, as you did about the Doe in the Adirondacks! There is no telling what you might accomplish by it. You might even prick through to Carl Schurz's heart.—I am going to try to set Gail Hamilton on the track. I did not expect ever to desire to lead her to unsling her vulgar tomahawk; but she can get at things nobody else can—and if she could once be roused on the question, her "dinging" would do good.

Mr. Jackson and I have been saying every day "we must go up or over and take tea with the Warners"—we have been to Boston & back twice—but there has never been a day when he could spare a minute, and now I am afraid he is chained tight here by the hour; but after he goes back to Col Dec. 1st, I shall come and stay a day with you, if you want me—and mean time—perhaps you will be here. Mrs. Runkle—whom I have not yet seen—wrote me that you might possibly come this week.—I hope so and that Mrs. Warner will come too—we shall be here for two weeks yet—: with hearty love to you both,

Your audacious friend<br>Helen Jackson

P.S. If youre "agin" the Indians, dont mention the subject when we meet.

## 1880: NOVEMBER 14
## CHARLOTTE HOWARD CONANT TO HER FAMILY

*The opportunities for women to pursue higher education in America—extremely limited before the Civil War—began to broaden during the second half of the nineteenth century. Vassar in 1865, and Smith and Wellesley in 1875, led the way for private women's colleges, and numerous state universities were open to women as well. By 1880, the year that Charlotte Howard Conant (1862–1925) sent this letter home from Wellesley, women represented a third of the country's college and university students.*

Charlotte Conant would grow up to become a teacher herself and, eventually, to co-found Walnut Hill, a girls' school in Natick, Massachusetts. "Goldsmith" was probably the British writer and philosopher Oliver Goldsmith.

Wellesley College, Wellesley, Mass.<br>Nov. 14, 1880.

My Dear Family,

...It does seem such a long time. I don't think the first of September <u>can</u> seem so far past to you as it does to me. However I do not wish to give you the impression at all that life here is a dreary waste or a "howling wilderness" as Papa says, though I do want to see you so much. Every hour, almost every minute, is occupied and this very occupation while it makes time almost fly yet as one looks back upon it seems like living a great deal and passing through a good while. There is so much to think about here....

Mr. Field's lecture was a good one, upon Goldsmith. He began, or rather prefaced, it by a kind of short sermon on perseverance and industry. On Goldsmith he spoke very interestingly. He is a social and entertaining rather than critical lecturer.

Thursday morning, Miss Howard gave us a lecture in chapel of another kind. Upon our short-comings and long-goings, mostly long-goings. She mentioned a number of things which we ought not to do. Slamming doors and whistling, especially whistling. She said she never knew but one <u>lady</u> who whistled and she had taken lessons and practised until her whistle was the sweetest music, so now the girls all want to know who the lady was. Running through the halls and talking above a whisper after the lights are out are also forbidden. Then idle and flippant words about the faculty are reprehended; neither is it advisable to write frivolous and idle letters to general correspondents on Sunday. This is a <u>good</u> place, no doubt of that, and if one obeys all the rules and <u>regulations</u>, I should think she was almost perfect.

Friday Miss Freeman lectured on the battle of Marathon and its causes. She is an enthusiast in history, and in hearing her speak you seem to have the whole scene before you and be one of those Grecian soldiers eighteen or twenty centuries ago, ready to charge upon the Persians in defence of home and country. The freshman class only are required to attend the history lectures but the girls all like to go, so last time there were as many as two hundred and fifty there. Saturday we had a very interesting lecture on the circulation of the blood. In the morning, Miss Nunn gave a frog chloroform and put his foot under the microscope so we could see the blood flowing in the veins and even the little corpuscles which, as M. P. knows, give color to the blood. All the lectures are interesting but the History lectures I think I like best. Have we not been well lectured this last week?

With the best love of your own
Charlotte Howard Conant

## CIRCA 1881

## A CALIFORNIA RESIDENT TO A BODIE OFFICER

*Despite its ever-rising popularity, California was still a rugged place in 1881. The town of Bodie, fifty miles south of Lake Tahoe, had boomed in the late 1870s with a short but ardent gold rush and a population of ten thousand. Notorious for its whiskey, its street fights, its robberies, and its killings, Bodie would begin a slow decline to ghost town starting in 1882, but fortunately one thing that survived was this memorable—and chillingly pragmatic—letter, written to a town officer.*

Kind and Respected Cir:

I see in the paper that a man named John Sipes was attacted and et up by a bare whose kubs he was trying to get when the she bare came up and stopt him by eating him in the mountains near your town.

What I want to know is did it kill him ded or was he only partly et up and is he from this plaice and all about the bare. I don't know but he is a distant husband of mine, My first husband was of that name and I supposed he was killed in the war, but the name of the man the bare et being the same I thought it might be him after all and I ought to know if he wasn't killed either in the war or by the bare, for I have been married twise and there ought to be divorse papers got out by him or me if the bare did not eat him up. If it is him you will know by his having six toes on his left foot.

He also had a spreadagle tattooed on his front chest and a anker on his right arm which you will know him by if the bare did not eat up these sines of it being him.

Find out all you kin about him without him knowing what it is for, that is if the bare did not eat him all up. If it did I don't see as you kin do anything and you needn't to trouble. Please ancer back.

P.S.—Was the bare killed? Also was he married again and did he have propty wuth me laying claim to?

## 1881: JULY 3
## HARRIET BLAINE TO MARGARET BLAINE

*James Garfield had served only four months when he became the second president to be killed in office. His assassin, Charles Guiteau, apparently unhinged because he had been denied a political appointment, shot the president in the back at the Washington, D.C., train station. Garfield lived for another eighty days, his doctors' germ-riddled attempts to find the bullet probably proving more damaging than the bullet itself, before dying of a heart attack on September 19. At his side on the first day was Harriet Bailey Stanwood Blaine (1828–1903), the wife of Secretary of State James Blaine. In this letter, written the day after the shooting, Harriet described the scene to her daughter Margaret (1867–1949).*

Walker, Alice, and Emmons were three of the Blaines' six children. "Tom" was Thomas Sherman, a Jesuit priest and the son of General William Tecumseh Sherman; the Shermans lived two doors down from the Blaines. Virginia MacVeagh was the wife of Attorney General Wayne MacVeagh.

Washington, July 3rd, 1881

Dear M.—

Your Father got up quite early yesterday morning, in order to drive the President to the Station, and at 9:30 Tom, the boys, Alice and I had breakfast. In the midst of it, the doorbell rang, and Tom was called out. Then he called Walker;

but as the house is besieged all the time, we, who were so fortunate as to remain unsent for, paid no attention to the prolonged absence of the absentees; but shall I ever forget the moment when Maggie Nurse came running into the room crying, "They have telephoned over to you, Mrs. Blaine, that the President is assassinated." Emmons flew, for we all remembered, with one accord, that his Father was with him. By the time I reached the door, I saw that it must be true—everybody on the street, and wild. Mrs. Sherman got a carriage and we drove over to the White House. Found the streets in front jammed and the doors closed, but they let us through and in. The President still at the station, so drove thitherward. Met the mounted police clearing the avenue, then the ambulance; turned and followed into that very gateway where, on the fourth of March, we had watched him enter. I stood with Mrs. MacVeagh in the hall, when a dozen men bore him above their heads, stretched on a mattress, and as he saw us and held us with his eye, he kissed his hand to us—I thought I should die; and when they brought him into his chamber and had laid him on the bed, he turned his eyes to me, beckoned, and when I went to him, pulled me down, kissed me again and again, and said, "Whatever happens I want you to promise to look out for Crete" the name he always gives his wife. "Don't leave me until Crete comes." I took my old bonnet off and just stayed. I never left him a moment. Whatever happened in the room, I never blenched, and the day will never pass from my memory. At six or thereabouts, Mrs. Garfield came, frail, fatigued, desperate, but firm and quiet and full of purpose to save, and I think now there is a possibility of succeeding.

Of course I don't know when we shall go home. There seems a purpose in our delay. I came from the White House at two this morning, and had been there all day, but not in the room. Emmons is here. I am writing in greatest haste, and may have to sit up to-night.

> With love,
> H. S. B.

## 1882: OCTOBER 18
## HANNAH WHITALL SMITH TO RICHENDA LOUISA BARCLAY

*Not until the twentieth century, when Americans truly understood the connection between bacteria and illness, did the infant mortality rates show a significant decline. In the meantime, childhood remained a precarious business, fraught with vulnerabilities and potential disaster. The consequent expectation of loss was the reason that the Quaker activist Hannah Whitall Smith (see pages 188 and 202) gave her friend Richenda Louisa Barclay (1827–1888) for a surprisingly modern maternal laxness—and attendant guilt.*

Hannah's first daughter had died at the age of five, and her first son at eighteen. Mary would eventually marry the art critic Bernard Berenson. A third daughter, Alys, would marry the philosopher Bertrand Russell.

Germantown, Oct. 18, 1882

I do not think myself it is any harm to be proud of our children, when our pride takes the form of thankfulness to our Heavenly Father for His goodness in giving us such lovely gifts. But I may tell thee confidentially that I do not expect any of my children to live many years. Whether this is because I have lost so many that I feel it natural they should die, or whether it is prophecy I do not know. It does not worry me at all, but I confess it <u>does</u> make me indulgent.

The other day when I was fixing up Mary's room at College, she wanted me to buy her a leather covered arm chair. I did not think she needed it, and was going to refuse, when she coughed. Immediately I thought "Now perhaps she will die of consumption, and then how I shall wish I had bought her the chair." So forthwith I bought it. And when it came home I said, "There, daughter, thee coughed up that chair." I tell thee this that thee may know just what a foolish mother I am. I tell the children that Heavenly Father will have to give them their discipline, for their earthly parents have not the heart to do it.

## 1883: AUGUST 16
## JULIA DANIELS MOSELEY TO CHARLES SCOTT MOSELEY

*In 1882, southwest Florida was still a largely unsettled wilderness when Julia Daniels Moseley (1849–1917) moved there from Illinois with her husband, Charles Scott Moseley (1828–1918). Alone for long stretches of time while he pursued business in the north, she struggled to make adjustments—in this case the timeless adjustment to life with a new baby.*

Every twelve hours that I rock back and forth with Hallock it is 26,650 times. I counted.

I've lived through this day better than any other since you left me. And yet I told Florence that if I could have my choice to see you this day for half an hour and then die, or wait until Christmas and live, I would say, "Let me die if I can but see and touch them once more." But I must be brave. I know I'm a miserable coward. I seem to have lost all power, save the torture of your absence.

## 1884: JANUARY 14
## MARY VAN ALLEN TO AN ORPHANAGE ATTENDANT

*The Gilded Age was one of enormous extremes. The counterpart of the great luxuries being enjoyed by the rich were the tremendous hardships being endured by the poor. Victory or not, the northern states in the years following Reconstruction faced financial panics, unemployment, illness, and urban overcrowding. For families who couldn't make ends meet, the orphan asylum was sometimes a short-term solution. At Albany Orphan Asylum in New York State, only about 15 percent of the children were actually orphans; the others had either one or two parents, and many families would be reunited once economic or personal conditions improved. For Mary Van Allen and her son, Robert, however, no such reunion was forthcoming. It would be decades before the two met again. Nonetheless, Mary tried to supervise from afar.*

Kind lady:

   will you please to watch Robbie A little. he has the piles real bad some times. if you could have the Doctor give you some thing for him his little body comes down A good deal some times. i suppose you know what the piles Are. now please dont have him forget that hes got A mother. talk with him about me. dont let him forget his prayers, the lords prayer & the little prayer, he knew the most of them. i hope and pray that he will grow up to be a Christian and love his mother. May god love and protect him All of his life. this is all. so good by from robbies mother, tell robbie that ma ma wants to see him and kiss him for me & may god bless you to take good care of my little boy. good by.

respectfully yours,
Mary Van Allen

## 1884: MAY 4
## CAROLINE O'ROURKE TO ALBERT FULLER

*Orphan asylums were sometimes seen not as a last resort but as a positive social invention that could allow children to be brought up free of their parents' problems or vices. In the case of a New York woman named Caroline O'Rourke, the problem was a contentious marriage, and the vice was apparently liquor. In March of 1884, the O'Rourkes' two daughters were taken from them by the Humane Society and placed in the Albany Orphan Asylum. Almost immediately, Caroline began to write to Albert Fuller (1850–1893), the head of the asylum, to try to get her daughters back.*

In October of 1887, Cora and Carrie O'Rourke were returned to their parents' care; in 1892, the local humane society intervened again, but further developments are unknown.

May 4, 1884

Mr. Fuller:

Will you please Write how my Children Cora & Carrie are getting along and Please Send me a Lock of their hair. O how i Wish i Could See them. please to Write me if they are going to School and if go to Sunday School. O may the Lord Forgive me for What i have done and if i Could have them Back i Would do Better and i Would Never give them Up again. me and my Husband are keeping house again and Can you not Let us have them and i will do all i Can to Bring them Up good and take . . . good Care of them. O Mr fuller Can you not let me have them again. do help me if you can. give them my love and tell them this letter is from their Mother. . . .

To my dear Children Cora & Carrie: Be good . . . girls and . . . Learn Fast So you Can Write me a Letter. O how i wish i could See you & take care of little Carrie. i send Both my Love. Please send me a lock of your Hair. good By darlings. . . .

## 1884: SEPTEMBER 12
## WILHELMINE WIEBUSCH TO MARIE KALLMEYER

*More than seven million women emigrated to the United States between 1880 and 1920, most of them destined for cities where they could count on getting industrial work. Among the millions was Wilhelmine Wiebusch (1859–?), who came from Hamburg with her friend Anna Beckermann. Within days of arriving both girls had found jobs—thanks to members of Beckermann's family—in the home of a Brooklyn businessman whose wife happened to speak some German.*
Marie Kallmeyer (1863–?) was both girls' friend and remained in Hamburg. The *Novellen Zeitung* (literally "novel newspaper") was popular in Hamburg. This letter was translated from the German, but the underlined words were written in Wiebusch's best attempts at English.

Brooklyn, 9/12/84

My dear Marie,

A long, long time ago it was that we left Hamburg, and in this time you, dear Marie, have often been expecting a letter from me. You mustn't be angry that I am only now writing, because in a foreign country you have all sorts of things to think about at the beginning. Oh, if only we could sit together for a while, then I could tell you many a little tale of adventure, but the endlessly vast ocean calls for writing. I am sure you have heard something about us from Anna's sister, but I'll still tell about our trip as well as I can....

So there we were in the land of milk and honey, then we stayed in a German hotel with several others we got to know on the ship, and during this time we got to see a bit of New York. The first day it rained so badly we couldn't do anything, the second day we went to find Anna's relatives, and after 4 hours of asking around everywhere in our elegant English we finally found the way. Dear Marie, you really ought to see New York, when you get your Sunday off, come on over for awhile, the city must be 3 times as big as Hamburg, the most beautiful and main street, Broadway, is more than 6 hours long, with about 300 side streets to the right and left and many many more streets, so you can't go on foot much, everything's so spread out, so you simply take the <u>Care</u> or railroad which runs in almost every street, way up high, as high as the second floor of the houses. Crossing the street is positively dangerous, one wagon after the next, so loud you can't hear yourself talk, business and money everywhere. On August 8 we had the dumb luck of both getting a job together in a very fine private house in Brooklyn. This town is only separated from New-York by water, you can go across in 5 minutes with the ferry, and most of the quality folks who have their business in new York live here, since Brooklyn is much prettier and the air is much healthier. Anna is the scullery maid and I'm the cook, we each get 12 dollars a month (50 marks)—what do you think, dear Marie, don't you have the slightest desire to come to <u>Kamerika</u>?

There's more work, of course, since the Americans live very lavishly, they eat 3 hot meals a day, and then we have to do all the laundry in the house, since it's so awfully expensive to send it out, we even have to iron the shirts and cuffs, here you have to understand everything, we do our best, but we can do things when we want, the <u>Ladys</u> don't pay much attention to the household, they don't do anything but dress up themselves 3–4 times a day and go out. The family is remarkably friendly, there are 8 persons all together, Mr. and Mrs. Moses, 3 grown-up beautiful daughters and 3 good-looking boys., the <u>Lady</u> herself speaks broken German, we can make ourselves understood quite well with her, the others want to learn it too, they like German a lot. You should just hear us speaking English, we just rattle off what we hear, whether it's right or not, the <u>Lady</u> says sometimes she almost dies laughing at us.

Our house consists of a ground floor and three more stories, but they don't do all that much scrubbing and cleaning here. The rooms are like a Chinese doll house, they're all covered with rugs and carpets, its not fashionable to have white lace curtains in the windows here, the best thing is the beds, they are big and wide. Because of the heat, they're only made up of a mattress, pillow and 2 sheets. At the moment it is very hot here, the ladies all wear real thin muslin dresses. Anna and I sometimes work up quite a sweat, we only wear a shirt and a dress and would like to take that off too. I have no complaints about the Americans, they are very friendly, gallant people, but I don't like the Germans here very much, they are all a bunch of snobs, act like they can't understand German anymore, act like they know nothing about their old homeland any more, but we won't forget, since even if it is nice in a foreign country, it'll never be home. . . .

There's still lots and lots to write you about, dear Marie, but another time, because for today it is (time to go to bed. I am wery tired. It is a quarter past one) translate that into German, and then write back soon how you are, do you have a little bit of news about your sweetheart? and a lot about Hamburg, I miss my wonderful Novellen Zeitung here a lot, I would really like to have it forwarded if it weren't so much trouble. I'd send you the money if you could arrange it for me. . . .

Now farewell dear Marie, warmest regards/from the faraway/west

Anni and Meini

my address is/Wilhelmine Wiebusch/ care. of. Mr Leionel Moses./751 Union-Street. Brooklyn. /New-York.

Please write and tell me when you get this letter. Oh blast it, I forgot to tell you what wonderful fruit there is in Kamerika, every day we eat peaches, melons and bananas, and then I also wanted to tell you if you have an old shoe or boot, don't throw it away, tie a red or blue bow on it and hang it on the wall in your room. You may think I'm crazy, but you ought to know, dear Marie, that here in America, that's what they call an antique.

I. put this Letter in the Letterbax, hve you undrstand Mary? You see I speak wery well Englisch, i believe it is anough.

I'll give you another little idea of how it is sometimes when we talk, this evening at dinner Mr Moses said to Anna, plase give me some breat. (bitte geben Sie mir ein wenig Brot) and Anna understood smal plaid [small plate] (kleine Teller) and came back with an empty plate, of course everyone laughed, that kind of thing happens to us a lot, but they don't take it badly, it's all right. Anna pulls a lot of such silly tricks, one time she wanted to go the drug store and get some chlorine, so she goes into the first drug store that comes along and says speak you Germain (sprechen Sie Deutsch), no (nein), na den geben Sie mir für 10 Ct. Chlorkalk, i do not undrstand you (ich verstehe Sie nicht), well then forget it, you dummy, and so she went to 4 different drug stores and finally she got so lost that the police had to bring her home.

I can't find the Fritz Stellen you told me about since there's no town hall here, for we live here like wild folks here in the land of freedom, we haven't needed any papers yet, no one has asked us about our names and origin.

But that's enough for now, if there's anything else you want to know about, just ask what you want to know and then I'll write and tell you what you want to know.

Now the American post office is closing.

Goodnight/ to be continued

## 1884: OCTOBER 4
## LUCY PARSONS TO TRAMPS

*Lucy Eldine (1853?–1942) claimed her ancestry as Indian and Mexican; her dark skin meant she was identified as black. In any case, her marriage to a former white Confederate soldier named Albert Parsons wasn't tolerated in Texas, and in 1873, they moved to Chicago. A decade later, they were identifying themselves as anarchists and atheists and were openly championing racial equality, sexual equality, the rights of the poor, and the overthrow of capitalism. Lucy Parsons's 1884 letter to tramps (a word that originally suggested more "vagabond" than "vagrant") was printed in the socialist newspaper* The Alarm. *Two years later, it would be offered as evidence that Albert had conspired with seven other anarchists to commit murder in Chicago's Haymarket Riot.*
Albert Parsons and three of his cohorts were executed in 1887.

To Tramps, the Unemployed, the Disinherited, and Miserable.

A word to the 35,000 now tramping the streets of this great city, with hands in pockets, gazing listlessly about you at the evidences of wealth and pleasure of which you own no part, not sufficient even to purchase yourself a bit of food with which to appease the pangs of hunger now knawing at your vitals. It is with you and the hundreds of thousands of others similarly situated in this great land of plenty, that I wish to have a word.

Have you not worked hard all your life, since you were old enough for your labor to be of use in the production of wealth? Have you not toiled long, hard and laboriously in producing wealth? And in all those years of drudgery do you not know you have produced thousands upon thousands of dollars' worth of wealth, which you did not then, do not now, and unless you ACT, never will own any part in? Do you not know that when you were harnessed to a machine and that machine harnessed to steam, and thus you toiled your 10, 13, and 15 hours in the 24, that during this time in all those years you received only enough of your labor product to furnish yourself the bare, coarse necessaries of life, and that when you wished to purchase anything for yourself and family it always had to be of the cheapest quality? If you wanted to go anywhere you had to wait until Sunday so little did you receive for your unremitting toil that you dare not stop for a moment, as it were? And do you not know that with all your squeezing, pinching and economizing you never were enabled to keep but a few days ahead of the wolves of want? And that at last when the caprice of your employer saw fit to create an artificial famine by limiting production, that the fires in the furnace were extinguished, the iron horse to which you had been harnessed was stilled; the factory door locked up, you turned upon the highway a tramp, with hunger in your stomach, and rags upon your back?

Yet your employer told you that it was overproduction which made him close up. Who cared for the bitter tears and heart-pangs of your loving wife and helpless children, when you bid them a loving "God bless you" and turned upon the tramper's road to seek employment elsewhere? I say, who cared for those heartaches and pains? You were only a tramp now, to be execrated and denounced as a "worthless tramp and a vagrant" by that very class who had been engaged all those years in robbing you and yours. Then can you not see that the "good boss" or the "bad boss" cuts no figure whatever? That you are the common prey of both, and that their mission is simply robbery? Can you not see that it is the INDUSTRIAL SYSTEM and not the "boss" which must be changed?

Now, when all those bright summer and autumn days are going by and you have no employment, and consequently can save up nothing, and when the winter's blast sweeps down from the north and all the earth is wrapped in a shroud of ice, hearken not to the voice of the hypocrite who will tell you that it was ordained of God that "the poor ye have always" or to the arrogant robber who will say to you that you "drank up all your wages last summer when you had work, and that is the reason why you have nothing now, and the workhouse or the woodyard is too good for you; that you ought to be shot". And shoot you they will if you present your petitions in too emphatic a manner. So hearken to them, but list! Next winter when the cold blasts are creeping through the rents in your seedy garments, when the frost is biting your feet through the holes in your worn-out shoes, and when all wretchedness seems to have centered in and

upon you, when misery has marked you for her own and life has become a burden and existence a mockery, when you have walked the streets by day and slept
upon hard boards by night, and at last determine by your own hand to take your
life,—for you would rather go out into utter nothingness than to longer endure
an existence which has become such a burden—so, perchance, you determine
to dash yourself into the cold embrace of the lake rather than longer suffer thus.
But halt, before you commit this last tragic act in the drama of your simple existence, Stop! Is there nothing you can do to insure those whom you are about to
orphan, against a like fate? The waves will only dash over you in mockery of your
rash act; but stroll you down the avenues of the rich and look through the magnificent plate windows into their voluptuous homes, and here you will discover
the very identical robbers who have despoiled you and yours. Then let your
tragedy be enacted here! Awaken them from their wanton sports at your expense! Send forth your petition and let them read it by the red glare of destruction. Thus when you cast "one long, lingering look behind" you can be assured
that you have spoken to these robbers in the only language which they have ever
been able to understand, for they have never yet deigned to notice any petition
from their slaves that they were not compelled to read by the red glare bursting
from the cannon's mouths, or that was not handed to them upon the point of
the sword. You need no organization when you make up your mind to present
this kind of petition. In fact, an organization would be a detriment to you; but
each of you hungry tramps who read these lines, avail yourselves of those little
methods of warfare which Science has placed in the hands of the poor man, and
you will become a power in this or any other land.

    Learn the use of explosives!

Dedicated to the tramps by
Lucy E. Parsons

## 1884: NOVEMBER 7
## BETSEY SHIPMAN GATES TO BETSEY GATES MILLS

*More than a century before the American people were confounded by the vote
counting in the presidential race between Albert Gore and George W. Bush, a similar state of confusion reigned. In the 1884 election, the contest was between Democratic nominee Grover Cleveland and Republican candidate James G. Blaine (see
page 385). In Marietta, Ohio, Betsey Shipman Gates (1853–?) wrote to her daughter about the debacle. After a smear-driven campaign that was considered the*

*absolute nadir of American politics, the election came down to the contest in New York, which Cleveland carried by just over a thousand votes, and which the Republicans promptly contested. It took a few days to count and recount the votes. Ultimately, of course, Grover Cleveland prevailed, becoming the first Democratic president since James Buchanan.*

Although Gates was casual about its use, the telephone had been patented only in 1876 and would not become truly widespread until the next century.

Marietta, November 7, 1884.

Here we are all torn to pieces over Indiana, what is the matter out there. We do have here the most ridiculous times you ever heard tell of celebrating victories, first the democrats and then the republicans. We went to bed last night thinking we had to tolerate Cleveland for President and then in the night between two and three we were aroused by the fellows firing cannon and bonfires and horns and all sorts of noises. Of course nobody but democrats would be such fools and I would hardly let the sound enter my ears but covered my head with the bed clothes. Well this morning before we ate our breakfast some one telephoned that Blaine was elected and that was the rejoicing we heard in the night. Then of course we had a little bit of a love feast on a small scale but before nine o'clock by the time your father had got to the Bank here was another telegram that New York and Indiana and Illinois had gone for Cleveland. What in the world was the matter with the men and the wires and the messages. We came into the library after dinner and the telephone rung saying that Blaine had got New York by 500 or more! Here were three different returns in less than twelve hours. I hope now we have got them for sure. If they change again the men better quit and let the women take hold of it and run the elections for awhile. But I am going to drop the subject and let the thing work itself out and I am going to Missionary meeting at Mother Mills.

Evening. The town is still agitated over the election and I am all mussed up and cannot tell a straight story to save my life, so I won't try to give you the latest news but we are probably given over to the democrats. If Cleveland beats, our people that work by the day or week will be apt to feel the difference to their disadvantage. They will find that free trade and free whiskey won't feed and clothe their families. I think I shall hardly spend two or three weeks in Washington this winter if Cleveland is at the White House. I don't seem to write about anything but the presidency. The whole country is as much disquieted about it as we have been about the College president. I believe they have got

their finger on somebody now. We shall probably know in time for his inauguration and then the whole country will know whether Blaine is president on the
fourth of next March. I am sorry about Indiana.

**1885: MARCH 12**

**LILLIAN WAITE FLEET TO HER FAMILY**

_____

*For the first part of the nineteenth century, childbirth occurred at home in America,*
*attended to by relatives or perhaps by midwives. By mid-century, however, the field*
*of obstetrics was gaining ground, and births would increasingly take place in hospi-*
*tals, under a doctor's care. In the case of a Washington State educator's wife named*
*Lillian Waite Fleet (1858–1939), however, it took three doctors to handle the*
*complications—both physical and moral—of an apparently life-saving abortion.*
David and Lillian Fleet would eventually have two children and stay married for more than
fifty years.

Montesano, March 12th 1885

Dear Mother and sisters,

For the first time I am propped up in bed, and feel that I can attempt a letter
to you. It seems almost like coming back from the other side to greet you and
my heart is very full. To say the least it makes one feel very strange to have been
so near death's door so many times. My heart is full of gratitude to God that he
has spared me to live for David. Oh can a life-time of devotion repay such love,
kindness and constant attention? Since I learned the depth and strength of his
love for me, I determined I <u>would live</u> for his sake; and I believe that it, with
prayer, has carried me through some of the crises. It has certainly been very surprising to see how kind the ladies of this place have been—nearly all have offered their services and for weeks until last Friday night, there have been night
watchers, generally two. On the 27th of Feb. I suffered such a severe attack, Dr.
Coleman said I couldn't live through another. David begged him to perform an
abortion but he refused, saying I would surely die during the operation, admitting I would die anyway. So he was dismissed and Dr. French was called. Dr.
French wanted Dr. Coleman to act with him, he taking responsibility for my
life. Dr. C. refused on account of professional jealousy we think, so we had to
wait until Sunday evening for Dr. Pearson from Aberdeen, one doctor not daring
to act alone for fear of the trouble which might ensue, should I die. During this
interim I was able to retain some beef broth and brandy stimulants—more than
I had taken during the five previous weeks.

I will spare you the details of the operation which lasted most of the night but when it was over, one doctor collapsed as soon as he reached another room and was kept from fainting only by whiskey being poured down his throat. The other did not even attempt to leave the room but sank completely exhausted into a chair by my bedside. One lady was deathly sick but the other did not give up at all. She is a noble woman—the wife of a Methodist minister. She has been with me day times for the last three weeks and says she knows the good Lord gave her strength to get through <u>that</u> night, as it has been years since she has done anything of that kind. Truly God has raised up friends for us in our time of need.

I am reduced in flesh until I don't believe I would weigh 100 lbs. My hair was cut very short by the barber. The cropped hair with the pinched, sallow face and skinny body make me look quite unlike the girl David married—and yet—God bless him! he seems so inexpressibly happy now that I am out of danger, and we are making great plans for our summer's work together. The great trials we have been called to pass through have knit our hearts <u>so much</u> the more closely together, and brought us humbly to an appreciation of the goodness and mercy of our Heavenly Father.

You will pardon me, I trust, if I close abruptly now. Many thanks for your kind sweet letters and love from

Lillian

## 1885: MARCH 22
## VICTORIA SACKVILLE-WEST TO AMY HEARD

*Victoria Josepha Dolores Catalina Sackville-West (1862–1936) enjoyed the gilded part of the Gilded Age. The future mother of the writer Vita Sackville-West, Victoria had come to the nation's capital as the daughter of the British minister, Sir Lionel Sackville-West. Despite the semiscandalous fact that her father had never been married, Victoria became a popular Washington hostess, and, as is clear from the way she exchanged gossip and stole servants, fit right in with the social scene. In this letter, translated from the French, she described her current concerns to a New York friend named Amy Heard (1860–1949).*

Theodore Justin Roustan was the French minister, rumored to be in love with Sackville-West. Frederick Frelinghuysen replaced James Blaine as secretary of state. Madame de Struve was married to the Russian minister. Reuterskiold was the minister from Sweden and Norway. Juan Valera was the Spanish minister. Chester A. Arthur was the president to whom West was referring.

22 March 85

My very dear Amy,

I am responding to you quickly because of your little box which Canfield will come to take next Tuesday or Wednesday. Have it ready, will you? I will return it to Mr. Roustan, and you tell me who he should send it to in Paris. You do not bother me by asking me to do your little errands, so do not bother yourself about it.

I am afraid that I can no longer go to N.Y., because of changes in our domestic servants; it is necessary that I be there to survey them myself, especially at the beginning. I definitely captured the maitre d'hotel of the Frelinghuysans and their laundress; there remains finding a good cook: a big affair! These difficulties of the household bore me to death! What's more, it is necessary to buy another horse. I have to therefore sacrifice my pleasure of going to N.Y. and of seeing you again, my dear friend. I hope that you have fun in Boston. If you could come back to spend a month in spring with us; for example, May with Mme de Struve and June with us.

Try to arrange that; it would be so nice!

Our dinner with the President was good, as was the small soiree which followed. Tomorrow we are giving tomorrow a dinner for the Reuterskiolds; Mme de Struve had the amiability to ask me if it was an engagement dinner! . . . She is incorrigible. Theo was much better than in the abominable play of Monday. The daughter of Tambour Major was charming. Au revoir, my dear; write me as soon as you have the time. We will send you often news of the house and your friends. Do not forget your errand for Mr. Valera, who now has the air of a body without a soul.

A thousand good memories to your mother.

Always your <u>best</u> friend.

Victoria

I hope that your <u>brother</u> succeeds well.

### 1885: SEPTEMBER 27
### ROSE WILLIAMS TO ALLETTIE MOSHER

---

*Different sorts of birth control had been around for centuries, but they were still the source of whispers and rumors when Rose Williams wrote to her friend Allettie Mosher about how to avoid getting pregnant. Such instruction was hardly routine: In 1873, the Comstock Act had made it illegal to publish, distribute, or possess information about contraception.*

It is unclear whether the pessary Williams was referring to was a suppository or a solid object; both were among the many only semisuccessful methods that women used to avoid unwanted pregnancies in the nineteenth century. "Dak" was Dakota.

Well now I should say & did say "who would have thought it." You better bet I was surprised when I read your letter, you never let a fellow know you even had a fellow. . . . You never sent a piece of your dress as you said you would. You want to know of a sure prevenative. Well plague take it. The best way is for you to sleep in one bed and your Man in another & bet you will laugh and say "You goose you think I am going to do that" no and I bet you would for I don't see any one that does. Well now the thing we [use] (when I say <u>we</u> I mean us girls) is a thing: but it hasn't always been <u>sure</u> as you know but that was our own carelessness for it is we have been sure. I do not know whether you can get them out there. They are called Pessairre or female prevenative if you don't want to ask for a "pisser" just ask for a female prevenative. They cost one dollar when Sis got hers it was before any of us went to Dak. She paid five dollars for it. The Directions are with it. . . . Reece just told me to tell you to wear a long night dress with a draw string at the bottom and a lock and key for if you was in separate beds you would crawl over together . . . & would not like to have someone else to get this. It would spook them sick I wouldent wonder . . . let me know if it does.

**1886: MAY**
**EMILY DICKINSON TO LOUISE AND FRANCES NORCROSS**

---

*On her deathbed, Emily Dickinson wrote her last letter, characteristic in its lightly ironic touch. The words would be her epitaph.*

Little Cousins,
    Called back—

                        Emily

**1887: JUNE 17**
**HELEN KELLER TO ANNA TURNER**

---

*Helen Keller (1880–1968) was six years old and locked in both silence and darkness when Annie Sullivan first came to teach her. Only three and a half months later, Keller wrote this letter to a cousin named Anna Turner. Keller would go on to show extraordinary talent, first as a student and later as a lecturer and writer.*

Tuscumbia, Alabama, June 17, 1887.
helen write anna george will give helen apple simpson will shoot bird jack will give helen stick of candy doctor will give mildred medicine mother will make mildred new dress

### 1888: MAY

### WOMAN'S CHRISTIAN TEMPERANCE UNION TO CONGRESS

*The term "the age of consent" refers to the age at which a person can legally consent to have sex. In the United States, at the end of the nineteenth century, that age was only ten or twelve in most states. The prevailing, if illogical, assumption was that any woman over that age who had engaged in sex must have done so willingly. Thus, in the event of an assault or rape, women had virtually no legal recourse. In this petition, similar versions of which were circulated nationally, representatives of the Woman's Christian Temperance Union turned their advocacy skills to the question of consensual sex.*

By 1920, the age of consent would be sixteen or eighteen in most states.

To the Senate and House of Representatives:

The increasing and alarming frequency of assaults upon women, and the frightful indignities to which even little girls are subject, have become the shame of our boasted civilization.

A study of the Statutes has revealed their utter failure to meet the demands of that newly-awakened public sentiment which requires better legal protection for womanhood and girlhood.

Therefore we, women of Chesening, State of Michigan, do most earnestly appeal to you to enact such statutes as shall provide for the adequate punishment of crimes against women and girls. We also urge that the age at which a girl can legally consent to her own ruin be raised to at least eighteen years; and we call attention to the disgraceful fact that protection of the person is not placed by our laws upon so high a plane as protection of the purse.

### 1889

### MARY COLLINS TO READERS OF THE AMERICAN MISSIONARY

*Thanks to the writings and speeches of advocates like Helen Hunt Jackson (see page 381), the plight of American Indians had gained greater visibility by the end of the nineteenth century, a time when there were ever more zealous attempts to convert Native Americans to the Christian religion. Despite spending years among the Dakota Sioux, missionaries such as Mary Clementine Collins (1846–1920) were still finding it difficult to persuade some of them to give up their traditions.*

Thomas Riggs was a Congregational minister who ran both the Oahe mission and an industrial school north of Pierre.

Last Sabbath, Mr. Riggs came up from Oahe and we had communion, and there were five children baptized and seven grown people, and seven more were examined and advised to wait till the next communion. It was a most interesting season.

Three of the young men were the leaders in the Indian dance. They have always been the head ones in all Indian customs. A year ago, one of them said in the dance that he should follow the Indian customs a year longer—give himself up to them wholly and try to be satisfied, and if he had in his heart the same unsatisfied feeling, the same longing, that he then had, he should throw it all away.

On last New Year's day, the same young man, "Huntington Wolcott," came to me and said—"Last night I arose in the dance and told them that I had given the old customs and the old Indians a fair trial, and that they did not satisfy, now I should leave them forever and give myself to God, and if any others were ready to follow to arise and so make it known. The other two leaders arose, stood silently a moment, and walked out." From that time they have given themselves up to singing, praying and studying the Bible. They had, for two years, been halting between two opinions, attending the school, church, etc., and the Indian feasts and dances, too. These three having come out so boldly on God's side, has made a great change in our work here.

Poor old Running-Antelope feels very sad. It is his desire to keep the young men from learning Christianity and civilization as long as he can. He wants them to have everything in common, and to feel that for an individual to accumulate anything is a disgrace. As long as they feel so, of course squalor and suffering will be the natural consequences.

The young men are working hard to build up homes and to accumulate something for their families during the winter. One young man has cut logs and is building a house. I try to teach them that long prayers and loud singing is not all of Christianity—that however regularly a man attends to his church duties, if he fails to provide for his family, his religion is vain; and if he gives all his goods to his friends and lets his wife and children cry for bread, that their cries will reach the ears of God, and his prayers and hymns will be lost in this round of wailing of the hungry. All this is very different from their old Indian doctrine and hard to understand.

Elias, our native teacher, has formed a class of young men who meet every Tuesday night and talk and pray and sing together, and he directs their thought. I think it will prove very helpful. Then on Thursday night I have my Bible class, which now numbers about twenty. It is formed of the young men and women who wish to follow Christ's example, and band themselves together to learn of him. It has been the <u>training school</u> of the young Christians.

### 1889: MARCH 13

### JANE ADDAMS TO MARY CATHERINE ADDAMS LINN

*The concept of the settlement house, borrowed from British social reformers, was that students and educated adults would settle in poor neighborhoods and provide social services directly. Having seen the British example during a trip abroad, Jane Addams (1860–1935) was determined to bring it to America, and she described her visits to the Chicago slums in this letter to her sister Mary Catherine Addams Linn (1845–1894). Later in the year, Addams and her co-founder, Ellen Gates Starr, would open the doors of the Charles Hull Mansion, dubbed Hull House, for a kindergarten, nursery school, and infant day-care center that would eventually expand to include thirteen buildings housing everything from a gym to a labor museum.*

Frank Gunsaulus was a Chicago minister who would give a famous sermon in 1890 about how, with a million dollars, he could build a technical school open to all. Frank Stauber was a German-born anarchist. London's Denison Club was a meeting place for workers.

4 Washington Pl.<br>
Chicago March 13, 1889

My dear Mary,

I have rather a disheartening impression that it is much more than a week since I wrote last, but I have been looking up different "slums" and usually when I come back am too tired to do any thing.

As I do not know where I left off in the journalistic account it may be well to go backward. I spent the morning with an Italian "attendance agent" (a man hired by the Board of Education to look up truant children) going through the Italian quarter of North Chicago—It was exactly as if we were in a quarter of Naples or Rome, the parents and the children spoke nothing but Italian and dressed like Italian peasants. They were more crowded than I imagined people ever lived in America, four families for instance of six or eight each, living in one room for which they paid eleven dollars a month, and are constantly afraid of being ejected. Yet they were affectionate and gentle, the little babies rolled up in stiff bands and the women sitting about like mild eyed Madonnas. They never begged nor even complained, and in all aspects were immensely more attractive to me than the Irish neighborhood I went into last week with a Mrs. Estes. Everything seems to indicate South Clark as our abiding place. Dr. Gunsaulus thinks it is the one spot in the city destined for us. Signor Mastro Valerio who took me this morning is an Italian of some literary note as a journalist. He has sent five hundred Italian children to school in the last three months and was delighted with my feeble Italian, poor as it was. He said there were many young ladies in Chicago who spoke Italian but they sang or were members of the Italian club, they did not visit the Italians. It is quite incomprehensible to me, for I feel exactly as if I had spent a morning in Italy, and enjoyed it just as much. Last evening I spoke to the young people missionary club of the New England church, about seventy-five young men and women who were spending the evening at a Mrs. Clark's house on State St. The invitation came from a young lady of the society, but Mrs. Clark had called the day before, and everything was done in conventional order. The young are usually enthusiastic, and hence it is well not to count too much in the enthusiasm expressed. Miss Blatchford professed herself converted to the "scheme" and its future slave, she may be valuable.

On Sunday afternoon I visited one of the anarchist Sunday schools. I had gotten a letter of introduction to a Mr. Stauber, one of the leading "anarchists" which I had presented the day before. I found a gentlemanly looking man at the head of a prosperous hardware store. He looked as if he was bearing the burdens of all humanity, a thin and spiritual face. He was pleased that I wanted to see the Sunday School, said that "Americans never come up there, except the reporters of the capitalist newspapers and they always exaggerate." I went on Sunday afternoon, to find about two hundred children assembled in a hall in back of a saloon with some young men trying to teach them "free thought without any religion or politics." The entire affair was very innocent—I was treated with great politeness and may take a class—it seems to me an opportunity to do a great deal of good—it was all in German.

I think I wrote of the WCTU experience and the Woman's Alliance. I am getting just a little tired talking about it and should quite prefer beginning a little bit. Looking up localities is certainly toward it. We discover so many similar undertakings, the "Neighborhood Guilds" in New York, the Denison Club in

London, but we still think we have a distinct idea of our own. I had planned for a longer letter but it is dinner time and after that the boys of the Moody School, so I should better get this off.

Mrs. Worrall and Mary went home last week. I spent one day with them, took lunch at Mr. Jenkins, they had their own carriage & afterwards rode in the park etc. They were on the verge then of giving up Kansas City then. I had a letter from Clara yesterday saying they had arrived in Phila. safely. I will try to write oftener next week. Always your loving Sister,

Jane Addams

I will inclose the circular of a similar thing in New York. We are modest enough to think that ours is better, is more distinctively Christian, and less Social Science. I have been corresponding with Miss Fine, she is discouraged over the few offers of service, plenty of money has come in. The little scrap is part of an article in the Chicago Tribune of March 8th you may have seen it. The reporter came twice and it was only by much browbeating that we finally got her to mention no names & keep to generalities. The first part of it I lost but it didn't amount to much. Will you please send the letter & scraps to Alice & Weber.

### 1890: JANUARY 19
### GRACE HENDERSON TO ED HENDERSON

*The growth of cities throughout the last half of the century meant more newspapers, and more newspapers meant an ever escalating war for readers. The 1880s and 1890s would be the heyday of sensationalist journalism, with Joseph Pulitzer and William Randolph Hearst always attempting to outdo each other's headlines. Even the staid* New York Times *ran its share of salacious stories and tearjerkers. The headline on one was "Looked in Vain for Work: Pathetic Instance of a Sensitive Woman's Fruitless Efforts to Get Honest Work in This City." The woman in question was named Grace Henderson; her husband, Ed, had become too ill to work and had moved to a farm to recuperate. Without work experience, she was rudely rebuffed in her search for a job. After writing this note to her husband, she slit her wrist, then jumped out a window.*

Sunday Evening

My Ever Beloved Ed:

I am not in a fit condition of mind to write you, because I am too despondent. I cannot get any employment, and what is going to become of me I know not. I was out in all that storm last week, and came in drenched and, as usual, unsuccessful, and I think will become a total wreck if I ever again hear the expression: "Have you any references?"

Women who were so ignorant that I felt sorry for them would not take me in their kitchens because I could not show "city references," and I tried to explain that I had never had to work before, but because I was not born and bred in the gutter I must starve.

Such is life in charitable New-York. There is help for all but the genteel poor, and they are the ones who suffer most; but I have the satisfaction of knowing that I have tried, and would have done any honest work, even to scrubbing. I could have got plenty of shady work. Widowers who advertise for housekeepers and then gently insinuate that you add wifely duties to domestic arrangements are very plenty in this city, but I do not approve of such economy. I have been so indignant that I would like to have shot the top of their heads off, <u>the old fools</u>.

### 1892: OCTOBER 20

### M. P. LEE TO <u>THE AMERICAN WOMAN'S JOURNAL</u>

*The dress reform movement of the mid-nineteenth century was relatively short-lived, and women who had adopted the "Turkish costume" (see page 206) soon abandoned it because they felt it was distracting people from the main issue of women's rights. After the war, spurred in part by health arguments offered in a variety of forums by Frances Willard (see page 408), the reform movement found new impetus.*

Ferris' Good Sense Corset Waists were an increasingly popular alternative to the rigid corset that, when used for "tight-lacing," had profound health repercussions. Said one Ferris advertisement: "It is the only waist that creates the perfection of contour demanded by particular women, without the slightest restricting or discomfort."

Minneapolis, Minn., Oct. 20, 1892

Dear Madam:

I was very much interested in Miss Willard's article upon Physical Culture and Dress Reform in the last number of the Journal, especially where she says that "the amount of force exerted at this moment to compress the waists of women by artificial methods, would if aggregated, turn all the mills between Minneapolis and the Merrimac." The illustration exactly expresses my feelings, when upon a few memorable occasions, I have put on corsets.

I can sympathize with the wheat at the mills, for my sensations must have

been very similar. I felt that I was being ground, compressed, and generally reduced to something impalpable. The only difference was that by this torture I
was hindered from, instead of being helped to future usefulness. I put on my
waist again—I have worn the Ferris' Good Sense Waist for five years—with a
blissful feeling of comfort that defies expression, and if I continue in a normal
state of mind I shall endeavor to keep my body in the same happy condition, by
clothing it in a "Good Sense" garment. Yours for health, happiness and a long life.

> Sincerely
> M. P. Lee

## 1893

### LOUISA DREW TO LIONEL BARRYMORE

*The daughter, wife, and mother of actors, Louisa Lane Drew (1820–1897) was an
actor herself, having been both a child and an adult star. For three decades, she also
managed Mrs. John Drew's Arch Street Theatre in Philadelphia. It was in that capacity that she wrote the following letter to her grandson, fifteen-year-old Lionel
Barrymore (1878–1954), who had just made his debut in a touring production of*
The Rivals. *He had trouble with everything from a breaking voice to a tangled
whip, but his performance and this letter notwithstanding, he would grow up to be
one of the most celebrated American character actors of all time.*

My dear Lionel,

I sincerely wish I did not have to write this letter, for I want to spare your
feelings. But, dear boy, I am compelled to inform you of the plain facts regarding
your portrayal of Thomas. You were somewhat inadequate, and it is with the
deepest regret that I convey the news that it is no longer necessary that you appear in the cast.

I shall see you in the morning, dear boy. Until then, good night, and God
bless you,

> Your affectionate grandmother,
> Mrs. Drew

## 1894

### OLIVIA CLEMENS TO SAMUEL CLEMENS

*Muse, editor, housekeeper, hostess, mother, nurse, cook, and of course wife, Olivia
Langdon Clemens (1845–1904) was married for thirty-four years to Samuel*

*Clemens (see page 314), and by most recent accounts it was she who most helped him to become and remain Mark Twain. Along with coauthor Charles Dudley Warner, he had introduced the term "The Gilded Age" to refer to the decadence and greed of the last part of the century, but he himself had not been immune to it. Seeing the possibility of a huge return, he invested in a publishing house and a typesetting machine (developed by partner James W. Paige) that never paid off. Beset by debt, Clemens traveled extensively, lecturing and writing. At one dark moment, when Livy and the family were in Germany and Twain in New York, she sent him this characteristically loving and encouraging note.*

"Youth" was Olivia's nickname for her husband. Clara and Susy were two of the Clemens's three daughters. Mark Twain published an 1894 article in the *North American Review* called "In Defence of Harriet Shelley," a review of a current biography. He had started writing *Personal Recollections of Joan of Arc* the previous year in Etretat, a fishing town on the coast of Normandy, which presumably was where he wrote the Shelley article as well.

Youth darling:

If you want to know what a lonely place is, just stay in it when you have gone away from it and see how you miss yourself. This long separation is depressing and it seems as if nothing could be worth it. Yet I know you will come to us as soon as it is possible to leave all the financial confusion over there. Once in a while I am oppressed by a consuming dread of catastrophe and the feeling that perhaps I shall never see you again. At these times it gives me a deep pang to see a woman pass in the street wearing a widow's cap. The other day Clara said to me, "If Father died, would you die, too?" "Unfortunately, no," I answered.

Now if anything happens that Paige does not sign, do not forget for one moment that you have done everything that a human soul could do and that you are in no wise yourself responsible for the failure of your plans. Do not let yourself experience a great reaction. Also do not forget for one moment that all the money this earth possesses could not repay us for any harm coming to you; and that without the money we can be happy and content if you are in good health. So if this whole business fails, pack your bag and come back to us. We will give you some literary work to do and every evening we will be happy together hearing you read what you have written during the day. You know I can learn to economize even better than I have been doing, as I get more and more experience. You know we have an income of about $6000 a year and with what you can comfortably earn in addition, without taxing yourself we can live perfectly well for our requirements. I write all this to let you know that if failure comes we shall not be cast down and you must not allow yourself to be. You know I love you yourself, much more than anything that you may be able to give me. So do take care of yourself and don't be discouraged whatever happens.

I am so sincerely and deeply gratified that your Shelley Etretat article has met with such warm praise. But it was sure to do that. It is a great cause for thankfulness to me that evidently others as well as I realize that your work grows stronger as you grow older. I feel certain that you will receive just as much praise for your Joan. I hope you will soon be so situated that you can go on and finish it. I feel how much you would enjoy this life here and I hate to have you losing it. We see few people and spend most of the day reading and writing by the fire. Susy and Clara take frequent donkey-rides. We all miss you continually.

## 1894: MAY 21
## IDA B. WELLS TO THE <u>WESTMINSTER GAZETTE</u>

*The daughter of slaves, Ida B. Wells (1862–1931) was thirty years old and had been teaching and writing for more than a decade when three of her friends were lynched, and her career of radical activism found its focus. An appalling side effect of Reconstruction, the increase in lynchings of black Americans reached a peak in the last decade of the century, and Wells tirelessly traveled America and Britain to organize antilynching campaigns. The interview she refers to in this letter was conducted by a British temperance leader, Lady Henry Somerset, with Frances Willard, the head of the Woman's Christian Temperance Union. Wells believed that Willard, while trying to use temperance to unite women from the North and South, was too complacent in her treatment of southern racism.*
*Fraternity was published by the Society for the Recognition of the Brotherhood of Man, a British antilynching group co-founded by Wells. In 1895, Wells married a Chicago lawyer named Ferdinand Barnett.*

SIR,—

The interview published in your columns to-day hardly merits a reply, because of the indifference to suffering manifested. Two ladies are represented sitting under a tree at Reigate, and, after some preliminary remarks on the terrible subject of lynching, Miss Willard laughingly replies by cracking a joke. And the concluding sentence of the interview shows the object is not to determine how best they may help the negro who is being hanged, shot, and burned, but "to guard Miss Willard's reputation."

With me it is not myself nor my reputation, but the life of my people, which is at stake, and I affirm that this is the first time to my knowledge that Miss

Willard has said a single word in denunciation of lynching or demand for law. The year 1890, the one in which her interview appears, had a larger lynching record than any previous year, and the number and territory have increased, to say nothing of the human beings burnt alive.

If so earnest as she would have the British public believe her to be, why was she silent when five minutes were given me to speak last June at Princes' Hall, and in Holborn Town Hall this May? I should say it was because as President of the Woman's Christian Temperance Union of America she is timid, because all these unions in the South emphasise the hatred of the negro by excluding him. There is not a single coloured woman admitted to the Southern W.C.T.U., but still Miss Willard blames the negro for the defeat of Prohibition in the South. Miss Willard quotes from Fraternity, but forgets to add my immediate recognition of her presence on the platform at Holborn Town Hall, when, amidst many other resolutions on temperance and other subjects in which she is interested, time was granted to carry an anti-lynching resolution. I was so thankful for this crumb of her speechless presence that I hurried off to the editor of Fraternity and added a postscript to my article blazoning forth that fact.

Any statements I have made concerning Miss Willard are confirmed by the Hon. Frederic Douglass (late United States minister to Hayti), in a speech delivered by him in Washington in January of this year, which has since been published in a pamphlet. The fact is, Miss Willard is no better or worse than the great bulk of white Americans on the negro questions. They are all afraid to speak out, and it is only British public opinion which will move them, as I am thankful to see it has already begun to move Miss Willard.

I am, &c.,
Ida B. Wells

**1896: FEBRUARY 28**

**MARY KINCAID TO MAMIE GOODWATER**

*No matter the decade or century or place, no matter that the Comstock Act still forbade them to possess any information about contraception, some pregnant women still had a way of mingling resignation with humor and hope.*

Mamie,

I got two hard months before me yet that if I count right. I just dread the time coming. I aint any bigger than Gwendoline was when she come home, but I am different shape that she was. I stick out in the back as much as I do in front, so you might know what kind of a looking thing I am. O Mamie I wish there was no such a thing as having babies. I wish I took George Willard's receipt and left the nasty thing alone. I will next time you bet I not have any more if I live through this time what I hope I will. Well Mamie it is there and it has to come out where it went in. Well might as well laugh as cry it be just the same.

### 1897: DECEMBER
### VIRGINIA O'HANLON TO THE EDITOR OF THE NEW YORK SUN

*This is the letter that inspired* New York Sun *editor Francis P. Church to write what is probably the most famous editorial in American history, "Yes, Virginia, There is a Santa Claus." In it, Church memorably affirmed the importance of faith in a skeptical age. Santa Claus, he wrote, "exists as certainly as love and generosity and devotion exist." The editorial was reprinted annually until the* Sun *folded in 1949.*

Virginia O'Hanlon (1899–1971) grew up to become a New York City teacher and principal.

Dear Editor—

I am 8 years old. Some of my little friends say there is no Santa Claus. Papa says, "If you see it in The Sun, it's so." Please tell me the truth, is there a Santa Claus?

Virginia O'Hanlon

### 1898: FEBRUARY 6 OR 7
### FANNIE REED TO ELIZA CRAWFORD

*In addition to the myriad ills besetting the poor and the disadvantaged at the end of the nineteenth century, tuberculosis reigned as the leading cause of death. Particularly rampant in situations where fresh air was scarce, TB was as feared as any incurable disease of any era. Two of its unfortunate victims were Orrock Reed and his wife, Fannie Perkins Reed (1866–1905), who had traveled to California from Minneapolis in the hope that the change in climate would lead to Orrie's recovery. Fannie herself would die of the disease at thirty-seven (see page 432), seven years after writing this letter to her twin sister, Eliza Crawford (1866–1960).*

The children Fannie mentioned, Edith and Allan, would eventually go to live with their aunt.

North Pasadena. Cal. 2/6 or 2/7, 1898

My dear bro. & Sister,

I will try to write to you of my awful sorrow. You got the card I suppose telling you of our darling Orrie's death. I have not fealt like writing before and I can not, Oh I can not tell you of my sorrow. No one can know until they have tried it. Dear Orrie failed right along very fast after I wrote you he was failing, He went <u>home</u> Tuesday morning at just ten. Never will I forget bro Mills words "Just ten", & I realized what it meant. He failed so during the night that we all fealt it would come that day. He said to me "dont leave me." I sat down by him and he held my hand quite a while. And every time I had to leave the room, they said he would look after me. That morning I said, You're going home, 'aint you darling. (Too weak to whisper) he nodded yes. I said are you happy & he nodded yes again. Soon he began to sink I sat by him. bro Mills had lain down. he had been up all night. Mrs. Caid came to the bed & said. He's most gone. Went right in & called bro Mills Mrs. Hentz came in with the children. Dear Sister Inarles was there too. He opened his dear eyes & looked at me & then closed them. And such a smile as he had on his face. As he passed over. O, if you all could have seen that smile, as he passed beyond. "We saw not the angels who met him there The gates of the city we could not see" but we know they <u>did</u> meet him. And they have taken him home. And O, how lonely it is without him. A few days before he died Bro. Langen was trying to comfort me. <u>He</u> Orrie said the 23 Psalm is for her.

And as he Bro Langen read—Though I walk through the valley of the shadow of death. he said thats for her. There is no shadow for me. Its all sunshine. Then he said to another. There's no river bro, there is no river. One day he said, as he looked at the children & I. "If it wasn't for this little circle how many more I have on the other side. Every one loved him. O, we have so many dear friends here, & they would not leave us alone for a minute Dear Mrs. Quarels said, "I said good morning here to him, the last words I spoke to him & I think it shall be the first words I shall speak to him over there. The house was full of dear friends all day & the next trying to comfort & help. & they had to do it all for I could'nt do any thing. They told me I must live for the little ones and I must I suppose but O, how I miss him. A few days before he died Mrs. Q. & Mrs. Norse sang, "My Jesus I love thee—I'll love the in life. I will love the in death," He raised his hand & whispered, "that's my testimony." They sang it at the funeral.

I wish you could have seen the many beautiful flowers. I made a reath of violets. & they laid it on his breast, there were two wreaths of lillys (Chinese) A wreath of green & white. And five or six bunches of violets. Roses lillys, &c. On the mat, a black, a black fur, that the coffin stood on was a cassir, blossoms woven several feet long. There were palm leaves with the word victory on them, made of flowers. Do you see, Palms of victory. The lady who fixed them said it so represented his life. I asked him if he had any message to send you and the rest of them, he said "Tell them to meet me, tell them to meet me . . . tell them to make no mistake." We buried him beside mother, in Mountain View cemetery. There were six ministers at the funeral. And all the friends the house & porch would accomodate. Bro. Crawford & Bro. Langen conducted the services. Will send an account. Bro. Hontz wrote up a very nice article but they had this in print before he got there with it. I am at their house now. I went home the day of the funeral, & staid that night. They put me to bed the minute I got home. got supper. & Mrs. Car staid with me that night. & Mrs. Stuntz came after me the next day. I have been there & here since but I have not felt like writing before. I have a very sore throat, & am so tired, while I am here they have fumugated & cleaned house took up carpets &c.

Monday morning. I was going home to-day, and Mrs. Hentz was going with me, to stay a few days, but it rains, so we will have to wait till tomorrow, It does not seem like home now, without my darling. Little Allan says I don't want to go home, I said why. He said, "Cause papa is not there." I could not wish him back to suffer again. Poor darling. he suffered so much, from his stomach. I never saw any one so patient and good. Always greet every one who came in with a smile and a "pretty well." He was so poor that a rinkle in the sheet would hurt him, & we had to handle him like a baby. His ear got raw where he had to lie on it, & his hip was sore.

Let Nellie read this too, and it will save me writing separate, as I must write to so many and feel so miserable.

I hope she will write soon, & you also. I read your letter to Orrie the night before he died. the last letter I ever read to him. Will have to close your sorrowing sister

Fannie

[Written in the margin of the first page]: No, do not let Nellie read this.

I will write to her. You asked if any one sent us any birthday present. No, no one, or Christmas but pa, though we got several Christmas presents from dear friends here, & a birthday present from Mrs. Q. Dear Orrie never wore the tie you sent him, or the one you sent last year but once or twice. As he had to wear a sweater most of the time.

I must close. I have a letter at home that I wrote before dear Orrie died to you making a proposition to you. about coming out.

### 1898: APRIL 5
### ANNIE OAKLEY TO WILLIAM McKINLEY

*The Spanish-American War was just weeks away when Annie Oakley (1860–1926) sent this offer to President William McKinley (1843–1901). Set off by Spain's repressive response to Cuba's attempts at independence, the war became a popular cause in the States and inspired a period of U.S. expansionism. Oakley (née Phoebe Ann Moses), who had been famous since her teens for her extraordinary marksmanship, would not be needed in the conflict, which would prove to be both lopsided and brief.*

Hon. Wm McKinley President

Dear Sir I for one feel Confident that your good judgment will carry America safely through without war—

But in case of such an event I am ready to place a Company of fifty Lady sharpshooters at your disposal. Every one of them will be an American and as they will furnish their own arms and ammunition will be little if any expense to the government.

> Very truly
> Annie Oakley

## EXCHANGE

### 1898: SUMMER
### "NORA" AND BEATRICE FAIRFAX

*The idea of writing an advice column came from Arthur Brisbane at William Randolph Hearst's New York Evening Journal. But the name for the columnist— Beatrice Fairfax—came from its author, journalist Marie Manning (1873–1945), who combined Dante's Beatrice with Virginia's Fairfax County, where her family had a home. Fairfax's motto was simple: "Dry your eyes, roll up your sleeves, and dig for a practical solution." And Manning's success with the column was both vast and quick, with thousands of letters arriving on her desk every day. One of the very first came from a woman who signed her letter "Nora"; like so many women who would turn the advice column into an institution, she sought wisdom on the subject of romance.*

## NORA TO BEATRICE FAIRFAX

Miss Beatrice Fairfax:

Dear Madam: I read that you will advise young persons concerning their love affairs. I want your advice. I came from Ireland six months ago. A young man whom I have known since I was a little girl asked me to promise to marry him.... It was breaking my heart to come away, and I loved him dearly when he asked me. So I said yes. He is to come over as soon as he gets enough money. When I reached this country I met another young man at my married sister's. I have been to some picnics with him, and I see him often, and I think I have fallen in love with him. It will kill my friend in Ireland if I am not true to him, and it will kill me if I have to be. Please advise me.

Nora

## BEATRICE FAIRFAX TO NORA

My Dear Nora:

I am glad that you are, although apparently fickle, at least conscientious enough to be troubled by your fickleness. That is a sign that your heart is pretty nearly in the right place....

Don't try to decide anything now. Don't see the new young man much. Avoid the occasions of inconstancy. Remember that as an honest girl, you cannot encourage him while you are pledged to another. And wait. Grow accustomed to your new surroundings and your new life. Then act as your heart directs. And be sure of this, Nora dear. It will not kill the young man if you should fail him. Death is not so easily accomplished.

## 1899: AUGUST
## MRS. CHARLES DUNMORE TO LYDIA PINKHAM

---

*For the woman seeking more physical and less psychological advice, there was Lydia Estes Pinkham (1819–1883), whose company thrived for decades after her death. Pinkham, who had used her likeness, her name, and a lot of her energy to create the ultimate female patent medicine, was a pioneering businesswoman who spoke directly to her consumers and, by soliciting their letters, asked them to speak directly to her. Her main product, introduced in 1875, was a mixture of herbs, roots, and about 18 percent alcohol. It was prescribed for "the worst form of Female Complaints, all ovarian troubles, Inflammation and Ulceration, Falling and*

*Displacements . . . faintness, flatulency . . . craving for stimulants . . . Bloating, head-aches, nervous Prostration, General Debility, Sleeplessness, Depression," among countless other woes. In the 1920s, with new regulations for consumer products, the company would reduce its claims and its product's alcohol content. In the meantime, ubiquitous ads included testimonials—however authentic can only be guessed—like the one below.*

To Mrs. Pinkham:

I was in pain day and night; my doctor did not seem to help me. I could not seem to find any relief until I took Lydia E. Pinkham's Vegetable Compound. I had inflammation of the womb, a bearing-down pain, and the whites very badly. The pain was so intense that I could not sleep at night. I took Lydia E. Pinkham's Vegetable Compound for a few months, and am now all right. Before that I took morphine pills for my pains; that was a great mistake, for the relief was only momentary and the effect vile. I am so thankful to be relieved of my sufferings, for the pains I had were something terrible.

Mrs. Charles Dunmore

**1899: DECEMBER 21**

**JEANNETTE LINN TO SANTA CLAUS**

---

*American children have been writing letters to Santa Claus since the end of the nineteenth century, when Thomas Nast's illustrations for the poem "An Account of a Visit From St. Nick" completed Santa's transformation from saint to portly gift-giver. This letter appeared in Ohio's* Sidney Daily News. *The author is as obscure as the recipient is famous.*

Dear Santa,

I thought I would drop you a few lines and tell you a few things what I want. Well, I want a pair of skates, because I think by the time Christmas comes it will be frozen up. And for another thing, I want a pair of leggings so that it will keep my feet warm and I want them so that they will come up above my shoe-tops, and I want a little slate like those that have pictures of cats and rabbits and dogs on and like those that are almost like a slate, and if it don't cost too much I would like a large doll, so large that it would look about four years old. I will tell you where to find it. If you look in the basement of the Arcade on the place where the dolls are, you will see a large doll with real long curly hair and it is jointed and it is as pretty as I am. And I don't think I want much, but dear Santa,

I know that I want more than you can afford to give, for there are more little boys and girls and they want something too. But I would like to have so much a nice tricycle that would cost three dollars and that is too much, I think, to pay for anything, but that is really the price of it because I saw the price on it and it said $3.00 as plain as this letter is written and I think it is written pretty plain. Well Santa, I must close because it is getting late and I think if I don't close you will not bring me anything. I have got as much as I can think of. Goodbye, dear Santa. Jeannette E. Linn, 509 south Walnut avenue.

# MODERN TIMES

# 1900

# ∼

# 1928

I keep thinking what a different world it will be to mothers; when you all come marching home again! And when you do come marching home old fellow bring me back the same boy I gave my country,—true, and clean, and gentle, and brave.

*—Kate Gordon to her son*
*Circa 1917*

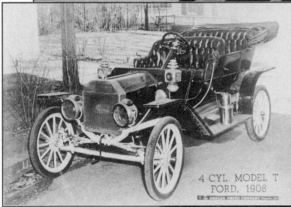

# BETWEEN 1900 AND 1928 ...

**1900:** The United States population is 76,212,168, more than 14 times larger than it was a century ago. ☆ Women occupy a third of all government jobs. ☆ L. Frank Baum publishes *The Wonderful Wizard of Oz;* the first printing—10,000 copies—sells out in two weeks. **1901:** Desperate for money that she hopes will come with publicity, 63-year-old Michigan teacher Anna Edson Taylor becomes the first person to go over Niagara Falls in a barrel and survive; after completing the 18-minute trip, she declares, "Nobody ought ever to do that again." ☆ President William McKinley is assassinated by anarchist Leon Czolgosz, who gives police his name as "Fred Nieman," meaning Fred Nobody. **1902:** Inspired by hearing that, on a hunting trip, President Theodore Roosevelt spared a bear that friends had tied down for him to shoot, Brooklyn store owners Morris and Rose Michtom create a soft toy they call "Teddy's Bear"; a nationwide craze ensues. ☆ The National Biscuit Company (Nabisco) introduces Barnum's Animals: cookies in circus-wagon boxes made with string so they can be hung as Christmas ornaments. **1903:** At Kill Devil Hills in North Carolina, with five citizens standing by as witnesses, Orville and Wilbur Wright take turns making the first sustained airplane

---

Clockwise from top left: World War I recruiting poster; Immigrants passing the Statue of Liberty; Teddy Roosevelt and the Teddy Bear; Margaret Sanger; Charlie Chaplin and Jackie Coogan in *The Kid;* Prohibition; Edna St. Vincent Millay; Jeannette Rankin (in hat); The Model T Ford; *The Letter* by Mary Cassatt.

flights.  ★  Thomas Edison's motion picture company produces the first narrative film; called *The Great Train Robbery,* it lasts 12 minutes and is touted in an Edison Films catalog as a "sensational and highly tragic subject [that] will certainly make a decided 'hit' whenever shown." **1906:** Will Keith Kellogg adds sugar to corn flakes and begins marketing them as breakfast cereal; he is promptly—if unsuccessfully—sued by his brother, Dr. John Harvey Kellogg, who had prescribed the sugarless version at the Battle Creek Sanitarium, believing that bland foods promoted health, cooled passions, and thus helped people resist what he saw as the dangerous temptation to masturbate.  ★  The San Francisco earthquake is felt as far south as Los Angeles and as far north as Coos Bay, Oregon.  **1907:** New York chemist Leo Baekeland creates a liquid resin that will not burn, boil, crack, fade, or melt; called "Bakelite," it will be used for products ranging from radios and jewelry to electrical insulation and weaponry.  **1908:** Henry Ford introduces the Model T.  **1909:** The National Association for the Advancement of Colored People is founded by W. E. B. DuBois, Mary White Ovington, Ida Wells-Barnett, and others.  ★  **1910:** There are 2,200 daily newspapers in the nation.  **1911:** Nearly 150 workers die when New York City's Triangle Shirtwaist factory catches fire; *The New York World* reports: "They jumped with their clothing ablaze. The hair of some of the girls streamed up aflame as they leaped. . . . It is a ghastly fact that on both . . . sides of the building . . . there grew mounds of the dead and dying."  ★  Some 100,000 people march down Broadway in a memorial parade for the Triangle workers.  **1912:** About 1,500 passengers die en route to America when the *Titanic* sinks on its maiden voyage.  **1914:** World War I begins in Europe.  ★  After using the U.S. mail to send out information about birth control, Margaret Sanger is indicted on obscenity charges.  **1916:** Los Angeles noodle maker George Jung invents the fortune cookie.  ★  Montana's Jeannette Rankin becomes the first woman elected to the House of Representatives.  **1917:** The United States enters the war in Europe; in two years, 4,734,991 Americans will serve, including some 30,000 women.    **1918:** An estimated 25 million people—including 550,000 Americans—die from influenza in a worldwide epidemic that lasts more than a year.    **1919:** The Eighteenth Amendment is ratified, banning the manufacture, sale, and transportation of "intoxicating liquors."    **1920:** The population of the United States exceeds 100 million for the first time.    ★ Among American women, .8 percent are divorced, 11.1 percent widowed, and 27.3 percent never married.    ★ The Nineteenth Amendment is ratified, granting women the vote.    ★ Edith Wharton publishes *The Age of Innocence*.    **1921:** *The Kid* is Charlie Chaplin's first full-length film and first major hit.    ★ The winner of the first Miss America pageant is 16-year-old Margaret Gorman, standing five feet, one inch tall and weighing 108 pounds.    **1922:** Appointed to fill a vacancy in the U.S. Senate, Georgia's Rebecca Latimer Felton takes the oath of office and serves for two days.    **1924:** Attempting to commit the perfect crime, teenagers Nathan Leopold and Richard Loeb murder 14-year-old Bobby Franks; "It was just an experiment," Leopold says. "It is as easy for us to justify as an entomologist in impaling a beetle on a pin."    ★ After a 33-day trial and in the midst of a 12-hour summation, attorney Clarence Darrow begs the judge to reject the death penalty for Leopold and Loeb: "I am pleading for life, understanding, charity, kindness, and the infinite mercy that considers all. I am pleading that we overcome cruelty with kindness and hatred with love"; the confessed murderers are sentenced to life in prison.    **1927:** *The Jazz Singer,* the first feature-length talking picture, premieres.    ★ The first transatlantic telephone call is made.    ★ Charles Lindbergh makes the first nonstop transatlantic flight.    **1928:** George Gershwin introduces *An American in Paris* and Walt Disney introduces Mickey Mouse.

*Elizabeth Cady Stanton (see page 195) celebrated her eighty-fifth birthday in the first year of the new century. In this note she thanked fellow women's rights crusader Clara Dorothy Bewick Colby (1846–1916) for her good wishes, but Stanton was two decades premature in her rejoicing. Neither woman would live to see passage of the Nineteenth Amendment, granting American women the right to vote.*

New York, November 12, 1900

Dear Mrs. Colby:

Many thanks to the Washington Suffrage Association for the kind words you sent on my birthday. I have had so many congratulatory letters and telegrams and gifts that the reproaches and ridicule of half a century ago are quite forgotten. The sweet words of affection that I am receiving from all points of the compass make the sunset of my life bright and cheering. We may already rejoice in the triumph of our cause. With equal political rights in four states of the American Union, the others must speedily follow suit. You may congratulate yourself that the <u>Woman's Tribune</u> has done essential service in securing this grand consummation.

Your friend as ever,

[Elizabeth Cady Stanton]

*Ideas about women's health would undergo radical changes in the twentieth century. In this letter, Heloise Edwina Hersey (1855–1933), who ran Miss Hersey's School for Girls, in Boston, put forth her relatively modern health advice—including instructions to exercise—to a young woman she called "Helen." This person, she wrote in an epistolary advice book called* To Girls, A Budget of Letters, *was someone*

*who has "decided not to go to college, but who is finding . . . an education in the bet-*
*ter sort of boarding-school. I think her problems are grave ones."*
A megrim was a migraine.

My dear Helen:

I am sorry to hear that you are ill, but I hope that you will find some comfort in the reflection that the illness is through no fault of yours. You must set that consolation over against the fact that nobody will give you much sympathy for your discomfort in one of the afflictions usual to the period of childhood. I wonder if you will like to read a dissertation upon health while you are shut up in the hospital.

There are two kinds of sickness in the world: the first is the one which you are at present enduring. You have no more responsibility for having mumps, or even for diphtheria, than I have for the colour of my eyes. Our Puritan fathers were used to speak of these things as "a dispensation of Providence," and the phrase was well chosen. These illnesses must be borne with a steady courage and an equally steady reticence. It requires fortitude to be tolerably silent about the pain of such a trial, and it takes courage to sustain one's self through the dull and dreary hours of the illness. Still, pain borne heroically is often an obvious blessing, not only to the victim, but to all the friends that see her heroism.

I doubt, however, if more than one-quarter of all the illness among our social class can properly be considered unpreventable by the victim. The truth is that most illness comes from ignorance or carelessness, or both. For this there is no philosophy, and perhaps there should be none. A heavy cold contracted by a moment's carelessness cannot be borne patiently in any such fashion as I expect you to bear your present sickness. Of course, this does not mean that you shall have license to complain and wear out all your family when you suffer for your own sins; but I do not see how one can be inwardly at peace under a scourge of one's own preparing. Perhaps one of the motives for better care next time is this very impatience with our own stupidity.

A girl at fifteen enters upon the management of a vast trust fund: it is her health. Next to the gift of time itself, it is the most precious thing she possesses. She never realises this until her treasure is somehow depleted. We never think how good it is not to have headache until the pain is upon us. Now the truth is that the girl who squanders this trust fund which we call "health" is as much a thief as is the man who misappropriates the property intrusted to him for widows and orphans. Health means not only strength for pleasure, but strength for social service. The world perhaps owes me a living; but I owe the world my life, and a healthy life as well. It is hard that one should be called to account for the care of so priceless a treasure when one has no experience in such care, but this is inevitable. Take such facts of experience as I have to offer you, and let them, if they may, ripen a harvest of their own in your wisdom and good practice.

Here are a few commonplace hints about the preservation of health for the ordinary girl. In the first place, she should have proper food, in proper quantities, at proper times, week in and week out. You will say the requirements are very vague. So they are, and must be. Regularity is an essential element in feeding the body, and good judgment is another. The truth is that all the maxims of health become foolish and useless unless they are applied by this same common sense. "What a pretty thing man is when he goes in his doublet and hose and leaves off his wit!" Half the time, when questions of health are concerned, we seem not to apply our own common sense to them. The sweetmeat habit, the nibbling habit, the starving habit, the stuffing habit, are about equally undesirable. Happy the girl who possesses a healthy appetite, and at whose mother's table common sense and good cooking prevail! If there is one practice more disastrous than another to the school-girl's health, I think it is the eating and drinking between meals. The seductive ice-cream soda is responsible for more muddy complexions and more megrims than you will believe. Use your own high intelligence to learn a little out of any ordinary text-book where are described the process of digestion, and the delicate and intricate machinery which carries it on. Then, without acquiring self-consciousness about the work which goes on in your own person, see if you cannot learn to be kind, at least, to your own stomach. Better five attacks of healthy hunger than one half-hour of that satiety and disgust which come from repletion.

We used to laugh at the girl who starved herself that she might remain slight, and ate slate-pencils and chalk to increase her interesting pallor. I suppose she has given place to the girl who has no self-control in the matter of eating, and who clogs and embarrasses all her intellectual and spiritual operations by gormandising in season and out of season. Neither to the one extreme nor to the other do I commend you. A healthy appetite is a great blessing. If it has not been given you, try to find out how to earn it. To this end you must consult your physician, not your teacher. But a reasonable self-control in matters of appetite is within the reach of any high-minded girl.

The second of my little maxims is the avoidance of needless exposure. Wet feet and wet skirts are sins: regard them as sins. The girl who forgets her overshoes, and inflicts the coughing and sneezing of a heavy cold upon the household, deserves all the pain she suffers, and more. That, however, does not cancel her indebtedness to the trust fund of health, which she has thoughtlessly incurred. Don't say now that I am preaching the policy of coddling. Far from it. Regular and sensible care of one's conditions, instead of rendering one soft and susceptible, makes one ready to withstand exposure when it is necessary. A series of severe colds leaves one ready to be a victim to any chance microbe which may be seeking shelter. On the other hand, a clean skin, free lungs, and a sound digestion are the most discouraging of foes to threatening disease.

In the third place, my healthy girl should have eight or nine hours of sleep, taken during the night. For once in a way sleeping late in the morning may be very well, but I have never been able to bring myself to believe that morning sleep had the same power for refreshment that comes when the world and nature share our rest. I like well the old-fashioned way of dividing our day: eight hours for sleep, eight hours for work, eight hours for recreation, this last including, of course, our eating. Nobody whose life is thus ordered should complain of overwork. I doubt whether inclination to sleep is reason enough for a girl to increase this allotment of hours; and I am sure that disinclination to sleep as much as this is a definite warning against overwork. The highly strung nerve does not readily relax.

Once more, we cannot be healthy without suitable exercise. You say again I use a vague adjective. Who is to determine what is suitable? Evidently, the person in question, and with such enlightened intelligence as she can command. About no physical requirement is there greater difference of opinion than in regard to this matter of exercise. Temperament and occupation have much to do with it. The woman who spends a large part of each day on her feet about her household cares certainly does not need the bicycle or golf or a long walk as does the woman who sits over book and pen hour after hour. I suspect that sometimes the need for fresh air is confused with the need for exercise, and the really tired woman makes herself the more tired for the sake of relieving the oppression which comes from breathing vitiated air. Cultivate a keen sense of poor ventilation, and try to correct it in your surroundings. Good work is seldom done where there is a lack of oxygen. The best advice one can give another person about exercise is that that person shall really take into serious consideration her own habits in this regard, and by experiment shall find out what is the surest path to the desired end of health.

I have already said that all rules for health presume intelligence on the part of the person that applies them. I think that I should add that they also presume the ability to keep one's self free from hobby-riding. I am very tired of all the folk who have discovered panaceas for disease. Neither oatmeal nor blue glass, nor Swedish gymnastics nor Christian Science, nor osteopathy nor abstinence from eating of breakfast, nor dress reform, nor cold water, nor vegetarianism, will secure health. The names of these "fads," and others like them, might be multiplied by twenty in the history of the last century of American life. Every one of them militates against that clear sanity which is the best preservative of human health. "A sound mind in a sound body" is a fine maxim; and, to preserve that balance, one must look out for the condition of the mind as well as of the body. It is curious and interesting, and I believe that it is true, that the great men of the world, from Napoleon to Edison, and from Socrates to Lincoln, appear to have been free from any of these hobbies in regard to personal practice in eating, drinking, and sleeping, and the other habits of life; whereas the dyspeptic clergyman, the anaemic teacher, and the consumptive clerk are often able to tell you, with positive certainty, the one specific for health and long life. They ignore the great fact that man is made for varied experiences. His superiority over the animals that eat flesh alone, as to those who live upon vegetables exclusively, is gained in this very demand for variety. He needs it in his life, in his habit, in his body, in his thought. He needs all this variety to demonstrate that it shall have a regularity of its own, and that both variety and regularity shall be his servants, not his masters.

If I were a poet, I would write an ode to health. If some of the poets had possessed this same homely blessing, we should have been spared their poems "written in dejection." Paradoxical as it may seem, health is the panacea for all the ills of life. It is also the enricher of all its joys. It paints the sky bluer, and the grass greener, and the snow whiter, and the mountains nobler. Wind and rain, and dust and cold, are grateful to it, since they all give fresh room for endurance and resistance. Even sorrow and failure borrow new courage from health. Without it the most fortunate life must seem hard and cruel. With it the severest life must have in it some brightness and hope.

**1901: SEPTEMBER 2**

**A "HEART-BROKEN MOTHER" TO CARRY NATION**

---

*The Woman's Christian Temperance Union (see page 400) had been in operation since 1874, but one of its most flamboyant members didn't join the movement until 1890, when Kansas's prohibition laws were softened by a court ruling in favor of importation of liquor. From that point on, Carry Nation (1846–1911) became feared and famous for descending upon barrooms with biblical zeal—and a hatchet. Arrests and assaults did not deter her, and this plea from a Paterson, New Jersey, woman was typical of the myriad requests she received for her intervention.*

Sept., 2nd, 1901

Dear Mrs. Nation:—

Will you come to this city before going home? The conditions here are worse than in any place in the whole country. One thousand saloons run day and night, every day in the year.

Come for God's sake. You can do so much good, and if you smashed fifty or sixty of the hell holes here you would be called an angel. Do Come! And save the young of both sexes.

Yours
A heart-broken mother.

## 1901: SEPTEMBER 17
## ELIZABETH CABOT TO FRANCES PARKMAN

*William McKinley was in the first year of his second term as president when he was shot on September 6 by an anarchist named Leon Czolgosz. Eight days later, McKinley died, the third United States president to be killed by an assassin, and Vice President Theodore Roosevelt assumed office. Writing to her niece just a few days later (and shortly before her own death), a Boston matron and frequent community volunteer named Elizabeth Dwight Cabot (1830–1901) revealed something of the country's deep need for reassurance.*

Beverly Farms, Sept. 17, 1901

My dearest Frances,—

It was a blessed comfort to see your dear handwriting this morning and read your precious words. The week has been so inexpressibly solemn and pathetic that we need to draw near first to God and next to our dearest ones, and feel the love that rules the world and makes life beautiful in spite of crime and suffering and death. How grandly the country has taken this shock! How much you feel the strength and the calmness of the nation in the midst of its tenderness and sorrow! McKinley himself set the standard by his own heroic and dignified behavior, and the country has responded. Still the oppression of such an awful deed remains; the power of evil even in this country of freedom and law is appalling, and every one feels the weight. Roosevelt has shown himself manly, respectful, and tender, and all that he has done has been well done. We liked his proclamation very much and are glad that he appointed a day of mourning immediately, while the people are full of real emotion and need legitimate expression.

We have had a series of private shocks here for the last two weeks in George Nickerson's, Frederick Warren's, Lillie Codman's, and Mrs. Charles Paine's deaths, and we need to take into our inmost lives what we believe, that death is only one step in life, but how difficult for those who are in the anguish of separation.

I still miss my morning visit to you and wish I could always begin the day with a sight of you.

Most lovingly,
Aunt Lizzie.

## 1902: MAY 5
## SUSAN HALE TO CAROLINE WELD

*The ability to transmit sound without wires was a revolutionary idea when Guglielmo Marconi filed his first patent in 1896. By 1902, when the Italian inventor was receiving radio messages over distances of 2,000 miles, wireless was still inspiring varying amounts of wonder, derision, and laughter all over the world. Susan Hale (1833–1910) was a painter, teacher, inveterate traveler, and a descendant of the patriot Nathan Hale. With Marconi's inventions gaining increasing renown, she wrote to her friend and traveling companion Caroline Weld, unable to resist a few of the kinds of comments that would later inspire Ira Gershwin to write the famous line: "They told Marconi wireless was a phony / It's the same old cry."*
"Comm" was Boston's Commonwealth Avenue. Susan's father, a newspaper editor also named Nathan Hale, had died in 1862, so the "Millennium" celebration she described here must have included some kind of memorial to him.

Matunuck, Rhode Island, May 5, 1902.

My Dear,—

I have waited to write this till the last moment before your arrival, that it may reach you warm and bubbling with freshness and all the glow of this raw sou'easter now raging. I had your *grand* letters, but no use answering out into space with no address short of 6 Comm. . . .

Speaking of space, and wireless Marconi, did you see about the mouse that wanted to go to a piece of cheese he saw? "Take care," said Ma Mouse, "it may be one of these wireless traps." Of course you know that I have long had a wire-less doorbell, the knob is still up in the garret some place. Nobody ever answers it, but it answers perfectly well itself, so I feel in advance of the invention. By the way, I have just invented wireless bird-cages, won't it be nice, all those little birds we saw in Mexico sitting round in the air on invisible perches, eating invisible seeds out of wireless glass. Of course they can't fly away, through fear of Marconi. I mean to have a quantity of them.

But this, you will remark, is neither here nor there. You will want to know some of my adventures since last I wrote, whether from Europe, Asia or Africa, I can't remember. Yet stay,—it was to Louisa I wrote last from May Moulton's lovely spare-room on March 18. Since then, ever since then, I've been fighting a barking, sneezing, catarrhal attack, such as you've seen me through with many a time. Oh! for Dr. Deahens' glorious spraying-machines! It was the change from lovely Algiers to cold raw London done it, and then the Voyage on the <u>Saint Paul</u> was colder and rawer (but lots of fun, I had my cabin to myself, dressed a doll, read a whole book, and mended all my stockings). Black and blue all over from bumping in and out of my berth, so rough. Then New York, Boston, coldest, rawest,—but Pa's Millennium had to be attended to, a glorious ovation it really was, and he was in fine shape throughout, all my boys, his sons, there, and we sate in a row to contemplate the apotheosis of Pa. . . .

Your loving Susie

### 1902: JUNE 23
### MOTHER JONES TO JOHN MITCHELL

---

*John Mitchell (1870–1919) was head of the United Mine Workers of America, one of the most powerful organizations in the growing labor movement, when he hired Mary Harris ("Mother") Jones (1830?–1930) as a union organizer. In doing so, he gained a dynamic and tireless colleague, a woman who once described herself by saying "I'm not a humanitarian. I'm a hell-raiser." Jones, who was already in her fifties when she began giving speeches and seeking followers around the country, was in West Virginia helping organize the anthracite coal strike of 1902 when she sent this report—characteristic in its feistiness—back to Mitchell.*

In Jones's autobiography, she told how miners Bernard ("Barney") Rice, Charles Blakely, and Jo Battley were on their way to a meeting about the Consolidated Coal Company when Battley was beaten up by members of the company. Rice and Blakely ran, shouting for help; "the poor Italian" may have been Battley. "Tom" was Tom Haggerty, a strike organizer. "T. L." might have been T. L. Lewis, vice president of the UMW.

Parkersburg W Virginia

My dear Comrade Mitchell

Just before I go back Jail which I expect to have to do after the old Zar of West Virginia gets through with me on Tuesday I will write you things as they are. you heard of the poor Italian getting beat up by the Corporation Thugs. of all the cowards that Barney and blakely are the worst   they ran away   left the poor Italian by himself to be beat up by the Corporation blood hounds   They ran away and left me. If you hunted the U.S. you could not get a gang of bigger cowards than you have got in here. everytime those dogs gets after them they wont Show a bit of fight   they have made up their mind   they have us all coward   I would not give Tom H—— for the whole Shooting match.

There are Some of Them would like that this thing would a failure for when ever anything happens that gives us a little back set the Silent glances exchange with a Smile of derision

Dont trust this fellow Blakely he wont do to bet on. he is a T. L. man dont be fooled in him.

This came over the Telephone Sat. I was in the jail office, heard all. T.L called Morgan up asked what he could do   Said he would like to come over here.   Where are you Said M—— in Bridgeport, doing any thing. No   Ill See Said M——   then he went up talked to Barney. B—— Said Tell him come on at once   he is to be here to day. I gave Barney H—— for tying your hands. he is no man for this place to deal with these tricksters   between you and I the Whole Shooting Match out side of Tom ought to have a Nursing Bottle,   keep up   dont worry I think the others will all go free   I will take my medicine gracefully   perhaps after it will better for the cause   I feel it will   take care of yourself   the cause would amiss you   God bless

Mother

## 1902: OCTOBER

## SUSAN B. ANTHONY TO ELIZABETH CADY STANTON

*They had first met in 1851, and for the next fifty years Susan Brownell Anthony (1820–1906) and Elizabeth Cady Stanton (see page 195) were friends, colleagues, and mutual inspiration. In the early years, they campaigned for both black and women's suffrage; after the Civil War, they ran a new periodical called* Revolution; *in 1869, they formed the National Woman Suffrage Association; in the 1870s, they traveled extensively, advocating women's suffrage in various states. Stanton died a few days after receiving this letter from Anthony.*

My dear Mrs. Stanton

I shall indeed be happy to spend with you November 12, the day on which you round out your four-score and seven, over four years ahead of me, but in age as in all else I follow you closely. It is fifty-one years since first we met and we have been busy through every one of them, stirring up the world to recognize the rights of women. The older we grow, the more keenly we feel the humiliation of disfranchisement and the more vividly we realize its disadvantages in every department of life and most of all in the labor market.

We little dreamed when we began this contest, optimistic with the hope and buoyancy of youth, that half a century later we would be compelled to leave the finish of the battle to another generation of women. But our hearts are filled with joy to know that they enter upon this task equipped with a college education, with business experience, with the fully admitted right to speak in public— all of which were denied to women fifty years ago. They have practically but one point to gain—the suffrage; we had all. These strong, courageous, capable young women will take our place and complete our work. There is an army of them, where we were but a handful. Ancient prejudice has become so softened, public sentiment so liberalized and women have so thoroughly demonstrated their ability as to leave not a shadow of doubt that they will carry our cause to victory.

And we, dear old friend, shall move on the next sphere of existence—higher and larger, we cannot fail to believe, and one where women will not be placed in an inferior position but will be welcomed on a plane of perfect intellectual and spiritual equality.

Ever lovingly yours,
Susan B. Anthony

## 1904: JANUARY 20
## FANNIE REED TO ELIZA CRAWFORD

*Widow of Orrock Reed (see page 410), Fannie Reed was herself only thirty-two when she too contracted the disease that had killed him. Dying of tuberculosis, as Fannie makes clear in this heartbreaking letter to her twin sister, could be not only extraordinarily painful, but also terribly lonely.*

Allan and Edith were Fannie's children. Mabel, otherwise unidentified, seems to have been a hired girl and was clearly the source of much bitterness. "Ma" was Fannie's stepmother. Jessie was Fannie's half-sister. The Bensonizer Sanitarium for Consumptives in St. Louis advertised the "Bensonizer treatment"; that may be what Fannie was referring to at the end of the letter. The "sure cure" could have been any of numerous patent medicines of the day.

Hammond, Jan. 20,1904

Dear Ones all,

I will try to write some to you. I haven't fealt like writing before. I have been feeling quite bad lately. My kidneys are awful bad and my right lung. My lungs feel better today. I found some matter on the plaster I took off last night. I have quite a number of plasters yet. May not need anymore. They don't seem to do much good anymore.

Thank you for those things you sent dear Sister. Wish I had some thing for you. And the drawings were very nice. Dear little girl. I'm glad you are learning so nicely. Poor Allan has bad luck with having to stay with me so much. Mrs. Gould swept for me one day. Yesterday she did part of the work.

I wrote Rowland to turn the business over to you. Every one says not to sell the place for what I gave for it. & I hate to. As I can get more rent than int. & I could sell it for that any time I guess. Disbrow told me I did not pay to much for it. And my taxes are always higher than yours & you ask $1500 for yours. I know the house is awful old, but I could not build much for $500 or $600 and they say the lot is worth $900 or $1000. I don't want to sell it less than $1400 would you. You know it is all I have got. and I want all I can get for it. D. & R. both said they would sell it for $25. If D. has a chance to sell it what can he get for it. Ask Anderson what he will give. Mabel has been gone a week and a half. Isnt it cute. She is fraid she will get it. I dont suppose she will stay long. Ma has been up twice to help me & the floor hasnt been mopped since week ago Saturday, but some people don't like to mop. If she did it for nothing it would be different. Allan's throat & cough is awful bad. I am so worried about him. He has staid out to help me this week as I can not get around but little. You were rather cranky because I mentioned Edith's coming home, wasnt you sister mine. I have had to give up so much I ought to know how to give every thing more gracefully I suppose. You have never had to give up your home husband, child and friends like I have yet.

I say friends, because nearly every one is so fraid of me that they cant hardly use me human. Carrie King is very low. Aunt K. & Irene's children are sick, J. Millers folks sick. Old Mrs. Carley sick (Suppose some one could help her as it isn't consumption). Yes those things came. 72c freight. Wish I had got my bed & springs. & lounge. this lounge is all to pieces. I am so thin & my kidneys & hip & chest hurt so on that old cord bed that I could not sleep for pain last night.

Mr. & Mrs. Holcomb were to see me one day last wk. I did not feel able to write on our birthday. Wonder if I will ever have another. I fealt for several days as if I wouldn't   feel some better in my chest today. but my kidneys are very sore & bad. Dear little Edith if you are not homesick you can stay longer if you want to.

Aunt K. is quite sick. They sent for Armenia today.

Ma cant stay <u>here</u>. Jessie cant get breakfast, but she can <u>there</u>.

G. was not very well Monday but is as well as usual again. I dont know what to do about that Bensonizer. Do you suppose it is any better. I have about 1 doz. "sure cure". Kiss each other for me for I cant even kiss my children <u>for fear</u>.

With love.<br>Fannie.

## 1905: NOVEMBER 11
## EDITH WHARTON TO WILLIAM ROSCOE THAYER

*One of the most gifted American writers of the twentieth or any century, Edith Wharton (1862–1937) had just published* The House of Mirth *when she wrote this letter to William Roscoe Thayer (1859–1923), a historian and author who lived in Boston. Much like her Pulitzer Prize–winning novel* The Age of Innocence, *which would be published in 1920,* The House of Mirth *took on the New York social world in which Wharton had lived for most of her life.*

Robert Minturn was part of an old New York family and was a linguist. The "Italian novel" was *The Valley of Decision,* published in 1902. Lily Bart is the doomed protagonist of *The House of Mirth.*

The Mount,<br>Lenox, Mass<br>November 11

Dear Professor Thayer,

By a pleasant coincidence, I was talking of you with Robert Minturn a few weeks ago, saying how much I admired your essay on historical methods in the "Atlantic," & how deeply I was indebted to "The Dawn of Italian Independence" for such light on that intricate & engrossing period as I needed in writing my Italian novel.

Judge then, how pleased & surprised I was to receive your letter the other day, & to learn that I had been able to make ever so slight a return for the great pleasure your admirable book has long given me.

I am particularly & quite inordinately pleased with what you say of my having—to your mind—been able to maintain my readers' interest in a group of persons so intrinsically uninteresting, except as a social manifestation. I knew that my great difficulty lay there, & if you think I have surmounted it, I shall go about with a high head.—But—before we leave the subject—I must protest, & emphatically, against the suggestion that I have "stripped" New York society. New York society is still amply clad, & the little corner of its garment that I lifted was meant to show only that little atrophied organ—the group of idle & dull people—that exists in any big & wealthy social body. If it seems more conspicuous in New York than in an old civilization, it is because the whole social organization with us is so much smaller & less elaborate—& if, as I believe, it is more harmful in its influence, it is because fewer responsibilities attach to money with us than in other societies.—

Forgive this long discourse—but you see I had to come to the defense of my own town, which, I assure you, has many mansions outside of the little House of Mirth.

I hope when I am next in Boston I may have the pleasure of thanking you in person for your letter, which I value more than anything my book has brought me.

Sincerely Yrs
Edith Wharton

I wish you felt a little more kindly toward poor Lily!

## 1906: MARCH 27

## HELEN KELLER TO SAMUEL CLEMENS

*By the time Helen Keller (see page 399) sent this thank-you note to Mark Twain (see page 314), she was an author herself, having published numerous magazine articles, as well as* The Story of My Life *in 1902 and* Optimism *in 1903. Among her other extraordinary accomplishments were graduating cum laude from Radcliffe in 1904 and penning this letter, in which she evoked with piercing clarity the world of the blind.*

Twain filled in for Keller, who was ill, at a public meeting of the New York State Association for Promoting the Interests of the Blind. Some years later, in a speech, he would describe her as "the most marvelous person of her sex that has existed on this earth since Joan of Arc." Joseph P. Choate was America's ambassador to Britain. A guerdon is a reward.

Wrentham, Mass. March 27, 1906

My dear Mr. Clemens:

It is a great disappointment to me not to be with you and the other friends who have joined their strength to uplift the blind. The meeting in New York will be the greatest occasion in the movement which has so long engaged my heart: and I regret keenly not to be present and feel the inspiration of living contact with such an assembly of wit, wisdom and philantropy. I shall be happy if I could have spelled into my hand the words as they fall from your lips, and receive, even as it is uttered, the eloquence of our Newest Ambassador to the blind. We have not had such advocates before. My disappointment is softened by the thought that never at any meeting was the right word so sure to be spoken. But, superfluous as all other appeals must seem after you and Mr. Choate have spoken, nevertheless, as I am a woman, I cannot be silent, and I ask you to read this letter, knowing that it will be lifted to eloquence by your kindly voice.

To know what the blind man needs, you who can see must imagine what it would be not to see, and you can imagine it more vividly if you remember that before your journey's end you may have to go the dark way yourself. Try to realize what blindness means to those whose joyous activity is stricken to inaction.

It is to live long, long days, and life is made up of days. It is to live immured, baffled, impotent. All God's world shut out. It is to sit helpless, defrauded, while your spirit strains and tugs at its fetters, and your shoulders ache for the burden they are denied, the rightful burden of labor.

The seeing man goes about his business confident and self-defendent. He does his share of the work of the world in mine, in quarry, in factory, in counting room, asking of others no boon, save the opportunity to do a man's part and to receive the laborer's guerdon. In an instant accident blinds him. The day is blotted out. Night envelops all the visible world. The feet which once bore him to his task with firm and confident stride stumble and halt and fear the foreward step. He is forced to a new habit of idleness, which like a canker consumes the mind and destroys its beautiful faculties. Memory confronts him with his lighted past. Amid the tangible ruins of his life as it promised to be he gropes his pitiful way. You have met him on your busy thoroughfares with faltering feet and outstretched hands, patiently "dudging" the universal dark, holding out for sale his petty wares, or his cap for your pennies; and this was a man with ambitions and capabilities.

It is because we know that these ambitions and capabilities can be fulfilled that we are working to improve the condition of the adult blind. You can not bring back the light of the vacant eyes; but you can give a helping hand to the sightless along their dark pilgrimage. You can teach them new skill. For work they once did with the aid of their eyes you can substitute work that they can do with their hands. They ask only opportunity, and opportunity is a torch in the darkness. They crave no charity, no pension, but the satisfaction that comes from lucrative toil, and this satisfaction is the right of every human being.

At your meeting New York will speak its word for the blind, and when New York speaks, the world listens. The true message of New York is not the commercial ticking of busy telegraphs, but the mightier utterances of such gatherings as yours. Of late our periodicals have been filled with depressing revelations of great social evils. Querulous critics have pointed to every flaw in our civic structure. We have listened long enough to the pessimists. You once told me you were a pessimist, Mr. Clemens, but great men are usually mistaken about themselves. You are an optimist. If you were not, you would not preside at the meeting. For it is an answer to pessimism. It proclaims that the heart and the wisdom of a great city are devoted to the good of mankind, that in this busiest city in the world no cry of distress goes up but receives a compassionate and generous answer. Rejoice that the cause of the blind has been heard in New York, for the day after it shall be heard around the world.

Yours sincerely,<br>Helen Keller

## 1906: APRIL 28
## MARGARET WRIGHT TO ETHEL PAPE WRIGHT

*It was five in the morning on April 18 when the first foreshock rattled the San Francisco Bay area. The earthquake itself, one of the most devastating in history, lasted for nearly a minute and was felt as far east as central Nevada. Three days of fire followed. More than 3,000 people died, more than 28,000 buildings were destroyed, and 225,000 people—more than half the city's population—were left without homes. Ten days after the earthquake, Margaret Wright described it to her sister-in-law.*

"The Works" was the Union Iron Works. Margaret's husband, Henry, was a U.S. Navy captain. Joseph was their four-year-old son. Julius was Ethel's husband. The panhandle is a thin strip of Golden Gate Park. Enrico Caruso was the great operatic tenor of the day.

1141 Arch St. Berkeley.<br>April 28, 1906

My Dear Ethel,

You need not feel any regret at not having experienced one of San Francisco's terrific earthquakes. They are not pleasant, neither are the fires that follow them. It is frightful to have your house swinging back and forth and glass and china and falling pictures about you. It was a very pleasant surprise to find the house still standing. Henry looked out the window, saw all the houses standing and with no apparent damage but fallen chimneys, decided it was a frequent San Francisco occurrence and went back to bed, but you may be assured I did not let him sleep. Every little while we would have a small quake and it was just as terrifying to me as the first heavy one, because I was sure each one was beginning of another terrific quake, and the house could not have stood another.

In spite of the fact that people were out in front of their houses waiting in abject terror for another earthquake and that fires had begun downtown, Henry walked down to the Works, where he was sure everything would be running as usual. Needless to say, it was not. The president of the works was there almost in tears over destruction of his floating dry dock and several ships that were on the building slips, besides minor injuries to the plant. The Naval vessels were out in the water and sustained no injury whatever.

When Henry returned, I had put up some canned things, and made up a roll of bedding and prepared for flight in case the fire should come too close. Dr. O'Neill came along to see if we were still in existence and advised me to go up to Buena Vista Park. Then took place hike one, we started out an interesting procession. Henry with a large box of provisions, and a roll of blankets, I with a small basket, and Joseph's hand in mine, Dr. O'Neill with a straw satchel, Chesu the Japanese maid with bedding and bundles, Chesu's husband, who had escaped from a burning hotel and come out to join her, with a carpet bag and bedding. We made our way to Buena Vista Park and met many other fugitives as picturesque as ourselves. We sat down and made some "elegant" sandwiches for Dr. O'Neill, who had not eaten anything all day. Then Dr. O'Neill and Henry went on a tour of exploration and decided that the fire was spreading too close to be either safe or comfortable at Buena Vista Park. So again we started out for home, and met Dr. O'Neill's cousin. His family were going out in the panhandle with a tent, so Dr. O'Neill went in and secured an invitation for me to share their tent, and Henry made me accept. Then we hiked to the panhandle. Up to six o'clock, P.M., it had been impossible to get water, so the fire department was helpless, and could do nothing but blast away buildings in front of the fire.

We spent the night in the panhandle. Joseph stirred away in the tent, with about twenty other people, among whom was a mother with a two weeks old baby. I slept out in the air on a mattress. Henry, Dr. O'Neill and the other men were coming and going all night watching the progress of the fire. The panhandle was lighted by the glare of the fire, and all night there was a mad rush of automobiles, panting horses, people walking and struggling along with bundles or pushing baby carriages, and play wagons piled with household goods. One man passed with evident pleasure at having rescued an empty bird carriage, and one woman had saved nothing but her Easter bonnet. Henry laughed and she replied yes "We got it safe." Many escaped only with their lives. All the hotels downtown were aflame and the fire was spreading rapidly through the mission. By morning an encouraging report was sent out and we went home and had cold breakfast of whatever we could find around the house that was eatable, but I went back out in the park, for the minute I came in the house I would be seized with wild terror of another earthquake, and at every shake would rush with Joseph to the stairs. The wind died down, ashes began to fall over us, and word was sent that in a few hours, the fire would reach our section of the city. Not having any fancy for being crisped in the panhandle, we began to make desperate efforts to get away. At the invitation of one of Dr. O'Neill's cousins, we went with her to her cottage on Ocean Beach. It took about the last penny of everybody in the party to get there. The first teamster Henry went to said he would move us five blocks for $25. At that rate we could not have gone two blocks. The morning of the earthquake we had fifty cents in the house. The next day Henry had managed to borrow $10 from a paymaster from Mare Island whose family lives near us. It was mere accident Henry found him. We stayed two days at the beach. On Saturday Henry went over to Mare Island for funds, and we came back to our flat and spent the night.

The fire by some miracle had been stopped before it went very much beyond Van Ness Ave. On some streets it reached Fillmore and D. By Sunday we were able to reach the ferry and came over to Berkeley. We had rented this house on the first April and were only waiting in the city in order to hear Faust, to be given by the Metropolitan Opera company on Saturday twenty-first. I do not know how the opera singers escaped the fire and got out of the city. Caruso and in fact nearly all of them were at the St. Francis. Caruso is said to have wept piteously after the earthquake. I felt better on hearing that, because the only time I cried was when Henry left me to go down to the Works. He asked where we should meet in case the house went to pieces or was damaged by fire before his return. I replied between sobs that it was not necessary to appoint a meeting place, for if he should ever return he would find my mangled body under the ruins of the house. Heartless creature, he thought it a great joke and went off laughing at me. He did not laugh anymore though, until we came out here.

In the city the lights are destroyed, fires not permitted in the chimneys, there is no sewerage, and street cars not yet running. Everybody there is cooking out of doors.

The business portion of the city is a mass of ruins. Market Street was swept its entire length to within one block of the ferries. Everything South of Market went, nearly all the mission district, and north of Market to Van Ness. There is not a trace left of China Town. I suppose every San Franciscan has suffered greatly from the fire. Many are destitute, and numbers are homeless. The earthquake of course did great damage to all brick buildings, and many frames are not fit for habitation. Some frame ones slid off the foundations. Henry thinks our flat will probably go to pieces when the Page street cars begin to run.

The Union Iron Works will begin work again Monday. Of course they will be much delayed by the damage done, and we are sure of being here another year even if the U.I.W. does not get another contract.

Henry has been going back to the city to get our things in the flat packed up. This house is completely furnished and exceedingly comfortable. We have a large back yard with prune trees in it, and beautiful in the front yard. The house faces Golden Gate and we can see every ship that comes into or leaves port. The view is beautiful. Joseph is wild with delight at the unaccustomed freedom.

I wish you had seen something of Berkeley. It is really a beautiful place, pretty homes and the greatest profusion of flowers everywhere.

I felt so contented and happy when I reached here last Sunday after all the turmoil of the week. But there are always snakes even Paradise, and the snakes in this Eden are the people who run the house. They live in a little house at the rear of the back yard, the lot runs through from street to street. I thought of course they had a separate exit but, no, they are all over the place. Mrs. comes out in the front yard and works the flowers, and this afternoon to my chagrin, I see they have swung their hammock and placed their chairs in what I had supposed was my back yard, and was one of the great considerations in renting the place. There is no excuse for it either, for they have just as large a yard on the other side of their house with much larger trees. They leave their doors spread open all the time and the minute I turn Joseph out in the yard, he makes a break for their house. I have been trying to keep him out but I am not going to do it any more, for maybe if he is very annoying they will move over to their side. I wish Mrs. would go away. She was away when we took the place and I supposed she was going to stay. I am so provoked and distressed that I could write reams on the subject, so I'll stop now, for I have subjected you as it is to a very illegible letter and a very incoherent one.

I think my nerves are not quite steady yet.

Much love to you and Julius from us all.

Lovingly yours,
Margaret.

## 1906: JULY 5
## GRACE BROWN TO CHESTER GILLETTE

---

*Grace Brown (1886?–1906) might still have been hoping that Chester Gillette (1885?–1908) would marry her when she begged him in this letter to take her on a promised trip to the Adirondacks. Brown, a twenty-year-old skirt factory worker, had become pregnant during an affair with the twenty-two-year-old Gillette, the nephew of the factory owner. On July 9, Gillette and Brown did leave Cortland, New York, and go away together, but sometime during the third evening of the trip, Brown drowned at Big Moose Lake. Gillette's nearly month-long murder trial made headlines all over the country, and the tale would eventually inspire Theodore Dreiser's* An American Tragedy *and the movie* A Place in the Sun. *Both the jury and the spectators wept when they heard this letter read. Gillette's defense lawyers tried to portray it as a suicide note, but the jury found him guilty, and the following year he died in the electric chair.*

Thursday night

My dear Chester—

I am curled up by the kitchen fire and you would shout if you could see me. Everyone else is in bed. The girls came up and we shot the last firecrackers. Our lawn looks as green as the Cortland House corner. I will tell you all about my Fourth when I see you. I hope you had a nice time.

This is the last letter I can write dear. I feel as though you are not coming. Perhaps this is not right, but I cannot help feeling that I am never going to see you again. How I wish this was Monday.

I am going down to stay with Maude next Sunday night, dear, and then go to DeRuyter the next morning and will get there about 10 o'clock. If you take the 9:45 train from the Lehigh there you will get there about eleven.

I am sorry I could not go to Hamilton, dear, but Mama and Papa did not want me to go and there are so many things I have had to work hard for in the last two weeks. They think I am just going out there to DeRuyter for a visit.

Now, dear, when I get there I will go at once to the hotel and I don't think I will see any of the people. If I do and they ask me to come to the house I will say something so they won't mistrust anything. Tell them I have a friend coming from Cortland, that we are to meet there to go to a funeral or a wedding in some town farther on. Awfully sorry, but we were invited to come and I had to cut my vacation a little short and go. Will that be all O.K. dear? Maybe that won't be just what I will say, but don't worry about anything for I shall manage somehow.

Only I want you to come in the morning. I don't want to wait there in the hotel all day, for if they should see me there, and all day, they would think it funny I did not go to the house. You must come in the morning for I have had to make—you don't know how many plans to fit your last letter—in order to meet you Monday. I dislike waiting until Monday but now that I have I don't think anything only fair that you should come Monday morning. But, dear, you must see the necessity yourself of getting there and not making me wait. If you dislike the idea of coming Monday morning and can get a train up there Sunday, you can come up Sunday night and be there to meet me. Perhaps that would be the best way. All I care is that I don't want to wait there all day or half a day. I think there is a train that leaves the Lehigh at six something Sunday night. I don't know what I would do if you were not there or did not come. I am about crazy now.

I have been bidding goodbye to some places today. There are so many nooks, dear, and all of them so dear to me. I have lived here nearly all of my life. First, I said goodbye to the spring house with its great masses of green moss; then the beehive, a cute little house in the orchard, and, of course, all of the neighbors that have mended my dresses from a little tot up to save me a thrashing I really deserved.

Oh dear, you don't realize what all of this is to me. I know I shall never see any of them again. And Mama! Great heavens, how I do love Mama! I don't know what I shall do without her. She is never cross and she always helps me so much. Sometimes, I think if I could tell Mama, but I can't. She has trouble enough as it is, and I couldn't break her heart like that. If I come back dead, perhaps, if she does not know, she won't be angry with me. I will never be happy again, dear. I wish I could die.

I am going to bed now dear. Please come and don't let me wait there. It is for both of us to be there. If you have made some plans for something Sunday night you must come Monday morning.

Please think, dear, that I had to give up a whole summer's pleasure and you will surely be brave enough to give up one evening for me. I shall expect and look for you Monday forenoon.

Heaven bless you until then.

Lovingly and with kisses,
The Kid

I will go to the Tabor House and you come for me there. I wish you would come up Sunday night, so as to be there, and, sweetheart, I think it would be easier for you. Please come up Sunday night, dear.

# EXCHANGE

*Ethel Waxham (1882–1959) was twenty-three years old when she embarked on the adventure of a lifetime. After growing up in Denver, graduating from Wellesley, and volunteering in New York City's slums for a summer, she went west to become a teacher in a one-room schoolhouse in Wyoming. There she met a sheep rancher named John Galloway Love (1870–1950), who routinely rode eleven hours for the chance to see her. When Waxham left to do graduate work at the University of Colorado, Love courted her by pen, and the letters that follow give some indication of his progress in winning her.*

The couple would be married on June 20, 1910, and would stay married—through flood, fire, and illness—for forty years.

Muskrat, Wyoming
September 12th, 1906

Dear Miss Waxham,

Of course it will cause many a sharp twinge and heartache to have to take "no" for an answer, but I will never blame you for it in the least, and I will never be sorry that I met you. I will be better for having known you. I know the folly of hoping that your "no" is not final, but in spite of that knowledge . . . I know that I will hope until the day that you are married. Only then I will know that the sentence is irrevocable.

Yours Sincerely,
John G. Love

November 12, 1906

Dear Miss Waxham,

I know that you have not been brought up to cook and labor. I have never been on the lookout for a slave and would not utter a word of censure if you never learned, or if you got ambitious and made a "batch" of biscuits that proved fatal to my favorite dog. . . . I will do my level best to win you and . . . If I fail, I will still want your friendship just the same.

Yours Sincerely,
John G. Love

February 15th, 1907

Dear Mr. Love,

I am fortunate in having two letters from you to answer in one. . . . The days have been comparatively dull. . . . I am too busy for dances here, if I care to go, which I do not. . . . The seven months I spent at the ranch I would not exchange for any other seven months in my life. They seem shorter than seven weeks, even seven days, here.

> Sincerely yours,
> Ethel Waxham

Dear Miss Waxham,

I for one am glad that your curiosity led you to drift up here to Wyoming, and now my supreme desire in life is to persuade you to come back.

> With love and kisses,
> Ever yours,
> John G. Love

Dear Mr. Love,

Since you began to sign your name as you do . . . you must have known that I would not like it and would not continue, since we are only friends. I wrote you not to expect any more letters from me unless you stopped it.

> Ethel P. Waxham

Dear Miss Waxham,

I will always sign all letters properly in the future. Please forgive my errors of the past. I suppose that I ought to be satisfied with your friendship, but I won't be.

> Yours sincerely,
> John G. Love

April 3, 1909

Dear Mr. Love,

There are reasons galore why I should not write so often. I'm a beast to write at all. It makes you—(maybe?)—think that "no" is not "no," but "perhaps" or "yes," or anything else. . . . Good wishes for your busy season

> From E. W.

P.S. I like you very much.

October 25th, 1909

Dear Miss Waxham,

There is no use in my fixing up the house anymore, papering, etc., until I know how it should be done, and I won't know that until you see it and say how it ought to be fixed. If you never see it, I don't want it fixed, for I won't live here. We could live very comfortably in the wagon while our house was being fixed up to suit you, if you only would say yes.

John Love

Dear Mr. Love,

Suppose that you lost everything that you have and a little more; and suppose that for the best reason in the world I wanted you to ask me to say "yes." What would you do?

E.

Dear Miss Waxham,

If I were with you, I would throw my arms around you and kiss you and wait eagerly for the kiss that I have waited over fours years for.

Yours Sincerely,
John G. Love

## 1908: DECEMBER 13
## SARAH ORNE JEWETT TO WILLA CATHER

---

*Willa Cather (1873–1947) published her first collection of stories,* The Troll Garden, *in 1905, and in the same year became managing editor of* McClure's. *She was clearly enjoying both her fiction and nonfiction callings when author Sarah Orne Jewett (1849–1909) offered her this slightly scolding but nonetheless timeless literary advice. Jewett, whose own fiction offered a signature blend of sympathy and realism, would have a profound impact on Cather. In 1912, the younger writer gave up her journalism work to become a full-time novelist.* Alexander's Bridge, O Pioneers!, *and* My Antonia *soon followed, and in 1922 Cather would win the Pulitzer Prize for her novel* One of Ours.

148 Charles Street, Boston, Mass.,
Sunday, 13th of December.

My Dear Willa,—

I have been thinking about you and hoping that things are going well. I cannot help saying what I think about your writing and its being hindered by such incessant, important, responsible work as you have in your hands now. I do think that it is impossible for you to work so hard and yet have your gifts mature as they should—when one's first working power has spent itself nothing ever brings it back just the same, and I do wish in my heart that the force of this very year could have gone into three or four stories. In the "Troll-Garden" the Sculptor's Funeral stands alone a head higher than the rest, and it is to that level you must hold and take for a starting-point. You are older now than that book in general; you have been living and reading and knowing new types; but if you don't keep and guard and mature your force, and above all, have time and quiet to perfect your work, you will be writing things not much better than you did five years ago. This you are anxiously saying to yourself! but I am wondering how to get at the right conditions. I want you to be surer of your backgrounds,—you have your Nebraska life,—a child's Virginia, and now an intimate knowledge of what we are pleased to call the "Bohemia" of newspaper and magazine-office life. These are uncommon equipment, but you don't see them yet quite enough from the outside,—you stand right in the middle of each of them when you write, without having the standpoint of the looker-on who takes them each in their relations to letters, to the world. Your good schooling and your knowledge of "the best that has been thought and said in the world," as Matthew Arnold put it, have helped you, but these you wish and need to deepen and enrich still more. You must find a quiet place near the best companions (not those who admire and wonder at everything one does, but those who know the good things with delight!). You do need reassurance,—every artist does!—but you need still more to feel "responsible for the state of your conscience" (your literary conscience, we can just now limit that quotation to), and you need to dream your dreams and go on to new and more shining ideals, to be aware of "the gleam" and to follow it; your vivid, exciting companionship in the office must not be your audience, you must find your own quiet centre of life, and write from that to the world that holds offices, and all society, all Bohemia; the city, the country— in short, you must write to the human heart, the great consciousness that all humanity goes to make up. Otherwise what might be strength in a writer is only crudeness, and what might be insight is only observation; sentiment falls to sentimentality—you can write about life, but never write life itself. And to write and work on this level, we must live on it—we must at least recognize it and defer to it at every step. We must be ourselves, but we must be our best selves. If we have patience with cheapness and thinness, as Christians must, we must know that it *is* cheapness and not make believe about it. To work in silence and with all one's heart, that is the writer's lot; he is the only artist who must be a solitary, and yet needs the widest outlook upon the world. But you have been growing I feel sure in the very days when you felt most hindered, and this will be counted to you. You need to have time to yourself and time to read and add to your recognitions. I do not know when a letter has grown so long and written itself so easily, but I have been full of thought about you. You will let me hear again from you before long?

## 1909: APRIL 5
## EMMA GUSTAFSSON TO HER MOTHER

---

*The wave of immigration that had started in the 1880s continued in full force through the early part of the new century, most of the newcomers now arriving from Italy, Russia, and Central Europe. In addition to the challenge of making a living in an unfamiliar and sometimes hostile land, they had to face their feelings about what they had left behind.*

Emma Huhtasaari Gustafsson had come to Hancock, Michigan, from Sweden in 1903.

5 April 1909, Hancock, Michigan
Ever-beloved Mother, far away in the dear homeland,

I always think of Mother and tears come to my eyes when I think that the seventh year has begun since I left the dear home of my birth. I am not so attached to America that I should forget the homeland. One always feels such a strange longing. Though now I have it very good. I have a good husband. He is no drinker like some of them are here. They drink so there's not enough to live on. My husband is called Valter Gustafsson from Juhonpieti, Pajala. Recently several people from Kuivakangas have been married here. . . .

Here we have beautiful summer weather already. The snow has melted, they are driving with wagons. Last week we had Good Friday off. The miners also had Sunday free then, didn't have to go to the mine.

Mother has not had a photograph taken of herself, since I have not gotten any photograph like I asked. I have no picture of Mother except that inside of me. I believe that I shall never be able to see Mother again in this life.

Valter is getting tired of digging in the mine the whole time, and emigrants keep arriving in crowds and there are also people without work. Last month ten thousand emigrants landed from the old country.

Don't have so much this time, but greetings to all, but first and foremost to dear Mother.

Signed your daughter
Emma Huhtasaari

## 1909: APRIL 7
## HELEN TAFT TO ELIZA SCIDMORE

*An enthusiastic adviser to her husband, Helen Herron Taft (1861–1943) had supported William Howard Taft in his roles as judge, Philippines governor, and secretary of war under Theodore Roosevelt. After Taft was elected president in 1908, Helen was responsible for elevating the social life of the White House—and for planting the cherry trees that would become one of the defining features of the nation's capital. Travel writer Eliza Ruhamah Scidmore (1856–1928) had been suggesting the cherry trees since visiting Japan in 1885, but she did not find a truly promising response until this letter from the new first lady.*

The White House, Washington.
April 7, 1909

Thank you very much for your suggestion about the cherry trees. I have taken the matter up and am promised the trees, but I thought perhaps it would be best to make an avenue of them, extending down to the turn in the road, as the other part is still too rough to do any planting. Of course, they could not reflect in the water, but the effect would be very lovely of the long avenue. Let me know what you think about this.

Sincerely yours,
Helen H. Taft

## 1909: SEPTEMBER 5
## SUSAN HALE TO CHARLOTTE HEDGE

*As news of the discovery of the North Pole reached Matunuck, Rhode Island, the irrepressible Susan Hale (see page 429) voiced her mock anguish to a friend.*
Robert Peary announced that he had discovered the North Pole in 1909; Frederick Albert Cook claimed he had reached it the year before. Some support remained for Cook until after World War I; in later years he would be imprisoned for mail fraud. Henry Hudson, John Franklin, Nils Nordenskiold (not Norgenscold), and Otto Sverdrup (not Swerdros) were all Arctic explorers. "Sarlots" was Hale's nickname for Charlotte.

Matunuck, Rhode Island, September 5, 1909.

Dear Sarlots,—

Isn't this a dreadful business about the North Pole being found, all the mystery, all the charm, gone out of the Geography? It's now just like any other old place, say Watchaalascatchkan, Iowa. And such a commonplace man discovering it, named Cook. He just made a hole in the ground and came away. Why didn't he see blue devils, salamanders, and shooting flames, and the shades of Hudson and John Franklin and Norgenscold and Swerdros hawking round and wringing their hands saying, "He done it"?

I'm forcing myself now to turn my thoughts to the Antarctic Pole—<u>there</u> remains mystery, romance, inaccessibility; and I can't get over my childish impression that it's warm there. I am hoping you will sympathise with me in this new aggression of the twentieth century. How flat the world seems! He, Cook, seems to have taken absolutely no comfort in the fact there was no longitude. Write your sympathy.

I noticed, last night, no perturbation in the Pole Star. I was fearing it might refuse to go round a Cooked Pole.

Yours,
Susy

## 1910: APRIL
## EDITH WHARTON TO W. MORTON FULLERTON

*Edith Newbold Jones (see page 434) had married Edward Wharton in 1885, when she was twenty-three and he was thirty-six. They shared wealthy backgrounds, residences in New York; Newport, Rhode Island; and Lenox, Massachusetts—and, apparently, little else. First careless, then underhanded, with her money, he was repeatedly unfaithful as well. By 1908, when they were living in Paris, Edith began an affair with William Morton Fullerton (1865–1952), a correspondent for the* London Times. *Despite her claim to be writing to him here from "a sense of my worth," this letter suggested that she felt otherwise—and proved that her extraordinary insight into the lives of her fictional characters did not always extend to her own. The affair with Fullerton ended the year she wrote this letter, and her marriage in 1913.*

Fâchée *means "angry,"* ballottée: *"tossed around,"* point de repère: *"reference point,"* à quoi s'en tenir: *loosely, "where one stands,"* love d'amour: *after* aimer d'amour, *meaning "to be madly in love with."*

Thursday

Don't think I am "fâchée," as you said yesterday; but I am sad & bewildered beyond words, & with all my other cares & bewilderments, I can't go on like this!

When I went away I thought I shd perhaps hear once from you. But you wrote me every day—you wrote me as you used to three years ago! And you provoked me to answer in the same way, because I could not see for what other purpose you were writing. I thought you wanted me to write what was in my heart!

Then I come back, & not a word, not a sign. You know that here it is impossible to exchange two words, & you come here, & come without even letting me know, so that it was a mere accident that I was at home. You go away, & again dead silence. I have been back three days, & I seem not to exist for you. I don't understand.

If I could lean on some feeling in you—a good & loyal friendship, if there's nothing else!—then I could go on, bear things, write, & arrange my life . . .

Now, ballottée perpetually between one illusion & another by your strange confused conduct of the last six months, I can't any longer find a point de repère. I don't know what you want, or what I am! You write to me like a lover, you treat me like a casual acquaintance!

Which are you—what am I?

Casual acquaintance, no; but a friend, yes. I've always told you I foresaw that solution, & accepted it in advance. But a certain consistency of affection is a fundamental part of friendship. One must know à quoi s'en tenir. And just as I think we have reached that stage, you revert abruptly to the other relation, & assume that I have noticed no change in you, & that I have not suffered or wondered at it, but have carried on my life in serene insensibility until you chose to enter again suddenly into it.

I have borne all these inconsistencies & incoherences as long as I could, because I love you so much, & because I am so sorry for things in your life that are difficult & wearing—but I have never been capricious or exacting, I have never, I think, added to those difficulties, but have tried to lighten them for you by a frank & faithful friendship. Only now a sense of my worth, & a sense also that I can bear no more, makes me write this to you. Write me no more such letters as you sent me in England.

It is a cruel & capricious amusement.—It was not necessary to hurt me thus! I understand something of life, I judged you long ago, & I accepted you as you are, admiring all your gifts & your great charm, & seeking only to give you the kind of affection that should help you most, & lay the least claim on you in return. But one cannot have all one's passionate tenderness demanded one day, & ignored the next, without reason or explanation, as it has pleased you to do since your <u>enigmatic change in December</u>. I have had a difficult year—but the pain within my pain, the last turn of the screw, has been the impossibility of knowing what you wanted of me, & what you felt for me—at a time when it seemed natural that, if you had any sincere feeling for me, you should see my need of an equable friendship—I don't say love because that is not made to order!—but the kind of tried tenderness that old friends seek in each other in difficult moments of life. My life was better before I knew you. That is, for me, the sad conclusion of this sad year. And it is a bitter thing to say to the one being one has ever loved d'amour.

**1911: FEBRUARY 23**
**MAIMIE PINZER TO FANNY HOWE**

---

*Even in the early twentieth century, there was no shortage of writing about the lives of prostitutes. Diaries and memoirs were frequent features in newspapers and magazines, but almost without exception, they were written by moralists, and their authenticity was dubious at best. One notable exception (not published, however, until 1977) was the correspondence of Maimie Pinzer (1885–?) and Fanny Quincy Howe (1870–1933). Howe was an upper-crust Bostonian and sometime writer. She had been asked by a Philadelphia social worker named Herbert Welsh to correspond with Pinzer, a prostitute who had lost an eye and fought a morphine addiction, and was trying to go straight. With uncommon gifts for language and observation, Pinzer wrote frequently to Howe over the course of a dozen years, thereby capturing the life of a working girl with very few options at the beginning of the century.*

Albert Jones was Pinzer's first husband, a man she had married at her low point "as a sort of anchor," but who proved to be nothing of the sort. "M" stood for morphine. *The Opal* was a novel Howe had written that had been published anonymously.

Ca. February 23, 1911

My trolley is twisted again; that is, I am "off again," and that means I can't think but that everything is going to the bow-wows. I think it's a scurvy trick on my part to write you in this mood, but I just can't or won't help it....

On Saturday of last week, Albert came home with the glad tidings that work was over, and I don't know of any time, before, that news broke me up so. You see, we have been here a month, and our rent was due today again. I had $12.00

saved, and as there was one more "pay day" before "rent day" (which was today), I expected to surely have it, and was comfortable, in consequence. The news that there was no work, of course, brought visions of the hurried exit from Broad Street and all its wretched details, due to not having the rent. My mind became filled with one idea, and that was how to get the remaining $8.00, and also to live, until Albert got to work—which I hoped would be the next day. The week passed and yet not a hopeful sign of work; and we had spent $2.50 of my $12.00—leaving $10.50 and then, today, the bill for the rent was shoved under our door. In the afternoon I went to Brother's, expecting to borrow the money from him, much as I hated to, and almost would prefer being dispossessed than admit to him my need. At any rate, I left there without borrowing it, although just one word would have done the trick; but his smug satisfied manner made the saying impossible. And while I was downright hungry when I got there, and there was food of every sort and description there, I ate nothing, because it was in-between their regular mealtimes, and I could not let them know I had no lunch nor breakfast. When I left them, I went to a restaurant—and while I had bought no food all that forenoon, knowing I was going and would eat there, when I didn't eat there and found myself in a restaurant, I attacked the menu card with a vicious delight, and ate 75 cents worth of food. Somehow it gave me new courage; and I looked up a man who wants to buy two of my puppies. And while they are much too young to sell, I suggested that if he paid for them now, I'd sell them for $15.00 for the two, instead of the $20.00 I had priced them, and would keep them for two months more. He could not be made to see it my way; and I came home Thursday night no better off, and if anything worse, due to my extravagant meal. Believe me, I was almost frantic. And Albert—I pitied him, for he seemed so frightened about what would happen on rent day, which was two days off. I wish I had gotten a letter from you Friday, but I didn't; so I just kept on going with no definite aim or reason in thinking I would be any better off by going out than by staying in—so I went out. I went to the Photographic Art Society's Exhibit, and on my return, I was terribly hungry for some good food; and as I had given over the money to Albert—for fear I would get another crazy notion to eat expensive meals—I only had a dime in my pocketbook, and my appetite felt that the 10 cents wouldn't even take the edge off of it. And then I felt I must eat some good steak in a first class place where they served sweet butter and sweet clean bread. Then I used a nickel to phone a young boy I used to know well, intending to get him to meet me—as he had often asked me to—and I was told he was in Salem Beach with his family. And then I just had to phone the man I had borrowed the $20.00 from. I don't try to excuse myself, but I was terribly hungry—and my appetite has a contemptible trick of getting very lively just when I am without funds. So he came to meet me at five o'clock and brought his brother, a young fellow of twenty-six years. The one I knew couldn't stay—a prior engagement—so the younger one did; and I frankly told him I was hungry, after he had bought two cocktails apiece. I did not know it at the time—but I do now—that liquor taken when one's stomach is empty is sure to knock one out. At any rate, I ate my dinner with an uncomfortable feeling, but did not recognize that it was due to the liquor—for I drink rarely, ever, but when I do, I can drink without much effect. That is, I used to; and since that was the first time I had tasted liquor since being rid of the M——, I attribute my not feeling the liquor, before, to being a M—— user. At any rate, some light wine went with the dinner, and then some liqueur—yellow chartreuse, I believe—and then I knew I was horribly, frightfully, disgustingly intoxicated. Thank goodness the man wasn't a rotter, but much of a gentleman, and tried to fix me up to send me home. But there wasn't any use—I just could not revive, though he walked with me blocks and blocks. I had all my faculties, but could not control my feet—and then, I was very sick. It grew late. . . . I disliked going home to Albert in that condition, for I did not know what to tell him, as he had never seen me in so sorry a plight before. But I did manage somehow to get to the third floor at 1:00 A.M.—and he was almost wild with worrying as to what had become of me. When he saw my condition, he grew angry and loud, at first. But I settled that in short order, and he helped to undress me. In the morning, I told him just what did happen, telling the unadulterated truth; and he has been crying and acting the fool all day today in consequence. Now I have told you—and you don't know how humiliating it all is. I wish I could have done without telling you—but somehow I couldn't. It is the first bad thing I've done since last March—a year, lacking a week—and I feel so small.

As a sequel, I must tell you that I lost in the shuffle, somewhere, a fur piece which belonged on my coat. You see, my coat is worn, directly in front, and last year when I had money, I purchased a big flat bow which I pinned across the front. It looked smart, and it covered the worn places—and now it is gone. Can you imagine how I hate myself? Today was spent in bed. I asked Albert to go out all afternoon, and stay out, as I wanted to be alone. He took some fool notion that I intended taking my life, which was never a moment in my thoughts. So after reassuring him, he went, and did not return until seven-thirty. About five o'clock I phoned my cousin Alex. He is a young boy of sixteen years who has been in this country, coming from Russia, thirteen months. He is really a "greenhorn," but a very eager boy to learn, and I have been giving him English lessons all winter, and it is marvellous how he progresses. I know that he has been saving a small sum out of his weekly earnings to save enough so that he might send the money to bring his widowed mother to this country. And altho he only earns $5.00 a week, I know he saves $1.00 each week by the most rigid economy. I frankly told him my plight—and without the slightest hesitation, he gave me the entire savings, which were $15.00. And I felt so cheap to take it. But he knows it is as safe as though it is in the bank, and before he has the whole amount, I will repay the $15.00. Doesn't it seem strange that I could not ask my own brother to lend me the money—and yet had no hesitation about asking Alex?

If I was "blue" all week, last night's sweet escapade has given me a monopoly on all the Blues in the world. Somehow I feel I ought not tell you all this, for I think it will pain you; but then, I don't want to keep that one ugly thing out. For I have said all along to myself that I was writing you—my other self—just as I would write were I keeping a faithful diary.

I would like to read your mind when you read this letter. I don't think you would be angry, but still you might be disgusted. It surely doesn't seem as though your and Mr. Welsh's encouraging letters helped me much. Well, there is no use sitting here condemning myself. I am to you what I am to myself; so it is rank waste of time expressing my opinion of myself, when you know my worth—or, rather, worthlessness—just as well as I do. I wonder whether you knew I was off again, when you did not hear from me.

I will go to bed now, as it is twenty-five minutes of five and I am sleepy; but I wish I could end this appropriately—cleverly I mean—as you do in the letter in <u>The Opal</u>.

Perhaps after all I had better say goodnight.


## 1912

## JULIETTE GORDON LOW TO GIRL SCOUTS

*Juliette Gordon Low (1860–1927) was a recent widow living in England when she met Sir Robert Baden-Powell, the founder of Britain's Boy Scouts and Girl Guides, and decided that America needed its own youth organization. The first troop—of eighteen girls from Low's Savannah, Georgia, hometown—met to go camping and play basketball in 1912. Just four years later, there would be 5,000 Girl Scouts, and by the time Low died there were more than 140,000 troops throughout the nation. In this early note to girls about the group's internal laws, Low listed some of the virtues she wished to instill.*

HONOR. This means that a girl is not satisfied with keeping the letter of the law when she really breaks it in spirit.

LOYAL. This means that she is true to her country, to the city or village where she is a citizen, to her family, her church, her school, and those for whom she may work or who may work for her.

HELPFUL. The simplest way of saying this for the very young Scout is to do a good turn to someone every day: that is, to be a giver and not a taker. This is the spirit that makes the older Scout into a fine, useful, dependable woman.

THRIFTY. The most valuable thing we have in this life is time, and most girls are apt to be rather stupid about getting the most out of it. Health is probably a woman's greatest capital, and a Girl Scout...doesn't waste it in poor diet... so that she goes bankrupt before she is thirty. Money is a very useful thing to have....A Girl Scout saves, as she spends, on some system.

FRIEND TO ANIMALS. All Girl Scouts take particular care of our dumb friends, the animals, and protect them from stupid neglect or hard usage.

PURE. A good housekeeper cannot endure dust and dirt; a well-cared-for body cannot endure grime and soot; a pure mind cannot endure doubtful thoughts that cannot be freely aired and ventilated.

To put yourself in another's place requires real imagination, but by doing so each Girl Scout will be able to live among others happily.

I am like the old woman who lived in the shoe! And now the shoe has become too small for the many children and we must have a building that will be large enough for us all.

I hope that during the coming year we shall all remember the rules of this Girl Scouting game of ours. They are: To play fair. To play in your place. To play for your side and not for yourself. And as for the score, the best thing in a game is the fun and not the result.

## 1912: SEPTEMBER 15
## MRS. SAMUEL FRIEDMAN TO DAVID BRESSLER

*Immigrants often faced opposition and prejudice, not only from descendants of the original colonists but also from more recent generations of immigrants, who worried that the newcomers would reinforce old stereotypes. The Industrial Removal Office was formed in 1901 by Americanized German Jews whose ostensible goal was to find work for new Jewish immigrants. The subtext was the assumption that all Jews would fare better if they were dispersed. Between 1901 and 1922, the IRO helped move approximately seventy-nine thousand Jews from New York to some seventeen hundred smaller cities around the country. Although some of the so-called removals wrote to the office for information or with thanks, many also wrote to complain about how they had been treated.*

David Bressler (1879–1942) was head of the Industrial Removal Office from 1901 to 1916. Nothing more is known about Mrs. Friedman.

September 15, 1912
823-15 Ave S.
Minneapolis, Min

Mr. Bresler;
Industrial Removal Office,

Dear Sir:

Inclosed please find ten dollars ($10), the ballance of the debt, which we contracted for my transportation to this city.

Allow me to thank you for your kind favor, which can really be called, "good deeds". You are reputed to be an educated and clever man, therefore you will not resent criticism that is extended to you. I mean to give mine in good intention.

There are different ways of doing things. The most important is courtesy, if the party that is looking for a favor should be refused gently, he will feel better then if he were granted the request and treated as if he was not among those that can be classed as human, and spoken to as if that party did not know the meaning of insult.

When I applied to you for transportation, I told you everything, and the truth only. Yet, it was not enough. You humiliated me by asking why I do not pawn my jewelry, which was pawned for the last five years, why I did not sell my furniture, which we did sell to pay my husbands way to Minneapolis. Then you went on asking me, why I do not borrow of friends, and when I told you I owe everybody, you suggested that I should leave my child some place with strangers and go to a hospital to have my second baby. At last, when I told you I intend to pay it all back as it is only a loan, you made me sign a note for $20. My husband had it all arranged with Miss Foxe to pay her $15 as soon as we are in position to do so.

Sir, I do not complain! In fact I am very grateful to you. But the reason I mention it all is because, you should not think everyone that comes into the office to ask for aid must be a cheat, a liar and ignorant. The few hours that I sat waiting,

I had a chance to study the characters that came in. Some may be such I admit, but there are exceptions and a man like you ought to know the difference.

You will excuse us for not settling the bill as promised, Because we paid the bills in turns. We are now clear from all debts. Nevertheless we are not less grateful to all our friends and good people, for their kindness.

Mr. Friedman would like to have the note if possible.

Respectfully Yours

Mrs. Samuel Friedman

## 1912: DECEMBER 2
## ELINORE PRUITT STEWART TO JULIET CONEY

*Elinore Pruitt (1876–1933) was eighteen when she was orphaned, and thirty when in 1906 she left or was left by a husband in Oklahoma. Later that year, she moved with her young daughter, Jerrine, to Denver, where she worked for several years as a laundress and a housekeeper. Eventually she answered an ad for a job as a house-keeper for Clyde Stewart, a Wyoming rancher whom she soon married. Her letters to a former employer, Juliet Coney, who arranged for them to be published in the* Atlantic, *gave a vivid account of the life of the homesteader in the early twentieth century.*

Becky Sharp, the heroine of William Makepeace Thackeray's *Vanity Fair*, was famously manip-ulative and selfish. Erysipelas is a bacterial infection of the skin.

December 2, 1912.

Dear Mrs. Coney,—

Every time I get a new letter from you I get a new inspiration, and I am al-ways glad to hear from you.

I have often wished I might tell you all about my Clyde, but have not because of two things. One is I could not even begin without telling you what a good man he is, and I didn't want you to think I could do nothing but brag. The other reason is the haste I married in. I am ashamed of that. I am afraid you will think me a Becky Sharp of a person. But although I married in haste, I have no cause to repent. That is very fortunate because I have never had one bit of leisure to repent in. So I am lucky all around. The engagement was powerfully short be-cause both agreed that the trend of events and ranch work seemed to require that we be married first and do our "sparking" afterward. You see, we had to chink in the wedding between times, that is, between planting the oats and other work that must be done early or not at all. In Wyoming ranchers can scarcely take time even to be married in the springtime. That having been settled, the license was sent for by mail, and as soon as it came Mr. Stewart saddled Chub and went down to the house of Mr. Pearson, the justice of the peace and a friend of long standing. I had never met any of the family and naturally rather dreaded to have them come, but Mr. Stewart was firm in wanting to be married at home, so he told Mr. Pearson he wanted him and his family to come up the following Wednesday and serve papers on the " wooman i' the hoose." They were astonished, of course, but being such good friends they promised him all the assistance they could render. They are quite the dearest, most interesting family! I have since learned to love them as my own.

Well, there was no time to make wedding clothes, so I had to " do up" what I did have. Isn't it queer how sometimes, do what you can, work will keep getting in the way until you can't get anything done? That is how it was with me those few days before the wedding; so much so that when Wednesday dawned everything was topsy-turvy and I had a very strong desire to run away. But I always did hate a "piker," so I stood pat. Well, I had most of the dinner cooked, but it kept me hustling to get the house into anything like decent order before the old dog barked, and I knew my moments of liberty were limited. It was blowing a perfect hurricane and snowing like midwinter. I had bought a beautiful pair of shoes to wear on that day, but my vanity had squeezed my feet a little, so while I was so busy at work I had kept on a worn old pair, intending to put on the new ones later; but when the Pearsons drove up all I thought about was getting them into the house where there was fire, so I forgot all about the old shoes and the apron I wore.

I had only been here six weeks then, and was a stranger. That is why I had no one to help me and was so confused and hurried. As soon as the newcomers were warm, Mr. Stewart told me I had better come over by him and stand up. It was a large room I had to cross, and how I did it before all those strange eyes I never knew. All I can remember very distinctly is hearing Mr. Stewart saying, " I will," and myself chiming in that I would, too. Happening to glance down, I saw that I had forgotten to take off my apron or my old shoes, but just then Mr. Pearson pronounced us man and wife, and as I had dinner to serve right away I had no time to worry over my odd toilet. Anyway the shoes were comfortable and the apron white, so I suppose it could have been worse; and I don't think it has ever made any difference with the Pearsons, for I number them all among my most esteemed friends.

It is customary here for newlyweds to give a dance and supper at the hall, but as I was a stranger I preferred not to, and so it was a long time before I became acquainted with all my neighbors. I had not thought I should ever marry again. Jerrine was always such a dear little pal, and I wanted to just knock about foot-loose and free to see life as a gypsy sees it. I had planned to see the Cliff-Dwellers' home; to live right there until I caught the spirit of the surroundings enough to live over their lives in imagination anyway. I had planned to see the old missions and to go to Alaska; to hunt in Canada. I even dreamed of Hono-lulu. Life stretched out before me one long, happy jaunt. I aimed to see all the world I could, but to travel unknown bypaths to do it. But first I wanted to try homesteading.

But for my having the grippe, I should never have come to Wyoming. Mrs. Seroise, who was a nurse at the institution for nurses in Denver while I was housekeeper there, had worked one summer at Saratoga, Wyoming. It was she who told me of the pine forests. I had never seen a pine until I came to Colo-rado; so the idea of a home among the pines fascinated me. At that time I was hoping to pass the Civil-Service examination, with no very definite idea as to what I would do, but just to be improving my time and opportunity. I never went to a public school a day in my life. In my childhood days there was no such thing in the Indian Territory part of Oklahoma where we lived, so I have had to try hard to keep learning. Before the time came for the examination I was so dis-couraged because of the grippe that nothing but the mountains, the pines, and the clean, fresh air seemed worth while; so it all came about just as I have writ-ten you.

So you see I was very deceitful. Do you remember, I wrote you of a little baby boy dying? That was my own little Jamie, our first little son. For a long time my heart was crushed. He was such a sweet, beautiful boy. I wanted him so much. He died of erysipelas. I held him in my arms till the last agony was over. Then I dressed the beautiful little body for the grave. Clyde is a carpenter; so I wanted him to make the little coffin. He did it every bit, and I lined and padded it, trimmed and covered it. Not that we couldn't afford to buy one or that our neighbors were not all that was kind and willing; but because it was a sad plea-sure to do everything for our little first-born ourselves.

As there had been no physician to help, so there was no minister to comfort, and I could not bear to let our baby leave the world without leaving any message to a community that sadly needed it. His little message to us had been love, so I selected a chapter from John and we had a funeral service, at which all our neighbors for thirty miles around were present. So you see, our union is sealed by love and welded by a great sorrow.

Little Jamie was the first little Stewart. God has given me two more precious little sons. The old sorrow is not so keen now. I can bear to tell you about it, but I never could before. When you think of me, you must think of me as one who is truly happy. It is true, I want a great many things I haven't got, but I don't want them enough to be discontented and not enjoy the many blessings that are mine. I have my home among the blue mountains, my healthy, well-formed children, my clean, honest husband, my kind, gentle milk cows, my garden which I make myself. I have loads and loads of flowers which I tend myself. There are lots of chickens, turkeys, and pigs which are my own special care. I have some slow old gentle horses and an old wagon. I can load up the kiddies and go where I please any time. I have the best, kindest neighbors and I have my dear absent friends. Do you wonder I am so happy? When I think of it all, I wonder how I can crowd all my joy into one short life. I don't want you to think for one moment that you are bothering me when I write you. It is a real pleasure to do so. You're always so good to let me tell you everything. I am only afraid of trying your patience too far. Even in this long letter I can't tell you all I want to; so I shall write you again soon. Jerrine will write too. Just now she has very sore fingers. She has been picking gooseberries, and they have been pretty severe on her brown little paws.

With much love to you, I am

"Honest and truly" yours,
Elinore Stewart.

## 1913?: MARCH 26
## MARY CASSATT TO ELLEN MARY CASSATT

*One of the most celebrated American women artists, Mary Cassatt (1844–1926) was a maverick in the 1880s when her work was exhibited in Paris along with the early Impressionists'. Though she lived abroad for most of her adult life, she had a profound effect on American art, not only inspiring other artists but also urging American collectors to buy Impressionist works. Most famous for her portraits of mothers and children, Cassatt was also known for her outspoken opinions and her generous estimation of her own talents. Both of these traits, as well as some passing anti-Semitism and one spectacularly inaccurate prediction, were evident in this letter to her niece.*

Ellen Mary Cassatt (1894–?) was the daughter of Cassatt's brother Gardner. "Brown" was apparently a nickname. Sarah Choate Sears was a photographer and painter; Helen was her daughter. Jean Jacques Henner was a French academic artist who died in 1905. *L'assiette de beurre* means "a plate of butter," in this case a cushy government post.

Villa Angeletto
March 26, 1913

Dearest Brown,

Yours of the 17th is just here; and as the weather is storming and a pouring rain has been our portion all night and likely to be all day, I have plenty of time before me to answer some of your questions about cubists and others. No Frenchman of any standing in the art world has ever taken any of these things seriously. As to Matisse, one has only to see his early work to understand him. His pictures were extremely feeble in execution and very commonplace in vision. As he is intelligent he saw that real excellence, which would bring him consideration, was not for him on that line. He shut himself up for years and evolved these things; he knew that in the present anarchical state of things— not only in the art world but everywhere—he would achieve notoriety—and he has. At his exhibition in Paris you never hear French spoken, only German, Scandinavian and other Germanic languages; and then people think notoriety is fame and even buy these pictures or daubs. Of course all this has only "un temps"; it will die out. Only really good work survives. As to this Gertrude Stein, she is one of a family of California Jews who came to Paris poor and unknown; but they are not Jews for nothing. They—two of the brothers—started a studio, bought Matisse's pictures cheap and began to pose as amateurs of the only real art. Little by little people who want to be amused went to these receptions where Stein received in sandals and his wife in one garment fastened by a broach, which if it gave way might disclose the costume of Eve. Of course the curiosity was aroused and the anxiety as to whether it <u>would</u> give way; and the pose was, if you don't admire these daubs I am sorry for you; you are not of the chosen few. Lots of people went, Mrs. Sears amongst them and Helen; but I never would, being to old a bird to be caught by chaff. The misunderstanding in art has arisen from the fact that forty years ago—to be exact thirty-nine years ago—when Degas and Monet, Renoir and I first exhibited, the public did not understand, only the "élite" bought and time has proved their knowledge. Though the Public in those days did not understand, the artists did. Henner told me that he considered Degas one of the two or three <u>artists</u> then living. Now the Public say— the foreign public—Degas and the others were laughed at; well, we will be wiser than they. We will show we know; not knowing that the art world of those days did accept these men; only, as they held "L'assiette de beurre," they would not divide it with outsiders. No sound artist ever looked except with scorn at these cubists and Matisse.

Mary Cassatt

1914

## "A FAITHFUL READER" TO THE "BINTEL BRIEF"

*On March 25, 1911, a fire in a building occupied by the Triangle Shirtwaist Company killed 146 people, most of them young women who were recent immigrants. Out of this tragedy came an increased awareness of the wretched conditions of sweatshops, and a new commitment to labor laws and health regulations. But for those who survived the fire, the personal devastation was often long lasting. Writing to the editor of the popular advice column "Bintel Brief" more than three years after the fire, one "Faithful Reader" asked for some kind of reassurance.*

The "Bintel Brief," which literally means "Bundle of Letters," was an advice column published in the Yiddish *Jewish Daily Forward,* a newspaper that was started on the Lower East Side of Manhattan in 1897. The editor's reply urged the young woman to begin her life over. "It is senseless for this girl to sacrifice her life in memory of her faithful bridegroom, since this would not bring him back to life," he wrote. "What the earth covers must be forgotten."

Worthy Editor,

I am a girl twenty-two years of age, but I've already undergone a great deal in my life. When I was born I already had no father. He died four months before my birth. And when I was three weeks old my mother died too. Grandmother, my mother's mother, took me in and soon gave me away to a poor tailor's wife to suckle me.

I was brought up by the tailor and his wife, and got so used to them that I called them Mother and Father. When I grew up I learned from the tailor how to do hand sewing and machine sewing too.

When I was sixteen my grandmother died and left me her small dilapidated house. The rabbi of the town sold it for me for three hundred rubles and gave me the money.

In time one of the tailor's apprentices fell in love with me, and I didn't reject his love. He was a fine, honest, quiet young man and a good earner. He had a golden character and we became as one body and soul. When I turned seventeen my bridegroom came to me with a plan, that we should go to America, and I agreed.

It was hard for me to take leave of the tailor's good family, who had kept me as their own child, and oceans of tears were shed when we parted.

When we came to America my bridegroom immediately started to work and he supported me. He was faithful and devoted. I'll give you an example of his loyalty: once, during the summer in the terrible heat, I slept on the roof. But it started to rain in the middle of the night and I was soaked through to the bone. I got very sick and had to be taken to the hospital. I was so sick that the doctor said I could be saved only by a blood transfusion. My bridegroom said immediately that he was ready to give me his blood, and so, thanks to him, I recovered.

In time I went to work at the "famous" Triangle shop. Later my bridegroom also got a job there. Even at work he wanted to be with me. My bridegroom told me then, "We will both work hard for a while and then we'll get married. We will save every cent so we'll be able to set up a home and then you'll be a housewife and never go to work in the shop again."

Thus my good bridegroom mused about the golden future. Then there was that terrible fire that took one hundred and forty-seven young blossoming lives. When the fire broke out, the screaming, the yelling, the panic all bewildered me. I saw the angel of death before me and my voice was choked in my throat. Suddenly someone seized me with extraordinary strength and carried me out of the shop.

When I recovered I heard calming voices and saw my bridegroom near me. I was in the street, rescued, and saw my girlfriends jumping out of the windows and falling to the ground. I clung to my bridegroom and rescuer, but he soon tore himself away from me. "I must save other girls," he said, and disappeared. I never saw him alive again. The next day I identified him, in the morgue, by his watch, which had my picture pasted under the cover. I fainted and they could hardly bring me to.

After that I lay in the hospital for five weeks, and came home shattered. This is the fourth year that I am alone and I still see before me the horrible scenes of the fire. I still see the good face of my dear bridegroom, also the black burned face in the morgue. I am weak and nervous, yet there is now a young man who wants to marry me. But I made a vow that I would never get married. Besides that, I'm afraid that I will never be able to love another man. But this young man doesn't want to leave me, and my friends try to persuade me to marry him and say everything will be all right. I don't believe it, because I think everything can be all right for me only in the grave.

I decided to write to you, because I want to hear your opinion.

Respectfully,
A Faithful Reader

\*      \*      \*

### 1914

### JESSIE EASTON TOWNSEND TO EDWIN J. WEBB

*The fight for women's suffrage, which had begun in the late 1840s, had endured—and been variously strengthened or weakened by—the Civil War, Reconstruction, temperance, race issues, westward migration, European immigration, and a huge schism within the ranks of feminist leaders. By the early twentieth century, women were regrouping, and the National American Woman Suffrage Association, now led during key periods by Carrie Chapman Catt, sought more followers. Among them was Jessie Easton Townsend, a Virginian who made the case in one very long, yet somehow efficient, sentence to a North Carolina congressman.*

Hon Sir:—

As a law abiding citizen; as a tax payer; as a graduate of a Kentucky High School where I took honors above every boy in my classes; as a mother of two sons, and mother-in-law of two fine men; as still the wife of one man (for thirty-two years); as a worker in the church all my life; as a worker in charitable and civic organizations for the betterment of the community; as one who finds at fifty-two years of age, more time, leisure, money, brains, health and strength to study and handle the questions of the day than ever before and probably twenty to thirty years left to live; as one who loves the good men of our country and has no other wish than to help them in the stupendous task of solving the many perplexing problems of these days; as one who believes in conservation and utilization of all good resources, especially such resources for good as lie in our matured womanhood; as a Democrat, who has inherited from Revolutionary fathers feelings of hot resentment against taxation without representation, and a firm belief in government by the people—all the people; and as a member of the Equal Suffrage League of Norfolk, representing a thousand such as myself in this town, I beg and implore you to vote favorably on the Woman Suffrage question now before you; and may I have the courtesy of a reply?

Sincerely yours,

Jessie Easton Townsend

### 1914: APRIL 9

### EMMA GOLDMAN TO MARGARET SANGER

*Protests, arrests, and the opposition of American authorities were all old news to Emma Goldman (1869–1940) by the time she wrote this letter to Margaret Sanger*

*(1879–1966). Goldman, an anarchist who had been outspoken since the 1890s on a variety of social, political, and artistic issues, was a natural ally of Sanger, the pioneering American proponent of birth control. In 1914, Sanger had begun publishing* The Woman Rebel, *a magazine that included information about birth control; she would indeed be indicted under the Comstock Act for using the mail to distribute "obscene" literature. Goldman herself would be arrested in 1916 for speaking out about birth control.*

Goldman was in Chicago and Sanger in New York when this letter was written.

April the Ninth, 1914

My dear Margaret:—

So the thing has happened before you have at all started on the way: But, then, we might have expected it, from the stupidity of the postal department. I only hope that it will prove a false alarm, because the law pertaining to "obscene" literature embraces almost every channel of distribution—the express and freight, and also those who circulate or sell so-called objectionable matter. Therefore, it would be almost impossible for you to continue the "Woman Rebel," if the authorities place their damnable seal upon it. However, meanwhile, I am pushing the paper all I can.

By the way, the first bundle contained only 37, and not 50 copies.

Let me know what your agent's prices are. You can send me another hundred by express to this city, and if you have sufficient copies on hand you may ship 200 to Denver to

Julia May Courtney<br>617 Fourteenth St.

It is too bad that you did not get out a very large edition of the first number, as we would at least have been able to circularize the first attempt, and thus arouse enough sympathy and interest.

I know you will be amused to learn that most of the women are up in arms against your paper; mostly women, of course, whose emancipation has been on paper and not in reality. I am kept busy answering questions as to your "brazen" method. They would not believe me when I told them that you were a little, delicate woman, refined and shrinking, but that you did believe in the daring and courage of woman in her struggle for freedom.

I am having good and interesting meetings and shall stay in this city all of next week. Write me again soon. I am keeping posted about the brutalities in New York. One so long in the revolutionary struggle as I have been is no longer surprised at anything that the police will do, but it is a pity that our boys must always be the victims.

> With much love.
>
> Emma

### 1914: OCTOBER 28
### MARGARET SANGER TO FRIENDS

---

*After being indicted for violating obscenity laws, Margaret Sanger (see previous letter) jumped bail and, under the name "Bertha Watson," sailed to England. Her parting orders were for her supporters to distribute one hundred thousand copies of a birth control pamphlet called* Family Limitation. *In 1916, Sanger would be arrested after opening America's first birth control clinic. The following year, she started a new monthly, the* Birth Control Review, *and in 1921, the American Birth Control League, which eventually became Planned Parenthood. In this letter, written just before her departure for England, Sanger succinctly—if hastily—laid out the essentials of the birth control movement.*

New York Oct. 28th 1914

Comrades and Friends

Every paper published should have a message for its readers. It should deliver it and be done. The Woman Rebel had for its aim the imparting of information of the prevention of conception. It was not the intention to labor on for years advocating the idea, but to give the information directly to those desired it. The March, May, July, August, September and October issues have been suppressed and confiscated by the Post Office. They have been mailed regularly to all subscribers. If you have not received your copies, it has been because the U.S. Post Office has refused to carry them to you.

My work on the nursing field for the past fourteen years has convinced me that the workers desire the knowledge of prevention of conception. My work among women of the working class proved to me sufficiently that it is they who are suffering because of the law which forbids the imparting of this information. To wait for this law to be repealed would be years and years hense. Thousands of un-wanted children may be born into the world in the meantime. Tousands of women made misserable and unhappy.

Why Should we wait?

Shall we who have heard the cries and seen the agony of dying Women respect the law which has caused their death?

Shall we watch in patience the murdering of 25000 women, who die each year in U.S. from criminal abortion?

Shall we fold our hands and wait until a body of sleek and well fed politicians get ready to abolish the cause of such slaughter?

Shall we look upon a piece of parchment as greater than human happiness greater than human life?

Shall we let it destroy our womanhood, and hold millions of workers in bondage and slavery? Shall we who respond to the throbbing pulse of human needs concern ourselves with indictments, courts and judges, or shall we do our work first and settle with these evils later?

This law has caused the perpetuation of quackery. It has created the fake and quack who benefits by its existence.

Jail has not been my goal. There is special work to be done and I shall do it first. If jail comes after I shall call upon all to assist me. In the meantime I shall attempt to nullify the law by direct action and attend to the consecquences later.

Over 100000 working men and woman in U.S. shall hear from me.

The Boston Tea Party was a defiant and revolutionary act in the eyes of the English Government, but to the American Revolutionist it was but an act of courage and justice.

Yours Fraternally
Margaret H. Sanger

## 1915: AUGUST 4
## EDITH GALT TO WOODROW WILSON

*One of three American presidents to be widowed in office (the others were Benjamin Harrison and John Tyler), Woodrow Wilson (1856–1924) was apparently devastated by the 1914 death of Ellen Wilson, whom he had married twenty-nine years earlier. But seven months later, while he was struggling with the question of war in Europe, Wilson met Edith Bolling Galt (1872–1961), a forty-two-year-old Washington widow. In short order, Galt provided the president with diversion and hope, love, affection, advice, and support. Though his political advisers urged him to keep the relationship secret with a campaign in the offing, Wilson ignored them and married Galt in December of 1915.*

Galt would prove an effective if controversial first lady, sheltering the president through a stroke and, by some accounts, taking on many of his duties while he was ill. At the time of this letter, she was staying with friends in upstate New York, and Wilson was at the summer White House in Cornish, New Hampshire.

10 Park Place,
Geneva, N.Y.
August 4, 1915

Dearest and best beloved—

I have missed, and wanted you so today that I know you have felt it. And I can hardly wait until tomorrow to get your blessed letter telling me of yourself and

August 5, 10 a.m.

My precious one—

I began writing this last night as you see but could not finish it on account of one of those rare, but awful headaches I have. I had to stop and go to bed—and so before anything prevents this morning am going to have a much-needed talk with my "other self."

I am quite well again this morning and think the headache was really neuralgia as it has been so damp and rainy for days but this morning is perfect, with floods of sunshine—and I am by a big window with my purple writing case beside me and everything to make me happy <u>but, one great lack</u>.

How I did long for your tender fingers last night to rub away the pain in my eyes. After all I wondered if it was all physical pain—or if the longing at my heart increased it ten fold. It was <u>our</u> anniversary of May 4th and that made the distance between us seem greater.

Just here the postman came—and I have just finished reading your beloved letter covering Tuesday and Wednesday—and also the enclosure in the other envelope. You were sweet to send me such a long messenger when you had so many guests and things to claim you and every word has brought me happiness. . . .

This is just the time we used to work, and I am wondering if you still take your work out on the porch, or if you sit in the study—or your room. I am always with you, and love the way you put one dear hand on mine, while with the other you turn the pages of history. . . .

As always
E

## 1915: OCTOBER 18
## "MADEMOISELLE MISS" TO A FRIEND

*The daughter of a former United States Navy medical director, the author of this letter was in France when World War I began in August of 1914. Inspired to help,*

*"Mademoiselle Miss" (as she would be known by her soldiers) finished her nursing training there with extraordinary speed and, after passing her oral exams, was given the rank of lieutenant. Beginning in the fall of 1915, she served in a French army field hospital near the Marne. Her moving letters home were first published (anonymously) in 1916.*

October 18, 1915.

Sitting in the sun outside my barracks.
Midday.

I have an hour of liberty—an unheard-of luxury.

I never dreamed what real work was before, of course; but now I know, and am learning mighty quick to accommodate myself to the revelation,—never to take two steps when I can arrive in one, never to bend over the low beds if I can sit, to relax everything but the occupied hand when I am feeding a patient. These seem little things, but just because of them I am as fit as possible, though I work always more than 14 hours per day.

It is a marvellous life; and strangely enough, despite all the tragedy, I call it a healthy one. One works, and when that is over one sleeps enough to keep in condition, and that is absolutely <u>all</u>, except a cold sponge bath (no bath-tubs here), and an eau de cologne rubdown in the morning, and the walk to and from the Hospital. In the morning now it is bitter cold and misty and half dark, and one gets weird glimpses of departing regiments, and white-capped old market-women, and pointed gables across the gloom; and at night the splendid stars, and now a great lustrous moon, and every day and night the boom, boom of the cannon which sounds very awesome these days. That is all I know of the world I live in.

## 1915: DECEMBER 22
## RUTH GORDON TO HER PARENTS

*By the end of 1915, Henry Ford had sent a much-publicized "peace ship" toward Europe, Albert Einstein had announced his general theory of relativity, and Alexander Graham Bell had made the first transcontinental phone call. But for nineteen-year-old Ruth Gordon (1896–1985), making her theatrical debut as one of the Lost Boys in* Peter Pan *was the only news item of interest. With the kind of enthusiasm she would carry through a career as both actress (*Rosemary's Baby*) and writer (*Adam's Rib*), Gordon declared her love of the theater in this exuberant letter home. The envelope she mentioned held a* New York Times *review by Alexander*

*Woollcott in which the famous critic wrote: "Ruth Gordon is ever so gay as Nibs."*
Maude Adams gave more than fifteen hundred performances as Peter Pan.

December 22, 1915

Dear Mama and Papa,

Well, it's all over and you can be proud of me. I wish you could have been there. That was truly the only thing missing. It was the worst day of my life and the greatest night. No matter how old I live I will never experience such emotions. I'll begin from the worst, it was my period and, Mama, you know what pains I have, but nothing could equal yesterday. Thank fortune I had a good sleep although how I had the courage to, the night before my first opening night, I don't know! I really think I am wonderful. But this horrible pain woke me up. I could just groan and our good colored maid looked in. She asked me if I ever had gin. Mama, I <u>didn't</u> drink any. Ida fixed me up some of the Penny Royal tea from Wollaston. I thought I would throw up, but I didn't and it worked.

That was my terrible day. My night made up for all that and for all the rest of my life. In a big envelope I am sending you something will prove why. I don't care how hard it is or how terrible, I would rather be an actress than live. In other words, if I could not be an actress, I would gladly take my life. I can say that without fear because I can be an actress and <u>will</u> be, as proven by what it says in the other envelope. Papa, I know you like the Boston Globe, but wait till you see this envelope!

At the Empire Theatre I dress one flight up with Angela Ogden, who kind of slips me little hints of what to do, without exactly letting on she's doing it. Also in the dressing room is Miss Keppel, who is sweet and subdued. They are all too old, except me, to play the Lost Boys, but most of them are friends of friends of Miss Adams or been with her since the year one. Angela Ogden is a very wonderful actress, who, they say, stole the show from Miss Adams when they played <u>Quality Street</u>, so Miss Adams won't put that one on any more, but will revive <u>The Little Minister</u> where Angela has a nice part that's no competition.

Well, I better get back to opening night. Did I write you I wear a suit of sort of like teddy bear fur? It goes all over me except my face and is quite hot and cumbersome, but the Lost Boys have to wear them. Well, the curtain went up and I thought I would die of fright, but the scenes in the Darlings' nursery are before I come on, so I recovered. Our scene started in the Never Never Land and I was in my place inside the tree trunk when I heard my cue and came out and said my line and got a huge laugh. I was so pleased. They tell me no one ever got that laugh before, so it made quite an impression.

All went swimmingly. It was a very fashionable audience, all the Fifth Avenue set. Miss Adams is a big society draw. They said all the men wore silk hats and white ties and tails and the ladies were quite decolleté and heavily jewelled. After my dance Miss Adams beckoned me to take three bows and our orchestra leader Henri Deering stood up and applauded. Gratifying after all I've been through. And Miss Adams has no jealousy like Alice Claire Elliot says many stars have. My cup runneth over and I guess when you read this yours will, too.

Then came the final curtain with Miss Adams alone in the treetop house after having waved goodbye to Wendy who flew home and everybody including the cast in the wings were crying when down came the curtain to thunderous applause and we all took our rehearsed bows, then rushed back and stood in the wings. That means just out of sight in the scenery. Miss Adams took one of her calls alone then came over and said 'Nibs' and led me on and while the audience applauded she broke off a rose from the immense bouquet that had been passed over the footlights and handed me a long-stemmed American Beauty rose that must have cost I don't know how much and I will treasure and preserve forever.

Well, that's about all. All the people in the dressing room including those I mentioned and Mrs. Buchanan, quite a swell, and Miss Clarens, extremely elegant, told me I had made a most auspicious start. And when you see the other envelope you will note they are right.

> Your loving actress daughter,
> Ruth Gordon
> (a name you will one day see in lights)

December 22, 1915, my favorite day of my life.

> R.


## 1916: MAY 15
## LELLA SECOR TO LORETTA SECOR

---

*As American women reacted to the outbreak of war in Europe, a "Mademoiselle Miss" (see page 468) was less typical than the thousands who dedicated themselves to trying to keep the United States out of the conflict. Lella Secor (1887–1966) had grown up in Michigan, homesteaded in Washington State, and worked as a journalist in New York. Committed by 1916 to the "war against war," she wrote to her mother, describing her passionate activism in the face of a growing commitment to American preparedness.*

Secor would marry Philip Florence, a teacher, and have two sons. After moving with them to England in 1921, she started the Cambridge Birth Control Clinic and remained vocal about women's rights. Benjamin Huebsch was a publisher and one of Secor's closest advisers in New York. A middy blouse was a buttoned shirt with a sailor collar. A hug-me-tight was a short, fitted jacket.

Monday
May 15, 1916

Dear Mother and All:

I feel as though I must stop and write a few lines before I go out this morning. . . . Unless I keep at my correspondence every day, it piles up until I don't know where I'm at. . . .

I am devoting every spare moment these days to the fight against preparedness, and if I neglect you, you will know it is because I am giving my minutes to a good cause. Last Saturday the Navy League—backed of course by the munitions makers and the political preparedness crowd—had a tremendous parade in New York. There were over 400,000 people in line, and it lasted from nine in the morning until ten o'clock at night. They have, of course, all the money they need, and there were bands and banners galore. Anne Herendeen, Mrs. Lane of the Woman's Peace Party, and a few other young women decided that the day ought not to pass without some protest on the part of those who see the thing as it is and are not deceived or scared by the munitions crowd. So we planned a little stunt which worked beautifully, and we were able to reach thousands of people with our ideas.

Needless to say, the experience was a brand new one for me, and one which I shall never forget. The plan was to have a crowd of girls all dress in white and with identical hats, so as to stand out from the mob, and circulate among the crowds distributing literature which would set forth the other side of the question. We wanted to carry sandwich boards—a sign which covers the person both front and back, the like of which I don't remember having seen out West—but we found that almost anything we might wish to do would infringe upon the law, and we had every reason to believe that the strictest censorship would be exercised over all those not with the preparedness crowd. It was I, fortunately, who finally struck upon a happy idea. I suggested that we paint the legend on the back of our middy blouses. Thus it would become part of our clothes, and policemen would be unable to do anything about it. Out of this suggestion evolved the final plan of using large black letters which were pasted on, and looked really quite startling. When we walked in front of anyone, he had to read this sign: "Real Patriots Keep Cool." We all wore white skirts and middies—I borrowed mine from Louise—and little ten-cent open-work sea-shore hats. Sort of hyphenated hats it would appear from this description.

I had to finish some work at home before going down Saturday morning, so that by the time I reached Fifth Avenue, the parade was well started. I have never had anything affect me more deeply. In spite of my best efforts, I could not keep back the tears, and for blocks down Fifth Avenue I wept over the pitiful spectacle. I could not look at those long lines of fine looking men, marching so gaily along, and with so little realization of what it all means, without a fresh outburst of tears. How little they realized that they were endorsing a system which means that great armies of splendid manhood shall go forth and slay other great armies. And why? Because stupid diplomats were too avaricious, too selfish, too ambitious to sanely handle the affairs entrusted to their care. All the lunatics turned loose from all the hospitals in the world could not have made so sorry a mess of things as have the diplomats of Europe. And yet we, blind and stupid as we are, are rushing into the same horrible cataclysm.

In a flash I was back in Europe, on the streets of Holland, watching the steady tramp, tramp, tramp of young men and boys being trained in the gentle art of murder. But their faces bore none of the lightness and frivolity which could be seen on the faces of those marchers Saturday. By the time I reached the peace headquarters, I was so wrought up that I could hardly control myself long enough to speak to anyone. Only those who have been to Europe during this brutal war, and have seen the horrible results of militarism, can realize or understand completely what it means. Anne Herendeen and I decided to go out together, but first we went for lunch, though I was scarcely able to eat anything.

Then, with white bags slung over our shoulders and filled with pamphlets, we started out. New York women, who have fought for suffrage and free speech and social betterment and every other thing, are accustomed to such stunts. But I confess that my heart was beating like a trip hammer. We started down Fifth Avenue, and almost the first person we met was Mr. Huebsch, with whom I have been carrying on a polite little quarrel over certain differences of opinion. He disapproved of our plan, and did not want me to go in on it. At first I pretended not to see him and was going to pass by, for I was in such a state anyway that I hardly felt fit to undertake anything more. Then I thought that very cowardly, and turned to overtake him and show him how I looked and what I was doing. As I turned, he turned also to come back to me. We exchanged just a few words, and then I went on. This morning I have a note from him telling me how charming I looked, etc., just by way of amelioration. But I am not so easily satisfied.

We began to hand out our pamphlets, and were astonished at the eagerness with which people took them and read them. We had 50,000 copies, and within a few hours they were all handed out. We met with courtesy on every hand, and only those violently pro-English or pro-German had anything to say against our program. On the other hand, when people read the signs on our back, they would often come up by the dozens, asking for our pamphlets, so that many times it was difficult to hand them out fast enough. There were many comments such as, "That's the dope!" "I sympathize with this idea!" "I'm interested in this; give me all the different kinds you have!" etc. By evening my spirits had risen. I began to feel that after all the preparedness parade did not represent such prodigious strength as it appeared to represent. As someone suggested, most of the preparedness people were marching, and the crowds on the street were either against preparedness or mildly indifferent.

Hundreds of those who marched did so not because they sympathize with the effort to line the munitions makers' pockets with more money, but because they were practically compelled to do so by their employers. A number of them came to our headquarters after their part was over, and signed a petition to Congress asking that no great preparedness program be entered into.

The "war against war"—as we peace people like to call ourselves—contingent has opened an exhibit on Fifth Avenue which is attracting much attention. At six o'clock, the woman who had it in charge, and who had already worked eight hours, announced that the place was to be closed. I felt that this was a big mistake, since the parade was still to be in progress for several hours. So Anne and Mr. and Mrs. Seltzer and a few others, with myself, offered to remain and keep the place open. Anne and her husband took me to a fine restaurant near by for dinner, and then we began our work of the evening.

Little groups gathered here and there for discussion, and the first thing I knew, I was the center of a large crowd which had gathered to listen to my debate with a man who favored preparedness. We thrashed the thing out, and the crowd agreed that I had won. It's thrilling work, and I love it, especially since I feel confident that whenever folks are started thinking on the right lines, they will see the thing for themselves as it really is. This idea that vast armaments is going to preserve peace is the biggest fallacy that was ever perpetrated on a reasonable people. But I must stop preaching on this subject. I am sending copies of our literature which we handed out. Oh how I wish that I might be financed so that I could simply devote my whole time to this work. I CAN grip the attention and interest of an audience. Everyone who has heard me speaks of it, and I feel it myself. So I think it seems like sort of a waste of talent which might be used to good advantage in this needed field. Over 11,000 people visited the exhibits on that one day. . . .

I have been having little spells of homesickness lately, which of course I must put out of the way. I cannot afford to waste any time mooning. But New York is such a deadly place to live in that I can't help sometimes longing for the green fields of home. There seems to be something about this place which saps my vitality. I am perfectly well—I'm sure I weigh more than I have for some time—but I seem to have no energy. I think it is because I do not get enough fresh air, so I am going to try to go into the country somewhere every Sunday as soon as the weather is better. This morning it is raining and cold, so cold that I am uncomfortable, even in my hug-me-tight. . . .

Don't stay home from prayer meeting to write to me, Mother. Of course I do miss your letters when they are long in coming, but I don't want you to deny yourself any pleasure in order to write.

. . . I don't believe I'll bother about piecing down that blue dress, for I only wear it around the house, and skirts are so short now anyway. . . .

Now I must stop, for the morning is slipping away, and I still have loads to do. . . .

Lovingly,
Lella

## 1916: OCTOBER 19

## A WYOMING MOTHER TO JULIA LATHROP

*A social reformer who had worked at Hull House with Jane Addams (see page 402), Julia Lathrop (1858–1932) was the first head of the U.S. Department of Labor's Children's Bureau. In addition to studying child labor laws and juvenile delinquency, the bureau investigated infant mortality and maternal health and aimed to educate American women about pregnancy, childbirth, and child care. One of its greatest accomplishments was the publication and wide distribution of two pamphlets,* Prenatal Care *(1913) and* Infant Care *(1914). The writer of this letter lived in Wyoming and was eventually visited by a public health doctor sent by the bureau.*

Dear Miss Lathrop,

I should very much like all the Publications on the Care of my self, who am now pregnant, also the care of a baby, both No. 1 and No. 2 series.

I live sixty five miles from a Dr. and my other babies (two) were very large at birth, one 12-lbs the other 10½ lbs. I have been <u>very</u> badly torn each time, through the rectum the last time. My youngest child is 7½ (and when I am delivered this time it will be past 8½ yrs). I am 37 years old and I am so worried and filled with perfect horror at the prospects ahead. So many of my neighbors die at giving birth to their children. I have a baby 11 months old in my keeping now whose mother died—when I reached their cabin last Nov It was 22 below zero and I had to ride 7 miles horse back. She was nearly dead when I got there and died after giving birth to a 14 lb. boy. It seems awfull to me to think of giving up all my work and leaving my little ones, 2 of which are adopted—a girl 10 and this baby. Will you please send me all the information for the care of my self before and after and at the time of delivery. I am far from a Dr. and we have no means, only what we get on this rented ranch. I also want all the information on baby care especially right young new born ones. If there is <u>anything</u> what I can do to escape being torn again wont you let me know. I am just 4 months along now but haven't quickened yet.

I am very Resp.

## CIRCA 1917
## KATE GORDON TO HER SON

In the middle of March, despite all efforts at diplomacy, three United States merchant ships were torpedoed by German submarines, and on April 2, Woodrow Wilson asked Congress for a declaration of war. In time, three children of a New York mother named Kate Gordon would go to fight. The youngest, eighteen-year-old Jimmy, was killed in battle. John and Luke would return home in 1919. Luke would die in 1922 as a result of a mustard-gas attack he had endured four years earlier. It is not known which of Gordon's three sons received this undated letter.
The quote is from Rudyard Kipling's dedication to his Barrack-Room Ballads: "He scarce had need to doff his pride or slough the dross of Earth— / E'en as he trod that day to God so walked he from his birth, / In simpleness and gentleness and honour and clean mirth."

My dear boy,

Your father says to tell you that he will give his son to his country, but that he will be ——— (never mind what!) if he will give all his new suspenders. He says you pinched three pairs from the top drawer of his dresser—he adds that he "is on to your curves."

Nora says you were very wise to take them, and she would give you all of hers, if she had any! Betty says to tell you that she hears Jack Ellis sails next week;—I know just how his mother will feel for those ten days while he is crossing. But she wouldn't have had him stay at home, any more than I would have had you! All the same, she won't have a good night's sleep until she hears he has landed. I keep thinking what a different world it will be to mothers; when you all come marching home again!

And when you do come marching home old fellow bring me back the same boy I gave my country,—true, and clean, and gentle, and brave. You must do this for your father and me and Betty and Nora;—and most of all, for the daughter you will give me one of these days! Dear, I don't know whether you have even met her yet,—but never mind that! Live for her or if God wills, die for her;—but do either with courage,—"with honour and clean mirth!" But I know you will come back to me—

Mother

### 1917: CIRCA JULY 2
### DAISY WESTBROOK TO LOUISE MADELLA

*America's entry into the war meant a boom in military industries, and in a movement known as the Great Migration, about a million black Americans came north in search of employment. In East St. Louis, Illinois, an estimated ten thousand blacks arrived between 1916 and 1917, and racial tensions became rampant. On July 2, one of the deadliest race riots of the twentieth century was responsible for about fifty deaths, thousands of injuries, and hundreds of thousands of dollars in property damage. High-school teacher Daisy Westbrook lived in the "Black Valley" section of the city along with her sister, mother, grandmother, and adopted baby. At first, their house was spared by white mobs, perhaps because of its stately appearance. From Missouri several weeks later, Westbrook described the ordeal in a letter to a friend.*

3946 W. Belle<br>St. Louis, Mo.

Dearest Louise:

Was <u>very</u> glad to hear from you. Your letter was forwarded from what used to be my house.

Louise, it was <u>awful</u>. I hardly know where to begin telling you about it. First I will say we lost everything but what we had on and that was very little—bungalow aprons, no hats, and sister did not have on any shoes.

It started early in the afternoon. We kept receiving calls over the 'phone to pack our trunks & leave, because it was going to be <u>awful</u> at night. We did not heed the calls, but sent grandma & the baby on to St. Louis, & said we would "stick" no matter what happened. At first, when the fire started, we stood on Broadway & watched it. As they neared our house we went in & went to the basement. It was too late to run then. They shot & yelled some thing awful, finally they reached our house. At first, they did not bother us (we watched from the basement window), they remarked that "white people live in that house, that is not a nigger house." Later, someone must have tipped them that it was a "nigger" house, because, after leaving us for about 20 min. they returned & started shooting in the house throwing bricks & yelling like mad "kill the 'niggers,' " burn that house.

It seemed the whole house was falling in on us. Then some one said, they must not be there; if they are they are certainly dead. Then some one shouted "they are in the basement. Surround them and burn it down." Then they ran down our steps. Only prayer saved us, we were under tubs & any thing we could find praying & keeping as quiet as possible, because if they had seen one face, we would have been shot or burned to death. When they were about to surround the house & burn it, we heard an awful noise & thought they were dynamiting the house. (The Broadway Theatre fell in, we learned later.) Sister tipped to the door to see if the house was on fire. She saw the reflection of a soldier on the front door—pulled it open quickly, & called for help. All of us ran out then, & was taken to the city hall for the night—(just as we were). The next morning, we learned our house was not burned, so we tried to get protection to go out & get clothes, & have the rest of the things put in storage. We could not, but were sent on to St. Louis. Had to walk across the bridge with a line of soldiers on each side—in the hot sun, no hats, & scarcely no clothing. When we reached St. Louis; we tried to get someone to go to our house, & get the things out, but were not successful.

On Tuesday evening at 6 o'clock our house was burned with two soldiers on guard. So the papers stated. We were told that they looted the house before burning it. We are in St. Louis now trying to start all over again. Louise it is so hard to think we had just gotten to the place where we could take care of our mother & grandmother well, & to think, all was destroyed in one night. We had just bought some new furniture & I was preparing to go away, & had bought some beautiful dresses. Most of my jewelry was lost also. I had on three rings, my watch bracelet and LaValliere—Everything else was lost. 9 rings, a watch, bracelet, brooch, locket, and some more things. I miss my piano more than anything else.

The people here are very nice to us. Several of our friends have brought us clothing, bed clothes etc.

Tell me how you got in the Gov. Printing Office. Do you take an examination, if so what does it consist of. I might take it. I have had a <u>good</u> position in E. St. L., but don't know whether there will be enough children to teach there this fall or not. People are moving out so fast. The papers did not describe all the horrors. It was awful. People we[re] being shot down & thrown back into fire if they tried to escape. Some were shot & then burned; others were dragged around with ropes about their necks, one man was hung to a telegraph post. We saw two men shot down. One was almost in front of our house. One man & his wife, a storekeeper, were burned alive, a cross in front of our house.

I must close now    it makes me blue to talk about it    Write again.

Tell Miss Black I received her card. Will you tell Florene & Mrs. Bowie, I haven't their address. Will expect to hear from you <u>real</u> soon. All send love.

Lovingly,<br>Daisy

**1917: JULY 25**

**JULIA STIMSON TO HER FAMILY**

---

*A native of Worcester, Massachusetts, and a graduate of Vassar, Julia Catherine Stimson (1881–1948) began her nursing career at New York Hospital in 1904 and by 1917 was serving at a base hospital in Rouen, France. She would go on to become chief nurse of American Red Cross Nursing in Paris and, later, superintendent of the Army Nurse Corps. She would receive the Distinguished Service Medal as well as honors from Britain, France, and the International Red Cross. But in 1917, when she wrote this letter to her family, she was coming face-to-face with the carnage of war for the first time.*

July 25, 1917.

I do not know how to write about our doings of the past few days, for I cannot write numbers, and it is only numbers that would give you any idea at all of what we have been doing. I wrote in my last letter, I think it was, that we were not working hard, well, we have begun our hard work, and for our own sakes we are glad of it. In the past 24 hours we have admitted more patients than the total capacity of the Barnes and Children's Hospital, not the average number of patients, but the total capacity. And all these patients have been bathed, fed, and had their wounds dressed. Some of course were able to walk and could go to the bath house and the mess tents, but most of them to-day are stretcher cases, and oh, so dirty, hungry, and miserable. The mere (I say mere, but it is really the most important part of the whole thing) proper recording of the names, numbers, ranks, nearest relatives etc., is in itself a huge task. Of course the nurses don't have all that to do, but they have a lot of it. The boys who are stretcher bearers must be so lame, they can hardly move, for just consider what it means to lift down out of ambulances as many patients as that, and then afterwards carry them as far sometimes as a city block, for we filled our farthest tents to-day. It is most remarkable how things have gone. There are many aching backs to-night, for all the beds are very low and the stooping is terrific, but every one has been a brick. Many of the nurses have worked 14 straight hours to-day, and many of the doctors had only two or three hours' sleep last night, and were working all day. The difficulty to-day was, that we had to put patients into rows of tents that have not been used for some time and were not equipped, and our warning was not long enough to prepare. We had the beds ready, but little else. To-night things have straightened out a lot, but it is going to be a busy night as we are to send out a convoy, and get another in. Three additional night nurses are on to-night, taken from the day force that has to stretch itself a little thinner.

Our nurses don't need any "Hate Lecture" after what we have seen in the past few days. We have been receiving patients that have been gassed, and burned in a most mysterious way. Their clothing is not burned at all, but they have bad burns on their bodies, on parts that are covered by clothing. The doctors think it has been done by some chemical that gets its full action on the skin after it is moist, and when the men sweat, it is in these places that are the most moist that the burns are the worst. The Germans have been using a kind of oil in bombs, the men say it is oil of mustard. These bombs explode and the men's eyes, noses, and throats are so irritated they do not detect the poison gas fumes that come from the bombs that follow these oil ones, and so they either inhale it and die like flies, or have a delayed action and are affected by it terribly several hours later. We have had a lot of these delayed-action gassed men, who cough and cough continuously, like children with whooping cough. We had a very bad case the other night who had not slept one hour for four nights or days, and whose coughing paroxysms came every minute and a half by the clock. When finally the nurses got him to sleep, after rigging up a croup tent over him so that he could breathe steam from a croupkettle over a little stove that literally had to be held in the hands to make it burn properly, they said they were ready to get down on their knees in gratitude, his anguish had been so terrible to watch. They said they could not wish the Germans any greater unhappiness than to have them have to witness the sufferings of a man like that and know that they had been the cause of it. It is diabolical the things they do, simply fiendish, and like the things that would be expected from precocious degenerates.

I cannot imagine what kind of change is going to take place in our minds before we get home. There are so many changes coming over our ideas every day. They are not new ideas, for many people have had them before, since the beginning of this war, but they are new to us. Human life seems so insignificant, and individuals are so unimportant. No one over here thinks in any numbers less than 50 or 100, and what can the serious condition of Private John Brown of something or other, Something Street, Birmingham, matter? One's mind is torn between the extremes of such feelings, for when a nurse takes the pulse of a wounded sleeping man and he wakes just enough to say "Mother," she goes to pieces in her heart, just as though he weren't only one of the hundreds of wounded men in just this one hospital.

This morning when the big rush was on, I was in the receiving tent when the last three men were unloaded: One had his head and eyes all bandaged up and seemed in very bad condition, so I went with the stretcher bearers to see if I could help get him into bed. The eye specialist was sent for at once, and got there in a few minutes. We untied the big triangular bandage that was keeping the wads of cotton on his head and eyes, and found his eyes in a terrible condition from being bandaged for over 24 hours without attention. We soaked off the dressings with some boric solution that I had procured from the Operating Hut. There was not even a single basin in the tent to which the man had been brought, not to mention a nurse or medicines. After a while we got the eyes open a tiny bit so that they could be examined and washed out a little, and then the doctor blew out: "It's a perfect crime to send a man down here in this condition, look at this puncture wound of this eye, and see what a terrible condition his eyes are in. A whole lifetime of blindness will probably be the result." The patient was delirious and quite incapable of understanding. Just then an older officer came along and heard the remark and said: "Crime! my dear boy, you've got absolutely the wrong point of view. How could they keep a man like this up there at the front, from which they have sent him? Don't you realize that at a place like that every wounded man is simply a hindrance and must be gotten out of the way? Just stop and think how well they are doing to get so many of them to us in any decent shape at all." Then the other one said: "Oh, I suppose so. War's the thing now, all right." After he was dressed, and things had been straightened out a bit, this patient was transferred to one of the lines that is better equipped to take care of such serious cases. He was put on the "Dangerously Ill," and word was sent to his mother! His head injury is bad, so maybe he wont live to be blind. (Later. He is much better now and will get well and probably have the sight of one eye.)

No man leaves here in his own clothes. It couldn't be done. All the things have to be sent to be disinfected and then they go to the clothes tent, and then are just drawn, as clothes for so many men, when the convoys go out. That is unless they are going to the Convalescent Camp or back to a base, then they are fitted as nearly as possible and given a full equipment, but the men going to England are fixed up just so that they can travel. They are lucky if they can stick to their little comfort bags in which are their little treasures. Just so many pins that must have so many moves is all they are. And they are so good and patient. They are so grateful, it just makes everybody wish she were a dozen people and could do twelve times as much as she can possibly do with her one set of arms and legs.

But what will we think when we get through with it all? How are we going to stand the mental strain? Yet others do, and go on being normal, cheerful human beings, teaching bayoneting one hour, and playing tennis the next, or having tea with pretty nurses. Oh, it's a queer world! as the orderly said who came to tell me of a few more hundred wounded expected in soon. "Isn't it a cruel world?"

### 1917: DECEMBER

### ROSE WINSLOW TO HER HUSBAND AND TO MEMBERS OF THE NATIONAL WOMAN'S PARTY

*With American men overseas, the war offered American women new possibilities— not only for hard and important work, but also for political leverage. In 1917, Alice Paul and a group of suffragists started picketing the White House on a nearly daily basis, demanding the vote. The presence of these self-named "Silent Sentinels," as well as their placards ("Mr. President How Long Must Women Wait for Liberty") was a constant affront to Woodrow Wilson and an embarrassment before visiting dignitaries. In June of 1917, the first six women were arrested, and eleven more on July 4, on charges of obstructing traffic. Rose Winslow was among one group sentenced to seven months in prison. After staging a hunger strike—in which the women asked to be treated as political, not criminal, prisoners—they were brutally force-fed. The letter below is comprised of a series of notes smuggled out from the prison hospital to Winslow's husband and her friends.*

If this thing is necessary we will naturally go through with it. Force is so stupid a weapon. I feel so happy doing my bit for decency—for <u>our</u> war, which is after all, real and fundamental. . . .

The women are all so magnificent, so beautiful. Alice Paul is as thin as ever, pale and large-eyed. We have been in solitary for five weeks. There is nothing to tell but that the days go by somehow. I have felt quite feeble the last few days— faint, so that I could hardly get my hair brushed, my arms ached so. But to-day I am well again. Alice Paul and I talk back and forth though we are at opposite ends of the building and a hall door also shuts us apart. But occasionally— thrills—we escape from behind our iron-barred doors and visit. Great laughter and rejoicing! . . .

My fainting probably means nothing except that I am not strong after these weeks. I know you won't be alarmed.

I told about a syphilitic colored woman with one leg. The other one was cut off, having rotted so that it was alive with maggots when she came in. The remaining one is now getting as bad. They are so short of nurses that a little colored girl of twelve, who is here waiting to have her tonsils removed, waits on her. This child and two others share a ward with a syphilitic child of three or four years, whose mother refused to have it at home. It makes you absolutely ill to see it. I am going to break all three windows as a protest against their confining Alice Paul with these!

Dr. Gannon is chief of a hospital. Yet Alice Paul and I found we had been taking baths in one of the tubs here, in which this syphilitic child, an incurable, who has his eyes bandaged all the time, is also bathed. He has been here a year. Into the room where he lives came yesterday two children to be operated on for tonsillitis. They also bathed in the same tub. The syphilitic woman has been in that room seven months. Cheerful mixing, isn't it? The place is alive with roaches, crawling all over the walls, everywhere. I found one in my bed the other day. . . .

There is great excitement about my two syphilitics. Each nurse is being asked whether she told me. So, as in all institutions where an unsanitary fact is made public, no effort is made to make the wrong itself right. All hands fall to, to find the culprit, who made it known, and he is punished. . . .

Alice Paul is in the psychopathic ward. She dreaded forcible feeding frightfully, and I hate to think how she must be feeling. I had a nervous time of it, gasping a long time afterward, and my stomach rejecting during the process. I spent a bad, restless night, but otherwise I am all right. The poor soul who fed me got liberally besprinkled during the process. I heard myself making the most hideous sounds, like an animal in pain, and thought how dreadful it was of me to make such horrible sounds. . . . One feels so forsaken when one lies prone and people shove a pipe down one's stomach. . . .

This morning but for an astounding tiredness, I am all right. I am waiting to see what happens when the President realizes that brutal bullying isn't quite a statesmanlike method for settling a demand for justice at home. At least, if men are supine enough to endure, women—to their eternal glory—are not. . . .

They took down the boarding from Alice Paul's window yesterday, I heard. It is so delicious about Alice and me. Over in the jail a rumor began that I was considered insane and would be examined. Then came Doctor White, and said he had come to see "the thyroid case." When they left we argued about the matter, neither of us knowing which was considered "suspicious." She insisted it was she, and, as it happened, she was right. Imagine any one thinking Alice Paul needed to be "under observation!" The thick-headed idiots! . . .

Yesterday was a bad day for me in feeding. I was vomiting continually during the process. The tube has developed an irritation somewhere that is painful.

Never was there a sentence like ours for such an offense as ours, even in England. No woman ever got it over there even for tearing down buildings. And during all that agitation <u>we</u> were busy saying that never would such things happen in the United States. The men told us they would not endure such frightfulness. . . .

Mary Beard and Helen Todd were allowed to stay only a minute, and I cried like a fool. I am getting over that habit, I think.

I fainted again last night. I just fell flop over in the bathroom where I was washing my hands and was led to bed when I recovered, by a nurse. I lost consciousness just as I got there again. I felt horribly faint until 12 o'clock, then fell asleep for awhile. . . .

I was getting frantic because you seemed to think Alice was with me in the hospital. She was in the psychopathic ward. The same doctor feeds us both, and told me. Don't let them tell you we take this well. Miss Paul vomits much. I do, too, except when I'm not nervous, as I have been every time against my will. I try to be less feeble-minded. It's the nervous reaction, and I can't control it much. I don't imagine bathing one's food in tears very good for one.

We think of the coming feeding all day. It is horrible. The doctor thinks I take it well. I hate the thought of Alice Paul and the others if I take it well. . . .

We still get no mail; we are "insubordinate." It's strange, isn't it; if you ask for food fit to eat, as we did, you are "insubordinate"; and if you refuse food you are "insubordinate." Amusing. I am really all right. If this continues very long I perhaps won't be. I am interested to see how long our so-called "splendid American men" will stand for this form of discipline.

All news cheers one marvelously because it is hard to feel anything but a bit desolate and forgotten here in this place.

All the officers here know we are making this hunger strike that women fighting for liberty may be considered political prisoners; we have told them. God knows we don't want other women ever to have to do this over again.

## 1918: NOVEMBER 29
## MAUDE FISHER TO MRS. HOGAN

*Like smallpox during the Revolutionary War, influenza was a foe without nationality. Between 1918 and 1919, it was responsible for the deaths of 550,000 Americans and, internationally, between 20 and 40 million people. During World War I the flu killed as many American soldiers (about 43,000) as combat did. One of the victims was Richard Hogan, whose Red Cross nurse, Maude Fisher, wrote this letter to his mother just days after the armistice was declared.*
Although Fisher didn't know it, Mrs. Hogan had already lost two other children to the flu epidemic back home in Massachusetts.

November 29th, 1918.

My dear Mrs. Hogan:

If I could talk to you I could tell you so much better about your son's last sickness, and all the little things that mean so much to a mother far away from her boy.

Your son was brought to this hospital on the 13th of November very sick with what they called Influenza. This soon developed into Pneumonia. He was brave and cheerful though, and made a good fight with the disease. Several days he seemed much better, and seemed to enjoy some fruit that I brought him. He did not want you to worry about his being sick, but I told him I thought we ought to let you know, and he said all right.

He became very weak towards the last of his sickness and slept all the time. One day while I was visiting some of the other patients he woke up and seeing me with my hat on asked the orderly if I was his sister come to see him. He was always good and patient and the nurses loved him. Everything was done to make him comfortable and I think he suffered very little, if any pain.

He laughed and talked to the people around him as long as he was able. They wanted to move him to another bed after he became real sick and moved the new bed up close to his, but he shook his head, that he didn't want to move. The orderly, a fine fellow, urged him. "Come on, Hogan," he said, "Move to this new bed. It's lots better than the one you're in." But Hogan shook his head still.

"No," he said, "No, I'll stay where I am. If that bed was better than mine, you'd 'a' had it long ago."

The last time I saw him I carried him a cup of hot soup, but he was too weak to do anything but taste it, and went back to sleep.

The Chaplain saw him several times and had just left him when he breathed his last on November 25th, at 2:30 in the afternoon.

He was laid to rest in the little cemetery of Commercy, and sleeps under a simple white wooden cross among his comrades who, like him, have died for their country. His grave number is 22, plot 1. His aluminum identification tag is on the cross, and a similar one is around his neck, both bearing his serial number, 2793346.

The plot of the grave in the cemetery where your son is buried was given to the Army for our boys and the people of Commercy will always tend it with loving hands and keep it fresh and clean. I enclose here a few leaves from the grass that grows near in a pretty meadow.

A big hill overshadows the place and the sun was setting behind it just as the Chaplain said the last prayer over your boy.

He prayed that the people at home might have great strength now for the battle that is before them, and we do ask that for you now.

The country will always honor your boy, because he gave his life for it, and it will also love and honor you for the gift of your boy, but be assured, that the sacrifice is not in vain, and the world is better today for it.

From the whole hospital force, accept deepest sympathy and from myself, tenderest love in your hour of sorrow.

Sincerely,
Maude B. Fisher

## 1919: MARCH 7
## AGNES VON KUROWSKY TO ERNEST HEMINGWAY

*No one seems entirely sure about the origin of the phrase "Dear John letter," although many researchers date it to World War II. Whatever she might have called it, Agnes von Kurowsky (1892–1984) was writing just that when she penned this letter to a young Ernest Hemingway (1899–1961). Hemingway, who was an ambulance driver in Italy in 1918, had been wounded and had fallen in love with Kurowsky, an American Red Cross nurse. He had just turned nineteen, and she was seven years older. The affair did leave one lasting result, however; namely, the character of Catherine in* A Farewell to Arms.

March 7, 1919

Ernie, dear boy,

I am writing this late at night after a long think by myself, & I am afraid it is going to hurt you, but, I'm sure it won't harm you permanently.

For quite awhile before you left, I was trying to convince myself it was a real love-affair, because, we always seemed to disagree, & then arguments always wore me out so that I really gave in to keep you from doing something desperate.

Now, after a couple of months away from you, I know that I am still very fond of you, but, it is more as a mother than as a sweetheart. It's alright to say I'm a Kid, but, I'm not, & I'm getting less & less so every day.

So, Kid (still Kid to me, & always will be) can you forgive me some day for unwittingly deceiving you? You know I'm not really bad, & don't mean to do wrong, & now I realize it was my fault in the beginning that you cared for me, & regret it from the bottom of my heart. But, I am now & always will be too old, & that's the truth, & I can't get away from the fact that you're just a boy—a kid.

I somehow feel that some day I'll have reason to be proud of you, but, dear boy, I can't wait for that day, & it is wrong to hurry a career.

I tried hard to make you understand a bit of what I was thinking on that trip from Padua to Milan, but, you acted like a spoiled child, & I couldn't keep on hurting you. Now, I only have the courage because I'm far away.

Then—& believe me when I say this is sudden for me, too—I expect to be married soon. And I hope & pray that after you have thought things out, you'll be able to forgive me & start a wonderful career & show what a man you really are.

Ever admiringly & fondly
Your friend
Aggie

## 1919: JUNE 21
## HILDA ROSE TO A FRIEND

*Hilda Rose was teaching school in Illinois when she contracted tuberculosis and moved west for her health. After five years in Montana, she married a man twenty-*

*seven years older than she was, whom she called "Daddy." She had a son, cared for two orphans—and became starved for intellectual stimulation. One winter she wrote to the* Chicago Tribune *asking for "books that nobody cared for any more." Volumes and letters followed, and gradually she became friends with some of the women who had responded. "I have no women to talk to, so I will write to ease my brain," she once explained. The letters that resulted captured a rugged, harsh life on a frontier that had changed little despite the new century.*

June 21, 1919

We are friends now, so we won't stand on ceremony. At last! At last! I am going to have friends who will be glad to see me when I go back to the world for a visit or to stay. Time will tell, but I presume that it will be when I am old and gray.

I can see one farmhouse from here, but it's about a mile off and the inmates are impossible. The nearest "shack," about as big as a henhouse on the easy, is inhabited by a crippled grandmother and her son. I tramp through the woods to see her once in a while. She is very poor and ignorant, but I like her, and she treats me like an equal.

On the west I am bounded by the woods, and also on the north. So there isn't much to see, as we live in a depression, or small valley, on this shelf or bench. I can't go anywhere very often, though I do get out for at least one picnic every summer, given by the Farmers' Union. I belong to it, but I have to go alone, as Daddy is so old he doesn't like to go anywhere any more. So whenever I can, I take the boy and go. But it's the winters that are trying. That is why I had to have something to read, or go crazy.

You don't know how anxiously I look in the glass as the years go by, and wonder if I'll ever get to look like the rest of the natives here. You have seen overworked farmers' wives, with weather-wrung and sorrow-beaten faces, drooping mouths, and a sad look.

I want to go back, I don't care where, and have friends once more. I must not look like that—No! No! I want to be elected president of a club, and go to socials, and I want to eat ice cream. I also would love to live for a few years in a college town. Would n't that be grand? And then I'd teach kindergarten a few years, and join a card club. But the truth of the matter is that I'll probably spend the rest of my life right here. But dreams don't hurt—nor do air castles, and maybe they'll come true.

For the third year we are having a drought. Each year has been a little dryer, until this summer, and I don't believe we'll get any hay at all. Daddy and I thought we were getting along well until the dry years came. Then we sold the old cow and bought feed for the calves. Last summer they went, all but a few head, to buy feed for the team, and food for us, and we got into debt besides. I could n't stand it. Daddy was nearly beside himself with worry, so I wrote to the <u>Tribune</u> for reading matter. All winter I have read aloud to Daddy and helped him to forget. We went through a siege of the flu also this winter, so our dear Daddy is practically an invalid. He may get stronger after a while. Ruth and I do the chores which are not many. What we are going to live on this winter I don't know. Something may turn up. We may get a rain before it is too late.

By religion I don't know what I am. I never could decide. Daddy says I'm an atheist, but I hope not. Sometimes I doubt if there is God. He seems so terribly cruel to his children. And what is he and where? My brother says I am an agnostic. They don't believe anything, you know.

### 1920: AUGUST
### FEBB BURN TO HARRY BURN

---

*The organized campaign for women's suffrage in the United States had been going on since the first convention in Seneca Falls in 1848 (see page 195); an amendment to the Constitution had been formally proposed in 1878 and again in 1914. In 1918, under the leadership of Carrie Chapman Catt and others, the amendment was finally carried in both houses, and it went back to the states for ratification. Thirty-six states were needed, and as of June 1920, thirty-five states had passed it. In Tennessee, the "War of the Roses" evolved, with prosuffrage voters wearing yellow roses, and antisuffrage voters wearing red. The Tennessee senate passed the amendment, but the initial vote in the house showed a 48–48 tie. Then Harry Burn (1895–1977), at twenty-six the youngest legislator in the state, received this letter from his mother, Febb King Ensminger Burn (1873–1945). Despite the fact that he had been wearing a red rose, he voted in favor of suffrage, and the Nineteenth Amendment passed.*

Dear Son:

Hurrah, and vote for suffrage! Don't keep them in doubt. I noticed some of the speeches against. They were bitter. I have been watching to see how you stood, but have not noticed anything yet. Don't forget to be a good boy and help Mrs. Catt put the "rat" in ratification.

Signed,
Your Mother

*Fan mail to the new silent movie stars was the rage when a Norton, Kansas, surgeon's wife wrote this paean to a different kind of idol: Thomas Edison (1847–1931). Holder of more than a thousand patents, inventor of the incandescent lamp, the phonograph, key elements of the telephone and the motion-picture system, Edison had arguably done more than any other individual to usher in the modern age. Though Lathrop still described her wifely role in traditional terms, she also evidently knew a revolution when she saw one.*

The "U.P." was the Union-Pacific Railroad. A mangle is an ironing machine with heated rollers. Fritz Kreisler was a popular Austrian-born violinist; Alma Gluck and Amelita Galli-Curci were singers.

Norton, Kans.
March 5, 1921

Mr. Edison.

Dear sir:

It is not always the privilege of a woman to thank personally the inventor of articles which make life liveable for her sex. I feel that it is my duty as well as privilege to tell you how much we women of the small town are indebted to you for our pleasures as well as our utmost needs. I am a college graduate and probably my husband is one of the best known surgeons between Topeka and Denver. I am an officer in the District of Women's Club as well as President of our Town Organization.

We have four children. The oldest lad expects to have a telegraph station in the Summer on the U.P. We have a large house so you see when doing practically all my own work, my duties are many and my activities most varied, yet I enjoy my labors and do not feel that I entirely neglect to get pleasure out of life. Positively as I hear my wash machine chugging along, down in the Laundry, as I write this it does seem as though I am entirely dependent on the fertile brain of one thousand miles away for every pleasure and labor saving device I have. The house is lighted by electricity. I cook on a Westinghouse electric range, wash dishes in an electric dish washer. An electric fan even helps to distribute the heat over part of the house. (at our private hospital electricity helps to heat some of the rooms). I wash clothes in an electric machine and iron on an electric mangle and with an electric iron. I clean house with electric cleaners. I rest, take an electric massage and curl my hair on an electric iron. Dress in a gown sewed on a machine run by a motor. Then start the Victrola and either study Spanish for a while or listen to Kreisler and Gluck and Galli-Curci in almost heavenly strains, forgetting I'm living in a tiny town of two thousand where nothing much ever happens but am recalled when the automatic in my stove releases and know my dinner is now cooking. The Doctor comes home, tired with a days work wherein electricity has played almost as much part as it has at home, to find a wife not tired and dissatisfied but a woman waiting who has worked faithfully believing that work is beneficial and who is now rested and ready to serve the tired man and discuss affairs of the day. To play him a beautiful piece on the Victrola and possibly see a masterpiece at the "Movies."

Possibly he brings in a guest without warning but electricity and a pressure cooker save the day for the hostess. Indeed, I've entertained the Governor of our State and a dozen of our rep. citizens at a little more than an hours notice—at luncheon, but that was one of my pleasures, unexpected but none the less a real one.

Please accept the thanks Mr. Edison of one most truly appreciative woman. I know I am only one of many under the same debt of gratitude to you and while I also know you must have received the thanks of other women before yet a word may not be unwelcome to you. I believe men are like women after all and like to know that their labor is appreciated and I do think the world is inclined to be too parsimonius in the praises of work and value.

Sincerely<br>Mrs. W. C. Lathrop

### 1924: JANUARY

### EDNA ST. VINCENT MILLAY TO EUGEN JAN BOISSEVAIN

*Though at times it haunted her, Edna St. Vincent Millay (1892–1950) became famous for writing a four-line poem: "My candle burns at both ends; / It will not last the night; / But ah, my foes, and oh, my friends— / It gives a lovely light!" She was already in her late twenties and the author of many other poems and several plays when "First Fig" was published in her book* A Few Figs from Thistles, *but it became a kind of signature for her—as well as for the rebellion and recklessness of youth in the Roaring Twenties. In 1923, she married Eugen Jan Boissevain (1880–1949), a Dutch businessman. The same year, she won the Pulitzer Prize for*

Ballad of the Harp-Weaver. *This letter, written while Millay was on a trip to Chicago, captured some of her spirit—as well as her frustration with fame.*
"Arthur" was probably the poet Arthur Davison Ficke, a friend and former lover. Abie the Agent was a Jewish comic-strip character.

Chicago & Northwestern Station<br>10: 25 A.M. Wednesday

Darling:

I have made my train, & here I sit. The thing is just about to pull out. The conductor has just called <u>all aboard</u> in the most musical & lovely way—sort of like this—

I put this down here not because it's done right, but because I want to remember how it goes, & this is near enough.

———————

Did you ever go from Chicago to Cedar Rapids on one of these Middle-Western so-called Parlor-cars?—Well, don't. The only difference I see between this & the day-coach is that in the day-coach you have one person at your elbow, & you see the backs of several people's heads, & if you are lucky you get a seat by the window & can look out:—whereas,—in the Parlor-Car you have two people at your elbow—one at the right & one at the left, you stare into the faces of a long row of people, and your chair is nailed with its back to the window so that you couldn't possibly see a thing, even if you should happen to want to, which I should say is unlikely; you have no place at all to put your luggage, because right in front of your feet is the aisle where people walk back & forth; you are squeezed together as tight as in seats at the theatre; you couldn't possibly lean your head on the back of your chair, because it isn't high enough,—also, it has no white towel on it—well, in fact it is just like the subway when the subway comes up for air at 137th Street. And I am to spend six hours in this chair. Though I imagine they have a diner. If it is as funny as this I shall die. Ask Arthur why he never told me about these terrible trains.

———————

My hands are so dirty it's almost theatrical. Everybody who looks at me wonders why such a nice girl, with such a beautiful gold pencil, & such expensive cuff-links, & such a refined & elegant address-book, has such dirty hands.—I don't care. I'm tired of washing my hands. It's a great waste of time. Besides, in the winter it's dangerous. It is likely to roughen the skin.

———————

The men's & women's toilets are directly opposite one another, at the end of the car. If a man & a woman started to come out of them at the same moment, & turned to shut the door, they would bump backsides.

I got through my two readings yesterday well enough—the one in the afternoon in Evanston was a great success—a crowded house, large audience, etc.— But the one in the evening was in a private house!—A bunch of wealthy people come together to see what I looked like, & bet with each other as to how many of my naughty poems I would dare to read.—My hostess herself & her children were sweet & real people, & intelligent. There were a few women who came up & talked to me who had really liked some of the poems besides the Figs from Thistles; & one man, who was motoring back to Chicago & brought me home, was really a delight, awfully nice & clever & amusing, & seemed to know all my books by heart.—He said his seventeen-year-old daughter also knows my poems by heart.—But on the whole—oh, Jesus!—If ever I felt like a prostitute it was last night.—I kept saying over & over to myself while I was reading to them, "Never mind—it's a hundred & fifty dollars."—I hope I shall never write a poem again that more than five people will like.

The two gentlemen opposite me have just decided to have a friendly little morning chaw of gum together.—The one on my right is following with much concern the fortunes of Abie the Agent in the Chicago Evening American.

———————

It's wonderful to write to you, my dearest. It takes the sting out of almost anything, I find. I wanted you so last night. I was pretty unhappy. And of course I was tired, too.—I had to get up early this morning, because I made a sudden decision to check out of the Hotel Windermere & never look upon its face again,—so I had to pack & it takes an hour to get from the hotel to the station, & I had to take a 10: 30 train. This is a hard-luck letter, so I'll just keep on, & tell you about the Windermere Hotel, which is the God-damndest place I ever set an unwary foot in. You know, it advertises itself as Chicago's Most Home-like Hotel. Well, that's it. It's so . . . home-like that if you want a cup of coffee you have to go down to the kitchen & make it yourself.—Yesterday morning my train was about two hours late getting into Chicago, & I was an hour getting from the station to the hotel, & when I finally got into my room & took down the receiver to order breakfast, this is the conversation which took place:

I:—Room service, please.

Voice:—Do you want it from the East or from the West?

I:—What?

Voice:—Do you want it from the East or from the West?

I:—How do I know?—I don't know what you're talking about. I'm a stranger here. I want a cup of coffee. I don't care where it comes from.

Voice:—Well, some people want it from the East. But of course it has to come through the tunnel then, & it's likely to get cold.

I:—Well, then, that settles it. I don't want it cold. So send it from the West.—Hello!—Hello!—Operator! (Silence.)

I:—(After a pause, taking down receiver) Operator, give me the West Room Service, please.

Voice:—There is no West Room Service.

I:—Well, but what am I going to do? I want a cup of coffee!—They told me—(sound of receiver being hung up).

Voice:—(after a pause) Room Service!

I:—Hello, this is Room 275 West speaking.—Will you kindly take an order for breakfast?

Voice:—This is the East, Madam. Do you want it from the East?

I:—I don't <u>know</u>!—I don't <u>care</u>!—I'm dying for a cup of coffee! Won't you please send it up?

Voice:—You want it from the East, then?

I:—(very calmly) Would you mind telling me what is the difference? Voice:—Well, some people like to have it from the East,—but of course there's a difference in price—

I:—I don't care anything about the price. Will you please send me at once a pot of coffee, half a grape-fruit & some Kellogg's Bran?—(Yes, I did, U-geen).

Voice:—Coffee, one half grape-fruit, Kellogg's Bran. (Receiver goes up.)

I:—(a few minutes later)—Operator, will you give me the Porter, please. I want to enquire about trains.

Voice:—Did you give in a breakfast order to the East, Madam?

I:—I did.

Voice.—Well, I'll give you the West.

I:—I don't <u>want</u> the West. I've got it all fixed up with the East. The East & I understand each other perfectly.—Operator!—Operator!

Voice:—Kitchen!

I:—Is this the East or the West?

Voice:—This is the West.

I:—Well, I'm sorry. The operator has called you by mistake. I've already given my order to the East Room Service.

Voice:—Is this Room 275?

I:—Yes.

Voice.—Well, you see, Madam, you're in the West, and—

I:—I know—I know all about that. You have me there.—But, <u>please</u>, won't you send me up a cup of coffee at once! I've just come in on the train, & I'm dying for a cup of coffee! Never mind the rest!— Just coffee!—Will you send it up at once?

Voice:—Sorry. But we work by rotation. You'll have to wait your turn.

I:—How long will that be?

Voice:—I couldn't say, Madam. You see, you're in the West, and—

I:—No, God help me, I'm in the Middle West! (I fall on the floor in a cataleptic fit.)

(Curtain)

I've just been into the diner & had my luncheon. I feel a little better. They certainly eat a lot of pork.

It's amusing to think how entirely, <u>totally</u>, ABSOLUTELY different everything would be if you were in this chair beside me.—It makes me laugh, it's so funny that there could be such a difference.—Oh, it will be so lovely when we go around the earth together!—I told some people yesterday that we are going to Java & China in March.—Why not?—For we are, we are!—Aren't we?

I will let you know as soon as I find another hotel in Chicago. It will be difficult, for everything's full up. But I won't go back to that Christless Windermere West if I have to sleep in the stock-yard. In the meantime, in case you didn't get my wire, address me <u>care of Margaret Burns, 1209 East 60th St., Chicago</u>.—I have given this address to the Windermere for forwarding.

There's a man getting off at this station, which is called <u>Sterling</u>. The porter just brushed him off, standing just in front of me. This is the porter's little trick. He brushes the dust from the man getting off at this station, onto the man getting off at the next station,—& business flourishes.—Well, darling, I have poured out all my troubles.—None of them matters, when I think of you.—

Edna.

*   *   *

### 1924: AUGUST

### MARY MacARTHUR TO JOHN J. PERSHING

*The world war was over, peace was at hand, and the country was in the midst of the Roaring Twenties. But for Mary Pinkney Hardy MacArthur (1852–1935), the ever-ambitious mother of a forty-four-year-old Douglas MacArthur, 1924 was no time for relaxing. MacArthur had served as chief of staff, brigade commander, and divisional commander in France during World War I; he had been named superintendent of West Point after the war. But in 1922, MacArthur married a woman with whom Chief of Staff General John J. Pershing (1860–1948) had had an affair, and Pershing sent him to the Philippines, possibly a semibanishment. Mary MacArthur, who had known Pershing since her husband and he had served together, sent this appeal to him. Apparently, it worked. Ten days after Pershing's resignation, MacArthur became the youngest major general in U.S. Army history. In 1930, he himself would be made chief of staff.*

Confidential My dear General Pershing:

It was a real joy to see you on Saturday looking still so young and wonderfully handsome!

I think you will never grow old. I have felt particularly unhappy since I had my little heart-to-heart chat with you. It is just because I know You to be such a noble, broadminded and just man and friend that I am presuming on long and loyal friendship for you—to open my heart in this appeal for my Boy—and ask if you can't find it convenient to give him his promotion during Your regime as Chief of Staff?

He now stands number 7th on the list. He made good on the battlefields in France—And I have your fine letter to him written in France, telling him that you had recommended him to be a Major General. The mear fact that he is younger in years than other deserving officers should not be sufficient reason for overslaughing him again—And of course you must know that every junior man the Department places above him, becomes an actual punishment to him that will last for a life time. Men of great prominence, as well as men at large—have told me that the whole country would approve his promotion. You are so powerful in all Army matters, that you could give him his promotion by the stroke of your pen! You have never failed me yet—and somehow I feel you will not in this request. Your own life is so full to overflowing with joys and happiness—and deserving success—that it may be hard for you to understand the heartaches and bitter disappointments in the lives of others. Won't you be real good and sweet—The "Dear Old Jack" of long ago—and give me some assurance that you will give my Boy his well earned promotion before you leave the Army? I would rather have this promotion from your hands—than from any other hands in the world. I pledge to keep absolutely to myself—in strictest confidence—any hope you may give me in this matter. If I had the power—there is nothing on earth I would not do for you to prove my loyalty and admiration for you. God bless You—and crown your valuable life—by taking you to the White House.

Faithfully your friend<br>Mary P. MacArthur

## 1925: CIRCA MAY
## LILLIAN AURORA TO JOHN SCOPES

*The trial of John Scopes (1900–1970) in Dayton, Tennessee, for teaching the theory of evolution would become famous for its dramatic clash between Clarence Darrow (for Darwin and the defense) and William Jennings Bryan (for the Bible and the prosecution). This telegram, from an actress to the defendant, captured some of the circus atmosphere that preceded the "Monkey Trial" and only intensified as the case went on.*

If the personal appearance of a highly educated chimpanzee will be of any assistance to you in arranging your defense, I tender you the services of "Smoky Ci," famous moving picture chimpanzee, without any fees.

Lillian Aurora

## 1925: JULY 9
## AIMEE SEMPLE McPHERSON TO WILLIAM JENNINGS BRYAN

*A wildly popular evangelist and radio preacher, Aimee Semple McPherson (1890–1944) sent this telegram of support to prosecutor William Jennings Bryan (1860–1925) on the day before the Scopes trial opened.*
The judge focused the trial on the specifics of the accusation, not the theory of the law. Scopes was found guilty and fined $100. Bryan died just days after the trial ended.

Ten thousand members of Angelus Temple with her missions of radio church membership send grateful appreciation of your lion-hearted championship of the Bible against evolution and throw our hats in the ring with you for God and the Bible as is. Constant prayer during week all night prayer Saturday night.

Sunday afternoon Bible parade. Mass meeting and trial with hanging and burial of monkey teachers Tennessee can count on us.

Aimee Semple McPherson

# EXCHANGE

### 1926: MARCH
### A <u>PHOTOPLAY</u> READER AND CAROLYN VAN WYCK

---

*The advice column that had been started by Beatrice Fairfax (see page 413) had spawned a host of imitators, including one "Carolyn Van Wyck," whose column (no doubt pseudonymous) appeared in the pages of* Photoplay *magazine. Petting (i.e., making out, necking) was just one of the decade's favorite bits of slang. Others included* let's blouse *for "let's go,"* butt me *for "give me a cigarette,"* handcuff *for "engagement ring," and* biscuit *for a flapper who would pet, possibly even with a young man who might call himself a* snugglepup.

The quote in Van Wyck's response is from the Bible, Matthew 10:16: "Behold, I send you forth as sheep in the midst of wolves: be ye therefore wise as serpents, and harmless as doves."

### A <u>PHOTOPLAY</u> READER TO CAROLYN VAN WYCK

Dear Miss Van Wyck:

Petting is my biggest problem. The boys all seem to do it and don't seem to come back if you don't do it also. We girls are all at our wits' end to know what to do.

All the boys want to pet. I've been out with nearly fifty different ones and every one does it. I thought sometimes it was my fault but when I tried hardest to keep from it they were all the worse. As yet I've never been out with anyone that got beyond my control. It may sound simple, but the minute I say that it is mean to take advantage because they are stronger they all seem to respect my wishes. I've tried getting mad but it doesn't do any good.

I don't seem to know what I want out of life. I want the thrills. I get a kick out of petting and I think all girls do no matter how much they deny it. What's to be done? The boys all like it and I can't seem to make myself dislike it and am not afraid of any of the men I know. Yet older people say, "Don't do it." Is it just because they are older and forget how they felt? I don't want it if it really is wrong.

It makes me wonder how on earth you are to get a husband who respects you because you don't pet if you get turned down everytime because you won't, before they have time to appreciate your sterling qualities. I'm quite sure that I don't want to marry anyone who is too slow to want to pet. But I want to discover what is right.

Please help me.

### CAROLYN VAN WYCK TO A <u>PHOTOPLAY</u> READER

To pet or not to pet.

That is the question that comes more and more often in my mail. To pet or not to pet. Poor, puzzled girls like the very nice girl who has written me above. You are only one of hundreds, my dear, though you are franker than most and face your problem more squarely.

"Petting" is the modern term that has replaced mother's "spooning" and grandmother's "sparking" and great-grandmother's "courting." Each term, it seems to me, is in itself indicative of the change in mood, the loss of romance in the approach between girl and boy to the reality of love.

In the last analysis, petting or spooning, or what you will, is the attempt to bridge the sex barrier. It should lead to marriage and life long happiness between husband and wife. But it doesn't always. That's the trouble.

Actually considering whether to pet or not to is like realizing that one's home would make a lovely bonfire and then considering whether to turn off the blinds for a neat little blaze, or to have a bigger blaze by burning the blinds and the porches or to have one marvelous fire by burning down the whole place. True, the house will be gone and there will be nothing but scorched fingers to remember the color of the flames and the heat. But one will have had the thrill of destruction and made a hit with the neighbors by lighting up the horizon.

I think petting is like that. At the risk of shocking the older generation, I must say that I see this not so much as a struggle between right and wrong as a judgment between good and bad values. Petting is of the moment. It is feverish and hectic and in more cases than any of us are willing to admit, disastrous to a girl's whole life.

It depends, then, on what one wants from life and the part one wants men to take in that life. If a girl is husband hunting, she must proceed very carefully and seriously, "as wise as a serpent and as soft as a dove." If she is after a career and only wants men sandwiched into that career from time to time, she can be much more casual in her contacts with the opposite sex. If she wants only the thrill, the petting and necking parties, the hip flasks and the parked car in the dark, that's up to her. But oh, what a shame to cheapen love so greatly, to pull it down on the level of chocolate sodas, and French pastry and chiffon hose, things from which one gets a momentary thrill of nonsensical indulgence and nothing more.

There is so much more than that in love and life. It seems to me much better to be known as a flat tire and keep romance in one's mind than to be called a hot date and have fear in one's heart.

To pet or not to pet. The choice is up to every girl. Choose wisely, then. Try not to let the glitter of the moment keep you from the gold of life.

### 1927: MAY 20
### ELINOR WYLIE TO HORACE WYLIE

*A poet and novelist, Elinor Wylie (1885–1928) was well known in her lifetime for her writing, her beauty, and her three marriages. In 1910, she left her first husband for a Washington lawyer named Horace Wylie (1868?–1950), and thirteen years later, left Wylie for William Rose Benét, also a poet and editor. She suffered from Bright's Disease, which may help explain the sense of life's brevity she conveyed in this letter to Wylie.*

Elinor died at home a year later, of a stroke.

Dearest Horace,

A strange thing is going to happen to you, for that thing is going to come true which undoubtedly you once desired, & for which you will now not care a straw. I am going to admit to you that I wish with all my heart I had never left you. I don't want you to keep this letter, & I hope—& trust—that you will tell no one, but although the admission may afford us both a certain pain, it is founded upon such deep principles of truth & affection that I feel it should be made.

You must not tell this, because the knowledge of it would give pain to Bill, who is one of the best people who ever lived & with whom I expect to pass the remainder of my days. But you & I know that that remainder is not long, & the entire past—which is so much longer—makes me wish to tell you the truth.

I love you, Horace, with an unchanged love which is far more than friendship, & which will certainly persist until my death. It is impossible for me to tell your present sentiments towards me, but it can hardly be a matter for regret that your former devotion should have bred a devotion in me which nothing could destroy.

In Paris I was constantly reminded of you, & although even if we had been together we should have been no longer young, no longer, perhaps, lovers, nevertheless I wished we were together. In England the same thing is true—you

are constantly in my thoughts, & remembered with an affection which is undoubtedly the strongest I shall ever feel.

It seems to me that our—shall we dignify it by the name of tragedy, or shall
we call it failure?—our whatever it was was one of the war's cruel mishaps—as
much so as my miscarriages or the loss of your money. I do not admire myself for
having fallen in love with the idea of freedom, & poetry, & New York, & any individual among them: the misery of Washington, of anonymous letters, of this &
that—your memory may supply the rest—spoiled what must always seem to me
the happiest part of my life—my life with you. It was not your fault in any way,
and mine only in my inability to stand the terrible alterations in that life which
Washington made.

If we had stayed in England? You will say—impossible. If we had stayed in
Bar Harbour? You will say I would have died—in some bad way. I doubt it, in
both instances. But this is because I wish we had never parted.

Well, my dear, do not think I am divorcing Bill or something like that. He is
the best boy imaginable. I suppose it is, in a way, devilish to write this. But I
loved you first, I loved you more, I loved him afterwards, but now, that I love you
both, I love you best. Surely you must, in some way, be glad to know this.

If you ever want me, I will come back to you openly. I have never cheated any
one, you know. But I don't suppose you do want it, & I think it is much better as
it is. Only—well, if you had been me, you would have written this letter from
this little house in Chelsea. Answer it.

> Yours truly,
> Elinor

## 1928: JULY 10
## ZORA NEALE HURSTON TO LANGSTON HUGHES

*Zora Neale Hurston (1891–1960) had only just graduated from Barnard College
but was already hard at work on some anthropological field studies when she wrote
this letter to Langston Hughes (1902–1967). Both writers were major figures in the
literary and artistic movement that came to be known as the Harlem Renaissance
and took place in the twenties and thirties. Hurston spent several years in the
South, studying the folklore of black Americans, and she would go on to write novels, stories, works of anthropology, and her autobiography.*

Hughes's second collection of poetry, *Fine Clothes to the Jew,* had been published in 1927. Its
title, as well as the lines quoted in this letter, came from his poem "Hard Luck." "Skinning," or
"skinball," is a fast-paced betting game in which one card at a time is dealt by a "banker" to any

number of players; the object is not to have the last card matched by the banker's card. Alain Locke had edited an influential anthology called *The New Negro*. "Godmother" was Charlotte Osgood Mason, who was financing both Hurston's and Hughes's work.

Magazine, Ala
July 10, 1928

Dear Langston,

I have been through one of those terrible periods when I cant make myself write    But you understand, since you have 'em yourself.

In every town I hold 1 or 2 story-telling contests, and at each I begin by telling them who you are and all, then I read poems from "Fine Clothes." Boy! They eat it up. Two or three of them are too subtle and they dont get it. "Mulatto" for instance and "Sport" but the others they <u>just eat up</u>. You are being quoted in R.R. camps, phosphate mines, Turpentine stills etc. I went into a house Saturday night (last) and the men were skinning—you remember my telling you about that game—and when the dealer saw his opponent was on the turn (and losing consequently) He chanted

> When hard luck overtakes you
> Nothin for you to do
> Grab up yo' fine clothes
> An' sell em to-ooo de Jew Hah!!

(slaps the card down on the table)

The other fellow was visibly cast down when the dealer picked up his money. Dealer gloating continued: "If you wuz a mule

> I'd git you a waggin to haul—
> But youse <u>so</u> low down-hown
> you aint even got uh stall."

So you see they are making it so much a part of themselves they go to improvising on it.

For some reason they call it "De Party Book." They come specially to be read to & I know you could sell them if you only had a supply. I think I'd like a dozen as an experiment. They <u>adore</u> "Saturday Night" and "Evil Woman," "Bad Man" "Gypsy Man"

They sing the poems right off, and July 1, two men came over with guitars and sang the whole book. Everybody joined in. it was the strangest & most <u>thrilling</u> thing. They played it well too. You'd be surprised. One man was giving the words out-lining them out as the preacher does a hymn and the others would take it up and sing. It was glorious!

Work going on well. I am getting much more material in a given <sup>area</sup> space & time than before because I am learning better technique. Getting more love letters too. Am keeping close tab on expressions of double meaning too, also compiling lists of double words. They—to give emphasis—use the noun and put the function of the noun before it as an adjective. Example, sitting-chair, suck-bottle, cook-pot, hair-comb.

Without flattery, Langston, you are the brains of this argosy. All the ideas have come out of your head.

I have about enough for a good volume of stories but I shall miss nothing. I shall go to New Orleans from here. Oh! almost forgot. Found another one of the original Africans, older than Cudjoe about 200 miles up state on the Tombighee river. She is most delightful, but no one will ever know about her but us. She is better talker than Cudjoe.

Had a letter from Alain. Wrote him at his Paris address.

Be here for two weeks more at least.

Lovingly,<br>Zora

I wanted to let your publishers know what a hit you are with the people you write about, but Godmother doesnt want <u>me</u> to say anything at present. But I shall do it as soon as this is over.

## 1928: JULY 12
## R. E. CONRAD TO MRS. E. W. LANTOW

*In the interests of full disclosure, we must admit that we were unable to find out whether "R. E. Conrad" was male or female, a public-relations invention or a flesh-and-blood secretary. But this letter was such a wonderful time capsule that we stretched a bit to include it. Max Factor, certainly a real person himself (born Max Faktor in Poland and renamed at Ellis Island), was responsible for changing the lives and appearances of untold millions of twentieth-century American women. Hitherto an under-the-counter trade associated with prostitutes on the one hand*

*and stage actresses on the other, cosmetics got its big break when Factor developed a makeup that didn't crack or cake. It was first used by film actors and then made available to average consumers. As this letter shows, the idea was truly novel.*

Dear Mrs. Lantow:

    Mr. Factor was indeed glad to make your analysis, because he feels that when you read his Make-Up Manual, which is enclosed, you will become a firm believer in his teaching.

    If you want to look your best at all times, by all means use cosmetics—but use them so that they will bring out in its full glory, your own natural charm. The Manual tells you how to use cosmetics correctly—how to put them on in their proper order, so that the use of one will help, rather than hinder, the other.

    This harmonious blending of cosmetics and its proper application, we call "Make-Up". It is far superior to the ordinary use of cosmetics and embodies the principles Mr. Factor has advocated to the profession and which have met with such wonderful success.

    Of course, if you want to take full advantage of Mr. Factor's advice, he suggests that for best results with make-up, you use the cosmetics which he has prepared with the knowledge he has gained in thirty years of experience.

    Mr. Factor's Society Make-up preparations are the same as those he made while cosmetician to the ladies of the Imperial Russian Court. These titled ladies, conscious of Mr. Factor's skill and fearing to lose him, held him a virtual prisoner. However, Mr. Factor escaped to America where he soon became Beauty Adviser to the Queens of America—the Movie Stars.

    To take full advantage of Mr. Factor's advice it is best to have his prescription filled complete. Of course, you needn't buy them all at once, if you don't wish to, but buy the ones you feel you have greatest need of now, and fill in with the others later.

    Mr. Factor's preparations although of the finest quality obtainable are not expensive. This is because Mr. Factor believes in a fair price for cosmetics, and wants to make real beauty available to every woman.

    Mr. Factor is always delighted to hear from those whom he tries to help. And if he can be of any further assistance to you in matters of beauty, don't hesitate to write him. You will receive a frank and prompt reply.

                             Sincerely,
                             R. E. Conrad
                             Sec'y to Mr. Factor.

# DEPRESSION AND WAR

# 1929
# ~
# 1945

I could have stayed forever in a spellbound world where I was young and you were there.

—*Isabel Kidder to her husband*
*Circa October 1942*

# BETWEEN 1929 AND 1945 . . .

**1929:** In a crime that will become notorious as the St. Valentine's Day Massacre, assassins hired on behalf of Al Capone dress as policemen and stage a mock whiskey raid at a Chicago warehouse, killing seven members of rival Bugs Moran's gang. "Who shot you?" police ask Frank Gusenberg as he lies dying from 22 bullet wounds; "No one," Gusenberg says, "nobody shot me." ✴ On "Black Tuesday," October 29, the stock market crashes as 16 million shares of stock are traded and all efforts to stem an 11-day fall in prices fail. ✴ Paying $10 a seat, 250 guests attend the first Academy Awards ceremony, in the Blossom Room of the Hollywood Roosevelt Hotel. **1930:** Chic Young creates the comic-strip character Blondie, whose maiden name is Boopadoop, and who will marry Dagwood Bumstead and earn lasting fame as his long-suffering suburban wife. ✴ Grant Wood paints *American Gothic,* with his sister and his dentist as models. **1931:** Irma Rombauer uses half her late husband's estate to self-publish *The Joy of Cooking,* which will eventually sell more than 14 million copies. ✴ Social reformer and anti–World War I activist Jane Addams becomes the first woman to receive the Nobel Peace Prize.

---

Clockwise from top left: Charles A. Lindbergh, Jr.; "The Stock Market Crash" by Rollin Kirby; Clara Bow; "Migrant Mother" by Dorothea Lange; Walt Disney and Mickey Mouse; Eleanor Roosevelt; World War II Rosie the Riveters; Amelia Earhart; "Hiroshima, Nagasaki to Come" by Robert Chesley Osborn; Seamen at Kaneohe Naval Air Station decorate the graves of their fellow sailors killed at Pearl Harbor.

★ The Empire State Building opens after a year and 45 days of construction and 7 million man-hours; at 103 floors and 1,454 feet (counting its radio antenna), it surpasses the recently completed Chrysler Building as the tallest in the world. ★ Ignoring testimony by doctors that they found no physical evidence of the crimes, an all-white jury convicts nine black men of raping two white women in Scottsboro, Alabama; all but the youngest, who is 12, receive the death sentence; throughout the ensuing decade, a series of appeals, reconvictions, and paroles will make the case a rallying point for the civil rights movement. ★ "The Star-Spangled Banner" is made the official national anthem by an act of Congress. **1932:** Charles A. Lindbergh, Jr., 20-month-old son of the famous pilot, is kidnapped and murdered; the crime attracts unprecedented amounts of publicity, especially with Bruno Hauptmann's subsequent trial and conviction, described by H. L. Mencken as "the greatest story since the Resurrection." ★ Franklin Delano Roosevelt is elected to the first of four terms as president. **1933:** Unemployment reaches a high of 24.9 percent. ★ Parker Brothers releases its first edition of Monopoly, a game that, in an earlier incarnation as "The Landlord's Game," had been rejected three decades before as too complicated and too hard to win. ★ Replacing opiates and other longer-lasting sedatives, sodium pentothal is introduced for pain relief during childbirth. ★ Frances Perkins becomes the first woman to serve as a cabinet member when FDR appoints her secretary of labor; the *New York Times* reports that the question of whether Perkins should sign the payroll as *Miss Perkins* or *Frances Perkins* "was settled ... after a solemn discussion of the matter that occupied time badly needed for more weighty matters in a crowded Congressional session" ("Frances Perkins" is the winning signature). ★ FDR launches the New Deal, inaugurating a majority of its programs within his first 100 days in office. **1934:** John Dillinger, Pretty Boy Floyd, and Bonnie and Clyde are all killed, in separate incidents, by law-enforcement agents. **1935:** A New York stockbroker named William Griffith Wilson and an Ohio surgeon named Robert Holbrook Smith meet to explore strategies for overcoming their drinking problems; the result is the formation of Alcoholics Anonymous, which will eventually spread to 150 countries and, in 2005, include more than two million members. **1936:** After witnessing the devastation caused by years of drought and decades of land misuse, reporter Ernie Pyle writes from Kansas: "If you would like to have your heart broken, just come out here. This is the dust-storm country. It is the saddest land I have ever seen." ★ *Life* magazine publishes its first issue, with a Margaret Bourke-White photograph of Fort Peck Dam on its cover. ★ Margaret Mitchell's *Gone with the Wind* sells 50,000 copies in one day and one million in six months. **1937:** The Golden Gate Bridge opens after four years of construction; chief engineer Joseph P. Strauss writes: "At last the mighty task is done; / Resplendent in the western sun / The Bridge looms mountain high; / Its titan piers grip ocean floor, / Its great steel arms link shore with shore, / Its towers pierce the sky." ★ Three-quarters of the way toward her goal of flying around the world, Amelia Earhart and her navigator, in a twin-engine Lockheed Electra, disappear near Howland Island in the central Pacific Ocean. **1939:** World War II begins in Europe. ★ A new synthetic fabric, nylon, is shown at the New York world's fair. **1940:** More than 750,000 pairs of nylon stockings are sold on the first day that they appear in stores. **1941:** The Japanese bomb American ships at Pearl Harbor in Hawaii. During the next four years, more than 16 million Americans—including some 400,000 women—will serve in World War II. **1942:** On the home front, the war effort includes rationing of sugar, coffee, butter, canned foods, gasoline, oil, and shoes. **1943:** *Oklahoma!* can be found on Broadway, *A Tree Grows in Brooklyn* in bookstores, and the jitterbug on dance floors. **1944:** New movies: *Gaslight, Meet Me in St. Louis, Going My Way.* ★ New songs: "I'll Be Seeing You," "Long Ago and Far Away," "Don't Fence Me In." **1945:** FDR dies at the age of 63 and is succeeded by Harry S. Truman. ★ Germany surrenders and Hitler commits suicide, ending the war in Europe. ★ The United States drops atomic bombs on Hiroshima and Nagasaki. ★ Japan surrenders.

---

*Before the nation was rocked by the stock market crash of October, much of America was reveling in its prosperity. But an undercurrent of poverty presaged the darker times to come. In the state of Washington, a widow named Alice Stewart wrote a particularly affecting appeal to Lou Henry Hoover (1875–1944), wife of the president-elect.*

Sumner Wash. Sta.
R. Rout #1
Feb 11—1929

Mrs Herbert Hoover

Miami Fla.

Kind Friend

I am a "civil war" widow. I am writing to you instead President-elect Hoover

Thinking perhaps he may be too busy just now, to pay attention and you could present this to him when he is not so busy

I know as he is a humanitarian   he will listen and help the old "War Widows" to get a better pension

I will be 75 next July, and have been a widow since 1914.

I had two sons in the "World war"   One came home with both legs off, after going through seven opperations in five months, a cripple for life, and general health broken, at the age of 19 years   He the youngest son should have been my support now.

I appeal to Mr Hoover to do what he can to get us war widows a "living pension" not less than $50.00 per month and let it come <u>very</u> soon as we <u>need</u> it <u>now</u>.

I fell and broke my arm last fall and then I could see how helpless I am. Put your own mother in my place.

At least give all over seventy a good pension for you or the Government wont have to give it very long. Thanking you in advance, and hope to get more pension very soon. My family put in a good vote for Mr Hoover

Yours Respt.

Mrs Alice M Stewart

## 1929: JULY 16
## CAROL TO HER MOTHER

*From Oberlin, Ohio, a troubled daughter wrote home to her mother in Pennsylvania. The phrases "sexual harassment" and "medical malpractice" were not yet everyday terms, but they would have been entirely appropriate.*

"Carol" and "Dr. Jones" are pseudonyms.

Tuesday Aft.

My dear mother:—

I received your letter and I want to tell you a few things or so. Perhaps I have been careless in regard to Dr. Jones but I think I have been perfectly justified in doing so. Furthermore, I wish you would send me the letter.

I went to him 2 weeks ago yesterday and he gave me an appointment for the following Friday, also one for the next Mon. Tues. Thurs. Friday provided I heard from you people in regard to my work. I went to him Friday (a week ago) and fully intended to tell him that you were of the opinion that I had better have the rest of my work done at home—but before the afternoon was over I changed my mind. He put in my gold inlay and then said he thought I could stand a good story and then he told me of a woman during labor having twins etc. I never said a word, I supposed I should have told him I didn't approve but I had my head back and I saw no reason, so I kept. Then a little later he offered me $15 a week to work in his office while his girl was on her vacation. I said I would if I didn't have to go to 3 classes every day, for I wanted to make some money. I told him I was tutoring getting $.50 an hour. When he was thru with my tooth—he said we always have a little extra to do when we put in a gold inlay—of course I believed him, he tilted the chair back and shined the tooth (gold inlay) and then he <u>kissed</u> me. I was so surprised I didn't know what to do. He said, "I fooled you, didn't I?" I suppose I should have acted mad—but I didn't for no one was around, not even an office girl, and I was afraid—and I didn't want him to know that I was, so I didn't say a word. When he said he would see me Monday I never said anything about him kissing me—I just said "yes." I was so frightened. I came out of the office, walked around the campus twice, then I still felt so terrible I went home & cried till I got it out of my system. I also told my room-mate. I think about it all the time. I dream about it and I'm so ashamed I don't know what to do.

When Monday came, I never went. Tuesday came—I didn't go. Wednesday the office girl called and Kay told the girl I decided not to have any more work done. That I had heard from my parents. In the meantime they had called for me Mon. & Tues. but I was at the library. I don't know why but yesterday when I came back from Kay's week-end party there was a note for me to be at Dr. Jones's office at 1:30. I didn't go but I called the office and I told him that I had found a note to come at the office at 1:30. He said "Oh yes, where have you been?" I told him my room-mate told the office girl that I wasn't having any more work done now. He said, oh, she (office girl) must have misunderstood. I felt like saying applesauce but I didn't, but I know she understood for I heard Kay tell her. Anyhow I said I couldn't have my work done until after Summer School because I had too much work to do but I would see about having it done later—he said he left on his vacation Aug 15th. He never said he had written to you.

Now, draw your own conclusions. Fair or unfair, I will not go to him or keep my appointments. Furthermore, I'll never <u>trust</u> a dentist or doctor. Never! I won't go to them—that is all.

I feel so tired and mean. I was supposed to be "off the roof" July 10 and as I told you the night I talked I had cramps, but as yet I haven't had the curse. I'm 8 days late now, so I guess that's why I feel so "blue."

Aunt Eva called last night & said Joe would probably be in bed 6 weeks more—is that the case? I certainly hope not. Please tell me more about him.

I'll write to him to-morrow. Bill was out to see me Sat. We had a party at Macbeths. They are so nice. I'm enclosing a picture of my room-mate—please don't loose it.

To-day, I received letter from Union Trust Co. of Cleveland. I was scared only to find an invitation to dinner in Akron next Sat. night by Bud Lodge—Harvard Graduate. I don't know whether I'll go or not. He is related to Marie.

I told you she was coming to see me—didn't I? When will suit us best? She will be one of the family—no trouble at all.

You don't need to get anything ready for me to come home. Please don't. You can't, that's all! I'll be awful glad to see you, but don't do anything extra for me. I have had a wonderful summer.

Mother, I wouldn't have written this letter to you, but of course I would have told you when I saw you. However, when you said I was unfair to Dr. Jones and hadn't treated him right, I was determined to tell you the truth. Please let the matter drop, as I'd die if any trouble was made—but I wanted you, my mother, to know the truth.

> Always your own—
> Love to all,
> Carol

## 1929: DECEMBER 11
## MARTHA SHRADER TO HER MOTHER

*In 1869, an English scientist named Francis Galton proposed a theory—eventually dubbed by him "eugenics"—that a better human race could be engineered through selective marriage between wealthy women and successful men. Partly embracing this theory, partly reflecting the rising fears that the recent waves of immigration had set off, the American Eugenics Society was founded in 1926. Eventually, with its urging, thirty-three states would enact some form of legislation that permitted the forced sterilization of thousands of American citizens deemed "socially inadequate." According to the model law, that meant the "feebleminded, insane, criminalistic, epileptic, inebriate, diseased, blind, deaf, deformed, and dependent... orphans, ne'er-do'wells, tramps, the homeless and paupers." In Virginia, after a U.S. Supreme Court case had upheld the legality of sterilization in 1927, a woman named M. M. Shrader sent a passionate plea regarding her daughter, Martha, to Governor Harry Byrd (1887–1966), writing: "I am sending her letter of her own hand writing to prove to you she is not feeble mind and they claim they have to sterlyize her before she can come home."*

Martha Shrader's fate is unknown. By 1944, forty thousand people had undergone sterilization procedures in America.

My dear Mother

I will take the pleasure of answering your sweet letter which I have just received a few minutes ago. I am well and I hope you are the same. I hadnt heard from you all for nearly two weeks. I was just worried to death for I thought maby something had happend for I always hear from you every week. Moma I declare I do wish I could come home for I know you need me if I could come home I would stay   if this werent the only trouble I had been in it would be diffrent but I do hate to be sterlized but it is the only way to come home   I absolutely would be willing for them to cut my head off if I could only come home once more and you relise it   I have been away from home in institutions for nearly three xmas   I do wish I could come home for xmas   I would be willing to come back   I hope you will get well and Father to   tell father I said hello and kiss the children for me   tell them all to send xmas presents as I know you will   Moma you all please come out here soon if you can for I have a lot of business to talk over with all of you    if I just thought I would come home for xmas I would be happy   I just worrie my self to death about you. I am so homesick I dont know what to do   I never did want to come home so bad in all of my life Well I will change the subject   the weather is fine out here and I hope so out their. I do wish it was Summer time   Ana Hunt said hello   she is a right good girl freind of mine   I wish you all to be good until we meet again   if I don't see you any more in this world I hope to meet you all in and other and hope God will help all of you and be with us   I will have to close for this time   answer real soon. XXXXXXX

From your daughter
Martha Shrader

Locks and keys may parts us. And we are far apart but your name in golden letters still lingers around my

H E A R T

## 1930: DECEMBER 4
## MRS. PETER STONE TO EDWARD STAEBLER

*The unemployment rate was climbing; by 1932, 23.6 percent of the population would be jobless. Like thousands upon thousands of other Americans who wrote to public officials for help, a Mrs. Peter Stone asked Ann Arbor mayor Edward Staebler (1872–1946) not for charity, but for work.*

Kind Sir:

I'm sending you this notice stating my case   I'm a resident of Ann Arbor the past 7 years   I have walked this town a dozen times looking for work with no success, and I know they are married woman employed where I have been who dont need the work as their husbands work. And I'm all discouraged. I lost my husband here in Ann Arbor and got along very well up until the hard times come. I have kept roomers & boarders since but now I have only 2 and I can't keep my expenses up. I'm in debt two hundred dollars, and I'm trying very hard to keep my home although I'm a renter. I never see a moments pleasure or enjoyment not even a picture show. Every penny I get I must save for expenses. I had a few dollars in the bank but I had use it up. I don't want charity but I would like some kind of lite work 6 or 7 hours a day or most    I would like to get out of debt. If I wasnt a hard honest working woman, I wouldnt state my case to you. And all who knows me can give you a good recommendation of me. I'm a real home woman. Coarse I don't care to have my name published, but if their is any way you can possibly help me I should shure appreciate it. trusting you will please do all you can for me I'm yours truly

Mrs. Peter Stone

## 1931: FEBRUARY 7
## AMELIA EARHART TO GEORGE PALMER PUTNAM

*Born in Atchison, Kansas, Amelia Earhart (1897–1937) was already a free spirit when she learned to fly, despite her family's protests, and in 1922 bought her first plane. She became world famous in 1928 as the first woman to fly across the Atlantic (albeit as a passenger), and made the flight alone in 1932. Her independence was also much in evidence on the morning of her wedding, when she handed this letter to her future husband, the publisher George Palmer Putnam (1887–1950). Later he would call it "brutal in its frankness but beautiful in its honesty." They were still married six years later, when her plane disappeared over the Pacific Ocean.*

Dear GP,

There are some things which should be writ before we are married. Things we have talked over before,—most of them.

You must know again my reluctance to marry, my feeling that I shatter thereby chances in work which means so much to me. I feel the move just now as foolish as anything I could do. I know there may be compensations, but have no heart to look ahead.

In our life together I shall not hold you to any medieval code of faithfulness to me, nor shall I consider myself bound to you similarly. If we can be honest I think the differences which arise may best be avoided.

Please let us not interfere with each other's work or play, nor let the world see private joys or disagreements. In this connection I may have to keep some place where I can go to be myself now and then, for I cannot guarantee to endure at all times the confinements of even an attractive cage.

I must exact a cruel promise, and this is that you will let me go in a year if we find no happiness together.

I will try to do my best in every way.

A. E.

## 1931: APRIL 24
## CLARA BOW TO B. P. SCHULBERG

*She was sixteen when she sent her photograph to* Motion Picture Magazine *and won its 1921 "Fame and Fortune Contest." Her victory allowed her to escape a horrible childhood of poverty and abuse, and throughout the next decade, Clara Bow (1905–1965) was one of the most famous people in America. Known as the "It Girl" (after starring in the film based on the novel* It*), she was the sexual icon of her day, the flapper liberated from the nineteenth century and prepared for anything in the twentieth. In addition to men, she attracted rumors, lawsuits, and a wild tabloid-style treatment by the press. A Brooklyn accent and fear of the microphone didn't help her transition to talking pictures. By the time she wrote this letter to producer B. P. Schulberg (1892–1957), she had reached the end of her rope—and her career.* Frederic Girnau was editor of the Coast Reporter, which published articles accusing Bow of everything from drug addiction to bestiality.

April 24, 1931

Dear Ben:

I was just finishing a letter addressed to you when I received your telegram. After reading it I tore the letter up. I will not tell you why, except that it was a heart to heart letter explaining many things and telling you of my high regard for you and Paramount.

I will tell you why you couldn't reach me to-day. My phone number was being changed and the men just finished a little while ago, hence the failure to reach me. I am not trying to dodge the studio and I don't take off receivers to avoid being reached by anyone.

I didn't come to the studio yesterday because I was at the beach house and didn't receive the message to report until four o'clock, which was rather late to start in and rehearse.

The other reason was the more important though. The truth of the whole matter is that I am a very sick girl. My physician tells me there is only one cure and that is a complete rest regardless of anything else. If my career must be sacrificed, I can't help it. My health comes first and you know it. I have been through so much the past year including the last vicious attack by Girnau, that my system can stand it no longer. I'm on the verge of a nervous breakdown and I don't intend to have one if I can help it. In the past I have always tried to do my best for Paramount and play square, thinking only of my employers, but the time has come when I am forced to think about myself first. The only reason I am not at the studio is because I am ill, please believe that. I told you once before that if I didn't work for Paramount I wouldn't care to make any more pictures. Paramount is my home, and if anything should happen to prevent my working there anymore, I would give up pictures altogether.

I want you to know I appreciate all you have done for me in the past and the hard work you and others have put in to this latest production for me. I think it is a corking story and a swell part, and I am just as disappointed as you in not being able to do it. I am not being tempermental or anything like that, you know me well enough to appreciate that. I am very sorry that I have caused you to worry, but you see I can't help it. I must obey my doctor's orders or suffer the consequences. Please don't be angry with me and try to understand my feelings. I am sick in heart as well as body and I am only going away to try and regain my health. I will be back as soon as I am able to resume my work at the studio, that is if you still want me. If you don't, well, thats up to you to decide.

You say in your telegram, you will be forced to take legal and financial safeguard to minimize your loss, well Ben go ahead. What little money I have is in a trust fund and the only property I have is my little home and the lot next door to it. If you take those two things away from me, I will have nothing left, but I guess I can take it with my chin up. I have been through so much trouble, I guess I can take a few more knocks without squawking. I have always tried to be decent and nice to everyone and I think the people who know me well understand the real Clara Bow.

By the time you receive this letter I will be far away. In case you care to know where I am, you can find me c/o Woolf Ranch, Nipton, California, seeking mental peace and rest, trying to get well again, far away from people's lies, and their efforts to destroy my reputation and health. I have found out that nothing else except happiness and health count in this life. I have never had much of either, but I am going to find them both.

In your wire you asked me to snap out of it again. You know I have in the past, and if I could at this time, don't you think I would, Ben? It is just physically impossible. Please let me hear from you, as I would not want anything to interfere

with our friendship of eight years, and as for suing me, you know that isn't necessary. You can have the little I have without going to law.

I know that any industry must keep going regardless of anything, or anybody,
still a human mind and body can only stand so much punishment, and if you
will just sympathize with me for a moment, you will realize my condition. It is
needless to say that the last vicious attack on me by Girnau was the last straw.
Please understand, and don't be angry with me.

Clara

## 1931: APRIL 25
## BABE DIDRIKSON TO TINY SCURLOCK

*Another star of the thirties—and well beyond—was Mildred "Babe" Didrikson
(1911–1956). A native of Port Arthur, Texas, she was one of the most gifted athletes
of the century, and probably the most versatile. In 1932, she competed as a one-
woman track-and-field team in the Women's Amateur Athletic Association meet
and easily outscored the second-place team, which consisted of twenty members.
She would break world records in myriad events and win three Olympic medals.
She was good at swimming, skating, basketball, baseball, football, billiards, and—
playing professionally from 1934 on—at golf. In this early letter to her friend and
would-be manager, William "Tiny" Scurlock, Didrikson revealed not only her drive
and rampant self-confidence, but also her cunning.*

When she wrote this letter, Didrikson was playing in Dallas for the Employers' Insurance Association's women's semiprofessional basketball team, coached by Melvin McCombs. Scurlock
was a sportswriter. Apparently he did not follow her instructions. In 1938, Didrikson would
marry a wrestler named George Zaharias.

Dearest "Tiny"

Why hello old top, how in the heck are you getting along. Now this is the
time that I need a manager. Tiny I think that I should be making more money so
I am asking you to write me a letter telling me of a better job that I can get and
more money about $125.00 a month, you see they have us under a twelve
month rule, that is if you played in the national tournament with one team you
can't change clubs until one year after the date of the last game that you played
with this one team, so if you will tell me it's a better job as proffessional and
more money. You know kinda shake 'em up a little.

They wouldn't want to let me go for nothing.

Colonel McCombs made that twelve month rule so that he could keep us in the Co. and make us work for nothing but he has another think coming. I know good and well I am worth a $150.00 and I am gonna get it out of this company, with your help.

All I want is a letter from you tell me all about a keen proposition that you have found for me. and kinda stretch it see, cause when I show it to him he will raise my pay to about what you say in that offer. This is just to make them break a loose and pay me a little more dough.

Put the price and everything make a keen contract form and make it plenty real—"C."

Tiny don't tell anyone about this will you, because I couldn't have it get to Dallas.

The president is giving me free Golf Lessons out at Dallas Country Club, and they are plenty nice so they won't have to raise my pay. When I get your letter I will take it in to Mr. McCombs and show it to him. I am the only prospect of him winning the National and he knows that, plenty of teams want me but can't get me on account of the 12 month rule, the only way out is to turn professional and that will make them chirp up any pay me what they ought to. All the rest of the teams get payed keen and a lots more than any of us do. So Tiny will you please do that for me.

Write me just as though I had never written to you—so they won't suspect.

Love,
Babe Didrikson

## 1931: MAY 8

## AN OREGON WOMAN TO KARL MENNINGER

*Part of a distinguished Topeka family of doctors who had a special interest in mental health, Karl Menninger (1893–1990) was the author of a popular book called* The Human Mind *when he began writing a column in* Ladies' Home Journal. *Thousands of letters from readers subsequently deluged him, letters he answered with a mixture of vivid, accessible metaphor and Freudian theory. Menninger was a pioneer in believing that mental health (or "hygiene," as it was popularly known) was an attainable and worthwhile goal for most people. Yet his definition of mental health excluded homosexuality and embraced heterosexuality as the mature phase of human relationships. With that in mind, he urged the author of the following letter not to berate herself, but to seek help from a psychoanalyst in getting rid of her "homosexualist" urge.*

Portland, Ore.
May 8, 1931

Dear Sir:

Please advise me. I am so disgusted with myself and so miserable. Until recently I didn't know there was such a thing as homosexualism and now that seems to explain my past and present unhappiness. It is too hideous.

My mother died when I was three. During childhood my craving for mother-love found an outlet in worshipping different women. I would "play" I was the loved child of whichever charming woman held my fancy at the time.

This unnatural make-believe continued through high school, where I had "crushes" on my teachers. I no longer pretended to be their child, of course, but wanted their friendship, their attention, even their love, more than anything in the world and was naturally very unhappy over real and imagined slights.

In college my infatuation turned to upper classmen, and I knew periods of exaltation and despondency over these "cases." It was late in my college life before I began to feel the normal interest in men.

After graduation from college there was a blessed period of five years—blessed because it was free from what now seems so perverted an emotional life. I had the usual friendships with men, and married.

Now, after two years of comparatively happy married life the old curse is back. I have fought against it this time in view of my later knowledge of psychology. Yet, even while I tell myself how revolting it all is, my interest in this older, charming woman supplies me with a satisfaction I cannot explain. It seems the one absorbing thing in life. Infantile as it is, I carry on imaginary conversations with her, and she is constantly on my mind.

I feel my love for my husband disappearing. I am critical of him. Perhaps I should say that he is not passionate and we have had sexual intercourse only at rare intervals. I have told him this is not normal.

This is all revolting to me and I hate myself more every day. Is there something I can do to rid myself of this complex, or whatever it is? Am I going crazy? Sometimes I think so. Am I really that awful thing, a homosexualist? Be frank with me. I need it.

Sincerely yours,

\*     \*     \*

### 1931: AUGUST
### ALINE BERNSTEIN TO THOMAS WOLFE

*As she predicted in the last line of this letter, the life of Aline Frankau Bernstein (1882–1955) would indeed someday be overshadowed by the work of Thomas Wolfe (1900–1938). In truth, that seems to have been the case even when she wrote this beautiful, seething, and ultimately futile letter to her former lover. Yet Bernstein was a remarkable woman in her own right. As an author and a theatrical set and costume designer, she worked with the likes of Lillian Hellman, James Thurber, and Lunt and Fontanne; she also won a Tony Award, published several works of fiction, and helped found the Metropolitan Museum of Art's Costume Institute. Her affair with Wolfe was excruciatingly volatile; it inspired him to dedicate* Look Homeward, Angel *to her, and inspired her own novel,* The Journey Down, *which was published the year he died.*

I cannot sleep, this is what I think, there is nothing in life that cannot be made beautiful. Years ago I bought a jar on Allen street, because it had a good shape. I paid 65 cents for it. I scraped and polished it, and found it was made of copper with circles worked all round the bowl. It comes from somewhere in the east. I had it made into a lamp and every night when I put on the lights, its surface gives me back fires. It gives me this because I knew and recognized its beauty under the grime of its wandering. Last Saturday when it was so ghastly hot I went to market early, to White Plains. The roads here about are all being repaired. It was so hot the men worked with only pants, no shirts at all. One big man breaking stones nearly as big as you are. I did not see his face, his back might almost have been yours, but nothing on God's earth would make me touch man's flesh that is not you. I thought if I put my hand upon a back, the tissue skin muscle is the same as yours, but nothing but you is you. So I am convinced that we are not nature's fools. We have soul, I review my life for you, and find I have come to a time so like the sadness of my childhood. I know now what I only feared then. If I show you this it is only so much stuff for you to use. You can't look into my heart. You have not the proper light to see. Time is not a dream, time has brought you to touch upon my life and now is moving you past in a widening arc. But what of time and me, I stay fixed in my circle like the planets.

Any plausible female will do for you, to spend the night or the day, or to lie with. Only Tom will do for me. Since you left me I passed through fire and hell, maybe before I am through even jealousy will be burned from me. Only loving pity will be left for you who do not see. You said I am maudlin, if that is what I am, you will live to see the day when you will stand ashamed at your use of such a word. It is true I am maudlin, only because of the strength of a love that confuses my mind. You would put upon my love the ugliness of your desertion and a fidelity, but that does not change my undying fire—Your book will be so great that possibly the sum of my entire life will be nothing compared to it. So something beautiful may come of this constant misery I live.

### 1931: SEPTEMBER 12
### MRS. HILLYER TO THE SEATTLE BUREAU OF PROHIBITION

*Prohibition had been in place since 1920, and bootleggers had flourished along with the black market for booze. The extent to which the laws were implemented—especially as hard times hit—varied from place to place, but cities tended to be more lax than small towns. In Seattle, one wife sought immediate enforcement from the Bureau of Prohibition.*

Dear Sir:

My husband is in the habit of buying a quart of wiskey every other day from a Chinese bootlegger named Chin Waugh living at 317–16th near Alder street.

We need this money for household expenses. Will you please have his place raided? He keeps a supply planted in the garden and a smaller quantity under the back steps for quick delivery. If you make the raid at 9³⁰ any morning you will be sure to get the goods and Chin also as he leaves the house at 10 o'clock and may clean up before he goes.

Thanking you in advance
I remain

Yours truly,
Mrs. Hillyer

### 1932: JANUARY 5
### RUBY BATES TO EARL STREETMAN

*It is impossible to know how many times southern courts had been used for dispensing vigilante justice. But around the country the question was asked with increasing urgency after nine black teenagers were tried in a Scottsboro, Alabama, courtroom just weeks after their arrest in March of 1931 and convicted of gang-raping two white teenage girls. All but the youngest of the "Scottsboro Boys" were sentenced to death, despite the fact that doctors who examined their accusers, Ruby Bates (1915–1976) and Victoria Price, testified that no rapes had occurred. At a second trial following appeal, Bates became a surprise witness for the defense, recanting her former testimony. The following letter, written to her then boyfriend, seemed further proof that she had lied in the first place. Although the origins of both her recantation and the letter were also called into question (one prosecutor asked in summation: "Is justice going to be bought and sold in Alabama with Jew money from New York?"), Bates maintained for the rest of her life that she had not been raped. There were numerous appeals, retrials, and protests, but the last of the Scottsboro Boys would not be released until 1960.*

*"Jazz" was a vulgarism for "have sex with."*

Jan 5 1932
Huntsville, Ala
215 Connelly Aly

Dearest Earl

I want to make a statment too you   Mary Sanders is a goddam lie about those negroes jassing me   those policement made me tell a lie   that is my statement because I want too clear myself that is all too if you want to believe, ok. If not that is ok. You will be sorry someday   if you had to stay in jail with eight Negroes you would tell a lie two. those Negroes did not touch me or those white boys. i hope you will believe me the law don't. i love you better than Mary does ore any body else in the world. that is why i am telling you of this thing. i was drunk at the time and did not know what i was doing. I know it was wrong to let those Negrroes die on account of me. i hope you will believe me. I was jazed but those white boys jazed me. i wish those Negores are not burnt on account of me. it is these white boys fault. that is my statement. and that is all i know. i hope you tell the law hope you will answer.

Ruby Bates

P.S. this is the one time i might tell a lie but it is the truth so god help me.

Ruby Bates

**1932: JANUARY 30**

**JESSIE LLOYD O'CONNOR TO POTENTIAL DONORS**

---

*The United Mine Workers of America was formed in 1890 and had about half a million members by 1920. But despite its many successful efforts to strike for better wages and working conditions in the lower Midwest and Pennsylvania, there were newer, less organized mines in West Virginia and Kentucky. Jessie Lloyd O'Connor (1904–1988) was a journalist and progressive who tried to bring the plight of the Kentucky miners to the attention of the rest of the country. Along with her husband, Harvey O'Connor, she used the wealth she had inherited from Chicago Tribune money to campaign for unions. Eventually she would serve on the boards of more than a dozen reform groups and help found an organization to abolish the House Committee on Un-American Activities.*

"Flux" was the common word for dysentery.

> 314 Marsonia St.
> January 30, 1932

Dear friend—

I have just returned from Harlan and other Kentucky and Tennessee counties where miners are striking in desperation against starvation. I have seen men and women gaunt and haggard, pale children fed on cornbread and beans—two meals daily, one meal, bad days none. Heavy food, rare and irregular, is killing the babies with "flux". They rarely see milk after weaning.

Two reporters looking into these conditions last summer were threatened and then shot in the legs. I was threatened several times by badged deputies. Now, however, the Harlan Relief Assn. itself admits, of miners on the job, "Already men have reached the physical condition in which it is dangerous for them to enter the mines due to malnutrition." (Harlan Daily Enterprise, Jan. 24.)

But it gives relief only to men who continue to slave for such rewards. Those who walked out in protest at the cheating on the weight of coal—shortweighting 10% to 25%—those who objected to prices in the company store, from 10% to 110% over outside rates, even in this time of acute poverty—those who tired of working in the black hole with a dinner pail full of water and their children crying for bread—such men are barred from relief as "not willing to work."

Because they sought comfort in union—strength to bargain like men instead of the ghastly need to underbid each other for jobs—these miners are excluded from succor, evicted from their homes, charged with "criminal syndicalism" for carrying strike leaflets. (21 years, $10,000 fine, or both).

Coal companies have fought organization, which might have stabilized costs: they have rivaled each other in cutting wages, at last below subsistence level. Shall we wait till the miners are pushed down another notch, and then dig up a few grudging pennies for eternal charity—or back them now, while they are struggling for their rights?

"We don't ask to <u>live</u>—just enough to get by till we get a union," say these skinny and incredibly courageous men and women. The miners at Wallins Creek showed me their books—they feed two hundred men, women and children on $7 a day. Will you help fill the desperate need in other mining towns?

> Sincerely and gratefully yours,
> Jessie Lloyd

Make your check payable to the Kentucky Miners Relief Committee, and mail to Room 414, 611 Penn Ave., Pittsburgh. Food and clothing may be sent direct to the Miners Warehouse, 155 Pine St., Pineville, Ky.

### 1932: JULY 19
### CAROLINE HENDERSON TO EVELYN HARRIS

*Born in Iowa, educated at Mount Holyoke College, Caroline Boa Henderson (1877–1966) was about thirty when she began homesteading in the Oklahoma panhandle and married Will Henderson. Together they started a farm, built a barn, had a daughter, and weathered the devastation of Depression and drought. The conditions Henderson described in this letter—the barren expanse of the 1930s Dust Bowl—forced thousands of people to leave their land as dust and dirt storms coated the landscape and years of drought offered no relief. Ultimately, Henderson and her family managed to stay. One modest contribution to her income came from magazine sales of letters she exchanged with Evelyn Harris, a widow who farmed in Maryland.*

Eleanor was Caroline's daughter.

My dear Evelyn,

I am sure you know enough about the uncertainties of farming not to have been unduly elated over my last more hopeful letter. It had hardly been mailed before trouble began.

One of our neighbors was trying to cut down tractor expenses by using horses to cultivate his crop. He lacked one team, so we let him have Ned and Star. Since we bought our tractor they have not had much to do, but Will has always said that the horses made for us the little we have, and that they were welcome to live out their old age in peace, helping us now and then in the lighter tasks. They worked well enough for a week, and our friend said they seemed all right when he turned them into the pasture Sunday evening. Monday morning Star lay there dead.

Some people say that animals do not suffer keenly and have no dread of death. I hope it is so, and certainly I am glad for gentle, faithful Star that there can be for her no more sweat and dust and tugging at loads the importance of which she could not understand. But horses hate to leave their homes; they know their friends; and I suppose it will always hurt me to think that perhaps Star wondered why we didn't come in her hour of need. I am afraid she will always seem a sacrifice to the demands of this cruel time.

How we should welcome a small part of your surplus rain! We have had none in a month. The extreme heat and almost constant high winds have destroyed all hope of a satisfying return from the garden. The potatoes were set back seriously by the early hail, and, though the vines grew out, they are now dying down, with little potatoes like marbles half cooked in the parched ground. Canada field peas, which we hoped would provide a late crop after the earlier peas were gone, blossomed fully, but, lik the tomatoes, were blighted by the withering winds. Cowpeas and peanuts are standing the heat the best of anything, and along with the field crops, <u>may</u> hold out until rain comes. No one knows. The cattle still have sufficient pasturage on the weeds and grasses among the ruined wheat, but the prairie grass is brown again and crackles under one's feet.

This has been another long day of wild wind and blistering heat. Tonight I am quite alone—a mile and a half from anybody. The wind has gone down and the quietness makes me think of Will's memories of his old cowboy days, of silences out on the open plains so intense that one's ears would ache with listening.

Will and Eleanor, with a neighbor's boy to help them, have gone with truck, car, tractor, combine, and oil wagon to harvest a half section of wheat for some people out in the adjoining county, seventeen miles from home. Money is scarcer than ever with us, and they are taking their pay in wheat at three bushels for the acre. Whether they will make anything to compensate for their exhausting effort and for the expense and depreciation of the machinery depends on the future wheat market.

The wheat yield is disheartening all through this part of the country; there is hardly one stalk where three or four grew last year. The man for whom our folks are harvesting counted on about twelve bushels to the acre and is getting less than five. It puzzles everyone to know how to manage these poor crops. They will not pay handling expenses. . . . Many fields will not be cut at all. On three sides of our own home farm are 330 acres left for the birds—potentially something like a thousand sacks of flour poured out on the ground in a hungry world!

People still toil amazingly and make a conscious effort to keep cheerful. But it seems to me that the effort grows more apparent. Behind the characteristic American nonchalance one detects a growing anxiety, especially about the coming winter. People speak openly of their dread of cold weather. I am told by a man who is familiar with neighborhood conditions that many farmers once regarded as well-to-do will not be able to put in another crop on their own resources. City folk talk lightly of the obvious remedy. "Let the farmers stop producing if they can market their stuff only at a loss," they say. But the thing is not as simple as that. When all of one's investment is in land and equipment for working it, there is nothing else to depend on for taxes, repairs, the upkeep of buildings and fences, and the maintenance and education of a family.

But it is useless to tackle that problem tonight. It is already late, and day comes soon. Tomorrow I must care for the new shorthorn I found this evening when I went for the cows; look over the winter-squash vines for bugs; go around a mile and a half of fence and put in missing staples; finish hoeing and working the ground around the small trees which we are trying to save through the drought. Why do people speak of "the monotony of farm life?"

### 1934: CIRCA MAY
### E. E. SMALLWOOD TO OKLAHOMA STUDENTS

*Bonnie Parker (1910–1934) and Clyde Barrow (1909–1934) were a couple from Texas who never stole more than $1,500 but were responsible for the deaths of at least three police officers. Mythic figures long before they were immortalized in the 1967 film* Bonnie and Clyde, *they were gunned down together in Louisiana. Some days later, a teacher named E. E. Smallwood tried to find a lesson in her former student's life.*

Bonnie Parker who now lies cold in death and whose spirit has been wafted away to the great beyond was once a pupil in my school and a beautiful and obedient little girl and possessed seemingly a desire to do good and build for an ideal station in life

But like many others who fell a victim to the wrong environments and not for lac of parental training, this should be a lesson to young girls & boys, they should strive to gain the highest Badge of honor for themselves and for their country

E E Smallwood

## 1934: DECEMBER 14
## A FLORIDA WIDOW TO ELEANOR ROOSEVELT

*Through a combination of determination, brains, and unaffected devotion, Eleanor Roosevelt (1884–1962) set a standard as first lady that few, if any, political wives have ever met. In August of 1933 she wrote a* Woman's Home Companion *article titled "I Want You to Write to Me," and in the first year alone, she received approximately three hundred thousand letters. In an article about her incoming mail, Roosevelt once recalled a woman who had written: "I am the farmer's wife who wrote you a year ago and you told me to write again when the Bill went through." When she first opened this letter, Roosevelt admitted, she found the assumption that she would remember the request amusing. "But I was to find as the years went by," she wrote, "that everybody thinks their situation unique. . . ."*

Miami, Fla.
December 14, 1934

Mrs. Franklin D. Roosevelt
Washington, D.C.
Dear Madam—.

I am a widow with a son fourteen years of age and am trying to support him and myself and keep him in school on a very small sum which I make.

I feel worthy of asking you about this: I am greatly in need of a Coat. If you have one which you have laid aside from last season would appreciate it so much if you would send it to me. I will pay postage if you see fit to send it. I wear size 36 or 38.

Please treat this confidentially and I shall do likewise in case you reply.

I assure you I am worthy of any help you render.

Sincerely

## 1935: SPRING
## ANONYMOUS SENDER TO FIVE FRIENDS

*Desperate times called for desperate measures. One example was the "send-a-dime" letter, also known as the Prosperity Club. Originating in Denver, it was spread, predominantly by women, throughout the country and even went overseas. Within a few months, the letter had been copied more than a billion times (and even parodied, with a listing of mock participants such as U. Kickum and E. Normus Foote).*

*Though chain letters of other sorts, promising luck or blessings, had existed before, the money chain letter was a child of the Depression.*

PROSPERITY CLUB—"IN GOD WE TRUST"

FAITH! HOPE! CHARITY!

This chain was started in the hope of bringing prosperity to you. Within three (3) days make five (5) copies of this letter leaving off the top name and address and adding your own name and address to the bottom of the list, and give or mail a copy to five (5) of your friends to whom you wish prosperity to come.

In omitting the top name send that person ten (10c) cents wrapped in a paper as a charity donation. In turn as your name leaves the top of the list (if the chain has not been broken) you should receive 15,625 letters with donations amounting to $1,536.50.

NOW IS THIS WORTH A DIME TO YOU?

HAVE THE FAITH YOUR FRIENDS HAD AND THIS CHAIN WILL NOT BE BROKEN.

## CIRCA 1936

## ZELDA FITZGERALD TO SCOTT FITZGERALD

---

*F. Scott Fitzgerald (1896–1940), one of the greatest of all American authors, was famous not only for his talent but for his life, which he lived with alcoholic urgency in a period he helped define as "The Jazz Age." He had married Zelda Sayre (1900–1948) in 1920, and for at least a decade, in both America and France, they tried to have a happy life. A dancer, a painter, and a talented author herself, she suffered the first of several breakdowns in 1930 and spent much of the rest of her life in mental hospitals. Fitzgerald once wrote of her: "I left my capacity for hoping on the little roads that led to Zelda's sanitariums." In this letter, she seemed to be longing for both the past and the future.*

"Scottie" was the Fitzgeralds' only child, Frances. Scott and Zelda had met when he was a lieutenant stationed at the army camp in her hometown of Montgomery, Alabama.

Highland Hospital, Asheville, North Carolina

Dearest, dearest Do-Do:

What a funny picture of you in the paper. I wish we had just been swimming together, the way it seems—I'll be so glad when you come home again. When will we be three of us again—Do you remember our meal in the Biltmore when you said "And now there'll never be two of us again—from now on we'll be three—" And it was sort of sad somehow and then it was the saddest thing in the world, but we were safer and closer than ever—Oh, I'll be so glad to see you on the tenth.

Scottie was as sweet as I had imagined. She's one inch shorter than I am and weighs four pounds more—and I am her most devoted secret admirer—

Maybe I can come home—

O my love  
O my darling } Yes, I mean it

That's what we said on the softness of that expansive Alabama night a long long time ago when you envited me to dine and I had never dined before but had always just "had supper." The General was away. The night was soft and gray and the trees were feathery in the lamp light and the dim recesses of the pine forest were fragrant with the past, and you said you would come back from no matter where you are. So I said and I will be here waiting. I didn't quite believe it, but now I do.

And so, years later I painted you a picture of some faithful poppies and the picture said "No matter what happens I have always loved you so. This is the way we feel about <u>us</u>; other emotions may be super-imposed, even accident may contribute another quality to our emotions, but this is our love and nothing can change it. For that is true." And I love you still.

It was me who said:

I feel as if something had happened and I dont know what it is

You said:

—Well and you smiled (And it was a compliment to me FOR you had never heard "well" used so before) if you don't know I can't possibly know

Then I said "I guess nobody knows—

And

you hoped and I guessed

Everything's going to be all right—

So we got married—

And maybe everything is going to be all right, after all.

There are so many houses I'd like to live in with you. Oh Wont you be mine—again and again—and yet again—

Dearest love, I love you

Zelda

Happily, happily foreverafterwards—the best we could.

\*　　\*　　\*

# EXCHANGE

**1936**

**KAY BROWN AND DAVID SELZNICK**

*Kay Brown (1902–1995) had been one of the first people hired by David O. Selznick (1902–1965) when he started his own film production company in 1935. As New York–based story editor, she was supposed to find him existing properties that might be turned into movies. In May of 1936, having received an early copy of* Gone with the Wind *from Margaret Mitchell's agent, Brown set about trying to persuade Selznick of something that the rest of the country—and soon the world—would know in a matter of months. The following telegrams, just a few of the dozens exchanged over several months, were part of the process.*
We have normalized the original uppercase text here and supplied punctuation for legibility.

### KAY BROWN TO DAVID SELZNICK

Val Lewton was the West Coast story editor. *Anthony Adverse* was a best-selling novel of 1933 that became a popular movie released in August of 1936 amid much hype. In 1936, Miriam Hopkins starred in *Men Are Not Gods;* Margaret Sullavan in *The Moon's Our Home.*

5/20/36

We have airmailed detailed synopsis of "Gone with the Wind" by Margaret Mitchell and also copy of book to Val. This is Civil War story and magnificent possibility for Miriam Hopkins or Margaret Sullavan. It will be the July Book of the Month Club and is over a thousand pages long and I guess that is why everybody thinks it is going to be another Anthony Adverse. All picture companies have definitely registered their interest one going so far as to make a 25,000 offer on hearing the story told to them by a person who was going to its review. We have told Macmillan the publishers that you have been looking for a Civil War story told from a different angle and asked them to do nothing on it before Monday of next week therefore would appreciate it greatly if you would give this your prompt attention

### KAY BROWN TO DAVID SELZNICK

Janet Gaynor had just starred in *Ladies in Love,* Clark Gable in *San Francisco,* Bette Davis in *The Petrified Forest,* Franchot Tone in *The King Steps Out,* and Ronald Colman in *Under Two*

*Flags.* John Hay "Jock" Whitney was chairman of the board of Selznick International Pictures; Merian Cooper was vice president. *Sparkenbroke* was a 1936 novel by Charles Morgan. Sylvia Schulman was Selznick's secretary.

May 21, 1936

I went over synopsis of "Gone with the Wind" again last night very carefully and I think this is an absolutely magnificent story and it belongs to us. I am fearful that my yesterdays wire may have given you the idea that this is primarily a Civil War story. This is not so. There are four main characters and the title role of Scarlet is made to order for Miriam Hopkins or Bette Davis. Melanie should be played by Janet Gaynor. Bret by Clark Gable. It is too bad Colman is English otherwise he would be perfect as to description. Ashley should be played by Franshot Tone. I have got an advance copy for Mr Whitney and one for myself and I have also airmailed a copy to you. I have had the agent in this morning and seen her before any other people and it is my feeling that the price on this book will be 50,000. The agent happens to be a sweet little person who doesn't know anything about racketeering prices on a book like this and in the hands of several other agents in town I bet my last cent that it would bring between 75,000 and 100,000 dollars. Metro is reported to have paid 40,000 for Sparkenbroke and the agent pointed this out to me this morning but I told her my guess was that Sparkenbroke was bought under option and not outright and that I thought 50,000 a very substantial figure for this book. As I told you yesterday they have rejected an outright offer for 25,000. in the line of my dual capacity I have informed Mr. Cooper of my liking for this book. You can see from the above that I am absolutely off my nut about this book and I would appreciate it if Sylvia would notify me the minute the synopsis arrives and when I can expect to hear from you either by teletype or telephone so I can leave number where I can be reached late tonight.

**DAVID SELZNICK TO KAY BROWN**

May 22, 1936

Will certainly read "Gone with the Wind" synopsis minute it arrives. Your cast looks swell except are there roles for Garbo and Chaplin whose names I think would help bolster it don't you. I think we ought to also be able to find a part for that "sweet little person" who does not know anything about prices and is so naïve as to ask only fifty thousand dollars. I think we ought to use her to sell our pictures.

### KAY BROWN TO DAVID SELZNICK

May 22, 1936

I think you're slipping. I can think of lots more names to bolster up my picture of Gone with the Wind. I knew I'd get an awful blast on that price quotation. I take it that the synopsis of Gone with the Wind has not yet arrived. It was sent seven o'clock plane Wednesday night.

### DAVID SELZNICK TO KAY BROWN

*So Red the Rose* was a 1934 novel and a 1935 film, also about the Civil War. Despite the discouraging tone of the last telegram in this sequence, by July, Brown had accomplished her goal, and Selznick purchased the film rights for $50,000.

May 25, 1936

Have gone over and carefully thought about "Gone with the Wind." I think it is fine story and I understand your feeling about it. If we had under contract a woman ideally suited to the lead, I would probably be more inclined to buy it than I am today but I do feel that its only important showmanship values would be in either such star casting or in a tremendous sale of the book. To pay a large price for it now in the hope we could get such a star and-or in the further hope book will have tremendous sale is I feel unwarranted. Perhaps one of the larger companies can afford buy it now in the hope or expectation of such casting opportunities and such a sale but I do not feel we can take such a gamble. If it is not purchased immediately then I know you will watch its sales carefully and if it threatens to become an Anthony Adverse—which however I frankly doubt—then we presumably will be in as close touch as any other company but if it is bought in interim, we must have no regrets. I feel incidentally that its background is very strongly against it as witness "So Red the Rose" which also threatened to have tremendous sale and which in some particulars was in same category and which failed miserably as a picture. Most grateful for your interest and early action on this and do not want discourage you from bringing to our attention this forcibly any new or old story which you run across and therefore most sorry to have to say no in face of your enthusiasm for this story.

✳    ✳    ✳

**1936: JANUARY 8**

**DORA HERSHKOWITZ TO PHILLIP LEAR**

---

*Dora Hershkowitz (1909–) was the daughter of Romanian immigrants, a native of Boston, a graduate of Simmons College, and, throughout much of the Depression, an employee of the Farm Security Administration in Washington. Her devotion to the New Deal and the Democratic Party was one obvious stumbling block (or sparring ground) in her relationship with Phillip Lear (1905–1998), a Yale graduate and New York medical school student who was a dyed-in-the-wool Republican. Although Dora may have fumbled in this letter for a definition of love, it seems clear that she already had the answer: She and Phillip were married in September of 1936 and stayed married for sixty-one years, until his death at the age of ninety-two. Fressing is Yiddish for "overeating."* The Agricultural Adjustment Act (AAA), enacted by Congress in 1933, paid American farmers to cut back production so that prices would not continue to fall. In 1936, the Supreme Court ruled the act unconstitutional. John Marshall was the fourth chief justice of the Supreme Court, and to a large extent shaped its powers.

January 8, 1936

Dear Phil:

Little Dodie here again. So—you big so and so—you don't think my communications are literary masterpieces!!!! I'll! I'll! I'll!!! You can't do-o-o that. In spite of your opinion it was good to hear from you, and to be assured that you are not interested in my limbs, and that you don't have nightmares.

No, I did not go bicycling Sunday—went room hunting with a friend instead, thereby managing to have my exercise.

Sunday evening proved to be interesting. It was spent with a group of musicians, all members of the National Symphony Orchestra. Their reactions to the broadcasts were broadening and amusing.

I had a delightful time at Dr. Nasserman's home Monday night. He played Beethoven's Emperor Concerto and the Kreutzer Sonata on his phonograph. The music was wonderful, the fire cozy, and as usual, the drinks plentiful. It was a very restful evening—I thought of you.

Tonight I am going to the Jackson Day dinner given by the Democratic Party. Mrs. Roosevelt and other prominent people will do the speeching while yours truly will do the fressing. I wonder what the menu will have to say.

What did you think of the Supreme Court decision regarding the A.A.A.? It sure has created tension in Washington. The sooner they declare everything unconstitutional the sooner there will be a showdown which we need. Think of it! Six old fogies, Republicans, steeped in the past and their legal technicalities, unaware of reality and the trend of the times, daring to declare aid to the farmer who has been suffering for decades and who can't help himself unconstitutional. The humorous part of the whole thing is that it is not constitutional for the Justices to declare Congressional legislation unconstitutional. They act only on precedent set by John Marshall.

As a result of the decision everyone, since Man is naturally a selfish animal, is wondering about the permanence and stability of his position. Sympathize with me. You'd feel bad, too, if the possibility of your being declared unconstitutional was imminent. Almost as bad as being declared immoral. Maybe I ought to start looking for another job. The opening you have—is the work interesting? I have always been a conscientious employee and actually enjoy working hard and overtime, mind you, if the work is interesting.

I am planning to come up to New York over the Feb. 22nd weekend. The holiday comes on a Saturday and so I will have two whole days in the big city. There is a possibility that mother may visit New York in January. If she does, I'll try to get down to see her.

Apropos to a postscript of one of your letters I thought I might attempt to relate some of my ideas on a very old, greatly misunderstood, and very much abused subject—love. (excluding mother love etc)

I would say it is a state or condition resulting from a relationship between a man and woman who are physically, mentally, and spiritually compatible. I conceive of it as a state that does not remain static, one that changes, ideally becoming more intense and richer as time passes. At first, the physical probably predominating, later, the latter two growing in importance. Therefore, I do not think it possible for two people to fall in love immediately on first sight of each other. They may be physically attracted, thereby becoming sexually intoxicated. (I become very annoyed when people use "love" in vain to describe that state. Don't misunderstand me, I don't object to the state—I object to the name.) I do not think it is possible for two people to have the sort of feeling for each other that I am trying to describe until they have lived together for some time.

If, in addition to possessing the above-mentioned requisites, two individuals, of different sex, are good friends, have respect for each other, understand each other, are cooperative, adaptable, willing to adjust, considerate of each other, they will have a beautiful, rare, and rich relationship. The idealist in me has spoken. (I am a paradox, a most peculiar paradox.)

The practicalist in me appreciates the state about which I speak is not an easy one to obtain, and that it requires intelligence, concentration, and conscious effort on the parts of the interested parties.

The optimist in me believes, in spite of Man's (meaning the Homo Sapian and not the male sex) limitations that the ideal can be attained.

Now, how does all this tie up with your question? In view of my ideas, I cannot, if I am truthful with you and myself, say "yes" to the question in question. (Don't you love the alliteration—humor—time out to Haw haw) "No" certainly is not a correct answer. My belief that great potentialities, for the growth of such a state for us exist would be answering your question more truthfully than anything else can think of at the present time.

In all fairness to yourself and myself I presume I should attempt to define my feelings for you. I trust you will not object to my frank and sincere desire to be honest. (I firmly believe that frankness and honesty is the only basis on which any relationship can operate successfully). Also, forgive my very serious mood. The weather, rain since Mon., must have brought it on. And since repression is bad I am attempting to express it (badly, I'll admit, but I am banking on your understanding).

I find you physically attractive. I have a great deal of respect for your background, your character (what I know of it) and your efforts to reach a goal. I think you have the capacity for friendship, in its finest sense, are considerate, cooperative, and perhaps adjustable. What more can I say?

My, this is lengthy. Forgive me if I have detained you too long from chopping legs.

Shall I hear from you soon?

As ever<br>Dora

On reading what I have written I realize how jumbled it all is, and am sending it on the chance that you will understand what I am trying to say. At least, I hope you will appreciate my attempt and desire to be honest and to give you an idea of some of my thoughts which I have had for a long, long time. I certainly should appreciate an expression of yours on any subject.

1937: FEBRUARY 6
MARGARET MITCHELL TO MORDECAI THURMAN

*A popular success on an unprecedented level,* Gone with the Wind *sold fifty thousand copies in one day, a million copies in six months, and eventually became one of the best-selling American novels of all time. For its author, Margaret Mitchell (1900–1949), the publication not only brought instant fame, a Pulitzer Prize, and a movie sale (see page 532), but also plenty of theories and armchair analysis. Mordecai Thurman (1908–1985) was rabbi at the Wilmington, North Carolina, Temple of Israel and had apparently suggested to Mitchell that* Gone with the Wind *had been written with the Great Depression in mind.*

Wilmington, North Carolina
February 6, 1937

Dear Doctor Thurman:

I only wish I were not pressed for time by illness in my family, for I would like to write you a long letter of appreciation of the wonderful letter you wrote me. You said so many things that were well calculated to warm this author's heart, and I thank you for all of them. I do not think you are "too ministerial" in your analysis. I thought it a very fair and broad minded summing up of the underlying currents of my story. I am happy to know that you intend to review it. . . .

I do not know if this will interest you but I will tell you about it. Many people have thought that I wrote "Gone with the Wind" as a parallel to the modern War and depression, but I had almost finished the book before the depression began. When I wrote it everyone thought the boom was here to stay. But I wrote about another world that blew up under the unsuspecting feet of our grandparents, without any idea that the world in which I lived would blow up shortly. Now that I look back on it I feel that the same qualities of courage are needed when, at any period of history, a world turns over. And the same qualities of gentleness and idealism are needed too.

1938: APRIL 17
J.I.A. TO ELEANOR ROOSEVELT

*Although unemployment had fallen somewhat by 1936, two years later it started to rise again—and would not be truly reversed until the American entry into World War II. In the meantime, the first lady (see page 529) continued to receive letters like the following one from Centerdale, Rhode Island. The response: "Mrs.*

*Roosevelt . . . is very sorry indeed that she cannot comply with your wishes, but owing*
*to the large number of similar requests it is impossible for her to do as you ask. . . ."*

April 17, 1938

Dear Mrs. Roosvelt

I am writing to you to ask a big favor, the biggest favor anybody can ask. I
would like to know if you would pay my way to Hollywood. You may think me
crazy but I not. I mean every word I say. I know you may write back and say, lots
of people ask you to pay their way to Hollywood or for some other reason, but
this is different   honest it is   you've just got to believe in me   your the only
one that can help. Or you may say what can I do child. Well you could tell them
that you sent me and you know I can act, I'm sure they would believe you, because you tell no fibes. Just think wouldn't you be proud if I became a great
movie Star and you would say to your friends, She's the little girl who wrote to
me and asked if she could go to Hollywood. And I've helped to make her a great
Star. I would like to tell you all this in person and then you could see me, but I
have no money for carfare and I don't want you to bother to give it to me. My
Little mother is a sickly lady, she is lovely so small and sweet   I love my little
mother dearly and I want to help her all I can so this is why I am writing to you,
It will also give me a future and bring proudness to my relatives. My Little
mother has something wrong with her heart which these small Doctors dont
know although they do try their best. So I thought if I went to Hollywood and
earned enough money I would be able to give my Little mother the best Doctors
and proper care. I am not writing this letter to Mr. Roosvelt because men don't
understand things like us laides do, so I am writing to you because I know you
understand. I have read and heard so many nice [missing text] I know I can act
because I make little plays which I get out of story books and act them out.
Please tell Mr. Roosvelt that I'm terribly sorry he lost that Bill. I think Mr.
Roosvelt is doing wonders. Please be sure and tell him this, it will make him feel
much better. I told some of my friends about my Idea but they only laugh at me,
and I get discouraged but when I look at my Little mother I run upstairs in my
room and cry. I have Mr. Roosvelt's picture in my room and his name in big read
and blue letters. And when I looked at his picture it gave me an Idea and my
Idea was writing to you. Please Mrs. Roosvelt answer my letter, and please oh
please say yes that you'll try your hardest. God will never forget you in the next
world. And what you do for your father and mother will never be forgotton. My
father is also a sickly man, he had two nervous breakdowns but never got over
the second one. But I am a healthy child. I am fourteen years old. blue eyes,

about sixty in. tall, weigh 105½ pds, hair is long and curly sort of natural   the
color is light brown   my complexion is very white. I have big eyes. Please trust
in me with all your heart and I will trust in you with all my heart. Please just for
my Little mother. (That's what I call her because she is so small.)

   If you the Secretary should open this letter Before Mrs. Roosvelt please give
it to her. Thank you.

> A Little Girl who is still
> Unknown and Just
> Became Your Friend
> J.I.A.

## 1939

## ANAÏS NIN TO ROBERT DUNCAN

*Born in France, educated in New York City, author Anaïs Nin (1903–1977) spent
her early career in Europe but returned to the United States at the beginning of
World War II. Unheralded as a writer for much of her life, she published her own
stories, wrote erotica for hire, and kept a journal that, in part because of its expressions of feminist independence, would eventually make her famous. In this letter to
the poet Robert Duncan (1919–1988), Nin made an argument against guilt and in
favor of honesty. Her position, insofar as it concerned Duncan's army service, was
rare at a time when homosexuality in the military was treated as a criminal act. One
of the quotes most often attributed to her is "The only abnormality is the incapacity
to love."*

Henry was Henry Miller, Nin's mentor and one of her lovers.

1939

To Robert

   You refuse to free yourself from serving in the Army by declaring your homosexuality. And by this you will live a double lie, for you are also against war. At
the same time you feel burdened with guilt. Our only prison is that of guilt.
Guilt is the negative aspect of religion. We lost our religion but we kept the guilt.
We all have guilt. Even Henry has it, who seems the freest of all. Only domestic
animals have guilt. We train them so. Animals in the jungle do not have it.

   Everything negative should die. Jealousy as the negative form of love, fear the
negative form of life.

   You speak of suffering, of withdrawal, retreat. Face this suffering, for all the
real suffering can save us from unreality. Real pain is human and deepening.

Without real pain you will remain the child forever. The legend of Ondine tells of how she acquired a human soul the day she wept over a human love. You were caught in a web of unreality. You chose suffering in order to be awakened from your dreams, as I did. You are no longer the sleeping prince of neurosis. Don't run away from it now. If you run away from it without conquering it (I say accept the homosexuality, live it out proudly, declare it), then you will remain asleep and enchanted in a lifeless neurosis.

### 1939: FEBRUARY 28
### ELEANOR ROOSEVELT TO MRS. HENRY M. ROBERT, JR.

*Marian Anderson had been performing in concert recitals since winning a 1925 competition, but her venues were limited by her race. When the Daughters of the American Revolution barred the great black singer from performing at its Washing-ton, D.C., Constitution Hall, Eleanor Roosevelt (see pages 529 and 538) sent this letter to the DAR's president general. Less than two months later, the federal gov-ernment organized a public Easter Sunday concert at the Lincoln Memorial, where Anderson sang before seventy-five thousand people.*

February 28, 1939

My dear Mrs. Henry M. Robert Jr.:

I am afraid that I have never been a very useful member of the Daughters of the American Revolution, so I know it will make very little difference to you whether I resign, or whether I continue to be a member of your organization.

However, I am in complete disagreement with the attitude taken in refusing Constitution Hall to a great artist. You have set an example which seems to me unfortunate, and I feel obliged to send in to you my resignation. You had an op-portunity to lead in an enlightened way and it seems to me that your organiza-tion has failed.

I realize that many people will not agree with me, but feeling as I do this seems to me the only proper procedure to follow.

Very sincerely yours

### 1939: SEPTEMBER 6
### ELEANOR ROOSEVELT TO CAROLA VON SCHAFFER-BERNSTEIN

*Eleanor Roosevelt was a champion of human rights, committed to helping women, children, blacks, coal miners, laborers, and refugees. But she was also a daughter of privilege, a member of a patrician class that was, in the 1920s and 1930s, fairly steeped in anti-Semitism. Both aspects of the first lady were evident in this letter to Carola von Schaffer-Bernstein, a former school friend who was living in Germany and seemed to support the Nazi regime. Mixed with the distaste Eleanor expressed for the megalomania and methods of Hitler was the quiet assumption that the "ascendancy of the Jewish people" was something that might need to be stopped.*

Arnold was Schaffer-Bernstein's son. This letter was written just five days after the German invasion of Poland, the beginning of World War II.

September 6, 1939

Dear Carola:

Your last letter, written on August 19, has just come to me and I realize even more how terribly sad you are, for evidently Arnold had meant a great deal to both you and his father. Anything as sudden as his illness seems to have been is a doubly hard blow.

I cannot say that I feel the present situation had a parallel in 1914. All of us, of course, are appalled at plunging the European continent into war, but I do not think there is any bitterness toward the German people in this country. There is an inability to understand how people of spirit can be terrified by one man and his storm troops to the point of countenancing the kind of horrors which seem to have come on in Germany, not only where the Jews are concerned, but as in the case of the Catholics and some of the liberal German Protestants.

I say this with knowledge, because I have actually seen many of the people who have reached this country from concentration camps. I realize quite well that there may be a need for curtailing the ascendancy of the Jewish people, but it seems to me it might have been done in a more humane way by a ruler who had intelligence and decency.

The radio makes a tremendous difference because one can actually hear these leaders make speeches, and I listened, knowing enough German, to Mr. Hitler's speech to the Reichstag. He never mentioned that there was a God whom we are supposed to have, nor did he show the slightest sympathy for the people whom he had plunged into war. There was a certain triumphant note through the whole of it which was never heard from the leaders of other nations.

You are wrong if you think the people of this country hate Germany. That is not so, but they hate Hitler and Nazism because of the evidence that have been placed before them. I do not think either France or England was anxious for war and I think that was shown by the fact that their first planes dropped no bombs but propaganda leaflets. They could easily have killed women and children in the same way that women and children have been killed in Warsaw and other Polish cities.

You who believe in God must find it very difficult to follow a man who apparently thinks he is as great as any god. I hope that we are not facing another four years of struggle and I hope that our country will not have to go to war, but no country can exist free and unoppressed while a man like Hitler remains in power.

I shall be thinking of you and yours with great sympathy until these horrors are passed.

Affectionately,

## 1940: OCTOBER 8
## MARY ANDERSON TO JOHN STUDEBAKER

*John Ward Studebaker (1887–1989) was commissioner of education when he received this letter from Mary Anderson (1872–1964), director of the Women's Bureau for the U.S. Department of Labor. What Anderson envisioned for women in defense work—the unfortunate racial distinction she made here aside—turned out to be extremely conservative. During World War II, jobs would be held by some twenty million women, seven million of whom had never worked; before the war was over, there would be such a large demand for production that women would enter virtually all fields of labor.*

In replying to Anderson, Studebaker wrote: "Women and girls are eligible for training on the same terms as men. . . . As soon as employers show an inclination to use women, training will be offered them."

October 8, 1940

My dear Dr. Studebaker:

I have received a great many letters asking what women can do to be trained for work in the defense program. I usually suggest in reply that they register at the nearest Public Employment Office and then apply through the Vocational Education Service for the same training that men and boys are getting.

I realize that women and girls are now getting training for the traditional women's jobs such as domestic science, dressmaking, and commercial courses, but during the last war women did all kinds of work in the defense industries, along with men, and demonstrated their ability creditably as machine operators, inspectors, and other operatives. With training women were able to work with blueprints and follow graphic instructions on the same basis as men on similar jobs. On some work, especially those with small parts, even more was accomplished by women because of their finger dexterity and quickness of motion. Studies of women's work in the World War proved their ability to operate machines such as drill presses, milling machines and many others.

The training that you are offering in vocational schools is such that it could be given with some adjustments to women. Courses in blueprint interpretation, the use of gauges and scales, shop mathematics, principles of mechanical drawing and machine shop practice will undoubtedly be as useful to many women in securing employment and helping in the emergency as to men. I trust, therefore, that you will see your way clear, if you have not already done so, to issue a recommendation to public trade schools offering industrial courses for defense production, that women who wish to take training be given consideration and allowed the same opportunities as men.

The Women's Bureau will be very glad to work with you on plans for women's defense training.

Sincerely yours,
Mary Anderson, Director.

Work for Women in Overhaul
(Airplanes)

1. Stripping old fabric from fabric covered airfoils preparatory to overhaul.
2. Fabric and upholstery work.
3. Cleaning and stripping of paint from hulls, fuselage and metal parts. (Recommended for colored women, especially vigorous physique). Work done now by colored laborers.
4. Limited amount of hand painting, not requiring special skill.
5. Hand brush doping of fabric-covered airfoils. (High temperature working conditions would permit use of women of excellent physique only.)
6. Electrical bonding of aircraft.
7. Specially qualified women on minor instrument repair.
8. Application of radium paint to instrument dials.
9. Overhaul of spark plugs.
10. Progressing and moving of parts between shops.
11. Shop storerooms—issuing, receiving and stocking supplies; clerical work in connection therewith.
12. Typists and clerks.

**1941: DECEMBER 7**

**DOROTHEA TAYLOR TO P. H. TAYLOR**

---

*The Japanese attack on Pearl Harbor killed twenty-three hundred Americans, in-jured more than a thousand, dismantled air and naval forces in the Pacific—and galvanized the country's entry into World War II. In Honolulu, Dorothea Taylor wrote this letter to her brother just hours after the bombing. Taylor was a nurse who had gone to Hawaii as a private companion to a woman named Jessie Miles Camp-bell. Campbell happened not to be in Hawaii at the time of the attack; Taylor would remain there throughout the war.*

Joseph Boyd Poindexter was governor of Hawaii. *The Keys of the Kingdom* was a popular novel by A. J. Cronin.

Honolulu, Dec. 7, 1941

This morning was as delightful a Sunday morning as ever. There was a cool breeze, for rain had fallen in the night. I wakened about seven. There was the sound of heavy firing in the distance as there so often is when our brave defend-ers are practicing. I thought it peculiar the paper was not in the box. When I stepped up to the street to look at the ocean I noticed heavy black smoke, as from oil rising from the region of Pearl Harbor. My first thought was that an ac-cident had set fire to one of the oil tanks, or worse still, aircraft, which did not amaze me as they are often shot for practice.

Calmly I sat down to my coffee and doughnuts to listen to the broadcast of the Salt Lake City Choir. The singing was interrupted by the announcer stating that a sporadic attack had been made on Pearl Harbor and one Japanese plane had been shot down. Civilians were forbidden to use the telephone or to go on the streets. We were advised to keep our radios on and bulletins would be given as fast as they came in. We were told to be calm and stay where we were, that everything was under control. The announcer had to repeat a number of times that this was a real attack, not practice maneuvers.

Bulletins and orders continued at intervals. All firemen were called to duty. All army and navy men told to report to their stations. Disaster wardens were sent to their districts and the meeting places named for each ward. Mine is at the Robert Louis Stevenson school, just down the steps from my gate. Explo-sions and anti-aircraft firing continued. I went to the top of the reservoir across the street where most of my frightened neighbors had congregated. With my binoculars I could see numerous large fires in Pearl Harbor and Hickam Field.

It made me sick at heart to see all the oil going up in clouds of black smoke, for of what good will our ships and planes be without oil? The loss is already disastrous. I heard two shells whistle overhead. The fire siren sounded every few minutes. KGU announced a bomb had hit about 50 ft. from their building, and there were some other craters elsewhere. As a precaution I packed up all the valuable things in the apartment in small baggage, so it could be moved easily. I filled everything with water, inside and out, and Miss Davis did the same, and asked everyone to draw water into every container in their apartments. There was smoke rising from two large fires in Makiki district, about a mile away, but I have not yet learned what started them or how much damage was done. Governor Poindexter spoke on the radio at 11 a.m., but unfortunately that is just when my set went bad so I could not get any broadcasts. It has been acting up for some time, and has not been serviced for a year. I had to depend on my neighbor's radio for further bulletins. One bomb fell on a place on Lillian Street, about two miles from me. No one hurt.

Parachute troops were reported to have landed on St. Louis heights—a mostly bare steep hill, far from any military objectives—and guards were directed by radio to deal with them. I never learned whether the suspects were our own men who had to bail out of a plane or whether they were enemies. By mid-afternoon there was no more smoke from fires that I could see, which was a relief because the wind was blowing quite strongly all day, and still is.

Most of my time was spent trying to calm and divert these young navy wives. They have husbands on cruisers and destroyers and in the air force, but they cooked meals with each other and insisted I eat supper with them, which I did. They packed their suitcases and stayed at home. About three o'clock martial law was declared, so we now have to obey all orders and give an account of our every mo[v]e. Two civilian men are left on the place and they were made Civilian Defense wardens and act as police in the neighborhood. Tonight there is a complete blackout. Millions of stars not otherwise seen make the heavens shine with a soft glow. I believe the moon rises about 10. I am sitting in my dressing-room closet with the door shut, and heavy green paper over the narrow high screened opening in the shower. Very little air gets in through the cracks, so I go out and cool off every few minutes. I am not excited, nor a bit afraid. I have plenty of food on hand. We were instructed to boil all our drinking water in case the open reservoirs had been meddled with.

I resort to my knitting when I get a little nervous. I am in the midst of Cronin's book Keys to the Kingdom, but it was hard to concentrate on any reading or study today. Now night has come, everything is silent and peaceful. It has been a tense day, and with no lights on, everyone seems to have retired. You people on the mainland have probably had a lot more news of this incident than I have while right on the spot. One announcement stated a naval battle was going on west of Oahu. It was said a Japanese ship flying the American flag with planes marked with U.S. insignia came within range and started all the trouble. It has been an Incident. We are all wondering what tomorrow will bring forth.

> Most affectionately,
> Dorothea

## 1941: DECEMBER 22
## MONICA CONTER TO HER PARENTS

*Also present during the Pearl Harbor attack, a United States Army nurse named Monica Conter described the scene to her parents.*

Tripler was the army medical center on Honolulu.

> Hickam Field, Honolulu, T.H.
> December 22, 1941

My Dearest Daddy and Mother,

...I understand we may write anything that has been published in the local paper concerning the raid and as I know you are curious to know my part in the "show" I will try to give an account.

Sunday A.M.—Dec. 7th I rushed on duty at CENSORED late for duty (overslept as we had quite a party the night before at the Pearl Harbor Officers Club)....While drinking coffee and tomato juice—I heard some planes real low—one sounded like it might crash on the hospital CENSORED. Just as I jumped up from my desk, I heard a <u>terrible noise</u>—I said, "A plane crashed"—and ran out on the screened porch, 3rd floor, overlooking Pearl Harbor. The music really started!—What I saw was a lot of black smoke and about CENSORED planes so low they looked as if they might be landing in the Harbor. Having lived on the air post I have learned to identify our different types of planes and I know we didn't have anything with big red circles on the side—I turned to some of the patients who know aircraft and the other nurses (Miss Boyd) who <u>knew</u> aircraft and said, "My G—— it's the Japs!" They laughed and said, "Don't be silly—It's maneuvers." I was beating Sgt. Holliday on the shoulder trying to make him confirm my statement and he laughed too—so I ran downstairs to the Commanding Officer, Capt. Lane, M.C. and asked him if it was the "real McCoy—the Japs." All he could do was shake his head in the affirmative and start making phone calls.

Then I got all my patients down stairs to the first floor and we "all" stayed there. I mean the entire medical personnel working.

Really, I never heard so much noise in my life, bombs, some 500 lbs.—machine guns, our anti aircraft—and in the middle of it all some of our CENSORED were just coming in from the mainland <u>without</u> radio or ammunition or guns. Naturally, a few were "ruined"....

The wounded started coming in 10 minutes after the 1st attack. We called Tripler for more ambulances—they wanted to know if we were having "Maneuvers." Imagine! Well, the sight in our hospital I'll never forget. No arms, no legs, intestines hanging out etc.... In the meantime, the hangars all around us were burning—and that awful "noise." Then comes the second attack—We all fell face down on the wounded in the halls, O.R., and everywhere and heard the bombers directly over us. We (the nurses and the doctors) had no helmets nor gas masks—and it really was a <u>"helpless"</u> feeling.—One of the soldiers who works for my ward saw me and so we <u>shared</u> helmets together. In the meantime, the bombs were dropping all around us and when a 500 lb. bomb dropped about CENSORED from the CENSORED, we waited for the plane to come in as it felt like it had hit us—then they were gone. CENSORED.

All our electric clocks <u>stopped</u> on the dot. The dead were placed in back of the hospital, the walking wounded went in trucks to Tripler, and the seriously injured in the ambulances. We used our place as an "Evacuation Hospital".... The mayor sent out 20 cases of whiskey so that helped some—that is, the uninjured who were going around in a daze.—Of course, it was used medicinally too. We worked, and worked, and worked—and when night came on "Blackout" (I'm used to it now).... For a week the nurses slept in uniform on the ward in one of the officer's rooms. Then we were moved downstairs to "the X-Ray dark room"....

Received another letter from A. D. Glad Daddy wired him. He was quite worried. And I do appreciate people's interest in my welfare. But, tell everyone I wouldn't have missed it for anything. You know, I always loved activity and excitement—For once, I had "enough"....

A happy, happy New Year to all—

> Your loving daughter—
> Monica

\*   \*   \*

## 1942: JANUARY 28
## CORNELIA FORT TO LOUISE FORT

*In Honolulu, Cornelia Fort (1919–1943) was giving a flying lesson to a young student when an unfamiliar aircraft seemed to be heading directly for her plane. Eluding the Japanese attacker, she looked back to see smoke rising from Pearl Harbor. Within weeks, she received an invitation to join the Royal Air Force Air Transport Auxiliary in Britain, and days later she wrote this letter to her mother, Louise (1885–1969), apparently believing she would soon be overseas. As it turned out, Fort instead joined America's Women's Auxiliary Ferrying Service (WAFS) and flew planes from factories to air bases. In the spring of 1943, one of her plane's wings was accidentally clipped in midair by another plane's landing gear, and she crashed. She was the first woman pilot in U.S. history to die for her country.*

Dear Mother,

In writing this letter, which if delivered will be my last, I'm filled neither with a sense of morbidity nor a prescience of disaster. But the ocean voyage I will be making shortly has elements of danger and if I lose my life before seeing you again, dearest, I wanted to say aloha and send you my love forever and forever.

I want you to know that except for not seeing you in the last weeks when I've ached for you so, my life has been exceedingly happy. Thanks to environment, both physical and spiritual that you and Dad gave me, my life has been rich and full of meaning.

I've loved the green pastures and the cities, the sunshine on the plains and the rain in the mountains. Springtime in New York and fog in San Francisco.

Books and music have been deeply personal things to me, possessions of the soul. I've loved the multitudinous friends in many places and their many kindnesses to me. I've loved the steak and red wine and dancing in smoky nightclubs, self-important headwaiters who bring reams of French bread and wine sauces in New Orleans.

I've loved the ice coldness of the air in the Canadian Laurentians, the camaraderie of skiing, and the first scotch and soda as you sit in front of the fire.

I loved my blue jeans and the great dignity of life on the ranches. I loved foxhunting even with its snobbishness, I loved the deep pervading tiredness after six hours of timber-topping.

I dearly loved the airports, little and big. I loved the sky and the planes and yet, best of all, I loved flying. For it too was a deeply personal possession of the soul. I loved Johnny, because he knew what I meant when we were flying and I suddenly grinned or clapped my hands because the inside excitement was too great not to grin. I loved it best perhaps because it taught me utter self-sufficiency, the ability to remove oneself beyond the keep of anyone at all—and in doing so it taught me what was of value and what was not.

It taught me a way of life—in the spiritual sense. It taught me to cherish dignity and integrity and to understand the importance of love and laughter.

For I have loved many people and many places and many things and best of all I have loved life, and especially American life—And if I can say one thing in truth, it is that to my friends and convictions I have brought all the loyalty and integrity of which I am capable.

If I die violently, who can say it was "before my time"? I should have dearly loved to have had a husband and children. My talents in that line would have been pretty good, but if that was not to be, I want no one to grieve for me.

I was happiest in the sky—at dawn when the quietness of the air was like a caress, when the noon sun beat down and at dusk when the sky was drenched with the fading light. Think of me there and remember me, I hope, as I shall you.

With love,
Cornelia

## 1942: JULY 15
## HANAYE MATSUSHITA TO IWAO MATSUSHITA

*After Pearl Harbor, Japanese Americans became, as far as the government was concerned, more Japanese than American. By the fall of 1942, more than one hundred thousand had been removed to ten remote internment camps between the Mississippi River and the Sierra Nevada. Some of them, including Japanese national Iwao Matsushita (1892–1979), were deemed the more dangerous "enemy aliens" and were moved to facilities run not by the War Relocation Authority but by the Immigration and Naturalization Service. Matsushita was arrested the night of Pearl Harbor and sent to Fort Missoula, in Montana. Meanwhile, his wife, Hanaye Matsushita (1898?–1965), presumably not considered as serious a threat, was sent to the Minidoka relocation camp in Idaho. Since their marriage in 1919, the couple had never been apart, and Hanaye found the separation, exacerbated by her unfamiliar surroundings, extremely hard to bear.*

This letter was translated from the Japanese.

July 15, 6 a.m.

To my husband:

Monday I received your letter. Thank you so much. I'm glad that your letters of late seem to be arriving quickly and safely. I'm glad to hear that your health is good. I'm doing well. I want to write more often but my eyesight seems to be going. It's probably my age. My nerves are also on edge, and when I take up a pen my heart leaps into my throat and I can't write. Forgive me. I've really gotten old and embarrassingly weak-spirited. Every day keeps me busy, with little free time to do what I want.

Uncle is as you left him although he has experienced some difficulties as well.

Please know that I'm working as hard as I can. I continue to pray to god that we will see each other as soon as possible. I'm overwhelmed with thoughts of how you spend each day. While I realize that I need to stay level-headed, it's depressing to feel as though I have to take care of everything myself. I've come to know the people next door and that helps, but I still spent the last two weeks in tears.

My neighbors on both sides are doctors. Do you know Dr. Kato from Tacoma? He lives next door. Lillian married Jack and moved in with him. Their quarters are in Area C, so we don't see much of each other. Wataru's place is in Area A, so I hardly ever see him either.

Since I didn't know a soul when I arrived after Uncle, I was constantly on the verge of tears and lost weight until I was nothing but skin and bones, but recently I've been trying to get over my loneliness and have gained some weight. . . . I'm not ill so don't worry. I have so many stories to tell you that although I may risk death, I won't die until we see each other and you've heard them in person.

Take heart. Whatever happens, pray to God and live on. No matter how sad I may feel, I'll keep going. I keep myself busy every day with this and that. With so many visitors coming and going, I don't have much time for reading. People I don't even know have been extremely charitable, while those I had counted on don't even give me a second glance. I now understand human nature. I sometimes think about how wonderful it will be when peace prevails and we can go back home to Seattle.

Doctors have to get up in the middle of the night to treat patients and are even busier in the afternoons, though things have gotten much easier for them with the completion of the hospital.

Shigeko's younger sister Chiyoko lives in the same flophouse. She's a nice girl.

I eat well every day, so don't worry. I imagine the move was hard on everyone over there. I'd like to send you something but am unable to reach anyone outside. Forgive me. If it's something insignificant I can buy it at the canteen. Let me know and I'll send it right away. Don't hesitate to request anything you might need.

Thank you so much for the stone talisman. Everyone enjoyed looking at it. I'll keep it with me forever. It will protect me I'm sure.

Sunday we were shown a movie and I was finally able to forget about everything for once. As long as I'm here, I'm safe, fed, and can buy things at the canteen.

From here on out, I plan to write you once a week. Stay in good spirits.

Hana

## 1942: SEPTEMBER 2
## DOROTHY PARKER TO ALEXANDER WOOLLCOTT

---

*Known for her wit and her writing, her seat at the Algonquin Round Table and the drinking she frequently did there, Dorothy Parker (1893–1967) was anything but glib in this description of her husband's departure for the army. Parker was eleven years older than Alan Campbell, an actor and screenwriter whom she had married in 1933 (they would divorce in 1947 and remarry in 1950). Apparently Parker urged him rather forcefully to enlist; one friend suggested that Campbell's watch, which was inscribed* Qui Sensat Acet–*"Who feels, acts"—should have read "Whose wife feels, acts." No hint of that subtext was evident in this remarkable letter to fellow Round Table writer Alexander Woollcott (1887–1943), who once described Parker as being "so odd a blend of Little Nell and Lady Macbeth."*
"Goodbye Dolly Gray" was an old Civil War song. A-, B-, and C-cards entitled civilians to increasing amounts of gasoline.

FOX HOUSE<br>Pipersville, Bucks County<br>Pennsylvania

September second.

Dear Alec,

Private Campbell has just gone, and I'm afraid I'm feeling a little like Dolly Gray. So I thought I would—Oh hell, I wanted to talk to you. So here's this letter.

I am this minute back from Philadelphia, where I went with him to see him off. Seeings-off are usually to be regretted, but I am so glad that I went. Twice before he had had a card with a date and had appeared with his bag, all ready, but each time—that cutting off of that dog's tail by those inches—they had told him to go home and wait. Even to-day, the sergeant said to him, "Are you <u>sure</u> you want to do this?" Yes. He was sure he wanted to do this.

The enlistment office in Philadelphia is in the customs house—it is a great, bare room, used, I suppose, as a sort of warehouse before. Along one wall are a couple of benches, packed tight with men sitting down, and beyond them is a line of men, moving up, man by man, as a man vacates the bench to go to the enlistment sergeant, and the sitting men move up to give another place, and the standing men move along a place for their turn. They are the men coming that day to enlist in the army. All the while we were there, that line kept lengthening, and men were still coming in when we left. That goes on every day, all day. Jesus, Alec, I guess we're all right.

Most of them look poor—I mean by that, they haven't got coats on, they have soiled shirts and stained pants, their working clothes. The Lord God knows, those men who have made up their minds don't look poor in any other way and aren't poor! The majority of them are very young—"heart-breakingly young", I read in a piece by a lady who watched the troops go by and threw them roses, which were their immediate need. They are not in the least heart-breaking, and I think if you called them that they would turn out to be neck-breaking. They are young, certainly—several even had women standing beside them in line, their mommas, come to give consent to a minor's enlistment—but they're all right. There were many older men, too, carefully dressed, and obviously prosperous in their businesses—which they were willing to leave. There was nothing whatever pathetic about them, either. There were numerous Negroes. And nobody avoided them, as they stood in line with the whites, nobody shied away from them or stood in silence. They all talked with one another, in the lowered voices you decently accord a big office full of busy men, but a man in line talked to the men on both sides of him.

(Look, Alec, I'm not going to make any more pencil corrections. I know you will know what I mean.)

The greater part of the room is for the men who are going to camp that day. They all have their bags, and the only time I busted was at the sight of a tall, thin young Negro—"lanky" I belive is the word always employed—carrying a six-inch square of muslin in which were his personal effects. It looked so exactly like a bean-bag. . . . And then I realized I was rotten to be tear-sprinkled. He wasn't sad. He felt fine. . . . I was ashamed of myself. And yet, dear Alec, I defy you to have looked at that bean-bag, and kept an arid eye. That, of course, has nothing to do with war. Except, also of course, that a man who had no more than that was going to fight for it. . . .

Well, anyway, there were a few camp-stools—not enough, many were standing—for mothers and wives and friends and various interested parties. Many women had brought their kids, certainly beacuse there were no nurses to leave them with, and the little ones pooped about and fought and whined and demanded drinks of water and in general conducted themselves like swine. But theirs was the only bad behavior. Not one woman but was fine. They were not quite of all classes. There were no stinking rich nor fantastically poor. They were lower-to-middle and middle-to-upper. There wasn't one that didn't look proud and respecting, both of herself and of the man because of whom she was there.

The men who were to go to camp—they didn't know where they were going, they are not told until they go, and that is, of course, quite right—stood in line, filed along to desks, filled out forms, and were finger-printed. They were not yet in the army. It was impressed upon them that they could get the hell out then, if they wanted to. No one went.

Then a sergeant called the roll of their names. I was astonished, Alec, at the preponderance of the short, quick English or Scottish or American names—Marsh, Kent, Brown, Downs, Leith. We think—due I am afraid to the newspapers—of factory workers, and most of these men were obviously those, as a mess of consonants. God knows that is nothing against them, but it just happens that this especial day, those men who had volunteered were of plain, familiar names. There were only a couple of Cazzonottis and Schecovitxixzes. But, as I say, this is only this day. There was also, God help us, only one to represent my side—a lone Levy. I am delighted to say he was a fine looking young man.

They formed in two blocks of thirty men each—six men across, five men down. Then they took the oath of induction into the army of the United States. I had never heard it before, never seen men take it. It was a fine and solemn and stirring thing. It is flat simple and direct, as to what they pledge themselves to do, and it is in the form of a question—it begins "Do you ———"? When the sergeant had finished reading it to them, those sixty men said "I do" as one man. I never heard a thing like that. There were no stragglers, no piping voices, no quavers. Precise and proud and strong it came, from sixty men—"I do". Jesus, Alec. I will not soon forget that sound.

Then the sergeant talked to them, as decent a talk as I have evr heard. Then he said, "men on the right are to go to Fort Cumberland, men on the left to Fort

Meade." Then he turned to the Fort Cumberland group and called "Private Campbell!" I had one horror-stricken moment when I thought he was going to say "stop biting your nails'." But it turned out, when our private stepped forward looking pretty sheepish, that Private Campbell was to have charge of his detail, that the men were to report to him at the station, and obey his orders on the way to camp. I saw Private Campbell for a moment before they left for the station. Private Campbell said only, "I'm going to see they don't leave the car messy." Dear Alec, he will be a brigadier-general by Tuesday.

Fort Cumberland, by the way, is where you go for a few days, to get your clothes and take your tests and be assigned to what they think is best for you. And I must say, I have the deepest respect for the way they seem to be trying to assign a man to his most useful job. From there, they are sent on some place else. I will let you know as soon as I know.

Then we went to the station. The Mothers and wives and friends all came too, and so did the kids, but the kids felt something and behaved superbly. The men were lined up in two rows, each man with his bag beside him—the varying kinds of bags, Alec! Ah, it really is a democratic war!—and Private Campbell, giving orders. I couldn't hear much—drat those acoustics in the Penn station at Philadelphia—but I did hear him say something and then add, "That is, if it's all right with you." I love Alan. Don't you, Alec?

In the station, it was a little bad. Oh, I don't mean everybody didn't go on being swell—but you know how it is, when a train's going out. The mothers and wives and girls all had tears in their eyes, and they all looked carefully away from one another, because you can be fine, yourself, but when you see tears, you're gone. Jesus, what fine people, Alec!

So while we were standing there, there came up to me a fat, ill-favored, dark little woman, who said to me, "Parn me, but aren't you Doorthy Parker? Well, I've no doubt you've heard of me, I'm Mrs. Sig Greesbaum, Edith Greesbaum, you'd probably know me better as, I'm the head of our local chapter of the Better Living Club, and we'd like to have you come talk to us, of course I'm still a little angry at you for writing that thing about men not making advances at girls who wear glasses, because I've worn glasses for years, and Sig, that's my husband, but I still call him my sweetheart, he says it doesn't matter a bit, well, he wears glasses himself, and I want you to talk to our club, of course we can't pay you any money, but it will do you a lot of good, we've had all sorts of wonderful people, Ethel Grimsby Loe that writes all the greeting cards, and the editor of the Doylestown Intelligenser, and Mrs. Mercer, that told us all about Italy when she used to live there after the last war, and the photographs she showed us of her cypresses and all, and it would really be a wonderful thing for you to meet us, and now when can I put you down to come talk to us?"

So I said I was terribly sorry, but if she didn't mind, I was busy at the moment. So she looked around at the rows of men—she hadn't seen them before, apparently; all they did was take up half the station—and she giggled heartily and said, "Oh, what are those? More poor suckers caught in the draft?"

And an almighty wrath came upon me, and I said, "Those are American patriots who have volunteered to fight for your liberty, you Sheeny bitch!" And I walked away, already horrified—as I am now—at what I had said. Not, dear, the gist, which I will stick to and should, but the use of the word "sheeny", which I give you my word I have not heard for forty years and have never used before. The horror lies in the ease with which it came to me—And worse horror lies in the knowledge that if she had been black, I would have said "You nigger bitch"—Dear God. The things I have fought against all my life. And that's what I did.

Well, so anyway, then they came down to the train, and then I left before the train pulled out, because flesh and blood is or are flesh and blood.

Alec, the private is a good man. He could have had a commission; he saw in Washington the men comissioned as majors and colonels and lieutenat colonels—cutters and directors and producers and assistants. He said—and that's all he ever said about it—"I don't think this is that kind of war." He enlisted without telling one soul. He had a job at which he was extremely good and at which he got a preposterous, in anybody's terms, salary. Just before he left, he had an offer of a six-months contract at Hollywood at twelve hundred and fifty dollars a week.

Of course it is right that he did what he has done—but no one told him what was right, except himself. He had had a bad time. When he was a kid, he liked his father; he has apparently always hated his mother. When he was fourteen, sensitive and cognizant, his mother divorced his father, took Alan, and never allowed him to see his father again. (His father died some three years after.) His resntment against his mother increased to the point where he cannot remain in the room with her—although she gives him some curious guilt, as only Southern mothers can, about his lack of filial duty. He went to New York after V.M.I—because his father went there; he himself loathed a military college—did what he could and damn near starved. Hollywood was all assurance to him. He was good at what he did, he did it with all his conscience, he said whatever it was, it was honest work—not what came out of it, but what he put into it.

And I behaved like a shit to him, Alec. I screamed about Hollywood. I had much right on my side, but I used all the wrong things. I yipped about lowering of standards and debasing of princilples. There was a lot in what I said. But there was nothing in what I thought I understood. Private Campbell's standards are not low.

He's given up a lot. His job, the house here he builded—no, I don't mean built, I mean Builded—which, I think, means more to him than anything. Anything, of course, except what he must do. I know other men have done as much, but sometimes I see the other side. I hear men who say, "Gee, I'd certainly like to do something in the war—but there's my business I've got to look after, and everything." I hear women who say, "Well, let them take everybody but George. Goodness knows they don't need him—they've got enough men." They are not the natives or the workers around here, who are all we've seen, day by day. But when we've been in to New York we've heard those things.

Now about Alan's mother. She always comes up to expectations, but this time she has outdone them and herself. When she heard Alan had enlisted, she made a scene that shook the oat fields. "Selfish", "heartless", "never thinks of me"—oh, it was great. Then when she found that did not induce him to desert the army, she found a happier—for her—role. She became the gold-star mother. Her heart was broken. She went all about the country side—she has a B card, I guess for being Southern—telling all the neighbors of the sacrifice she was making for her country. In most cases the act flopped; their sons had gone before hers. But she got some of them. There was a little delegation that came up here and talked to Alan and me about that poor sick woman living all alone. Alan spoke to them. We ended friends.

Then she tried heart attacks. We brought our doctor, who pronounced her in perfect shape. She then, of course, hated him and us. I am not a vengeful woman, no matter what you have said—possibly for the perfectly working reason that if you just sit back and wait, the bastards will get theirs, without your doing anything about it, and it will be fancier than anything you could ever have thought up. But I would, for the sake of immedaite action, give quite a large bit of my soul if something horrible would happen to that woman for poisoning Alan's last days here.

You see, there is no basis for it, Alec, but her insane selfishness. It isn't that she is not going to see him for a while. When he was in Hollywood for a year or so at a crack, when he was in New York, when he first came, for four years without once seeing her, that never worried her. Nor can it be the dread of immediate or even eventual danger for him. When he was in Spain, being bombed and shelled and machine-gunned and sniped at, she sat under a magnolia tree and waved her fan. (I may say, when we came back from Spain, she said to me, "well, that old war wasn't goin' on while you were there, was it?" So I said, with what I thought was blasting irony, "Oh, no, they stopped the war while your son was there". So she said, smiling elegantly, "Well, I tho't so.") It's just that she must do everything to make everything wretched for everybody but herself and her importance. I know. I know it is pathetic that she can achieve importance in no other way. Only, you know, it isn't.

She lives perhaps five miles from us, in a most horrible little house, horrible because of her decor. ("Awways sayude ah could be inteya decraytuh") It is however, a little house, if you consider four bedrooms, three baths and the usuals little, which I do not. She refers to it as her "rotten lil ole shayukah". (That is meant to spell the way she says "shack", but I guess it doesn't actually convey it.) The fact that Alan and I bought her the shayukah at great expense, and keep it going at greater, means nothing. She wants to come live here. I don't know what the hell she would do here. Here I am with no servants, no telephone, no gasoline—even if I could drive. The farmer and his wife and children live over in the barn, a good stone's throw if you had a pitching arm. I can't stay on here. In the first place, I've got to root up some work, and in the second nobody could do it. But she is obsessed to move in here, and settle. And if you say "Why not?" I can only say we tried that once, while we were in Hollywood, and she fired our farmer—and oh boy, are they hard to replace—fired our servants, and set fire to our drawing-room.

This isn't lousy. She could go back to Richmond, where she lives with an enormous family of brothers and sisters all of whom she has buffaloed, and a circle of illiterate friends. But she won't do it. She wails about her horrible loneliness here, and when Alan—who is afraid of her, there's no good saying he isn't and so for that matter am I—suggests that she go back home, she says that Richmond is too dangerous—she's just sure they're goin to bomb it. She says she'd only feel real safe in this house. . . .

Oh, the hell with her. I don't want to talk about her any more. Anyway she'll be here any minute—because she'll always be here any minute, no matter what time—and I'll have to face it.

And who am I to talk about people's families? On the way back from Philadelphia, I telephoned my brother and sister—whom I had neglected to inform that I was back in the East. I got my sister, and said Alan had enlisted and had gone. She said, "Oh, isn't that terrible? Well, it's been terrible here, too, all Summer. I never saw such a Summer. Why, they didn't even have dances Saturday nights at the club."

So then I tried my brother, who is not bad, but I got my sister-in-law. I told her about Alan. She said, "Oh, really? Well, of course, he's had a college education. That's what's holding Bertram back—he never had a college education". (She has a son named Bertram, approximately thirty-five) "He'd just love to be an aviator, but of course he hasn't got a college education." I skipped over Bertram's advanced age for the aviation corps, and explained that the college-educated Alan had enlisted as a private. "Oh, really?" she said. "Oh, listen, Dot, we're going to take a new apartment, the first of October. It's got two rooms that the sun simply POURS in—and you know how I love sun!" I don't, Alec.

Honestly, if you were suddenly to point a finger at me and say, "Dorothy Parker, what is your sister-in-law's opinion of sun?" I should be dum-founded.

Jesus Christ. People whose country is at war. People who live in a world on fire, in a time when there have never before been such dangers, such threats, such murders. . . .

Well. On the other hand, and so far outbalancing them, thank God, there are those boys in their sweat-stained shirts streaming in to enlist, there are those sixty men saying "I do" in one strong voice, there is Private Campbell, U.S.A.

I think I'd like to write a story about that enlistment place. That isn't being phoney, is it?

I've got to write a lot of stories—if, of course, I can. I've got the farm to keep going, I've got myself, I've got Alan's mother. I've been feeling pretty guilty about not doing any war work. But if I can keep all this swinging, I'll be releasing a man for the front just as much as if I were welding in a factory. I am proud to think that and to know it.

Dear Alec, I'll be here for a few days, and then I'm going in to the Ritz Tower. Alan knew the manager and got me a room, much less expensive than you think, though still too expensive. I will, though, as often as the hired man can spare gas to meet me at the station, come out here, because there are alterations going on, and I should say a few words. This address is always the one for me. Please, dear Alec, please. I'll be embarassed when this letter is sent. It's so long. I can only say, if I had had more time, it would have been longer. I think you know that my friendship could not be deeper and higher than writing you this, and knowing you understand why and to whom I write it.

Dear Alec—

Dorothy—

*    *    *

*Maurice Kidder (?–1975), an army chaplain, was waiting to be sent to England when he received this letter from his wife, Isabel Alden Kidder (1913?–1989), who would spend the next three years without him.*

The Kidders had two young children; their son Joel was six.

Durham, New Hampshire

The First Day,

My darling, I call this the first day, for it is the first day in which I do not know where you are. If your ship slipped out into the wideness of ocean last night, tonight, or tomorrow I shall not know until after the war probably. Maybe there will be many details which I shall never know, and that seems hard to bear. It must seem equally hard to you to feel that there are things which are going to happen to "we three" which you cannot know. But I shall attempt to write as many of them down as possible.

If you could see me now, pleased as punch because down in the cellar the fire is burning and it is of my creating. I am determined to master that imperturbable monster. Otherwise, it just isn't decent to have it there. But I say burning with a good deal of relief. For I was afraid it was roaring. My coal came this afternoon and I got a fire built. . . . But it got away from me. The house got so hot I shut all the radiators and opened the front door, and I felt as if I'd let the genie out of the bottle. . . .

This was one of October's perfect afternoons. We put our lunch in a bag— two peanut butter sandwiches apiece, an apple, two cookies, and a napkin full of those little bittersweet chocolate drops they put in cookies and took to the road. We sat on yellow leaves in a group of little trees and watched the water spreading into pools below the dam. It made a rippling sound coming over the rocks around the bend, but right in front of us it was clear and still enough to reflect the trees. . . . Even the off-red of a glowing tree colored the water like the reflection of a fire. Everywhere the water-spiders glanced along over the surface and as we sat there thistledown was forever passing us and skimming out over the water. Joel thought it was exactly like the milkweed fairies in <u>Fantasia</u>.

I could have stayed forever in a spellbound world where I was young and you were there. . . .

Good night you nut.

Isabel

## 1942: OCTOBER 9

## ROSE KENNEDY TO HER CHILDREN

*Matriarch of the most famous and most publicly tragic American family, Rose Fitzgerald Kennedy (1890–1995) wrote this letter to her children two years before the eldest—Joseph, Jr.—died when his bomber exploded over the English Channel. Rosemary (1918–2005) had been institutionalized since 1941. Kathleen would die in a plane crash in 1948. John (1917–1963) would become president in 1961 and be assassinated in 1963. Bobby would be killed while campaigning for the presidency in 1968. In addition to Rosemary, Eunice (1921–), Patricia (1924–), Jean (1928–), and Teddy (1932–) outlived their mother, who died at the age of 105. The cheerful author of this letter would one day say: "Birds sing after a storm; why shouldn't people feel as free to delight in whatever remains to them?"*

Bobby was at Milton Academy. Joe, Jr., was in Norfolk, Virginia, having just received his navy wings. JFK was in Portsmouth, Rhode Island, for a PT boat training program. Pat was at Rosemont College. Jean was at Eden Hall, the Convent of the Sacred Heart. Torbert Macdonald had been JFK's Harvard roommate.

Hyannisport, Mass.

October 9, 1942

Dear Children:

I have been home all the week and it has been lovely here. I have been working in my own little way, trying to get all your clothes sorted out, etc. Dad came home from New York on Wednesday as it was our twenty-eighth anniversary.

We expected darling Teddy home over this weekend, but it seems the little angel got into a water fight in the lavatory and "after he knew his way around he got full of biscuits" and got himself into quite a little trouble, so he was put on bounds for two weeks. It seems quite unfair because I am sure the boys who were there before provoked him to mischief. Also, these are our last two weekends when he might come home as we now expect to close the house about the 19th. I suppose he has learned his lesson, but a little too late.

Bobby did not expect to get off for the holiday as I can quite understand that they are steeping their brains in study. He will have to keep on his toes to get used to the new school and the new masters and the new requirements because everyone is going at a rapid clip in order to get into college as soon as possible.

Joe wrote to us this morning and it seems his latest concern is over a new mustache which he is raising. He has promised to have some photos taken later and so you will see him all in his mustache glory. He is still busy with his students and general flying business.

Jack, you know, is a Lieutenant, J.G. and of course he is delighted. His whole attitude about the war has changed and he is quite ready to die for the U.S.A. in order to keep the Japanese and the Germans from becoming the dominant people on their respective continents, believing that sooner or later they would encroach upon ours. He also thinks it would be good for Joe's political career if he died for the grand old flag, although I don't believe he feels that is absolutely necessary.

Dolly von Staden was down over last weekend and seemed to be a very pleasant, happy-go-lucky girl. I say happy-go-lucky, as when she left here Sunday night she was not quite sure whether she would get a sleeper on the train to New York, or whether she would get the midnight train for Boston, where she would awaken her brother, but neither predicament seemed to upset her very much.

Torb Macdonald has been in a dreadful mess again. It seems some woman, who signed herself "A Conscientious Taxpayer" complained that one Torbert Macdonald was using a Navy Station Wagon to call at a certain number on a certain street every day. The woman represented the fact that her tax money was put to such a use. The above-mentioned street and number turned out to be Polly Carter's house. Torb disclaimed that he had ever called for Polly in the Navy Station Wagon, but he had to get the affidavit of two policemen on the beat, plus numerous other legal signatures in order to explain it to the Navy. It all was very complicated and upset his weekend no end. It seems he is always in some sort of physical or mental dilemma.

Kathleen wanted very much to get to Hot Springs this weekend. It seems Zeke thought of going down, too. She was trying to get Betty or Charlotte to go with her, but they had other plans and I could not allow her to go down there without a chaperone. We scanned the register for some mutual friend but could find no one and so I do not know what her presents plans are. She said everyone and his brother was to be at LaRue in New York this weekend. Your father, by the way, said New York is a mad house. You cannot get near the Copa Cabana. They are just standing on the street so the Maitre d'hotel cannot see you even if you have an ambassadorial air. On some instances, even the beaming countenance of Ted O'Leary can not affect an entrance and so it is all too complicated. Jack is going over this weekend and your father has warned him and as usual has been making life easy for him by preparing the way at the various hot spots.

I do hope you will have a good time this weekend, Pat. I do not blame you for being bored and I wish you knew a few exciting swains in Cambridge or New Haven. It is really not your fault that you do not, as we really should make a few contacts for you and then you might follow them up. I am certainly going to do something about it pretty soon as there is no reason why you cannot be having your share of debutante excitement. By the way, I hear you are an excellent bridge player and I cannot understand how you accomplished that art.

I am sorry if you have to wear your old clothes, Jean, and I am quite ashamed that I have not been able to buy you any new ones, but I am going to New York in about another week. Your father and I are going to visit the Convent and I hope I shall have the pleasure of meeting Reverend Mother as I missed her last year. I also hope I shall hear words of praise for your application and industry. And please do not put on a lot of weight. It is so silly at school to eat that long bread roll, etc.

Mrs. Daly is here as usual, and arrives nightly with her little bag. She always brings a gift and is so generous. Her latest kind deed was to ask her sister-in-law to send Joe a cake from Georgia. Marie made one for Jack down here, but someone came in the front door and she had to remove the frosting before it was finished and so the cake could not be sent but was presented to me. Our Josephine also made an angel cake here last Sunday to send to Jack but there were not enough eggs in it so I got that. Josephine also made another one on Tuesday, during which Stevens slammed the back door and spoiled that one, whereupon it also was given to me. I have had angel food the last week until I must be ready for the golden gates.

Pat, do keep up your good work because as I said, there is always a record of your marks sent for every college year to whatever school or position you are taking. When I was applying for a secretary myself, I had complete records from Simmons College and Boston University of applicants who had studied there, their courses and their marks during the four years, with recommendations from their Professors or teachers as to their eligibility.

Much love to you all. Off for the 4 o'clock mail

Mother

## 1943: FEBRUARY 10
## HAZEL GALLANT TO J. CLIFFORD GALLANT

---

*The idea of sacrifice came with evident clarity to Hazel Gallant, who had married J. Clifford Gallant just two months before writing this letter. All we know about Hazel is that until the war, she had worked in several Boston department stores, selling cosmetics; during the war, she would work at the Industrial Union of Marine and Shipbuilders of America in Boston and head the women's auxiliary of Boston's National Maritime Union. We know nothing about Cliff.*

February 10, 1943

To My Dear Husband:

I am writing now in hopes when you arrive, at whatever far distant port, this will be awaiting you. I have waited these few days since your last telephone call in hopes I could formulate those things I feel in my heart so strongly.

Along with the sadness and heartache of your going away is also a feeling of pride in the job you are doing. When moments of loneliness descend I suddenly throw my head high and walk with a more determined step forward. Not only are we of one heart but one mind, we know this beast we are fighting and what he stands for, we know what we are fighting for, and every sacrifice gives us a share in that great day when we march hand in hand with the millions throughout the world, when we try these barbarians for every life, every broken heart, and every act of barbarism they have committed. We would not have it otherwise, we are where we belong, each in our own field fighting for victory and so will we take our place in rebuilding the future, stronger, and greater, and ours will be the voice of the jurors to see that justice is meted out.

As regards our own selfs Cliff, I want you to feel about this war as I do. I can't fight on the battle front, that is your priviledge, but I can fight here with every hour I can keep awake. I am lonely and miss you and that will intensify for us both in the long months ahead, but we feel these present emotions only to preserve and protect the greater ones. We are preserving the right for two people to feel this great emotion of love for one another we have, we are protecting the right to build and plan a future of dignity, a home and children to be surrounded by kindness, human brotherhood, culture, and love. A future cleansed of greed, intolerance, hunger, want, degradation, and bitterness. A future full of a thirst for knowledge and opportunity, where there is a place for all of us side by side around the globe to build, build, and build. This is the heritage of mankind and we have the priviledge of being a part of assuring it.

Dear Cliff I cannot find it in my heart to bewail my unhappiness in our being separated. Rather I feel a deep and burning hatred for this monster and those forces throughout the world who allowed its birth and growth to threaten the life of the world, its utter distruction must be first accomplished in order for our being together to have a lasting foundation. I love you very much and want you home to start our new life as soon as possible, but without victory there will be no love or future for anyone. And so we leave one another with a job determined to do and do well, helping those who aren't quite as clear as we are with understanding, a positive note to our voice and step, and a clear and alert mind. We know where we are going and why and to the extent do we keep this clearly before us to that extent do we preserve and protect those things dear to us.

And so darling in some small way in this letter I hope I have made you understand how I feel. It is so much harder for you, so isolated from all these things, but perhaps this will help to see the glorious years ahead for us by carrying out this assignment. By writing all this I feel stronger and in turn I hope you do by reading it. And so until my next letter—smooth sailing—.

### 1943: MARCH 5
### MADGE RUTHERFORD TO IRENE AND E. V. RUTHERFORD

*Madge Rutherford (1920?–2004) was already a trained pilot when America entered the war. Turned down for advanced flight courses because she was a woman, she wrote to Eleanor Roosevelt and in 1943 received an invitation to join the Women Airforce Service Pilots (WASP) being organized by Jacqueline Cochran in Texas. The all-women's base soon caused a sensation, and male pilots from neighboring bases started to make a suspiciously large number of "emergency" landings to check out the personnel. Those distractions aside, the women still had work to do. For Rutherford, as she made clear in this letter to her parents, Irene (1894–1970) and Elmer Virgil (1893–1988), that meant virtually around-the-clock training.*
In October of 1944, Madge married Sherman Minton. Together they would have three daughters and coauthor several books about reptiles.

Friday, A.M. 3/5/43

Dearest Mother & Dad:

Well, little 6'3" Mr. Jones admitted yesterday in his Texas drawl that "Baby, you're doin' bettah! But there's a H—— of a lot room for a H—— of a lot more improvement." He is mildly profane as all Texans seem to be here in Sweetwater. We took P.T. 114 off the line at 10:00, trundled her through clouds of dust and sand down to the take-off line and I took off from a half-ground loop along with 3 other planes simultaneously. The traffic here is terrific. I haven't made a landing "solo" yet. It can't be helped with 40–50 planes going off and coming back at approximately the same time in our flight and as many cadets in flight at the same time, also. You have to feed in right rudder on your sewing machine during takeoff until you're holding it on all the way when she leaves the ground.

Well, we got off, and trudged manfully up into the air at about 90 knots, turned at 300 ft, at 500 ft and brushed off various sister bugs to rise to 2500 where I stalled and stalled and banked and stalled until I thought surely he would wash me out of the course for lack of coordination. But he simply snap-rolled it a few times to loosen me up and I did much better after that. When I would skid turns, etc. he'd sing to the tune of "I can't give you anything but love, Baby" "Oh, How I'd like to see you shake your bank, baby." I feel better about the whole thing today. But I can't fly because about 20 ships are in the shop for minor repairs and since I have as many hours as any, they are taking girls who are behind in their time.

Last night spring came to Texas. We had a real old-fashioned thunder storm which brought the first dampness here since last November. It was just like home to see the lightning, etc. Everyone in the barracks was at the doors or windows. We were very excited about it all. For the first time, I woke up without sand in my mouth and the damp odor of clay and old rain permeates the flight room here as I write. The sunrise this morning was chiefly green.

Another navigation test this afternoon but I think I'm ready for it. If someone wants to send me a box of stationery for my birthday, it would be greatly appreciated.

I've written you'all almost every day. You are getting my letters O.K., aren't you? Sometimes the mail doesn't go out here and we all are very irritated about that.

Say! How about that box of candy you mentioned. I'm afraid I can't hold myself much longer.

To clear our minds and refresh our souls, some of us congregate for 40 minutes + or − every evening in the canteen to hold a good gripe session. That + sunsets + letters from home + the airplanes compensate for army discipline which I do not like. Forgive me please.

It's good to have all the details, mother. Don't let the submarine get you under too far.

Love,<br>Madge

## 1943: MARCH 24
## AUDREY MITSCHER TO ALLEN FERGUSON

*War speeded up some marriages and delayed others; there were couples who felt that making a lifelong commitment in the face of great risk was a reckless, even a selfish, thing to do. Audrey Mitscher (1921–) was one woman who forcefully rejected that reasoning. She had met Allen Ferguson (1919–) in the autumn of 1940 when they were both at Brown University. By 1943, already sworn in as a marine, she wrote him the letter below while she was home in New Jersey awaiting her orders and he was at boot camp in Tennessee. By coincidence, her letter crossed one of his saying much the same thing. They married in January of 1944. Ferguson went on to become a second lieutenant, and Mitscher a technical sergeant. After the war, he would work for the CIA, the RAND Corporation, and the U.S. Department of State. They would have four children, eight grandchildren, and two great-grandchildren.*

The stickers were for faster but more expensive airmail postage.

Wednesday nite
March 24, 1943

Hi Darling

Allen darling, I want to tell you something which I may not ever mention again. I may, but the important thing is, please please remember it just in case I shouldn't actually say it, because it will always hold true—as long as I love you & that's forever. It concerns our getting married or not getting married during the war. Neither one of us are "marryable" right now any way and it'll look pretty hopeless & impossible in the months to come I'm sure. We'll both be terrifically busy & we may hardly have time to write each other let alone anything else. Someday we may both get commissions (you will & I can live in hopes). In any event, while you're still here we might have more time and a few more priviledges then. But this is what I want to say. If we don't get married during the war—for whatever reasons there may be—don't you ever ever ever have this reason for not getting married—that I might be better off if we weren't married. Sweetheart, I just couldn't be. And that's an absolute fact & not a romantic notion. You read it in books, but I've talked with lots of girls & anyone who really loves a fellow would rather a million times be married to him—even if & <u>especially if</u> he were killed in action overseas. It's just true. I really mean it. Darling, please remember that & don't ever consider it for a moment as a reason for not getting married during the war. I'd feel terrible if you did. I'd just rather 10 million times to be married to you before you went overseas than anything else. Don't even think it would be better for me not to be married 'cuz you were risking your neck & the possibility existed that you might not return. It just wouldn't be that way. Maybe it'll be hard for you to realize that. It's just a fact about a woman that's all. And sweetheart—I love you so much. Oh I do.

Darling, darling—oh you are one. Mmmmm to you too. And if you outrank me, I refuse flatly & absolutely to say yes sir—I may salute you but I won't say yes sir—I'll say yes, sweetheart darling so loudly that anyone that hears will stare us down & I'll laugh & you'll be embarrassed & want to tickle me but that wouldn't be dignified either so you'll just walk along with me calmly until we're alone which is when you'll kiss me instead of tickling me and we'll both be completely happy. Darling I love you. Oh I do.

Sweetheart please don't forget that very serious & very much meant part of this letter—

Darling. I love you. I love you. I'll always be just your very own

Private Snoogles

P.S. This letter I'm sending Air Mail 'cuz I got those pretty stickers & I have to try them out. I'll try to refrain sending you an air mail letter until I get my orders. So then you'll know before you open the envelope.

I love you,
Audrey

### 1943: APRIL 9
### LOUISE OGAWA TO CLARA BREED

*Louise Ogawa was a teenager in the spring of 1942, when the War Relocation Authority (see page 550) moved her from her home in San Diego to the internment camp at Poston, Arizona. A year later, she shared her feelings about that upheaval in this letter to Clara Breed (1906–1994). Breed, the children's librarian at the San Diego Public Library, corresponded with numerous relocated teenagers and young adults, providing books, care packages, encouragement—and a kind of touchstone throughout the war.*

April 9, 1943

Dear Miss Breed,

Yesterday marks my first year in camp. Time certainly flies!

As I sit listening to my history teacher, Miss Warvarovsky, talking about the problems of today, a tidal wave of memories came rushing before my eyes. That feeling of sorrow and the emptiness of my tummy comes back to me every time I think of how I left San Diego. I shall never forget how I spent that night of April 7th sleeping on the train. My sister and I stuck our heads out the window never peeling our eyes off the direction of our home. We filled our eyes with the sight of San Diego to the limit until my pupils gave in and I dozed off.

Today marks my first full day of camp life. Oh, how busy we were—hurrying and scurrying about—making the beds, sweeping the asphalt floor, running back and forth getting scraps of wood. Oh my! What a busy day that was. When I awoke this morning one year ago, I looked up at the ceiling and a funny strange feeling came over me. I knew I was not at home and had a terrible yearning to go home. A little boy next door was crying asking his mother to take him home. That day I felt so lost I was as blue as the deep blue sea. But the sight of a friend certainly cheered me up even though it was just for the moment I saw her. Today that homesickness still is within me but that lost feeling has disappeared. I often wonder how I have changed in thought, actions, knowledge, and facial and physical features during the short memorable one year.

April 10, 1943

This morning was a very disgusting day one year ago. When I saw that the legs of my bed had sunk into the asphalt, I began looking at mothers, fathers, sisters, and brothers. They were all like that. Then I knew my weight had nothing to do with it. But it was such a disgust.

Yes memories—through experiences and hardship we become wiser.

Now Poston—it may seem strange to you when I say—it is like winter again. I just wrote you and said it was very hot. Well, it was until two days ago. Today the wind is blowing, and it rained yesterday. I guess by now, you believe me when I say Poston weather is unpredictable. For certain it is!!!

April third was the Sr. Prom. The Camp I Orchestra came to play for us. The leader of the band is still a young boy. He plays the trumpet as well as the drums. Back home, he use to be a pupil of Gene Krupa. (a well-known orchestra leader.) He, I mean the leader of the Camp I band, is very good. The dance was held in 305 mess hall. It was beautifully decorated with orchid and white crepe paper. The reception was grand. But was so hot I felt sorry for the boys (they wore ties).

By the way, are Kleenex frozen on the outside? It is no longer available here. I have always been wondering about laundry soap. Is it frozen too?

After a long letter, I always seem to ask favors. I am such a troublesome correspondent.

I have tried and tried to purchase a radio tube but I seem to have no luck. I wrote to San Diego to the dealer I purchased the radio from, but he joined the army and no longer has his shop. Then I wrote to Sears and Montgomery but they do not carry that kind of tube. So as my last resort I am asking you. You are the most reliable source I have. I have been trying to purchase the tube ever since Dec. of last year. Every once in a while I turn on the radio and then remember one of my tube is dead. Will you purchase the following tube for me. The number is 12SA7 G.T. Also a box of Lux soap. I just can't seem to get along without it. I'd like a few cards of that scarce thing called bobbie pins and shower caps.

I am enclosing $2.00 in money order.

Please pardon me for troubling you so. Please do not rush this.

Most sincerely,

Louise Ogawa

### 1943: AUGUST 14
### JUNE WANDREY TO HER FAMILY

*June Wandrey (1920–) was a combat nurse who served in Europe and North Africa and would receive eight battle stars. From her post in Italy, she sent this letter home to her family in Wisconsin.*

Poor Sicily

Dearest family,

Working like slaves. Too tired to write and it's always too dark to see when I get off duty. We were so close to the lines we could see our artillery fire and also that of the Germans. The Jerries have poor aim today. Shells landed in front of us and behind us. I'm well and as happy as one could be in this set up. Glad I have lots of energy. Don't know how the older nurses stand the pace. I finally got the slack suit and it fits perfectly. I love it. Our ingenious men made a shower out of a 250 gallon drum, a piece of hose and a shower head, and plopped some wooden duckboards on the ground and wrapped a latrine screen around it. Heaven smiled on me briefly.

Overtired, overworked and totally exasperated I blundered by asking the chief nurse today how she ever got her job. For years she taught school, tired of that, took up nursing and graduated just a year before I did. Her dad had a friend in Washington, a Pentagonite with pull. She stood outside the surgery tent, her nervous tic was to pick at her left elbow when she spoke. "My, you certainly are capable." She has never, ever helped care for a patient, no matter how rushed we are. Maybe it's not part of her job description. She's a paper shuffler.

In our pell-mell existence, we received our first naval casualties. A ship right off shore from us was bombed and strafed. Even our dentists were doing minor surgery we were so swamped. We have surgical priorities that must be operated on first: belly or chest wounds take precedence over orthopedic surgery or some simple debridement. Even if the patients are the enemy, if they fit the category, they come before our soldiers. We have surgical auxiliary teams that come to our unit to do the surgery. They work non-stop 'til the shock wards are emptied of patients. The doctors were specialists in chest, belly, or orthopedic surgery.

At first, we used to line the inside of the surgery tent tops with clean sheets; it was supposed to keep the dirt from falling into the wounds. It was cumbersome work for the enlisted men and so time-consuming. We needed a sewing machine to sew the sheets together, but when the machine arrived, there weren't any needles for it. Our infection rate was almost nil, despite the wounded coming to us from straight off the battlefield. Many times there were maggots in their wounds and when you carried them on the litter, the maggots would roll out of the wounds onto the canvas.

Working in the shock wards, giving transfusions, was a rewarding, but sad, experience. Many wounded soldier's faces still haunt my memory. I recall one eighteen year old who had just been brought in from the ambulance to the shock ward. I went to him immediately, he looked up at me trustingly, sighed and asked, "How am I doing nurse?" I was standing at the head of his litter. I put my hands around his face, kissed his forehead and said, "You are doing just fine, soldier." He smiled sweetly and said, "I was just checking up." Then he died. Many of us shed tears in private. Otherwise, we try to be cheerful and reassuring.

I've seen surgeons work for hours to save a young soldier's life, but despite it they die on the operating table. Some doctors even collapsed across the patient, broke down, and cried. There are many dedicated people here giving their all. Very tired,

June.

**1943: AUGUST 29**
**MARGE TO WALTER**

---

*The identities of "Marge" and "Walter" have long since been lost. All we know is that he was a crew member on the World War II Liberty Ship* John W. Brown, *one of many vessels built for carrying wartime equipment and supplies.*

Dear Walter,

I hope this finds you doing well. I have been keeping busy. I work at Martin's Aircraft factory. I started in March and I like it.

I don't know how to tell you this but you need to know! I met this really nice guy, he drives a blue ford convertible. He takes me dancing and he's a real gentleman. I don't know what the future might hold so, it's only fair to return your ring, and picture. I don't mean to hurt you! I know you'll meet a wonderful girl, when this horrible war is over. Have a good life and please don't hate me!!

Take Care of Yourself,
Marge

### 1943: OCTOBER 31
### ALICE CLARK TO FRED CLARK

*All we could learn about the author of this moving and unusually explicit love letter is that she was living in Commerce, Oklahoma, when she wrote it. Her husband was in McCaw General Hospital in Walla Walla, Washington.*

Miami, Oklahoma, is about three miles south of Commerce. *Mr. Lucky* is a film starring Cary Grant. "Alice," "Fred," "Bill," and "Gail" are pseudonyms.

Sunday afternoon
Oct 31, 1943

My Most Darling Fred

There are so many things in my heart I hardly know where to begin. First thing I must tell you that when I got home yesterday afternoon I had 3 letters from you. One written Mon. Tues. and Wed. Each was filled with sweet things and of your love for me. Sweetheart you make me so happy when I read of your love and devotion and Darling each letter holds a fascination for me that no other piece of paper could. Money written in checks could not begin to be as interesting. Fred if I was rich and did not have you life would be empty. Fred if you could only know how very much I love and worship you.

Fred why haven't you gained weight? You should. You said you were feeling OK and you have plenty of food and rest. Is it because you worry about home and when you'll get to see us? Could it be because you want me so much that it keeps down your weight? My sweetheart please take good care of your self. Maybe you are worse off than you think. I mean your back. Of course I know you think that you are in a bad shape elsewhere but you can soon get over that.

I'm not as worried about that as your back. I can fix that in one evening's time but I can't mend vertebras.

It is a beautiful day. I'd love to drive out somewhere and look at the pretty leaves and do a lot of strenuous necking with my honey. Boyee what I couldn't do to you. Sweetheart how grand it would be. If you were here we couldn't go very far because about all of my gas tickets are used. 3 gal. don't go very far.

Honey I fixed you a box of candy today and in it is some of your birthday cake that I made in June. I still have the rest of it. I have always kept it wrapped up in wax paper and it is still moist. I cut the pieces & wrapped them separate so you could eat them when you wanted. You will find the first layer is candy then the next is fruit cake and the last layer is chocolate. I hope you enjoy it. The cake has already had one trip to Seattle. It is 5 months old. It isn't as good perhaps as it was when it made its first trip but I've always kept it for you. No one else has taken any of it.

Bill is sending you a white flying scarf with this box. They bought white flying scarfs for all the instructors out there & he thought you might like to wear one with your bath robe. That is if you ever have one to wear up there. If you can't use it take good care of it because it will sure go good with your top coat. Bill thought you might get to use it. He ran up home & got it when he saw me packing the candy.

In a seperate cover I'm sending you another funny book. I sent you one last week. Did you get it? I read this one through before sending it to see if it was OK for you to read <u>ha ha</u>.

Honey I went to church this morning. This ended the first month of the red & blue contest at church & our side won. It's the blue side. We beat Bill's side by 3 points & they've got to give us a party. The contest begins all over for next week with the same people only different captains. When you come home you are to be on the blue side with me. Honey I don't want to ever be on any side opposite of you. Your mother & Dad went to-day. It's nice and warm and hard to stay in side.

My darling seems like Sundays are so long. I never did think so when you were here. They just flew. This is Sunday night. Gail Bill & I went to the show tonight & saw Pat O'Brien in "Bomerdier." Sure was good. Your Mother & Dad rode down to Miami & went to church and came home with us. They seemed to enjoy it very much going to church down there.

I'm in bed and honey for the last hour there has been the awfullest roar and whistling noise. Papie thinks that the gas line has bursted over on the new state road. The noise gets on my nerves. Boyee, we'll sure have to pay for all this extra gas that's going to waist.

Sweetheart I'm in bed laying on my back writing this and as I lay here partly uncovered one breast is out    it makes me wish for the past and how I'd enjoy having you lay on my arm and with you loving and sucking on my right breast as I laid on my side real close to you. Honey I can almost imagine the thrill & how hot I'd get if you were doing it. Honey I dreamed of you loving me last night & you didn't leave anything undone.

I'm glad you bought a shirt if its an army shirt they cost from $3 to $5 here. Wish you could buy some pants especially if you plan to work at Spartans if you come home. Fred I keep planning that you'll come home. You have me doing it. I hope you're not wrong. If you are I'm sure riding for a fall. I'll be able to take it tho if you are.

Fred I'm going to get see Mr. Lucky after all. It's on at the Coleman next Sunday. You said it was so good & to be sure & see it. Just think this is the last day of Oct. It doesn't seem possible that the year is almost over. My Darling we're getting old aren't we. Sweetheart let's grow old together. I believe with you I'll be able to stay young. My Darling the noise has stopped. Guess they have the gas line fixed. I'm glad. It was getting on my nerves. I guess I'd better go to sleep. I've been off for so long I'd almost forgot I've got a job to take care. I love you Fred with all my heart. Wish you were laying here beside me ready to love me as soon as I got this written. In fact I wouldn't be writing this. I'd already be loving you. Boy oh Boy how I'd love to lay on your arm. It's been so long but I'll not forget how it was done. If I don't go to sleep now I'll be so wide awake wanting you. I won't be able to go to sleep. I do hope you are sleeping better than you were. Good night Fred, I love you more than life and I'll always be your Darling. Just hold on a little longer and we'll make the grade. Take good care of your self and don't worry. I love you and that's all that matters.

Your Darling wife always
Alice

## 1943: DECEMBER 24
## GRETCHEN KROCH TO HER FAMILY

*Gretchen Kroch was stationed in France when she sent this letter home to her parents in Chicago.*

Darlings—

This is War—and War Is Hell. It's Christmas Eve—and instead of being at home with you, amidst gaiety and happy clamor, I'm in the bleak waiting room of the railroad station in Maxton, waiting to put a coffin on the train. A nice young flyer was killed last night when his glider plummeted to the ground. He was to have been married tonight. . . . He will not celebrate Christmas. But because he died . . . perhaps some year we will again have a Merry Christmas.

. . . War Is Hell. I whom you brought up carefully and tenderly, sheltering me from life's vicissitudes, look now upon broken bodies and bloody corpses without flinching. . . .

War Is Hell. I long for your comforting presence tonight. I am bitterly lonely. Instead of being gathered into the warm circle of the family, I will return to my bare little apartment, brave with holly and a Christmas tree. I will sip my eggnog and open my presents, and perhaps I will forget for a moment that I am an officer, and remembering that I am alone, will cry a little.

Yes, this is War.

All my love,<br>Grey

## 1944: CIRCA JUNE
## DORA SAMUELSON TO HYMAN SAMUELSON

*Dora Samuelson (1921–1944) married Hyman Samuelson (1919–) in 1941, three months before he shipped out. Dora gave birth to their son, Ian, in October of 1942. From New Guinea, where he served as a southern white Jewish officer commanding a battalion of African American troops, Hyman wrote to her about training, bureaucracy, racism—and his occasional dalliances with other women. To her family in New Orleans, Dora privately expressed her misery about this last subject. But she wrote to her husband in a far different tone.*

Hymie was still in the army in 1944 when Dora died of cervical cancer. He writes: "I was coming home . . . on emergency leave because Dora was not expected to live much longer. I did not learn of her death until I got off that train. And when I asked 'where is she now?' and they told me that she had been buried already—well, I never have been able to fathom how I felt. Not then. Or now."

. . . And about your going out with women—well, really at first when I heard about it it did sound "funny" to me—I can't explain how I felt—but really I can't and never could imagine you doing anything "bad." And do you think for one minute that that is what is bothering me—about your being "unfaithful" to me as you put it? How can you know me so little, you stinker? All I ask is for you to come home to me—for you to keep loving me. All I want is a chance to see you again, to hold you close to me—to make you happy again. That seems to me to be the most important thing. And I understand, really I do—I never know quite what to say when you tell me about this woman—or that, but I do understand about them. And as far as your doing anything "bad," I don't know what you mean. What you may think is bad, I might not. And really no matter how bad you are I don't think you could do anything worse than not come out in the open with me.

You're such a child, Hymie, that I feel as though I have to mother you more than anything else. You've had it hard—all your life you've had to face things that were heartbreaking and you've been bruised up pretty well. But you aren't as hard-boiled as you think you are. Just wait until you meet your baby, until you see him smile and he puts his little arms around you and puts his little nose close to yours and says "Di deee. Di deee." You'll feel just like a human being again. You'll feel alive.

### 1944: JUNE 7
### CHARLOTTE COLBURN TO HER FAMILY

*D-day—June 6, 1944—was the beginning of the Allied invasion of western Europe. After unprecedented planning, 156,000 troops—mainly British and American— crossed the English Channel to France by sea and 23,500 by air. Back in England, a young American Red Cross worker named Charlotte Colburn (1914–) described the events to her family. Since the year before, Colburn had been part of the American Red Cross Clubmobile Service, a fleet of converted buses and trucks that drove to towns near army installations, offering free doughnuts and coffee, cigarettes, gum—and conversation.*

The GMC trucks were slightly smaller versions of the original clubmobiles. "ETO" stood for European Theater of Operations. Air Force Lieutenant Jim Colburn, Charlotte's brother, died in an air battle over France on D-day—the day before this letter was written.

June 7, 1944

Hello darlings,

The great day finally arrived and it doesn't take much imagination to know that all the Colburn radios have been blaring night and day and typical every other minute American broadcasts and news analyzations are keeping you posted on all developments. Honestly, I think it is more difficult for you there than for those of us who are so close. We have known the very imminence of it for quite sometime and it is our boys, all of whom we have grown to know and like so much, the paratroopers and airborne, who were the first—the very first. Some of our best friends were the pathfinders and these boys land fully an hour before anyone else. We have been "sweating out" the moment with them for the past three weeks and now we are keeping ourselves as busy as possible "sweating out" the fates of this one and that one. Already the dead and wounded are being flown back, but we don't know details—the only consolation is that we will be the first to know. I'm so anxious to see Jim because I know that he will be able to describe the amazing spectacle. The night before, the continuous drone of planes was over our heads for endless hours. I can't describe fully the feelings I had but the terrific tension is heart bursting. The calmness and philosophy of the boys are wonderful—they are so brave, the classic gripes and cracks that have been made in the past weeks would fill a book—I love these boys—everyone, but to me the best part is that even though they are wonderful fighters "the great warriors", actually they do not have that bloodthirsty outlook and almost everyone—to a man—wants to get this hellish business over with and get back to Brooklyn, or Chicago, or Los Angeles or Milford. Which reminds me—I met another boy from Oneonta this week—Bob Searles from West End. He went to school with Marion McKinney, Peg Hatch, and Peg Ford. He gave me a couple of Stars, but the Milford news was very deficient.

The last time I wrote I was headed for London town to meet Erna and we had a super deluxe weekend. She is splendid and is doing a perfectly marvelous job in her little Aero club. Next to my clubmobile I would like the position Erna has because where we service a greater number of boys, we cover a greater expanse of territory and are the very first to move into new places, Erna's work is concentrated on a definite group of boys. She gets to know each individual and sweats out each mission with them—when they crash—she does and Erna is a wonderful girl to be in that position although the strain I really think is more difficult for her than for us.

Marianne, Mary and I went in by train Friday A.M. and met Erna at the Park Lane Hotel—a very nice one where we had reserved two double rooms with sumptuous beds. Mary and Marianne had appointments for permanents so Erna and I did a few errands and found a cocktail lounge where we talked and talked about everyone home and what each of us has been doing. It was so good to see her. If Jim could have made it things would have been perfect, but he could not. We met the girls at 5:30, had dinner at Maxims, a Chinese restaurant, fair and then saw Ginger Rogers in "Lady in the Dark", which you said you enjoyed so much and so did we. I saw Gertrude Lawrence do it on the stage in New York. Saturday AM we slept late, luxury of luxuries and had breakfast in bed about 11. After lunch we saw a British play "The Lisbon Story" and frankly "she steenks". It was comparable to a fair high school production and has been running here since last summer, why and how I don't know. It was the lousiest production I have seen in the legitimate theater in many a year. After this we drowned our disappointments at the American bar at Park Lane, where we ran into a couple of friends from our old air base. As we had to take a 9:30 train back, we departed for the Dorchester to have a good dinner, said goodbye to Erna and arrived here about 11:45.

How I wish you could wrap up a gallon of icecream and ten quarts of milk. You've no idea how we miss them. Marianne can practically make me writhe by chanting out different foods that we would like. The British can't cook, they don't know how and have little to work with. We eat at the Army mess but one gets pretty sick of the chow and we see all too much, how it is prepared.

From now on we sit tight and wait for our next <u>big move</u>. We know little except that as soon as establishment across the pond is complete enough we go and our gang will be in the first ARC move, and as far as we are concerned, the sooner we can catch up with the boys, the better we like it.

Our groups we have been visiting this week are fairly small in comparison to the thousands we have had some days. We are wonderfully independent with our GMC's. Night before last we visited the grandest gang, arrived just in time for chow, stayed for the baseball game—they rode us on bicycles, danced on the grass. They really enjoy having us there more than receiving coffee and doughnuts. More than one CO has told us that our visits are looked forward to more than anything else and the days we are expected they all shave and dress up. When we don't arrive the scheduled day, they bawl us out when we do get there—they are crazy and we love it.

Yesterday we visited one of the paratrooper groups that have just come from Italy. We stayed for supper and afterwards drank beer with them—they are a crazy wild gang, taught us how to jump from a dummy plane. The entire gang of eight are escorting four of us to a dance tomorrow, and so it goes, the rough life in the ETO.

Love,
Charlotte

\*   \*   \*

1944: JULY 8

FRANCES PERKINS TO JANE GRANT

---

*Frances Perkins (1882–1965) was serving the second to last of her dozen years as secretary of labor when she wrote this letter to Jane Grant (1892–1972), an ardent feminist and supporter of the Equal Rights Amendment. First presented to Congress in 1923, the amendment would finally be approved by the House in 1971 and by the Senate in 1972, but would fall three states short of the thirty-eight needed for ratification and is still awaiting passage. In explaining why she disapproved of the measure, Perkins here laid out the basic argument that would continually prevent the amendment's passage: that women needed the protections—such as financial support and exemptions from combat duty—that went hand-in-hand with separate, if unequal, treatment.*

Grant married Harold Ross, helped start *The New Yorker*, partied hard through the twenties, married again in the thirties, became an avid gardener, and then wrote her memoirs.

Dear Jane:

Thank you for your letter of June 12th about the Equal Rights Amendment.

I think you know that I have given that amendment a great deal of consideration and have thought about it for a long time. The more I think of it, the more I am convinced that it is the wrong way to go about removing such handicaps as remain to women at this time. No one has been more gratified than I have at the excellent showing which women have made in the war industries. I knew, of course, that they would do it. There has never been any doubt in my mind about the capacity of women to work and their skill and intelligence has always made them very capable, but they have been successful in industry <u>only when the industrial conditions have been adapted to their needs</u>. Those women who have worked so well in the war industries have worked under the protection either of State laws which limit their hours and establish certain working conditions designed to make them comfortable and relieve their strain, or they have worked under rules and regulations promulgated by the War Department, the Navy Department, based on recommendations of the Women's Bureau of the Department of Labor for hours, shifts, sanitary facilities, rest periods, special provision of time off for performing household duties, and for their peculiar forms of illness, including pregnancy and menstruation. Intelligent employers desiring to get as much work as possible from their employees, particularly in this manpower shortage, have sought advice of this sort and have readily agreed to put such rules into operation, and they have not put such rules into operation for the men. Women do excellent work when the conditions of industry are modified to make it possible for them to do so, and they earn good wages under those circumstances too.

At the suggestion of the Women's Bureau of the Department of Labor and the War and Navy Departments, men's jobs have been broken up into parts so that they would not be so heavy and so that they might be done by groups of women who had not previously done, and perhaps could not have done, some of the heavier tasks which had always been regarded as men's work. It is my belief that women will earn more money, maintain their health, their poise, their dignity and their peace of mind within the family if they work under conditions which are favorable to them, and that is why I am in favor of, and shall continue to be in favor of, labor legislation tending to establish minimum wage laws for women to limit the hours of labor of women, provide for some regulation of the shifts on which they work, require certain sanitary facilities, certain health protection devices, and certain provisions for their comfort and convenience, such as seats. You, I am sure, are aware of the fact that the increase in the number of women employed has been greatest in those States which have good labor legislation, not only during the war but for the last 25 years, and that under those conditions also the earnings and average wages of women in industry have steadily increased.

Yes, I am aware that there are some states that do not provide for the service of women on juries. I see, however, that their number is declining. I am aware that there are certain other matters which are regarded as disabling by the Woman's Party and which they seek to remove by the blanket amendment method. I have always thought it was unintelligent to proceed blindly, and an amendment to the Constitution is a matter so complex as this has results which are unforeseeable. The civil disabilities of women are being removed gradually by legislation—indeed quite rapidly, and I see no reason why we should not proceed in that method, knowing what we are doing, rather than knocking out blindly not only the industrial legislation which I feel is so essential, but also some of the laws and judicial interpretations of common law which protect the family as an institution and stabilizes in fact a woman's status in the family relationship. Some of these old common-law provisions are, of course, outmoded, but gradually the Courts, proceeding in the regular Anglo-American method of treatment of the common law, are interpreting and reapplying the ancient principles to modern times.

And may I say, my dear Jane, that I thought the pamphlet which you enclosed to me was particularly inept. I read it carefully, thinking I might find something new in it, but I didn't. I am afraid that it is an appeal to prejudice, pride and publicity, so, under the circumstances, I am sure that you will forgive me if I do not subscribe to the Woman's Party fund of $25,000. I hope your amendment will never be carried, but I, nevertheless, with deepest affection for you, gladly admit your right to differ with me in this or other matters.

Sincerely yours,<br>Frances Perkins

### 1945: APRIL 14

### DOROTHY DOW BUTTURFF TO AMIE TAPPAN DOW

*On April 12, 1945, thirty-nine days into his fourth term, FDR died of a cerebral hemorrhage at his cottage in Warm Springs, Georgia. Dorothy Dow (1904–) had started at the White House in 1933 as one of the secretaries who handled the mail, but she had gone on to become an all-around assistant, sometime hostess, dance partner, swim coach, and extra woman at dinner for the Roosevelts. Like many Americans who knew the president far less well, Dow experienced FDR's death not only as a national tragedy but also as a personal loss. From her vantage point inside the White House, she sent her mother this vivid description of the days immediately following his death.*

Malvina Thompson was Eleanor Roosevelt's private secretary. "Bob" was Robert Butturff, Dorothy's husband. Henry Morgenthau, Jr., was secretary of the treasury.

Sat. p.m. 4/14/45

Dear Mom,

I suppose you can guess what a terrific shock the President's death was to all of us. I don't know when I have ever felt as stunned and completely bowled over as I was Thursday night. Everything was as usual when we left the office Thursday night at 5:30 and stopped at the grocery store on the way home and Pete said he had heard there was a report that the President was dead. I passed it off as such rumors come a nickel a dozen around here all the time, but he turned the radio on and it almost took me off my feet. I went right on home and called up Miss Thompson to see if there would be anything I could [do] back at the office but she said No. Mrs. Roosevelt was to leave at 7:00 for Warm Springs and she would stay here to take care of things at this end. Bob and I just sat and listened to the radio until after midnight—and when the immensity of the thing began to sink in, it was more unbelievable than anything. At first I could only think—what would happen to the world in general—then gradually it began to sink in that there would be no more Mrs. Roosevelt or Miss Thompson to work for—everything I had left on my desk was completely dead—we could answer no more mail as Mrs. Roosevelt was no longer our boss and had any right to use White House stationery or speak with White House background—everything we have in the office, files, gifts, manuscripts, books, stuff in the Xmas closet—everything would have to be moved out of here.

The next day when we came to work there was certainly a pall over everything. Every one who worked in the White House had a real personal affection for the Roosevelts and we all felt as though we had lost a friend besides a world personality. There wasn't much we could do all day except answer the telephone and tell people they couldn't come to the funeral, etc. I started to clean out some books and things in the afternoon just to keep busy as the gloom was so thick you could cut it with a knife. Today, Saturday, they brought the President's body back and I have been to lots of different things in this town and at the White House, but nothing that was as solemn or stirring as the processional and whole occasion. Of course, we can't go to the funeral as it is to be in the East Room and there is only room for the officials and family, but they let us go out this morning and stand along the drive by the front portico when the body was taken in. As far as you could see across Lafayette Park, across the street from the White House, it was just a sea of faces—at 10:00 a.m. when the train pulled in the station St. John's Church near the White House began tolling the bell—the parade route was lined all the way with service men and policemen in mourning—and the procession was something I shall never forget. With the thousands of people we could see, there wasn't a sound among them even long before the procession arrived, a guard of honor of marines, soldiers, and sailors came and were stationed on the grounds in front of the portico and also a band. The procession was led by a service band, then came divisions of Marines, Army and Navy—then some armored equipment, more bands, Waves, Wacs, and Spars, then finally the guard of honor with flags, and the caisson with the flag-covered casket drawn by six horses. Everything was just ghastly still except for the distant roll of drums and the solemnity and immensity of the thing was almost overwhelming. I think especially for us who had so often seem him drive in the driveway there waving his hat and smiling and bowing to every one with people cheering and hollering that the contrast was indescribable. They stopped the caisson right in front of the portico—Mrs. Roosevelt, Anna, and Gen. Elliott Roosevelt were in the next car and they had to get out and stand for the photographers—then the four daughters-in-law were in the next car—and the following cars all pulled into the driveway and the people got out. The

Cabinet members, secretaries, and old friends of the President slowly walked up to the house and just stood outside while the armed forces presented arms, the band played the Star Spangled Banner and then the coffin was taken into the house. Josephus Daniels was standing right by me—he was Sec. of the Navy during the 1st World War when the President was Assistant Sec. of the Navy and he was Roosevelt's "boss" and has been a close friend and adviser ever since. He is an old, old man—well in his 80s, and he looked completely beaten. Sec. Morgenthau was next to him—and he also is a close personal friend—and others who were so closely connected with Roosevelt. The grief was something terrible to see and it just didn't seem as though it all could be real—it seemed that you were looking at something that was just a dream. During the procession, formations of big bombing planes flew over the route.

What it will all mean to us here I don't know. We will probably stay on just as before, but personally I simply can't imagine not working for Mrs. Roosevelt and Miss Thompson. One thing I know, that whatever happens to me the rest of my life, I feel privileged beyond words to have the close contact to people such as the Roosevelts. It does something to you to know people like that and it has been an experience that I shall always be grateful for. There has never been, and probably never will be, a more colorful administration, nor ever a time when so much history has been made, and to even have been a small part of it is a privilege.

It is about 2:00 p.m. now, and people are still milling around the park across the street—they just come and stand and look although there is nothing to see. At noon yesterday I went down town for a few minutes, and every one on the street was terribly solemn—small groups of people would gather and talk, but you couldn't help but sense that some great calamity had occurred. I think people in Washington were particularly fond of the President as a person as he always gave every one the feeling that he was glad to be here and was always so friendly.

Well, enough of this—you probably don't share my feelings about the Roosevelts—but if you don't, the only reason is that you never knew them.

Love,

Do

Miss Thompson said that they were trying to get out as soon as possible and I suppose next week we will be in it head over heels trying to get things packed up. I can't imagine what Mrs. Truman will be like. She probably will be just nothing after Mrs. Roosevelt and who her secretary will be will be anybody's guess. Things won't be the same again as there is a great deal of difference in just working, and working for some one because you have a real affection and admiration for them. Nobody could have been finer than Miss Thompson, nor more considerate, and the activities Mrs. Roosevelt was always engaged in were interesting and brought in a wealth of correspondence and information that you couldn't help but absorb. I don't imagine Mrs. Truman will do anything of that sort—she just isn't the caliber to do it, nor do I think she would have the drive that Mrs. Roosevelt had. However, I have a daughter to work for, so shall go on come what may.

### 1945: MAY 2
### JANE POULTON TO JACK POULTON

---

*Jack Poulton (1914–1987) had joined the navy in August of 1942 and had been stationed in the Pacific. In April 1945, he was allowed home for a leave with his wife, Jane Weaver Poulton (1926?–), who was attending college at the Richmond Professional Institute, a school for social work and public health. A month later, he received this letter, which he would keep, behind a photograph of Jane, for the rest of his life.*

The quote was from a song called "The Two Grenadiers." The Poultons' son was born in January of 1946.

May 2, 1945   Wednesday

Listen here, You! This is no time for you to be running around after Red Cross girls under tropical moons. You may be going to be a father and you had better behave. I wasn't going to tell you until I was sure but things look pretty good.

No, I am not angry with you for disrupting my life. I am only scared that something will happen to the baby and I want it more than anything in the world. I have picked out a good doctor and am to see him next week and feel fine except for a distaste for food.

I had to tell Nadia and Dr. D. about the possibility because they were going to offer me a job. Dr. D. says this comes under the heading of field work in population and Nadia has been telling me what to do in order to prevent problems.

I have everything figured out so don't worry. I will tell the family when I am sure and I will go on to summer school if I feel well enough. I want to get as much done as I can now and will try to go back part time when the baby comes.

There is to be a nursery school at RPI next year so it will only be a question of time before I can finish. I have to get the degree at RPI. My credits are weird. I never was a freshman and other colleges might not accept my transcript if I had to finish elsewhere.

After the baby I will retire for a while and maybe have another one when you get home. Meanwhile the degree is important now although the baby comes first.

Now that I am in a delicate condition, I don't feel generous about you so stay away from flight nurses and Red Cross girls. You belong to me and I am jealous.

Don't worry about me. I am fine and very happy. Only I am not as happy as Nadia who believes firmly in babies. She wants part interest.

I am glad I am to hear where you are. You are damn right I am interested. And you be careful with a wife and child at home who "without you would fare badly."

P.S. If it is a girl I am going to name it something wild.
P.S.S. Don't get too excited. Just get a little excited.

### 1945: JUNE 4
### JUNE WANDREY TO HER FAMILY

*Camp Allach, five miles north of Munich, had been liberated in April and turned into a hospital for displaced persons. There were four hundred patients when nurse June Wandrey (see page 570) was assigned to the area.*

Dearest family,

I'm on night duty with a hundred corpse-like patients, wrecks of humanity . . . macerated skin drawn over their bones, eyes sunken in wide sockets, hair shaved off. Mostly Jewish, these tortured souls hardly resemble humans. Their bodies are riddled with diseases. Many have tuberculosis, typhus, enterocolitis (constant diarrhea) and huge bed sores.

Many cough all night long, as their lungs are in such terrible condition. They break out in great beads of perspiration. Then there is the roomful of those that are incontinent and irrational. It sounds like the construction crew for the tower of Babel . . . Poles, Czechs, Russians, Slavs, Bulgarians. Dutch, Hungarians, Germans. What makes it so difficult is that I understand only a few words. Their gratitude tears at my heart when I do something to make them more comfortable or give a little food or smile at them.

One of the day nurses had a patient that kept leaving his cot and crawling under it to sleep on the bare wooden floor. She decided to put his mattress, sheets and pillow under there too as it seemed to be his favorite place.

The odor from the lack of sanitation over the years makes the whole place smell like rotten, rotten sewage. We wear masks constantly, though they don't keep out the stench. There are commodes in the middle of the room. Patients wear just pajama shirts as they can't get the bottoms down fast enough to use the commodes. God, where are you?

Making rounds by flashlight is an eerie sensation. I'll hear calloused footsteps shuffling behind me and turn in time to see four semi-nude skeletons gliding toward the commodes. God, where were you?

You have to gently shake some of the patients to see if they are still alive. Their breathing is so shallow, pulse debatable. Many die in their sleep. I carry their bodies back to a storage room, they are very light, just the weight of their demineralized bones. Each time, I breathe a wee prayer for them. God, are you there?

In the morning the strongest patients have latrine detail, it takes two of them to carry a commode pail and dump it. They also sweep the floors and carry out the trash. Many patients are only seventeen.

Our men sprayed the camp area to kill the insects that carried many of the diseases. We were told that the SS guards who controlled the camp used to bring a small pan of food into the ward and throw it on the floor. When the stronger patients scrambled for it, like starving beasts, they were lashed with a long whip. It's a corner of hell. Too shocked and tired to write anymore.

Love,

June

## 1945: AUGUST 6
## PRISCILLA HOLLOWAY TO JOHN HOLLOWAY

*It would be days before the true force of the Hiroshima blast became known, and years before its long-term effects began to be clear. On the day the United States dropped its first atomic bomb, Priscilla Kohn Holloway (1910–2002) had no way of knowing that some eighty thousand people had been killed in an instant. But after focusing on more mundane financial concerns, she expressed her worry, her dread, and her search for religious and patriotic comfort.*

Priscilla was in Milwaukee when she wrote this letter. Her husband, John Holloway

(1908–1988), was in the South Pacific. They numbered their letters to keep track of them. Saint Andrew Bobola was a seventeenth-century Polish cleric who was killed by enemies of the Catholics. *Herrenvolk* means "master race."

August 6, 1945

Cheri,

After a silence of ten days your second # 323 written July 28th came to me. The first # 323 came on July 27th (you wrote it on the 20th). We seem to have had the same difficulty, each of us, for you tell me in the letter received today that at its writing you hadn't had a letter from me for ten days—nothing after the first letter I wrote you from Hartland.

It always makes me feel badly when your mail doesn't go through—I suppose it is the feeling of helplessness that gets me. If there were something more I could do besides writing and sending them air mail I could consume my energies in that way. But inasmuch as the army insists on taking care of the mail itself there is nothing for me to do but get mad when yours doesn't go through— and then pray to St. Andrew Bobola for help. Which I will do pronto. I have for the past several nights been asking him to hurry up a letter to me—and presto! today I got one. Maybe I can turn the trick for you too.

I seem to be a very expensive proposition for you this month—for you tell me your pay was minus $66 to cover the allottment portion for June, July and August 1942. The army finance office seems to have a mind like an elephant. I hadn't even known they neglected to deduct the allottment back then. But old Uncle Sam always manages to come in on the collecting end, doesn't he? It is too bad they took it all at once—that must have been a mighty heavy blow for you. As I figure it you got less than $30 with that extra deduction. I still think they should have given you a little advance notice, or let you pay it back in installments or something. But accountants are notoriously heartless—even in the army, aren't they?

It seems almost more than coincidence that you should discuss in your latest letter President Truman's notice to Japan to surrender or face total destruction. For it came to me on the same day in which official announcement was made of the atomic bomb which was loosed on the Japanese army base at Hiroshima. The first two pages of tonight's paper carry no other news but the different releases of the years of experiment, the secrecy, the precautions that went into the planning and execution of the bomb that fell on Japan. Except for the report of the clouds of dust that rose from Hiroshima no knowledge is had yet of what the bomb did. But on the night radio news they described to us the experimental bomb that was set off in New Mexico last month as a test. They said the bomb was hoisted up to the top of a steel tower and when the bomb had exploded the tower had simply disappeared with no trace. All that showed where it had stood was a vast crater in the earth.

Reading about this harnessing of some of the "unknown" powers of the world made my blood run cold. In the hands of unscrupulous knaves like the late Nazi herrenvolk—the civilization we know today could be wholly destroyed. Secretary Stimson said that if the secret can be kept by Britain and the United States (who united in the work to produce this frightening force) we can force peace on the world—willing or not. Frankly I cannot now imagine either Britain or the United States using it for ill. With all our many faults of selfishness and greed, I think we stand out in the world as the most humane of any people.

Perhaps one is being a little theatrical in saying a man or group of men could destroy the world—as one army officer is reported to have said in speaking of the atomic bomb. God created the world and only God can destroy it—or permit its destruction. Perhaps if we keep on with our brutalities and our sins and our lack of devotion to Him he will see fit to wipe our civilization out as He wiped out the civilization extant at the time of the Flood; perhaps He will look upon us with disgust as He looked upon Sodom and Gomora. And perhaps He will give us another chance.

I am thinking back on what I have read of the promises of Our Lady of Fatima. I think I sent you some stories about the appearance of Our Lady at Fatima in Portugal after the last war. And she promised at that time that unless the world returned to God another and more horrible war would be loosed upon the earth. And we certainly are in the throes of a horrible war, are we not? But she also promised that if she were heeded Russia would be converted and a long era of peace would descend on the world. It remains now to be seen whether we are to have peace or further punishment. It is useless, and perhaps sinful, to speculate. We have to wait and find out.

But it is true, isn't it, that the Church flourishes most under difficulties and declines under too much prosperity. You have witnesses to that in the Phillipines—the Church had no opposition and decayed; you have the same example in France and Spain and Mexico. Maybe the world needs a few lessons to make it mend its spiritual fences, eh? It takes adversity to purify the soul.

I can't help but wonder what the reaction to this atomic bomb will be in your neck of the woods—certainly its use cannot help but shorten the war. Not that I think it will be used anywhere but in Japan itself—I doubt if our commands would consider destroying Chinese by a lavish use of such a destructive force. But used solely against Japan it can shorten the war by making it necessary to fight Japanese land forces only in China and Manchuria—where our superior armor will be a big force.

I begin to sound suspiciously like an armchair general so I will stop pronto! I have no use for armchair generals, you see.

Wisconsin lost its No. 1 hero today when Major Richard I. Bong was killed testing a Lockheed jet propelled plane. The Japs couldn't get him but imperfection did. One always hates to see a man killed—especially one who came through so much fighting unscathed. It must have been an awful blow to his family and his bride of less than six months. It seems rather ironic that he was kept out of combat areas so that he would not be killed—and then to have him lose his life on home soil. You can't keep the angel of death at bay forever, can you? Or just by wishing it. Proving again that senseless fear is a weakness. I keep hammering that item into my own brain to cure myself of worrying about silly trifles. And I think I'm succeeding, what's more to the point.

My, my. What a solemn owl I am tonight. Too much reading about atom smashing I guess. And considering I know absolutely nothing about science and less about physics—I ought not to try speculating about either!

Good night honey. I love you and I'll pray hard to our St. Andrew to get the mail through to you. I can see you, like me, are not quite so cheerful when there is a long wait between letters. I'll get St. A on the job right away!

Priscilla

### 1945: AUGUST 15
### MARJORIE HASELTON TO RICHARD HASELTON

*Six days after the American attack on Nagasaki, V-J (for Victory over Japan) Day was finally announced. From Athol, Massachusetts, Marjorie Kenney Haselton (1916–2004) wrote to her husband, Richard (1915–1975), who was serving in the U.S. Navy behind Japanese lines in the last months of the war.*

Marjorie didn't mention which song Bing Crosby was singing on the radio when she wrote this letter, but within a month, his version of "It's Been a Long, Long Time" would reach the top of the charts, with its fitting lyrics: "Kiss me once, then kiss me twice, then kiss me once again / It's been a long, long time / Haven't felt like this, my dear / Since I can't remember when / It's been a long, long time."

Athol, Massachusetts
V-J Day—August 15, 1945

My Darling,

I'm listening to the radio and I have a feeling that somewhere, right now, you are listening, too. Bing is talking to our hearts, as only he can do it, and the top talent of the USA is contributing its bit. The songs they are singing have me alternating between laughter and tears. . . .

You and I were brought up to think cynically of patriotism—not by our parents, but the books, plays, movies and magazine features written by the bitter, realistic writers of the twenties and thirties. They called patriotism a tool of the demagogues, a spell binder to blind our eyes to the "real" truth. We thought they were right—at least, I know, I did. I hated everything in music, books, movies, etc. that stressed love of country. That was for the yokels. The uninitiated, but not for anyone who was really in the know. Maybe I was right—I don't know. One thing I AM sure of—a thing this war has taught me—I love my country and I'm not ashamed to admit it anymore. Perhaps I am only thinking along the lines the nation's propagandists want me to think. But I know I am proud of the men of my generation. Brought up like you and I, in false prosperity and degrading depression, they have overcome these handicaps. And shown the world that America has something the world can never take away from us—a determination to keep our way of life. . . . You boys proved that you had a fighting spirit and team work that couldn't be beaten. Call it Yankee ingenuity or whatever you will, it still is the one force that won the war—the thing the enemy never believed we had. That is why, tonight, I am proud to be an American, and married to one of its fighting men. None of you fellows wanted the deal life handed you—but just about every one of you gritted your teeth and hung on. . . . I think the President sounded tonight as if he felt that way, too. Proud enough to bust. And, Gee, what other country in this world would let an insignificant Private introduce over the air, the head man of the country? Thank God for letting us live and bring up our family in a country like this. It's not perfect, I know, but it's the best there is—and away ahead of the rest! . . .

I've been hoping your special assignment is one that the surrender will make unnecessary. Wouldn't it be grand if you were heading home right now! I know that's too much to expect, but I hope I get a letter Tuesday with real news cause I want my chance to show you in person how much.

I love you.

Me

**1945: AUGUST 18**

**CONSTANCE JONES TO DONALD SWARTZBAUGH**

---

*Amid the jubilation and relief of victory, Constance Hope Jones sent this letter to Donald Swartzbaugh, whom she later married. Writing from Missouri, she looked ahead not only to the coming conflicts with Russia but also, quite prophetically, to the peculiar challenges of peace.*

Kirkwood, Missouri

August 18, 1945

Donnie,

Here I am again. How'd you celebrate the great news of the Japanese surrender? I'll never forget how things happened around here. Pop got out his 45 and 38 and blasted away his long saved shells. He was just like a kid playing with a new toy! (They tell me that men are always little boys, anyway, and I believe it.) In addition to that the church bells rang, whistles blasted loud and long, kids got out drums, pots and pans, flags, etc. and paraded the streets, people let loose of their tires and gas and paraded thru the streets until well into the night. Thousands crowded the streets in St. Louis. At Memorial plaza, 40,000 kissed and danced their way on the streets all night long. The next day everything closed up tight. Today most of the war plants are closed up and people are wondering about jobs. . . .

I think our family has been lucky in that both of our "warriors" are safe and sound. There are thousands of families not quite so lucky. . . .

Now, I suppose President Truman and Congress really have a big job of getting things and people adjusted to peace time ways of hiring and doing! Perhaps the biggest job is yet ahead.

Over the radio yesterday, I heard the starting of another war! All about how the US was developing new and secret weapons and how we should keep our secrets from the Russians! . . . Talk like that is a betrayal of those who died or were wounded in this war and of those who are working to make it possible for nations to live in peace with each other! . . .

Till later,

Connie

# THE WORLD OF
# THE BABY BOOM

# 1946
# ~
# 1979

I woke at 7 am the next morning and recall remarking to the nurse that it was a beautiful day to have a baby. I started timing my pains which were averaging then around 7 to 10 minutes apart. I just laid around, smoked and read a magazine for most of the morning. . . . Later on I was given stuff they call Scopolamine which believe me is the greatest.

*—Alice Crowther to her best friend*
*June 2, 1954*

WOODSTOCK

3 DAYS OF PEACE
AND MUSIC...AND LOVE

WARNER BROS.

JUDY GARLAND
JAMES MASON

A Star is Born

CINEMASCOPE

TECHNICOLOR

JACK CARSON · CHARLES BICKFORD

CBS
TELEVISION

# BETWEEN 1946 AND 1979 . . .

**1946:** Dr. Benjamin Spock publishes his *Common Sense Book of Baby and Child Care,* with the famously reassuring first sentence: "You know more than you think you do." **1947:** *Howdy Doody* and *Meet the Press* both debut on television. ⭐ While flying over the town of Victorville, California, pilot Chuck Yeager breaks the sound barrier. ⭐ Jackie Robinson joins the Brooklyn Dodgers, becoming the first black major-league baseball player of the twentieth century. **1948:** The game Scrabble—first called Lexico, then Criss-Cross Words—is trademarked by inventor Alfred Mosher Butts and his partner, James Brunot. ⭐ Andrew Wyeth paints *Christina's World*. ⭐ In Salinas, California, starlet Marilyn Monroe is named Artichoke Queen after posing with some of the produce at Cal Choke. **1949:** For the first presentation of television's Emmy awards, sculptor Louis McManus models the "golden girl" statuette after his wife, Dorothy. **1950:** In Wheeling, West Virginia, Senator Joseph McCarthy declares: "I have here in my hand a list of 205, a list of names made known to the secretary of state as being members of the Communist Party and who nevertheless are still working and shaping policy in the State Depart-

---

Clockwise from top left: Elvis Presley; Billie Jean King; Helen Gurley Brown; Woodstock poster; Rosa Parks being fingerprinted after refusing to move to the back of the bus in Montgomery, Alabama; Poster for *A Star is Born* with Judy Garland; Senator Joseph McCarthy; "Jacqueline Kennedy" by Elliott Erwitt; Nixon in a Watergate tape web by Robert Pryor; Dr. Benjamin Spock and friend.

ment." **1951:** The CBS eye logo, designed by William Golden, makes its first appearance; it will remain unchanged for the next five decades. **1952:** The first successful open-heart surgery is performed at the University of Minnesota by Dr. F. John Lewis. **1954:** Polio kills more than 1,300 Americans and cripples more than 18,000. **1955:** In Des Plaines, Illinois, the first McDonald's opens, offering French fries, coffee, and soft drinks for 10 cents each; hamburgers for 15 cents; cheeseburgers for 19 cents; and milk shakes for 20 cents. ★ Rosa Parks refuses to give her bus seat to a white passenger and is arrested, setting off the Montgomery bus boycott, which lasts for more than a year and ultimately leads the Supreme Court to rule that segregated seating is unconstitutional. **1956:** Seven mothers in a Chicago suburb form the La Leche League to promote and offer each other support for breast-feeding. ★ The top three songs, "Love Me Tender," "Hound Dog," and "Heartbreak Hotel," are all sung by Elvis Presley. **1959:** The Barbie doll, created by Ruth Handler and named for her daughter, goes on the market for $3, sporting a black-and-white-striped bathing suit and a ponytail; 350,000 are sold in the first year. ★ **1960:** The FDA approves the birth-control pill. **1962:** David Wagner, an Illinois engineer, receives a patent for a round birth-control pill dispenser that rotates one day at a time and is designed to look like a makeup compact. ★ Helen Gurley Brown publishes *Sex and the Single Girl,* with its semishocking— and, as it turns out, best-selling—assertion that marriage need not be a prerequisite to sexual activity. **1963:** On the steps of the Lincoln Memorial in Washington, D.C., the Reverend Martin Luther King, Jr., declares: "I have a dream that one day this nation will rise up and live out the true meaning of its creed: 'We hold these truths to be self-evident: that all men are created equal.' " ★ President John F. Kennedy is assassinated. **1964:** 24,000 rolls of Beatles wallpaper arrive in the United States. **1965:** After the widespread use of the Salk and Sabin vaccines, only 61 cases of polio are diagnosed in the U.S. ★ Black separatist Malcolm X is assassinated. ★ Reporting on a controversy within theological circles, *Time* magazine runs a cover story with the headline "Is God Dead?" **1966:** Hit songs: "The Ballad of the Green Berets," "You Can't Hurry Love," "Strangers in the Night." **1968:** Martin Luther King, Jr., is assassinated. ★ U.S. troop buildup in Vietnam reaches its height, at 541,000. ★ Billed as "The American Tribal Love Rock Musical," *Hair* premieres on Broadway, offering audiences frontal nudity, electric guitars, and the memorable lyrics "I want it long, straight, curly, fuzzy / Snaggy, shaggy, ratty, matty." ★ Robert Kennedy is assassinated. **1969:** Neil Armstrong walks on the moon. **1970:** 200,000 miles from earth, and 55 hours into the Apollo 13 mission, an oxygen tank explodes, and command module pilot Jack Swigert tells ground controllers: "Houston, we've had a problem here." ★ National Guardsmen open fire during an antiwar protest at Kent State University in Ohio and kill four students. **1972:** Seven men working for the Committee to Reelect the President break into the National Democratic Committee's headquarters at the Watergate complex, prompting a scandal that will ultimately lead to the resignation of Richard Nixon. **1973:** Some 50 million people watch the televised tennis match between Billie Jean King and Bobby Riggs in "The Battle of the Sexes," which King wins in three straight sets. ★ By a 7–2 vote, the Supreme Court rules in *Roe* v. *Wade* that the government cannot interfere with a woman's right to an abortion. ★ The last American fighting troops leave Vietnam. **1974:** Bar codes are used for the first time on products in American stores. **1975:** Bill Gates and Paul Allen form Microsoft to develop computer software. **1976:** Incumbent Gerald Ford is defeated by Jimmy Carter, who becomes the first president from the Deep South since 1865. **1979:** In the bookstores: Norman Mailer's *The Executioner's Song,* Tom Wolfe's *The Right Stuff;* at the movies: *Kramer vs. Kramer, Norma Rae, Apocalypse Now.*

---

*The war was over, but for some representatives of the Allied countries, there was un-finished business in the form of the Nuremberg Trials. Convened at the end of 1945, the trials were held by the International Military Tribunal in the German city that had been a center of Nazi activity. Katherine Fite (1905?–1989) served as an assistant to Robert Jackson, a U.S. Supreme Court justice who was chief prose-cutor. But being in Nuremberg, as she explained here to her parents, Alice (1875–?) and Emerson Fite (1874–1953), involved more than her work preparing evidence.*

The day after Fite wrote this letter, Hitler's former deputy, Herman Goering, committed sui-cide. Ten of his codefendants, including Wilhelm Frick, were hanged a day later. Aline Chalu-four was listed as a civilian among the Nuremberg Military Tribunal's personnel. UNRRA was the United Nations Relief and Rehabilitation Administration. Heinrich Himmler, former head of the SS, had committed suicide in May of 1945.

Dearest Mother and Daddy,

I believe last week I wrote you that your letter of Oct. 1 reached me Oct. 6. Well, it was followed on Oct. 9 by one written, I believe, on Sept. 28 or maybe even Sept. 26. So there's no telling.

To you probably the most interesting experience of this week will be my meeting with a woman lawyer on the French staff. She sat next me on the bus and seemed so pleasant and intelligent that I suggested we have lunch together. In the course of the lunch she said that her name was Aline Chalufour. I re-marked that I had seen her name in international law periodicals and had won-dered if she were related to André Chalufour. She looked astonished and said—Why, that's my own brother. She is a woman I suppose a few years older than I and really very intelligent and congenial—and I lack congenial femi-nine companionship. She speaks fluent English. André is now married and has

3 small children and a "very nice little wife" (no enthusiasm). He appears to have traveled in the U.S., to have worked in banks and I think travel bureaus, and to have been in the Army and a PW for a while. And is currently engaged in going around France establishing the offices in which the French Gov't repays the luxury taxes paid by the American soldiers. She also knows Cecile Thureau-Dangin—still keeps in touch with her. Believes that she and André were a little in love with each other, but, characteristically French, André was "young and not established". Cecile has had several operations, has had one leg removed, has a wooden leg which no one would ever know. But if anyone pays her court, malicious friends tell him she has a wooden leg. She has been brave but is somewhat bitter. Lives alone in a big house in Paris, coming from a wealthy family. And so we gossiped about Chateau d'Oex which she had visited. She remembered having heard of Mrs. Shackelton who "took a great interest in André". And also vaguely remembered having heard of our taking the ice cream freezer up the mountain. This afternoon another Chalufour sister arrived— working with UNRRA south of Munich, somewhat less attractive, but very pleasant and intense about DP's (displaced persons). The Chalufours must be quite a family. As a matter of principle none of them has ever patronized the black market. Aline was working for DeGaulle in Canada during the war.

Drove out with them to the French quarter in a village some miles out, in a little German car in which the sister had driven up here, alone and without a gun, some 150 miles across country. The village in question is so picturesque, so clean. Why couldn't the Germans have been satisfied? They rather terrify me. This city is coming to life so quickly—street lights, railroad trains running, etc. I suppose that's the result of American energy, but the Germans are energetic too. And they have so many, many babies—fat well-fed, well clothed little Krauts. They say the French babies are thin and scarce.

This afternoon to a concert by the same orchestra I heard in July—was larger and very good. The Opera House is freezing cold—being open to the air in its upper unseen regions. So as it gets colder, it will be less and less pleasant. That's where they have their USO shows and movies and the GI's stand in lines around the block to get in.

Yesterday I engineered an interrogation of Frick, formerly Minister of Interior later pushed out by Himmler. I mean I set the wheels in motion and we gave our questions to the interrogator. He's a ratty shifty looking man. You find yourself feeling sorry for the devils because you have them at bay, but then you stop and think of the fiendish mass exterminations they engineered. Goering was being questioned the same morning and I saw the back of his head through a door. They say the palms of his hands are great paunches of flesh. He is extremely clever in his answers.

Last night I met some of the Russian officers at our night club. One talked bad French. The General only Russian, but he informed me through his interpreter that I looked like a Russian, which is undoubtedly the highest compliment a [illegible] General knows how to pay you. And so we clicked glasses.

And so our narrow life proceeds. But narrow as it is, it is history and it is fascinating which we tend to forget as the novelty wears off and we get used to it all and get on each other's nerves. The Justice asked me the other night at a dinner at his house, how I liked Nuremberg. Which stumped me. Which of course he understood. We create our own pleasures—the interesting part is thrust on us—and the discomfort is at least interesting. You simply can't answer I'm having a wonderful time, because you don't have a marvellous time in a ruined city, in a hostile country, at a criminal trial where you look out a window at a jail all day and interrogate men you hope to hang.

This week I received via London, via Dr. Ecer, the Czech representative on the United Nations War Crime Commission, a letter from Lida Srbkova from Prague. She was in my class at V.C. She asks me to visit her in Prague—which probably the Russians would never let me do. She says "all Vassar girls are very anxious to see you", which sounds as tho none were missing. Prexy might be interested. He has probably heard already.

The towels haven't come.

I am fine and don't work the London hours. If I work at night, I bring it home to the hotel.

> Lots and lots of love,
> Titter

## 1949: FEBRUARY 22
## LILA MacLEOD TO LUCILE ALLEN

*From 1937 to 1958, Lemo Rockwood (1896–1982) taught a marriage course at Cornell University that, according to an early course catalog, covered topics including "scientific information which has promoted the study of mate choice . . . the development of affection in the individual, and the achievement of heterosexuality; substitutes for mate love and the adjustment of the single person. . . ." For the time, she was considered progressive, and her relatively frank approach made for plenty of controversy. In this letter, the head of Cornell's student Women's Self Government Association registered her protest with Lucile Allen, the dean of women. Just two decades later, some of Cornell's dormitories would become coed, but in the meantime, Cornell students had not yet experienced the sexual revolution—or even, as is clear below, the mysteries of dating in anything more private than "relative seclusion."*

Dear Dean Allen,

I would like to call to your attention a condition which has caused several difficult situations for the officers of the Women's Self-Government Association this year.

In September Dr. Rockwood, of the College of Home Economics, spoke to the Freshman Women's Camp on social adjustments and dating in college life. I felt at the time that her talk was based on the plane of a college Senior rather than Freshman and that it was open for misinterpretation on this account, as well as for her statements about the need for having seclusion for the development of courtship relations, and the strong implication that women's dormitories were at fault for not providing these conditions. My reaction was corroborated by the feeling of the Freshman class itself, as exemplified by their remarks to each other and on their camp evaluation sheets.

Dr. Rockwood's marriage course has been the root of another problem similar in nature to this first one. Her statements and implications there about courtship, seclusion and the inadequacy of the dating facilities of Cornell University dormitories in this respect are evidently open to the same interpretation; for just last week a member of the House of Representatives who is taking Dr. Rockwood's course came up to me and delivered a sharp criticism along these lines of the dorm living-room arrangements and pressured me to get a system established which would allow girls to get permission from parents to sign out to men's rooms for evenings.

Perhaps Dr. Rockwood has [a] mistaken impression of the dorm living-rooms. They are not heavily-trafficked, nor devoid of all privacy. Couples can find relative seclusion where they can talk quietly and uninterrupted, without the feeling that they are in the public eye. There are Senior rooms, too, which afford more privacy than the living-rooms. It is my opinion that Cornell provides all the facilities that a university can to make dating pleasant. I do not feel that a university or WSGA can sponsor any absolute, or even "more absolute" conditions of privacy for couples.

I call these conditions to your attention in hopes that there is some way in which they can be improved. I should be very glad to discuss the matter with you at any time.

> Sincerely,
> Lila MacLeod
> President of Women's Self-
> Government

## 1949: FEBRUARY 26

## AN EXPECTANT MOTHER TO GRANTLY DICK-READ

*As American women returned from their wartime work to the traditional home sphere, motherhood became not just a predictable outcome but a patriotic goal. The inevitable baby boom (the term was apparently coined in a 1953 report to Harry Truman) also had a medical aspect, as hospital deliveries—often with forceps—were now the norm, and mothers were either drugged or anesthetized by their (usually male) obstetricians. The notion that women could control the childbirth process and might even prefer to be conscious participants was a long time in coming. Dr. Grantly Dick-Read (1890–1959) was a pioneer; in a series of books and in his London practice, he insisted that childbirth need not be painful, an assertion that eventually would influence a generation of expectant mothers on both sides of the Atlantic. For the Illinois woman who wrote this letter, just finding an American doctor to help her was the first challenge.*

> February 26, 1949
> Illinois

Dear Dr. Read,

We have one child, and I should have another in seven months. Because of this first child, however, I hesitate to go very far afield in my search for an obstetrician who is using your "normal childbirth" (as I like to call it) technique. The strength of our desire to find such a person within a practicable distance prompts me to bother you with this request. Have you been in contact with, or do you know of any obstetrician in St. Louis, Missouri, or Chicago, Illinois, (or the intervening areas) who is advocating your method where possible?

It must seem strange that I cannot find anyone who will use your method but I have lost faith in my ability to convince a nonbeliever that the surgical-anesthesia-and high-forceps routine is not wanted. Seven obstetricians turned down the method as "taking too much time" before our first child was born; the eighth (who is in the employ of my father-in-law ——— an M.D.) said that I needn't have anesthesia if I didn't want it.

When I was having 2-minute "pains," however, (having been unattended in the labor room for two hours—my husband being barred), the obstetrician entered with a nurse and forcibly (I mean that—I didn't want anything, except some company) administered Demerol, scopolamine, (and later ether), and I didn't regain consciousness for 12 hours.

He later answered my protests by explaining bitterly that my request had been the result of a "pregnancy hallucination": that <u>men</u> were too intelligent to let women suffer because of their "notions"—and wasn't I lucky that he had been wise enough to humor me along until delivery time?

The fact that the child's skull was terribly (and needlessly—no complications were present) deformed, that he had a hematoma the size of a man's fist, that the placenta retained in part (I found this out the hard way—104 degree temperature and bleeding for some months)—all these things did not shake his faith in the wisdom of extracting the baby.

I apologize for bothering you with details, but do want you to know how important it is that we find someone who truly believes that childbirth is normal—not pathological.

That line—"Oh to be in England"—keeps running through my mind but I'm afraid coming to you is impossible. But please, Dr. Read, if you <u>do</u> have a known "disciple" over here, will you give us his name?

Yours sincerely

### 1950: NOVEMBER
### JUDY GARLAND TO HER FANS

---

*The child of vaudevillians and the mother of future singers Liza Minnelli and Lorna Luft, Judy Garland (1922–1969) was also a member of all her fans' families, the embodiment of the Hollywood star who belonged to everyone. Already famous as a teenager, Garland starred in a series of MGM movies, most famously* The Wizard of Oz, *during the 1930s. With her extraordinary voice and her winsome manner, she transcended her juvenile roles to make films throughout the 1940s, including* Easter Parade *and* The Harvey Girls. *By 1950, addicted to amphetamines and barbiturates, Garland was near collapse, and MGM terminated her contract. The same year, she published this letter—a faint foreshadowing of the celebrity confessionals that would be more ubiquitous and more direct in the coming decades—in the popular fan magazine* Modern Screen. *Comebacks and failures and more comebacks followed. In 1969, she died—as famously as she'd lived—from an overdose of barbiturates.*

Dear Friends,

This is a thank-you note.

At a time when I've been gossip's victim and the target of a thousand lies, you people have stood by me. I won't ever forget that.

You've judged me not on the basis of headlines, rumor and innuendo but on my performances as an actress and an entertainer.

Ever since the release of my last picture, <u>Summer Stock</u>, thousands of you have had the kindness to write to me. You've congratulated me, encouraged me, and pledged me your support. And for all this—let me repeat—I'm eternally grateful.

Inasmuch as it is impossible for me to reply individually to your more than 18,000 letters, I'm using this space in <u>Modern Screen</u> to answer those questions most frequently asked.

I have a responsibility to you friends. Rather than let you be misguided by the flood of nonsense printed about me by reporters and uninformed writers who know none of the facts, I intend to fulfill my responsibility by telling you movie-goers the truth.

I am not quitting motion pictures. Movies are my life's blood. I love making motion pictures and always have ever since I was a little girl.

I do not intend, however, to make any films for the next six months. I'm just going to relax, take things easy, and regain my peace of mind.

For a while I expected to go to Paris with my daughter, Liza, and my husband, Vincente Minelli—but his studio has decided to film all of <u>An American in Paris</u> in Hollywood, and since he is directing that picture and plans shortly to direct the sequel to <u>Father of the Bride</u>, we all plan to remain in California.

I love to work, I love to sing, I love to act—I get restless when I don't—and it's entirely possible that I will do a few broadcasts with Bing Crosby or Bob Hope before six months are up.

My health is fine. As I write this, I've just returned from a vacation in Sun Valley and Lake Tahoe. I'm sun-tanned, I weigh 110 pounds, and my outlook on things is joyful and optimistic.

Many of you have written and asked what was wrong with me in the past.

The honest answer is that I suffered from a mild sort of inferiority complex. I used to work myself up into depressions, thought no one really cared about me, no one outside my family, that is.

Why I should have ever gotten depressed, I certainly don't know. You people have proved to me that I've got thousands of friends the world over, that you care about my welfare and my career.

It's perfectly normal for people to have their ups and downs. I know that now, but a year or so ago, these depressions of mine used to worry me, and the more I worried about them, the lower I felt.

Anyway, all of that is gone and done with. The slate of the past is wiped clean. Insofar as I'm concerned, the world is good, golden and glorious. My best years and my best work lie ahead of me, and I'm going to give them everything I've got.

Many of you have asked if I realized how closely you followed my career and behavior. I certainly do, and that's why I want all of you to know, especially the youngsters, that I'm not in the slightest embittered about Hollywood and that I still think a motion picture career is one of the finest ambitions any girl can have.

It means hard work and it has its pitfalls but so has every other occupation.

If my daughter, Liza, wants to become an actress, I'll do everything to help her.

Of course, being a child actress and being raised on a studio lot is not the easiest adjustment a young girl can make. You don't go to baseball games or junior proms or sorority initiations, but every success has its sacrifices, and these are the ones a very young girl must make if she wants a career at a very early age.

The girl who finishes her schooling, however, and then wants to become an actress is facing a thrilling, rewarding career.

If I had to do it all over again, I would probably make the same choices and the same errors. These are part of living.

A lot of fanciful stories have depicted me as the victim of stark tragedy, high drama, and all sorts of mysterious Hollywood meanderings. All that is bunk.

Basically, I am still Judy Garland, a plain American girl from Grand Rapids, Minnesota, who's had a lot of good breaks, a few tough breaks, and who loves you with all her heart for your kindness in understanding that I am nothing more, nothing less.

Thank you again.
Judy Garland

## 1951: APRIL 30
## HELEN STEVENSON TO HER FAMILY

*Just five years after the end of World War II, Americans were back on the front lines, this time in Korea, where postwar attempts to unify the country had devolved into chaos. When the North Koreans, supported by the Chinese and Soviets, moved south across the thirty-eighth parallel, President Truman ordered the United States into South Korea for what the United Nations called a police action but was, of course, a devastating war. Helen Day Stevenson (1928–1997), the daughter of two devoted Red Cross leaders (Bill Stevenson had headed the ARC in Great Britain), arrived in Korea in April of 1951. Like Charlotte Colburn (see page 576), she served with a Clubmobile unit, providing doughnuts, coffee, and encouragement to the UN troops. From time to time, in a way that foreshadowed some of the growing American attitudes toward war, she also questioned the motives and behavior of her own side.*

In 1957, Stevenson married New Jersey governor Robert Meyner. In later years, she would write a column, host a television talk show, and, beginning in 1974, serve two terms in the U.S. House of Representatives. The ellipses were in the original text.

April 30, 1951

Dearest Mom, Pop, Peekie et al:

First I'd like to say that you had better not give any more of my letters to the News Tribune or if you do they had better be very well censored. Ginnie Griffeth just happened to read a copy,—the one about all the self-inflicted wounds—and she didn't like it. She said the hospital where I had worked would not have liked it and also Red Cross headquarters wouldn't like it. They are my <u>own</u> ideas you see, but when people read the articles they think they express what Red Cross thinks and that is not always true. It is not good to have people writing to the editor like one joker did and saying that Red Cross workers ought to be better indoctrinated! Oh Lordy!! Anything from now on that you give to the paper better be sent to me first for approval. Lots of my statements are private observations. People will think what are the matter with those hospitals that they don't have better supervision to see that men don't tear open their wounds or hold lights under their thermometers. . . . O.K.? Hope you understand. You know Red Cross, everything has to go through channels and then too they are so conscious of poor publicity. . . .

War news is very bad again and everyone here is down in the dumps over it. It looks as if Seoul had fallen again and as one officer said rather cheerfully last night "Well, it isn't the first time." Lots and lots of talk around here of an air raid because Pusan is so important and all the men and supplies come into this town to go up north. We have been having many alerts and complete black-outs at night and the ack, ack guns are forever shooting to practise. The other night they had an alert and we were told it was the real thing. It turned out to be three unidentified enemy planes, they didn't drop any bombs though. Thank Heaven!

We do feel that Pusan is the first thing they would hit. You can just picture yours truly under a cot with a mattress over her. But 'tis no use crossing bridges until we come to them.

I lead such a fascinating life. We feel all the time that we are right in the thick of things. It is a hectic life and you give and give and give until sometimes you never want to see another person again. Our living quarters are so nice that men stream in and out. If you were to walk into our small sitting room you could find gathered together colonels, privates, sergents, and Captains. There is a rule out that no officer can drive his own jeep and so when they come to see us we make them bring their drivers in. We drink beer and sometimes whiskey but the latter is almost impossible to get and there is much talk of how and where to get it. Not only will you find all ranks but all nationalities. I thought you might be interested in the different countries the men I have known here come from. It is quite an impressive list. Sweden (from the Swedish Red Cross Hospital here), Denmark (from the Danish Hospital ship here in Pusan harbor), English, Scotch, Irish, Australia, New Zealand, S. Africans, Belgiums, French, Dutch, Thailand, Turkey, Puerto Rico. . . . Lots of British troops and I must say that the foreign troops are ever so much more polite and appreciate on the whole than our own G.I.'s. American soldiers are treated better than any soldiers in the world. The foreign soldiers just can't believe that we have such a nice club and that they can come in. They have never seen anything like it in all their military experience.

We do not let South Korean soldiers come into the club. It seems that the higher-ups feel that we would be completely taken over by them. (Of this I am not convinced.) I am glad you can't see the way we as Americans treat the S. Koreans who work for us. It nearly kills me when I see some of the things they do to the S. K's who work for the army, and there are a great many of them. In the first place we treat these people as if we were occupying them, as if we were or had been at war with them. That is not the case at all, as you know. One day an American Major friend of mine took me out of town to see the S. Korean Officers training school. Some American officers work out there with the S. K. officers teaching them American ways, tactics, etc. This Major told me that he had talked to these S. K. officers and the general opinion among them was that they resented very much the Americans being here. And that they wanted to see their country united and as long as it was UNITED they did not care under what kind or type of government. They also told this major that they knew full well that the Americans were here for their own interests and not in any way for the interests of Korea as a whole. The S. Koreans who work for us get about four dollars a month pay. They do not get any time off and they work over 12 hours a day. The price of their own food and clothing is terribly high and all the workers are so thin and sickly looking. We scream at them in English and then get furious when they don't understand. The other day I was in the clubmobile and the G.I. Driver tooted his horn at a Korean who was in the middle of the street. The Korean did not hear the horn I guess, and so didn't get out of the way very fast. The G.I. driver stopped the clubmobile and hit the Korean very hard on the jaw. I was just furious. I couldn't believe my eyes and I told the driver that as long as I rode with him that would never happen again. But I am afraid that that experience is typical. We have taken over all the best Korean buildings (which, by the way are none too good). Every Korean who works for the Americans is searched when he leaves his place of work to go home. Imagine! In their own country too, and they are our allies.... I think it is deplorable but I guess it is just one of those things. I'll have to learn to accept it.

While I'm on a more or less depressing vein I might add for your information that the V.D. rates are as high here as they have ever been in any war. Right next to the club is a house of prostitution. Isn't that cute?? We put a volley ball net up in what used to be a rice paddy right out in front of the club and the other day when I was out playing volley ball with a group of G.I.'s several of "The Girls" stood by the Barb wire fence that seperates the club from the Korean houses and yelled at the boys that I was trying to engage in a nice out-door healthy sport. Never a dull moment. We hear that 60 percent of the soldiers (Officers included) have active V.D. That figure may be wrong, I really couldn't say for sure. You sure learn about LIFE when working over-seas with the great white mother....

I just love Club-mobile and we work like dogs on it. Last Saturday I stood in the pouring rain down at the very grim Pusan railroad station and served 2,000 men coffee and donuts. They had just come in on a ship and were on their way up north by train. You pour coffee until you think your arm may drop off and all the while you keep up a witty line of chatter. If I have yelled "Who here is from Ohio" once I have yelled it a hundred times in the last week. The men are so cute and very thrilled to see Red Cross that it makes it all such a wonderful experience. There are only three of us doing clubmobile (The club comes first at all times) and so I think I told you we have to go out alone, one girl with a driver and a Korean boy to help mix the sugar and cream in the coffee, load up, etc. We have been very busy, for beside the regular runs to various out of the way outfits north of here who don't have the chance to come into the club, we have been serving all these replacements that keep swarming in. Lots of 3rd division men, Mom, who went all through North Africa and Italy. Lots of reserves coming in straight from the States. Poor kids. Many of them can't believe that here they are right in the middle of it again. We get men who come down from the front for a bit of rest and we get men on their way up again. They are always coming and going. It is so sad to see them on their way up again. A darling Captain friend of mine was just killed in action. It nearly killed me but I'm afraid it won't be the last time I will have an experience such as that. I am careful in my social life to have "buddies" and not get all emotionally involved with some guy. We do things in groups and every night, night after night we are at parties. They seem to break up early. Thank the dear lord! Because we are the only women around, we are always, always, in demand. The men are so nice to us, they are forever bringing us little snacks or some little presents. I just love this life and it is all fascinating, even if at times very depressing. I just hope that the time will not come when we have to be evacuated. But, from the looks of things it well might. A week ago at staff meeting we were told that it was definate that we would go into a big clubmobile operation (no more clubs) and that by June there would be 70 more ARC girls in Korea and 20 clubmobiles being built. Ginnie, Libby, and Helen Woleck were to take off this past weekend for Taegu and Inchon to start setting up kitchens and arranging for billets for this big operation to go into effect, and Mr. Janeway was coming over from Tokyo to help set up but now the situation has changed again and it looks doubtful. Boy how frustrating this all is. Poor Ginnie and Louise Wood. You never know from day to day what may happen and you can't seem to plan ahead. We have been trying to get this big operation set up since October and have gotten no place. Those 3 girls can't go north yet. I'm grateful I got the chance to come over when I did. Don't know if those other club gals in Japan will get the opportunity now.

Last Tuesday I took the clubmobile about 30 miles north of here over the most awful roads (make anything you travelled over in Italy look like the Merritt Parkway . . . ha, ha). (Can't wait to get home and rub it in about the sissy war in Italy. What a brat your daughter is.) You can't imagine the dust and the mud it was unbelievable. I went out to a huge base full of Marines (1st marine division) and also went to an air port 35 miles away which was full of Marine fliers (1st Marine Air wing). I am afraid that the Marines are my favorites. I had such a nice day and I must have served 3,000 men and had to miss some because our donuts gave out. It was the first time we had visited them and they were so cute and excited. They have absolutely nothing in the way of recreation out there and they could hardly believe their eyes when they saw a white woman. They took a million pictures of me and made such a fuss over me that you might have thought I was Lana Turner. I guess I seemed like Lana to them. It was wonderful every moment of it and I went right out on the air field and served a lot of fighter pilots who had just come from a mission. They couldn't believe their eyes when they stepped off the fighter planes and saw me there. I recommended to Ginnie that we open a canteen out there boy it sure is needed. May be we will be able to do it. I now go out a[nd] serve the Marines every Tuesday all day and it is my favorite run. . . .

I love the Club work I do too, you get more chance to sit down and talk to the men much more so than in the clubmobile. Phylis Williams seems very happy here. She is in charge of the Korean help and is so good with them and feels just the way I do about treating them well. We have a good staff of gals here. . . . Must run. . . . Write often. I long to know all the news and gossip.

Much, much love,<br>The Clubmobile Kid

P.S. I never find time to write a single letter except to you all so please send these on—

## 1951: OCTOBER 8
## SYLVIA PLATH TO AURELIA PLATH

*Long before her suicide at the age of thirty-one, Sylvia Plath (1932–1963) was a vivacious, eloquent, and obviously very popular Smith College student who sent this letter recounting a classic 1950s college party to her mother, Aurelia (1907–1994). Plath had published her first poem at the age of eight and would become famous for the volumes* Ariel, The Colossus, *and* Crossing the Water, *as well as for her novel,* The Bell Jar, *which was published the year of her death.*

The occasion Plath described was a coming-out party for a friend named Maureen Buckley. "Mrs. Jack's patio" was a reference to Boston's Isabella Stewart Gardner Museum.

Sharon, Connecticut<br>October 8, 1951

Dear Mother,

How can I ever, ever tell you what a unique, dream-like and astounding weekend I had! Never in my life, and perhaps never again, will I live through such a fantastic twenty-four hours. Like years, it seems—so much of my life was involved.

As it is, I'll start out with an attempt at time sequence. Saturday afternoon, at

2 p.m., about 15 girls from Smith started out for Sharon. Marcia and I drew a cream-colored convertible (with three other girls and a Dartmouth boy). Picture me then in my navy-blue bolero suit and versatile brown coat, snuggled in the back seat of an open car, whizzing for two sun-colored hours through the hilly Connecticut valley! The foliage was out in full tilt, and the hills of crimson sumac, yellow maples and scarlet oak that revolved past—the late afternoon sun on them—were almost more than I could bear.

At about 5 p.m. we rolled up a long drive to "The Elms." God! . . . Great lawns and huge trees on a hill, with a view of the valley, distant green cow pastures, orange and yellow leaves receding far into blue-purple distance.

A caterer's truck was unloading champagne at the back. We walked through the hall, greeted by a thousand living rooms, period pieces, rare objects of art everywhere. On the third floor (every room was on a different level) most of the girls slept. Marcia and I and Joan Strong (a lovely girl, daughter of a former headmaster of Pomfret) had the best deal. We lived across the way at "Stone House," a similar mansion. Marcia and I had a big double bed and bath to ourselves in a room reminiscent of a period novel, with balconies, gold drapes, and another astounding view. We lay down under a big quilt for an hour in the gray-purple twilight, conjecturing about the exciting, unknown evening fast coming.

Joan, Marcia, and I were driven in a great black Cadillac by one of the Buckley chauffeurs to the Sharon Inn where a lovely buffet supper was prepared for the 20–30 girls. After supper, Marcia, Joan, and I skipped and ran along the lovely dark moonlit road to our mansion. Another hour of lying down (reminding me of Scarlett O'Hara before the ball) and then the dressing. I struck up a delightful conversation (while ironing my black formal) with the Filipino houseboy.

Again the chauffeur. Up the stone steps, under the white colonial columns of the Buckley home. Girls in beautiful gowns clustered by the stair. Everywhere there were swishes of taffeta, satin, silk. I looked at Marcia, lovely in a lilac moiré, and we winked at each other, walking out in the patio. Being early, we had a chance to look around. The patio was in the center of the house, two stories high, with the elm treetops visible through the glassed-in roof. Remember Mrs. Jack's patio? The same: vines trailing from a balcony, fountains playing, blue glazed tiles set in mosaic on the floor, pink walls, and plants growing everywhere. French doors led through a tented marquee built out on the lawn. . . . Two bars and the omnipresent waiters were serving champagne. Balloons, Japanese lanterns, tables covered with white linen—leaves covered ceiling and walls. A band platform was built up for dancing. I stood open-mouthed, giddy, bubbling, wanting so much to show you. I am sure you would have been supremely happy if you had seen me. I know I looked beautiful. Even daughters of millionaires complimented my dress.

About 9:30 we were "announced" and received. There was a suspenseful time of standing in fluttering feminine groups, waiting for the dancing to begin, drinking the lilting, bubbling, effervescent champagne. I began to wish I had brought a date, envying the initial security of the girls that had, wondering if I could compete with all the tall, lovely girls there.

Let me tell you, by the end of the evening, I was so glad I hadn't hampered my style by a date and been obligated like the girls who did.

I found myself standing next to a bespectacled Yale Senior. (The whole Senior class at Yale was there—it was just about All-Yale to All-Smith!)

Maureen's brother is a senior. (Ten children in the Catholic family, all brilliant, many writers!)

I decided I might as well dance instead of waiting for a handsome man to come along. The boy was . . . a scholarship Philosophy major, admitting a great inferiority complex. We got talking over champagne, and I had just about convinced him that he should be a teacher when we went back to dance. "Darn," I thought, "I can see me bolstering inferiority complexes all night."

At that point a lovely tall hook-nosed freshman named Eric cut in. We cooled off on a terrace, sitting on a couch, staring up into leaves dramatically lighted. Turned out we both love English. Great deal in common.

Back to floor with Carl, who asked me to Cornell weekend. I refused: nicely. Eric cut in.

Next I had a brief trot with the Editor of the Yale News. No possibilities there. About then the Yale Whiffenpoofs sang, among whom was one of Dick's old roommates, who grinned and chatted with me later.

Now, suddenly, a lovely grinning dark-haired boy cut in. "Name?" I asked. The result was a sort of foreign gibberish. Upon a challenge, he produced a card bearing the engraved "Constantine Sidamon-Eristoff " . . .

He was a wonderful dancer and twirled so all I could see was a great cartwheel of colored lights, the one constant being his handsome face. Turned out his father was a general of the Georgian forces in the Russian Caucasus Mountains. He's a senior at Princeton.

I was interrupted in a wild Charleston (champagne does wonders for my dancing prowess. I danced steps I never dreamed of and my feet just flew with no propulsion of mine) by a tall . . . boy, who claimed his name was Plato. By that time, I was convinced that everyone was conspiring against me as far as names were concerned. Turned out he really was—Plato Skouras whose father is a

Greek—head of 20th Century Fox productions. Plato did the sweetest thing anyone has ever done. In the midst of dancing on the built-up platform amid much gay music, he said, "I have a picture I want to show you." So we crossed through the cool, leaf-covered patio, the sound of the fountain dripping, and entered one of the many drawing rooms. Over the fireplace was a Botticelli Madonna.

"You remind me of her," he said.

I was really touched. . . . I learned later that he has traveled all over the world. Speaks several languages, including Greek . . . A devout Catholic, I learned that he believes in the Divine Revelation of the Bible and in Judgment Day, etc. You can imagine how much I would like to have really gotten into an intense discussion with him. As it was, I had a lovely dialogue. Imagine meeting such fascinating, intelligent, versatile people! At a party, too.

From there followed a few more incidental people, and, saving best to last, my Constantine. Again he cut in, and we danced and danced. Finally we were so hot and breathless that we walked out on the lawn. The night was lovely, stars out, trees big and dark, so guess what we did—Strauss waltzes! You should have seen us swooping and whirling over the grass, with the music from inside faint and distant.

Constantine and I really talked. I found that I could say what I meant, use big words, say intelligent things to him.

Imagine, on a night like that, to have a handsome, perceptive male kiss your hand and tell you how beautiful you were and how lovely the skin was on your shoulders!

I would have taken it all with several grains of salt had we not gone farther. I came out with my old theory that all girls have lovely hair, nice eyes, attractive features and that if beauty is the only criterion, I'd just as soon tell him to go and pick someone else and let me out.

He said he'd take me home, and so we drove and drove along in the beautiful night. I learned a great deal about him, and he said the most brilliant things. I learned about Jason and the Golden Fleece—the legend having been written about the Georgian people—who were a civilized culture, like China, while the Russians were "still monkeys." I learned about his ideas of love, childbirth, atomic energy . . . and so much more.

I asked him what happened when a woman got old and her physical beauty waned, and he said in his lovely liquid voice, "Why she will always be beautiful to the man she married, we hope."

. . . when I asked him what I should call him, he told me three names.

"I like Constantine best," I said. "I like to say it, because of its good sound."

"I have a dear Grandmother who is 92 years old," he said, "and she always calls me Constantine. I do believe it's because she likes the feeling of the name rolling from her tongue."

He sang for a while, and then the bells struck four o'clock in a church tower. So I asked if I could tell him my favorite poem. I did, and he loved it.

Oh, if you could have heard the wonderful way he talked about life and the world! That is what made me really enjoy the dear remarks he made about me.

Imagine! I told him teasingly not to suffocate in my long hair and he said, "What a divine way to die!" Probably all this sounds absurd and very silly. But I never expressed myself so clearly and lucidly, never felt such warm, sympathetic response. There is a sudden glorying in womanhood when someone kisses your shoulder and says, "You are charming, beautiful, and, what is most important, intelligent."

When we drove into the drive at last, he made me wait until he opened the door on my side of the car and helped me alight with a ceremonial "Milady . . ."

"Milord," I replied, fancying myself a woman from a period novel, entering my castle.

It was striking five when I fell into bed besides Marcia, already asleep. I dreamed exquisite dreams all night, waking now and then to hear the wind wuthering outside the stone walls, and the rain splashing and dropping on the ivy-covered eaves.

Brunch at Buckleys' at 1 p.m. on a gray, raining day: About 30–40 of the girls and a few men had the most amazing repast brought in by colored waiters in great copper tureens: scrambled eggs, bacon, sausages, rolls, preserves, a sort of white farina, coffee, orange juice. Lord, what luxury! Marcia and I left, went back to our mansion and lay snuggled side by side in the great double bed under a warm quilt in the gray afternoon, talking and comparing experiences, glowing with happiness and love for each other and the world!

At 3 p.m. the chauffeur picked us up. Five girls drove back in the big Cadillac. I sat up front beside the driver and wrapped myself in silence for two hours of driving through rain and yellow leaves.

Back here. I can't face the dead reality. I still lilt and twirl with Eric, Plato, and my wholly lovely Constantine under Japanese lanterns and a hundred moons twining in dark leaves, music spilling out and echoing yet inside my head.

To have had you there in spirit! To have had you see me! I am sure you would have cried for joy. That is why I am spilling out at such a rate—to try to share as much as I can with you.

I wonder if I shall ever hear from Constantine again. I am almost afraid he was a dream, conjured up in a moment of wishful thinking. I really loved him that evening, for his sharing of part of his keen mind and delightful family, and for listening to me say poetry and for singing—

Ah, youth! Here is a fragmentary bit of free verse. What think you?

> gold mouths cry with the green young
> certainty of the bronze boy
> remembering a thousand autumns
> and how a hundred thousand leaves
> came sliding down his shoulderblades
> persuaded by his bronze heroic reason.
> we ignore the coming doom of gold
> and we are glad in the bright metal season.
> even the dead laugh among the goldenrod.
>
> The bronze boy stands kneedeep in centuries,
> and never grieves,
> remembering a thousand autumns,
> with sunlight of a thousand years upon his lips
> and his eyes gone blind with leaves.

Very rough. But I've got an evolving idea. Constantine is my bronze boy, although I didn't know him when I wrote it.

I've got to work and work! My courses are frightening. I can't keep up with them. See you the 19th.

Love,

    love,

        love,

                Sivvy

## 1952: JANUARY 20
## LOUISE DUQUETTE TO NORMAN DUQUETTE

*From Iowa, two years into the Korean War, came the timeless and simple longings of a lonely air force wife. This letter, unopened, would be returned to Louise Wilson Duquette (1927–) when Norman Duquette (1926–) was reported missing. He spent 587 days in a North Korean prison, but returned to Louise in 1953.*

January 20 1952

Good afternoon

It's a bright cold beautiful day here in Iowa. How are you today, my sweet hubby? Jan is snoozing in her afternoon nap & Jay plays cowboy all day long & he hardly even takes a nap anymore. I think it is high time you are coming home because Jan is beginning to call every man she sees in a magazine "Daddy."

It will be wonderful to have you home again. You can come home at night to a nice comfy chair & Jay will bring you your slippers & pipe (?!) & I will bring you a nice tall glass of something cold in one of our new iced tea glasses.

The shadows are growing long on the lawn. It's 4:30 & soon will be dark again & your day just beginning. . . .

Take good good care of yourself, Sweetie.

All our love to you always,
Lou, Jay, & Jan

## 1952: APRIL 28
## MARILYN MONROE TO DR. MARCUS RABWIN

---

*Screen legend Marilyn Monroe (1926–1962) had just been dubbed "the genuine article . . . a sensational glamor girl" by* Life *magazine when she went into Los Angeles's Cedars of Lebanon Hospital to have her appendix out. Before the surgery, she taped this handwritten note to her stomach so that her doctor, Marcus Rabwin, would find it in the operating room. Her desire to become a mother was one she frequently expressed and never fulfilled.*

<u>Most important</u> to Read Before <u>operation</u>.
Dear Doctor,

<u>Cut as little as possible</u>   I know it seems vain but that doesn't really enter into it—the fact that I'm a <u>woman</u> is important and means much to me. Save please (can't ask you enough) what you can—I'm in your hands. You have children and you must know what it means—<u>please Doctor</u>—I know somehow you will! thank you—thank you—for Gods sake Dear Doctor No <u>ovaries</u> removed— please again do whatever you can to prevent large <u>scars</u>. Thanking you with all my <u>heart</u>.

Marilyn Monroe

\*    \*    \*

## 1952: MAY 19

## LILLIAN HELLMAN TO JOHN WOOD

*Korea was obviously a hot war, but a cold war was going on as well, and with ever increasing tension the Soviets and Americans eyed each other. High up in the echelons of the anticommunist fight was Senator Joseph P. McCarthy, who in 1950 announced—without proof—that 205 members of the State Department were "card-carrying communists." The Red Scare quickly enveloped Hollywood as well. Eventually, with a blacklist in full force, the House Committee on Un-American Activities (HUAC) came knocking on the door of Lillian Hellman (1905–1984). An essayist, reviewer, playwright, and screenwriter who had gained considerable fame for such works as* The Children's Hour *and* Watch on the Rhine, *Hellman was also known for her left-wing politics. This was her response, with its justly famous line about "cutting her conscience," to the committee's request that she testify.* HUAC ended up rejecting Hellman's proposal; she took the Fifth Amendment and was blacklisted. John S. Wood (1885–1968) was chairman of HUAC from 1949 to 1953.

May 19, 1952

Dear Mr. Wood:

As you know, I am under subpoena to appear before your Committee on May 21, 1952.

I am most willing to answer all questions about myself. I have nothing to hide from your Committee and there is nothing in my life of which I am ashamed. I have been advised by counsel that under the Fifth Amendment I have a constitutional privilege to decline to answer any questions about my political opinions, activities and associations, on the grounds of self-incrimination. I do not wish to claim this privilege. I am ready and willing to testify before the representatives of our Government as to my own opinions and my own actions, regardless of any risks or consequences to myself.

But I am advised by counsel that if I answer the Committee's questions about myself, I must also answer questions about other people and that if I refuse to do so, I can be cited for contempt. My counsel tells me that if I answer questions about myself, I will have waived my rights under the Fifth Amendment and could be forced legally to answer questions about others. This is very difficult for a layman to understand. But there is one principle that I do understand: I am not willing, now or in the future, to bring bad trouble to people who, in my past association with them, were completely innocent of any talk or any action that was disloyal or subversive. I do not like subversion or disloyalty in any form and if I had ever seen any I would have considered it my duty to have reported it to the proper authorities. But to hurt innocent people whom I knew many years ago in order to save myself is, to me, inhuman and indecent and dishonorable. I cannot and will not cut my conscience to fit this year's fashions, even though I long ago came to the conclusion that I was not a political person and could have no comfortable place in any political group.

I was raised in an old-fashioned American tradition and there were certain homely things that were taught to me: to try to tell the truth, not to bear false witness, not to harm my neighbor, to be loyal to my country, and so on. In general, I respected these ideals of Christian honor and did as well with them as I knew how. It is my belief that you will agree with these simple rules of human decency and will not expect me to violate the good American tradition from which they spring. I would, therefore, like to come before you and speak of myself.

I am prepared to waive the privilege against self-incrimination and to tell you anything you wish to know about my views or actions if your Committee will agree to refrain from asking me to name other people. If the Committee is unwilling to give me this assurance, I will be forced to plead the privilege of the Fifth Amendment at the hearing.

A reply to this letter would be appreciated.

Sincerely yours,
Lillian Hellman

## 1953: JUNE 19
## ETHEL ROSENBERG TO MICHAEL AND ROBERT ROSENBERG

*Ethel Greenglass Rosenberg (1915–1953) and her husband, Julius (1918–1953), were arrested in the summer of 1950 and charged with espionage for disclosing military secrets to the Soviet Union. In the spring of 1951, the Rosenbergs were found guilty under the Espionage Act of 1917 and sentenced to death. Despite two years of appeals and massive publicity, they became the first U.S. civilians ever executed for espionage. Their children, Michael and Robert, were ten and six at the time. Ethel wrote this letter to them from Sing Sing prison on the day of the execution.*

"Julie" was signed in Julius's handwriting.

June 19, 1953

Dearest Sweethearts, my most precious children,

Only this morning it looked like we might be together again after all. Now that this cannot be I want so much for you to know all that I have come to know. Unfortunately I may write only a few simple words; the rest your own lives must teach you, even as mine taught me.

At first, of course, you will grieve bitterly for us, but you will not grieve alone. That is our consolation and it must eventually be yours.

Eventually, too, you must come to believe that life is worth the living. Be comforted that even now, with the end of ours slowly approaching that we know this with a conviction that defeats the executioner!

Your lives must teach you, too, that good cannot really flourish in the midst of evil; that freedom and all the things that go to make up a truly satisfying and worthwhile life, must sometimes be purchased very dearly. Be comforted, then, that we were serene and understood with the deepest kind of understanding, that civilization had not as yet progressed to the point where life did not have to be lost for the sake of life; and that we were comforted in the sure knowledge that others would carry on after us.

We wish we might have had the tremendous joy and gratification of living our lives out with you. Your Daddy who is with me in these last momentous hours sends his heart and all the love that is in it for his dearest boys. Always remember that we were innocent and could not wrong our conscience.

We press you close and kiss you with all our strength.

Lovingly,

Daddy and Mommy—

Julie Ethel

---

## 1954: JUNE 2
## ALICE CROWTHER TO DEE COX

---

*Unlike the expectant mother who wrote to Dr. Grantly Dick-Read (see page 603), Alice Ebdon Crowther (1927–) had no apparent objections to the usual approach to childbirth in the 1950s. After giving birth to daughter Wendy (the first of her three children), she described the experience in this letter to her best friend, Dee Sweat Cox (1926–). The timelessness of Crowther's joy (not to mention the all-too-familiar worry about her figure) mingles here with some classic fifties artifacts: cigarettes, tranquilizers, and a five-day hospital stay.*

Dear Dee,

It was awfully sweet of you to send the baby her first little dress. Believe it or not, but it's the only dress I have other than a couple my sister sent on from Chicago which her little girl had worn. She wore it home from the hospital and looked so feminine and cute.

I'm terribly anxious to hear about you. I hope you've had your baby by now and that everything is well. When it's all over for you, I'd love to be able to talk to you on the phone and compare notes. It's fun talking about it to someone who has just recently gone through the same thing.

I was staying at mothers the night I went to the hospital as Bill was out of town on business. He had left on a Sunday & expected to be home the following Wednesday. He was furious when he left but I promised I'd try to hold off 'til he got home. However, all day Monday I felt kind of crampy and at 8:15 p.m. I got my first pain. I wasn't even sure if it was labor because they didn't bother me very much but when they started coming at 15 minute intervals I decided I'd better call the Doctor. I found him at the Glen Cove Hospital where he was almost ready to deliver a baby. He was expecting to deliver another one at the same hospital in the morning. However I was planning to go to North Shore Hospital in Manhassat which made things a little rough for him. At any rate, he told me to try to get some sleep & that they'd probably go away & come back in the a.m. but that if they should continue and become 5 minutes apart I was to call him. At 2 a.m. I called him & he arranged for me to be admitted to the hospital. Mother & I were calm as cucumbers. (Daddy was also out of town) We drove to the hospital, she kissed me goodbye and into the examining room I went. In the meantime my pains had completely disappeared & I felt like a complete fool. I felt for sure I'd be sent home but after all the preliminary work was finished they gave me a couple of pills and put me to bed in my own private labor room. I watched as one woman was wheeled away and shortly after wheeled back having delivered her baby already. Boy was I envious. I woke at 7 am the next morning and recall remarking to the nurse that it was a beautiful day to have a baby. I started timing my pains which were averaging then around 7 to 10 minutes apart. I just laid around, smoked and read a magazine for most of the morning. My Dr. arrived about 11:30 and said I had a long way to go. He went back to his office as he had office hours that afternoon. Later on in the afternoon I asked for a sedative & was given 2 little pills. Every once in awhile some strange person would come in to see how much I had dilated. By that time I didn't care if Clark Gable came in to examine me. I had no thoughts of modesty.

Later on I was given stuff they call Scopolamine which believe me is the greatest. I believe it's used a great deal now. It makes you forget almost everything from the time they shoot it into you. I have just a vague recollection of certain things & with the little I do remember I associate no pain although it is not a pain relieving drug. I don't remember going to the delivery room but I remember being on the delivery table when I was asked to bear down. From that point on I knew nothing until I came to in the recovery room & was told I had a baby girl at 5:20 p.m. The sense of relief that comes over you can't be put into words. A flat stomach at last. I was wheeled through the reception room where Bill's mother was waiting. She was exstatic. She had already seen the baby before it was taken to the nursery & told me she was beautiful. She was waiting for Bill to arrive at any minute. My mother had called him earlier that day & he started home from Pennsylvania. I was then wheeled passed the nursery where they held up my baby—a precious doll with a lot of very dark brown hair. That was the last I saw of her for 24 hours as they don't give them to you to feed until they're 24 hours old. Shortly after I was delivered to my room this white face appeared at the door—Bill. To me—that's a very wonderful moment—when you see your husband for the first time. You probably know by now, yourself. Bill said later I acted half drunk. Just talked all over my face as the effects of the gas still hadn't entirely left me. We had about a half hour to ourselves & then visiting hours started so mother and dad came over. It was wonderful seeing them too.

I spent five days in the hospital and got a good rest. My only problem was that I developed a few hemroids during my pregnancy which became irritated from the delivery so between that and the stitches my poor little bottom was quite sore. Nothing short of dynamite could make me go to the bathroom.

At any rate it's all over & in another 2 years I think I'll try it again.

I'm at mothers now & will be for at least another week. My aunt who does practical nursing is here & is taking care of the baby for me. I've been trying different things each day so that by the time I get home I'll have some idea how to take care of her. She's been a very good baby so far. Lives pretty much according to her schedule.

Bill is a riot. I had no idea he'd be so interested in her. At the hospital I think he spent more time looking in the nursery window than with me. He's the type that starts out by saying—"I always hated people to talk about their children but my baby is the smartest thing. Why she's only one week old and practically crawling already." I'm delighted with the way he carries on about her.

Well kiddo, write me all about your delivery. I'm very interested. It's really a wonderful thing, isn't it. Gosh I hope you've had yours by now.

Thanks once again for the darling dress. Let me know as soon as you can about your baby so I can get him or her something from Aunt Alice & Uncle Bill. <u>And write soon.</u>

Love

Alice

## 1954: JUNE 19
## KATHARINE McCORMICK TO MARGARET SANGER

*While millions of American women were playing their indispensable part in the postwar baby boom, Margaret Sanger (see page 464) was still trying to discover ways for birth control to be more effective as well as more available. In 1953, she found a research scientist named Gregory Pincus who, with the backing of a remarkable philanthropist named Katharine Dexter McCormick (1875–1967), would develop the world's first birth control pill. McCormick, a wealthy Chicagoan, had been the first woman to graduate from MIT with a degree in biology; she married a man who became mentally ill, and she soon turned to activism. As a young woman, she campaigned for the vote and helped Sanger smuggle diaphragms into the country. As an older woman, she was almost single-handedly responsible for funding the research that led to the Pill. In this letter, she gave Sanger an update on what she was hearing from Pincus.*

Dr. John Rock was a fertility specialist. Although a U.S. territory, Puerto Rico had no laws against birth control; that fact, plus its proximity and dense population, made it an ideal site for human trials. Dr. Hannah Stone was head of Sanger's research clinic. Hudson Hoagland and Pincus had created the Worcester Foundation for Experimental Biology in 1944.

June 19, 1954

Dear Mrs. Sanger:

I had a fine talk with Dr. Rock for two hours on the 16th. This visit was more than valuable to me—it was invaluable. It is always so hard to get all the facts one needs about any particular matter. I suppose it is because one does not ask the right questions necessary to reach the heart of the matter. In this talk with Dr. Rock I learned a great deal that I should have known before but evidently had not clearly understood. He took a lot of trouble to show me just what their difficulties are with the progesterone testing work. I had not realized that these were so formidable.

Dr. Pincus is imaginative and inspirational. Dr. Rock is informative and very realistic about medical work. Both he and Dr. Pincus are very exacting in regard to the progesterone test examinations for they consider that the proof of progesterone's effectiveness rests on these examinations—is made or broken by them. The two critical ones are (1) the vaginal smears and (2) the urine. At the Brookline Lying-in Hospital Dr. Rock's married daughter does the vaginal smears and he sent her to New York for special training with a vaginal-smears-examination expert in order that this work might be of the first order. I expect to learn more this week of the details of all the progesterone test examinations so that you and I can be more fully informed concerning them.

It is the considered opinion of both Drs. Pincus and Rock (and repeats their opinions of last year) that the best way to enlarge their investigation of progesterone would be to open a station in Puerto Rico's Welfare Department. I went over this pro and con with Dr. Rock and had already discussed it with Dr. Pincus. The reasons they are in favor of Puerto Rico are as follows:

1. It is near enough so that the vaginal smear slides and the urine collections can be sent here for examination. It is only one night by plane so that material and doctors can go back and forth easily.

2. The Puerto Rico medical personnel is thoroughly acquainted with Dr. Pincus' work and he has complete confidence in them. This personnel has assured them that sufficient selected patients can be easily secured.

3. They are convinced there would be no religious interference.

It was a surprise to hear from Dr. Rock how necessary the patient's cooperation was—that none with families can be used as they would not be able to give the necessary time to this cooperation. I was surprised to hear that 25 cases took the whole time of one woman doctor (Conant) at the Brookline Lying-in Hospital. I was very surprised to realize that Pincus wished to have the smears and urine examined here instead of in Puerto Rico and I cannot understand it for I think no such arrangement exists with Dr. Stone in New York.

I expect to be able to clear up these details before long as I shall see Dr. Hoagland as well as Drs. Pincus and Rock again soon. However, it is already clear to me that for an enlargement of the testing work of Drs. Pincus and Rock the Welfare Department in Puerto Rico is considered by them to be the most practical place. I had not thought of Puerto Rico at all seriously as you know but may have to. I will keep you informed of course.

Yours,
K. D. Mc
Mrs. Stanley McCormick

## 1955: APRIL 12
## RUTH GOTTLIEB TO JONAS SALK

---

*On the day that a New York woman named Ruth Gottlieb wrote this letter, the announcement was made that a team at the University of Pittsburgh led by Jonas Salk (1914–1995) had developed an effective vaccine for polio. Between 1950 and 1954, there had been an average of 12,500 cases a year of paralysis caused by polio in the U.S. The promise of a vaccine that was both safe and potent made Salk a national hero.*

Within five years, the incidence of polio would be reduced by more than 90 percent.

April 12, 1955

Dear Dr. Salk,

I am not one to write to the "great" men of this world—their greatness is usually far above my life and thought. Today, however, more than I have ever known, I feel that I can write. You, Dr. Salk, have given something to all of mankind, and as one of the "common people" who will be rewarded by this gift, I do so want to send thanks to you.

I wish I could in some way describe the feeling I had as I learned that your vaccine had beaten Polio. As a young adult who someday hopes to marry and raise a family, I could only feel that your genius had given me an assurance that those close to me would be free from one of man's most cruel enemies.

I know that prominent men in all walks of life are congratulating you today, but I did want you to know too, that the rest of us are sincerely grateful.

Sincerely,
Ruth Gottlieb

## CIRCA 1956
## DIANA SHAPIRO TO ROSA PARKS

---

*On December 1, 1955, Rosa McCauley Parks (1913–) boarded a bus in Montgomery, Alabama, ignored the driver's request that she give up her seat for a white passenger, and was promptly arrested. In the year that followed, forty-two thousand black citizens led by Martin Luther King, Jr., boycotted the Montgomery buses, and the Supreme Court ruled city-bus segregation unconstitutional. A working seamstress, Parks was also an active member of the National Association for the Advancement of Colored People. Along with the author of this letter, she had recently*

*attended a summer workshop at Highlander, an education and research center*
*where participants learned and planned strategies for nonviolent protests.*

Starting in 1950, the American Jewish Society for Service (AJSS) ran summer work camps throughout the United States for social service volunteers. John's Island, in South Carolina, was a place of extreme poverty, and a rallying point for some civil rights leaders.

Dear Rosa:

I hope you won't mind my calling you by your first name, but that is the way I think of you. As you were at Highlander.

I can't tell you how pleased I was to receive your letter. Of course, we all knew about the bus strike but none of us associated it with you. Lately, the northern newspapers have said practically nothing about what has been happening so your news was quite a shock.

All of us are so very proud of you, and of having known you, brief though the acquaintance was.

To us outsiders the purpose of Highlander remained rather vague no matter how many times it was explained. We were aware of the excitement surrounding the workshops, we were aware that they were unique and were accomplishing a great deal. But, nonetheless, after returning to the north we tended to lapse into the old attitude of "my, oh, my, but isn't that all fine! But what is all that talk doing."

Now we know, or at least, understand, some of the reason for Highlander. Not just the academic value of writing the "Guide for Community Action" but the wonderful feeling it must give to southerners to be able to air out the problems that have been hidden behind the closed doors of fear and prejudice, and to find that other people are willing to join you in the last battle of the Civil War. People who are in the same position you are in.

We had talked about the cooperation you had received from all those who refused to ride the buses and who had been supporting the car pool before I received your letter and every one of us was beaming with pleasure at the unified action. We, all the members of the A.J.S.S. work camp, hope that the strength of this strike will succeed in giving you a vantage point in your stand against segregation.

Perhaps sometime in the near future you will give me a complete guided tour of Montgomery, Alabama. The information that I asked of you originally arrived too late, however, I did write a lengthy theme on segregation and integration on your side of the Mason-Dixon line. The information I gathered together was rather shocking even after what I had heard about John's Island.

Irene Osborn was very nice about sending me some of the details on Washington and I included the Guide after a chapter on Highlander. All of us were so very impressed that each of us has become a sort of self-appointed defender of integration and the methods discussed and listed during the workshop. Of course, we are all homesick for Tennessee and Highlander.

I hope to hear from you as soon as you find time because we are all thirsty for any direct information about what is actually happening in Montgomery, and all the other places where minor revolts are changing the entire picture of the south.

I wish you success in this struggle and in all the others that are bound to come, and I hope that we will meet once again after the "times that try men's souls" are passed.

> Yours truly,
> Diana Shapiro

## 1956: FEBRUARY 22
## PATSY CLINE TO TREVA MILLER

*One of the enduring voices of the era, country singer Patsy Cline (1932–1963) was still balancing the family ironing with her recording plans when she wrote this letter to Treva Miller (1938?–1960), the president of her first fan club. Cline would become a star the following year, when she sang "Walkin' After Midnight" on* Arthur Godfrey's Talent Scouts.
Cline and her first husband, Gerald Cline, divorced in 1956. (She married Charlie Dick in 1957.) Like Cline, who was thirty when she died in a plane crash, Miller died terribly young: in a car crash at the age of twenty-two.

> Frederick Md.
> Feb 22/56

Dear Treva:

I guess you think I'm never going to answer your letter, but there are two reasons why I haven't written sooner.

I was moving to Frederick, and the other, I just didn't have the money to send you yet. I still don't have it until next <u>Thursday</u> the 30th or 31st or whatever it is. I just moved in a 56, 33ft trailer, but I still can't say I'm satisfied. Don't mention this in your letters, but you know already (I think I told you) I've been married 3½ years and in 55 in June I left him because he's just so jealous of my singing, and I was separated six months. This past Nov. we went back together but I'm

afraid things aren't going to work out. He's 33, and I'm 23, which I don't think
has anything to do with it but he has been married before. I'm his 3rd wife, and
he doesn't want any children. Now he's starting about my singing again. So I'm
afraid things are not going to be the same as they are now in the next 6 months.
I've tried 3 times and still can't seem to get what ever it is straightened out. If
things do come to a point as a divorce I'm certainly not going to marry again.

Oh! Well, I'm just telling you my troubles so I'll stop for now.

How are things with you?

They cancelled my Ozark appearance again. But the Opry called me the
other day and they want me back for 2 T.V. shows either in June, April, or Aug.
I'll let you know the date when I get it.

The Apple Blossom Fest which is in my home town, Winchester, is going to
have me in the grand feature parade as the T.V. personality (the only one,) of the
Shenadoah Valley, sort of a <u>lady grand marshal</u>, I guess you would call it. Next
Thurs. I'm starting at Quantico for the Marines. A 3 hour show there. Just for
the base and the fellows. I use to play there with The Melody Boys and they ask
for me back to sing for them. So I guess I'm going back, and they sure are a fine
bunch of fellows. Maybe we can get them to join my fan club. Some of them
any way. About the picture I'll send you a copy about next week for the <u>picture
fan club card</u> for the fans. In the mean time you can maybe use this little one for
something.

The one I'm sending later will be in my new costume. I'm working on a new
one with white horses in rhinestones on it, in deep purple, with white fringe.
Maybe I told you about it already. I'm so mixed up lately.

Well, I'm going to close and get busy ironing, so write soon Treva and thanks
for waiting so long for me, I'll sure send you the money as soon as I get it.

How is Max and how is he doing? Tell him hello for me.

And I'll write again soon. You write too. If you can give me a little advance,
write to 608 S. Kent St. Winchester.

Love,
Pat.

## 1957: MARCH 11
## CHARLOTTE JONES TO GEORGE SOKOLSKY

*Elvis Presley hit the big time in 1956 with "Love Me Tender," "Hound Dog," and
"Don't Be Cruel." Wherever he went, teenage girls, in a kind of group hysteria,
would swoon and scream. The charms of his extraordinary voice and unique moves*

*were lost on most members of the older generation, which led one young woman in
Dallas to try to explain things to syndicated columnist George Sokolsky (1893–1962).*

Dear Mr. Sokolsky:

There are too many people saying that Elvis is going to die out. When Elvis
dies out is when the sun quits burnin.

You say everybody is forgotten that is once great: George Washington has
never been forgotten and nobody can ever be as great a president or as long remembered as he. Nobody can ever take his place or do what he did. Well, it's
the same with Elvis. He'll always be remembered and nobody has ever or ever
will do the same thing as Elvis has. Elvis is the king of popularity and we (teens
of America) love him and we'll see he lives forever. Not his body but his name.
Adults won't admit he's so great, because they're jealous! They know that their
top singers weren't as great as Elvis. They're mad because their taste isn't quite
as good as ours.

Look at James Dean, been dead for a year and he's bigger now than he ever
was.

God gifted Elvis to us and you oughta thank him, not tear down the greatest
thing the world has ever known: Elvis Presley!!!!!!

Scornfully yours,
Charlotte Jones

P.S.: And if you're over 30, you're old. You're certainly not young.

## 1957: MAY 31

## JEAN McCARTHY TO MR. BALDWIN

*Particularly reviled by liberals and Democrats, officially censured by the Senate in
1954, Joseph McCarthy remained in office until his 1957 death from liver complications brought on by alcoholism. In this response to a condolence letter from an
unknown source, the senator's widow, Jean Kerr McCarthy (?–1979), made it clear
that the man who had been demonized by so many Americans was to her if not a
saint, then at the very least a martyr.*
Appleton, Wisconsin, was McCarthy's hometown. Adam Grill was pastor of St. Mary's Roman
Catholic Church in Appleton, and presided over McCarthy's burial mass.

You were so kind to take time to send words of comfort to me. I only wish in
some way I could comfort you, for we do indeed share a loss.

Joe gave his life, as Father Grill said at St. Mary's, "principally because he exhausted himself physically for love of his fellow beings." This is so very true that I, as his wife—having known this for a long, long time—never thought before that anyone else would understand.

When Joe came home to Appleton, the heart and soul of this country was standing along the roadside on the 30 mile drive from Green Bay. It was all of that that made Joe and all of that to which he dedicated his life. It was the reason for his sacrifice of personal comfort, the reason for his courage to withstand being alone at times.

I cannot help but feel, however, that his sacrifice of personal comfort, his aloneness at times—along with that of many unknown and unheralded men— will have been for nought unless we see the purpose of the immense drive that was his. Knowing Joe as I do, I know he would be impatient with the thought that we simply mourn his passing or praise his life. God had purpose in both of these. The battle Joe fought so fearlessly and with such insight is not over. It will only end, as Joe so often said, with victory or death for our civilization.

Joe once said in answer to the question: 'What can I do to help?'—Look to your schools, search behind the printed word, give purpose to and demand a contract from the men you send to man the watchtowers in Washington. If everyone of Joe's friends took that suggestion to heart, I would then know God's purpose has been done.

May I add an afterthought I know Joe would share. That is, never underestimate your power as a citizen. When Joe walked into his first open clash with the wrecking crew of our nation, he had in his mind—and this he has written—the "thought of those real people who are the heart and soul and soil of America; thoughts of the young people in my office, toiling night and day . . . thoughts of the many young men, friends of mine, who went to their death in the Pacific for what they thought was a better world—those thoughts convinced me that this fight I had to win."

Perhaps now a few more will stop to think that a man with the intellect and the courage, the drive and the honesty, a man such as Joe—with his love for life—could not have spent all that without reason. Perhaps a few more will search their minds and step with decision to the side of right.

With sincere personal regards,

\*    \*    \*

**1963: FEBRUARY 17**

**RACHEL CARSON TO BARNEY CRILE**

*Rachel Carson (1907–1964) was diagnosed with breast cancer in 1960 and under-*
*went, as was common at the time, a radical mastectomy. The National Book*
*Award–winning author of* The Sea Around Us *and the maverick who in* Silent
Spring *questioned the environmental impact of pesticides and other chemicals,*
*Carson was known for her thoroughness as a scientist and her courage as a writer. In*
*response to her candid questions about her own health, her surgeon had apparently*
*been less than forthcoming—also typical of the time. Searching for straight an-*
*swers, she wrote to her friend Dr. George (Barney) Crile, Jr., (1907–1992), a sur-*
*geon at the Cleveland Clinic. Crile's own wife, Jane, had died of breast cancer in*
*January. Carson would die fourteen months after writing this letter.*

Dear Barney,

You have been much in my mind. . . . I am glad you have the book to work on,
and above all, glad you and Jane had those months to work on it together, giving
it form and substance. It may be emotionally hard in some ways for you to carry
it through to completion, and yet I think it will be a satisfaction.

Jane meant many things to me—a friend I loved and greatly admired, and a
tower of strength in my medical problems. When she wrote me, after my visit
with you two years ago, that she shared my problem, it was as though a great
tide of courage flowed into me. If she, so vibrant, so gay, so full of the love of
life, could live with the problem so fearlessly, I could at least try to do the same.
Over the months since then the feeling I've had could best be explained by an
analogy. Once, years ago, my mother and I were driving at night in uninhabited,
unfamiliar country near the North Carolina coast. For the 50 or more miles
through those wooded lowlands we were able to follow the lights of a car ahead.
As long as it progressed smoothly I knew our way was clear. Jane was that kind
of reassuring light to me. Now, without that light to follow, I admit my courage
is somewhat shaken.

But you, Barney, for different reasons, are also a great source of strength. So
now I'm writing you of my current problems. I didn't want to bother you while
Jane was ill, and for that matter the more important ones have just happened, or
at least have just been noticed.

First: I finally saw a cardiologist, Dr. Bernard Walsh, about three weeks ago. I
definitely have angina (even the cardiogram is now abnormal, but he said the di-
agnosis was perfectly clear from symptoms alone) of the less common type in

which the pains come on without physical provocation, the worst ones during sleep. Dr. Walsh said frankly the implications are serious and it is most important to get the situation under control. So—I'm virtually under house arrest, not allowed to go anywhere (except as you will see later) no stairs, no exertion of any kind. I had to rent a hospital bed for sleeping in a raised position. . . .

The second problem is in your department. About two weeks ago I noticed a tender area above the collar bone on the left (operated) side, and on exploring found several hard bodies I took to be lymph nodes. Dr. Caulk was just going out of town for several days and said he would come to the house on his return. By that time I was so sure I was going to need treatment that I just had myself taken down to see him. . . . They are definitely lymph nodes "gone bad," some lying fairly well up in the neck. This is the side opposite last year's trouble spots and is an area never previously treated. So we have begun—5-minute treatment 3 days a week to keep my hospital trips to a minimum.

Now there is a further complication. At the time I went in about my back in December I kept making remarks about having "arthritis" in my left shoulder, but no one paid much attention. It has been increasingly painful, and now there is some difficulty about certain arm movements. I had begun to have suspicions, so now I've tackled Dr. Caulk about it again. They took a picture Friday and there does seem to be trouble. He let me see the x-rays. It is the coracoid process of the scapula—the edge of it looks irregular and sort of eroded. For some reason Dr. Caulk seems rather puzzled—says he wants some of his associates to look at it and may want a picture from another angle, but on the whole he does feel it is a metastasis.

Well, all this brings questions in my own mind, which leaps to conclusions that may or may not be justified. Oh—the back trouble cleared up, but so slowly that Dr. Caulk had about decided it wasn't a metastasis. Treatment was begun just before Christmas and completed December 31. I was still in considerable pain in mid-January. Then rather rapid improvement set in and now it's ok. But now this bone deterioration in the shoulder makes me think all the more I had a metastasis in the spine. Dr. C. says not necessarily, but I think he's just trying to reassure me.

Barney, doesn't this all mean the disease has moved into a new phase and will now move more rapidly to its conclusion? You told me last year that it might stay in the lymph nodes for years, but that if it began going into bone, etc., that would be a different story. If this is the correct interpretation I feel I need to know. I seem to have so many matters I need to arrange and tidy up, and it is easy to feel that in such matters there is plenty of time. I still believe in the old

Churchillian determination to fight each battle as it comes. ("We will fight on the beaches—" etc.) and I think a determination to win may well postpone the final battle. But still a certain amount of realism is indicated, too. So I need your honest appraisal of where I stand.

Jane continues to give me courage. Kay told me of her question to the doctors: "Which of you is in charge of not giving up?" How like her! Well, I nominate you to that post. I would like so much to discuss some of this with you, and wonder if you'd call me some day soon. . . .

My love to the children. As ever,
Rachel

### 1963: FEBRUARY 18
### BOBBIE LOU PENDERGRASS TO JOHN KENNEDY

---

*Along with other riddles surrounding the presidency of John F. Kennedy (1917–1963) is the question of his intentions in Vietnam. By 1963, there were already some fifteen thousand military advisers in South Vietnam, the first several hundred of them having been sent there in 1955 by Dwight D. Eisenhower. On January 11, 1963, seven of them died in a helicopter crash, and Bobbie Lou Pendergrass, the sister of one of the victims, asked the president a question that would soon be on the minds of many Americans: "If a war is worth fighting—isn't it worth fighting to win?" The following month, JFK answered Pendergrass's letter, asserting the global importance of fighting Communism in North Vietnam, assuring her that her brother had not died in vain, and declaring: "full scale war in Viet Nam is at the moment unthinkable."*

James Delmas McAndrew's name appears on the Vietnam Memorial. He served in the army for ten years, having joined in Reno, Nevada. He was thirty-four when he died.

February 18, 1963

Dear President Kennedy,

My brother, Specialist James Delmas McAndrew, was one of the seven crew members killed on January 11 in a Viet Nam helicopter crash.

The Army reports at first said that communist gunfire was suspected. Later, it said that the helicopter tradgedy was due to malfunction of aircraft controls. I've wondered if the "malfunction of aircraft controls" wasn't due to "communist gunfire." However, that's neither important now, nor do I ever care to know.

My two older brothers entered the Navy and the Marine Corps in 1941 immediately after the war started—they served all during the war and in some very important battles—then Jim went into the Marines as soon as he was old enough and was overseas for a long time. During those war years and even all during the Korean conflict we worried about all of them—but that was all very different. They were wars that our <u>country</u> were fighting, and everyone here <u>knew</u> that our sons and brothers were giving their lives for their country.

I can't help but feel that giving one's life for one's country is one thing, but being sent to a country where half <u>our</u> country never even <u>heard</u> of and being shot at without even a chance to shoot back is another thing altogether!

Please, I'm only a housewife who doesn't even claim to know all about the international situation—but we have felt so bitter over this—can the small number of our boys over in Viet Nam possibly be doing enough good to justify the <u>awful</u> number of casualties? It seems to me that if we are going to have our boys over there, that we should send enough to have a <u>chance</u>—or else stay home. Those fellows are just sitting <u>ducks</u> in those darn helicopters. If a war is worth fighting—isn't it worth fighting to <u>win</u>?

Please answer this and help me and my family to reconcile ourselves to our loss and to feel that even though Jim died in Viet Nam—and it isn't our war—it wasn't in vain.

I am a good Democrat—and I'm not criticizing. I think you are doing a wonderful job—and God Bless You—

Very sincerely,<br>Bobbie Lou Pendergrass

## 1963: DECEMBER 1
## JACQUELINE KENNEDY TO NIKITA KHRUSHCHEV

---

*The week after her husband's assassination, Jacqueline Kennedy (1929–1994) wrote this extraordinary letter to the premier of the Soviet Union, Nikita Khrushchev (1894–1971). It was a reflection not only of one woman's grace, but also of an entire country's Cold War fears.*

December 1, 1963

Dear Mr. Chairman-President:

I would like to thank you for sending Mr. Mikoyan as your representative to my husband's funeral.

He looked so upset when he approached me, and I was very touched by this.

I tried that day to tell you some things through him, but it was such a horrible day for me that I do not know if my words were received as I wanted them to be.

Therefore now, on one of the last nights I will spend in the White House, in one of the last letters I will write on this White House stationery, I would like to write my message to you.

I am sending it only because I know how much my husband was concerned about peace and how important the relations between you and him were to him in this concern. He often cited your words in his speeches: "In the next war, the survivors will envy the dead."

You and he were adversaries, but you were also allies in your determination not to let the world be blown up. You respected each other and could have dealings with each other. I know that President Johnson will make every effort to establish the same relations with you.

The danger troubling my husband was that war could be started not so much by major figures as by minor ones.

Whereas major figures understand the need for self-control and restraint, minor ones are sometimes moved rather by fear and pride. If only in the future major figures could still force minor ones to sit down at the negotiating table before they begin to fight!

I know that President Johnson will continue the policy my husband believed in so deeply—the policy of self-control and restraint—and he will need your help.

I am sending you this letter because I am so deeply mindful of the importance of the relations that existed between you and my husband, and also because you and Mrs. Khrushchev were so kind in Vienna.

I read that she had tears in her eyes as she was coming out of the American embassy in Moscow after signing the book of condolences. Please tell her "thank you" for this.

Sincerely,
Jacqueline Kennedy

## 1963: DECEMBER 7
## MARINA OSWALD TO GREG OLDS

*Two days after JFK's assassination, nightclub owner Jack Ruby shot Lee Harvey Oswald, who had been arrested and charged with the murder. For Marina Oswald (1941–), the end of 1963 was only the beginning of a struggle to come to terms with what had happened, and over the years she would change her opinion several times about the guilt of her husband. Greg Olds was head of Dallas's Civil Liberties Union and had written to express his concern.*

Marina and her young daughters had been staying with Ruth Paine in Dallas at the time of the assassination.

Dear Mr. Olds—

I would like to thank you for your attentiveness toward me, and for the fact that you are worried about my fate.

Your concern is quite unnecessary, although, if one is to judge by what appears in the papers, it would seem justified.

I have no complaints about the Secret Service personnel who are "protecting" me. Except for thankfulness that they are taking care of my well-being and security in the present circumstances, I have nothing more to say. I am completely free to go where I want and to see whom I want. My isolation is due to my own state of mind; after all that has happened, I just don't want to see anybody, especially when it could remind me of what has happened. I hope you will understand my position and excuse my isolation. When I feel that life has more or less returned to its former course, I will be very glad to see Ruth Paine, who is a very fine person and who has been only helpful to me. I hope you will also understand that, since I am living in another person's house, it is just embarrassing for me to bother people with lots of visits from my friends and from other people who want to talk to me. And, besides, I am busy with the children and with visits from FBI people—and this takes up a lot of time and energy.

Once again thank you for your concern about me. I assure you quite sincerely that I am in as good a position as is possible, after all that has happened.

I also ask you to tell Ruth Paine that I am very obliged to her for her attentiveness toward me and of course consider her to be my friend.

Best regards
Marina Oswald

**1963: DECEMBER 8**
**KATHRYN HOHLWEIN TO PAT LAMB**

*Kathryn Hohlwein (1930–) and Patricia Frazer Lamb (1931–) met in 1950 as students at the University of Utah. With Pat living abroad, they corresponded for years afterwards—about their husbands and children, about travels and politics, and, so movingly in the case below, about America in the days following the president's assassination.*

Kathryn was teaching at Ohio State University in Columbus.

Columbus
December 8, 1963

Dear Pat,

Beloved friend in history and space! How I would love to embrace you in sorrow. Oh, Pat, your letters have articulated so passionately my grief as well as yours, and the grief of millions. You expressed my experience exactly in saying, "I have never grieved so deeply and for so long." In addition to grief, I have known a corollary depression so intense as to inhibit my proper functioning. I could write no one, and only now, to you, do I begin to articulate, to cease weeping and waking in the predawn stillness, to horror or anguish. What will become of us? The only amazing and heartwarming, though in no degree reconciling, aspect of this has been the deep genuineness of the mourning across America (oh, Amerika!) and around the world.

The students, generally so apathetic and callous from sheer ignorance, have been deeply touched. Never have I seen more massive and uninhibited sorrow. One boy student broke down and wept on my shoulders. The Negro janitor, tears in his eyes, stared at me shaking his head for a full two or three minutes. Infuriating students who'd been brainwashed to think Kennedy was Satan and Goldwater God saw clearly, in proportion, but in grief. The old professors, the good ones, whose lives have been directed against madness and meaninglessness, were stooped and shaken. And of course, Jackie Kennedy was as regal as Antigone. I've never, I mean <u>never</u>, seen any human gestures so eloquent as those of this beautiful woman in bereavement. Her control, her pain, her sense of history and of this nation, of her motherhood to those two small wounded children, and of her wifehood to a husband and a man of great eminence—all pulled together into the elegance and pure dignity of all she did. It was truly remarkable.

But oh! that interminable weekend. The sound of the drums, the rocking of the caisson, the riderless horse. My God! We've all been ripped from our daily trivia and placed firmly in the scroll of recorded history, and having been brought so close to the abyss, I cannot but look on this sometimes as from a place in eternity, acknowledging it as one of the momentous tragedies of time past. I love you, my dear friend, and I embrace you across water, lands and many peoples.

[Kathryn]

\*    \*    \*

## 1964

## JOAN BAEZ TO THE INTERNAL REVENUE SERVICE

*In August, after reports that a U.S. destroyer had been fired on in the Gulf of Tonkin, Congress authorized Lyndon Johnson to take "all necessary measures to . . . prevent further aggression," and Johnson ordered the U.S. Navy to begin bombing North Vietnam. The antiwar movement intensified with the war. Among its most visible leaders was folk singer Joan Baez (1941–),who sent the following letter to the Internal Revenue Service.*

In response, the IRS put a lien on Baez's property and occasionally sent representatives to her concerts, where they confiscated cash to cover the taxes she owed.

Dear Friends

What I have to say is this:

I do not believe in war.

I do not believe in the weapons of war.

Weapons and wars have murdered, burned, distorted, crippled, and caused endless varieties of pain to men, women, and children for too long. Our modern weapons can reduce a man to a piece of dust in a split second, can make a woman's hair to fall out or cause her baby to be born a monster. They can kill the part of a turtle's brain that tells him where he is going, so instead of trudging to the ocean, he trudges confusedly toward the desert, slowly blinking his poor eyes until he finally scorches to death and turns into a shell and some bones.

I am not going to volunteer the 60% of my year's income tax that goes to armaments. There are two reasons for my action. One is enough. It is enough to say that no man has the right to take another man's life. Now we plan and build weapons that can take thousands of lives in a second, millions of lives in a day, billions in a week.

No one has the right to do that.

It is madness.

It is wrong.

My other reason is that modern war is impractical and stupid. We spend billions of dollars a year on weapons which scientists, politicians, military men, and even presidents all agree must never be used. That is impractical. The expression "National Security" has no meaning. It refers to our Defense System, which I call our Offense System, and which is a farce. It continues expanding, heaping up, one horrible kill machine upon another until, for some reason or another, a button will be pushed and our world, or a good portion of it will be blown to pieces. That is not security. That is stupidity.

People are starving to death in some places of the world. They look to this country with all its wealth and all its power. They look at our national budget. They are supposed to respect us. They do not respect us. They despise us. That is impractical and stupid.

Maybe the line should have been drawn when the bow and arrow were invented, maybe the gun, the cannon, maybe. Because now it is all wrong, all impractical, and all stupid.

So all I can do is draw my own line now. I am no longer supporting my portion of the arms race....

> Sincerely yours,
> Joan C. Baez

## 1964

## "DONNA" TO JOHN LENNON AND GEORGE HARRISON

*About five thousand fans greeted the Beatles when they arrived in the United States for the first time on February 7. Two nights later, they were seen by seventy-three million Americans when they appeared on* The Ed Sullivan Show. *And presumably some time after that, one fan sent this letter.*

Dear John,

Please Forward this letter to GEORGE.

I think you are wonderful too.

DEAREST Darling BEATLE GEORGE

I was very disappointed when you came to the U.S.A. and didn't come to see me. You don't know what you missed. I'm really a beautiful doll. I am 5'3" tall and slender and very good looking. I would make some Beatle a very lovely wife. Since I consider you the prettiest one, I'm giving you first choice. If you decide that you will be my lucky husband, then I will know that not only are you pretty, but also very intelligent.

Every night before I go to sleep, I say, "Goodnight, Georgie. I love you. Yeah, yeah, yeah!

So think it over my love and give me your answer. If you are stupid enough to decline my offer, forward this letter to Ringo and Paul. Forget about John, he's married you know.

I think you are the most.

All my love,
Your Donna

## 1964: JUNE 30
## NANCY ELLIN TO LILLIAN AND MARTIN ELLIN

*In the summer of 1964, Nancy Bowles Ellin (1936–) and her husband, Joseph, left their home in Kalamazoo, Michigan, to become Freedom School teachers in Hattiesburg, Mississippi. Along with thousands of other civil rights activists, many of them northern college students, they were participants in what became known as "Freedom Summer," organized by a coalition of groups including the Congress of Racial Equality (CORE) and the Student Nonviolent Coordinating Committee (SNCC). The ostensible goal was to help black citizens register to vote, but the thirty Freedom Schools established in Mississippi also drew three thousand students from the poorly funded black public school system. The Freedom Schools' programs emphasized black history and leadership training as well as remedial reading and math, and became a model for later programs like Head Start. Nancy Ellin had just arrived in Mississippi when she sent this report to her mother- and father-in-law in Brooklyn.*

Training for the volunteers took place at the Western College for Women in Oxford, Ohio.

Dear Dr. and Mrs. Ellin,

It was nice to get your letter today; we hope you will write often. I'm sure Joe will write to you any minute now, but I thought I might as well, too.

We got here OK, though we were frightened most of the way, quite unnecessarily. It was the people who came down in integrated cars who had the unpleasant time—refused service, cars following them, etc. We came down with a very nice girl who just graduated from Smith and who did quite a bit of driving.

We are currently hard at work getting the Freedom Schools organized. Joe and another boy have everyone typing up stencils of the Constitution, the Declaration of Independence, etc. The school enrollment is over 150; we are having official registration Thursday. The philosophy is to take everyone who comes; we will be teaching adults in the evening. There are 10 teachers, 8 more expected from New York City on Thursday. We also intend to recruit a few local people.

I, too, am sorry things came to such a pass. We felt terrible about causing you all such anguish, but we felt the decision was ours to make, and though we were very afraid and doubtful at Oxford, we made the decision to come. You must know that you were not the only parents who were worried, and some kids did drop out, one from our group, in fact, who was underage and couldn't get his parents' consent. Now that we are here we feel more than ever that coming here was the right thing to do. Even if we don't teach a single child (and I think the odds are heavily against that) we still will have accomplished something in showing the people of Hattiesburg that they should not hate whites. Even our own group leaders, Carolyn and Arthur Reese, who are Detroit Negroes (school-teachers), were very anti-white until Oxford, Ohio. (Carolyn has been extremely frightened much of the time we have been here.) The people of Hattiesburg are militant and eager; our landlady told us last night about a woman who had at-tempted to register to vote 17 times before she made it.

Things here are pretty horrible. The Negro section, where we are, smells and looks more than a little like India. The house we are staying in (free) is pretty good-sized but very delapidated—creaky floors, etc. It has a bathroom—some don't. Our landlady is registered; her husband has tried but hasn't made it yet. Everyone agrees that things here would be much worse right this minute if it weren't for our presence and the pressure exerted on the govt. on our behalf by our rich Northern parents. Negroes in the movement tend to lose their jobs. We feel—rightly or wrongly—that our place is here, in the heart of the struggle. No man is an island . . .

Otherwise, there isn't much news. We have been to one mass meeting and are cutting another one tonight to make stencils. Another job we have before us is organizing the library—there are tremendous quantities of books. We haven't had much contact yet, aside from smiles and handshakes, with the regular Negro community, so I haven't much else to report. The leaders we have met are terrific.

Thank Mary and everyone for praying for us.

Love,
Nancy

Thank you very much for your letter. What you say makes me feel much better. I hope we can make you feel more at ease too.

\*    \*    \*

### 1964: AUGUST 25
### LADY BIRD JOHNSON TO LYNDON JOHNSON

*Despite the fact that he was almost certain to win the 1964 election, Lyndon John-son (1908–1973) hesitated about his candidacy—even after the opening of the Democratic convention in Atlantic City. "I have a desire to unite the people," LBJ told his press secretary, George Reedy, "and the South is against me, and the North is against me, and the Negroes are against me, and the press doesn't really have an affection for me." Then his wife, Lady Bird (1912–), wrote him this letter.*

*Time magazine had just published a critical article about Lady Bird.*

Beloved—

You are as brave a man as Harry Truman—or FDR—or Lincoln. You can go on to find some peace, some achievement amidst all the pain. You have been strong, patient, determined beyond any words of mine to express.

I honor you for it. So does most of the country.

To step out now would be wrong for your country, and I can see nothing but a lonely waste land for your future. Your friends would be frozen in embarassed silence and your enemies jeering.

I am not afraid of Time or lies or losing money or defeat.

In the final analysis I can't carry any of the burdens you talked of—so I know its only <u>your</u> choice. But I know you are as brave as any of the thirty-five.

I love you always

Bird

### 1964: NOVEMBER 29
### A HIGH SCHOOL STUDENT TO THE <u>NEW YORK TIMES</u>

*For the younger generation, the 1960s made questioning authority a full-time job. That meant challenging the status quo in government, in church, at home, in the military, in college—and even in high school. One student at the Emma Willard School in Troy, New York, described her workload with a classic mixture of rebelliousness and self-pity.*

*Its postscript notwithstanding, the letter was published in the New York Times Magazine.*

To the Editor:

I'm a student in the oldest girls' school in the country. I love my school, but your recent article on homework really hit home ("Hard Day's Night of Today's Students," by Eda J LeShan).

I came to this school not thinking I could ever keep up with the work. I was wrong. I can keep up. I can even come out on top. My daily schedule's rough: I get up at 6:30 and have classes from 8:15 to 3:00 and stay in study hall or engage in activities until 5:30. I have five majors, plus religion, speech, music and art once or twice a week. I have gym four times a week. All this I can take. The homework I can't. I work from 3:00 until 5:30 in school.

After dinner I work until midnight or 12:30. In the beginning, the first two weeks or so, I'm fine. Then I begin to wonder just what this is all about: Am I educating myself? I have that one all answered in my own mind. I'm educating myself the way they want. So I convince myself the real reason I'm doing all this is to prepare myself for what I really want. Only one problem. After four years of this comes four years of college and two of graduate school for me. I know just where I'm going and what I want, but I'm impatient.

Okay, I can wait. But meanwhile I'm wasting those years of preparation. I'm not learning what I want to learn. I don't care whether $2 + 2 = 4$ anymore. I don't care about the feudal system. I want to know about life. I want to think and read. When? Over weekends there are projects and lectures and compositions, plus catching up on sleep.

My life is a whirlpool. I'm caught up in it but I'm not conscious of it. I'm what you call living, but somehow I can't find life. Days go by in an instant. I feel nothing accomplished in that instant. So maybe I got an A on that composition I worked on for three hours, but when I get it back I find it means nothing. It's a letter you use to keep me going.

Every day I come in well prepared. Yet I dread every class; my stomach tightens and I sit tense. I drink coffee morning, noon, and night. At night, after my homework I lie in bed and wonder if I've really done it all. Is there something I've forgotten?

At the beginning of the year I'm fine. My friends know me by my smile. Going to start out bright this year. Not going to get bogged down. Weeks later I become introspective and moody again. I wonder what I'm doing here. I feel phony; I don't belong. All I want is time; time to sit down and read what I want to read, and think what I want to think.

You wonder about juvenile delinquents. If I ever become one, I'll tell you why it will be so. I feel cramped. I feel like I'm in a coffin and can't move or breathe. There's no air or light. All I can see is blackness and I've got to burst. Sometimes I feel maybe something will come along. Something has to or I'm not worth anything. My life is worth nothing. It's enclosed in a few buildings on one campus; it goes no further. I've got to bust.

Name Withheld

P.S. I wrote this last night at 12:15 and in the light of day I realize this will never <u>reach</u> you.

## 1965: JULY 28
## JUDY FINN TO LYNDON JOHNSON

---

*By the end of 1965, 180,000 Americans would be serving in Vietnam. From New York City, one teenager sent this telegram to the president.*

President Johnson I am 15 years old. I have my whole life to live. Every day you stay in Vietnam you put my life on a line. I want to live. I want to have children. Stop killing me and my children. Peace doesn't mean weakness. Get out of Vietnam.

Judy Finn.

## 1965: OCTOBER 6
## JANIS JOPLIN TO PETER DeBLANC

---

*In this letter to her then boyfriend, a young and decidedly not yet famous Janis Joplin (1943–1970) revealed her romantic insecurity, her artistic progress—and the fact that she had a father who preferred classical music. Just two years after writing this, Joplin would stagger the audience at the Monterey Pop Festival with her classic performance of "Ball and Chain." In 1970, she died from a heroin overdose, and in 1971, her album* Pearl *and her single "Me and Bobby McGee" became number-one hits. She was still living at home in Port Arthur, Texas, and was a sometime student at nearby Lamar State College, when she wrote this letter.*
Laura is Janis's sister. The ellipses were in the original.

Dear Peter,

I've decided to make this a precedent—my Wednesday morning letter written in the Union. I didn't get to write you yesterday, I'm sorry. I had homework to do & then Philip & Diane came over & we played bridge. And I just didn't have time to write. So I'm going to try & write you every Wednesday at this time—I usually feel good, I'm dressed up & confident, and I haven't gone home yet to see that I haven't gotten a letter which usually depresses me.

After I got that letter from you last week, I had a feeling I was to be in for a dry spell. Letter-wise I mean. Which is decidedly unfair I think—you write me one letter telling me how bad things are & then, no word. Jesus Christ what am I supposed to think. But actually I'm faring quite well. I worry & I'm sort of depressed all the time, but I'm really not panicking (although I do have to admit that I tried to call you last night. Twice. But no one answered...). I've decided to try & maintain this same leaden level until I hear from you, and not to presume changes—good or bad. Although to be honest, most of my presumptions have been for the better—I keep figuring things are bound to be better than you felt they would be when I last heard from you.

We're kind of half-way expecting your cousin this weekend. This is to be the 9th & 10th which is what you said. And so did gruff-voiced Roger when I talked to him, but he also said she would undoubtedly call us at least a week before she came & so far, no word. What the fuck's going on up there? I've been quite anxious to talk to her. I want to know how you are! Damn, it's been a long time since I've <u>seen</u> you & I don't know what's going on. I don't know how you are physically <u>or</u> mentally and I really want to talk to her. But now it doesn't look like she's going to come. Phoo.

I get both of my tests back today I think & I'm really excited. I think I did pretty good.

I haven't gotten very much done on your sweater yet—I've changed colors though. I think you'll like this one much better. It sure is going to be pretty. I hope you like it.

My guitar playing is growing by leaps & bounds though. I do a really great version of a blues called "Come Back, Baby" in G. I really wail on it. If you can call it wailing when you do it all alone in your bedroom w/ your doors closed. I call it wailing. I've got a high spade-type falsetto part in it that is too much! I wish I had fans that thought I was as good as <u>I</u> do. So far, this is my best thing. I'm working on some others & I do them fairly well but I still don't have enough to do a set or anything. Besides, where would I do it? Poor dad is being driven to distraction by my practicing. Laura's guitar playing didn't bother him too much—she plays quietly & sings softly. But me! I've got a big thumb pick & I really play & really sing too. And he sits in the living room feverishly trying to be calm & placid & listen to Bach. Poor thing. But there's nothing else I <u>can</u> do. I try & practice when no one's home, but there's usually someone there all the time. He's pretty glad I didn't get that guitar.

Which reminds me. Did I tell you I put $200 in a savings account? I did. So, whenever I need it...

Mother is getting worried about me because I stay at home too much. She doesn't think I spend enough time with "people my own age." So I think I'm going to have a bridge party. Doesn't that sound like madcap fun!? I thought I'd have Philip & Diane of course and another girl I know named Kristin. She's the daughter of my father's & mother's best friends & I've known her, literally, all my life. She has a degree in Art Education & wants to teach. She was in New York last year & <u>adored</u> it! She applied all over Long Island but no job yet, so she's here taking 4 advanced English courses, trying to pick up a minor. So these are my social plans... Don't I lead an exciting life? Whee.

Sure do hope to hear from you soon. You mentioned that you would call before Debbie came—before next week-end, that is, so I've been straining my ears in anticipation of a phone call. But then I might get a letter today! Don't be so negative, Janis.

Did you get my package? Are you getting my mail? Oh fuck, this is driving me to distraction not knowing what is going on! Please call me or write me or something! I'm really sorry to be such a drag but I can't help it! Until I <u>know</u> that everything's going well, I'll worry. And probably after, too...

Guess I ought to do my homework. 'Bye, I love you. Let me hear from you, please? I love you & everything will be okay.

Love XXXXXXX

J

### 1967: AUGUST 11
### ELIZABETH HOFFMAN TO <u>TIME</u> MAGAZINE

*Over five days in July, race riots in Detroit left forty-three people dead, more than a thousand injured, and more than seven thousand arrested. Lyndon Johnson sent in federal paratroopers and National Guardsmen, and, when the dust had cleared, one teenager wrote this letter to Time.*

Because I am a mere 17 years of age and am one person in a country of millions, what I say doesn't make much difference to anyone else. But what I have witnessed in the past week makes me feel somewhat sorry that I am even the small part of it that I am. I have seen my city, the fifth largest in the U.S., reduced by one-sixth its original size. Not by a tornado or flood, or any other act of nature or God, but because of people who somehow seemed to lose every bit of their sanity and proceeded to loot, burn and murder innocent citizens. Why? I don't know, maybe someone does, but all we who do not know see is smoldering rubble, homeless people, and the corpses of those who were the sniper's prey. There is nothing more frightening than seeing what appeared to be a sane world turn into a grotesque horror picture. I am sad; I cannot even begin to describe how sad I am to see what has happened to my people. I will be proud to tell my children that I was alive when the first astronaut went up into space, and how I saw science and medicine advance at an unbelievable speed, but it will be nearly impossible for me to look at them and say that I was here when my city went mad, when the people arose, took all the good and peace in my city, and destroyed it.

> Elizabeth Hoffman
> Detroit

## 1968: SPRING
## MARIJANE DILL DUNCAN TO NANCY GURI DUNCAN

*A number of factors converged to create the sexual revolution. The birth-control pill was introduced in 1960 (see page 623). Masters and Johnson came out with their study of human sexuality in 1966. And bit by bit the taboos that had dominated the Eisenhower years were first relaxed and then forcibly rejected. For Marijane Dill Duncan (1920–1990), the news that her first daughter, Nancy (1944–), was planning to live with a man without marrying him occasioned a remarkably enlightened and loving response. Yet between the lines the confusion and wistfulness of the generation gap is also evident.*

Nancy and Freddie lived together for six years, first while attending New York University, later in Singapore, his home. They parted in 1972, but remain friends.

I have been pondering your last letter—it is so often difficult to know exactly what is being conveyed when there is no chance for face to face exchange. I think you are telling me you have decided to live with Freddie but have not decided on marriage. Whether I approve or disapprove is not germane any longer. You are a woman and a free agent. But I must be concerned about you still, for you are my child, if grown and gone—and I love you no less because you are far away. I want your happiness and your feeling contented about your way of life more than I want your acceptance of our standards. I realize that marriage does not have the same importance to your generation as it did to mine. However, it is going to be a long long time before we are ready to bypass this ceremonial entirely, if only because of the great advantage to children who have thereby mother, father, home, stability, and legal status. No doubt you have considered this and planned accordingly.

There is no longer the stigma attached to extramarital relationships that once existed, particularly if you live, as you and Freddie do, in a large city. There are, however, your personal lives and futures—there is, for instance, the question: if marriage is not indicated now, will it be next time—or the time after? The way you order your lives now may establish a pattern that—particularly for the woman involved—could mean instability and insecurity in future relationship. None of this has anything to do with differences in background or temperament—I am assuming compatibility, at least for the present. I have not touched on the most important component of a strong and lasting relationship. You say you love Freddie—but your definition is not mine, for if I were nearly twenty-four and loved a man enough to live with him and to look forward to a continuing intimacy and sharing, I would want, by the same token, to be married to him. But you and I are different, and you must respond to your feelings and work out your situation according to your own lights.

If and when you do decide to marry, your husband will be welcomed into our family by all of us. Freddie sounds like a fine and good person. I hope, whatever decision you reach, you will not hurt him, nor he, you.

### 1968: SEPTEMBER 11
### PATRICIA ROBINSON AND BLACK SISTERS TO BROTHERS

*At times, the movements for black power and women's liberation collided head-on. Among some radical black men, the birth control pill, which had been on the market since 1960, was decried as a means for whites to limit the black population. But for the women who signed this letter, effective birth control was a way to assert power over their own bodies and lives, and to protect themselves against domination by black men. After members of the Black Unity Party—a Peekskill, New York, group—released a statement calling on black women not to take the Pill, they received this response.*

September 11, 1968

Dear Brothers:

Poor black sisters decide for themselves whether to have a baby or not to have a baby. If we take the pills or practice birth control in other ways, it's because of poor black men.

Now here's how it is. Poor black men won't support their families, won't stick by their women—all they think about is the street, dope and liquor, women, a piece of ass, and their cars. That's all that counts. Poor black women would be fools to sit up in the house with a whole lot of children and eventually go crazy, sick, heartbroken, no place to go, no sign of affection—nothing. Middle class white men have always done this to their women—only more sophisticated like.

So when whitey put out the pill and poor black sisters spread the word, we saw how simple it was not to be a fool for men any more (politically we would say men could no longer exploit us sexually or for money and leave the babies with us to bring up). That was the first step in our waking up!

Black women have always been told by black men that we were black, ugly, evil, bitches and whores—in other words, we were the real niggers in this society— oppressed by whites, male and female, and the black man, too.

Now a lot of the black brothers are into a new bag. Black women are being asked by militant black brothers not to practice birth control because it is a form of whitey committing genocide on black people. Well, true enough, but it takes two to practice genocide and black women are able to decide for themselves, just like poor people all over the world, whether they will submit to genocide. For us, birth control is freedom to fight genocide of black women and children.

Like the Vietnamese have decided to fight genocide, the South American poor are beginning to fight back, and the African poor will fight back, too. Poor black women in the U.S. have to fight back out of our own experience of oppression. Having too many babies stops us from supporting our children, teaching them the truth or stopping the brainwashing as you say, and fighting black men who still want to use and exploit us.

But we don't think you are going to understand us because you are a bunch of little middle class people and we are poor black women. The middle class never understands the poor because they always need to use them as you want to use poor black women's children to gain power for yourself. You'll run the black community with your kind of black power—you on top!

> Mt. Vernon, N.Y.
> Patricia Haden—welfare
>     recipient
> Sue Rudolph—housewife
> Joyce Hoyt—domestic
> Rita Van Lew—welfare recipient
> Catherine Hoyt—grandmother
> Patricia Robinson—housewife
>     and psychotherapist

*In this letter to FBI head J. Edgar Hoover (1895–1972), a mother of five seemed to be expressing the reaction of an entire generation to the changing culture. Sounding perhaps a bit unhinged, she railed about the incomprehensible gyrations of Elvis, bemoaned the violence of movies and television, and offered a solution that had at best a kind of* Music Man *logic to it.*

Dear Honorable Sir,

Thank goodness you are still in Washington, still serving us all as no one else has or can. Congratulations!

Quite a few years ago I wrote to you about the repulsive antics of Elvis Presley. Look at the money he is making to-day! Still harming our youth! I believe he has done more harm in his style of dancing, to our young people than any one element in our society. It put the suggestive ideas into more young people because he was before them on television so much! This sort of thing had not been seen by many, many of our young people; before this time, it could only been seen at side-shows, so this was something new, something very thrilling to our boys and girls. It spread like wild-fire. It opened up something very daring and catching.

So much for Elvis. You were very kind, understanding and really did all you could about this guy. That's why I am coming to you now.

I am a mother of five daughters, seventeen grandchildren so my keen interest in young people, my own and others, is intensely keen.

Now! Praise the Good Lord, they are beginning to wonder—out loud—if these killer movies, war movies, obscene movies are having an effect on our young people! I wish I had time, I'd write a book!

Let me say right here. I do believe you are very much in accord with the fact that these movies and pictures certainly have and make a sad impression on some of our youngsters. Let me tell you just what a four year old granddaughter said to her mother one day after they had been in a store in the city. Her mother said, why didn't you speak to Mrs. ——— when she spoke to you?" "You told me not to speak to strangers mommy and I was afraid she might kidnap me like that little girl on TV." A four year old little girl! Impression?

Another mother told of her little boy not wanting to speak to a man (an acquaintance of the father) because he was afraid he might kidnap him and take him away and turn him into a tiger. Impression?

I will say this—my daughter selects, very carefully the pictures or programs her children shall watch. Sometimes this is a problem because—maybe the child wants to watch after school, right after supper etc. and nothing to look at but KILLING!

Oh, yes, indeed these programs affect our young people. AND adults are giving it to them!

Let's take music. College presidents have said it is "the greatest mind-trainer on the list".

A large part of a child's education is affected by music. Let's think that thru together, Mr. Hoover.

Let's take someone who says I am all wrong on this theory. Alright. A marching band goes by. They stop and play to a group of school children. While that band is in their midst, are they not watching the drummer, the trumpeter, whoever happens to be nearest—and wishing they could play like that. Are they not keeping time with their feet, perhaps clapping their hands in time with the music? Are their thoughts not of the highest education and emotional order? An impression!

Now let's take Elvis Presley and some of the other singers whom he has influenced. Compare impression.

We can never say that music does not have an effect on the mind.

If it did not—we could play a wedding march at a funeral, we could have jazz music in our churches, chants and hymns in our dance halls. There is no chance for argument.

All this leads me to this: if our country would come forth and realize the importance of musical training for EVERY child I do believe the crime in our country would be greatly erased!

You and many others may say that every child is not musical, does not care for music. That's where our trained teachers can MAKE it enjoyable and appealing. It can be done with very rewarding results. SO MANY WAYS TO MAKE GOOD MUSIC!

Our beloved Madame Kordica, the world's greatest Wagnerian singer began when she was a very little girl sitting beside a brook on their farm and listening to the birds, the water as it flowed over the rocks and she tried to imitate them. She did!

I do hope you will use your influence to ban, discard, throw out these horrible, destructive programs they are showing on TV, every day!

Thanks if you have stayed with me and we are so thankful for YOU!

A friend,

_Two years before writing this letter, Anne Harvey Sexton (1928–1974) won the Pulitzer Prize for poetry, a reflection of her power as a confessional poet. In her work, she frequently confronted her own psychological struggles and revealed a vulnerable yet wry spirit. Having battled depression for much of her adult life, she wrote this haunting letter, a kind of farewell, to her daughter, Linda Gray Sexton (1953–). Anne would kill herself five years later._

Wed—2:45 p.m.

Dear Linda,

I am in the middle of a flight to St. Louis to give a reading. I was reading a New Yorker story that made me think of my mother and all alone in the seat I whispered to her "I know Mother, I know." (Found a pen!) And I thought of you—someday flying somewhere all alone and me dead perhaps and you wishing to speak to me.

And I want to speak back. (Linda, maybe it won't be flying, maybe it will be at your own kitchen table drinking tea some afternoon when you are 40. Anytime.)— I want to say back.

1st I love you.

2. You never let me down.

3. I know. I was there once. I too, was 40 and with a dead mother who I needed still. . . .

This is my message to the 40-year-old Linda. No matter what happens you were always my bobolink, my special Linda Gray. Life is not easy. It is awfully lonely. I know that. Now you too know it—wherever you are, Linda, talking to me. But I've had a good life—I wrote unhappy—but I lived to the hilt. You too, Linda—Live to the HILT! To the top. I love you, 40-year-old Linda, and I love what you do, what you find, what you are!—Be your own woman. Belong to those you love. Talk to my poems, and talk to your heart—I'm in both: if you need me. I lied, Linda. I did love my mother and she loved me. She never held me but I miss her, so that I have to deny I ever loved her—or she me! Silly Anne! So there!

XOXOXO
Mom

1969: JULY 24

LYNDA VAN DEVANTER TO HER FAMILY

*Lynda Van Devanter (1947–2002) joined the 71st Evacuation Hospital in Pleiku in 1969, becoming one of the more than seven thousand American women who served in the Vietnam War. In this letter home, she gave a glimpse of the horrors she saw, and also of the loneliness she and so many others faced as they learned of the antiwar protests at home. In the years after the war, Devanter would become the national women's director of the Vietnam Veterans of America, leading seminars and counseling other veterans, but also suffering from post-traumatic stress and possibly the effects of Agent Orange. In 1983, she wrote a memoir,* Home Before Morning, *which became the inspiration for the television series* China Beach.

*Montagnard* is French for "mountain man," a catchall word for Vietnamese people who inhabited the highlands. "Frag" wounds come from fragmentation bombs, which splinter upon impact.

Dear Family,

Things go fairly well here. Monsoon is very heavy right now—haven't seen the sun in a couple of weeks. But this makes the sky that much prettier at night when flares go off. There's a continual mist in the air which makes the flares hazy. At times they look like falling stars; then sometimes they seem to shine like crosses.

At 4:16 a.m. our time the other day, two of our fellow Americans landed on the moon. At that precise moment, Pleiku Air Force Base, in the sheer joy and wonder of it, sent up a whole skyful of flares—white, red, and green. It was as if they were daring the surrounding North Vietnamese Army to try and tackle such a great nation. As we watched it from the emergency room door, we couldn't speak at all. The pride in our country filled us to the point that many had tears in their eyes.

It hurts so much sometimes to see the paper full of demonstrators, especially people burning the flag. Fight fire with fire, we ask here. Display the flag, Mom and Dad, please, every day. And tell your friends to do the same. It means so much to us to know we're supported, to know not everyone feels we're making a mistake being here.

Every day we see more and more why we're here. When a whole Montagnard village comes in after being bombed and terrorized by Charlie, you know. These are helpless people dying every day. The worst of it is the children. Little baby-sans being brutally maimed and killed. They never hurt anyone. Papa-san comes in with his three babies—one dead and two covered with frag wounds. You will try to tell him the boy is dead—"fini"—but he keeps talking to the baby as if that will make him live again. It's enough to break your heart. And through it all, you feel something's missing. There! You put your finger on it. There's not a sound from them. The children don't cry from pain; the parents don't cry from sorrow; they're stoic.

You have to grin sometimes at the primitiveness of these Montagnards. Here in the emergency room, doctors and nurses hustle about fixing up a little girl. There stands her shy little (and I mean little—like four feet tall) papa-san, face looking down at the floor, in his loin cloth, smoking his long marijuana pipe. He has probably never seen an electric light before, and the ride here in that great noisy bird (helicopter) was too much for him to comprehend. They're such characters. One comes to the hospital and the whole family camps out in the hall or on the ramp and watches over the patient. No, nobody can tell me we don't belong here.

Love,
Lynda

### 1970: APRIL

### MARY HAISE TO FRED HAISE

*Neil Armstrong walked on the moon in July of 1969. Nine months later, partway through the Apollo 13 mission to the moon, an oxygen tank exploded, and the crew's survival became the only goal. With the outcome still completely in doubt, astronaut Fred Haise (1933–) found this note from his wife, Mary, as well as photographs of his children, which floated out into the weightlessness of the lunar module.*

Dear Fred:

By the time you read this, you will already have landed on the moon, and hopefully, be on your way back to Earth. This is to let you know how much we love you, how proud we are of you, and how very much we miss you.

Hurry home!

Love,
Mary

**1970: MAY 5**

**BERYL TUFFYAS TO THE <u>DAILY KENT STATER</u>**

*As war deepened, so did protests. At Kent State University in Ohio, students set fire to the ROTC building after learning that President Richard Nixon had ordered U.S. troops into Cambodia. Two days later, on May 4, there was another demonstration, and members of the National Guard opened fire, killing four students and injuring nine others. One sophomore, writing to the campus newspaper, captured some of the horror felt both on and beyond the campus.*

May 5, 1970

Dear Sirs:

The reason that I came to Kent State University was for an education. And I'm getting one! I am referring, of course, to the tragic incidences that occurred on our campus Monday, May 4, 1970. Though the practicality of this "educational experience" may be disputed—the reality cannot be.

Seeing those khaki green tents and trucks on the football field, men carrying <u>real</u> M-1 rifles loaded with <u>real</u> ammunition—then witnessing some of my fellow students bleeding and hysterical, left a far deeper impression within me than my most effective professor could have done.

It was real. It was shocking. It was a totally devastating experience.

From it, I have observed that violent confrontation results <u>only</u> in impertinent deaths and unwarranted destruction. It is my feeling that this is much too high a price to pay for any "unknown" cause.

Beryl Tuffyas

**1971: DECEMBER**

**A MOTHER TO HER DAUGHTER**

Womankind *was a monthly newspaper published from 1971 to 1973 by the Chicago Women's Liberation Union, a vocal and well-organized women's rights group. An article in one of the first issues, signed "Erica," revealed the author's recent discovery about her own sexuality. It inspired the following letter from Erica's mother.*

In his immensely popular book *Summerhill*, A. S. Neill had written: "The function of a child is to live his own life—not the life his anxious parents think he should live."

Dear Daughter,

A few weeks ago you wrote an article for WOMANKIND on Gay Liberation. I read it and enjoyed reading it because I've read a lot of your writing and like it. Ever since your first story appeared in a nursery school bulletin—"I saw a bird and another bird"—I loved reading your writing. As much as I loved reading, I haven't ever stooped to reading anything you haven't permitted me to read.

In the same way I have always permitted you to read some of my letters, but not all.

I really have no comments on anyone's sex life which may be part of my growing up with all the taboos or an enlightened idea that sex is not the single most important issue in the world that interests me.

In watching and helping you grow up, I followed a basic rule. Whenever you told me you were ready to do something on your own—you did it, but as long as you wanted help it was given. So, in your growing up I came across A.S. Neil's Summerhill which reinforced my ideas of children being allowed to develop at their own speed. Gibran's The Prophet with the advice to parents that they can't control their children's thoughts or lives in their own images.

The pill came into existence during your teen years. I was appalled at a few parents of your friends who supplied their daughters with the pill. It seemed to me that they were encouraging their daughters to enter relationships with boy friends earlier than they were prepared for emotionally. I was appalled because it seemed to be license and parental approval, but I knew that these parents also feared raising babies of their babies. But I never openly judged the parents too harshly.

On the other hand, interracial marriages were more close and I had to think out an answer of what I really thought. So, my answer that a man and woman can mate as a natural law whether their skin colors coordinate or their languages do, has nothing to do with the man-made laws of civil marriages.

So I've read a lot of writing on gay and not so gay liberation and my ideas are still pretty much unformed, but like any other union, it's a decision between two people and needs no approval or disapproval from me.

You may have been born from my body (with a little help from Daddy) but you grew up outside of my body and you are not mine in a selfishly possessive sense. You are you.

Do you think I am avoiding the discussion of sex? I am not. Our whole relationship is just that. A whole. I really trust your judgment on what you want to do. When you want to do it. With whom you do it. This goes for the books you read, the food you eat, the clothes you wear, the people you know, the liquors you drink and your sleeping partners. And the mistakes, too. The whole shit. I love you very much.

Mama

## 1972: APRIL 19
## JOAN GANZ COONEY TO WILMA SCOTT HEIDE

*By the 1960s, television was ubiquitous in American life, but it had not yet been tested as an educational medium, and certainly not as a medium addressed to inner-city youth. All that changed in 1968 when Joan Ganz Cooney (1929–), with the help of Carnegie Corporation vice president Lloyd Morrisett, launched the Children's Television Workshop, soon to be best known as the home of* Sesame Street. *With a format based on fast pacing, mock advertisements, familiar characters, lovable Muppets, and preschool lessons, the show became a landmark in broadcast history. It also became a target of the National Organization for Women, whose head, Wilma Scott Heide (1921–1985), suggested that the show's depiction of women was not nearly progressive enough. With this letter, Cooney attempted to soothe Heide while reminding her that there was a bigger agenda at hand.*

Anne Grant West was head of NOW's education committee, which had threatened to boycott General Foods, one of *Sesame Street*'s early patrons. *The Electric Company,* which ran for seven years, was CTW's second show. Action for Children's Television (ACT) was a grassroots advocacy group founded in 1968.

19 April 1972

Dear Ms. Heide:

Thank you very much for your thoughtful letter of April 3.

Happy as I am to hear from you and other members of NOW about the importance of the feminist movement and the portrayal of females on TV, I can't help but be reminded of the story about Clare Boothe Luce visiting the Pope and his being overheard to say, "But, Mrs. Luce, I already <u>am</u> a Catholic". To summarize: I'm <u>with</u> you.

However, I would like to advance a few thoughts which, perhaps, you and some of the other members of NOW might wish to consider:

1. The way NOW has gone about its educational program at CTW has certainly left something to be desired. For example, Ms. Anne Grant West's threatening letter to General Foods last year and her recent threatening and offensive letter to Jon Stone and me really set the feminist cause back in this organization. Further, the threats of picketing and so on which we have received do not

help this organization achieve our mutual goals. Indeed, such threats and the recent letter-writing campaign only cause a counter-reaction that I must work very hard to dispell, and it seems a waste of energy.

2. I couldn't agree more that NOW would be derelict in its duties if it did not point out, and continue to point out, to us where we might be performing a dis-service to little girls in this country. However, I don't know how useful it is to look at "Sesame Street" solely through feminist eyes when, clearly, it is trying to do a number of things for young children. For example, we consider our primary aim of reaching and teaching the disadvantaged child a life and death matter, for education determines whether these disadvantaged youngsters enter the economic main stream of American life or not. At the same time, we are trying to correct the sexism that exists on "Sesame Street". (I am quite shocked that you mention "The Electric Company" as a sexist show. Since women are about equally represented with men and perform all roles on the show, it is hard to see what you are talking about unless you and other viewers have misunderstood some of the spoofs of sexist commercials that the show sometimes indulges in.)

3. While I certainly don't object to having our faults pointed out to us, (and God knows, everyone is doing it), I wonder if NOW is really performing a ser-vice by concentrating so much public attention and energy on one of the few really decent programs for young children on television. Perhaps you are not aware that preschool children watch up to eight hours a day and that the num-ber of baldly sexist commercials and situation comedies they are exposed to during that time is not to be believed. Further, I don't know of a single cartoon that is popular with children that portrays females as other than dopey, med-dling, and objects of ridicule. Shouldn't NOW begin to address itself to the male-dominated media of commercial TV and advertising that have created this situation on TV and which brainwashes children day in and day out, year in and year out? NOW members keep saying that they direct so much fire at us be-cause we are so influential. I have not noticed anyone copying us (TV, alas, for children and adults has not changed very much since we went on the air) and so I really doubt the kind of influence NOW members are talking about.

4. I continue to be disturbed by the strong belief held by some prominent whites, as well as Blacks, that the feminist movement, and NOW in particular, is displaying anti-Black attitudes. In a recent letter to me, Ms. Anne C. Hall said: "The majority of NOW members that I have discussed 'Sesame Street' with feel that change has not occurred as fast as they would like to see and the program has shown greater responsiveness to the needs of Blacks than women. . . ." Perhaps Ms. Hall is not aware that "Sesame Street" was funded to

serve the needs of disadvantaged children in this country, with particular emphasis on the inner city poor. Naturally, then, their needs come first, though I see no conflict between their needs and feminist goals on "Sesame Street". We acknowledge that we can and should change our portrayal of women and girls on "Sesame Street", but we don't like to see the issue cast in racial terms nor compared with the nightmare of racism and poverty. And, certainly, our Black staff—men and women—harbor resentments against the feminist movement when it speaks in such terms, making it more difficult for us to achieve our mutual aims. I think your continuing to focus so much criticism on "Sesame Street", which is trying to meet the needs of disadvantaged youngsters, appears to add substance to the feelings of some that they must make a choice between the feminist cause and the case for equal rights for Blacks.

5. If NOW had taken on the advertisers who create those highly offensive commercials, they might have achieved less success than by focusing on "Sesame Street", which was already committed to its goals. But at least it would have signified that you are even handed and know where the real problems and real intransigence exist. Had you taken on the real offenders, you could have quietly pointed out to us that we had a long way to go ourselves, and might have been able to join with you informally in the feminist cause, as we have with ACT in its crusade to upgrade children's TV. As it is, you have placed us in the position of an adversary and made cooperation more difficult than it might have been.

6. I am asking Ms. Chase and Ms. Eaton to meet with our Production staff in late May to help them prepare materials which might, as you suggest, overcompensate for some of the older materials which we will have to go on using.

Again, I would like to assure you that there is no opposition at CTW to your goals.

Sincerely,
Joan Ganz Cooney

# EXCHANGE

## 1972
## PAT AND HER PARENTS

*Like the new music, the new attitudes toward sex and marriage were foreign to a lot of parents. For Pat, who was raised in Ohio, and her mother, the rift became all too apparent when Pat announced that she was moving in with her boyfriend.*

"Pat" is a pseudonym.

## PAT TO HER PARENTS

1 August 1972

Dear Mom and Dad,

. . . I'm not moving back home after I graduate. There is really nothing for me there (aside from being with the family). I am contented, happy, and settled down in a place where I don't mind living. What would you rather have: me as a mature adult, handling my own affairs and making my own decisions . . . or me as a "child" depending on you for everything? I want to be able to handle my own financial matters after I graduate. It is time for me to stop accepting money from you and start supporting myself. I don't want to limit my world to one thing or one place or one set of ideals.

My roommate is moving out at the end of this term. There is a possibility that Tony will move in. We have talked about it and it seems like the logical thing to do since we might as well be living together anyway. I hope you have realized by now that I am not a little girl any more. I firmly believe we have made the right decision and so does Tony. We are happy together and we have much to learn and gain, and much to experience by doing this. Also, if I am living with a man I will feel safer living in an area where rapes and robberies are a common occurrence.

I assume you think that living together is morally wrong as opposed to marriage which is morally "right". I feel that two people can be just as close and happy living together, and they do not need a marriage contract to make theirs a "legal" partnership. If marriage is a form of "security", then I don't want that form of security. Security alone is not a valid reason for two people to be together. This is what I believe and I want you to be able to accept it and be aware that this is what I really am.

Much love,<br>your daughter, Pat

## HER PARENTS TO PAT

Pat did move in with Tony. Sharon was Pat's sister. A family snapshot was enclosed.

8 August 1972

Dear Pat,

I don't know what reaction you expected from us after reading your Air Mail letter to us this week. Naturally we are disappointed at your apparent lack of appreciation and respect for us, as well as respect for yourself. We did the best we could for both our girls, and expected to see you graduate, as did Sharon, knowing where you were going and with both feet on the ground. As it is, you seem to be in a confused state, changing your major for the third time and not knowing exactly what you want or where you are going.

When you gave us the snow job several months ago, convincing us that you wanted to move from the dorm into an apartment, even though we had a few misgivings as to the advisability of it, our trust and confidence in you overruled our doubts and we gave our consent. At that time you seemed to be acting with mature judgement with goals firmly set. We are now convinced that you weren't as prepared as we thought you were to handle the outside world.

You always prided yourself on dating fellows who respected you. What happened along the way that you can no longer demand such respect? Aren't you able to look ahead and visualize what may be in store for you in two, five, or ten years? When this fellow has finished with you and moves on to someone else, and when you meet THE ONE you will want to spend the rest of your life with, will he want to settle for secondhand, used merchandise?

No Pat, we didn't expect you to move here after graduation. You had wanted to go to grad school, and we had made plans to see you thru after your graduation. We wanted to give you every opportunity to fit yourself for self support. If you are willing to throw all this away, there is nothing we can do about it since you are now an adult and must make your own decisions. If you believe Tony is THE ONE in your life, then he will be willing to wait for you to attain your goals. You have your whole life ahead of you and one more year or less shouldn't make any difference.

Naturally we are disappointed that you do not want to spend your quarter break with us, but you know what is best so far as your studies are concerned. We do want you to be able to retain your good grades and graduate when you planned, and hope that you will reconsider what you proposed in your letter so that we will want to put you through this last quarter. Of course you realize that would be impossible if you should go through with it.

How about Tony's sweet mother, the one who mailed the violin to you? Are you a girl whom he would like to take home to meet his mother? Would she condone such an arrangement? Is he considering her feelings? I'm leaving the remainder to be said by your daddy.

Your loving
Mom

P.S. Whatever will I do with the pretty blue print corduroy bedspread I have just made for you?

Honey, anytime you want to come home for a visit, your room will be waiting for you. Your husband, if and when you get one, will also be welcome. Here is a picture of the happy family that once was.

[Note from her father:]

Pat, as you can well understand from what your mother has written, you know we do not condone your proposal to shack up with Tony. You stated in your letter that you wanted to be independent and make your own decisions. We have let you do just that. However, if you decide to go through with your proposal, God pity you. Here are some of my proposals:

1. Be sure and get some insurance.

2. Get acquainted with income tax rules and regulations.

3. Don't expect any more financial assistance from us.

4. Straighten up and fly right. You will be all the better off if you do.

If you are going to live with a man I will expect him to support you. I pray that you will give this matter some serious thought. Let us know your decision so we can know where we stand financially.

Daddy

### 1972: AUGUST 14
### HELEN GURLEY BROWN TO ERIC RAYMAN

Cosmopolitan *magazine had been around since 1886, but it was completely rein-vented in 1965 as the decidedly outspoken, decidedly female, child of Helen Gurley Brown (1922–). Author of the best-selling* Sex and the Single Girl *(1962), Brown used her magazine to showcase and inspire young women, both single and married, who were trying to balance work and love in a newly open world. When* Cosmo *ran the first male centerfold in 1972, it proved irresistible to editors of* The Harvard Lampoon, *who promptly created a parody, complete with a Henry Kissinger center-fold. The letter that follows, to editor-in-chief Eric Rayman (1951–), was Brown's reaction to the planned* Lampoon *cover.*

Having been told of the parody, Brown had requested that she see the cover in time to make sure its color scheme was not too similar to her magazine's. According to Rayman, the original cover girl had been dressed as a hooker, and Brown's reaction was entirely persuasive. "We should have known," Rayman recalls. "That wasn't a *Cosmo* girl." The reshot cover featured a beautiful girl in tasteful clothes—with crossed eyes.

Dear Eric,

As I mentioned in our telephone conversation, our feeling is that COSMOPOLI-
TAN is such a self-help magazine in <u>many</u> areas that it isn't quite true to us to
bear down so heavily on sex in your cover lines. I would hope that you could
change at least fifty per cent of them. The two I object to most are 10 WAYS TO
DECORATE YOUR UTERINE WALL and TURN YOUR PERIOD INTO A DASH. I'm enclosing the September issue of COSMO so you can see how few of our <u>own</u> cover
lines are sexy.

Regarding the cover illustration, as you know, I think it's just generally not
very pretty and won't sell as many magazines for you as something more attractive would. She looks gloomy, which is always a put-off and I don't think <u>any-
body</u> is going to be attracted to that bosom! You have told me how expensive it is
to try another cover but I would hope very much that you might be able to do so.
May I hear from you soon?

## 1972: NOVEMBER 3
## KATHARINE GRAHAM TO JOHN EHRLICHMAN

*One of Richard Nixon's chief advisers, John Ehrlichman (1925–1999) was responsi-
ble for the group of White House "plumbers" whose assignments included the break-
in at the National Democratic Committee headquarters in the Watergate. Ultimately,
Ehrlichman would be found guilty of conspiracy, perjury, and obstruction of justice
for having helped to plan the ensuing cover-up. While the story was unfolding, however, Katharine Graham (1917–2001) sent him this letter. Graham had succeeded
her husband, Philip (who committed suicide in 1963), as publisher of the* Washington Post *and* Newsweek. *With legendary clarity, she oversaw the* Post's *coverage of
Watergate, even as much of Washington was doubting the paper's approach and as
Republicans tried to explain it away with accusations of personal animosity.*
Robert Dole was chairman of the Republican National Committee; he would later become
Senate majority leader and make one successful and two unsuccessful bids for his party's
presidential nomination.

November 3, 1972

Dear John:

A short while back you threw me a message over the fence, and I genuinely
appreciated it. Here is a message I want to send you.

Among the charges that have been flying over the past few weeks, many have disturbed me for the general misunderstanding they suggest of the Post's purposes in printing the stories we do. But none has disturbed me more than an allegation Senator Dole made the other day. It was that the Post's point of view on certain substantive issues was explained by me as proceeding from the simple fact that I "hate" the President.

There are so many things wrong with this "anecdote," that one hardly knows where to begin in correcting them. But I would begin with the fact that I cannot imagine that the episode ever took place at all or that I ever expressed such a childish and mindless sentiment—since it is one that I do not feel.

I want you to know that. And I also want you to know that the fiction doesn't stop there. For the story suggests, as well, that somehow editorial positions on public issues are taken and decisions on news made on the basis of the publisher's personal feelings and tastes. This is not true, even when the sentiments attributed to me—unlike this alleged and unworthy "hate" for the President—may be real.

What appears in the Post is not a reflection of my personal feelings. And by the same token, I would add that my continuing and genuine pride in the paper's performance over the past few months—the period that seems to be at issue—does not proceed from some sense that it has gratified my personal whim. It proceeds from my belief that the editors and reporters have fulfilled the highest standards of professional duty and responsibility.

On this I know we disagree. I am writing this note because I think we have enough such areas of sharp and honest disagreement between us not to need a harmful and destructive overlay of personal animosity that I, for one, don't feel and don't wish to see perpetuated by misquotation! (My turn, it seems.)

Best regards to you and Jean,

### 1974: MAY
### TERESA MANNING TO MS. MAGAZINE

*Among the many innovations of the 1970s women's movement were the revival of the term "Ms." (it had originally been introduced in the 1940s), the introduction of the magazine Ms. (under the leadership of Gloria Steinem, among others), and the now less-than-shocking notion that women might want to reclaim or retain their maiden names.*

"Give Yourself Your Own Name for Christmas" (December 1973) provided me with the final assurance I needed: I really wasn't so weird for wanting my original name back. On December 26, I went to court and in a few short minutes was once again Teresa Manning.

I have found the experience to be totally exhilarating. With my husband's name, I felt tied to roles I didn't want and social expectations I could never live up to. With my own, I am my own person again—free, independent, and happy. Changing my name back was the best thing I've done since I gave it up.

I have included a copy of the announcement I sent out. I have since had my consciousness raised even further and regret that I used the term <u>maiden name</u> instead of <u>birth name</u> or <u>original name</u>. Indeed, consciousness-raising is a continuing process—with new discoveries every day. That's what's so great about the women's movement—one cannot stay involved in it and not grow.

> By order of the
> Superior Court of the State of Washington
> King County, Washington
> Teresa M. Shoemaker resumed
> the use of her maiden name
> Teresa Mary Manning
> on December 26, 1973.
> This action in no way affects the
> validity of the marriage vows
> she exchanged with Dean Shoemaker
> > Teresa M. Manning
> > Eau Claire, Wisconsin

## 1974: AUGUST

## JULIE NIXON EISENHOWER TO RICHARD NIXON

*As revelations about Watergate grew, so did the pressure on Richard Nixon (1913–1994) to resign. Just days before he did, the president's younger daughter, Julie (1948–), left this note for him. In later years, Nixon would write that if anything could have changed his mind, it would have been this.*

Dear Daddy—

I love you. Whatever you do I will support. I am very proud of you.

Please wait a week or even ten days before you make this decision. Go through the fire just a little bit longer. You are so strong!

> I love you,
> Julie
> Millions support you.

## 1974: OCTOBER 24
## RITA MAE BROWN TO BETTY FRIEDAN

*Long before Ellen DeGeneres brought lesbianism to prime time, Rita Mae Brown (1944–) spoke out about her sexual orientation and campaigned for gay rights. In 1967, she started the first college gay group (NYU's Student Homophile League). In 1969, she was one of the few women to take part in the Stonewall Riot, when gay men fought back against a police raid at the Stonewall Inn in New York City. And in 1970, Brown resigned her membership in the National Organization for Women (NOW) when Betty Friedan (1921–) led a movement to exclude lesbians, whom she called "the Lavender Menace."*

The year before writing this letter, Brown had gained considerable renown with the publication of her first novel, *Rubyfruit Jungle*. Ivy Bottini, also an activist, designed the famous NOW logo.

Dear Ms. Friedan,

You founded NOW in 1966 on the belief that women deserved something more than housework. NOW's goal is to change the societal pressure placed on women to stay at home and neglect their career potential by remaining house-wives. At a time when women are discriminated against and treated unfairly, I would expect you and your fellow members of NOW to unite with all members of our gender, regardless of sexual orientation, against a male dominated society.

Instead of welcoming our support as fellow women's rights activists, you have expelled Ivy Bottini and myself simply because of our sexual orientation. Yes, we are lesbians, Ms. Friedan, but is it fair to deny us membership on this premise?

There is contention among you, and fear that lesbian members will confuse your cause in the media. I ask you, have women ever been fairly represented in the media? Doesn't the media, which is run by middle class males, always represent women unfairly? And isn't the media's image of women exactly what one of NOW's goal is to change? Why not accept our help and the added force our identity brings so we can join our forces and double our strength together?

I find it strange that you have decided you no longer desire our support despite the influence and leadership powers we possess. Ms. Bottini has been a prominent figure in gay activist groups. Have you forgotten her contribution as founder of the first chapter of NOW? She went on to design and introduce feminist awareness to N.O.W. in 1968. I recall that Ms. Bottini organized the takeover of the Statue of Liberty in 1970 and she held that statue for near three hours. She helped organize and lead the Women's Strike for Equality and 50,000 women marched behind her in the streets of New York that day. Despite these tremendous achievements, you treat her as if she were expendable. A woman like Ivy Bottini is not a liability, Ms. Friedan, she is a reliable and powerful asset to all women's rights groups.

I have remained politically active and continued to speak out in support of my cause even after my dismissal from NOW. In 1967, I helped start the Student Homophile League at Columbia, which was a promising organization and unfortunately did not survive. However, I started another, more successful organization at Washington Square College in New York University, which has gained hundreds of supporters and whose power is undeniable. From this group, several political homosexual groups have sprung—proving that there is certainly a magnetic force behind my movement, and that my own leadership skills have allowed me to capably handle a group of this size.

I ask you, in light of my and Ms. Bottini's accomplishments, are you willing to maintain that you made the correct choice in dismissing us? Look around you—discrimination and unfairness abound. Your cause is weakened by your own prejudice, not homosexual supporters. We have so much to offer that is denied because of the fear that is attached to our sexuality. With all we have accomplished separately, our success would have been tripled had we been able to work together.

My interest is in the successful future of the feminist movement, and I hope that my remarks will persuade you to reconsider your position.

Sincerely,
Rita Mae Brown

# EXCHANGE

## 1974: OCTOBER–NOVEMBER
## JAN AND DOROTHY

---

*Abortion became legal nationwide in 1973 when the U.S. Supreme Court ruled in* Roe v. Wade *that a statute criminalizing abortion violated women's constitutional right to privacy. A year later, eighteen-year-old Jan made the choice that* Roe *had made possible, and she wrote this letter to her mother, Dorothy, describing her experience.*

"Jan" and "Dorothy" are pseudonyms.

## JAN TO DOROTHY

October 1974

Dear Mom,

Health-wise I'm OK but I've been through some unfortunate experiences as of late. Day before I left for my New York visit I went to the doctor for a check-up. He examined me and told me I was 6 weeks pregnant. I was shocked. He offered to give me an abortion that day but I knew I had to prepare myself emotionally and I also wanted to continue with my New York trip.

My first thoughts were that I could never have an abortion, but the more I thought it over and the more Al and I discussed it I realized it was the only thing I could do.

The day of the abortion Al and I went to the clinic at 10 a.m. I saw a counselor; we discussed my feelings and she felt my decision was carefully thought over and one I believed in. She also explained the actual procedure: dilation, suction and then a scraping of the womb.

I can only feel fortunate that I live in a time when abortion is legal and I did not have to suffer through an unwanted pregnancy or find means of an illegal, unsafe abortion. The other women there—one 35, one 50, one 15; all making an important decision about their lives.

I was pretty calm about it. The counselor was there with me as well as a doctor and a nurse. I was given a local anesthetic but I swear I never knew such physical pain existed. I thought I would die or leap off the table (they said my cramping was much worse than usual). But when it was over so was the pain.

Immediately after, they led me into a small room where Al was allowed to come sit with me. It was then I cried and I haven't cried since. The feeling was mostly of relief—the pain was gone but most of all the pregnancy.

I knew from the start that I would tell you, but I waited till now to give you the reassurance that I'm alright. I'm too close to you not to tell you. I guess I still fear that I'm the little girl that will be punished. I just want to be understood. I know you will feel sad but don't feel disappointed. Just understand.

The night after the abortion I had a dream. I dreamt that I was walking down a street in New York. A young boy, 16 or so, offered me a ride. We drove and drove all the way to Mississippi and gradually he became younger until he was about 8 years old. He lived in a big house by a lake. Then Al was in the dream—

we were telling the boy we wanted to make love with him to show him how much we loved him. Then his mother came home and we left. To me, that symbolized our love for the child even though we had to leave it behind and realizing that it had found another place.

Please write me of your feelings. I'm glad that I felt I could write you of this. I will see you and talk to you soon.

Much Love,

Jan

**DOROTHY TO JAN**

November 1974

Dearest Daughter,

Your adolescent years have provided us with the usual tense moments that all parents must associate with "growing-up". Your wailing despair with hair and figure. Your ups and downs with "first-lover" and the gradual moving away from the once close companionship that you shared with your father.

As you know the "new sexuality" was not hard for me to accept. I think I was relieved to know that we were now living in an era that allowed a young woman to explore her sexual curiosity without the shame of feeling <u>ruined</u> or the necessity of having to "marry the boy". You are not a promiscuous girl and when you did lose your virginity we discussed it thoroughly along with the responsibilities it entailed.

I think my only real days of despair came when you entered into this "live-in" relationship with Al. It was neither the "live-in" that bothered me nor the fact that he is almost twice your age but the knowledge that he is a deeply <u>disturbed</u> person. I was afraid for you.

During the weekend that dad and I spent with the two of you, we were so shaken by his violent moodswings. On our long drive home the silence was broken only by my tears and dad's laments of disbelief.

Now I have before me the letter telling of your recent abortion. It's difficult to explain how very saddened I am—not by the loss of a grandchild but by the necessity to deny some spark of human potential, its existence. I, who would not knowingly step on an ant, do understand how you have done what you <u>had</u> to do. At eighteen, with your life before you, you are not ready for a child nor are you ready for marriage to its father. This unfortunate "flying Dutchman" who drifts from coast to coast, crashing with friends until they can no longer abide his temper could provide neither emotional nor financial support for a "family".

I think my real sorrow stems from the fact that you had to undergo this traumatic experience. That you had to make this decision, endure the physical pain and mental anguish; the knowing loss. And finally that I should, somehow, have "been there" to comfort, to hold you in my arms and tell you (although we would both know, deep inside that it wasn't) that everything was all right—

With my love,
Dorothy

### 1978: NOVEMBER 18
### ANNIE MOORE

*Jim Jones was the founder of the People's Temple, a congregation that had begun in Indianapolis, Indiana, in the 1950s, moved to California in the 1960s, and by 1977 attracted thousands of devoted followers. That year, many of them followed Jones to the small South American country of Guyana, where they formed a colony that embraced Jones's mix of apocalyptic visions, communal living, faith healing, and revival-style worship. In 1978, a group of disaffected former members brought California congressman Leo Ryan to visit the compound; he and four others were assassinated when they prepared to leave four days later. Jones then exhorted his followers into mass suicide and murders that left more than nine hundred dead. Some of them had drunk poison-laced Kool-Aid; others had been shot. Annie Moore (1954–1978) died of a gunshot wound. She had been Jones's personal nurse and was thought to be one of the last to die. This was her final letter, written in a spiral notebook and found next to her body.*

I am 24 years of age right now and don't expect to live through the end of this book.

I thought I should at least make some attempt to let the world know what Jim Jones and the Peoples Temple is—OR WAS—all about.

It seems that some people and perhaps the majority of people would like to destroy the best thing that ever happened to the 1,200 or so of us who have followed Jim.

I am at a point right now so embittered against the world that I don't know why I am writing this. Someone who finds it will believe I am crazy or believe in the barbed wire that does NOT exist in Jonestown.

It seems that everything good that happens to the world is under constant attack. When I write this, I can expect some mentally deranged fascist person to find it and decide it should be thrown in the trash before anyone gets a chance to hear the truth—which is what I am now writing about.

Where can I begin—JONESTOWN—the most peaceful, loving community that ever existed, JIM JONES—the one who made this paradise possible—much to the contrary of the lies stated about Jim Jones being a power-hungry, sadistic mean person who thought he was God—of all things!

I want you who read this to know Jim was the most honest, loving, caring, concerned person whom I ever met and knew. His love for animals—each creature, poisonous snakes, tarantulas. None of them ever bit him because he was such a gentle person. He knew how mean the world was and he took any and every stray animal and took care of each one.

His love for humans was insurmountable and it was many of those whom he put his love and trust in that left him and spit in his face. Teresa Buford, Debbie Blakey—they both wanted sex from him which he was too ill to give. Why should he have to give them sex?—And Tim and Grace Stoen—also include them. I should know.

I have spent these last few months taking care of Jim's health. However, it was difficult to take care of anything for him. He always would do for himself.

His hatred of racism, sexism, elitism, and mainly classism, is what prompted him to make a new world for the people—a paradise in the jungle. The children loved it. So did everyone else.

There were no ugly, mean policemen wanting to beat our heads in, no more racist tears from whites and others who thought they were better. No one was made fun of for their appearance—something no one had control over.

Meanness and making fun were not allowed. Maybe this is why all the lies were started. Besides this fact, no one was allowed to live higher than anyone else. The United States allowed criticism. The problem being this and not all the side tracks of black power, woman power, Indian power, gay power.

Jim Jones showed us all this—that we could live together with our differences, that we are all the same human beings. Luckily we were more fortunate than the starving babies in Ethiopia, than the starving babies in the United States.

What a beautiful place this was. The children loved the jungle, learned about animals and plants. There were no cars to run over them; no child-molesters to molest them; nobody to hurt them. They were the freest, most intelligent children I had ever known.

Seniors had dignity. They had whatever they wanted—a plot of land for a garden. Seniors were treated with respect—something they never had in the United States. A rare few were sick, and when they were, they were given the best medical care....

We died because you would not let us live in peace.

Annie Moore

### 1978: NOVEMBER 21
### A RESIDENT OF LOVE CANAL TO PHILIP HARPER

*Love Canal, in western New York, was the site of one of the worst environmental disasters in the United States, but the damage did not occur overnight. The canal had been the dump site for more than twenty thousand tons of chemical waste during the 1940s and 1950s; after that, it had been filled in, and the city of Niagara Falls had encouraged residential building there. Not until the 1970s did officials begin to acknowledge that chemical waste had contaminated the soil, air, and water. As this letter from a worried resident to a department of health investigator makes clear, the medical implications were far from benign.*

A swale is a swamp or low-lying land.

November 21, 1978

Dear Mr. Harper:

The medical data on my family which you requested is attached. For your information, our home seems to be located on a swale coming out of Love Canal. My husband's blood test results show that the entire enzyme study is elevated as is his white count. My tests show only an elevated liver enzyme. My daughter's results are still not available. Air sampling of the house showed 87 benzene, 182 toluene and 2 tetrachloroethene.

Based on advice we received pertinent to the readings and the fact that our health has been poor for the past three years, we will be vacating our home early December. If you need to contact us, we will still pick up our mail at ———— Avenue.

It appears that my husband, daughter, and myself share the following ailments which we never experienced before living at our present address, except for minor colds.

|                                            | [Husband] | [Daughter] | [Self] |
|--------------------------------------------|-----------|------------|--------|
| Severe respiratory problems                | X         | X          | X      |
| Painful and irritated eyes                 | X         | X          | X      |
| Rectal bleeding (no reason found)          | X         | X          |        |
| Depression                                 |           | X          | X      |
| Skin Disorders                             | X         | X          | X      |

Very truly yours,

# JUST YESTERDAY

# 1980

~

# 2005

In a million years, for a million dollars, I could not do
what you have done. Once, we had pride in the two towers
that gallantly scraped the sky. Now, we have pride in *you*.

—*A schoolgirl to New York City firefighters*
*September 12, 2001*

# BETWEEN 1980 AND 2005 . . .

**1980:** Ronald Reagan, former California governor and star of such films as *Bedtime for Bonzo*, wins 489 electoral votes in a landslide victory to become America's fortieth president. ★ CNN starts broadcasting. ★ The first Rubik's Cubes are imported from Hungary. **1981:** IBM introduces the personal computer. ★ Sandra Day O'Connor is appointed to the Supreme Court, becoming the 102nd justice and the first woman. ★ John Hinckley, Jr., attempts to assassinate Ronald Reagan; wounded in the chest, the president tells his surgeons, "I hope you are all Republicans" and—quoting the legendary boxer Jack Dempsey—tells his wife, "Honey, I forgot to duck." **1982:** Michael Jackson's album *Thriller* sells 25 million copies. **1983:** Scientists discover the virus that causes AIDS. **1984:** After winning her second Academy Award, for her performance in *Places in the Heart*, Sally Field tells the audience: "I wanted more than anything to have your respect. The first time I didn't feel it, but this time I feel it and I can't deny the fact that you like me. Right now, you really like me!" ★ Jay McInerney's *Bright Lights, Big City* is a bestseller. **1985:** Rock Hudson

---

Clockwise from top left: Bill and Hillary Clinton; Yoko Ono, John Lennon, and friend; Bill Gates and Paul Allen; The *Challenger*; Nicole Simpson; Lyndie England; George W. Bush; Oprah Winfrey; the World Trade Center; AIDS prevention poster.

dies of AIDS. **1986:** The space shuttle *Challenger* explodes 74 seconds after liftoff, killing all seven crew members, including high school teacher Christa McAuliffe; for more than an hour, debris falls into the Atlantic Ocean. **1989:** The Berlin Wall comes down. **1990:** Iraqi president Saddam Hussein's forces invade Kuwait. **1991:** Congress authorizes the use of force against Iraq. ★ The Gulf War ends six weeks after it was begun. **1992:** James Carville posts the sign "It's the economy, stupid" on the wall of the campaign "war room" of William Jefferson Clinton, who is elected, beating incumbent George H. W. Bush. **1994:** AIDS and related illnesses are the leading cause of death for adults in the United States between the ages of 25 and 44. **1995:** After less than four hours, a jury finds O. J. Simpson not guilty of murdering his ex-wife, Nicole Brown Simpson, and her friend Ronald Goldman. ★ Pierre Omidyar and Jeff Skoll found eBay. ★ Amazon debuts on the Web; before the end of the first month, books have been shipped to all 50 states. ★ Roughly 17 percent of all families are headed by women. **1997:** Amazon founder Jeff Bezos flies to Japan to hand-deliver an order for the company's millionth customer. **1998:** In his appearance before the grand jury, President Bill Clinton is asked whether he was lying about intern Monica Lewinsky when he told top aides "there's nothing going on between us." Clinton responds: "It depends on what the meaning of the word 'is' is." ★ There are an estimated 300 million sites on the World Wide Web, with 1.5 million added daily. **1999:** As the millennium approaches, some Americans prepare for the end of time, and many more worry that the Y2K bug will crash computer networks everywhere. **2000:** The millennium arrives without apocalypse, and with computer systems intact. ★ For the first time, the Barbie doll is manufactured with a belly button. ★ Roughly two-thirds of Americans own their homes, an all-time high. ★ The phrase "getting voted off the island" enters the American lexicon as the television show *Survivor* becomes a huge hit and reality TV the reigning trend. ★ Upon learning that George W. Bush is fewer than 1,000 votes ahead of him in the pivotal state of Florida, vice president and Democratic contender Al Gore telephones him to say that, contrary to an earlier call, he is not ready to concede the presidential election. "Let me make sure I understand," Bush says. "You're calling me back to retract your concession?" Gore replies: "You don't have to get snippy about this." ★ Thirty-six days and numerous court decisions later, Gore announces on TV: "I accept the finality of this outcome, which will be ratified next Monday in the Electoral College, and tonight, for the sake of our unity as a people and the strength of our democracy, I offer my concession." **2001:** More than 3,000 people die when two hijacked airplanes crash into New York City's World Trade Center towers, a third crashes into the Pentagon, and a fourth goes down in Pennsylvania. ★ After being told that America is under attack, George Bush remains in the grade school classroom he is visiting for a full seven minutes, listening to students read a story about a pet goat and then asking them questions. ★ On October 7, 2001, the United States and an international coalition begin bombing terrorist targets in Afghanistan. **2003:** Citing the continuing development of "weapons of mass destruction" by Iraqi president Saddam Hussein, Bush launches a fierce air and ground war in Iraq on March 19; on May 1, he appears under a banner that reads "Mission Accomplished" and says, "Major combat operations in Iraq have ended." **2004:** U.S. troops remain mired in Iraq as an insurgency led by Saddam loyalists and international Islamic extremists continues. ★ George W. Bush is elected to a second term. **2005:** After serving five months in a federal prison for obstruction of justice and conspiracy, professional homemaker Martha Stewart is released into house arrest. ★ The chairman of New York's Republican Party launches a "Stop Hillary Now!" initiative on the theory that a defeat in her 2006 Senate reelection campaign will make it that much harder for the former first lady to run for president in 2008.

## 1980: FEBRUARY 22
## JUDY NAPIER TO JIMMY CARTER

---

*Jimmy Carter (1924–) had become president in 1977 and was beset by challenges that included rising inflation, an energy crisis, and the taking of American hostages in Iran. In the last month of 1979, Soviet troops invaded Afghanistan. Responding first with economic sanctions, Carter next led fifty-nine other nations to boycott the Moscow summer Olympics. It was a gesture that met with considerable support, even among some of the athletes who had trained so hard to make the games. But as this telegram suggests, there were many other Americans—including Judy Napier, wife of an Olympic hopeful—who were frustrated and disappointed.*

My husband has trained for 8 years in a garage to make U.S. weight lifting team in Moscow. We have sacrificed our time, energy, personal income and emotions to have this dream come true. He is not alone. There are thousands of other athletes like him. Please reconsider your boycott. We are not politicians. The differences between countries should not be manifested in athletics. Our sacrifices have been many. We count too.

Judy Napier

## 1980: MARCH 8
## JEAN HARRIS TO HERMAN TARNOWER

---

*The headmistress of a private girls' boarding school in Virginia, Jean Struven Harris (1923–) wrote this letter two days before she killed its recipient, her longtime lover, Herman Tarnower (1910–1980). On the professional front, Harris had just learned that drug paraphernalia had been found in the dorm rooms of several respected students. On the personal front, Tarnower—author of the best-selling Scarsdale Diet book—had just told her that he did not want her sitting beside him at an upcoming banquet in his honor; like her romantic rival, Lynne Tryforos, Harris would be seated instead at a separate table. Unable to reach Tarnower by phone, Harris descended into depression and rage. At the trial, one of the most notorious of the decade, the defense would claim that Harris had intended to kill herself, not Tarnower. The jury nonetheless found her guilty of murder in the second degree; she was sentenced to fifteen years to life in prison. There, she published several books, taught parenting classes to inmates, and, after two heart attacks, had her sentence commuted in 1992.*

"Vicious, adulterous psychotic" referred to Tryforos. "The boys" were Harris's two sons from a previous marriage. Henri and Suzanne van der Vreken were Tarnower's live-in staff.

Hi:

I will send this by registered mail only because so many of my letters seem not to reach you—or at least they are never acknowledged so I presume they didn't arrive.

I am distraught as I write this—your phone call to tell me you preferred the company of a vicious, adulterous psychotic was topped by a call from the Dean of Students ten minutes later and has kept me awake for almost 36 hours. I had to expel four seniors just two months from graduation and suspend others. What I say will ramble but it will be the truth—and I have to do something besides shriek with pain.

Let me first say that I will be with you on the 19th of April because it is right that I should be. To accuse me of calling Dan to beg for an invitation is all the more invidious since it is indeed what Lynne does all the time. I am told this repeatedly. "She keeps calling and fawning over us. It drives us crazy."

I have and never would do this—you seem to be able to expiate Lynne's sins by dumping them on me. I knew of the honor being bestowed on you before I was ever asked to speak at Columbia on the 18th.

Frankly, I thought you were waiting for Dan's invitation to surprise me—false modesty or something. I called Dan to tell him I wanted to send a contribution to be part of those honoring you and I assured him I would be there.

He said, "Lee and I want you at our table." I thanked him and assured him I would be there—"even if that slut comes—indeed I don't care if she pops naked out of a cake with her tits frosted with chocolate."

Dan laughed and said, "And you should be there and we want you with us."

I haven't played the slave for you. I would never have committed adultery for you—but I have added a dimension to your life and given you pleasure and dignity, as you have me.

As Jackie says, "Hi was always such a marvelous snob. What happened?"

I suppose my check to Dan falls into the "signing of masochistic love" department. Having just, not four weeks before, received a copy of your will with my name vigorously scratched out, and Lynne's name in your handwriting written in three places, leaving her a quarter of a million dollars and her children $25,000 apiece—and the boys and me nothing.

It is the sort of thing I have grown almost accustomed to from Lynn—that you didn't respond to my note when I returned it leaves me wondering if you send it together. It isn't your style—but then Lynn has changed your style. Is it the culmination of 14 years of broken promises, Hi—I hope not—"I want to buy you a whole new wardrobe, darling." "I want to get your teeth fixed at my expense, darling." "My home is your home, darling." "Welcome home, darling." "The ring is yours forever darling. If you leave it with me now, I will leave it to you in my will." "You have of course been well taken care of in my will, darling." "Let me buy an apartment with you in New York, darling."

It didn't matter all that much, really—all I ever asked for was to be with you—and when I left you to know when we would see each other again so there was something in life to look forward to. Now you are taking that away from me too and I am unable to cope—I can hear you saying, "Look, Jean—it's your problem. I don't want to hear about it."

I have watched you grow rich in the years we have been together, and I have watched me go through moments when I was almost destitute.

I have twice borrowed fifty cents from Henri to make two of the payments on the Garden State Parkway during these five years you casually left me on my hands and knees in Philadelphia.

And now—almost ten years later—now that a thieving slut has the run of your home you accuse me of stealing money and books, and calling your friend to beg for an invitation.

The many things your whore does openly and obviously (to your friends and your SERVANTS! Sadly not to you) you now have the cruelty to accuse me of.

My father-in-law left me a library of over 5,000 books. I have given away in the past ten years more books than you own. I have thanked you most sincerely and gratefully for the books you have given me.

Ninety percent of them have been given to a school library and on at least four different occasions I have asked you if you wouldn't like a letter on school stationery that you could use as a tax deduction.

Each time you have airily refused and now, for God's sake, you accuse me of stealing your books. It borders on libel.

Any time you wish to examine my home or the school library you are certainly welcome to do so—a surprise raid might be most convincing for you.

Twice I have taken money from your wallet—each time to pay for sick damage done to my property by your psychotic whore.

I don't have the money to afford a sick playmate—you do. She took a brand new nightgown that I paid $40.00 for and covered it with bright orange stains. You paid to replace it—and since you had already made it clear you simply didn't care about the obscene phone calls she made it was obviously pointless to tell you about the nightgown.

The second thing you paid for (I never replaced it) was a yellow silk dress. I bought it to wear at Lyford Cay several years ago.

Unfortunately, I forgot to pack it because it was new and still in a box in the downstairs closet. When I returned it was still in the box, rolled up, not folded now, and smeared and vile with feces.

I told you once it was something "brown and sticky." It was, quite simply, Herman Tarnower, human shit!

I decided, and rightly so, that this was your expense, not mine. As for stealing from you, the day I put my ring on your dresser my income before taxes was $12,000 per year.

I had two children in private school. They had been on a fairly sizable scholarship until I told the school I wouldn't need it because we were moving to Scarsdale. It was two years before we got it back.

That more than anything else is the reason David went to Penn State instead of the University of Pa. He loathed every minute of it, and there is no question that it changed his life.

That you should feel justified and comfortable suggesting that I steal from you is something I have no adjective to describe.

I desperately needed money all those years. I couldn't have sold that ring. It was tangible proof of your love and it meant more to me than life itself.

That you sold it the summer your adulterous slut finally got her divorce and needed money is a kind of sick, cynical act that left me old and bitter and sick.

Your only comment when you told me you had sold it (and less than two months before you had assured you would get it from the safe so I could wear it again) was "Look, if you're going to make a fuss about it you can't come here anymore. I don't need to have anyone spoil my weekend."

Too bad Somerset Maugham didn't get hold of us before he died. He could have come up with something to top the Magnificent Obsession.

You have never once suggested that you would meet me in Virginia at your expense, and so seeing you has been at my expense—and if you lived in California I would borrow money to come there too if you would let me.

All my conversations are my nickel, not yours—and obviously rightly so because it is I, not you, who needs to hear your voice.

I have indeed grown poor loving you, while a self-serving ignorant slut has grown very rich—and yet you accuse me of stealing from you. How in the name of Christ does that make sense?

I have, and most proudly so—and with an occasional "Right On" from Lee and others ripped up or destroyed anything I saw that your slut had touched and written her cutesie name on—including several books that I gave you and she had the tasteless, unmitigated gall to write in.

I have refrained from throwing away the cheap little book of epigrams lying on your bed one day so I would be absolutely sure to see it with a paper clip on the page about how an old man should have a young wife.

It made me feel like a piece of old discarded garbage—but at least it solved for me what had been a mystery—what had suddenly possessed you to start your tasteless diatribe at dinner parties about how everyman should have a wife half his age and seven years.

Since you never mentioned it to anyone under 65, it made the wives at the table feel about as attractive and wanted as I did.

Tasteless behavior is the only kind Lynn knows—though to her credit she is clever and devious enough to hide it at times. Unfortunately, it seems to be catching.

The things I know, or profess to know about Lynn—except for what I have experienced first hand I have been told by your friends and your servants, mostly the latter—I was interested to hear from Vivian and Arthur's next door neighbor in Florida. I don't remember her name though I'm sure Lynn does.

"I took her to lunch she seemed so pathetic" that you sat at table while I was there and discussed Lynn and her "wonderful family—brother a Ph.D."

I can't imagine going out to dinner with you and telling my dinner partner how grand another lover is.

I told the woman to ask you sometime why if her family is so fine, Lynn decided to sell her kids to the highest bidder and make you and your family the guardian of her children if she should die before they do.

It must go down as a "first" for a splendid family to do.

My phone tells me this—that "mysterious" caller—I hope to God you don't know who it is! Who pays him?

When my clothes were ripped to shreds Suzanne said, "Madame, there is only one person who could have done it. You must tell him."

In my masochistic way I tried to down play it in my note to you, although in all honesty I thought it was so obvious you would know who did it. Instead you ignored it and went happily off to Florida with the perpetrator. Suzanne told me—and I think would say so in court.

1. The clothes were not torn when she went into the closet to find something of Henri's on "Wednesday or Thursday" while we were away.
2. On the Sunday morning before we came home Henri and Suzanne both saw Lynn drive hurriedly up to your house. They were outside and she did not see them. They saw her go in but not out.
3. Lynn knew you were coming home that evening and that she would see you by 8:00 the next morning. What business did she have at your home that morning?
4. When I discovered the clothes destroyed Suzanne was sitting in the dining room at the wooden table right next to the door. I said, "My God—Suzanne come look!" and she was right there.

When I called your slut to talk to her about it and see what she was going to do about it she said "You cut them up yourself and blamed it on me."

That was the first time it occurred to me they had been "cut" not ripped. Only someone with a thoroughly warped mind would decide that a woman with no money would ruin about one-third of her wardrobe for kicks.

Suzanne still believes Lynn did it and I most certainly do too. I think there is enough evidence to prove it in court!

The stealing of my jewelry I can't prove at all—I just know I left some things in the white ash tray on your dresser, as I have for many years. When I thought of it later and called, Lynn answered the phone.

When I called again and asked Suzanne to take them and put them away they were gone. I only hope if she hocked them you got something nice as a "gift"—Maybe I gave you some gold cuff links after all and didn't know it. I don't for one instant think Henri or Suzanne took them.

I had never called Lynn at the office anonymously as you accused me that grim November day in 1977. I had in fact called her at the office before I left and said, since I did not have her number and could not get it I would call her at the office every time I got an anonymous phone call if she did not immediately stop them.

Within two weeks my "mysterious" caller told me her number. I have had it ever since then. Every single time she changes it I get it.

And yet though I was the one being wronged, you refused to let me come see you that month because a lying slut had told you I was calling her. The thought of it had never crossed my mind. Her voice is vomitous to me.

The next month I called her virtually every single night only because of your rotten accusation while she sat simperingly by letting you make it.

Not once did Lynn answer the phone. At one, two, or three in the morning it was her children who answered, very quickly, TV playing.

Where does mumsie spend her nights. That she "totally neglects her children" is something Henri and Suzanne have told me. That you admire her for it is sad.

"Stupid" is certainly not the word for Lynn. In that I was totally wrong. "Dishonest, ignorant and tasteless" but God knows not stupid.

It would have been heartbreaking for me to have to see less and less of you even if it had been a decent woman who took my place.

Going through the hell of the past few years has been bearable only because you were still there and I could be with you whenever I could get away from work, which seemed to be less and less.

To be jeered at, and called "old and pathetic" made me seriously consider borrowing $5,000 just before I left New York and telling a doctor to make me young again—to do anything but make me not feel like discarded trash—I lost my nerve because there was always the chance I'd end up uglier than before.

You have been what you very carefully set out to be, Hi—the most important thing in my life, the most important human being in my life and that will never change.

You keep me in control by threatening me with banishment—an easy threat which you know I couldn't live with and so I stay home alone while you make love to someone who has almost totally destroyed me.

I have been publicly humiliated again and again but not on the 19th of April. It is the apex of your career and I believe I have earned the right to watch it—if only from a dark corner near the kitchen.

If you wish to insist that Lee and Dan invite Lynn, so be it—whatever they may tell you they tell me and others that they dislike being with her.

Dan whispers it to me each time we meet "Why weren't you here? Lee hates it when it's Lynn."

I always thought that taking me out of your will would be the final threat. On that I believed you would be completely honest. I have every intention of dying before you do, but sweet Jesus, darling, I didn't think you would ever be dishonest about that.

The gulf between us seems wide on the phone but the moment I see you it's as though we had been together forever.

You were so absolutely perfect over David's wedding and I will always be grateful.

I wish 14 years of making love to one another and sharing so much happiness had left enough of a mark that you couldn't have casually scratched my name out of a will and written in Lynn's instead.

But for God's sake don't translate that into begging for money. I would far rather be saved the trial of living without you than have the option of living with your money.

Give her all the money she wants, Hi—but give me time with you and the privilege of sharing with you April 19th—There were a lot of ways to have money—I very consciously picked working hard, supporting myself, and being with you.

Please, darling—don't tell me now it was all for nothing.

She has you ever single moment in March—for Christ's sake give me April— T.S. Eliot said it's the cruelest month. Don't let it be, Hi.

I want to spend every minute of it with you on weekends. In all these years you've never spent my birthday with me—There aren't a lot left—it goes so quickly.

I give you my word if you just aren't cruel I won't make you wretched. I never did until you were cruel—and then I just wasn't ready for it.

## 1984: DECEMBER 27
## ABORTION CLINIC BOMBER TO THE EDITOR OF THE
## PENSACOLA NEWS

*The Supreme Court recognized the constitutional right to abortion in 1973, and the decision roused a protest movement that its followers called pro-life and its opponents called anti-abortion. Citing their belief that the procedure was a form of murder, some extremists began to use violence as a deterrent. The National Abortion Federation would record 2,540 acts of violence against abortion providers between 1977 and 2000. The following letter was printed in the* Pensacola News *two days after Christmas, when pipe bombs exploded at a Pensacola, Florida, abortion clinic and at the offices of two doctors known to perform the procedure.*

Dear Editor:

So you want to know who bombed the 3 abortion clinics, huh?

I did.

Let me tell you why.

When I was stationed here in the waves, before I got married, I got pregnant. Everyone had told me that a fetus was just a little shapeless blob anyway, so I got an abortion. I was almost 6 months pregnant by then.

Later, after it was too late, a friend gave me some literature one day showing how the baby developed at different stages. I never realized that at that stage, a fetus is so much a baby that some of them have been born at that point and LIVED!

Well, you cannot imagine what that did to me, knowing that I had not just "had an unwanted intra-uterine growth "removed," but had KILLED MY BABY! It just about ruined my life. Even today, several years later, I lay awake at nights sometimes crying about it.

So maybe you can understand my reason for doing what I did.

It was not because of religious fanaticism . . . I don't even go to church.

It was because I have seen for myself what the psychological effects of an abortion can do to a woman, and I didn't want what happened to me to happen to anyone else.

I did not act alone. And if these clinics reopen, we will see that they are closed again.

Some will say that it is wrong to use violent means to put an end to the killing. Well, we used a lot of violence in World War II to stop the killing of the Jews.

It is a well-established principal of justice that force, even deadly force, is justified in order to save innocent lives if necessary. So, I do not feel that I have done anything wrong.

We will stop the slaughter of the innocents. We WILL put an end to the murder of babies. And we WILL prevent any more lives from being ruined.

Signed,<br>A Woman Who Knew What She Was Doing

# EXCHANGE

## 1985–1986

## LYNNE SIPIORA AND BARBARA SHULGOLD

*After decades of research, the first "test-tube baby"—conceived outside a woman's body—had been born in 1978. Seven years later, fertility enhancement techniques had become relatively common, and Resolve, a national organization for infertile people, was reporting in its newsletter on developments in the field. Lynne Sipiora was just embarking on a quest for fertility when she read a letter there from Barbara Shulgold, who had been trying unsuccessfully to become pregnant with the help of the fertility drug Pergonal. The women soon began a correspondence, finding a bond in the emotional and technical aspects of their common goal.*

Eventually they had four children between them, three adopted and one the product of Sipiora's successful in vitro fertilization. They wrote to each other often and spoke on the phone, but despite the plan to meet mentioned in Shulgold's letter, many years would pass before they actually did.

### LYNNE SIPIORA TO BARBARA SHULGOLD

May 5, 1985

Barbara,

Wonderful to receive your second letter—it arrived on the same day that I had a lengthy consult with my infertility specialist, so I suppose fate is <u>sometimes</u> on my side. I have not yet started Pergonal and probably will not for at least three more cycles. First I have to get rid of an infection I recently contracted, and then my doctor is insisting upon a <u>second</u> laparoscopy. She has an excellent reputation but is rather conservative in her approach. Though I'm anxious to get started, I'm also kind of relieved to be able to put it off for a while. Frankly, at this point I have no idea how I'll manage Pergonal. As you now, the Pergonal treatment requires going to the doctor for endless blood tests and ultrasounds during the first seven to twelve days of each menstrual cycle. My job requires me to travel, and my daily schedule is very unpredictable. I explained all of this to my doctor, and she said, "It's your choice." And so, once again I find myself angry! My career has been my salvation through all of this, and yet now I'm told rather plainly to choose between maintaining my career or risking it for a long shot on a baby. Actually there is no choice—I will opt for the latter and somehow or another work out the schedule—but <u>damn</u> it's just not fair!

Funny, but I knew you'd understand when I attempted to define the other me. I think I did it more for myself because I have to keep remembering that there <u>is</u> another me! Infertility <u>is</u> all consuming!

Re: adoption. Do you have any idea when you may get a baby? I am not opposed to the idea at all—but have been scared by a variety of stories on the unavailability of babies. Is this true? Are you going through an agency? How long have you been told you must wait? As usual, I have so many questions . . .

Know that I'll be thinking of you as your neighbor's baby arrives on the scene. I face a similar situation. My husband has a nine-year-old daughter from a previous marriage. She is a sweet kid and we get along well—but she is <u>not</u> mine. Ann is with us every other weekend, and sometimes just looking at her is difficult. I find myself consumed with jealousy that my husband was able to have a child with another woman, but not with me! From time to time she asks very normal questions about when she was born, and when Ken tells the story of the trip to the hospital, etc., I really cannot bear it! I had not intended to get into yet <u>another</u> of my problems, but somehow I think you'll understand.

You're right—the statistics on Pergonal are encouraging, but like you, I am cautious. Ovulation <u>and</u> cervical mucus are a problem for me—the ultimate double whammy! While I await Pergonal, I continue to take 100 milligrams of Clomid a day for five days per month, and I continue to hope. Despite many, many disappointments, I continue to feel symptoms of pregnancy—every month—right up to the day my period arrives. Crazy, I know.

I've tried to take your advice about being good to myself and it does help. I also talk to no one (except Ken) about my problem—I think that helps me keep it in perspective. Also, I could not stand the monthly requests for progress reports. I did speak to my mother once, who only said, "Oh well you're a career woman, not the maternal type anyway." Needless to say, we've not discussed it again. I think that's why writing to you has become very important—not only do I feel free to say exactly what I feel but, wonder upon wonder, you know what I'm talking about. Yes, Barbara, there just are not many people who can intelligently talk cervical mucus and the luteal phase—pity to be so uninformed! The last line of your recent letter confirmed what I've always believed—I do <u>deserve</u> a baby. I know you do too. I will anxiously await all the details of your soon-to-arrive "preciousness," because I feel confident that when the baby is in your arms you'll be able to put all of this aside. I hope I, too, have such a happy ending. I also hope I end up half as well adjusted as you are!

Keep in touch. My thoughts are with you.

Lynne

P.S. I <u>hate</u> Mother's Day!

### BARBARA SHULGOLD TO LYNNE SIPIORA

February 10, 1986

Dear Lynne,

It's taken two tall glasses of wine in the middle of the afternoon to help me get up the courage to write this to you. I came extremely close to calling you the other night, but figured you didn't need to hear my voice for the first time in a state of wild hysteria. Anyhow, you are the only person who is going to get this—all of this—in writing. If you feel the need, now is a good time for a glass of wine.

By now you have received our mourning note, which has apparently crossed with a note you sent me. I have not opened it and will not until we have a baby. There is just so much pain a body can take, and warm congratulations from you, after all we have been through together, would be too much.

Our precious baby was with us for five days before the birth-mother changed her mind. Five days was just long enough for BOTH of us to realize that a new life is indeed as breathtakingly, achingly wonderful as we had dreamed. We fell in love, could not keep our eyes or hands off her, and even loved the exhaustion of the 3:00 A.M. feedings. She was an easy baby, which of course makes our pain harder to bear. She would quiet instantly when we held her, and we held and cuddled and loved her all the time. We took rolls of pictures (I am afraid I sent you one with the birth announcement). We called everyone and told everyone, and I took a child-rearing leave, and my class sent me congratulations—tinged with sadness, as they did not know I was leaving—and the faculty (also kept totally in the dark) called endlessly with congratulations and—well, you get the picture. The most beautiful week of our lives was followed by the worst. Everyone has been extraordinarily wonderful, as they always are when someone dies (and this is as close to a death as I can imagine). The women in my adoption group have been super: fixing us meals, holding our hands, notifying all our friends, offering country homes for a getaway—you name it. They were here when the baby was taken away, and they held me and cried with us. I am so grateful. TIME OUT FOR A GODDAM KLEENEX.

So, they say, this happens about 5 to 10 percent of the time, particularly when the mother has no family support system (Nancy had tons), when she doesn't bond with the adoptive parents (we spent hours and hours and hours with her), when she is young (Nancy is thirty), or when she has no children of her own (she has a son). Big deal statistics. I don't think she was conning us; I think she was just one of those people who are not introspective and do not genuinely know their own minds until it is too late. I feel betrayed, raped, empty, and enraged.

Part of me worries about you and Melissa, a woman in my school district who keeps approaching and avoiding the idea of adoption, saying, "I'll believe it works when I see you holding your baby." I fear this has set her back a few steps.

And YOU: I know how strange and risky and expensive everything I have been writing to you about these many months has sounded. I know how badly you want to give birth to your own baby, but think about adoption "just in case." Hope it makes a hell of a lot of difference to you to know that here, in the midst of this hellish pain, albeit numbed a bit by alcohol, I am far more certain than ever that I will NEVER NEVER give up my search for a baby. This pain is worth it: I will be a mother. So will you.

As to Rich: He underwent the most amazing transformation. At first he was so scared to care for her that he almost threw up. Then the nurse came to give us parenting lessons, told us we were doing just fine and were the kind of people who would make great parents, showed us a few tricks, and left. And from then on there was no stopping him. HE became the expert on diapering techniques, burping, poop analysis—you name it. I took dozens of photos (gone now) of him kissing and cuddling her and just touching her cheek. SHIT, he really went for her hook, line, and sinker.

The night they took her, I watched him cry for the first time in the nine years I have known him. And he wept and wept and wept. I have awakened in the middle of the night to hear him crying. The difference is now he says, "Now I understand what you have been fighting for all these years. I will not rest until we have another baby, and it must be a newborn: they are nature's greatest creation." Well, I coulda told him. But, better late than never.

So, what now? Well, as the book title goes: first you cry. I am crying a lot, sleeping a lot, watching a lot of TV, and having a little too much wine. Also, ignoring the telephone and letting the machine take the condolence messages. Can't take it. I am retreating for a week, going back to my therapist who got me through the infertility crisis (I went to see her the morning after, and she cried more than I did; I was the one screaming—really screaming—in rage). I don't think I will be able to go back and face the class and the hundreds of kids at my school who know me and will ask what happened to my baby and the faculty . . . so, I am not going back. It may be a mistake, but I am going to look for temporary work away from children: working in a little store, or as a secretary or something. I need a break.

Needless to add, this is probably the worst time financially for me not to be working. The adoption cost us $3,500, and we just don't have an equivalent sum to start again. Our wonderful lawyer is beginning a campaign to try to get the money back, but since Nancy doesn't really have money or a job, I am hoping a guilt trip or two on her mother (a college professor, for God's sake) will get her to reimburse us. I will stop at nothing to get the money back, including taking her to court, although I am as yet unsure if the agreement was legally binding. But my rage is real, and I have no intention of just giving up. THAT is impossible.

Ellen Roseman, upon whom all our hopes are now placed, assures us we are at the top of her list. I would not be surprised if we have a baby in three months. She is marvelous. She has had all sorts of former clients who have gone through the same heartbreak call us. All but one have babies now and were so comforting. Sometimes I think I would be a basket case were it not for the Resolve/adoption group/Ellen Roseman networks.

You will be here in early March, yes? Spending time with you in person has now become an important future event for me. I guess, friend, there will be time for the two of us to talk uninterrupted by a baby's squalls, dammit. I do look forward to it, believe me.

My therapist says she admires me for enduring what I have endured, says that she sees me as a strong woman and that I will survive. You know, even now I can see that she is right. But, dammit, I would like to be weak for a while, and I would like to be a mother.

I know, I feel, how you hurt for me, Lynne. And it is a comfort.

Love,

Barbara

## 1985: SPRING
## PEGGY NOONAN TO STRASBOURG SPEECH COMMITTEE

*Peggy Noonan (1950–) had been a radio news writer and TV producer for about a decade when she was hired in 1984 as a speechwriter and special assistant to Ronald Reagan. Responsible for many of his memorable speeches, Noonan was as committed to conservative politics as she was to graceful metaphor. In the spring of 1985, Reagan was planning a European trip to coincide with the annual economic summit conference and the fortieth anniversary of V-E Day; his big speech would be delivered at the European parliament in Strasbourg. Noonan wrote a first draft and then, in response to various worries, quibbles, edits, and policy disagreements from the National Security Council and the State Department, several more. This is the memo she wrote to accompany yet another draft.*

SDI, the Strategic Defensive Initiative, was a hallmark of Reagan's foreign policy. "The C word" referred to "Communist," which Noonan had been criticized for using too often in previous drafts. Ted Sorenson had been John F. Kennedy's speechwriter.

MEMORANDUM FOR STRASBOURG SPEECH COMMITTEE

FROM: NOONAN, WRITER OF THE SPEECH

SUBJECT: Strasbourg Address

Gentlemen, this is the latest and as you read it I believe you should keep this in mind:

1) State/NSC directives on the economic section have been included. State/NSC directives on S.D.I. have been included. State/NSC directives on treaty compliance, on the suffering of a divided Europe, on Nicaragua, on the new democratic forum, and on the people of the communist countries have been included. In addition, we no longer use the "F" phrase; we no longer say Free Enterprise. We have cut down on use of the "C" word also.

2) [Your] memorandum of 11:00 a.m. this date contends that we should not call the communist system and the Soviet Union the most destabilizing force in the world. This was argued out back and forth at the 4:30 meeting Friday, and it was decided that we WOULD so characterize the Soviet Union provided we also include a section on the human suffering caused by the division of Europe. This section has been included. . . .

3) I ask you all to remember that this is a speech that attempts to communicate a sense of history, a sense of the flow of time. Just as it is appropriate that the President begin by remembering the happiness of VE Day, the horror of Europe after the war, and the triumph that followed, it is appropriate that the President address the realities of TODAY—Europessimism, etc. This is bold—it is the kind of thing great leaders are not afraid to do. And, as most of you have noted, Europessimism is a subject among Europeans themselves.

We cannot bolster Europe and inspire her at the end of the speech if we do not paint her predicament somewhere within. My position here is dictated not only by a concern for the content of the speech but also a concern for what is known, in the field of drama, as "the unities." Drama may seem to you an odd thing to mention here, but a speech is a form of theatre.

Similarly, it is important that we be frank regarding the Soviet Union. You will note there are no empires that happen to be evil in this speech, but there is, to an extent, a clearness and candor about who and what the Soviets are. Some of Young Europe's blues is traceable to a confusion, as we note in the speech, about what threatens us and what we can do about it. The speech attempts to state who threatens us and what, together, we can do about it. I believe this is necessary to the political logic of the speech.

4) [As for] the section on a reunited Europe . . . I do not think it in the interests of the President that you dull this passage and render it insipid. I am sure this is not your intention but it will likely be the result of your endeavors, because that's what happens to rhetoric when committees vote on it.

If Ted Sorensen had had to deal with your Committee in the writing of the 1961 Berlin speech, he would have submitted for your consideration the phrase "Ich bin ein Berliner." [It] would have been edited out by the Committee and replaced with "We in the United States feel our bilateral relations with West Germany reflect a unity that allows us to declare at this time that further concessions to the Soviet Union are inappropriate."

You would not have been serving your President well with this edit. But you would have made it because a) "Ich bin . . ." was an inherently dramatic statement, and dramatic personal declarations serve as red flags to Committees (sorry I said "red," that must be the 11th communist reference in this memo); b) The Official Worrier on your Committee would have pointed out, "A statement that strong really paints us in a corner when it comes to negotiations down the road. The press'll pick up on it and use it against us in the trade talks"; and c) the Literal Mind on your Committee would have pointed out, "The President isn't from Berlin and everyone knows it. He's from Massachusetts." . . .

8) The speech has already been weakened somewhat in various ways and to varying degrees. But it still has enough spring, I think, to make an impression. If you make serious changes now I think you will find, in time, that you have produced an address that does indeed make history but perhaps not the kind of history you intend. It will be the famous Strasbourg Hammock Speech of 1985. The speech that had a nice strong tree holding it up at one end, at the beginning, and a nice strong tree holding it up at the other end, at the coda, and in the middle there was this nice soft section where we all fell asleep.

Thank you all, and God bless you, and your children, and your children's children.

## 1986: APRIL 21
## MARGARETTE GOOS TO R. J. REYNOLDS TOBACCO

*The first warning labels had appeared on cigarette packages in 1965. In 1971, broadcast ads for cigarettes were banned. And throughout the early and middle 1980s, Surgeon General C. Everett Koop warned the public about the harms of smoking and secondhand smoke. By 1986, the movement to make smoking difficult for smokers—through restrictions in public places and higher taxes on cigarettes—*

*had begun to take off. Margarette Tucker Goos (1920–) was living in Liberal, Kansas, when, like millions of other Americans, she received a direct-mail letter from R. J. Reynolds Tobacco. The letter urged her to protest the federal government's proposed tax increases on cigarettes and to send enclosed, prestamped cards to key senators in Washington. No doubt there were some consumers who did just that, but Goos happened to be the wife of a smoker who had emphysema, congestive heart failure, and no plans to quit.*

We crossed out your message & asked for even higher tax. NO MORE LETTERS FROM YOU TO US.

Rather than send these cards off I would rather *sue* you. My darling husband Warren has emphysema, congestive heart failure, and chronic bronchitis <u>all</u> from the filthy weed you are pushing. Yes he still smokes "the non-habit-forming cigarettes." And you have the gall to ask us to endorse you! No way. Not even Warren the smoker is against taxing of poison. Look up how much nicotine is a fatal dosage. Warren also suffers from impaired circulation all thanks to you tobacco people. We have a friend who lost her 24 year old son from "Harmless smokeless tobacco." Thanks for our sorrow.

Remember whether you believe in God or not—you will stand before him one day and have a lot of deaths on your hands to try to justify. God Pity you.

## 1986: JULY 13
## RACHEL SILVERMAN TO JANE AND IRA SILVERMAN

---

*Since the beginning of the twentieth century, when the idea of summer camp first took hold, roughly 10 percent of all American children have attended one. Rachel Silverman (1974–), at the age of twelve, wrote this fairly classic letter of complaint from her camp in Maine to her parents, Jane (1945–) and Ira (1945–1991).*

Dearest mater et pater,
  Hola!; Howdy!; Hi!
  The weather at camp has been awful—Freezing air and water (which we have to swim a ¼ mile "triangle" in), and nonstop rain. Mr. Sunshine is sleeping on the job. Please note—this is Treetops stationary. Please send more stationary, a sleeping bag, my black sweatshirt (!) and the addresses.
  A square dance was yesterday and it was fun. The 2nd years (I'm one) hosted it, and our theme was tropical fever. We're probably having 3 more.
  Camp has gotten better, but next week (Wednesday) our tent has to go on a

camp-out with 4 NERDS. I dread it, mainly because they want to play* "truth or dare" with kissing bleccch. I think (actually I'm sure) that I'll refuse.

Yesterday we got our showers, which we haven't had in 8 days, and our laundry (they lost my sweatshirts). Also, my ears are infected and I have to take medication. They hurt a lot.

Thanks a lot for sending me pictures, and the pin. I wish that I was there to enjoy the 4th of july with you. We did absolutely nothing for the 4th of July.

> Love,
> Rachel

P.S. WRITE BACK
P.P.S. The weather is making me in a pathetic mood. Excuse this letter
P.P.P.S. Our goats just had kids.
P.P.P.P.S. MOM, please catch me up on the comics. You still haven't and I'm dying to know.
*It seems as if all the kids are so much more mature than I am. They are very nice but they kiss, shave, wear make-up, etc. I REALLY miss my friends, please send addresses.

## 1986: NOVEMBER 14
## JOAN GANZ COONEY TO TIMOTHY COONEY

*Joan Ganz Cooney (see page 657) was head of the Children's Television Workshop (now the Sesame Workshop) and already one of the nation's most prominent business-women when she wrote this letter to her ex-husband, Timothy Cooney (1930–1999). Cooney was a onetime civil defense chief for New York mayor John Lindsay. In 1985, he had published a book called* Telling Right from Wrong, *but he submitted it to publishers with a Harvard professor's letter of endorsement that was later discovered to have been forged.*

> November 14, 1986

Dear Tim:

I am drawing up a new separation agreement to reflect the following arrangement, beginning December 1st:

Every month—on the 1st and 15th—I will send you a check for $900.00.

I will continue to pay, in addition, your rent, gas and electricity bill, cable TV, medical and dental bills, medical insurance, prescription drugs and your Federal, State and City taxes.

The total package for me comes to around $45,000 or more in a bad medical year.

If $200 a month more would put you in heaven, as you said, then I suggest you cut your phone bill and Block's Drugstore by $100 each or alternatively, write some articles for The Nation and other magazines, or freelance for publishing companies writing dust jacket copy or something. Surely a writer with your talents could make $2,400 per year if he wished to.

The $1,800 per month includes a basic $50 for your phone bill which you will now pay direct, and Block Drugstore which you will also pay direct. Send me a copy of the bill if it contains prescription drugs and I will reimburse you.

If something happens to me, you will not have as much income as you now have. Lee Schoenberg and David Britt of CTW are the trustees of my estate and you would have to talk to them about the amount of income you have from a trust that would be set up.

At 65, you can begin collecting social security and medicare which will help some.

I really don't want further involvement in your spending and charging problems.

This whole thing is bizarre and excessive and if I were you, I would not push me any further.

> Best regards,
> Joan

## 1986: NOVEMBER 22
## SUSAN FISHMAN ORLINS TO HER PARENTS

---

*In 1979, China introduced a "one-child policy" to control the growth of its population. The result was a noticeable decrease in births, but also an increase in the number of abandoned baby girls. By 1994, the Immigration and Naturalization Service would report the adoption of more than four thousand Chinese babies by U.S. citizens, but in the 1980s it was still an extremely rare practice. As far as she knows, Susan Fishman Orlins (1945–) and her then husband, Steve, were only the third Caucasian couple to adopt a Chinese baby. But to Orlins, who had lived in China between 1979 and 1981 because Steve had business there, an instinctive kinship with its people and its culture made adoption seem perfectly natural. In the following letter, she described for her parents and her in-laws the early days of life with daughter Sabrina, while they were still in Beijing.*

Eliza ("Lizie") was the couple's older daughter. Adoption had become a consideration when Susan was told that another pregnancy might not be viable for her. As it turned out, she would give birth to her youngest daughter, Emily, sixteen months later.

Sat Nov 22, 1986

Dear Moms and Dads,

I'd like to write one of my marathon letters, but between feeding Sabrina, playing with Lizie, napping, and arranging the baby's documents; there is time for little else. I must say that adopting puts very little physical strain on the mom compared to giving birth. That may be due, in part, to the fact that I have two nannies just about full time. The one who is 45 calls the one who is 50 "Lao Tai Tai," meaning the Old Lady.

Sabrina is the model baby. She eats when she's supposed to, sleeps when she's supposed to and seems to enjoy being with us on the floor when we play games with Eliza. She's a pleasure and Lizie wants to include her in everything; although every now and then she gives the baby a good jab. So far I've taken the girls out twice—once to the park with Sabrina in her stroller and once on a walk near the hotel with the Snugli which drew stares from every passerby. These were very big events for us. So far, it seems as though we are still a family of three since Steve has had to work almost around the clock. His business should lighten up at Thanksgiving time. Some of the joint venture hotels are offering turkey dinners, so I'm sure we'll try to go in the hope of having a satisfying meal.

Wednesday night we arrived, and after dropping our bags at the hotel went to meet our darling new baby. It was around midnight and the doctor led us through the hospital's dark empty halls to the nursery. She was not as happy to see the three of us as we were to see her. She was wrapped tight as a drum and wailed when I took her picture with a flash.

The following afternoon, I simply went to the hospital and picked her up. Nothing to sign, they just handed her over. The head nurse permitted me to hire one of her staff for 2½ days for about $2.50 a day. I can't say she was worth much more. But I did learn some of the Chinese approach to caring for newborns. I was instructed to take the baby's temperature everyday. She should drink water midway between feedings. For a month, she should not go anywhere, and people should not come to see her.

So there we were; three in help, the four of us and twenty-some unpacked bags in a two-room suite. We stayed that way for a week until we moved to larger quarters where we are now quite comfortable. I have spent much of my free time working on Sabrina's adoption papers and visa. I received the adoption certificate on Friday—it was effective exactly six weeks after we arrived in early October and I began my effort to adopt a Chinese baby. The Chinese passport application went smoothly other than trying to get passport photos taken of a 2-week old sleeping baby where you want her eyes open and she shouldn't be crying. We should have the passport within a week. That leaves only the U.S. visa to contend with—the biggest obstacle. I have received verbal agreement that my Chinese documents are acceptable and we are only awaiting word from the immigration service in N.Y. I'm told that after 60 days, we can proceed without hearing from N.Y. if so, we'll return sometime around mid-January. I'm hoping for mid-December, however, although I'm reluctant to give up the leisurely life here. The good news on the visa front is that Sabrina will not have to make the round trip to Canton as we had previously thought. Instead, Steve can go as her representative.

Eliza continues to live the life of Eloise, wreaking havoc in the Peking Hotel. Everyday she visits her dad's office where no fewer than ten Chinese are ready to drop everything and play with her. A couple of times she has gone to a play-group where one Malaysian woman has 15 children running around her living room. Either a nanny or I will stay the whole time because she wants us to, and I think it's a good idea to improve the adult child ratio. Every night we go to a different restaurant for a different bad meal. Sometimes we shop at the outdoor free market where clothing made for export is sold at a small fraction of the foreign retail price. Eliza has a few playmates her age which is nice, but she misses her friends at home. One big event of the day is the 6:00 cartoon on TV

The good thing about not sleeping much for our 12 days in N.Y. is that I had no jet lag when we returned here. Eliza says Sabrina is more fun than her doll, Folly, but not as much fun as a cat because a cat licks your toes.

Happy Thanksgiving. Ours certainly is!

Love,
Susan

## 1987: AUGUST 2
## JOAN QUIGLEY TO RONALD REAGAN

---

*Astrologer Joan Quigley met Nancy Reagan in the 1970s after an appearance on* The Merv Griffin Show. *Sometime after the March 30, 1981, assassination attempt on Ronald Reagan, the first lady apparently began to consult Quigley on a regular basis. In time, Quigley offered advice on, among other things, the timing of the president's speeches, announcements, and trips. Though the eventual disclosure*

*of this arrangement gave rise to scandal—as well as to exaggeration on all sides—
the first lady would concede: "While I was never certain that Joan's astrological advice was helping to protect Ronnie, the fact is that nothing like March 30 ever
happened again."*

SDI, the Strategic Defense Initiative, was popularly known as "Star Wars."

Dear Ronnie,

With the exception of Washington, America's most outstanding presidents
have been Aquarians. Lincoln, Roosevelt and Reagan. They occupy a very special place in their people's hearts but they have had their problems as well. It is
said, "A great man, great problems."

It is also said that the only lasting evil a bad experience can do to anyone is to
warp their judgment. This has not happened to you. You have borne up nobly
during a period when your astrological transits could be likened to the adverse
weather conditions that threaten to destroy a farmer's carefully planted crops.
But you, the farmer unaltered by adversity, will come through your trials intact,
and mindful of the rich harvests of past years, will surpass past successes. . . .

You have remained firm and balanced as your personal good aspects indicate
and have gone about your business with a smile and now, having passed the test
by so doing, you will emerge triumphant.

Already you have in place three brilliant strategies: the missiles in Europe,
the development of SDI and the strong military.

It is my conviction that of the American presidents, Lincoln and Reagan will
go down in world history as the very greatest. Both have Jupiter rulers. Lincoln's
in Pisces, gave him the problem of slavery. Your ruler in Scorpio gave you the
problem of war. And as Lincoln abolished slavery, you, Ronald Reagan, will
bring peace to the world. Your vision will be vindicated, your role in history unparalleled.

As your astrologer, your steadfastness and courage, your true spiritual strength
did not surprise me. They are only what I expected.

With admiration,

Joan

## 1988: MARCH 5
## ANGELA GOMEZ TO MARIANA GARCIA CHAVEZ

*During the 1980s, immigration reached its highest peak, with some ten million
legal and illegal immigrants entering the United States. By far the largest group*

*came from Mexico, and nearly half settled in nearby California. Though life was better there for many than in their native land, Mexican Americans still faced daunting challenges: getting an education, finding a decent job, and, for those in the country illegally, evading the ever present immigration agents, or migras. To Angela Gomez and countless immigrants from other lands, learning English was a hoped-for ticket to a better life.*

This letter was translated from the Spanish.

March 5, 1988

Hello Mariana!

Receive this letter, wishing that it finds you very well. A little late, you know I'm a little lazy about writing, but here it is, one of the first letters I write.

Right now I'm studying English, it's a little hard to find work, but at least I'm not wasting time. I go to a school for adults where it's just about pure Chinese, Japanese and Iranians, almost pure Asian, in one of the groups I go to I'm the only Mexican woman, two other Mexicans go besides me, and like some 50 Chinese, so imagine, me there in the middle of a fuckload of Chinese. I'm learning quickly, I go every day and I take six hours a day. Aside from this I go to another school 3 days a week for just 2 hours a day. In this other school I have a black teacher who is really good people. So in a little while I'm going to be more or less speaking English, in the long run it's going to be useful to me somehow. Fresno, it's beautiful, it's a big city and has very few inhabitants, it's a very clean city, it has very beautiful parks (I was thinking of just writing a little . . .)

Mariana, tell me how the girls are (Alma, Georgina, Cristy), as for Alma, how it's gone for her, how are things with her baby, I think she's had it by this time.

How's it been going for you at school? What have you done? Haven't you seen Marco there? I'd really like to see that idiot. Listen, what's the wave with Leobardo? How's it been going for you with him? And Chema?

Mariana, what have you found out about the hassle over Elia's handicap, what happened? Tell me how it's been going for Georgina at school, and for Cristina?

There's a community radio station here in Fresno that's called <u>Radio Bilingue</u>, they give some courses for volunteers, they train you as an announcer, after the courses they give an exam and if you pass it they give you an announcer's credentials, all you have to do is program one day a week as a volunteer, you can program whatever you want (Canto Nuevo, etc.) I think I'm going to take these classes.

At the moment it's really boring here because it gets dark really early, and it's really dangerous to wander the streets, there are tons of crazies, a mountain of robberies, murders, rapes, and everything you can imagine, it's a really hostile environment, and more so for latinos.

About 22 days ago, in a city near here called Madera, an agent from <u>la migra</u> killed a 17 year-old boy, the agent came around asking for his papers, so the boy tried to run away, but the <u>migra</u> agent (almost 2 meters tall) grabbed him by the shirt and smashed him to the ground (the boy, Mexican, was very short and thin); the agent, even seeing the boy was bleeding, wasn't so good as to call an ambulance, but took him to jail instead, until later when they could see he was really hurt they took him to the hospital, but it was already too late, because a few hours later he died.

You hear about a mountain of abuses by the <u>migra</u> against latinos all the time.

The <u>Radio Bilingue</u> people are really aggressive in questions of defending the rights of immigrants, in this case of the death of the boy they held a vigil outside the offices of the <u>migra</u>, there was a mountain of undocumented people in the group that did the vigil, and so imagine, with the risk that they'd be caught.

Mariana, write me soon, I'm always looking in the mailbox to see if there's a letter for me.

Tell Georgina, Alma, Cristy to write me, give them my address. It's a pleasure to receive news from there. Give them a hug on my behalf.

Greet me to those who remember me. Well, Mariana, I leave you now because I'm writing in the air.

Write.

I love you,<br>Angelita

# EXCHANGE

### 1990: OCTOBER
### SHAWN CRIBARI AND WENDY CROWTHER

*In 1976, Wendy Crowther (1954–) graduated from Marymount College in Tarry-town, New York, without having told any of her friends that she was gay. She wasn't yet sure of it herself, but she was sure that her friends would reject her if she said she thought she might be. Fourteen years later, she happened to be speaking on the phone one night with her college friend Shawn Kennedy Cribari (1954–) when, without exactly planning to, she broke the news. It was Wendy's first "coming out"*

*experience with an old friend, and, as this letter makes clear, Shawn was more re-*
*lieved than surprised.*

### SHAWN CRIBARI TO WENDY CROWTHER

October 19, 1990

Dear Wendy,

I want to reassure you that I still treasure you as a friend and that I appreciate your honesty.

Last night, I found myself thinking about you, and tears came to my eyes. "Why?" I thought. I'm not sad. I realized they were tears of happiness.

Happiness that you confided in me—because I've always sensed you were holding something back. And happiness that you've experienced the joy of loving.

I remembered a conversation we had a <u>long</u> time ago. It was shortly before or after Arnold & I got married, so it was around 12 years ago. You said you couldn't imagine caring for someone so much that you could make the kind of commitment involved in marriage (I think you said "someone." You might have said "a guy.") I couldn't understand it—Wendy's not a cold and selfish person, I thought. I felt so sad for you.

Of course, now I understand what you were saying. You might not have understood what you were saying at the time—you may have still been thinking of "male-female" relationships as the only option. That's how I interpreted it at the time, of course.

Well, as I said on the phone, I'm glad to know you're not living a one-dimensional existence—that you can care for another person very deeply.

So—I hope I can get to meet your significant other soon. If she's special to you she must be a terrific person.

Love,
Shawn

### WENDY CROWTHER TO SHAWN CRIBARI

October 25, 1990

Dear Shawn,

Talk about tears coming to eyes—your note brought tears to mine. "Coming out" is never easy, no matter how many times I do it and no matter how confident I feel. Its difficult, not because I'm ashamed, embarrassed, ambivalent, or guilty—far from it. What's hard, at least for me, is the millisecond of silence that follows the announcement. During that silent moment, I empathize with the listener who I know must desperately be trying to balance intellect, morality, loyalty and emotion. It took me years to come out to myself and yet the listener has only that tiny moment in which to process a reaction and come out to me. I've always felt bad about that inequity.

Your note was so meaningful to me because it reassured me that your reaction following that "silent moment" was not simply polite but heartfelt. That sort of affirmation is something we are so often denied and, when it comes, the warm, bonded feeling it provides is precious. You are a dear friend, Shawn, I know that now more than ever. Your acceptance and support mean so very much to me.

You have such a wonderful memory. I'd forgotten that I'd expressed my confusion about marriage to you although now I remember our conversation well. At the age of 24 I was still trying to convince myself that I simply hadn't met the right man. What I was failing to recognize at the time (and two years hence) was that the depth of emotion that enables one to want to share a lifetime with another human being was something I wasn't experiencing in my relationships with men. Yet, I felt a warmth, genuineness, commitment, level of communication and an emotional bond for/to/with my women friends—something I denied out of fear for far too long. The pain and depression I began to feel in thinking that I was some sort of emotional eunuch drove me at last to do some serious soul-searching. I still remember the day I finally said to myself, "Wendy, you are a good person, allow yourself to feel, open yourself up to the beauty and fulfillment that your emotions can bring you, share yourself, allow yourself to be shared, love yourself, let go of your fears, let it be." Years of anguish came down to a moment of enlightenment that I have rejoiced ever since. So you see, twelve years ago, you recognized that something was at odds within me. I wish I had had your insight back then.

I feel so lucky to have family and friends who can see beyond the labels and stereotypes. Each time I've broken the news to someone, I've always prepared myself for the rejection that might follow (the rejection can be very subtle). At the very least, I hope for a "so what" or "no big deal" reaction which expresses a tolerance but perhaps not a full acceptance. Beyond tolerance and acceptance is what you offered in your note; your happiness. As happy as I am with my life, I've learned not to expect others to feel happy for me. Your sentiments were so positive and welcoming—I simply can't express how much that means to me.

It's funny, as we began our conversation last week, I had no idea that I was going to reveal myself to you. In fact, it was only at the last minute that I decided to take the risk. It felt right, somehow,. I'm so glad now that you were my first Marymounter to know. And, should the moment feel right for you as you chat with Kathy or others, I have no doubts that you'll pass on the story in a sensitive, positive way. Oh, and thanks for asking for my permission to do so. The potential for misrepresentation and gossip is great. Keeping a confidence is a difficult burden for anyone. I know this well because, for the most part, my life is kept a secret. Telling someone else relieves some of the pressure and helps to sort out and confirm your own feelings. So, it's o.k. with me, I know you'll do it well.

Lastly, I don't mind talking about my life. Its not a topic from which you or anyone should feel compelled to steer clear for fear that I'll think you are too curious or intrusive. Obviously, I love my life like most everyone else. To be able to have conversations without my mental editor constantly checking my pronouns or slashing out whole paragraphs is a tremendous freedom. Someday maybe I'll be able to come to one of our reunion parties and be "all me" to everyone. Its a nice thought.

Thank you, Shawn, for caring enough to write. I'm very lucky to have you as a friend.

## 1991: JANUARY 22
## SANDY MITTEN TO ETHEL MAE CAMPS

---

*On August 2, 1990, Iraqi president Saddam Hussein dispatched his army to invade Kuwait, and the United Nations Security Council promptly imposed a worldwide trade embargo on Iraq. Five months later, in keeping with the UN's deadline for Iraqi withdrawal, a multination coalition led by George H. W. Bush launched Operation Desert Storm. More than forty thousand U.S. women were deployed in the war (along with roughly half a million men), including forty-nine-year-old Sandy Mitten (1941–), who was already a grandmother when she wrote this letter home to her aunt.*

The United States would drive the Iraqis out of Kuwait after a month of air strikes and only four days of ground combat, but it would be another twelve years before Saddam Hussein was removed from power, during the presidency of a second Bush. Scuds were ballistic missiles first deployed by the Soviets in the 1960s. MOPP (for Mission Oriented Protective Posture) gear is a protective suit. Tom Mitten is Sandy's husband, and Carrie Eisenhauer is her daughter.

22 Jan. 1991

Dear A. Ethel,

Happy New Year. Yes, we are 5 days into war and I don't know just when you'll receive this. Our mail has almost stopped since the breakout.

Today is 30 days from our leaving here. That is if we still have rotation set. Our CO says we do, so we'll have to see. I guess it will depend what happens in the next month or so and also what the President does with us Reservists.

By the time you get this, you probably shouldn't write anymore because I may not get it. I don't know how long it will take to get to you and I'm sure with our situation over here the mail will be almost non-existent. Since our "war" has started, things have really been jumping over here. We are all fine. There have been some close calls because the SKUDS have gotten close. Daharan is not far from us. When the Patriots went off the other night it was right from our Port. I was inside, but the boat people saw it intercept. Simply amazing. The shock we felt when it took off and when it broke the sound barrier was tremendous. It shook windows & bldgs. and scared the shit out of all of us. We of course had our MOP gear & gas masks on. This is something else. Let me tell you. So far the attacks have been at night except for this morning. At 0720 this morning, 4 SKUDS were launched into Saudi Arabia. We heard the Patriots take off, but that was from Daharan, so the shock was nothing. We just heard boom, boom.

It's really something to be here. I know no one will ever understand this. You just have to be here. Before this all started, it's like you have the attitude this is just another exercise. Like so many I've been on before. Only much longer. Our duties were basically the same type that we always did before and sort of like playing a war game. Now in the past 5 days, all those hours and hours of practice go into effect without even realizing it. It's like we were awakened at 2:30 A.M. the first day to sirens and people screaming, running, getting real panicy. What a mess. Now, it's almost old hat. Now people are completely paranoid. We've been awakened so much and gone through so many of these episodes of putting our MOP gear, gas mask & gloves on that we can do it pretty fast now. In fact, most of us sleep in our uniforms. It's much easier and faster. All of us women have moved over to the men's barracks for night time. The barracks we live in goes absolutely crazy when these things happen. So it was decided we sleep with the men. We are completely separated from them otherwise because we are on the other end of the compound. These are our friends & compatriots; so we made the move 5 days ago. It's more comforting. We're altogether now. When this all happens, if we are at the barracks, we get into our gear and go in the passageways and sit on the floor and just hold hands and look at each other. Some cry, some sleep, some are just in a daze and all are scared. But we have each other.

This morning, while I was on watch we had a SKUD alert. It lasted about 1 hour before the "all clear" came. You hear those sirens and you know immediately what is happening. I'm on 12 hr. watches now and by the time I get back to the compound it's usually 7:30–7:45 P.M. Then hope you can get a shower in before an alert happens. You worry about eating the last thing. Then you just go to bed and know in an hour or so, you'll be awakened to "SKUD ALERT, MOP LEVEL 2 or 4 or 3 or WHATEVER. EVERYONE OUT IN THE HALLS!!" Then you know that is the beginning of the end of getting sleep for the night. If we have one, we usually have 3 or 4. They are usually about 2 hrs. apart, so you just get back to sleep and you're awake again. I get up at 4:30 to go on watch at 5:30 so in the past days I haven't gotten much sleep.

So, on a lighter note, I guess I'm a star. I haven't seen the article for People Magazine, but I hope it's good. I hope none of us were misquoted. They spent around 4–5 hours with me and it was undoubtedly the most exciting day in my whole life. Never in a hundred years did I ever imagine I'd come over here and I'd be interviewed on down the road. I haven't been able to call Tom and I won't be able to, but I hope he is pleased also. I got a letter from Carrie and she said they interviewed her about 20 min. Don't worry, tell everyone, I'll remember them when I get back!! Ha! Ha!

Anything else to say seems sort of meaningless. We have to see how this whole conflict develops. Today is the 30th day before we're supposed to go home. Our CO—I just realized I said that already. I'm tired, so I'll close for now. By the time you receive this I will soon be preparing to leave, so don't write after you receive this. I may not get this.

Another helicopter went over. That's a common occurrence now. I'm safe and I plan on staying safe. We will get out of here, believe me.

Take care and God Bless you. Read this to everyone else, because I may not get a chance to write them.

> I love you all.
> Love,
> Sandy

*     *     *

---

*Long before the night of June 12, 1994, O. J. Simpson (1947–) was one of the most famous Americans, having been a Heisman Trophy–winning running back, a National Football League star, a sports commentator, a charismatic pitchman, and a sometime actor. After June 12, he became infamous as well. Arrested for the murder of his former wife Nicole Brown Simpson (1959–1994) and her friend Ronald Goldman, O. J. was tried in an eight-month-long case that divided the nation clearly and disturbingly along color lines. Ultimately he was acquitted in the criminal trial and found liable in a civil suit brought by the Goldman family. The following letter, written by Nicole sometime in 1992, was never allowed as evidence in the criminal trial. It was introduced in the civil suit in 1997, although Simpson claimed he had never received it, and the defense suggested that it had been written at the request of Nicole's divorce lawyers.*

Sydney and Justin are the Simpsons' children.

O. J.—

I think I have to put this all in a letter. Alot of years ago I used to do much better in a letter, I'm gonna try it again now.

I'd like you to keep this letter if we split, so that you'll always know why we split. I'd also like you to keep it if we stay together, as a reminder.

Right now I am so angry! If I didn't know that the courts would take Sydney & Justin away from me if I did this I would [expletive] every guy including some that you know just to let you know how it feels.

I wish someone could explain all this to me. I see our marriage as a huge mistake & you don't.

I knew what went on in our relationship before we got married. I knew after 6 years that all the things I thought were going on—were! All the things I gave in to—all the "I'm sorry for thinking that" "I'm sorry for not believing you"—"I'm sorry for not trusting you."

I made up with you all the time & even took the blame many times for your cheating. I know this took place because we fought about it alot & even discussed it before we got married with my family & a minister.

OK before the marriage I lived with it & dealt with [illegible] mainly because you finally said that we weren't married at the time.

I assumed that your recurring nasty attitude & mean streak was to cover up your cheating & a general disrespect for women & a lack of manners!

I remember a long time ago a girlfriend of yours wrote you a letter—she said well you aren't married yet so let's get together. Even she had the same idea of marriage as me. She believed that when you marry you wouldn't be going out anymore—adultery is a very important thing to many people.

It's one of the 1st 10 things I learned at Sunday school. You said it [illegible] some things you learn at school stick! And the 10 Comandments did!

I wanted to be a wonderful wife!

I believed you that it would finally be "you & me against the world"—that people would be envious or in awe of us because we stuck through it & finally became one a real couple.

I let my guard down—I thought it was finally gonna be you & me—you wanted a baby (so you said) & I wanted a baby—then with each pound you were terrible. You gave me dirty looks looks of disgust—said mean things to me at times about my appearance walked out on me & lied to me.

I remember one day my mom said "he actually thinks you can have a baby & not get fat."

I gained 10 to 15 lbs more than I should have with Sydney. Well that's by the book—Most women gain twice that. It's not like it was that much—but you made me feel so ugly! I've battled 10 lbs up & down the scale since I was 15—It was no more X-tra weight than was normal for me to be up   I believe my mom—you thought a baby weighs 7 lbs & the woman should gain 7 lbs. I'd like to finally tell you that that's not the way it is—And had you read those books I got you on pregnancy you may have known that.

Talk about feeling alone . . .

In between Sydney & justin you say my clothes bothered you—that my shoes were on the floor that I bugged you—Wow that's so terrible! Try I had a low self esteem because since we got married I felt like the paragraph above.

There was also that time before Justin & after few months Sydney, I felt really good about how I got back into shape and we made out. You beat the holy hell out of me & we lied at the X-ray lab & said I fell off a bike . . . Remember!??

Great for my self esteem.

There are a number of other instances that I could talk about that made my marriage so wonderful . . . like the televised Clipper game & going to [illegible] before the game & your 40th birthday party & the week leading up to it. But I don't like talking about the past It depressed me.

Then came the pregnancy with Justin & oh how wonderful you treated me again—I remember swearing to God & myself that under no circumstances would I let you be in that delivery room.

I hated you so much.

And since Justin birth & the mad New Years Eve beat up.

I just don't see how our stories compare—I was so bad because I wore sweats & left shoes around & didn't keep a perfect house or comb my hair the way you liked it—or had dinner ready at the precise moment you walked through the door or that I just plain got on your nerves sometimes.

I just don't see how that compares to infidelity, wife beating verbal abuse—

I just don't think everybody goes through this—

And if I wanted to hurt you or had it in me to be anything like the person you are—I would have done so after the [illegible] incident. But I didn't even do it then. I called the cops to save my life whether you believe it or not. But I didn't pursue anything after that—I didn't prosecute, I didn't call the press & I didn't make a big charade out of it. I waited for it to die down and asked for it to. But I've never loved you since or been the same.

It made me take a look at my life with you—my wonderful life with the superstar that wonderful man, O.J. Simpson the father of my kids—that husband of that terribly insecure [illegible]—the girl with no self esteem [illegible] of worth—she must be [illegible] those things to with a guy like that.

It certainly doesn't take a strong person to be with a guy like that and certainly no one would be envious of that life.

I agree after we married things changed—we couldn't have house fulls of people like I used to have over & barbque for, because I had other responsabilities. I didn't want to go to alot of events & I'd back down at the last minute on fuctions & trips I admit I'm sorry—

I just believe that a relationship is based on trust—and the last time I trusted you was at our wedding ceremony. it's just so hard for me to trust you again. Even though you say you're a different guy. That O.J. Simpson guy brought me alot of pain heatache—I tried so hard with him—I wanted so to be a good wife. But he never gave me a chance.

## 1994

## PRISCILLA PERKINS TO COLLEAGUES

---

*In 1978, a television ad for Enjoli perfume had offered viewers the sight of a woman in a business suit belting: "I can bring home the bacon, fry it up in a pan, and never, never, never let you forget you're a man." A decade and a half later, after major in-roads had been made by women in the business world, some retrenchment had begun, and a slower-paced "mommy track" became the chosen path for some women who wanted to spend more time with their children. This memo, from Michigan management consultant Priscilla Perkins (1960–) to her colleagues at the professional services firm Plante & Moran, gave voice to the growing pride in the world of motherhood.*

Stephen Covey published a best-selling book in 1990 called *The 7 Habits of Highly Effective People.* Perkins did not return to the paid workforce but, in addition to raising her two sons, has been an avid volunteer for organizations including the YES foundation, the Cub Scouts, and the William Beaumont Hospital.

To:     P&Mers
From:  Priscilla Perkins
Re:     Hiatus

"To every thing there is a season, and a time to every purpose under the heaven..."

Ecclesiastes 3:1

I never envisioned a time where I would not be reporting to an office on a daily basis. I had always thought that maintaining an overflowing day planner, attending meetings, making and accepting phone calls, serving clients, traveling, and training sessions would always be a part of my day-to-day existence. After all, what else was there?

Well, to my pleasant surprise parenthood has exposed me to a whole new world filled with challenges and responsibilities that would test even the most ardent follower of Covey's Seven Habits. So, I began with the end in mind (Habit 2) and thought about the kind of parent, spouse, associate, sister, daughter, community servant I wanted to be. The answers left me overwhelmed, but certain that the season in which I now find myself asks that I give more of my time to Huel, Jared and me. Habit 3 states, "put first things first."

It was not an easy decision to take this break from the P&M work I enjoyed so well. Dennis, Liz, Melanie and Sheldon are the best people with whom I have ever worked. Plante & Moran is one of the finest organizations with which I have ever been affiliated. I will miss them and being a constant part of the P&M family more than I could ever describe in this letter.

I do not view this as a permanent farewell, but merely a break in the routine I have established over the past four years. I will keep in touch. Thanks to all who made my P&M experience a great one.

Sincerely,<br>Priscilla Perkins

---

*The earliest cases of AIDS in the United States had been reported in 1981. By 1995, researchers at the Centers for Disease Control were aware of more than three hundred thousand Americans who had died from the disease. Some were intravenous drug users, others recipients of blood transfusions. Most were gay men, and North Carolina Senator Jesse Helms (1921–) believed they had only themselves to blame. Patsy Clarke (1929–), the mother of a gay AIDS victim, wrote this anguished letter to the senator after her son's death. Helms responded by saying: "I wish he had not played Russian roulette with his sexual activity." A month later, he declared that AIDS was caused by gay men's "deliberate, disgusting and revolting conduct." Not until 2002 would he reverse his stance on funding for AIDS research.*

June 5, 1995

Dear Jesse,

This is a letter I have wanted to write for a long time. I do it now because its time has come.

When my husband (and your strong friend), Harry Clarke died in a plane crash at the Asheville airport on March 9, 1987, you called me in the night. You told me of your sorrow at our loss and of what Harry had meant to you as a friend. You placed your praise for him and his principles in the Congressional Record. You sent me the flag flown over the Capitol in his memory. You did all of these things and I am grateful.

Harry and I had a son, Mark who was almost the image of his father, though much taller. He was blessed with great charm and intelligence, and we loved him. He was gay. On March 9, 1994, exactly seven years to the day that his father died, Mark followed him—a victim of AIDS. I sat by his bed, held his dear hand and sang through that long last night the baby song that I had sung to all of our children. "Rock-a-bye and don't you cry, rock-a-bye little Mark. I'll buy you a pretty gold horse to ride all around your pasture . . ."

A few days before he died, Mark said these words: "This disease is not beating me. When I draw my last breath I will have defeated this disease—and I will be free." I watched him take his last breath and claim his freedom. He was 31.

As I write these words I relive the most difficult time of my life. The tears will smudge this if I don't take care. No matter, I will type it so it is legible. My reason for writing to you is not to plead for funds, although I'd like to ask your support for AIDS research; it is not to ask you to accept a lifestyle which is abhorrent to you; it is rather to ask you not to pass judgment on other human beings as "deserving what they get." No one deserves that. AIDS is not a disgrace, it is a TRAGEDY. Nor is homosexuality a disgrace; we so-called normal people make it a tragedy because of our own lack of understanding.

Mark gave me a great gift. A quote returns to me from long ago: "I have no lamp to light my feet save the lamp of experience . . ." I think Patrick Henry said it. Mark's life and death have illuminated my own, and I am grateful for him.

So, that's what this letter is about, and I hope I have written it well. I wish you had known Mark. His life was so much more eloquent than any words I might put on paper. I ask you to share his memory with me in compassion.

Gratefully,

Patsy M. Clarke

## 1996: JANUARY 27
## TINA BROWN TO LAWRENCE WESCHLER

---

*An Oxford graduate who became editor of Britain's* Tatler *magazine at the age of twenty-five, Tina Brown (1953–) was named editor of the American* Vanity Fair *in 1984. With uncanny twin instincts for detecting and creating heat, Brown became famous herself, with a reputation as a demanding, unpredictable, and brilliant editor. In 1992, she was put in charge of* The New Yorker, *where some of the staff occasionally bristled at her demands—especially for stories shorter than the ones they were accustomed to writing. In this memo to staff writer Lawrence Weschler, Brown gave a glimpse of her temper, but also of her standards.*

Weschler's proposed article had been about the Museum of Jurassic Technology in Los Angeles, a quirky institution that became the subject of his book *Mr. Wilson's Cabinet of Wonder.* Robert Gottlieb was Brown's predecessor at *The New Yorker.*

Dear Ren,

Thank you for your letter. I have been waiting for an explanation of your remarks in the Observer. I can understand why you were chagrined, as you say, to find "off the record" remarks made in Seattle reproduced in New York. I am also glad to hear that they don't reflect your current feelings.

I have to say, however, that I am not sympathetic. Your trashing of me and the magazine has been pretty consistent in the last three years according to many mutual friends and TNY writers who have found it unsettlingly beyond the normal grousing when a piece gets killed. In your "off the record" accounts of what happened on the Jurassic piece you leave out a few vital truths in your desire to promote your book on the back of gossip that demonizes me. If I was so obsessed with the piece being "hot" why would I have commissioned it in the first place, for instance? I commissioned it because I do want the kind of quirky material that interests you. It supplies an important strand in the magazine, one I have fostered with such brilliant and unexpected pieces as Nick Baker's library cards, your own Vermeer piece, the upcoming contribution by Simon Schama's friend who collects crack vials, etc.

I commissioned the Jurassic story at department length. It came in much longer than assigned, but that is not why I didn't read it. You are misinformed. I have read many pieces which came in much longer than assigned and will continue to do so and on many occasions I have published them at the greater length—because of their extraordinary quality. Larry Wrights Remembering Satan assigned at 10,000 words ultimately ran at 27,000 words in two parts. Mark Danner's piece on El Salvador was assigned at 8,000 and ultimately ran at 30,000 in one issue. So why did I not read your Jurassic piece? The answer, Ren, is because I was told by the editors to whom you showed it that the piece was "impenetrable", "boring" and "Ren at his most pretentious." I was told "not to waste time reading it" because, they told me, you refused to do what they felt needed to be done by way of cuts. Of course I am now aware that when you were rejected you were not given that explanation. Alas, I now see that this seems to be an old New Yorker tradition. The other day when you asked John to read your Milosovic piece, he told you he liked it when, in fact, he had already dispensed the opinion that it was sophomoric and we should not publish it. John has done the decent thing, I gather, in now telling you his real opinion. A great deal of this kind of soft soaping of writers has gone on at The New Yorker, wrongly construed as supporting them but in fact actively misleading them.

It is so much easier to blame me (or Gottlieb, no doubt, when he was there) than have a candid and uncomfortable conversation with an in house writer. The form these days is to play into the old gossip stereotyping: "I tried to persuade Tina to run it but unless it's about Michael Ovitz she doesn't give a damn. I fought for it, Ren!" What a joke! I often wish in the last three years I had a tape recorder in the editorial meetings as editors "fought" for pieces they were describing to me as unpublishable garbage.

I read every piece I am recommended to read and a great many that I am not.

At the time of the Jurassic piece I was trying to promote a greater sense of responsibility and commitment in the editors who seemed very often to see themselves as postmen, handing over material to me with a shrug. I want editors to be editors, to work with a writer to complete a draft so that it is improved enough for them to present it, with conviction, as ready for publication. Editors have to believe in the writers they are editing. They have to have the ability to recognise the potential that is sometimes latent in a piece that needs more work and the energy to see it through. If they cannot see the diamond in the dust heap, then I am going to be given the wrong signals and pieces that shouldn't die, do. Sandy Frazier's book, I discovered too late, was rejected in the same botched process that rejected you.

After nearly four years at the magazine I now have a system that works very much better than the one I inherited. I have a group of editors who support their writers not by handing the editor a chaotic draft but present a manuscript in which they have confidence. Sometimes they are unsure that we will agree on a piece in which case I read it anyway and we discuss it. These editors I am delighted to report are not in the habit of telling the writer they like a piece when they don't. In Jeff Frank, I have given you one of the best editors I've ever worked with, because I do believe in your work, Ren, and think you should have better support and greater conviction behind you. I am pleased that your book has had such excellent reviews and will be rooting for you in the National Critics award.

So much for the Jurassic saga. But even if the history were not the one I have described, trashing the new new New Yorker on back ground and describing what we publish as "shit," is frankly unconscionable. When I think of the material we've published in the last months by your colleagues like Jane Kramer, Janet Malcolm, Skip Gates, John McPhee, David Remnick, Adam Gopnik, David Denby, Simon Schama, Joan Accoccella, and Anthony Lane, and so many more, I marvel at your arrogance and at your destructiveness. In 1996, TNY has a good chance of breaking even for the first time in twelve years. Do you think what you did is appropriate conduct—even "off the record?" You are a writer who has many benefits from the New Yorker, including an office with all that goes with it.

I accept your apology, but in turn I ask you to consider what you now owe to your colleagues and the magazine which sustains you. Do not imagine for one minute that if you continue to trash our work on or off the record—I will tolerate it. It would just not be fair to have you in an office at West 43rd Street alongside those writers who are working so hard to protect the future of the magazine we love.

Yours,
Tina

### 1996: APRIL 11
### DANA REEVE TO CHRISTOPHER REEVE

---

*On May 27, 1995, the actor Christopher Reeve (1952–2004) was thrown from a horse and paralyzed from the chest down. He went from being a popular actor, most famous for his role as Superman, to being an object of pity and then—as his strength and resolve became evident—a source of extraordinary inspiration to people with disabilities and those without. By his side throughout the transformation was his wife, actress and singer Dana Morosini Reeve (1961–), who, roughly a year after the accident, wrote him this memorable note.*

My darling Toph,

This path we are on is unpredictable, mysterious, profoundly challenging, and, yes, even fulfilling. It is a path we chose to embark on together and for all the brambles and obstructions that have come our way of late, I have no regrets. In fact, all of our difficulties have shown me how deeply I love you and how grateful I am that we can follow this path together. Our future will be bright, my darling one, because we have each other . . . and our young 'uns.

With all my heart
and soul
I love you,
Dana

### 1997: SEPTEMBER 30
### MONICA LEWINSKY TO BILL CLINTON

---

*Almost halfway through his second term as president, William Jefferson Clinton (1946–) was impeached by the House of Representatives for perjury and obstruction of justice. Under the relentless scrutiny of Independent Counsel Kenneth Starr, Clinton was shown to have lied about the nature of his involvement with a twenty-two-year-old White House intern named Monica Lewinsky (1973–). When the intimate details of the affair emerged, they included a series of e-mails and letters that revealed the expectations and the disappointments that Lewinsky harbored.*

Betty Currie was Clinton's personal secretary. Clinton was acquitted of the charges by the Senate in 1999.

30 September 1997

MEMORANDUM FOR        HANDSOME

SUBJECT        The New Deal

A proposition for you: You show me that you will let me visit you sans a crisis, and I will be on my best behavior and not stressed out when I come (to see you, that is).

I'd like to come for a visit this evening. According to my calendar, we haven't spent any time together on the phone or in person in six weeks. You'll be gone the next few weekends so if we don't get together tonight, by the time I do see you it will have been over two months.

What do you think of maybe planning ahead with Betty that you would leave at seven so everyone else goes home, and then you could come back around 7:30 or later. I'll be tied up until about 7:30. any time after that is good for me.

Oh, and Handsome, remember FDR would never have turned down a visit with Lucy Mercer!

MSL-DC-00001050

*** JUST A REMINDER TO THROW THIS AWAY AND NOT SEND IT BACK TO THE STAFF SECRETARY!

## 1999

## KARIN COOK TO JOAN BARRETT COOK CARPENTER

*In 1999, according to the American Cancer Society, roughly 175,000 American women were diagnosed with breast cancer, and 43,300 died. Although survival rates were steadily improving at the end of the twentieth century, roughly one in every eight American women could expect to have breast cancer at some point in her life. A decade after her mother, Joan Barrett Cook Carpenter (1937–1989), died from the disease, novelist Karin Cook (1969–) wrote this letter.*

Dear Mom,

What time was I born?

When did I walk?

What was my first word?

My body has begun to look like yours. Suddenly I can see you in me. I have so many questions. I look for answers in the air. Listen for your voice. Anticipate. Find meaning in the example of your life. I imagine what you might have said or done. Sometimes I hear answers in the echo of your absence. The notion of mentor is always a little empty for me. Holding out for the hope of you. My identity has taken shape in spite of that absence. There are women I go to for advice. But advice comes from the outside. Knowing, from within. There is so much I don't know.

What were your secrets?

What was your greatest source of strength?

When did you know you were dying?

I wish I had paid closer attention. The things that really matter you gave me early on—a way of being and loving and imagining. It's the stuff of daily life that is often more challenging. I step unsure into a world of rules and etiquette, not knowing what is expected in many situations. I am lacking a certain kind of confidence. Decisions and departures are difficult. As are dinner parties. Celebrations and ceremony. Any kind of change. Small things become symbolic. Every object matters—that moth-eaten sweater, those photos. Suddenly I care about your silverware. My memory is an album of missed opportunities. The loss of you lingers.

Did you like yourself?

Who was your greatest love?

What did you fear most?

In the weeks before your death, I knew to ask questions. At nineteen, I needed to hear your hopes for me. On your deathbed, you said that you understood my love for women, just as you suggested you would have fought against it. In your absence, I have had to imagine your acceptance.

There are choices I have made that would not have been yours. Somehow that knowledge is harder for me than if I had you to fight with. My motions lack forcefulness. I back into decisions rather than forge ahead. This hesitancy leaves me wondering:

Did you ever doubt me?

Would you have accepted me?

What did you wish for me?

I know that my political and personal choices threatened you. Your way was to keep things looking good on the outside, deny certain feelings, erase unpleasant actions. Since your death, I have exposed many of the things that you would have liked to keep hidden. I can no longer hold the family secrets for you.

I search for information about your life. Each scrapbook, letter, anecdote I come across is crucial to my desire to understand you and the choices you made. I have learned about affairs, abuse, all things you would not have wanted me to know. Yet they explain the missing blanks in my memory bank and round out your humanity.

Who did you dream you would be?

Did you ever live alone?

Why did you divorce?

Did you believe in God?

One thing you said haunts me still. When I asked about motherhood, you said that children don't need as much as you gave. "Eighty percent is probably plenty." I was shocked by your words. Did you regret having given so much of yourself? Now, those words seem like a gift. A way of offering me a model of motherhood, beyond even your own example.

Becoming a mother is something I think about a great deal, almost to the point of preoccupation. I have heard it said that constant dreaming about birth often signals a desire to birth one's self, to come into one's own. My process of grieving the loss of you has been as much about birthing myself as letting you go.

What were your last thoughts?

Were you proud?

Were you at peace?

What is it like to die?

How frightened you must have been shouldering so much of your illness alone. The level of your own isolation is a mystery to me. In my life, I try hard to reach out, to let others in. I fear loss more than anything. I turn on my computer. Make things up. I tell the truth. My daily work is toward connection. All these questions move me to search, less and less for your answers and increasingly for my own.

Love,
Karin

## 1999: APRIL 27

## AN OKLAHOMA MOTHER TO A COLUMBINE WEB SITE

*Dylan Klebold and Eric Harris were students at Columbine High School in Little-
ton, Colorado, part of a group—known as the "Trench Coat Mafia"—who affected
Nazi trappings and voiced frequent threats. On April 20 (Hitler's birthday) they
opened fire in the school cafeteria and, in a rampage that extended throughout the
school, killed a dozen students, one teacher, and themselves. Among the countless*

*Americans who tried to make sense of the event was an Oklahoma mother who, a*
*week later, shared her thoughts on an online Columbine message board.*
The ellipses were in the original.

   The night of the shooting in Littleton, Co., my 3 children ages 8, 9, and 11 were sitting on the couch discussing the news that was unfolding in front of us. My 9 year old son looked deep into my eyes (as if searching for answers) and said after a long sigh...."Momma, what do I do if a gunman comes to my school?" I was searching for the right answer...I mean what do you say to that? So I simply said...."son, You run and hide! Hide anywhere you can...!" (never thinking I would ever have to explain to my children this scenario) Then after staring at me (you could tell he was in deep thought) he said...."Mom, I couldnt run and hide...I would have to help my brother and sister and teachers and friends..." I grabbed him and hugged him...and tears welling up in my eyes and heart...then he said (after a long silence) "Momma?...There is a lot of kids with Jesus tonight, huh?" I put him on my lap and layed his head on my chest and said. "Yes, Boston, there is..." He was obviously wanting to make something good from all this...he continued by saying...."There happy now, huh, mom?"...I reassured him that they were in the best place they could be... and we sat on the couch for a long time just holding each other. I wish I had the answers for my children, for the children who are around the world...wondering...."Will this happen to them"...It saddens me to explain unnecessary evil, senselessness, and death to my children. But, my kids were comforted in knowing that those people who died in a school in Co. will be with their Maker today and always. I felt compelled to share this story with you.

In Christ's Love,
Lisa

## 1999: JUNE 27
## JERRI NIELSEN TO HER FAMILY AND FRIENDS

*In 1998, Jerri Nielsen (1952–) was an emergency room doctor and recent divorcée whose teenage children had sided with their father in a bitter breakup. Seeking both escape and challenge, she signed on as physician for a polar mission to Antarctica. Once there, she faced the expected obstacles of cold and isolation, and the unexpected discovery of a lump in her breast. Unable to leave until the weather warmed, Nielsen performed her own biopsy and treated herself with air-dropped chemotherapy. She also sent regular updates to her family and friends—and lived to tell the tale.*

From: Jerri Nielsen
To: Family and friends
Date. Sun, Jun. 27,1999, 7.51 p.m.
Subject. Winter

Here we are looking down the hill at the other side of winter. Our astronomer is sending us e-mails explaining what to expect at dawn. Dawn... what a concept. The new dawn, what will it hold for me? Will I receive some of the best news in my life, or the worst?

Although we are halfway through the winter, we have not yet seen the worst of the worst place on earth. The coldest months are yet to come. And then, just as the sun peeks over our horizon, we are hit by the terrible Antarctic storms of spring.

Today was cold. It surprises me, as I walk out of my dear little hospital and my hands freeze and my washed hair turns to ice. It really shouldn't surprise me, at this point, but it does. At other times it seems so normal that it is so cold, and that my home has a floor of ice 9,300 feet thick. Then I wonder what would possess 41 people to sign up for a mission to the bottom of the earth, to live in small orange refrigerators that keep out the cold.

Deep down, I always know the reason: "We" are why we are here. People I wouldn't talk to in the world, I relish seeing in this place. We come to understand and rely on each other in a way that is not of this century, not of this time. This is how human beings were meant to live, in tribes.

The tribe is all that we have here and it makes its own laws, customs, rules of interaction, and concept of duty. Here, duty is everything. How beautiful and simple that is. It is my duty to love and accept and care for everyone, and worry about their mental, physical, and spiritual health, all the time—just like those who have done my job since the beginning of time.

And now, in my unique situation of being the most sick and the only healer it is my duty to never let the fear or concern for my condition become real. And in doing so, I heal myself.

Love from the Ice,
Doc

## 1999: OCTOBER 8
## KATIE THOMSON TO TED KACZYNSKI

---

*In the course of his seventeen-year run as the Unabomber ("Una" for universities and airlines, among his early targets), Theodore Kaczynski (1942–) mailed or*

*planted sixteen bombs, killing three victims and wounding twenty-two others. Fi-*
*nally arrested in 1996, he was found to be a Harvard graduate, a former Berkeley*
*math teacher, and a Montana resident who lived in a tiny cabin, forcibly rejecting*
*the world that technology and industry had wrought. The year after being sentenced*
*to four consecutive life terms, he gave one interview, which ran in* Time. *In an age*
*of celebrity journalism, he was promptly courted by numerous other news organiza-*
*tions, including 20/20, where editorial producer Katie Thomson made the case for*
*an interview with Barbara Walters.*

Kaczynski accepted no other offers for interviews.

October 8, 1999

Dear Mr. Kaczynski,

I am writing to again request an interview with you for the ABC News program 20/20. Barbara Walters, one of the world's most respected journalists,
would conduct the interview.

We have been following your case closely, and await the publication of your
book. However many Americans think your case is closed, and that you were
fortunate to escape the death penalty. They do not know that you have launched
a legal appeal and are fighting for the right to have your day in court.

Although your appeal may mean that you are not free to discuss in detail all
the allegations against you, anything you say will be of enormous interest to our
audience. We could explore the themes raised in your book and allow you to address what you think are misconceptions about you. No one else could more
powerfully express your views, and this interview would help bring more readers
to your book and a better understanding of your legal appeal.

Barbara Walters will provide a fair forum for you to express your views, and
you could reach the most people by appearing on 20/20, one of the most-
watched programs on television. We would welcome the opportunity to discuss
this further, and you can phone here collect at _____. We could also meet with
you in Colorado to discuss the possibility of an interview with no commitment
on your part.

I know that you have had many interview requests, and I appreciate your
continued consideration of this one.

Sincerely,<br>Katie Thomson<br>Editorial Producer<br>20/20

## 1999: NOVEMBER
## KRISTIN KINKEL TO JACK MATTISON

*About a year before the Columbine School shooting (see page 721), a fifteen-year-old boy named Kipland Kinkel had been expelled from Thurston High School in Springfield, Oregon. That same afternoon, he shot and killed his father; in the evening, he shot and killed his mother; the next day, at school, he killed two students and wounded twenty-five others before being tackled to the ground. He was charged with fifty-eight felony counts, including four of aggravated murder. After pleading guilty in September of 1999, he was given a sentencing hearing before Lane County Circuit judge Jack Mattison. The hearing featured testimony from victims and psychologists as well as the following letter, from Kip's older sister, Kristin (1976–).*
Kip was sentenced to 111 years in prison, without possibility of parole.

Dear Judge Mattison.

I am shaken by how difficult this letter is for me to write. I was told that you may need it to better understand my little brother. I wish there was an ideal place to begin. But where does one start when a loved one's life is laid across someone else's table?

What keeps me believing in him and loving him is the fact that he is a good person that came from a good home. I feel silly writing that, because it seems so contradictory, looking at what actually took place. However, it's the truth, and it keeps me alive. I wish more than anything that you, the man who decides his fate, could know him like I do. So a little bit of the Kip Kinkel that I know is where I will begin.

Growing up with him was very average. I was the typical big sister, and he seemed like every other little brother I had ever had any contact with. only with hindsight do I truly see the signs of someone who was in desperate need of help, different help than any of us knew how to give.

Kip was a very compassionate person. Like my mother, the norm for him was to put others first. He absolutely loved animals and treated them better than most. He was a people pleaser. He found ways to learn what those around him wanted and made every effort to become it. I believe that is how he dealt with his illness so well and with such subtlety for so long.

He was genuinely concerned about the same issues kids his age are, and unusually devoted to those that meant something extra special to him. When asked about his interests and opinions, he was able to rationally explain his ideas about them in ways far beyond those which someone his age would be capable of. He was very likeable and had a great sense of humor. He loved to make people laugh and did it well. My mother and I used to say that he would be a wonderful boyfriend because of his sensitivity and his devotion to what he loved. Kip had a lot of potential, and to see that die absolutely crushes me.

That is who I remember Kip to be, and let me tell you about who he is today. He's extremely bright, and the potential I mentioned before is still there, buried inside. He is hurting more than any of us can imagine, and yet is adapting to an extremely unpleasant situation better than most ever could. He is polite and considerate to those that have contact with him. He is realistic about his situation, yet remains hopeful that he will find something positive in it.

He does have plans for the future and has discussed with me his ideas of becoming a productive member of society, even from behind bars. All of his hopes and dreams have to do with getting an education and using it to help people without one. He already has passed the GED with very high scores.

I believe what he needs is the hope that he has a chance of achieving these goals. My first visit with him after this happened was at Skipworth and consisted of only crying. It took weeks for him to make eye contact with me, and even longer to say something. When he finally did, it was, "I am so sorry."

I believe he is aware of the pain that he has caused, and is just as shocked as the rest of us that he was capable of such horror. We were talking last week about the upcoming hearings and preparing ourselves for the things that we would have to listen to. I told him to do what I do, and just tune out that which you don't want to hear. I told him to go to a safe place in his memory, and not listen to the victims when they talk, because they are angry and going to say things they really don't mean. He stopped me and said, "No, I owe it to them to listen."

I share this story because I think it emphasizes the kind of person Kip was and still is. I think it also shows that there really should be no concern for this kind of thing to happen again.

I love my brother more than I ever thought possible. And not because he needs me to, but because I need to. It is a difficult concept for an outsider to understand, but it comes from what is inside us.

He will need support, love, medical help, et cetera. But most of all right now, he needs hope. In twenty-five years, we will be well into the Twenty-first Century. Our society will be very different. The technology and knowledge we will have then is mind boggling. The advances we will have made in psychological research and medication will amaze us. Kip will be forty.

Thank you for your time in reading this. I wanted to speak from my heart and hope you will forgive the informality of this letter. I realize you have a huge amount of things to consider in this case, and I hope I haven't sounded like a nagging sister. Thanks again for your attention.

## 2000: FEBRUARY
## BETTE LANDMAN TO THE BEAVER COLLEGE COMMUNITY

*Two trends at the turn of the twentieth century laid the groundwork for the following letter. The first was the rapidly spreading phenomenon of political correctness, that brand of censorship and self-censorship that targeted all language deemed derogatory or offensive. The second was the proliferation of sexually explicit Internet sites and junk e-mail—as well as the filters for blocking them. Bette Landman (1937–) was president of Beaver College in Glenside, Pennsylvania, when she sent this letter to past and current students, employees, and parents.*

In November 2000, Beaver College changed its name to Arcadia University.

I am writing today about a matter of great importance to the college and to me.

I have been asked to consider changing the name of the college. The word "beaver" too often elicits ridicule in the form of derogatory remarks pertaining to the rodent, the TV show <u>Leave It to Beaver</u>, and the vulgar reference to the female anatomy. The latter is of growing concern. We have found that computer access to information about the college, obtained from the increasingly popular Internet, is often screened out by sensitivity filters used by many parents, libraries, and schools. Furthermore, these filters have even blocked delivery of email messages originating from Beaver.

In addition, market research has shown conclusively that the college appeals to 30 percent fewer students solely because of its name. Also there are alumni reports that our name presents an obstacle when seeking employment and that some have chosen not to display their diplomas in order to avoid unkind remarks from colleagues. Accounts of this happening are more widespread in areas of the country where the name recognition of the college is not strong.

There has never been a time when I have had a greater need to hear from the alumni of Beaver about questions so important for the future of the college. Please complete your survey when it arrives.

Sincerely,
Dr. Bette E. Landman

## 2000: JULY 14
## COURTNEY PULITZER TO HER GRANDPARENTS

---

*In New York City alone, an estimated eight thousand Internet start-up companies took shape between 1994 and 2001, offering everything from consulting to content to streaming media. In a rapidly changing world, the dot-com boom created great idealism, as well as dizzying wealth. Before the tech bubble burst in late 2000 and early 2001, the city's "Silicon Alley" was the scene of frenetic networking and near-perpetual partying among its creative, technological, and financial players. Web designer-turned-party-and-events-planner Courtney Jane Pulitzer (1969–) captured the fin-de-siècle excitement in this explanatory letter to her grandparents, Marjorie Jane (1920–) and William Vertrees (1920–).*

HTML, Hypertext Markup Language, is a collection of formatting commands used to create Web pages.

July 14, 2000

Dear Grandma and Grandpa,

Hello there! I hope this letter finds you well, and Grandma—I hope you have a wonderful birthday today! Since today is a significant date for you, I wanted to catch you up on some significant things happening here. I am sorry I haven't written sooner, but things have been really busy here with my business in these wild times! You may remember the printouts of the Web pages I designed, with the supporting document showing the HTML code so you could begin to understand a little bit about the work I've been doing. And since you don't have a computer, I'm also sending along some pictures from some of my more recent press. You'll see, Grandpa, what's come of this "hearty peasant stock," as you used to say!

As you know, New York City has always been a great theater town. And over the last four years, the new media drama has become the best show in town! Were you to wander a ways down from Times Square and the Theater District, you would see a very different set of theatrics occurring. Sure, there are flashing lights, winning designs, costumes, stars and the hum of machines whirring to support the productions, but now Grandma, the flashing lights are modem lights flickering, the winning designs are award winning websites and the costumes are the garb of East Village creative types and Armani suits of the newly rich dot-com business owners. These "stars," one-time bit-players who worked in small, dusty offices, are now considered sexy geeks ("microstars" is a new term to describe them) who work in large, grand and newly designed lofts.

What's so neat about meeting all these founders of these new companies is that they came to Silicon Alley and helped create what it is today. (This little nickname for NYC was drummed up by a friend of mine, Mark Stahlman. He was quoted in a <u>Business Week</u> article several years ago and coined it in contrast to Silicon Valley, which as you know is where developments in silicon (and computers) goes on in California. Well Silicon Alley both describes the technology activity here in the city and an actual (growing) neighborhood, which extends down Broadway starting in the 20's (the Flatiron District) to Soho (an area South of Houston Street) and then ending in the Wall Street area.) It was created by people who came into it from all over the place. Some were actors, some were historians, some were philosophers, musicians, designers and some were programmers. But all were fascinated by this new medium and they had an insatiable desire to communicate both online (through computer-based bulletin board systems—which would be similar to the bulletin boards in your local supermarket, and which were considered an online community—and email) and in a F2F (face-to-face) setting in cafes and bars. (I know—what a concept! An actual meeting!)

Very few of these movers and shakers had any formal training in this business because it is so new no one had yet written a textbook. Look at myself! I came back down to my birthplace, Manhattan, to pursue acting after I graduated from NYU. But I soon realized acting was not the vehicle for my creative expression. I wasn't sure what was, but being the next Sarah Bernhardt wasn't it. So, as you may remember, in 1994 I began working for a corporate identity consultant and switched from doing analysis of characters in a play to analysis of companies and their branding. My entrée to the World Wide Web was like a flash of lighting that showed up one morning bright and early at my job. My boss rushed in the door after having attended an AIGA (American Institute of Graphic Artists) conference the night before and exclaimed, "I want a website! We've got to get Mosaic!" (Mosaic was one of the first Web browsers). And as you know, I was his only employee, so it was up to me to figure out what this meant and do it, which I did!

And I am so happy as a result! My Web career thus far has been infinitely more rewarding than acting would have been. There were a few groups where I met most of my friends and where lots of people went to network: East Coast Hangout (ECHO), the World Wide Web Artists Consortium (WWWAC), the New York New Media Association (NYNMA) and Webgrrls. I was really involved in the WWWAC group in the beginning as I learned HTML and how to build more effective websites. Most of the people in WWWAC and Echo are more of the down-in-the-trenches type of computer geeks, graphic designers, consultants and freelancers. NYNMA, which got started in one of my favorite Mexican restaurants in Tribeca, El Teddy's, was started by a slightly older, more professional crowd and has a slightly more corporate-business personality to it. Although, one of the founders, my friend Mark, is a <u>very</u> theatrical fellow. He throws his own brand of wild parties (salons) where I hear there are a lot of fun antics going on! The NYNMA also began their style of parties called Cyber-Suds, which were basically big bashes where lots of young guys in suits showed up, not really knowing anything about the Internet but wanting to cash in on it somehow (and who drank as much beer as they could get their greedy hands on!) Then there was Aliza Sherman, who I'm also friends with, and who created a name and splash for herself when she formed Webgrrls. She had gatherings too, but they were tamer (no boys allowed!) and had potluck snacks and unlike the other organizations, Aliza formed her organization so that women around the world could establish chapters of their own. Now there are hundreds of chapters in countries all around the world!

People began working crazy hours (me included!): sometimes 18 or 20 hours a day, sometimes they wouldn't even go home at night—they'd just curl up under their desk, after consuming cans of Jolt soda, Pringles, slices of pizza, coffee and whatever else they could get delivered at all hours of the day. (Although I still tried to be healthy by running along the Hudson in the mornings).

So these little one-and two-person shops cropped up everywhere in town and some grew, some folded, others merged and some changed their strategy. The deals being cut between companies increased in size and stake too. When Site Specific and Siteline worked on producing the Duracell website, that was news in '95. Today, CNNfn is forming alliances with Discovery Brokerage, NBC is buying into part of iVillage and FortuneCity is reaching across the seas to Asia joining the Online Technologies Consortium. Agency.com, which was started by another acquaintance of mine and who founded WWWAC—Kyle Shannon—and Chan Suh, acquired a bunch of companies after they received a major investment from another major firm, Omnicom.

One of Agency's competitors, Razorfish, which was started by two high-school friends Craig Kanarick and Jeff Dachis, became well known for cutting-edge designs and really fun parties. These two fellows were always being written up for their wacky style. Their company went public on the stock exchange and they became billionaires overnight! One of them even bought his dream car—a baby blue '65 corvette!

The parties actually became a major way of doing business, which was great for me since my whole business thrives on writing about them and throwing them myself! (The <u>New Yorker</u> magazine dubbed me as the "Liz Smith of the Internet." Isn't that funny? And I've been on cable shows on <u>CNN, Oxygen Media</u> and <u>Plugged In</u> reporting on technology trends and topics. I was even on <u>Live! With Regis and Kathie Lee</u> talking about gardening websites!)

Back to my original analogy, like the theater community, the cyber scene (which incidentally is the name of my newsletter) is a close-knit group of people. So they were always getting together to discuss new things or celebrate successes. Whenever a firm launched a great new website, there was a party! When two firms formed an alliance, there was a party! When a company got significant funding, there was a party! It seemed like there was a party for any reason, and they ranged in raucousness too. This one company, Pseudo, created a name for itself because of their wild 400 person parties. Their parties would start as a typical networking beer, chips and salsa affair from 6:00–9:00 PM. But then at nine o'clock, the pretzels and tablecloths went away and the "chips" would change into gambling chips on a blackjack table! I think the police came a few times too because they had some let's say scantily-clad (if at all) dancers and there were many rumors of substance abuse. Of course, I was just there to report it, so I never partook or even stayed very long for that matter!

But that company really went crazy when they got a $14 million investment. They had a "rave" party in 1999 that literally lasted three days! I went by on the 2nd day, August 20, to see what this was about and let me tell you, $14 million buys a lot of craziness. After telling the guard at the door of a former wax factory (353 Broadway) the password ("Pseudo") I walked into an airline security-check type gate, had to sit down in a chair and be video-taped as some guy barked questions at me! Fortunately I got off easy: my name, email and birth date were all I had to reveal. One guy told me he was asked "Who is the president of Microsoft?" Pseudo was always trying to capture free (read unpaid) content for their online TV and radio shows and they even had guys filming girls in skirts as they walked up the stairs. One woman pranced around in a dress made entirely of credit-cards, while another group wore sea-creature-headdresses. There was also this man who gyrated in front of a paint-splattered wall with a fish on his head! Yes, I know, times <u>have</u> changed, haven't they!

Upstairs another man in a 20'-long sea creature–lizard–dragon costume slithered along the floor as another guy held his tail and pretended it was a whip. And then down in the basement (Dante's Inferno as they called it) there was a white plastic-like group of tents in a row with different things going on in them. One "tent" had a woman giving shiatsu massages, another had a naked man examining himself with a digital camera, a woman was giving Mendhi tattoos in a third. In the back of the space a young man screeched out his tormented comedy monologue as other bored participants stared blankly ahead. Well. You can imagine my reaction, having grown up surrounded by girls and boys who revered <u>The Official Preppy Handbook</u> as a Bible!

Anyway, I wanted to also let you know about some <u>very positive</u> things I've been doing! I did my first black tie benefit last December (1999) at the fabulous Metropolitan Club for the Fresh Air Fund and their computer labs at their camps. It was literally Silicon Alley's First Annual Black tie Benefit! We had an amazing turnout and although he was confirmed, Mayor Guiliani couldn't come at the last minute. So he sent a representative from his office instead who read a letter from the mayor stating, "I'd like to thank Manhattan's own breath of Fresh Air, Courtney Pulitzer!" Isn't that amazing?!

This year I just did my second Silicon Alley Black tie Benefit at Central Park's Boathouse, which was so lovely. We even had gondola rides in the pond! This benefit was where I announced the creation of my fund that I am in the process of establishing with City Cares (a national non-profit in cities around the US). So my fund is going to be a national coffer of sorts to provide money for their Partners in Technology Program (PITP), which is directly focused on the digital divide problem. (and one that I'm really concerned about)

Well, I'm sure you can confidently say I've come a long way from ballet recitals in Skaneateles! It certainly has been an interesting ride, and the amazing thing is that it's still just at the beginning of it. Sure, there'll be ups and downs, but progress must have that. And I'm just so happy to be in the midst of all this enthusiasm, excitement, innovation and renaissance for our world.

You know, thousands of people flock to New York every year to realize their dream. Put this inherently busy town together with the hyper-enthusiasm of the new media scene and Silicon Alley is like a race-car on jet-fuel! It's one of the hottest places to be! And none of this activity looks to be slowing down anytime soon. This is the place where anyone can seize the day and grab opportunity by the horns and realize their potential. I write this as I sit on the precipice of my own potential. And hope too, to see it realized even more!

Well Grandma! I hope this little story about me and my world was interesting to you. Big hug and kiss to you and Grandpa (and little Charlie too!). I hope to be able to come Upstate and see you very soon. I wish I could be there with you today to celebrate your birthday. And I hope you have many, many more!

With much love for you both,
today and always,
Courtney

2000: AUGUST 8

SHARON O'CONNOR TO MIMI PARKER

---

*The care and keeping of children—especially by women who had been well edu-*
*cated and well employed outside the home—developed a new intensity in the post-*
*women's liberation years. In this letter to a friend, Vermont mother Sharon Higbee*
*O'Connor (1970–) described her daughter Mazie with wonder, worry, and insight.*

Cabot, Vermont
August 8, 2000

Dear Mimi,

As I sit down to write this, Mazie is up in her room screaming through the grate down into the kitchen, "Mom, I want you out of this house!" She is not even five, but already she sometimes has the wrath of a misunderstood teenager.

Yesterday we went to the local carnival—a midway, about five rides, barrel races, a petting zoo, and cotton candy. It was fun. I took the girls on the merry-go-round and stood between their two horses while it spun around. I held each girl in the small of her back, my almost five-year-old to my right, my two-year-old on my left. They bounced up and down like some crazy scale, unable to level out, me in the middle. And somehow it seemed both sweet and melancholy. All I could think of was the days invested in these lives. Mazie is nearing on 2,000 days—Clementine not even 800. When I looked at Mazie she literally looked to me like she could have floated right off the ride into the clouds.

I guess I've been trying to decode Mazie's sensitive nature more now that she's making the leap from pre-school to kindergarten. Her teachers have brought it to our attention that she's academically exceptional but emotionally fragile. Duh. I mean don't get me wrong, I love that she's at a small school where they notice the students. But the other night Charles and I were talking about our weird suburban school experiences and how if you were a freak, which we were, you kind of got by, and in the end I think it was character-building. Mazie is and will be a freak. Her old pre-school director called her "eccentric" in her meetings with me. On the other hand Clementine, even at two, seems oddly normal, suspiciously normal. I have weird little flashes of her as a teenager playing field hockey with a healthy glow, like some J. Crew catalog person. There is no question that she's well adjusted to being Clem.

Mazie's teachers said that she was "overly sensitive," and said that they thought that she should stay in pre-school next year, instead of moving on to kindergarten. That way, they said, she would get a chance to mature socially and gain confidence. I said that I thought it would actually be a real blow to her confidence to see the children she had started getting used to move on without her. She already wanted to be in kindergarten, and she's the only one in the class who knows how to read and do math (she gets multiplication and negative numbers already). The kindergarten teacher said, "Oh, she might mind for a week or so, but then she'll be fine." That's when I knew I had to try and explain Mazie to them, because they didn't really know her at all.

Charles and I think her sensitivity has to do with the way she's wired. She's brought to tears by so much, but her tears are never really inappropriate. I think she just has this brain that fills in the gaps too rapidly. She can become paralyzed by even the potential of a tragedy. When we try to watch movies these days, even ones she knows turn out all right, she gets agitated and turns off the TV. If I'm sweeping and a toy or sticker ends up in the pile she is frantic to collect it before I might absent-mindedly throw it away. Recently she woke up from a dream saying, "We have to get the bath toys out! We have to get the bath toys out before they go down the drain!" I tried to get her to describe the dream more but by the time she was fully awake it had left her. But now, if I don't get every single bath toy out before I drain the tub, she's frantic.

If a glass or dish breaks she is in tears, reassuring me that, "It's okay, Mom, Jill can fix it." (Jill is our friend the art restorer, who fixes broken art for rich people.) It's not worth telling her that something isn't fixable, or isn't worth fixing, because she just chokes up with a new wave of tears.

She reminds us almost daily that we're all young and that we won't die for a long time. Just the other day when we were gardening she asked me why plants die in the winter but then come back in the spring and people don't. I didn't know exactly where to begin but I started to tell her something along the lines of some people believe that the body is kind of like clothes and there's something called a soul that's the you inside of you, that can come back to a new life with a different body. Her reaction to this was to put her hands over her ears and say, "I don't want to talk about this any more."

The deaths of both of her grandfathers has really affected her. One of the episodes that disturbed her teachers the most was when she became very upset about a book they read aloud in school, in which a boy's parents pretend he's a pizza and lay him down on a table to put on the cheese and sauce. The page that made her flip looked suspiciously like the laid-out body she saw at Charles's father's viewing last year, when she was three. And my father's car accident, which happened four years before she was even born, still consumes her. Mazie fixates on the fact that he was fifty-four, and she asks us to tell her the ages of all of her nearest and dearest so that she can figure out some mathematical formula that absolves us from the inevitable.

We wrote this three-page letter to the school in hopes that they'd understand she isn't going to all of a sudden be this happy-go-lucky, eager-for-the-next-task type of kid. In the letter, we told them about this night that we got a cord of wood delivered. There were a few people here, and we got into this line and lifted it up the steps and stacked it. Mazie had a gray wool scarf wrapped around her neck, her face all wrinkled up with the concentration necessary to maneuver up the steps with her heavy load. We named her Queen of the woodpile at the end and lifted her on top. I have pictures of the girls from that night. Mazie absolutely glows with happiness. Charles and I have analyzed that night so often. We don't know if it was the teamwork, the physical effort, or the sensation of a job well done. But she felt so good, and in daily life, reaching that state of satisfaction is a struggle for her.

Anyway, the whole picture, if truth be told, is that her sensitivity, while it breaks my heart sometimes, is who she is. She's incredibly sweet and insightful, and I don't want to numb that out of her. Not that the school was suggesting that. But the implication is that who she is is not normal, and she picks up on that.

I'm probably struggling with the heavy truth that we've chosen this little piece of land, and a house, in a small village where both girls will go to the same school from pre-school to senior year. As well as celebrate every holiday, eventually get drunk at the shelter up at the rec. field, and have sex in some kid's pickup truck. It's small here. People know your business. They'll know Mazie's.

I keep thinking about the merry-go-round: watching Mazie, with her fragility around her like a cloak, and Clem, so solid and densely content, rising back and forth with their accumulated days, leaving me as the fulcrum of a scale weighing things not measurable, the component that does indeed balance them but that cannot control what each side will do.

> All my love,
> Sharon

## 2000: OCTOBER

## YOKO ONO TO THE NEW YORK STATE DIVISION OF PAROLE

*Mark David Chapman shot and killed Beatle John Lennon on December 8, 1980. Charged with murder, Chapman pleaded guilty and was sentenced to twenty years*

*to life in prison. At the time of Chapman's first parole hearing, the parole board received this letter from Lennon's widow, Yoko Ono (1933–).*
Chapman was denied parole in 2000 and again in 2002 and 2004.


Ladies and Gentlemen of the Parole Board:

This is my reply to the petition of parole made by Mark David Chapman, from here on called "the subject."

It is not easy for me to write this letter to you since it is still painful for me to think of what happened that night and verbalize my thoughts logically. Forgive me if I fall short of your expectation of giving you a satisfactory opinion. But these are my sincere thoughts.

My husband, John Lennon, was a very special man. A man of humble origin, he brought light and hope to the whole world with his words and music. He tried to be a good power for the world, and he was. He gave encouragement, inspiration and dreams to people regardless of their race, creed and gender. For me, he was the other half of the sky. We were in love with each other like the most vehement of lovers to the last moment. For our son, Sean, he was the world. That world shattered when the "subject" pulled the trigger. For Julian, it was losing his father twice. For the people of the world, it was as though the light went out for a moment and darkness prevailed. With his one act of violence in those few seconds, the subject managed to change my whole life, devastate his sons, and bring deep sorrow and fear to the world. It was, indeed, the power of destruction at work.

At first, I had refused to acknowledge John's death. I announced that, "there is no funeral for John." In my mind, I was saying, "BECAUSE HE IS NOT DEAD!" "Tell me he is not dead, tell me he is not dead," I was screaming inside myself. But then, I started to hear that young girls were jumping off buildings to kill themselves. I realized then that it was not a time for me to simply wallow in my own pain. I organized a world vigil with the prayer that, together, we would somehow get through.

For the past twenty years, I've carried the torch John and I once carried together to try to let the darkness go. I asked the fans to remember John's birthday, not the day of his passing. When people asked how I felt about the killer of my husband, I have always told them that I didn't think about that day anymore. I wanted to look to the future, and not to remember that horrible moment. But in actual fact, the memory of that night has never left me for the last twenty years.

It was so cruel. So unjust. My husband did not deserve this. He was in no way ready to die. He was feeling good with the prospect of doing a concert tour after making the album which became his last. He would have gladly changed his position with the subject, and live the life of protection that the subject enjoys now. Even in confinement, my husband, John, would have cherished hearing voices of people he loved, enjoyed creating songs, and simply appreciated watching the sky and its changes through the seasons. John cannot do any of that now.

His family and the world rested because justice was finally done by the court. The subject was imprisoned. If he were to be released now, many will feel betrayed. Anger and fear would rise again.

It would also give a "go" signal to the others who would like to follow in the footsteps of the subject to receive world attention. I am afraid it will bring back the nightmare, the chaos and confusion once again. Myself and John's two sons would not feel safe for the rest of our lives. People who are in positions of high visibility and outspokenness such as John, would also feel unsafe.

Finally, it will not be safe for the subject himself. He will cease to have the security that the state provides him now. I understand that he has been isolated from other prisoners because of the threat of possible harm to him. Well, there are more people in the outside world who are strongly distressed about what he has done. They would feel that it is unfair that the subject is rewarded with a normal life while John lost his. Violence begets violence. If it is at all possible, I would like us to not create a situation which may bring further madness and tragedy to the world.

I thank you in advance for your wise and just decision. I am,

Sincerely yours,
Yoko Ono Lennon

## 2000: OCTOBER 4
## KATHY FITZGERALD SHERMAN TO MICHAEL SHERMAN

*Writer Kathy Fitzgerald Sherman (1956–) was a veteran of at least a half-dozen approaches to improving her seventeen-year marriage when she decided to call it quits. As it turned out, this letter to her husband, Michael (1957–), accomplished for her what other methods had not: after receiving it, he asked for another chance, and four years later, the couple were still married.*

"S" and "L" referred to the Shermans' children; "R" was Kathy's therapist.

October 4, 2000

Dear Michael,

This is the hardest letter I've ever had to write, and probably the hardest one you'll ever have to read. I'm putting my thoughts and feelings on paper because I want you to hear me out fully before you react.

I have come to a decision that I believe serves the best interests of S——, L——, and myself. I wouldn't presume to speak for you, but I predict that my decision will serve your best interests as well.

Michael, I have decided to divorce you. The decision fills me with sadness—a deep, deep mourning for what might have been, but never was. I had so much hope for us in the beginning. But, as I look back on our history, I can see that that hope has been chiseled away, year after year, until now there is nothing left. For me, our marriage is empty. Yes, we are great intellectual partners, and we provide each other fantastic support in our entrepreneurial efforts. But that's not enough for a marriage. Large parts of myself have died (or, more accurately, are lying inside me, dormant, in a near-death state) and I'm no longer willing to live that way. I may not be living till the year 2100 like you, but at 43 I'm far too young to extinguish so many important parts of myself.

There are many things I appreciate about you, including your intellect and the fine financial support you've provided for all of us. Above all, you love S—— and L—— and they love you. You've had many wonderful moments with them and I know you'll have many more. But I believe that they are being harmed by the environment in which they're living. They witness the suppression of their mother's spirit on a daily basis and it hurts them. And they witness a continuous undercurrent of hostility between their parents which confuses and disorients them. I believe they need healthier relationship models. I'm hoping we can give them one in separation that we couldn't give them in marriage.

As I write this, I wonder how you'll be reacting. With anger? That's both my fear and my expectation. With sadness? I hope so, because I'm sad too. With at least a little relief? I believe that, if you're telling yourself the truth, the answer will be yes.

First, I want you to know that this decision was not encouraged or even influenced by R——. He supports me in the decision (and has been probing to discover any uncertainty, which doesn't exist) but I reached the decision on my own about two weeks ago.

Second, I want you to know that I have taken no legal steps yet. I felt that if I filed for divorce and had the papers served before speaking to you, it would set off an adversarial pattern that would benefit no one. As parents to our kids, we are a team and will be forever, married or not. I want to make sure we remain a team that works together rather than at cross-purposes.

My hope is that we can talk to each other in a civilized fashion and work out a dissolution that is fair, optimal, and, above all, protects the kids in every aspect of their lives. Ending our marriage will be further complicated by the fact that we each have a business that is located at ———. Neither of us can move our business on the spur of the moment and it's imperative, for our futures and our kids', that both enterprises continue to function throughout this process.

Michael, let's not be vindictive with each other. I can hear your voice in my head saying, "I've always known you would divorce me." Please believe me when I tell you that I didn't know it myself until two weeks ago. If you saw divorce on the horizon, then it's because you saw the pieces of me dying and knew that I would eventually call a halt to that process. I couldn't allow myself to see that process because if I had, I would have called it quits a lot sooner. I have been fully committed to our marriage (until my decision point) and have tried everything I know to make it work—est, therapy, sex therapy, more therapy, a housekeeper, religion (pastoral counseling), more therapy, even caving in and giving up all expectations. The fighting was hard, but the caving in became intolerable. Please don't allow yourself to believe that this is something I was plotting.

There is a lot more that needs to be said, but the rest has to be two-way, so I will stop writing now. Let's be a team, Michael. There's too much at stake not to.

> With deepest sadness and regret,
> K———

## 2001
## MARY TO CHRISTIAN BROTHERS AND SISTERS

*The "True Love Waits" movement began in the early 1990s among Southern Baptist churches, then spread to other Protestant denominations. During the nineties, more than two million teenagers took a pledge to abstain from sex until marriage, signing a "commitment card" that said, "Believing that true love waits, I make a commitment to God, myself, my family, my friends, my future mate and my future children to be sexually abstinent from this day until the day I enter a biblical marriage relationship." By 2001, a study published in the* American Journal of Sociology *found that teens who had made the pledge remained virgins an average of eighteen months longer than those who had not. This letter, from a teenager who came a little late to the idea of abstinence, showed the intensity with which believers sought the favored state of purity.*

Dear brothers and sisters in Christ,

My name is Mary, and I'm writing to explain the life of a "new virgin" to those that may have lost their virginity, and to tell them how they can become a "new virgin". I'm sorry to say this, but there is no magic potion that can ever turn back time so you can fix what you have done in the past. But, there is something better. God. I am 16 years old right now, and I lost my virginity when I was 13. It was the biggest mistake of my life, but at the same time, it was also the best lesson I have ever learned. For two years I totally hated myself for what I did. Not only did I take away practically the one most important thing I could have given my husband, I let God down. That was probably the worst part. For two years I pleaded with God to forgive me. I would have even cried myself to sleep. It is very painful knowing you lost something you can never have back. It wasn't until the summer of 98, that I understood the meaning of forgiveness of all sins.

I had attended a Christian youth camp in the mountains with my church youth group. Little did I know what was going to happen. Since I had lost my virginity, I had been carrying around this huge burden that hung over me, weighing me down, and keeping me from being closer in my walk with God. While I was there, I talked to a youth leader and explained my situation. They told me if I ask for forgiveness, God would forgive me. He (God) would even make me pure in His eyes, and pure in my husband's eyes. I wanted so desperately to believe them, but Satan was still pulling at me, telling me I would never be clean enough for anyone.

A few days after coming home from camp, I was having my usual prayer before bed and asking God to show me He had forgiven me. When I was finished praying, God told me to open my Bible to John 15.3. I thought I was just guessing a scripture, so I turned to it. It said: "You are already clean because of the word I have spoken to you". I couldn't believe it!!! God had spoken to me so clearly! I cried tears of thanks that night. I couldn't and still can't thank Him enough.

Just because you lost your virginity, doesn't mean you are worthless and don't have anything to give your future spouse. If you will ask God to forgive you, and are totally serious about it, He WILL forgive you. Now, I am in no way saying you can go out and be sexually active and ask God to forgive you and everything will be okay. I am just saying for those of you that may have already lost it, God will forgive you. You don't need to live with the burden anymore. Just ask God. You will be a totally new person.

I first learned about True Love Waits when someone came up to speak to us about it. Immediately after mass, I signed the pledge and made that commitment to God and I have not regretted it since. There has been temptation and pressure. The only thing that's keeping me back from making that big mistake is my promise to God.

## 2001: APRIL 23
## BETH PACITTI TO PARTY PLANNERS

*As Internet investors' fortunes evaporated, a darker side of the 1990s boom years began to emerge. Prosecutors and journalists began to uncover evidence of accounting fraud, self-dealing, and tax evasion at such firms as Enron, Global Crossing, and ImClone. But no scandal matched that of Tyco chief executive L. Dennis Kozlowski when it came to out-and-out greed. Investigators alleged that more than $100 million of corporate funds went to benefit Kozlowski, covering everything from a $13.5 million Boca Raton mansion to a $6,000 shower curtain to half of the $2.1 million bill for his wife's fortieth birthday bash in Sardinia. Beth Pacitti, a Tyco staffer, detailed the elaborate plans in this memo to party planners.*

"LDK" was L. Dennis Kozlowski. The criminal case against him on multiple business-corruption charges ended in a mistrial in 2004, and a new trial date was set. "K." referred to his wife, Karen, and "HBK" was for "Happy Birthday, Karen." Ecliff and the Swingdogs were a dance band from Nantucket.

BJ, Ellen, Herni & Jimmy:

Guests arrive at the club starting at 7:15 p.m. The van pulls up to the main entrance. Two gladiators are standing next to the door, one opens the door, the other helps the guests. We have a lion or horse with a chariot for the shock value. The guests proceed through the two rooms. We have gladiators standing guard every couple feet and they are lining the way. The guests come into the pool area, the band is playing, they are dressed in elegant chic. Big ice sculpture of David, lots of shellfish and caviar at his feet. A waiter is pouring stoli vodka into his back so it comes out his penis into a crystal glass. Waiters are passing cocktails in chalices. They are dressed in linen togas with fig wreath on head. A full bar with fabulous linens. The pool has floating candles and flowers. We have rented fig trees with tiny lights everywhere to fill some space. 8:30 the waiters instruct that dinner is served. We all walk up to the loggia. The tables are all family style with the main table in front. The tables have incredible linens with chalices as wineglasses. The food is brought out course by course, family style, lots of wine, and it's starting to get dark. Everyone is nicely buzzed. LDK gets up and has a toast for K.

Everyone is jumping from table to table. E Cliff has continued to play light music through dinner. They kick it up a bit. We start the show of pictures on the screen, great background music in sync with the slides. At the end Elvis is on the screen wishing K a Happy Birthday and apologizing that he could not make it. It starts to fade and Elvis is on stage and starts singing happy birthday with the Swingdogs. A huge cake is brought out with the waiters in togas singing and holding the cake up for all to see. The tits explode. Elvis kicks it in full throttle. Waiters are passing wine, after dinner drinks, and there is dancing. 11:30 light show starts. HBK is displayed on mountain, fireworks coming from both ends of the golf course in sync with music. Swingdogs start up and the night is young.

Here is the invitation:

Ottima Festa

Ottima Amici

Our summer party is moving from Nantucket to Sardinia. Please join us in the celebration of friendships and Karen's 40th birthday in the scenic Costa Smeralda.

Accommodations have been arranged at the Hotel Cala di Volpe Resort. We look forward to seeing you there—the fun begins the evening of June 10th.

Buon viaggio e felice arrivo—a presto!

Karen & Dennis

The best present for my birthday is your company so please, no gifts.

## 2001: SEPTEMBER 11

## GINA MORRISON TO HER FAMILY

*On September 11, four commercial airplanes were hijacked by the terrorist network al-Qaeda. One plane crashed in Pennsylvania; another slammed into the Pentagon, and two more hit the twin towers of the World Trade Center in New York City. In all, more than three thousand Americans died because of the crashes that day, and for millions of others, so did a sense of safety that had survived until then, despite previous attacks on U.S. property overseas. Like countless other New Yorkers, Gina Morrison spent a sleepless night, simultaneously counting her blessings and mourning the city's losses.*

Morrison was living in Melville, New York.

Dear Family,

It is 4am and I can't sleep. I have to go to work tomorrow but I can't sleep. What happened today was the most horrific tragedy that any of us could have imagined. I can't imagine ever feeling the same about our safety here in the U.S.. I guess this is what it feels like to live in less fortunate countries where terrorism is something they live with. For so long we felt invincible and untouchable.

Today was the first time I thanked God that you have all moved away from New York. And that Aunt Reggie was not in the city on this tragic day.

My heart bleeds for the people who were lost in this mess. All the fire fighters and cops, and all those people who are still hoping to see their friends and family members again.

I am wondering what it will be like for you to come home and see the skyline forever changed. I am wondering what it will be like for me to see it for myself. I don't think I will be going to see it for a while. It is too sad.

I have tried to call Dad and Aunt Jo but couldn't get through. So I stopped trying to make long distance calls.

I was able to call locally and was able to reach Mom. I wonder if Alexi and Dave will still be able to come back to the U.S. from Bahrain? I am sure Dave has a lot to do now. I wish Dave all the safety in the world. I hope he will not be needed in any battles.

I always knew that our city could be a target for this kind of thing. But who would think that anything this huge would happen?

Thank God I don't know anyone that was working in those buildings. But I know many people who had friends there.

Work today was awful. I was sitting at my desk when Kevin called me with the news that a plane had crashed into one of the Twin Towers. I got off the phone and found the first person I saw and told them what I had learned. They told me to go to the conference room where the news was showing on a television. As I watched the flames coming from the first building I never imagined what was coming next. I was shocked as the second plane crashed into the next tower. I prayed to myself that everyone would get out of the buildings. I was certain at this point it was no accident and that we were being attacked. When the first tower fell I just remember crying. I knew that many had died at that point. When the second building fell I was in shock. I was holding my breath waiting for another attack. I was worried about my boss who was in the city that day. But we soon got a call from him as he walked out of the city over one of the bridges.

Everyone around me in that room was in shock. Some people were crying others ran out of the room to make phone calls.

One girl was hysterical saying her cousins were N.Y. fire fighters.

It was just awful. As we learned about the Pentagon attack and the plane that crashed in the field and we tried to digest what was happening. We stared at that television waiting for the next unbelievable and unthinkable event to happen.

We got to leave work early. I tried to find an American Flag somewhere on my way home. I was having no luck. I felt bad that it took this tragedy for me to buy a flag. I just felt a need to get one. I went to many stores. Than I saw a guy outside of Sears. He had a big flag tied to the back of his truck. He was also holding a small flag in his hand. I asked him where he got it. He said I got it in Sears but it was the last one. He said "Here you take it".

I did and thanked him. I held it out the window all the way home. People blew their horns and gave me thumbs up. As I sat at a light in front of a school there was a Mother walking with a her young daughter. Her Mom pointed to me and said to her "look the American flag". And she waved to me. A man marched up and down Deer Park Avenue holding a big flag and yelled to me to join him. I didn't, I had to get home. The best thing about our flag today is that it made people smile. It made people realize that we are Americans and together we will stand.

After I went home I headed to a blood bank. The line was so long. The blood bank was in the same strip mall where the Aide Auto Store used to be. And the line reached all the way back to the Melville bowling alley. People kept on coming. We put our names on a list. They couldn't handle the amount of people who showed up. The spirit was good. People comforted each other and really pulled together. Many people donated water, orange juice and cookies to the blood bank. They handed it out to the people on line. As we stood there, a car drove past us with 2 young guys and one of them yelled "kill the Arabs!" Nobody cheered.

I want to cry but I know it won't do any good. It is so sad. I am left just hoping that this is all over. I want to tell you that I love you very much. I don't think there will be any more of this.

Kevin and I had dinner with our landlords. They were very upset too. Tom is a teacher and started to cry when he explained to us what it was like having to tell his students what had happened. Many of their parents work in the city.

You could see the smoke all the way out here on the Island. Tonight the sky is so clear. I am left with a horrible feeling that this is not the end. I pray it is. I just want to share with you what it was like to be here. I feel that even though it is the most horrible thing that could happen. The people here are joining together. It is amazing thing to witness. I love you and will talk to you soon.

Love,
Gina

## 2001: SEPTEMBER 12
## A NEW YORK CITY SCHOOLGIRL TO NEW YORK FIREFIGHTERS

*On September 12, in schools all over the country, teachers used class time to have their students write to members of the police and fire departments, who had shown so much courage and lost so many comrades. This was one such letter.*

Dear Fire Fighters,

My name is ———. I go to the ——— School, and I am nine and-a-half. It seems quite pointless to describe my everyday life to you, when you have just risked your life to save people like me. However, I think that my praise would mean more to you, if I did describe myself. My mother is [her name]. My father is [his name]. I have a brother who I cherish, named ———. Enough about me, I think that it is time to talk about you.

Your courage is outstanding. In a million years, for a million dollars, I could not do what you have done. Once, we had pride in the two towers that gallantly scraped the sky. Now, we have pride in you. I am determined to support you, and donate whatever I can to you. I think that you are the most courageous people in the world, because you are the ones who have risked your lives, to save the lives of others.

I am not only writing to firewomen and firemen; I am writing to heroes and heroines. Standing in the rubble, at ground zero, I would be very afraid. Were you afraid? I hope that your heroic team will always remain in the minds of all Americans. Thank you so much.

Sincerely,

## 2001: CIRCA SEPTEMBER 12
## ANN TO A POLICE OFFICER

*The collapse of the twin towers brought destruction, chaos, and many large and small acts of heroism. For the author of this letter, one emotion that lingered was gratitude.*

To the Police Officer who helped me on September 11th:

You literally picked me up off the sidewalk that day. I was on the east side of City Hall Park and after the second WTC collapse I was running from the wall of dust and flying debris when I fell. I was terrified—people were running over me and past me. You lifted me off the ground and said "run with me". After a few blocks when I said I didn't think I could run anymore, you said run just a little further and then if you can't run I'll carry you. You got me to a safe place and went back to help others. I didn't get your badge number or your name but I will <u>never</u> forget you. I pray that you are safe. You and your brother and sister officers are one of the great things about this city.

> With love and gratitude,
> Ann (the lady in the gray dress
> and yellow sweater)

## 2001: SEPTEMBER 17
## JILLIAN LEHMANN TO KATHLENE NAZARIO

*For weeks after the World Trade Center attacks, the smell from the fire lingered, along with emotions that included shock, disbelief, and, as a woman named Jillian Lehmann (1966–) described it to her friend Kathlene Nazario (1968–), occasional bouts of panic as well.*

Subject line of e-mail: burnt smell

Kath—

I can't begin to explain the smell. Right now I have all the windows closed and the air condition on with the temp. in the 60's. It's like burnt wire and paper with a little...ummm...I can't place it, but it is so disturbing. Not that it smells everyday, just when the wind is right. I actually have one of those masks. But there is so much asbestos in the air it doesn't help.

I panic every night at sundown, because that's when I can see the planes. I went home (Commack) and felt like a coward, letting the terrorists have their way with me. Being back I am so unsure, so frightened, my father is the only one who can talk me down from the panic that rips through me. (Right now I can hear the planes working their approach to Laguardia and the hair on the back of my neck is standing on end.) Nice way to live, huh?

What you see on the news is sanitized. I am next door to the staging area at St. Vincent's hospital. I have met families of the "missing" and rescue workers. I don't want to repeat their stories. I wish they wouldn't tell me. Because it is these accounts that paralyze me in fear. When family members came up to me and gave me a flyer asking me if I had seen their brother, I didn't know what to do. I just said I would look. Sometimes I feel like I am stuck in this really intense episode of the Saturday morning cartoon, SUPER FRIENDS. Like some diabolical creature has attacked New York City and all these wounded people are walking around in Brooklyn somewhere saying, "Who am I?" "What am I?" with amnesia and the Super Friends are going to save us and round up the amnesia victims and give them back to there families. Something along the lines of, "I would've gotten away with it if it wasn't for you meddling kids." No . . . wait that was SCOOBY DOO. Whatever—you get the point. We are stuck in a real life action movie but there is no real action hero. Get it?

Flying has never been safer. You'll be fine.

I'll write more later.

I Love You,<br>
Jill

## 2001: OCTOBER 8
## ERIN LEARY TO TIM SWAN

---

*President George W. Bush responded to the September 11 attacks by calling for an immediate war on terrorism. By October, a massive bombing campaign had begun against targets in Afghanistan, where the Taliban government was accused of aiding and abetting Osama bin Laden and the al-Qaeda network. Erin E. Leary (1976–) had been commissioned as a naval officer after taking part in ROTC at Pennsylvania State University. From her ship in the Persian Gulf, she wrote this letter to her then fiancé after watching the first Tomahawks launched into Afghanistan.*

Leary served on active duty in the navy for four years. She and Tim were married in 2003.

Hi, sweetpea.

I was looking forward to calling you this weekend, but our phones and emails were turned off about a day before the strikes happened. Did you know before it happened? I was on watch last night and saw the destroyer about six miles away launch two Tomahawk missiles. When I joined the Navy, I never really expected to be a part of anything like this. We found out yesterday morning that the bombers were on their way. About 45 minutes after the missile shots, it came on CNN. It was strange to know about something before seeing it on the news. I think this is something that is going to last a long time. Even after the Taliban are gone, we will have to help set up new government and support it while we help rebuild this country. This could be a part of the rest of our lives.

Like I said in the email, I am really understanding what you said "Everything has changed". I've been thinking more about our plan to get around waiting for the wedding. With everything that has happened and will happen, I want to be your wife as soon as I can be. Let's talk a little more about that. I love you very much.

Erin.

## 2001: NOVEMBER 24
## AMBER AMUNDSON TO GEORGE W. BUSH

*By November, strategic cities in Afghanistan had been captured, and by December, the remaining Taliban surrendered or fled. In the United States, opinion polls showed the vast majority of Americans had favored attack. But that preference was hardly unanimous. One woman who was decidedly antiwar was Amber Amundson, a recent widow whose husband, Craig Scott Amundson, had died at the Pentagon on September 11.*

Dear President Bush,

My name is Amber Amundson. I am a 28-year-old single mother of two small children. The reason I am a single mother is because my husband was murdered on September 11, while working under your direction. My husband, Craig Scott Amundson, was an active duty multimedia illustrator for your Deputy Chief of Staff of Personnel Command, who was also killed. I am not doing well. I am hurt that the U.S. is moving forward in such a violent manner. I do not hold you responsible for my husband's death, but I do believe you have a responsibility to listen to me and please hear my pain.

I do not like unnecessary death. I do not want anyone to use my husband's death to perpetuate violence. So, Mr. President, when you say that vengeance is needed so that the victims of 9/11 do not die in vain, could you please exclude Craig Scott Amundson from your list of victims used to justify further attacks? I do not want my children to grow up thinking that the reason so many people died following the Sept. 11 attack was because of their father's death. I want to show them a world where we love and not hate, where we forgive and not seek out vengeance. Please Mr. Bush, help me honor my husband. He drove to the Pentagon with a Visualize World Peace bumper sticker on his car every morning.

He raised our children to understand humanity and not fight to get what you want. When we buried my husband, an American flag was laid over his casket. My children believe the American flag represents their dad. Please let that representation be one of love, peace and forgiveness. I am begging you, for the sake of humanity and my children, to stop killing. Please find a nonviolent way to bring justice to the world.

Sincerely,<br>Amber Amundson

## 2003: FEBRUARY 15
## ROBYN DeSANTIS RINGLER TO AL PACINO

*Despite initial predictions that the September 11 attacks would forever change the cultural landscape in America, frivolity made a slow but steady comeback in the months that followed. By the winter of 2003, celebrity was again celebrity, and fans were fans. The day after Valentine's Day, Robyn DeSantis Ringler (1957–), a nurse, lawyer, and writer living in Ballston Lake, New York, sent this letter to actor Al Pacino (1940–).*

February 15, 2003

Dear Mr. Pacino,

You walked into Joe Allen's, moving faster through a restaurant than anyone I had ever seen. Your fast stride made me notice you. Your oversized black coat also made me look. I knew right away that you were wearing the same coat that enveloped you on the beach in the movie, The Insider.

Your eyes stared intensely yet appeared not to see anything. Was it really you?

I asked the waitress, "Isn't that Al Pacino?"

"I'm not supposed to say, but it is."

"Sue," I said to my sister-in-law. "Get up. Leave your stuff. C'mon lets go."

I don't know why I felt the urge to hurry. It was instinctual, kind of like an adrenaline reaction.

As we approached your table, Mr. Pacino, I became painfully aware that you were not only a celebrity, but a man, like any other man and that I had made a terrible mistake. When you saw us striding toward you, your head jerked to the side and your face grimaced as if you were in pain.

Despite what I interpreted as your anguish, it was too late to turn back. We were already standing at your table and I had already thrust a used cocktail napkin and pen at you, which you seemed to accept automatically.

"Mr. Pacino," I said, "we just wanted to tell you . . . how much . . . we have enjoyed your movies . . ."

"We don't get out much," Sue said, trying to explain our behavior.

When the corners of your mouth turned up in a perfunctory half smile and you looked like you might vomit, I tried to take the napkin back.

"Oh please, Mr. Pacino," I begged. "You don't have to sign that—really! Really, PLEASE DON'T SIGN IT. We just wanted to tell you we are great fans . . ."

For the first time, our eyes made contact. You began to laugh and your whole body seemed to relax. Mine did too. You signed my battered napkin, then reached out to shake our hands—a firm, friendly handshake offered with a wide grin.

Even though I cannot read what you wrote on the cocktail napkin (hopefully, it's not an obscenity—that's not why you were laughing, is it?) I will cherish it always because it reminds me that celebrities are human beings and that fame is only a perception.

At first, we thought that nothing could be more memorable than meeting you, Mr. Pacino. But we were wrong.

There were more memorable moments during this rare visit to New York City.

A man died on the sidewalk in front of our eyes. Minutes earlier, he had been laughing at a table next to ours in Charley O's Restaurant. But on the way to the theatre, we passed his body on the sidewalk. People just walked by as two firemen pumped on his chest. His blonde companion stamped her spiky black high heels, repeating, "C'mon, c'mon, c'mon." But he continued to lie there unresponsive.

We went on to Edward Albee's play The Goat, about a man who was having an affair with a goat named Sylvia. The wife, played brilliantly by Sally Field, spent much of the play enraged, breaking dishes and vases and talking and yelling about love and hurt and pain and how could he be having an affair with a goat? The story stunned us with grief and hysterical laughter and we craved a chance to read or hear the lines again.

Okay, I'll admit it. I spent $95 on a black velvet scarf with red, green, and gold flowers that change colors with the light. I've never bought anything so extravagant, but hey, it was New York City and it was Saks.

I saw my best friend from law school who has breast cancer and no hair. I got to wrap my arms around her and hug her like I've wanted to everyday since she started chemo.

I returned home to my husband and daughter who I am rarely away from. Getting home was the best part of the trip.

So Mr. Pacino, I just wanted to tell you that I understand now what Anna Scott was trying to tell Will in Notting Hill when she said, "The fame thing isn't real, ya know." Life and death are real. Love is real. New York City is real. And you are real.

It was nice meeting you.

Sincerely,
Robyn D. Ringler

# EXCHANGE

**2003: MARCH**

**LEZA KNIGHT AND JOHN KNIGHT**

---

*With the Taliban forced from power in Afghanistan, President Bush turned his attention to Iraq, where, he claimed, Saddam Hussein had continued—despite UN resolutions—to develop weapons of mass destruction. On March 19, after repeated warnings, threats, inspections, ultimatums, and deadlines, the United States launched its first strikes against the Iraqi leadership and strategic targets. A week or so before the fighting began—and thanks to the technical ingenuity of a soldier named Dustin Price, who was stationed at Kuwait's Camp New York—Lieutenant John Knight and his wife, Leza, managed to communicate by instant message.*
Bailee was the couple's five-year-old daughter. Leza had just moved to the U.S. Army base at Fort Campbell, Kentucky.

JOHN: are you there?
LEZA: I'm here
JOHN: great!
JOHN: i love you
LEZA: did you get my e-mail?
JOHN: what are you wearing? (laugh)
JOHN: yes i go t your email
JOHN: i miss you
LEZA: I miss you more
JOHN: is the housing that bad?
LEZA: it's not great
JOHN: do we have a garage
LEZA: and it's small
LEZA: we have a carport right next to the neighbors

JOHN: they would not work with you for something else

LEZA: What time is it there?

JOHN: did you tell them I am a O-1E, not a new 2LT and we have alot of stuff

JOHN: it is 735 in the morn

LEZA: yeah, I argued with them over it.

LEZA: We won't be here that much longer.

LEZA: we miss you so much

JOHN: i will im you every night before I goto bed. you are 9 hours behind me; so it will be about 1200–1300 your time when I am able to talk

JOHN: it is next to impossible to get on the phone; this is the easiest way to keep in touch

LEZA: This is fine

JOHN: i can also send pictures to you by digital cam. I will send some today

LEZA: that would be good

JOHN: we will not be here much longer; so if a day goes by that i dont email you or im you; you can assume we are gone, so watch the news

LEZA: I'm just happy I can talk to you right now

JOHN: everyone is doing fine. there was no plane crash; chaplain hart said a rumor was going around about that

LEZA: Yeah, I know. I just found that out tonight

LEZA: I don't know where that one came from

JOHN: i am keeping a journal for you. i will keep you informed on what is going on so you can stop rumors. i knew this would happen once we left

JOHN: while I am thinking about it; tell dad I need a GPS—and fast (the smaller the better)

LEZA: so you'll mostly e-mail me around 12 or 1 in the afternoon here

LEZA: Did you get your key?

JOHN: yes, IM around 1200–1300, (be ready to talk), no I have gotten no mail

LEZA: They say mail will take up to two weeks.

LEZA: packages may take longer.

JOHN: Great—that means i will not get a GPS before I really need it

LEZA: probably not

LEZA: who do you hang out with

JOHN: already being interrupted by sick-call

JOHN: mostly the staff; CPT Avilla, CPT Sparkman, Rich, Cowden

LEZA: that's good

JOHN: Rich, Dr Fagbuyi, and I sleep in back of aid station

LEZA: Is it better there?

JOHN: we still have no medical equipment as of yet. all we have is what we carried. our stuff hasnt arrived yet

JOHN: it is a challenge to do anything. you have to walk ½ mile to go anywhere

LEZA: so what do you do.

JOHN: so far, I bummed some meds off of a PA from 3rd Infantry Div; but that was a challenge. they have been told by their leaders not to help us out

JOHN: they are very bitter at 101st for taking this camp from them

JOHN: we have 24hr guards in camp to watch our camp. it is surrounded by wire to keep them out.

LEZA: have there been any close calls

JOHN: nothing yet; there is nothing going on yet; all of our things are not here yet; so we can do nothing. alot of bullshit time; but that should change today or tomorrow

LEZA: Are you ready for war?

JOHN: myself?

LEZA: it may begin next week

JOHN: yeah; they are keeping us informed on what is going on. we have our mission; we will begin planning soon

JOHN: how is my baby, bailee?

LEZA: I'd hate to know the plan.

LEZA: Bailee is doing well. She talks back a little more than usual.

LEZA: She asks when are you coming home

LEZA: She wears you slippers and she'll give them back when you come back.

JOHN: Tell her i love her and I carry patrick everywhere I go. I will send some pics today. Tell dad about the GPS, add me to your IM list in case you catch me online; you will know. Tell Bailee I love her and miss her and keep my slippers warm for me. I need to go. Sickcall

has started and DR Fagbuyi is nowhere to be found. I will talk with
you later today. I love you and miss you.

LEZA: we love you and miss you more

JOHN: Good bye. I love you.

LEZA: l love you too, Bye

The following message could not be delivered to all recipients:

l love you too, Bye

LEZA: I love you!!!!!!!!!!!!!!!!

The following message could not be delivered to all recipients:

I love you!!!!!!!!!!!!!!!!

## 2003: MAY 22

## AN AMERICAN IDOL VIEWER TO MICHAEL POWELL

_____

*A glorified talent show notable for the viciousness of its instant judgments, Ameri-can* Idol *debuted in the summer of 2002. It offered viewers the chance to root, wince, empathize, and even help choose the winner by phone. But when the second season ended with the selection of singer Ruben Studdard over Clay Aiken, Federal Communications Commission head Michael Powell (1963–) received a flurry of complaints, including this one.*

I wish to issue a formal complaint with regard to the American Idol competi-tion on Fox network which concluded last evening. I believe this was an unfairly judged and voted competition for several reasons . . . one being that many people including myself were unable to cast our vote for Clay Aiken due to inability to access their phone lines. Furthermore, it's been said that some who did get through to vote for Clay received a message that thanked them for voting for contestant #1 which was Ruben Studdard. What's up with all this? I am not a teenager. I am a 56 yr. old business woman from Broomfield, Colorado who has now wasted many nights watching a competition which in my opinion has been mishandled in some way. Why was it impossible for so many of the Clay Aiken fans like myself to be unable to cast their votes? I tried for over 3 hours without success! I would like an explanation. Furthermore, I for one will not be watch-ing American Idol again as I feel as cheated as Mr. Clay Aiken.

Sincerely,

\*   \*   \*

## 2004: JULY 15

## MARTHA STEWART TO MIRIAM GOLDMAN CEDARBAUM

---

*Famous for her homemaking tips, her perfectionism, and her inexorable energy, Martha Kostyra Stewart (1941–) was the creator and head of a billion-dollar media empire and a target of parody long before her legal troubles began in 2002. That January, government regulators started examining a suspiciously well-timed stock sale, and her subsequent arrest and trial—on charges of lying to investigators—took place in an inevitable celebrity spotlight. She wrote this appeal to Judge Miriam Goldman Cedarbaum the night before her sentencing.*

Cedarbaum gave Stewart the minimum, according to sentencing guidelines: five months in prison and five months of home confinement.

Dear Judge Cedarbaum:

We have never had the opportunity to speak one on one, you and I, despite the fact that I sat before you for five weeks. I am sorry that the legal system is such that even when a person's life is at stake—and for me that means my professional and personal life, not my physical being—the constraints prohibit conversation, communication, true understanding and complete disclosure of every aspect of the situation. I am not a lawyer, I am not skilled in legal processes, I am not even knowledgeable about many legal terms and legal procedures. I am still, after two and a half years of legal maneuverings and countless hours of preparation and trial time, abysmally confused and ill prepared for what is described to me as the next step in this process.

I am a 62 year old woman, a graduate of the excellent Nutley, New Jersey public school system and Barnard College. I have had an amazing professional life and several exciting careers, and I am grateful for that. I have a lovely family and a beautiful, upright, intelligent daughter (also a graduate of Barnard College), and I feel blessed and proud.

For more than a decade I have been building a wonderful company around a core of essential beliefs that are centered on home, family values and traditions, holidays, celebrations, weddings, children, gardening, collecting, home-making, teaching and learning. I have spent most of my professional life creating, writing, researching, and thinking on the highest possible level about qualify of life, about giving, about providing, so that millions of people, from all economic strata, can enjoy beauty, good quality, well made products, and impeccably researched information about many hundreds of subjects which can lead to a better life and more rewarding family lifestyle.

I have been so fortunate to have collected around me a large and vital group of like-minded, wonderfully creative and highly motivated colleagues who also wished to fashion and build a company devoted to promoting these same values. By 2002 Martha Stewart Living Omnimedia was a young, highly respected public company, with more than 650 employees, a group of extraordinary strategic partners, and a future filled with hope and great potential for growth. The company was fast growing, well run, well managed, and without debt and it was productively creating how-to information and consumer products centered on my original ideas.

I was often chided for being a "perfectionist" by my competitors, peers, and the press, but the way we looked at our business was that we were "teachers" and what we taught had to be based in fact, truth and "highest standards of perfection," a phrase I adopted from the American Poultry Association's handbook, The Standard of Perfection. I have also been accused of being arrogant (as lately as this week on page 11 of the government's answer to our request for downward departure), and I apologize for that. Perhaps, in my enthusiasm and in my quest for jobs well and quickly done I did not always take time to pat backs, or offer thanks for good work. I have been extra hard on myself and my work ethic and performance and I sometimes forgot that others need a bit more praise than I remembered to give. I am sorry for that and I wish I could always be polite, humble, respectful and patient. That said, many of the talented people who started my company with me still work with me, and many have been at my side for more than fifteen years. One of the two original producers of our one hour daily television show, Carolyn Kelly, was buried this past Tuesday, a victim of a cancerous brain tumor. She was just 43 and the mother of three young children. The other original producer spoke proudly at the funeral of their joint contributions and their helping to shape the vision, with me, of a pioneering, Emmy award winning, and how-to television show. Carolyn's death put my problems in perspective: she could no longer hope, no longer create. I could.

As a child I was drawn to the novels of Willa Cather, Upton Sinclair, Dostoevsky and Gogol. I loved Cather's My Antonia and decided early on that even if I could not be a pioneer in a true "Westward Ho!" manner, I could attempt to forge new territories for American business. I knew what American homemakers needed and wanted, because I listened. Moreover, I was one of them, and very serious about the subject matter. I was not afraid to be curious, not hesitant to try new things. My books, all written after I turned 40, filled giant voids. They were widely read and the ideas within were happily emulated.

My vacations have never been restful sojourns, but always information gathering expeditions. Oftentimes I would take friends and children with me so they, too, could experience the wonders of the exotic, the beauties of nature, and the hunt for new ideas. My frequent trips to Japan resulted in the creation of a viable and wonderful omnimedia business in Japan. My trips to the Galapagos, to Egypt, India, Africa, Mexico, Brazil, Panama and Peru have afforded me and the company with myriad product ideas, countless columns for our publications, and masses of materials for cookbooks and articles, and even flower sources for Marthasflowers.com.

Because I intend to appeal the verdict, it is inappropriate for me to discuss the facts of my case in this letter but it is very important for me to inform you that I never intended to harm anyone and I am dreadfully sorry that the perception of my conduct has caused my family, my friends and especially my beloved company so much damage.

And here we come, of course, to the conundrum, the problem, the Kafkaesque confusion. What to do?

The problem is yours, but it is also mine. For you there are difficult decisions to make, complicated problems to solve, vast challenges to meet. For me, there are your conclusions to accept and consequences to deal with. And with all such massive decision making and problem solving come further challenges.

I ask that in judging me you consider all the good that I have done, all the contributions I have made and the intense suffering that has accompanied every single moment of the past two and a half years. I seek the opportunity to continue serving my community in a positive manner, to attempt to repair the damage that has been done and to get on with what I have always considered was a good, worthwhile and exemplary life.

My heart goes out to you; my prayers are with you, and my hopes that my life will not be completely destroyed lie entirely in your hands.

Respectfully and most sincerely,
Martha Stewart

## 2004: SEPTEMBER
## FARNAZ FASSIHI TO HER FRIENDS

*By the end of September 2004, U.S. casualties in the Iraq war stood at more than a thousand dead and more than four thousand wounded. Although formal political control of the country had been returned to the Iraqis in June, insurgents had stepped up their attacks on coalition soldiers and civilians and also on Iraqis being trained by the American-led forces. As this e-mail from* Wall Street Journal *correspondent Farnaz Fassihi (1971–) dramatized, the situation on the ground was worse than many Americans understood, and so perilous to journalists that they could barely do their jobs. When Fassihi's e-mail was forwarded by a recipient and widely posted on the Internet, readers were disturbed not only by the conditions she described, but also by the fact that they learned so much more from this personal e-mail than they had from their usual sources of news.*

Iraq's three main groups are the majority Shiite Muslims, the Sunnis—the Islamic minority that had ruled the country under Saddam Hussein—and the Kurds. The Iraqi city of Fallujah was held by Sunni insurgents until U.S. troops ousted them in November 2004. Moqtada Sadr is a radical Shiite cleric who established a militia group, the Mehdi Army, in June 2003. Baathists belonged to Saddam Hussein's ruling party. Elections took place in Iraq in January of 2005.

Being a foreign correspondent in Baghdad these days is like being under virtual house arrest. Forget about the reasons that lured me to this job: a chance to see the world, explore the exotic, meet new people in far away lands, discover their ways and tell stories that could make a difference.

Little by little, day-by-day, being based in Iraq has defied all those reasons. I am house bound. I leave when I have a very good reason to and a scheduled interview. I avoid going to people's homes and never walk in the streets. I can't go grocery shopping any more, can't eat in restaurants, can't strike a conversation with strangers, can't look for stories, can't drive in any thing but a full armored car, can't go to scenes of breaking news stories, can't be stuck in traffic, can't speak English outside, can't take a road trip, can't say I'm an American, can't linger at checkpoints, can't be curious about what people are saying, doing, feeling. And can't and can't. There has been one too many close calls, including a car bomb so near our house that it blew out all the windows. So now my most pressing concern every day is not to write a kick-ass story but to stay alive and make sure our Iraqi employees stay alive. In Baghdad I am a security personnel first, a reporter second.

It's hard to pinpoint when the "turning point" exactly began. Was it April when the Fallujah fell out of the grasp of the Americans? Was it when Moqtada and Jish Mahdi declared war on the U.S. military? Was it when Sadr City, home to ten percent of Iraq's population, became a nightly battlefield for the Americans? Or was it when the insurgency began spreading from isolated pockets in the Sunni triangle to include most of Iraq? Despite President Bush's rosy assessments, Iraq remains a disaster. If under Saddam it was a "potential" threat, under the Americans it has been transformed to "imminent and active threat," a foreign policy failure bound to haunt the United States for decades to come.

Iraqis like to call this mess "the situation." When asked "how are things?" they reply: "the situation is very bad."

What they mean by situation is this: the Iraqi government doesn't control most Iraqi cities, there are several car bombs going off each day around the country killing and injuring scores of innocent people, the country's roads are becoming impassable and littered by hundreds of landmines and explosive devices aimed to kill American soldiers, there are assassinations, kidnappings and beheadings. The situation, basically, means a raging barbaric guerilla war. In four days, 110 people died and over 300 got injured in Baghdad alone. The numbers are so shocking that the ministry of health—which was attempting an exercise of public transparency by releasing the numbers—has now stopped disclosing them.

Insurgents now attack Americans 87 times a day.

A friend drove thru the Shiite slum of Sadr City yesterday. He said young men were openly placing improvised explosive devices into the ground. They melt a shallow hole into the asphalt, dig the explosive, cover it with dirt and put an old tire or plastic can over it to signal to the locals this is booby-trapped. He said on the main roads of Sadr City, there were a dozen landmines per every ten yards. His car snaked and swirled to avoid driving over them. Behind the walls sits an angry Iraqi ready to detonate them as soon as an American convoy gets near. This is in Shiite land, the population that was supposed to love America for liberating Iraq.

For journalists the significant turning point came with the wave of abduction and kidnappings. Only two weeks ago we felt safe around Baghdad because foreigners were being abducted on the roads and highways between towns. Then came a frantic phone call from a journalist female friend at 11 p.m. telling me two Italian women had been abducted from their homes in broad daylight. Then the two Americans, who got beheaded this week and the Brit, were abducted from their homes in a residential neighborhood. They were supplying the entire block with round the clock electricity from their generator to win friends. The abductors grabbed one of them at 6 a.m. when he came out to switch on the generator; his beheaded body was thrown back near the neighborhoods.

The insurgency, we are told, is rampant with no signs of calming down. If any thing, it is growing stronger, organized and more sophisticated every day. The various elements within it—baathists, criminals, nationalists and Al Qaeda—are cooperating and coordinating.

I went to an emergency meeting for foreign correspondents with the military and embassy to discuss the kidnappings. We were somberly told our fate would largely depend on where we were in the kidnapping chain once it was determined we were missing. Here is how it goes: criminal gangs grab you and sell you up to Baathists in Fallujah, who will in turn sell you to Al Qaeda. In turn, cash and weapons flow the other way from Al Qaeda to the Baathists to the criminals. My friend Georges, the French journalist snatched on the road to Najaf, has been missing for a month with no word on release or whether he is still alive.

America's last hope for a quick exit? The Iraqi police and National Guard units we are spending billions of dollars to train. The cops are being murdered by the dozens every day—over 700 to date—and the insurgents are infiltrating their ranks. The problem is so serious that the U.S. military has allocated $6 million dollars to buy out 30,000 cops they just trained to get rid of them quietly.

As for reconstruction: firstly it's so unsafe for foreigners to operate that almost all projects have come to a halt. After two years, of the $18 billion Congress appropriated for Iraq reconstruction only about $1 billion or so has been spent and a chunk has now been reallocated for improving security, a sign of just how bad things are going here.

Oil dreams? Insurgents disrupt oil flow routinely as a result of sabotage and oil prices have hit record high of $49 a barrel. Who did this war exactly benefit? Was it worth it? Are we safer because Saddam is holed up and Al Qaeda is running around in Iraq?

Iraqis say that thanks to America they got freedom in exchange for insecurity. Guess what? They say they'd take security over freedom any day, even if it means having a dictator ruler.

I heard an educated Iraqi say today that if Saddam Hussein were allowed to run for elections he would get the majority of the vote. This is truly sad.

Then I went to see an Iraqi scholar this week to talk to him about elections here. He has been trying to educate the public on the importance of voting. He said, "President Bush wanted to turn Iraq into a democracy that would be an example for the Middle East. Forget about democracy, forget about being a model for the region, we have to salvage Iraq before all is lost."

One could argue that Iraq is already lost beyond salvation. For those of us on the ground it's hard to imagine what if any thing could salvage it from its violent downward spiral. The genie of terrorism, chaos and mayhem has been unleashed onto this country as a result of American mistakes and it can't be put back into a bottle.

The Iraqi government is talking about having elections in three months while half of the country remains a "no go zone"—out of the hands of the government and the Americans and out of reach of journalists. In the other half, the disenchanted population is too terrified to show up at polling stations. The Sunnis have already said they'd boycott elections, leaving the stage open for polarized government of Kurds and Shiites that will not be deemed as legitimate and will most certainly lead to civil war.

I asked a 28-year-old engineer if he and his family would participate in the Iraqi elections since it was the first time Iraqis could to some degree elect a leadership. His response summed it all: "Go and vote and risk being blown into pieces or followed by the insurgents and murdered for cooperating with the Americans? For what? To practice democracy? Are you joking?"

# Sources and Permissions

"A Faithful Reader." Letter to the editor of the "Bintel Brief." 1914. In *A Bintel Brief: Sixty Years of Letters from the Lower East Side to the Jewish Daily Forward,* ed. Isaac Metzker, pp. 129–31. New York: Schocken Books, 1971.

"A Heart-Broken Mother." Letter to Carry A. Nation. September 2, 1901. In Carry A. Nation, *The Use and Need of the Life of Carry A. Nation,* Chapter 13. Online at http://www.webroots.org/library/usabios/tuanocn4.html. April 13, 2005.

"A Lady." Letter to Abraham Lincoln. February, 1861. In the Abraham Lincoln Papers, American Memory Collection, the Library of Congress. Online at http://memory.loc.gov/cgi-bin/query/r?ammem/mal:@field(DOCID+@lit(d0757000)). October 2, 2001.

"A Lady of Louisiana." Letter to Gen. P.G.T. Beauregard. April 23, 1862. In *A Woman's War: Southern Women, Civil War, and the Confederate Legacy,* ed. Edward D. C. Campbell, Jr., and Kym S. Rice, pp. 77–78. Richmond: The Museum of the Confederacy and Charlottesville: University Press of Virginia, 1996.

"Mademoiselle Miss." Letter to a friend. October 18, 1915. In *Mademoiselle Miss: Letters from an American Girl Serving with the Rank of Lieutenant in a French Army Hospital at the Front,* pp. 24–25. Boston: W. A. Butterfield, 1916.

A. V. Letter to Maria. 1792. In "A Letter from a Lady to her Niece, on her expressing great uneasiness at the loss of her Beauty by the Small-pox," *The Universal Asylum and Columbian Magazine.* November, 1792, p. 306. Online in database: American Periodicals Series Online, 1740–1900. July 3, 2002.

Abortion clinic bomber. Letter to the editor of the *Pensacola News.* December 27, 1984. In *Abortion: A Reader,* ed. Lloyd Steffen, pp. 447–48. Cleveland, Ohio: Pilgrim Press, 1996. Reprinted by permission of the *Pensacola News Journal,* Pensacola, Florida.

Adams, Abigail. Letter to John Adams. November 27, 1775. In Abigail Adams, *Letters of Mrs. Adams, the Wife of John Adams,* pp. 62–64. Boston: Wilkins, Carter, & Company, 1848.

———. Letter to John Adams. March 31, 1776. In Adams Papers, The Massachusetts Historical Society. Online at http://www.masshist.org/adams/apmanuscripts/apselected_1_text.html. February 21, 2005.

———. Letter to John Adams. July 21, 1776. In *Familiar Letters of John Adams and His Wife, Abigail Adams, During the Revolution,* ed. Charles Francis Adams, pp. 204–5. Freeport, N.Y.: Books for Libraries Press, 1970.

———. Letter to John Quincy Adams. June 1778. In Abigail Adams, *Letters of Mrs. Adams, the Wife of John Adams,* pp. 94–96. Boston: Wilkins, Carter, & Company, 1848.

Addams, Jane. Letter to Mary Catherine Addams Linn. March 13, 1889. In "Urban Experience in Chicago: Hull-House and Its Neighborhoods, 1889–1963," University of Illinois at Chicago. Online at http://tigger.uic.edu/htbin/cgiwrap/bin/urbanexp/main.cgi?file=new/show_doc_search.ptt&doc=760. October 13, 2004.

Alcott, Louisa May. Letter to Thomas Niles. June 1868. In *The Selected Letters of Louisa May Alcott,* ed. Joel Myerson and Daniel Shealy, p. 116. Boston: Little, Brown & Company, 1987.

Allen, Sarah. Letter to her sister. July 2, 1816. In *A Narrative of the Shipwreck and Unparalleled Sufferings of Mrs. Sarah Allen (late of Boston) on Her Passage in May Last from New-York to New Orleans,* pp. 3–24. Boston: Printed for M. Brewster, 1816.

Alston, Theodosia Burr. Letter to Aaron Burr. August 12, 1812. In *Correspondence of Aaron Burr and His Daughter Theodosia,* ed. Mark Van Doren, pp. 339–40. New York: Covici-Friede, 1929.

*American Idol* viewer. Letter to Michael Powell. May 22, 2003. In "Mike Powell—Regarding *American Idol* Outcome," The Smoking Gun Archive. Online at http://www.thesmokinggun.com/archive/idolletters8.html. July 21, 2004.

Amundson, Amber. Letter to George W. Bush. November 24, 2001. In "Amber Amundson's Letters," *NOW* with Bill Moyers. Online at http://www.pbs.org/now/transcript/transcript_amberletters.html. March 11, 2005.

Anderson, Mary. Letter to John W. Studebaker. October 8, 1940. In National Archives and Records Administration, Record Group 86, Records of the Women's Bureau, 1892–1971. Online in database: LexisNexis Primary Sources in U.S. American History. October 12, 2004.

Andrews, Sarah. Letter to James Andrews. April 9, 1865. In *Postmarked Hudson: The Letters of Sarah A. Andrews to Her Brother, James A. Andrews, 1864–1865. With a*

*Chronology of the Andrews Family,* ed. Willis Harry Miller, pp. 51–52. Hudson, Wis.: Star-Observer Printer, 1955. Online in database: The American Civil War: Letters and Diaries. October 23, 2002.

Ann. Note to a police officer. September 12, 2001[?]. In Ragsdale Flyer Collection, 911 Digital Archive. Online at http://www.911digitalarchive.org/lowresflyers/ragsdale/c8.jpg. July 25, 2004.

Annie. Letter to Mark Twain. 1865. In *Appletons' Journal: A Magazine of General Literature,* vol. 3, no. 60, May 21, 1870, p. 585. Online in database: Making of America. April 11, 2001.

Anonymous sender. Letter to five friends. May 1935. In Daniel W. VanArsdale, "Chain Letter Evolution." Online at http://www.silcom.com/~barnowl/chain-letter/evolution.html. January 13, 2003.

Anthony, Susan B. Letter to Elizabeth Cady Stanton. October 1902. In *The Elizabeth Cady Stanton–Susan B. Anthony Reader: Correspondence, Writings, Speeches,* ed. Ellen Carol DuBois, pp. 298–99. Boston: Northeastern University Press, 1992.

Aurora, Lillian. Telegram to John Scopes. May 1925[?]. In L. Sprague de Camp, *The Great Monkey Trial,* p. 82. New York: Doubleday & Company, Inc., 1968.

Baez, Joan. Letter to the Internal Revenue Service. 1964. In Joan Baez, *And a Voice to Sing With: A Memoir,* pp. 120–21. New York: Summit Books, 1987.

Barnes, Christian. Letter to Elizabeth Inman. April 29, 1775. In Nina M. Tiffany, *Letters of James Murray, Loyalis,* pp. 187–88. N.p.: privately printed, 1901. Online in database: North American Women's Letters and Diaries. January 28, 2002.

Barton, Clara. Letter to Elvira Stone. December 12, 1862. In "Clara Barton Letter," National Park Service. Online at http://www.nps.gov/frsp/barton.htm. March 30, 2000.

———. Letter to Stephen Barton. July 22, 1861. In William Eleazar Barton, *The Life of Clara Barton: Founder of the American Red Cross,* vol. 1, pp. 119–21.

Bates, Ruby. Letter to Earl Streetman. January 5, 1932. In "Scottsboro: An American Tragedy." Online at http://www.pbs.org/wgbh/amex/scottsboro/filmmore/ps_bates.html. January 12, 2003.

Bedell, Grace. Letter to Abraham Lincoln. October 18, 1860. In the Abraham Lincoln Papers, American Memory Collection, Library of Congress. Online at http://memory.loc.gov/cgi-bin/query/P?mal:2:./temp/~ammem_eurG::. February 23, 2005.

Beecher, Catharine. Letter to Zilpah Grant Banister. 1849[?]. In Beecher Family Papers, Archives and Special Collections, Mount Holyoke College. Online at http://clio.fivecolleges.edu/mhc/banister/a/2/491022/01.htm. September 7, 2004.

Bernstein, Aline. Letter to Thomas Wolfe. August 1931. In *My Other Loneliness: Letters of Thomas Wolfe and Aline Bernstein,* ed. Suzanne Stutman, pp. 334–35. Chapel Hill: University of North Carolina Press, 1983. Online in database: North American Women's Letters and Diaries. February 14, 2002. Reprinted by permission of Michael F. Cusick for the estate of Edla Cusick.

Bird, Isabella. Letter to Henrietta Bird. September 7, 1873. In Isabella L. Bird, *A Lady's Life in the Rocky Mountains,* pp. 17–22. Norman: University of Oklahoma Press, 1960.

Blackwell, Antoinette. Letter to Lucy Stone. 1850[?]. In *Friends and Sisters: Letters between Lucy Stone and Antoinette Brown Blackwell, 1846–93,* ed. Carol Lasser and Marlene Deahl Merrill, p. 105. Urbana: University of Illinois Press, 1987.

Blackwell, Elizabeth. Letter to an unknown recipient. November 9, 1847. In Elizabeth Blackwell, *Pioneer Work in Opening the Medical Profession to Women,* pp. 67–69. New York: Longmans, Green, 1895.

Blaine, Harriet. Letter to Margaret Blaine. July 3, 1881. In *Letters of Mrs. James G. Blaine,* vol. 1, ed. Harriet S. Blaine Beale, pp. 209–11. New York: Duffield & Company, 1908.

Boon, Mary. Letter to William Boon. December 1778[?]. In E. Arnot Robertson, *The Spanish Town Papers: Some Sidelights on the American War of Independence,* p. 79. London: Cresset Press, 1959.

Bow, Clara. Letter to B. P. Schulberg. April 24, 1931. In David Stenn, *Clara Bow: Runnin' Wild,* pp. 229–30. New York: Doubleday, 1988. Copyright © by David Stenn. Reprinted by permission of the William Morris Agency on behalf of the author.

Boyd, Virginia. Letter to Rice Carter Ballard. May 6, 1853. In "Letters to R. C. Ballard regarding slave woman abuse," Africans in America, Part 4. Online at http://www.pbs.org/wgbh/aia/part4/4h3436t.html. April 24, 2000.

Brown, Addie. Letter to Rebecca Primus. August 30, 1859. In *Beloved Sisters and Loving Friends: Letters from Rebecca Primus of Royal Oak, Maryland, and Addie Brown of Hartford, Connecticut, 1854–1868,* ed. Farah Jasmine Griffin, pp. 20–21. New York: Alfred A. Knopf, 1999.

Brown, Grace. Letter to Chester Gillette. July 5, 1906. In Craig Brandon, *Murder in the Adirondacks: 'An American Tragedy' Revisited,* pp. 108–9. Utica, N.Y.: North Country Books, 1986.

Brown, Helen Gurley. Letter to Eric Rayman. August 14, 1972. Printed by permission of Helen Gurley Brown.

Brown, Kay and David O. Selznick. Five teletypes. 1936. In "My Enthusiasm for this Property Has Never Wavered . . . ," Ransom Center, University of Texas. Online at http://www.hrc.utexas.edu/exhibitions/online/gwtw/book/. May 22, 2002. Printed by permission of Kay Brown's daughters and by Daniel Selznick.

Brown, Rita Mae. Letter to Betty Friedan. October 24, 1974. Online at http://www.English.ilstu.edu/hesse/bradway/stuweb/murphy1.html. February 1, 2003. Printed by permission of Rita Mae Brown.

Brown, Sargry. Letter to her husband. October 27, 1840. In *Major Problems in American Women's History: Documents and Essays,* ed. Mary Beth Norton, p. 153. Lexington, Mass.: D.C. Heath & Company, 1989.

Brown, Tabitha. Letter to Noyes and Polly Brown. January 1817. In Ella Brown Spooner, *Clark and Tabitha Brown: The First Part of Their Adventures and Those of Their Three Children in New England, Washington and Maryland,* pp. 97–99. New York: Exposition Press, 1957.

Brown, Tina. Memo to Lawrence Weschler. Janurary 27, 1996. Printed by permission of Tina Brown.

Bryant, Emma. Letter to John Bryant. August 6, 1873. In Emma Spaulding Bryant Letters, an On-line Archival Collection, Special Collections Library, Duke University. Online at http://scriptorium.lib.duke.edu/bryant/1873-08-06.html.

————. Letter to John Bryant. August 7, 1873. In Emma Spaulding Bryant Letters, an On-line Archival Collection, Special Collections Library, Duke University. Online at http://scriptorium.lib.duke.edu/bryant/1873-08-07.html.

Bull, Mary Lucia. Letter to Susanna Stoll. Summer 1779. In "A Woman's Letters in 1779 and 1782," *South Carolina Historical and Genealogical Magazine,* vol. 10, no. 2, April 1909, pp. 125–27.

Bullock, Mary. Letter to the Confederate War Office. September 21, 1862. In *A Woman's War: Southern Women, Civil War, and the Confederate Legacy,* ed. Edward D. C. Campbell, Jr., and Kym S. Rice, pp. 81–82. Richmond: The Museum of the Confederacy, and Charlottesville: University Press of Virginia, 1996.

Burn, Feb. Letter to Harry Burn. August, 1920. In Paula Casey, "A Legacy of Leadership: Tennessee's Pivotal Role in Granting All American Women The Vote," American Women's Issues Advocate, Gifts of Speech at Sweetbriar College. Online at http://gos.sbc.edu/c/casey.html. August 6, 2001.

Butler, Frances. Letter to an unknown recipient. April 12, 1866. In Frances Butler Leigh, *Ten Years on a Georgia Plantation,* pp. 16–24. London: Richard Bentley & Son, 1883. Electronic edition: Documenting the American South, University of North Carolina at Chapel Hill Libraries. Online at http://docsouth.unc.edu/leigh/leigh.html. October 30, 2002.

————. Letter to an unknown recipient. June 23, 1867. In Frances Butler Leigh, *Ten Years on a Georgia Plantation,* pp. 66–71. London: Richard Bentley & Son, 1883.

Electronic edition: Documenting the American South, University of North Carolina at Chapel Hill Libraries. Online at http://docsouth.unc.edu/leigh/leigh.html. October 30, 2002.

Butturff, Dorothy Dow. Letter to Amie Dow. April 14, 1945. In Dorothy Dow Butturff Papers, Box 1, Folder 2, Georgetown University Library, Special Collections, Washington, D.C. Printed by permission of Barbara Delaney.

Cabot, Elizabeth. Letter to Frances Parkman. September 17, 1901. In Elizabeth Cabot, *Letters of Elizabeth Cabot,* vol. 2, pp. 344–45. Boston: privately printed by Rockwell & Churchill Press, 1905.

California resident. Letter to a Bodie officer. 1881[?]. In W. A. Chalfant, *Gold, Guns and Ghost Towns,* pp. 47–48. Stanford: Stanford University Press, 1947.

Carson, Rachel. Letter to Barney Crile. February 17, 1963. In Ellen Leopold, *A Darker Ribbon: Breast Cancer, Women, and Their Doctors in the Twentieth Century,* pp. 140–42. Boston: Beacon Press, 1999. Letter copyright © 1998 by Roger Allen Christie. Reprinted by permission of Frances Collin, Trustee.

Cary, Sarah. Letter to Sam Cary. June 16, 1806. In Caroline G. Curtis, *The Cary Letters, edited at the request of the family,* pp. 174–75. Cambridge, Mass.: Riverside Press, 1891.

Cassatt, Mary. Letter to Ellen Mary Cassatt. March 26, 1913[?]. In *Cassatt and Her Circle: Selected Letters,* ed. Nancy Mowll Mathews, p. 310. New York: Abbeville Press, 1984.

Chace, Elizabeth. Letter to Samuel Chace. April 3, 1854. In *Virtuous Lives: Four Quaker Sisters Remember Family Life, Abolitionism, and Women's Suffrage,* ed. Lucille Salitan and Eve Lewis Perera, pp. 143–44. New York: The Continuum Publishing Company, 1994.

Champion, Deborah. Letter to Patience. October 2, 1775. In the Miscellaneous Manuscripts Collection, Archival Manuscript Material, Library of Congress Manuscript Division, Washington, D.C.

Cherokee woman. Letter to a government official. January 15, 1818. In *The Religious Intelligencer . . . Containing the Principal Transactions of the Various Bible and Missionary Societies, with Particular Accounts of Revivals of Religion (1816–1837),* vol. 3, no. 49, May 8, 1819, pp. 786–87.

Child, Lydia Maria. Letter to Anna Loring. February 6, 1845. In the Child Papers, William L. Clements Library, University of Michigan. Printed by permission of the library.

———. Letter to Henry Wise. October 26, 1859. In *Correspondence Between Lydia Maria Child and Gov. Wise and Mrs. Mason, of Virginia.* New York: The American Anti-Slavery Society, 1860. Online at http://womenshistory.about.com/library/etext/bl_lmc_as1_01.htm. February 24, 2005.

Christian, Anne. Letter to Patrick Henry. May 22, 1777. In William Wirt Henry, *Patrick Henry: Life, Correspondence and Speeches,* vol. 2, pp. 72–73. New York: Charles Scribner's Sons, 1891.

Church, Angelica Schuyler. Letter to Philip Schuyler. July 11, 1804. In Allan McLane Hamilton, *The Intimate Life of Alexander Hamilton, Based Chiefly Upon Original Family Letters and Other Documents, Many of Which Have Never Been Published,* pp. 404–5. New York: Charles Scribner's Sons, 1910.

Clappe, Louise. Letter to Molly Smith. November 25, 1851. In Louise Amelia Knapp Smith Clappe, *The Shirley Letters: Being Letters written in 1851–1852 from the California Mines by "Dame Shirley,"* pp. 74–82. Salt Lake City: Peregrine Smith Books, 1985.

———. Letter to Molly Smith. September 30, 1851. In Louise Amelia Knapp Smith Clappe, *The Shirley Letters: Being Letters written in 1851–1852 from the California Mines by "Dame Shirley,"* pp. 42–46. Salt Lake City: Peregrine Smith Books, 1985.

Clark, Alice. Letter to Fred Clark. October 31, 1943. Printed by permission of Steven S. Raab Autographs, Ardmore, Pennsylvania.

Clarke, Patsy. Letter to Jesse Helms. June 5, 1995. In "A Letter From Jesse," The Independent Weekly. Online at http://indyweek.com/durham/2002-02-27/cover2.html. April 9, 2002. Printed by permission of Patsy M. Clarke.

Clemens, Olivia. Letter to Samuel Clemens. 1894. In Clara Clemens, *My Father, Mark Twain,* pp. 108–9. New York: Harper & Brothers, 1931.

Cline, Patsy. Letter to Treva Miller. February 22, 1956. In Cindy Hazen and Mike Freeman, *Love Always, Patsy: Patsy Cline's Letters to a Friend.* New York: Berkley Books, 1999.

Cocks, Judith. Letter to James Hillhouse. March 8, 1795. In *Slave Testimony: Two Centuries of Letters, Speeches, Interviews, and Autobiographies,* ed. John W. Blassingame, pp. 7–8. Baton Rouge: Louisiana State University Press, 1977.

Colburn, Charlotte. Letter to her family. June 7, 1944. In "Women of World War II Red Cross Clubmobile." Online at http://www.clubmobile.org/L079June7_44_1.html. January 20, 2003. Printed by permission of Charlotte Colburn Gasperini.

Collins, Mary. Letter to *The American Missionary.* 1889. In "The Indians: Letter from Miss Collins," *The American Missionary,* vol. 43, no. 8, August, 1889, pp. 225–26. Online in database: Making of America. September 17, 2004.

Conant, Charlotte Howard. Letter to her family. November 14, 1880. In *A Girl of the Eighties at College and at Home from the Family Letters of Charlotte Howard Conant and from Other Records,* ed. Martha Pike Conant, pp. 109–11. Boston: Houghton Mifflin, 1931.

Conrad, R. E. Letter to Mrs. E. W. Lantow. July 12, 1928. The Adlers' collection.

Conter, Monica. Letter to her parents. December 22, 1941. In the United States Army Medical Department Museum, Fort Sam Houston, Texas. Printed by permission of the museum.

Cook, Karin. Letter to Joan Barett Cook Carpenter. 1999. In *Letters of Intent: Women Cross the Generations to Talk About Family, Work, Sex, Love and the Future of Feminism,* ed. Anna Bondoc and Meg Daly, pp. 184–86. New York: The Free Press, 1999. Letter copyright © Karin Cook. Reprinted by permission of International Creative Management Inc.

Cooney, Joan Ganz. Letter to Timothy Cooney. November 15, 1986. Printed by permission of Joan Ganz Cooney.

————. Letter to Wilma Scott Heide. April 19, 1972. University of Maryland National Public Broadcasting Archives. Printed by permission of Joan Ganz Cooney.

Craft, Ellen. Letter to *The British Anti-Slavery Advocate.* October 26, 1852. In James L. Smith et al., "Letters to Antislavery Workers and Agencies, Part 5," *Journal of Negro History,* vol. 10, no. 3, 1925, p. 449. Online in database: JSTOR.

Cribari, Shawn and Wendy Crowther. Two letters. October, 1990. Printed by permission of Shawn Cribari and Wendy Crowther.

Crowther, Alice. Letter to Dee Cox. June 2, 1954. Printed by permission of Wendy Crowther.

Davis, Varina. Letter to Montgomery Blair. June 6, 1865. In Words and Deeds in American History, American Memory Collection, Library of Congress. Online at http://memory.loc.gov/cgi-bin/query/r?ammem/mcc:@field%28DOCID+@lit %28mcc/005%29%29. April 12, 2000.

De Hart, Abigail. Letter to Peggy Marshall. April 1871. In Margaret Armstrong, *Five Generations: Life and Letters of an American Family, 1750–1900,* pp. 17–18. New York: Harper & Brothers, 1930.

Deming, Sarah Winslow. Letter to Sally Coverley. April 1775[?]. In *Journal of Sarah Winslow Deming,* pp. 46–49. Washington, D.C.: National Society of the Daughters of the American Revolution, 1894. Online in database: North American Women's Letters and Diaries. August 8, 2001.

Dickinson, Emily. Letter to Thomas Wentworth Higginson. April 16, 1862. In *Letters of Emily Dickinson,* vol. 2, ed. Mabel Todd Loomis, p. 301. Boston: Roberts Brothers, 1894.

————. Letter to Thomas Wentworth Higginson. April 26, 1862. In *Letters of Emily Dickinson,* vol. 2, ed. Mabel Todd Loomis, pp. 301–3. Boston: Roberts Brothers, 1894.

————. Note to Louise and Frances Norcross. Spring 1886. In "1884–1886: Called Back," Emily Dickinson, Sparknotes from Barnes & Noble. Online at http://www.sparknotes.com/biography/dickinson/section10.rhtml. October 28, 2004.

Dickson, Annie. Letter to Mary Todd Lincoln. May 21, 1860. In the Abraham Lincoln Papers, American Memory Collection, Library of Congress. Online at http://memory.loc.gov/cgi-bin/query/r?ammem/mal:@field(DOCID+@lit(d0280100)). October 2, 2001.

Didrikson, Babe. Letter to Tiny Scurlock. April 25, 1931. In Mary and John Gray Library Special Collections and Lamar University Archives, Accession number 11.1.14.10, Beaumont, Texas. Reprinted by permission of the library.

Dodd, Mary. Letter to frontier widows. September 5, 1817. In *Second to None: A Documentary History of American Women,* vol. 1, *From the Sixteenth Century to 1865,* ed. Ruth Barnes Moynihan, Cynthia Russett, and Laurie Crumpacker, p. 369. Lincoln: University of Nebraska Press, 1993.

Donna. Letter to John Lennon and George Harrison. 1964. In Derek Taylor, *Fifty Years Adrift,* ed. George Harrison, p. 204. Guildford, Surrey, England: Genesis Publications Limited in association with Hedley New Zealand and Hedley Australia, 1984.

Donner, Tamsen. Letter to a friend. June 16, 1846. In Dale Morgan, *Overland in 1846: Diaries and Letters of the California–Oregon Trail,* vol. 2, pp. 561–63. Lincoln: University of Nebraska Press, 1993. Online in database: North American Women's Letters and Diaries. January 23, 2002.

Dorothy and Jan. Two letters. October–November 1974. In *Between Ourselves: Letters Between Mothers and Daughters, 1750–1982,* ed. Karen Payne, pp. 70–72. Boston: Houghton Mifflin, 1983.

Douglass, Sarah Mapps. Letter to William Basset. December 1837. In "Letter to William Basset," Africans in America, Part 3. Online at http://www.pbs.org/wgbh/aia/part3/3h99t.html. April 24, 2000.

Doyle, Mahala. Letter to John Brown. November 20, 1859. In Oswald Garrison Villard, *John Brown, 1800–1859: A Biography Fifty Years After,* p. 164. Gloucester, Mass.: Peter Smith, 1965.

Drew, Louisa. Letter to Lionel Barrymore. 1893. In Bill Homewood, *Theatrical Letters: 400 Years of Correspondence Between Celebrated Actors, Actresses, Playwrights, Their Families, Friends, Lovers, Admirers, Enemies, Producers, Managers and Others,* p. 192. London: Marginalia Press, 1995.

DuBarry, Helen. Letter to her mother. April 16, 1865. In *We Saw Lincoln Shot: One Hundred Eyewitness Accounts,* ed. Timothy S. Good, pp. 52–55. Jackson: University Press of Mississippi, 1995.

Duchesne, Philippine. Letter to William Carr Lane. Spring 1828. In Louise Callan, R.S.C.J., *Philippine Duchesne: Frontier Missionary of the Sacred Heart, 1769–1852*, p. 475. Westminster, Md.: The Newman Press, 1957.

Duncan, Marijane. Letter to Nancy Guri Duncan. Spring 1968. In Marijane Dill Duncan, *My Mother's Arm Swings the Broom with Mine*, ed. Nancy J. Guri Duncan, pp. 458–60. Oregon: Driftwood Press, 1994. Reprinted by permission of Nancy Guri Duncan.

Dunmore, Mrs. Charles. Letter to Lydia Pinkham. August 1899. In "The Dawn of Womanhood," *Los Angeles Times*, August 22, 1899, p. 10. Online in database: ProQuest Historical Newspapers. October 24, 2004.

Duquette, Louise. Letter to Norman Duquette. January 20, 1952. In "The American Experience: War Letters." Online at http://www.pbs.org/wgbh/amex/warletters/filmmore/pt.html. January 27, 2003. Printed by permission of Norman E. Duquette.

Dwight, Marianne. Letter to Frank Dwight. September 18, 1844. In Brook Farm records, 1842–1901, the Massachusetts Historical Society. Reprinted by permission of the Massachusetts Historical Society.

Earhart, Amelia. Letter to George Palmer Putnam. February 7, 1931. In *Letters From Amelia: 1901–1937*, ed. Jean L. Backus, pp. 104–5. Boston: Beacon Press, 1982. Copyright © 1982 by Jean L. Backus. Reprinted by permission of Beacon Press, Boston.

Eisenhower, Julie Nixon. Note to Richard Nixon. August 1974. In Stephen E. Ambrose, *Nixon*, vol. 3, *Ruin and Recovery, 1973–1990*, pp. 420–21. New York: Simon & Schuster, 1991. Reprinted by permission of Julie Nixon Eisenhower.

Elizabeth. Letter to her mother. August 1830. In "A Trip to Ellicott's Mills," *The Young Ladies Journal of Literature and Science*, vol. 1, 1830, pp. 21–23. Online in database: The Gerritsen Collection. August 9, 2001.

Ellin, Nancy. Letter to Lillian and Martin Ellin. June 30, 1964. In the Joseph and Nancy Ellin Freedom Summer Collection, Civil Rights in Mississippi Digital Archive. Online at http://anna.lib.usm.edu/~spcol/crda/ellin/ellin005-trans.htm. April 10, 2002. Printed by permission of Nancy B. Ellin.

Emerson, Ellen. Letter to Lidian Jackson Emerson. April 15, 1861. In Ellen Tucker Emerson, *The Letters of Ellen Tucker Emerson*, vol. 1, ed. Edith E. W. Gregg, pp. 239–41. Kent, Ohio: Kent State University Press, 1982. Online in database: North American Women's Letters and Diaries.

———. Letter to Ralph Waldo Emerson. February 3, 1862. In Ellen Tucker Emerson, *The Letters of Ellen Tucker Emerson*, vol. 1, ed. Edith E. W. Gregg, pp. 265–67. Kent, Ohio: Kent State University Press, 1982.

Emerson, Lidian Jackson. Letter to Lucy Jackson Brown. April 23, 1838. In Lidian Jackson Emerson, *The Selected Letters of Lidian Jackson,* ed. Delores Bird Carpenter, pp. 74–75. Columbia: University of Missouri Press, 1987.

———. Letter to Ralph Waldo Emerson. February 17, 1843. In Lidian Jackson Emerson, *The Selected Letters of Lidian Jackson,* ed. Delores Bird Carpenter, pp. 129–31. Columbia: University of Missouri Press, 1987.

Emily. Telegram to her father. November 24, 1863. In "A Romantic Incident," *Daily Intelligencer,* November 5, 1863, p. 2, Online at http://www.uttyl.edu/vbetts/daily_intelligencer.htm. October 18, 2002.

Expectant mother. Letter to Grantly Dick-Read. February 26, 1949. In *Post-War Mothers: Childbirth Letters to Grantly Dick-Read, 1946–1956,* ed. Mary Thomas, pp. 52–53. Rochester, N.Y.: University of Rochester Press, 1997.

Fannie. Letter to Norfleet. December 28, 1862. In Randolph B. Campbell and Donald K. Pickens, " 'My Dear Husband': A Texas Slave's Love Letter, 1862," *Journal of Negro History,* vol. 65, no. 4, Autumn 1980, pp. 363–64. Online in database: JSTOR. October 4, 2001.

Fassihi, Farzi. Email to her friends. September 2004. In "From Baghdad," Common Dreams News Center. Online at http://www.commondreams.org/views04/0930-15.htm. November 18, 2004. Printed by permission of Farzi Fassihi.

Finn, Judy. Telegram to Lyndon Johnson. July 28, 1965. In Folder 19, Box 02, Larry Berman Collection (Presidential Archives Research), the Vietnam Archive, Texas Tech University. Online at http://star.vietnam.ttu.edu/scripts/starfinder.exe/4040/v.virtualarchive.txt. November 11, 2004.

Fisher, Maude. Letter to Mrs. Hogan. November 29, 1918. In *War Letters: Extraordinary Correspondence from American Wars,* ed. Andrew Carroll, pp. 170–71. New York: Scribner, 2001.

Fitch, Mrs. Edwin J. Letter to Joseph Brown. April 16, 1861. In *Georgia: History Written By Those Who Lived It,* ed. Mills Lane, p. 141. Savannah, Ga.: Beehive Foundation, 1995.

Fite, Katherine. Letter to her parents. October 14, 1946. In "Truman and the Holocaust," Truman Presidential Museum and Library. Online at http://www.trumanlibrary.org/photos/hcaust3a.jpg. January 23, 2003.

FitzGerald, Emily. Letter to her mother. February 19, 1875. In *An Army Doctor's Wife on the Frontier: Letters from Alaska and the Far West, 1874–1878,* ed. Abe Laufe, pp. 95–96. Pittsburgh: University of Pittsburgh Press, 1962.

———. Letter to her mother. July 16, 1876. In *An Army Doctor's Wife on the Frontier: Letters from Alaska and the Far West, 1874–1878,* ed. Abe Laufe, pp. 203–4. Pittsburgh: University of Pittsburgh Press, 1962.

Fitzgerald, Zelda. Letter to F. Scott Fitzgerald. 1936[?]. In *Zelda Fitzgerald: The Collected Writings,* ed. Matthew J. Bruccoli, pp. 478–79. New York: Simon & Schuster, 1981. Reprinted by permission of Simon & Schuster and Harold Ober Associates.

Fleet, Lillian Waite. Letter to her family. March 12, 1885. In *Green Mount after the War: The Correspondence of Maria Louisa Wacker Fleet and her Family, 1865–1900,* ed. Betsy Fleet, pp. 211–12. Charlottesville: University Press of Virginia, 1978. Online in database: North American Women's Letters and Diaries. September 8, 2004.

Florida widow. Letter to Eleanor Roosevelt. December 14, 1934. In Robert S. McElvaine, *Down and Out in the Great Depression: Letters from the Forgotten Man,* p. 57. Chapel Hill: University of North Carolina Press, 1983.

Forbes, Elizabeth. Petition to the North Carolina Assembly. May 6, 1782. In Cynthia A. Kierner, *Southern Women in Revolution, 1776–1800: Personal and Political Narratives,* p. 31. Columbia: University of South Carolina Press, 1998.

Forbes, Rose. Letter to Edith Perkins. January 1865. In Charles Elliott Perkins and Edith Forbes Perkins, *Family Letters: 1861–1869,* pp. 217–18. Boston: privately printed, 1949.

Fort, Cornelia. Letter to Louise Fort. January 28, 1942. In Rob Simbeck, *Daughter of the Air: The Brief Soaring Life of Cornelia Fort,* pp. 236–38. New York: Atlantic Monthly Press, 1999. And first lines of the letter in "Air Combat 1996 Schedule." Online at http://www.geocities.com/Nashville/7348/cornelia1.html. January 15, 2003. Reprinted by permission of Dudley Fort.

Friedman, Mrs. Samuel. Letter to David Bressler. September 15, 1912. In Robert A. Rockaway, " 'I Feel as if Newly Born': Immigrant Letters to the Industrial Removal Office," *American Jewish Archives,* vol. 45, no. 2, Fall/Winter 1993, pp. 164–65.

Frix, Matilda. Letter to the Freedmen's Bureau. August 27, 1867. In *Georgia: History Written by Those Who Lived It,* ed. Mills Lane, pp. 221–22. Savannah, Ga.: Beehive Foundation, 1995.

Fuller, Margaret. Letter to Samuel Ward. September 1839. In *The Letters of Margaret Fuller,* vol. 2, *1839–1841,* ed. Robert N. Hudspeth, pp. 90–91. Ithaca: Cornell University Press, 1983.

G. Letter to Paulina Wright Davis. September 1854. In "Extracts from Correspondence," *The UNA: A Paper Devoted to the Elevation of Woman,* vol. 2, no. 9, September 1854, p. 32. Online in database: The Gerritsen Collection. September 9, 2001.

Gallant, Hazel. Letter to J. Clifford Gallant. February 10, 1943. In *Letters Home,* ed. Mina Curtiss, pp. 141–42. Boston: Little, Brown & Company, 1944.

Galt, Edith Bolling. Letter to Woodrow Wilson. August 4, 1915. In *A President in Love: The Courtship Letters of Woodrow Wilson and Edith Bolling Galt,* ed. Edwin Tribble, pp. 104–5. Boston: Houghton Mifflin, 1981.

Garfield, Lucretia. Letter to James Garfield. September 19, 1870. In *Crete and James: Personal Letters of Lucretia and James Garfield,* ed. John Shaw, pp. 269–70. East Lansing: Michigan State University Press, 1994.

———. Letter to Sara Spencer. Spring 1879. In *Crete and James: Personal Letters of Lucretia and James Garfield,* ed. John Shaw, pp. 354–55. East Lansing: Michigan State University Press, 1994.

Garland, Judy. Letter to her fans. November 1950. In "An Open Letter from Judy Garland," *Modern Screen,* November 1950. Online at http://www.jgdb.com/article6.htm. April 13, 2005.

Gates, Betsey Shipman. Letter to Betsey Gates Mills. November 7, 1884. In *Grandmother's Letters: Being for the most part selections from the letters of Betsey Shipman Gates to her daughter Betsey Gates Mills,* ed. Mary Dawes Beach, pp. 137–39. N.p.: privately printed by Henry M. Dawes, 1926.

Gay, Elizabeth. Letter to Abigail Hopper Gibbons. August 13, 1863. In *Life of Abby Hopper Gibbons: Told Chiefly through Her Correspondence,* vol. 2, ed. Sarah Hopper Emerson, pp. 58–59. New York: G. P. Putnam's Sons, 1896. Online in database: North American Women's Letters and Diaries. January 23, 2002.

Goldman, Emma. Letter to Margaret Sanger. April 9, 1914. In *The Margaret Sanger Papers Electronic Edition: Margaret Sanger and The Woman Rebel, 1914–1916,* ed. Esther Katz, Cathy Moran Hajo, and Peter Engelman. Columbia, S.C.: Model Editions Partnership, 1999. Online in database: Model Editions Partnership. April 10, 2001.

Gomez, Angela. Letter to Mariana García Chavez. March 5, 1988. In *Between the Lines: Letters Between Undocumented Mexican and Central American Immigrants and Their Families and Friends,* ed. Larry Siems, pp. 93–95. Hopewell, N.J.: Ecco Press, 1992. Reprinted by permission of HarperCollins.

Goos, Margarette. Letter to R. J. Reynolds Tobacco. April 21, 1986. In "Rather Than Send These Cards Off I Would Rather Sue You," Legacy Tobacco Documents Library, R. J. Reynolds Collection, University of California, San Francisco. Online at http://legacy.library.ucsf.edu/tid/muq15d00. April 5, 2002.

Gordon, Kate. Letter to her son. 1917[?]. In *War Letters: Extraordinary Correspondence from American Wars,* ed. Andrew Carroll, p. 130. New York: Scribner, 2001. Reprinted by permission of Patricia Nicholson.

Gordon, Ruth. Letter to her parents. December 22, 1915. In *Theatrical Letters: 400 Years of Correspondence Between Celebrated Actors, Actresses, Playwrights, Their Families, Friends, Lovers, Admirers, Enemies, Producers, Managers and Others,* ed. Bill Homewood, pp. 187–88. London: Marginalia Press, 1995.

Gottlieb, Ruth. Letter to Jonas Salk. April 12, 1955. Printed by permission of Jonas Salk.

Graham, Katharine. Letter to John Ehrlichman. November 3, 1972. Printed by permission of Donald Graham for the estate of Katharine Graham.

Grant, Abigail. Letter to Azariah Grant. August 19, 1776. In *The Huntington Letters in the Possession of Julia Chester Wells,* ed. W. D. McCrackan, pp. 174–75. New York: Appleton Press, 1897.

Greenhow, Rose. Letter to William Seward. November 17, 1861. In Rose O'Neal Greenhow Papers. Online at http://scriptorium.lib.duke.edu/greenhow/1861-11-17/1861-11-17.html. July 27, 2001.

Grierson, Alice Kirk. Letter to Benjamin Henry Grierson. December 20, 1871. In *The Colonel's Lady on the Western Frontier: The Correspondence of Alice Kirk Grierson,* ed. Shirley A. Leckie, pp. 62–64. Lincoln: University of Nebraska Press, 1989. Online in database: North American Women's Letters and Diaries. September 7, 2004.

Grimké, Angelina. Letter to Theodore Weld. February 17, 1838. In *Letters of Theodore Dwight Weld, Angelina Grimké and Sarah Grimké, 1822–1844,* vol. 2, ed. Gilbert H. Barnes and Dwight L. Dumond, pp. 553–54. New York: D. Appleton-Century Company, 1934. Reprint, New York: Da Capo Press, 1952.

———. Letter to William Lloyd Garrison. August 30, 1835. In "An American Time Capsule: Three Centuries of Broadsides and Other Printed Ephemera," American Memory Collection, Library of Congress. Online at http://memory.loc.gov/cgi-bin/query/r?ammem/rbpe:@field(DOCID+@lit(rbpe05601500)). March 2, 2003.

Grimké, Mary. To Angelina Grimké. April 4, 1838. In "Angelina Grimké's Mother Expresses Her Opinion, Letter," Old Sturbridge Village, Online Resource Library. Online at http://www.osv.org/Welcome.php?L=/education/LessonPlans/Lesson List.php. February 22, 2005.

Griswold, Eleanor. Letter to Arvine Wales. August 24, 1863. In "Eleanor Griswold Letter to Arvine C. Wales Regarding Quantrill's Raid on Lawrence, Kansas," Ohio Memory Online Scrapbook. Online at http://worlddmc.ohiolink.edu/OMP/New Details?oid=1089012&format=list&fieldname=xml&results=10&sort=title&search status=1&hits=1&searchmark=0&searchstring=eleanor+griswold&searchtype= kw&count=1. September 13, 2004.

Gustafson, Emma. Letter to her mother. April 5, 1909. In *Letters From the Promised Land: Swedes in America, 1840–1914,* ed. H. Arnold Barton, p. 237. Minneapolis: University of Minnesota Press, 1975.

Haise, Mary. Note to Fred Haise. April 1970. In Jim Lovell and Jeffrey Kluger, *Apollo 13* (previously titled *Lost Moon*), p. 324. New York: Pocket Books, 1994.

Hale, Sarah Josepha. Letter to Abraham Lincoln. September 28, 1863. In the Abraham Lincoln Papers, American Memory Collection, the Library of Congress. Online at http://memory.loc.gov/cgi-bin/query/r?ammem/mal:@field(DOCID+@lit (d2669900)). September 6, 2004.

Hale, Susan. Letter to Caroline Weld. May 5, 1902. In Susan Hale, *Letters of Susan Hale,* ed. Caroline Atkinson, pp. 369–70. Boston: Marshall Jones, 1919.

———. Letter to Charlotte Hedge. September 5, 1909. In Susan Hale, *Letters of Susan Hale,* ed. Caroline Atkinson, pp. 450–51. Boston: Marshall Jones, 1919. Online in database: North American Women's Letters and Diaries. February 25, 2002.

Hall, Carrie. Letter to Christian Raushenberg. August 1, 1867. In Lee W. Formwalt, "A Case of Interracial Marriage During Reconstruction," *The Alabama Review,* vol. 45, no. 3, July 1992, pp. 220–22.

Hampton, Sally Baxter. Letter to William Makepeace Thackeray. April 5, 1862. In *A Divided Heart: Letters of Sally Baxter Hampton, 1853–1862,* ed. Ann Fripp Hampton, pp. 117–19. Spartanburg, S.C.: Reprint Company, 1980.

Hancock, Cornelia. Letter to an unknown recipient. November 15, 1863. In *Letters of a Civil War Nurse: Cornelia Hancock, 1863–1865,* ed. Henrietta Stratton Jaquette, pp. 31–32. Lincoln: University of Nebraska Press, 1998.

———. Letter to her cousin. July 7, 1863. In *Letters of a Civil War Nurse: Cornelia Hancock, 1863–1865,* ed. Henrietta Stratton Jaquette, pp. 7–8. Lincoln: University of Nebraska Press, 1998.

Harper, Frances Ellen Watkins. Letter to an unknown recipient. December 1870. In William Still, *The Underground Rail Road: a Record of Facts, Authentic Narratives, Letters, &c: Narrating the Hardships, Hair-breadth Escapes, and Death Struggles of the Slaves in Their Efforts for Freedom,* p. 771. Philadelphia: Porter & Coates, 1872. Online in database: North American Women's Letters and Diaries. October 30, 2002.

———. Letter to William Still. December 15, 1859[?]. In *American Women Activists' Writings: An Anthology, 1637–2002,* ed. Kathryn Cullen-DuPont, p. 137. New York: Cooper Square Press, 2002.

Harris, Jean. Letter to Herman Tarnower. November 8, 1980. In Shana Alexander, *Very Much a Lady: The Untold Story of Jean Harris and Dr. Herman Tarnower,* pp. 193–99. Boston: Little, Brown & Company, 1983.

Haselton, Marjorie. Letter to Richard Haselton. August 15, 1945. Judy Litoff and David C. Smith, *Since You Went Away: World War II Letters from American Women on the Home Front,* pp. 276–77. New York: Oxford University Press, 1991. Reprinted by permission of Stephen S. Haselton.

Hayden, Maria Trenholm. February 12, 1851. In "Communication with the Spirit of his dead daughter Jane Elizabeth Pierce," American Centuries . . . view from New England, Memorial Hall Museum Online, Pocumtuck Valley Memorial Association, Deerfield, Massachusetts. Online at http://www.memorialhall.mass.edu/collection/itempage.jsp?itemid=16275&img=0&level=advanced&transcription=1. October 11, 2004.

Hellman, Lillian. Letter to John Wood. May 19, 1952. In Lillian Hellman, *Scoundrel Time,* pp. 92–94. Boston: Little, Brown & Company, 1976.

Henderson, Caroline. Letter to Evelyn Harris. July 19, 1932. In Caroline Henderson, *Letters from the Dust Bowl,* pp. 114–16. Norman: University of Oklahoma Press, 2001. Reprinted by permission of Eleanor Grandstaff.

Henderson, Grace. Letter to Ed Henderson. January 19, 1890. In "Looked in Vain for Work," *New York Times,* vol. 39, no. 11,981, January 21, 1890, p. 8, col. 3.

Hersey, Heloise Edwina. Letter to Helen. Circa 1901. In *To Girls, A Budget of Letters,* pp. 214–22. Boston: Atheneum, 1901. Online in database: North American Women's Letters and Diaries. September 7, 2004.

Hershkowitz, Dora. Letter to Phillip Lear. January 8, 1936. Printed by permission of Dora Hershkowitz Lear.

Higginson, Anna. Letter to Mrs. Mark Skinner. November 10, 1871. In "Library: An Anthology of Fire Narratives," The Eyewitnesses, The Great Chicago Fire and the Web of Memory, Chicago Historical Society. Online at http://www.chicagohs.org/fire/witnesses/higginson.html. September 20, 2001.

High-school student. Letter to the *New York Times.* November 29, 1964. In "I've Got to Bust," *New York Times Sunday Magazine.* pp. 48–49.

Hillyer, Mrs. Letter to the Seattle Bureau of Prohibition. September 12, 1931. Online in database: National Archives and Records Administration. Online at http://arcweb.archives.gov. April 30, 2001.

Hine, Mrs. James. Letter to her mother. December 20, 1833. In *Georgia: History Written By Those Who Lived It,* ed. Mills Lane, pp. 86–89. Savannah, Ga.: Beehive Press, 1995.

Hodgdon, Sarah. Letter to Mary Hodgdon. June 1830. In *Farm to Factory: Women's Letters, 1830–1860,* ed. Thomas Dublin, p. 42. New York: Columbia University Press, 1981.

Hodgkins, Sarah and Joseph Hodgkins. Four letters. January 5, 1778 to April 26, 1778. In Herbert T. Wade and Robert A. Lively, *This Glorious Cause: The Adventures of Two Company Officers in Washington's Army,* pp. 233–40. Princeton: Princeton University Press, 1958.

Hoffman, Elizabeth. Letter to *Time* magazine. August 11, 1967. In *Dear Editor: Letters to Time Magazine, 1923–1984,* ed. Phil Perman, p. 205. Salem, N.H.: Salem House, 1985.

Hohlwein, Kathryn. Letter to Pat Lamb. December 8, 1963. In Patricia Frazer Lamb and Kathryn Joyce Hohlwein, *Touchstones: Letters Between Two Women, 1953–1964,* p. 305. New York: Harper & Row, 1983.

Holley, Mary Austin. Letter to Charles Austin. December 1831. In Mattie Austin Hatcher, *Letters of an Early American Traveller: Mary Austin Holley, Her Life and Her Works, 1784–1846,* pp. 167–70. Dallas: Southwest Press, 1933.

Holloway, Priscilla. Letter to John Holloway. August 6, 1945. In the John and Priscilla Holloway Papers, Marquette University Libraries. Online at http://www.marquette.edu/library/collections/archives/projects/holloway/pmh-1945-08-06.html. November 8, 2004.

Howe, Julia Ward. Letter to James Fields. December 1861. In Deborah Pickman Clifford, *Mine Eyes Have Seen the Glory: A Biography of Julia Ward Howe,* pp. 146–47. Boston: Little, Brown & Company, 1978.

Hulton, Anne. Letter to Elizabeth Lightbody. April 22, 1775. In Ann Hulton, *Letters of a Loyalist Lady,* pp. 76–80. Eyewitness Accounts of the American Revolution, series 3. New York: *New York Times,* 1971, © 1927.

Huntington, Rachel. Letter to Lucy Huntington Brown. May 28, 1797. In *The Huntington Letters in the Possession of Julia Chester Wells,* ed. W. D. McCrackan, pp. 151–56. New York: The Appleton Press, 1897.

Huntington, Susan Mansfield. Letter to her son. September 19, 1823. In Susan Mansfield Huntington and Benjamin B. Wisner, *Memoirs of the Late Mrs. Susan Huntington, of Boston, Mass., Consisting Principally of Extracts from her Journal and Letters; with the Sermon Occasioned by her Death,* pp. 362–63. Boston: Cocker & Brewster, 1826. Online in database: North American Women's Letters and Diaries. February 15, 2002.

Hurston, Zora Neale. Letter to Langston Hughes. July 10, 1928. In *Zora Neale Hurston: A Life in Letters,* ed. Carla Kaplan, pp. 121–23. New York: Anchor Books, 2003. Reprinted by permission of the Zora Neale Hurston Trust and Victoria Sanders & Associates.

Inman, Elizabeth Murray Smith. Letter to John Innes Clark. January 4, 1777. In Nina M. Tiffany, *Letters of James Murray, Loyalist,* pp. 260–61. Boston: privately printed, 1901. Online in database: North American Women's Letters and Diaries. August 9, 2001.

J.I.A. Letter to Eleanor Roosevelt. April 17, 1938. In New Deal Network. Online at http://newdeal.feri.org/search_details.cfm?link=http://newdeal.feri.org/eleanor/jia0438.htm. October 13, 2004.

Jackson, Charlotte Ann. Letter to an unknown recipient. 1863[?]. In Henry L. Swint, *Dear Ones at Home: Letters from Contraband Camps,* p. 252. Nashville: Vanderbilt University Press, 1966. Online in database: North American Women's Letters and Diaries. January 23, 2002.

Jackson, Elizabeth. Letter to Andrew Jackson. November 1781. In *Letters in American History,* ed. H. Jack Lang, pp. 28–29. New York: Harmony Books, 1982.

Jackson, Helen Hunt. Letter to Charles Dudley Warner. November 18, 1879. In *The Indian Reform Letters of Helen Hunt Jackson, 1879–1885,* ed. Valerie Sherer Mathes, p. 22. Norman: University of Oklahoma Press, 1998.

Jackson, Lethe. Letter to Virginia Campbell. April 18, 1838. In "Hannah Valentine and Lethe Jackson, Slave Letters in the Campbell Family Papers," Special Collections Library at Duke University. Online at http://scriptorium.lib.duke.edu/campbell/1838-04-18/1838-04-18.html. March 28, 2000.

Jackson, Mary Anna. Letter to Stonewall Jackson. April 1863. In Stonewall Jackson Papers, Virginia Military Institute Archives. Online at http://www.vmi.edu/archives/jackson/mj1863nd.html. September 20, 2001.

Jacobs, Harriet. Letter to Ednah Dow Cheney. April 25, 1867. In "Letter from Harriet Jacobs," Africans in America, Part 4. Online at http://www.pbs.org/wgbh/aia/part4/4h2925t.html. April 24, 2000.

Jewett, Helen. Letter to Richard Robinson. August 1835. In Patricia Cline Cohen, *The Murder of Helen Jewett: The Life and Death of a Prostitute in Nineteenth-Century New York,* pp. 262–63. New York: Alfred A. Knopf, 1998.

Jewett, Sarah Orne. Letter to Willa Cather. December 13, 1908. In *Letters of Sarah Orne Jewett,* ed. Annie Fields, pp. 247–50. Boston: Houghton Mifflin, 1911.

Johnson, Hannah. Letter to Abraham Lincoln. July 31, 1863. In *The Columbia Documentary History of Race and Ethnicity in America,* ed. Ronald H. Bayor, p. 294. New York: Columbia University Press, 2004.

Johnson, Lady Bird. Letter to Lyndon Johnson. August 1964. In President's Decision to Run in 1964, Family Correspondence, Lyndon B. Johnson Library and Museum, Austin, Texas. Printed by permission of Mrs. Lyndon B. Johnson.

Jones, Carol. Letter to her mother. July 16, 1929. In the Adlers' collection.

Jones, Charlotte. Letter to George Sokolovsky. March 11, 1957. In "Elvis Presley," Department of Justice, Freedom of Information Act, Part 01. Online at http://foia.fbi.gov/foiaindex/presley.htm. January 30, 2003.

Jones, Constance. Letter to Donald Swartzbaugh. August 18, 1945. In Judy Litoff and David C. Smith, *Since You Went Away: World War II Letters from American Women on the Home Front,* pp. 279–80. New York: Oxford University Press, 1991. Reprinted by permission of Judy Barrett Litoff.

Jones, Eva. Letter to Mary Jones. June 13, 1865. In Robert Manson Myers, *The Children of Pride: Selected letters of the family of the Rev. Dr. Charles Colcok Jones from the years 1860–1868, with the addition of several previously unpublished letters,* pp. 549–50. New Haven: Yale University Press, 1972.

Jones, Martha Selden. Letter to Martha Gibson. August 25, 1814. In C. G. Chamberlayne, "Letter of Martha Selden Jones," *William and Mary College Quarterly Historical Magazine,* series 2, vol. 18, no. 3, July 1938, pp. 291–93. Online in database: JSTOR. October 4, 2001.

Jones, Mary "Mother." Letter to John Mitchell. June 23, 1902. In "Mother Jones Collection," Catholic University of America. Online at http://libraries.cua.edu/MotherJones/mj020623jm.html. February 7, 2002.

Joplin, Janis. Letter to Peter DeBlanc. October 6, 1965. Steven S. Raab Autographs, Ardmore, Pennsylvania. Copyright © by Fantality Corporation. All rights reserved. Printed by permission of Laura Joplin.

Keller, Helen. Letter to Anna Turner. June 17, 1887. In Helen Keller, *The Story of My Life,* p. 145. New York: Doubleday, Page & Company, 1903.

———. Letter to Samuel Clemens. March 27, 1906. In Helen Keller Papers, Personalities T–Z, American Foundation for the Blind. Online at http://www.afb.org/section.asp?Documentid=1115. February 6, 2002. Reprinted by permission of the American Foundation for the Blind, Helen Keller Archives. Copyright © by American Foundation for the Blind.

Kendall, Keziah. Letter to Simon Greenleaf. 1839. In *Root of Bitterness: Documents of the Social History of American Women,* ed. Nancy F. Cott et al., pp. 128–31. Boston: Northeastern University Press, 1996.

Kennedy, Jacqueline. Letter to Nikita Khrushchev. December 1, 1963. In "Jackie's Letter to Russia After Assassination." Online at www.jfk-info.com/rus-jackie.htm. October 13, 2004.

Kennedy, Rose. Letter to her children. October 9, 1942. In collection JFK-JFKPP, John F. Kennedy Personal Papers, 1917–1963, John F. Kennedy Library (NLJFK), Columbia Point, Boston, National Archives and Records Administration. Online at http://arcweb.archives.gov. March 9, 2005.

Kidder, Isabel. Letter to Maurice Kidder. October 1942. In *Since You Went Away: World War II Letters from American Women on the Home Front,* ed. Judy Barrett Litoff and David C. Smith, p. 11. New York: Oxford University Press, 1991. Reprinted by permission of Judy Barrett Litoff.

Kincaid, Mary. Letter to Mamie Goodwater. February 28, 1896. In *Read This Only to Yourself: The Private Writings of Midwestern Women, 1880–1910,* ed. Elizabeth Hampsten, p. 106. Bloomington: Indiana University Press, 1982.

Kinkel, Kristin. Letter to Jack Mattison. November 1999. In "Frontline: The Killer at Thurston High: 111 Years Without Parole—Kirsten's Letter." Online at http://www.pbs.org/wgbh/pages/frontline/shows/kinkel/trial/letter.html. January 27, 2003.

Knight, Leza and John Knight. Instant message exchange. March 10, 2003. In "Soldiers and Families Connect Via Email," The Wall Street Journal Online. Online at http://online.wsj.com/article_print/0,,SB104854574091255900,00.html. March 26, 2003.

Knox, Lucy. Letter to Henry Knox. August 23, 1777. In "Revolutionary Ideology and Women" and "Treasures of the Collection, 1763–1777, the Revolutionary Era," The Gilder Lehrman Institute of American History. Online at http: //www.gilderlehrman. org/collection/document.php?id=278. February 4, 2003. And online at http://www. gilderlehrman.org/collection/treasures_popknoxknox.html. October 30, 2004.

Kroch, Gretchen. Letter to her parents. December 24, 1943. In *With Love, Jane: Letters from American Women on the War Fronts,* ed. Alma Lutz, p. 78. New York: John Day Company, 1945. Online in database: North American Women's Letters and Diaries. January 15, 2003.

Landman, Bette. Letter to the Beaver College community. February 2000. In "Uneager Beavers," *Harper's,* August 2000, p. 29.

Lathrop, Mrs. W. C. Letter to Thomas Edison. March 5, 1921. In "Thank You, Mr. Edison: Electricity, Innovation and Social Change," American Memory Collection, Library of Congress. Online at http://memory.loc.gov/ammem/ndlpedu/lessons/99/edison/images/mrs2.gif. January 6, 2003.

Leary, Erin. Letter to Tim Swan. October 8, 2001. Courtesy of Andrew S. Carroll, the Legacy Project. Printed by permission of Erin E. Leary Swan.

Lee, Elizabeth Blair. Letter to Samuel Phillips Lee. July 21, 1861. In the Blair–Lee Family Papers, Bx 7, F 7, Collection Number C0614, Department of Rare Books and Special Collections, Princeton University Library.

Lee, M. P. Letter to *The American Magazine.* October 20, 1892. In "She Believes in Dress Reform," *The American Magazine,* vol. 5, no. 2, p. 110. Online in database: The Gerritsen Collection. October 10, 2004.

Lee, Mary Custis. Letter to Elizabeth Stiles. February 9, 1861. In "Document of the Month, February 2000," Stratford Hall Plantation: The Birthplace of Robert E. Lee. Online at http://www.stratfordhall.org/feb00doc/letter.html. October 15, 2002.

———. Letter to Lettie. November 15, 1870. In "Mary Anne Randolph Custis." Online at http://www.civilwarhistory.com/custis.htm. October 24, 2001.

———. Note to Union soldiers. May 11, 1862. In Mary P. Coulling, *The Lee Girls,* p. 102. Winston-Salem, N.C.: John F. Blair, 1987.

Lehmann, Jillian. Email to Kathlene Nazario. September 17, 2001. Email #852, The September 11 Digital Archive. Online at http://www.911digitalarchive.org/email/details/852. Printed by permission of Jillian Lehmann.

Lester, Vilet. Letter to Patsey Patterson. August 29, 1857. In "Vilet Lester Letter," Joseph Allred Papers, Special Collections Library, Duke University. Online at http://scriptorium.lib.duke.edu/lester/lester.html. April 21, 2000.

Leverett, Mary Maxcy. Letter to Milton Leverett. February 24, 1864. In *The Leverett Letters: Correspondence of a South Carolina Family, 1851–1868,* ed. Frances Wallace Taylor, Catherine Taylor Matthews, and J. Tracy Power, pp. 384–87. Columbia: University of South Carolina Press, 2000.

Lewinsky, Monica. Letter to Bill Clinton. September 30, 1997. In *The Starr Report: The Evidence,* ed. Phil Kuntz, p. 428. New York: Pocket Books, 1998.

Lincoln, Mary Todd. Letter to Mary Harlan Lincoln. March 22, 1869[?]. In Mark E. Neely, Jr., and R. Gerald McMurtry, *The Insanity File: The Case of Mary Todd Lincoln,* pp. 153–55. Carbondale: Southern Illinois University Press, 1986.

Linn, Jeannette. Letter to Santa. December 21, 1899. In "A Letter to Santa—1899," Traveling Through Time with the Shelby County Historical Society. Online at http://www.shelbycountyhistory.org/schs/archives/events/santaltreventa.htm. November 16, 2002.

Liston, Henrietta. Letter to James Jackson. December 19, 1799. In Bradford Perkins, "A Diplomat's Wife in Philadelphia: Letters of Henrietta Liston, 1796–1800," *William and Mary Quarterly,* series 3, vol. 2, no. 4, October 1954, p. 628. Online in database: JSTOR. October 4, 2001.

————. Letter to James Jackson. February 24[?], 1797. In Bradford Perkins, "A Diplomat's Wife in Philadelphia: Letters of Henrietta Liston, 1796–1800," *William and Mary Quarterly,* series 3, vol. 11, no. 4, October 1954, pp. 608–9. Online in database: JSTOR. October 4, 2001.

Logue, Sarah. Letter to J. W. Loguen. February 20, 1860. In Frederick Douglass et al., "Letters to Antislavery Workers and Agencies, Part 3," *Journal of Negro History,* vol. 10, no. 3, July 1925, pp. 401–2. Online in database: JSTOR. October 4, 2001.

Lovejoy, Julia Louisa. Letter to the *New Hampshire Independent Democrat.* September 21, 1857. In "Letters of Julia Louisa Lovejoy, 1856–1864: Part Two, 1857," *Kansas Historical Quarterly,* vol. 15, no. 3, August 1947, pp. 306–8.

Low, Juliette Gordon. Letter to Girl Scouts. 1912. In "Juliette Low's Notes on the Laws, 1912," Juliette Gordon Low. Online at http://billb.i8.com/girlscout/JGL.htm. October 23, 2004.

MacArthur, Mary. Letter to Gen. Pershing. August 1924. In "From Mother's Pen: Letter #3," MacArthur, The American Experience. Online at http://www.pbs.org/

wgbh/amex/macarthur/filmmore/reference/primary/pinky03.html. April 4, 2002. Reprinted by permission of the General Douglas MacArthur Foundation, Norfolk, Virginia.

MacLeod, Lila. Letter to Lucile Allen. February 22, 1949. In "From Domesticity to Modernity: What Was Home Economics?" Rare and Manuscript Collections, Cornell University. Online at http://rmc.library.cornell.edu/homeEc/1g/to_lemo_letter Alt.htm. New York State College of Home Economics Records, 1875–1970. Courtesy of the Division of Rare and Manuscript Collections, Cornell University Library.

Madison, Dolley. Letter to Anna Cutts. August 23, 1814. In "The Washington Years," The Dolley Madison Project, Virginia Center for Digital History. Online at http://moderntimes.vcdh.virginia.edu/madison/exhibit/washington/letters/082314.html. February 22, 2005.

Manning, Teresa. Letter to *Ms.* May 1974. In *Letters to* Ms.: *1972–1987,* ed. Mary Thom, p. 32. New York: H. Holt, 1987.

Marge. Letter to Walter. August 29, 1943. In "Great Lakes 2000 Cruises," Project Liberty Ship. Online at http://www.liberty-ship.com/. February 5, 2002.

Mary. Letter to Christian brothers and sisters. 2001. In "Youth Arise." Online at http://www.arnold-komala.com/gki/kpr/confession.htm. March 12, 2005. Printed by permission of True Love Waits and LifeWay Christian Resources.

Matie, Julia. Letter to Mrs. A. M. Thomas. January 8, 1861. In the Abraham Lincoln Papers, American Memory Collection, Library of Congress. Online at http://memory.loc.gov/cgi-bin/query/r?ammem/mal:@field(DOCID+@lit(d0593900)) October 2, 2001.

Matsushita, Hanaye. Letter to Iwao Matsushita. July 15, 1942. In Louis Fiset, *Imprisoned Apart: The World War II Correspondence of an Issei Couple,* pp. 155–56. Seattle: University of Washington Press, 1997. Iwao Matsushita Papers, University of Washington Libraries. Reprinted by permission of the library.

Mauzy, Mary. Letter to Eugenia Burton. October 17, 1859. In "The Mauzy Letters on John Brown's Raid," Notable People, Harpers Ferry Historical Park. Online at http://www.nps.gov/hafe/mauzy.htm. March 30, 2000.

McCarthy, Jean. Letter to Mr. Baldwin. May 31, 1957. In "History for Sale: The Autograph and Manuscript Leader." Online at http://www.historyforsale.com/html/prodetails.asp?documentid=34618&start=1. January 15, 2003.

McCarthy, Margaret. Letter to her family. September 22, 1850. In Diarmaid O. Muirithe, *A Seat Behind the Coachman: Travellers in Ireland, 1800–1900,* pp. 138–42. Dublin: Gill and Macmillan Ltd., 1972.

McClendon, Sarah. Letter to family and friends. April 1797. In "Dear Mother, Daddie, Bruthurs, Susters, All our People, nebors and frunds," Henderson County,

Kentucky, TNGenWeb Project, Letters From Forgotten Ancestors. Online at http://www.tngenweb.org/tnletters/ky/hndky003.htm. September 20, 2001.

McCord, Louisa. Letter to Mary Dulles. October 9, 1852. In *Louisa S. McCord: Poems, Drama, Biography, Letters,* ed. Richard C. Lounsbury, pp. 293–94. Charlottesville: University Press of Virginia, 1996.

McCormick, Katharine. Letter to Margaret Sanger. June 14, 1954. In "The American Experience: The Pill." Online at http://www.pbs.org/wgbh/amex/pill/filmmore/ps_letters.html. March 11, 2003. Printed by permission of the Institute Archives and Special Collections, MIT Libraries, Cambridge, Massachusetts.

McDowell, Rebecca. Letter to Francis Smith. June 1, 1863. In "William H. McDowell, the 'Ghost Cadet,' " Virginia Military Institute Archives. Online at http://www.vmi.edu/archives/Civil_War/mcdr1.html. September 20, 2001.

———. Letter to Francis Smith. October 3, 1863. In "William H. McDowell, the 'Ghost Cadet,' " Virginia Military Institute Archives. Online at http://www.vmi.edu/archives/Civil_War/mcdr2.html. September 20, 2001.

———. Letter to her aunt. July 25, 1864. In "William H. McDowell, the 'Ghost Cadet,' " Virginia Military Institute Archives. Online at http://www.vmi.edu/archives/Civil_War/mcdr4.html. September 20, 2001.

McDowell, Sally and John Miller. Three letters. November 1855. In *"If You Love That Lady Don't Marry Her": The Courtship Letters of Sally McDowell and John Miller, 1854–1856,* ed. Thomas E. Buckley, S. J., pp. 432–39. Columbia: University of Missouri Press, 2000.

McIntosh, Peggy and Susannah. Letter to Duncan Campbell and James Meriwether. May 3, 1825. In "Selected Creek Letters, 1825–1829, Abstracted by Thelma Nolen Cornfeld." Online at http://www.rootsweb.com/~usgwnar/creekletters.html. August 22, 2002.

McPherson, Aimee Semple. Telegram to William Jennings Bryan. July 9, 1925. In L. Sprague de Camp, *The Great Monkey Trial,* p. 155. New York: Doubleday & Company, Inc., 1968.

Megquier, Mary Jane. Letter to Milton Benjamin. November 11, 1849. In *Apron Full of Gold: The Letters of Mary Jane Megquier from San Francisco, 1849–1856,* ed. Polly Welts Kaufman, pp. 41–44. Albuquerque: University of New Mexico Press, 1994, © 1949.

Michie, Mary. Letter to James Minor. February 4, 1857. In "Liberian Letters: Mary Michie to Dr. James H. Minor 1857 February 4," Electronic Text Center, University of Virginia Library. Online at http://etext.lib.virginia.edu/etcbin/toccer-new2?id=L570204.sgm&images=images/modeng&data=/texts/english/modeng/parsed&tag=public&part=1&division=div1. April 10, 2001.

Millay, Edna St. Vincent. Letter to Eugen Jan Boissevain. January 1924. In *Letters of Edna St. Vincent Millay*, ed. Allan Ross Macdougall, pp. 180–83. Westport, Conn.: Greenwood Press, 1952. Copyright © 1952, 1980 by Normal Millay Ellis. All rights reserved. Reprinted by permission of Elizabeth Barnett, literary executor.

Mitchell, Margaret. Letter to Mordecai Thurman. February 6, 1937. In Richard Harwell, *Margaret Mitchell's Gone With the Wind Letters, 1936–1949*, pp. 114–15. New York: Macmillan & Company, 1976. Online in database: North American Women's Letters and Diaries. January 8, 2003. Reprinted by permission of Eugene M. Mitchell and Joseph R. Mitchell.

Mitscher, Audrey. Letter to Allen Ferguson. March 24, 1943. Printed by permission of Audrey I. Ferguson and Allen R. Ferguson.

Mitten, Sandy. Letter to Ethel Mae Camps. January 22, 1991. In *War Letters: Extraordinary Correspondence from American Wars*, ed. Andrew Carroll. New York: Washington Square Press, 2002. Reprinted by permission of Sandy Mitten.

Monroe, Marilyn. Note to Dr. Marcus Rabwin. April 28, 1952. In Anthony Summers, *Goddess: The Secret Lives of Marilyn Monroe*, p. 62. New York: Macmillan, 1985.

Moore, Annie. Suicide note. November 18, 1978. In Rebecca Moore, *The Jonestown Letters: Correspondence of the Moore Family, 1970–1985*, pp. 76–78. Lewiston, N.Y.: Edwin Mellen Press, Studies in American Religion, vol. 23, 1986. Reprinted by permission of Rebecca Moore.

Morrison, Gina. Letter to her family. September 11, 2001. In "Stories of September 11," 911 Digital Archive. Online at http://www.911digitalarchive.org/stories/details/7711. November 16, 2004. Printed by permission of Gina Morrison.

Moseley, Julia Daniels. Letter to Charles Scott Moseley. August 16, 1883. In *Come to My Sunland: Letters of Julia Daniels Moseley from the Florida Frontier, 1882–1886*, ed. Julia Winifred Moseley and Betty Powers Crislip, p. 69. Gainesville: University Press of Florida, 1998. Online in database: North American Women's Letters and Diaries. September 8, 2004.

Mother. Letter to her daughter. December 1971. In "A Mother and Daughter Talk About Sexuality." Online at http://www.cwluherstory.com/CWLUArchive/mother daughter.html. February 2, 2003. Printed by permission of Elaine Wessel.

Mother of five. Letter to J. Edgar Hoover. March 13, 1969. In "Elvis Presley," Department of Justice, Freedom of Information Act, Part 02. Online at http://foia.fbi.gov/foiaindex/presley.htm. January 30, 2003.

Mott, Lucretia. Letter to Elizabeth Cady Stanton. July 16, 1848. In "Letter to Elizabeth Cady Stanton," Elizabeth Cady Stanton Papers, General Correspondence, Folder 1814–1849, Library of Congress. Online in database: LexisNexis Primary Sources in U.S. American History. October 12, 2004.

Murphrey, Elizabeth. Last will and testament. October 25, 1788. In James M. Creech, *History of Greene County, North Carolina: Compiled from Legends, Hearsay, Records Found There and Elsewhere.* Baltimore: Gateway Press, 1980, pp. 684–85.

Napier, Judy. Telegram to Jimmy Carter. February 22, 1980. In "Olympics, Cables, Important," Jimmy Carter Library, Atlanta, Georgia.

New York City schoolgirl. Letter to New York firefighters. September 12, 2001. Adler collection.

Nielsen, Jerri. Letter to her family and friends. June 27, 1999. In "Ice Bound," *Talk,* February 2001, p. 133. Reprinted by permission of Jerri Nielsen.

Nin, Anaïs. Letter to Robert Duncan. 1939. In *The Diary of Anaïs Nin: 1939–1944,* ed. Gunther Stuhlmann, pp. 114–15. New York: Harcourt, Brace & World, 1969. Reprinted by permission of the Anaïs Nin Trust, c/o Barbara W. Stuhlmann, author's representative. All rights reserved.

Noonan, Peggy. Memo to Strasbourg speech committee. Spring 1985. In Peggy Noonan, *What I Saw at the Revolution: A Political Life in the Reagan Era,* pp. 220–22. New York: Random House, 1990. Reprinted by permission of Peggy Noonan.

Nora and Beatrice Fairfax. Two letters. Summer 1898. In Lynne Olson, "Dear Beatrice Fairfax . . ." *American Heritage,* May/June 1992. pp. 90–92.

O'Connor, Jessie Lloyd. Letter to potential donors. January 30, 1932. In "Sophia Smith Collection: Agents of Social Change—Jessie Lloyd O'Connor, An Online Exhibit Displaying New Resources on 20th Century Women's Activism." Online at www.smith.edu/libraries/libs/ssc/exhibit/oconnor.html. January 31, 2003. Printed by permission of the Sophia Smith Collection, Northampton, Massachusetts.

O'Connor, Sharon. Letter to Mimi Parker. August 8, 2000. In "Open Letters: Parenthood (and Childhood)," vol. 1, no. 8, August 13, 2000. Online at http://www.open letters.net/000807/oconnor000808.html. August 6, 2001. Printed by permission of Sharon O'Connor.

O'Hanlon, Virginia. Letter to the editor of the *New York Sun.* December 1897. In "Yes, Virginia, there is a Santa Claus," Newseum: The Interactive Museum of News. Online at http://www.newseum.org/yesvirginia/. March 6, 2005.

O'Rourke, Caroline. Letter to Albert Fuller. May 4, 1884. In Judith A. Dulberger, *Mother Donit Fore the Best: Correspondence of a Nineteenth-Century Orphan Asylum,* p. 107. Syracuse, N.Y.: Syracuse University Press, 1996.

Oakley, Annie. Letter to William McKinley. April 5, 1898. In item AGO33879(2441), record group 94, series PI17E12, National Archives and Records Administration. Online at http://media.nara.gov/media/images/15/23/15-2293a.gif. June 29, 2000.

Ogawa, Louise. Letter to Clara Breed. April 9, 1943. In "Forwarding Address Required," Smithsonian National Postal Museum. Online at www.si.edu/postal/exhibits/onlineexhibits.html. January 8, 2003. Clara Breed Papers, Gift of Elizabeth Y. Yamada, Japanese American National Museum, 93.75.31EM. Printed by permission of the museum.

Oklahoma mother. Email to a Columbine message board. April 27, 1999. In "Columbine Memorial Guestbook." Online at http://redhare.com/columbine/guestbook/guestbook.html. April 26, 2002.

Ono, Yoko. Letter to the New York State Division of Parole. October 2000. In "In Opposing Parole, Ono Cites Safety," *New York Times,* vol. 150, no. 51,531, October 4, 2000, p. B6.

Oregon woman. Letter to Karl Menninger. In *Dear Dr. Menninger: Women's Voices from the Thirties,* ed. Howard J. Faulkner and Virginia D. Pruitt, p. 30. Columbia: University of Missouri Press, 1997.

Orlins, Susan Fishman. Letter to her parents. November 22, 1986. Printed by permission of Susan Fishman Orlins.

Oswald, Marina. Letter to Greg Olds. December 7, 1963. In *Warren Commission Hearings,* vol. 18, p. 547. Online at http://history-matters.com/archive/jfk/wc/wcvols/wh18/html/WH_Vol18_0281a.htm. January 25, 2003.

Pacitti, Beth. Memo to party planners. April 23, 2001. In The Smoking Gun Archive. Online at http://www.thesmokinggun.com/archive/tyco1.html. April 23, 2003.

Palfrey, Anna. Letter to John Gorham Palfrey. February 15, 1856. In *A Legacy of New England: Letters of the Palfrey Family,* vol. 2, ed. Hannah Palfrey Ayer, pp. 223–24. Portland, Maine: privately printed by the Anthoensen Press, 1950.

Parker, Dorothy. Letter to Alexander Woollcott. September 2, 1942. In Dorothy (Rothschild) Parker Letters, bMS Am 1449 (1278), Houghton Library, Harvard University, Cambridge, Mass. Copyright © 1999 by the National Association for the Advancement of Colored People. Reprinted by permission of the NAACP.

Parsons, Lucy. Letter to tramps. October 4, 1884. In "Word to Tramps," Act I: Subterranean Fire, The Dramas of Haymarket, Chicago Historical Society." Online at www.chicagohistory.org/dramas/act1/fromTheArchive/L27Large.jpg. November 7, 2002.

Pat and her parents. Two letters. August 1972. In *Between Ourselves: Letters Between Mothers and Daughters, 1750–1982,* ed. Karen Payne, pp. 33–34. Boston: Houghton Mifflin, 1983.

Patten, Ruth. Letter to William Patten. February 21, 1820. In Ruth Wheelock Patten, *Interesting Family Letters of the Late Mrs. Ruth Patten, of Hartford, Conn.,* pp. 195–96. Hartford, Conn.: D.B. Moseley, 1845.

Pendergrass, Bobbie Lou. Letter to John F. Kennedy. February 18, 1963. In the John F. Kennedy Library and Museum. Online at www.cs.umb.edu/~rwhealan/jfk/treasures-12.html. January 28, 2003.

Perkins, Frances. Letter to Jane Grant. July 8, 1944. In "Jane Grant: Life as a Lucy Stoner." Online at http://libweb.uoregon.edu/speccoll/exhibits/JaneGrant/lucy/perkins.html. October 7, 2004.

Perkins, Priscilla. Memo to colleagues. 1994. In "A Different Public Accounting: One Firm's Parting Tradition," *The Wall Street Journal* Online, August 1, 2002. Online at http://online.wsj.com/public/resources/media/memo1-073102.pdf. August 1, 2002. Printed by permission of Priscilla Perkins.

Peters, Lois. Letter to Nathan Peters. June 20, 1775. In Nathan Peters, *The Correspondence of Captain Nathan and Lois Peters,* ed. William H. Guthman, pp. 12–13. Hartford: The Connecticut Historical Society, 1980.

*Photoplay* reader and Carolyn Van Wyck. Two letters. March, 1926. In "Girls' Problems: Friendly Advice from Carolyn Van Wyck," *Photoplay* Magazine, vol. 29, no. 4, March, 1926, p. 96.

Pierce, Jane. Letter to Benny Pierce. January 23, 1853. In Manuscript Sampler, Tuck Library, New Hampshire Historical Society. Online at http://www.nhhistory.org/libraryexhibits/manuscriptcollection/mom/5-01janepierce/janepierce3.html. August 5, 2002.

Pinzer, Maimie. Letter to Fanny Howe. February 23, 1911. In Maimie Pinzer, *The Maimie Papers: Letters from an Ex-Prostitute,* pp. 29–32. New York: The Feminist Press, 1977.

Plath, Sylvia. Letter to Aurelia Plath. October 8, 1951. In Sylvia Plath, *Letters Home,* pp. 75–81. New York: Bantam, 1977. Reprinted by permission of HarperCollins and by Faber and Faber.

Porter, E. E. Letter to the corresponding secretary of the New York Female Moral Reform Society. April 21, 1838. In *Advocate of Moral Reform,* June 15, 1838. Online in database: Women and Social Movements in the United States, 1830–1930. May 30, 2000.

Poulton, Jane. Letter to her husband. May 2, 1945. In *A Better Legend: From the World War II Letters of Jack and Jane Poulton,* ed. Jane Weaver Poulton, pp. 226–67. Charlottesville: University Press of Virginia, 1993. Reprinted by permission of the University of Virginia Press.

Pulitzer, Courtney. Letter to her grandparents. July 14, 2000. Printed by permission of Courtney Pulitzer.

Quigley, Joan. Letter to Ronald Reagan. August 2, 1987. In Joan Quigley, *"What Does Joan Say?": My Seven Years as White House Astrologer to Nancy and Ronald Reagan,* pp. 167–68. New York: Carol Publishing Group, Birch Lane Press Book, 1990.

Copyright © 1990 by Joan Quigley. All rights reserved. Reprinted by arrangement with Kensington Publishing Corp. www.kensingtonbooks.com.

Quincy, Eliza. Letter to Mary Todd Lincoln. January 2, 1863. In the Abraham Lincoln Papers, American Memory Collection, Library of Congress. Online at http://memory.loc.gov/cgi-bin/query/r?ammem/mal:@field(DOCID+@lit(d2092400)). October 21, 2002.

Ramsay, Martha Laurens. Letter to David Ramsay, Sr. December 17, 1792. In David Ramsay, *Memoirs of the Life of Martha Laurens Ramsay, who Died in Charleston, S.C. on the 10th of June, 1811, in the 52d Year of her Age,* pp. 216–19. Boston: Samuel T. Armstrong, 1812. Online in database: North American Women's Letters and Diaries. February 25, 2002.

Randolph, Martha Jefferson. Letter to Thomas Jefferson. April 16, 1802. In *The Family Letters of Thomas Jefferson,* ed. Edwin Morris Betts and James Adam Bear, Jr., pp. 222–23. Columbia: University of Missouri Press, 1966.

Rawle, Anna. Letter to Rebecca Shoemaker. June 30, 1780. In Letters and Diaries of Rebecca Shoemaker and her daughters Anna and Margaret Rawle, Transcript Am. Historical Society of Pennsylvania, Philadelphia. Online in database: Women and Social Movements in the United States, 1600–2000. April 4, 2002.

Reed, Esther. Letter to George Washington. July 31, 1780. In *The Life of Esther De Berdt, afterwards Esther Reed, of Pennsylvania,* ed. William Bradford Reed, pp. 322–24. Philadelphia: privately printed by C. Cherman, 1853.

Reed, Fannie. Letter to Eliza Crawford. February 6 [?], 1898. In "Sister to Sister: Letters Written by Fannie Reed to Her Twin Sister Eliza Crawford, 1894–1904," *Turn-of-the-Century Women,* vol. 4, no. 1, Summer 1987, pp. 32–33.

———. Letter to Eliza Crawford. January 20, 1904. In "Sister to Sister: Letters Written by Fannie Reed to Her Twin Sister Eliza Crawford, 1894–1904," *Turn-of-the-Century Women,* vol. 4, no. 1, Summer 1987, pp. 36–37.

Reed, Virginia. Letter to Mary Keyes. May 16, 1847. In Marian Calabro, *The Perilous Journey of The Donner Party,* pp. 165–70. New York: Clarion Books, 1999.

Reeve, Dana. Letter to Christopher Reeve. April 11, 1996. In Dana Reeve, *Care Packages.* New York: Random House, 1999. Reprinted by permission of Dana Reeve.

Resident of Love Canal. Letter to Philip Harper. November 21, 1978. In Love Canal Collection, University Archives, University Libraries, State University of New York at Buffalo. Online at http://ublib.buffalo.edu/libraries/projects/lovecanal/disaster_gif/records/matsu9.html. April 10, 2002.

Revere, Rachel. Note to Paul Revere. April 18, 1775[?]. In "Spy Letters of the American Revolution," Collections of the Clements Library. Online at http://www.si.umich.edu/spies/letter-1775apr-large.html. March 27, 2000.

Reynolds, Maria. Letter to Alexander Hamilton. Circa February 1792. In Alexander Hamilton, *Observations on Certain Documents Contained in No. V and VI of "The History of the United States for the Year 1796," in which the Charge of Speculation against Alexander Hamilton, Late Secretary of the Treasury, is Fully Refuted,* pp. xvi–xvii. Philadelphia: Printed Pro Bono Publica, 1800.

Ringler, Robyn. Letter to Al Pacino. February 15, 2003. Printed by permission of Robyn DeSantis Ringler.

Robinson, Patricia and black sisters. Letter to brothers. September 11, 1968. In Rosalyn Baxandall and Linda Gordon, *Dear Sisters: Dispatches from the Women's Liberation Movement,* p. 135. New York: Basic Books, 2000.

Roosevelt, Eleanor. Letter to Carola von Schaffer-Bernstein. September 6, 1939. In *It Seems to Me: Selected Letters of Eleanor Roosevelt,* ed. Leonard C. Schlup and Donald W. Whisenhunt, pp. 33–34. Lexington: The University Press of Kentucky, 2001.

———. Letter to Mrs. Henry Robert, Jr. February 28, 1939. In Papers of Eleanor Roosevelt, Franklin D. Roosevelt Library, Hyde Park, N.Y. Online at http://www.archives.gov/exhibit_hall/american_originals/eleanor.html. January 20, 2003.

Ropes, Hannah Anderson. Letter to Alice Ropes. November 1862. In *Civil War Nurse: The Diary and Letters of Hannah Ropes,* ed. John R. Brumgardt, pp. 104–5. Knoxville: University of Tennessee Press, 1980.

———. Letter to Eliza Chandler. December 2, 1855. In Charles L. Chandler, "Two Letters From Kansas, 1855–1856," *The Mississippi Valley Historical Review,* vol. 29, no. 1, June, 1942, pp. 77–79. Online in database: JSTOR. October 4, 2001.

Rose, Hilda. Letter to a friend. June 21, 1919. In "The Stump Farm: A Chronicle of Pioneering," *The Atlantic Monthly,* vol. 139, no. 2, February 1927, pp. 145–46.

Rosenberg, Ethel. Letter to Michael and Robert Rosenberg. June 19, 1953. In *The Rosenberg Letters: A Complete Edition of the Prison Correspondence of Julius and Ethel Rosenberg,* ed. Michael Meeropol, pp. 702–3. New York: Garland, 1994. Printed by permission of the copyright holders, Michael and Robert Meeropol.

Rutherford, Madge. Letter to Irene and E. V. Rutherford. March 5, 1943. In "Excerpts from Madge Rutherford Minton's letters home," Fly Girls, The American Experience. Online at http://www.pbs.org/wgbh/amex/flygirls/filmmore/reference/primary/letters articles02.html. April 24, 2000. Printed by permission of the Madge Rutherford Minton Collection, the Woman's Collection, Texas Woman's University.

Sackville-West, Victoria. Letter to Amy Heard. March 19, 1885. In "Amy Heard: Letters from the Gilded Age," Professor Robert M. Gray course website, Stanford University. Online at http://www-ee.Stanford.edu/~gray/html/amy/amy_19.html. November 1, 2002.

Samuelson, Dora. Letter to Hyman Samuelson. June 1944[?]. In *Love, War, and the 96th Engineers (Colored): The World War II New Guinea Diaries of Captain Hyman Samuelson,* ed. Gwendolyn Midlo Hall, pp. 268–69. Urbana: University of Illinois Press, 1995. Reprinted by permission of Hyman Samuelson.

Sanger, Margaret. Letter to supporters. October 28, 1914. In *The Margaret Sanger Papers Electronic Editions: Margaret Sanger and The Woman Rebel, 1914–1916,* ed. Esther Katz, Cathy Moran Hajo, and Peter Engelman. Columbia, S.C.: Model Editions Partnership, 1999. Online in database: Model Editions Partnership. April 10, 2001.

Secor, Lella. Letter to her mother. May 15, 1916. In *Lella Secor: A Diary in Letters, 1915–1922,* ed. Barbara Moench Florence, pp. 69–74. New York: Burt Franklin & Company, 1978.

Sexton, Anne. Letter to Linda Gray Sexton. April 1969. In *Anne Sexton: A Self-Portrait in Letters,* ed. Linda Gray Sexton and Lois Ames, p. 424. Boston: Houghton Mifflin, 1977. Copyright © by Ann Sexton. Reprinted by permission of SLL/Sterling Lord Literistic, Inc.

Shapiro, Diana. Letter to Rosa Parks. 1956[?]. In the Rosa L. Parks Collection, Walter P. Reuther Library of Labor and Urban Affairs, Wayne State University.

Shepherd, Julia Adeline. Letter to her father. April 16, 1865. In *We Saw Lincoln Shot: One Hundred Eyewitness Accounts,* ed. Timothy S. Good, pp. 55–57. Jackson: University Press of Mississippi, 1995.

Sherman, Kathy Fitzgerald. Letter to Michael Sherman. October 4, 2000. In *Hell Hath No Fury: Women's Letters from the End of the Affair,* ed. Anna Holmes, pp. 161–63. New York: Carroll & Graf, 2002. Reprinted by permission of Kathleen Sherman.

Shippen, Alice Lee. Letter to Nancy Shippen. September 22, 1777. In *Nancy Shippen, Her Journal Book: The International Romance of a Young Lady of Fashion of Colonial Philadelphia with Letters: to Her and About Her,* ed. Ethel Armes, pp. 40–41. Philadelphia: J. B. Lippincott, 1935. Online in database: North American Women's Letters and Diaries. August 17, 2004.

Shrader, Martha. Letter to her mother. December 11, 1929. In Byrd Box 29, Office of the Governor, Letters Received and Sent, 1906–1998 re: the Lynchburg Colony, Library of Virginia. Printed by permission of the library.

Silverman, Rachel. Letter to Jane and Ira Silverman. July 13, 1986. Printed by permission of Rachel Emma Silverman.

Simpson, Nicole Brown. Letter to O. J. Simpson. 1992[?]. In "Nicole Brown Simpson's letter to O. J. Simpson," Doug Linder, Famous American Trials. Online at http://www.law.umkc.edu/faculty/projects/ftrials/Simpson/brownletter.html. May 19, 2003.

Sipiora, Lynne and Barbara Shulgold. Two letters. 1985–1986. In Barbara Shulgold and Lynne Sipiora, *Dear Barbara, Dear Lynne: The True Story of Two Women in Search of Motherhood,* pp. 8–10 and 49–51. Reading, Mass.: Addison-Wesley, 1992. Copyright © 1992 by Barbara Shulgold and Lynne Sipiora. Reprinted by permission of Felicia Eth.

Smallwood, E. E. Letter to Oklahoma students. May 1936[?]. In "Bonnie Parker's Schoolhouse." Online at http://texashideout.tripod.com/schoolhouse.html. January 9, 2003. Printed by permission of Sandy Jones, the John Dillinger Historical Society Collection.

Smith, Hannah Whitall. Letter to Richenda Louisa Barclay. October 18, 1882. In *Philadelphia Quaker: The Letters of Hannah Whitall Smith,* ed. Logan Pearsall Smith, p. 65. New York: Harcourt, Brace & Company, 1950.

Smith, Juliana. Letter to Betsey. Winter 1779. In Helen Evertson Smith, *Colonial Days and Ways As Gathered from Family Papers,* pp. 291–97. New York: The Century, 1900.

———. Letter to John Smith. 1782. In Helen Evertson Smith, *Colonial Days and Ways As Gathered from Family Papers,* p. 238. New York: The Century, 1900.

Smith, Margaret Bayard. Letter to Susan B. Smith. March 4, 1801. In Margaret Bayard Smith, *The First Forty Years of Washington Society in the Family Letters of Margaret Bayard Smith,* ed. Gaillard Hunt, pp. 25–27. New York: Frederick Ungar, 1965.

Smythe, Mrs. A. M. Letter to her cousin. February 17, 1837. In "Letter from Mrs. A. M. Smythe to her cousin, Feb 17, 1837 concerning the sale of a family of slaves," Electronic Text Center, University of Virginia Library. Online at http://etext.lib.virginia.edu/toc/modeng/public/SmyLett.html. April 10, 2001.

Southgate, Eliza. Letter to Mary Southgate. March 1, 1802. In Eliza Southgate Bowne, *A Girl's Life Eighty Years Ago: Selections from the Letters of Eliza Southgate Bowne,* pp. 92–97. New York: Charles Scribner's Sons, 1887.

Spaulding, Mrs. E. A. Letter to Abraham Lincoln. September 23, 1861. In the Abraham Lincoln Papers, American Memory Collection, Library of Congress. Online at http://memory.loc.gov/cgi-bin/query/r?ammem/mal:@field(DOCID+@lit(d1198100)). October 2, 2001.

Spooner, Bathsheba. Letter to the Council of the State of Massachusetts Bay. June 16, 1778. In Deborah Navas, "Notes and Documents: New Light on the Bathsheba Spooner Execution," *Massachusetts Historical Society Proceedings,* vol. 108, 1996, pp. 117–18.

Stanton, Elizabeth Cady. Letter to Clara Bewick Colby. November 12, 1900. In Elizabeth Cady Stanton Papers, Library of Congress. Online in database: Lexis-Nexis Primary Sources in U.S. American History. October 12, 2004.

————. Letter to the Akron Falls Women's Convention. May 16, 1851. In *The Proceedings of the Woman's Rights Convention, held at Akron, Ohio, May 28 and 29, 1851,* pp. 33–35. Cincinnati: Ben Franklin Book & Job Office, 1851. Online in "Votes For Women: Selections from the National American Woman Suffrage Association Collection, 1848–1921," Library of Congress, at http://lcweb2.loc.gov/cgi-bin/ampage?collId=rbnawsa&fileName=n8317/rbnawsan8317.db&recNum=29&itemLink=D?naw:20:./temp/~ammem_SZAT::%23n8317030&linkText=1. February 24, 2005.

Stevenson, Helen Day. Letter to her family. April 30, 1951. In Robert B. and Helen Stevenson Meyner Papers, Skillman Library, Lafayette College, Easton, Pennsylvania. Printed by permission of Diane Windham Shaw.

Stewart, Alice. Letter to Lou Henry Hoover. February 11, 1929. In "Hoover Online! Digital Archives," Herbert Hoover Presidential Library and Museum. Online at http://www.ecommcode.com/hoover/hooveronline/text/86.html. April 5, 2002.

Stewart, Elinore Pruitt. Letter to Juliet Coney. December 2, 1912. In Elinore Pruitt Stewart, *Letters of a Woman Homesteader,* pp. 184–92. Boston: Houghton Mifflin, 1982.

Stewart, Martha. Letter to Judge Miriam Goldman Cedarbaum. July 15, 2004. In "Stewart's Letter to Judge," The Smoking Gun Archive. Online at http://www.thesmokinggun.com/archive/0716043martha1.html. November 14, 2004.

Stimson, Julia. Letter to her family. July 25, 1917. In Julia C. Stimson, *Finding Themselves: The Letters of an American Army Chief Nurse in a British Hospital in France,* pp. 78–84. New York: The MacMillan Company, 1918.

Stone, Lucy. Letter to Antoinette Blackwell. February 20, 1859. In *Friends and Sisters: Letters between Lucy Stone and Antoinette Brown Blackwell, 1846–93,* ed. Carol Lasser and Marlene Deahl Merrill, p. 150. Urbana: University of Illinois Press, 1987.

Stone, Mrs. Peter. Letter to Edward Staebler. December 4, 1930. In "The Great Depression in Ann Arbor," Students on Site, the Arts of Citizenship Program, University of Michigan. Online at http://www.artsofcitizenship.umich.edu/sos/topics/depression/. January 8, 2003.

Stowe, Harriet Beecher. Letter to Calvin Stowe. 1852. In Annie Fields, *Life and Letters of Harriet Beecher Stowe,* pp. 138–39. Boston: HoughtonMifflin, 1897. Online in database: North American Women's Letters and Diaries. September 17, 2002.

Strong, Betsy. Letter to Sarah and Nathan Strong. Winter 1846[?]. In *America's Families: A Documentary History,* ed. Donald M. Scott and Bernard Wishy, p. 183. New York: Harper & Row, 1982.

Taft, Helen. Letter to Eliza Scidmore. April 7, 1909. In "History of the Cherry Trees in Washington, D.C." National Park Service. Online at http://www.nps.gov/nacc/cherry/history.htm. January 19, 2000.

Taylor, Dorothea. Letter to P. H. Taylor. December 7, 1941. In Mary Dewhurst Miles Papers, Illinois State Historical Library, Springfield, Illinois. Printed by permission of the library.

Thomson, Hannah. Letter to John Mifflin. September 17, 1786. In "Letters of Hannah Thomson, 1785–1788," *The Pennsylvania Magazine of History and Biography (1877–1906)*, vol. 14, no. 1, 1890, p. 28. Online in database: American Periodicals Series Online, 1740–1900. July 3, 2002.

Thomson, Katie. Letter to Ted Kaczynski. October 8, 1999. In "The Unabomber's Media Pen Pals," The Smoking Gun Archive. Online at http://www.thesmokinggun.com/unabomber2/thomson1.html. November 9, 2004.

Thurston, Lucy. Letter to her daughter. 1855. In Lucy Goodale Thurston, *Life and Times of Mrs. Lucy G. Thurston, Wife of Rev. Asa Thurston, Pioneer Missionary to the Sandwich Islands, Gathered from Letters and Journals Extending over a Period of More than Fifty Years*, pp. 168–75. Ann Arbor, Mich.: S. C. Andrews, 1882.

Tilghman, Molly. Letter to Polly Pearce. August 5, 1785. In "Letters of Molly and Hetty Tilghman: Eighteenth Century Gossip of Two Maryland Girls," ed. J. Hall Pleasants. *Maryland Historical Magazine*, vol. 21, no. 2, June 1926, pp. 129–33.

Topsy Turvy. Letter to *The Woman's Journal*. September 22, 1870. In "Letter From Kansas," *The Woman's Journal*, vol. 1, no. 40, October 8, 1870, p. 315. Online in database: The Gerritsen Collection. August 9, 2001.

Townsend, Jessie Easton. Letter to Edwin J. Webb. 1914. In Virginia and the New South, 1875–1925, Primary Source Documents, the Library of Virginia. Online at http://www.lva.lib.va.us/whatwedo/k12/psd/newsouth/townsend.htm. April 12, 2002.

Truth, Sojourner. Letter to Rowland Johnson. November 17, 1864. In Suzanne Pullon Fitch and Roseann M. Mandziuk, *Sojourner Truth As Orator: Wit, Story, and Song*, pp. 195–97. Westport, Conn.: Greenwood Press, 1997.

Tuffyas, Beryl. Letter to *The Daily Kent Stater*. May 5, 1970. In May 4 Collection, Box 173, Department of Special Collections and Archives, Kent State University, Ohio Memory. Online at http://worlddmc.ohiolink.edu/OMP/NewDetails?oid=2556524&format=list&fieldname=creator&results=10&sort=title&searchstatus=1&hits=1&searchmark=1&searchstring=%22Tuffyas%2C+Beryl%22&searchtype=kw&count=1. September 13, 2004.

Underhill, Julia. Letter to her husband. July 26, 1864. In *Root of Bitterness: Documents of the Social History of American Women*, ed. Nancy F. Cott et al., pp. 272–73. Boston: Northeastern University Press, 1996.

Van Allen, Mary. Letter to an orphanage attendant. January 14, 1884. In Judith A. Dulberger, *Mother Donit fore the Best: Correspondence of a Nineteenth-Century Orphan Asylum,* p. 58. Syracuse, N.Y.: Syracuse University Press, 1996.

Van Devanter, Lynda. Letter to her family. July 24, 1969. In Lynda Van Devanter, *Home Before Morning: the Story of an Army Nurse in Vietnam.* New York: Beautfort Books, 1983. Reprinted by permission of C. Thomas Buckley.

Von Kurowsky, Agnes. Letter to Ernest Hemingway. March 7, 1919. In *Hemingway in Love and War: The Lost Diary of Agnes von Kurowsky, Her Letters, and Correspondence of Ernest Hemingway,* ed. Henry Serrano Villard and James Nagel, pp. 163–64. Boston: Northeastern University Press, 1989.

Wakeman, Rosetta. Letter to Emily and Harvey Wakeman. June 5, 1863. In *An Uncommon Soldier: The Civil War Letters of Sarah Rosetta Wakeman, alias Private Lyons Wakeman 153rd Regiment, New York State Volunteers,* ed. Lauren Cook Burgess, pp. 31–32. Pasadena, Md.: Minerva Center, 1994.

Wandrey, June. Letter to her parents. August 14, 1943. In June Wandrey, *Bedpan Commando: The Story of a Combat Nurse During World War II,* pp. 54–55. Elmore, Ohio: Elmore Publishing Company, 1989.

———. Letter to her parents. June 4, 1945. In June Wandrey, *Bedpan Commando: The Story of a Combat Nurse During World War II,* pp. 204–6. Elmore, Ohio: Elmore Publishing Company, 1989.

Warren, Mercy Otis. Letter to Catharine Macauley. September 20, 1789. In "Dear Madam: Letters Between Catharine Macaulay and Mercy Warren," Gilder Lehrman Online Exhibits. Online at http://www.gliah.uh.edu/exhibits/dearmadam/01800-04p1.html. August 24, 2001.

———. Letter to James Warren. November 25, 1776. In Alice Brown, *Mercy Warren,* pp. 133–34. New York: Charles Scribner's Sons, 1896.

———. Letter to James Warren. September 21, 1775. In Alice Brown, *Mercy Warren,* pp. 78–80. New York: Charles Scribner's Sons, 1896.

Washington, Harriot. Letter to George Washington. April 2, 1790. In "GW: Life and Times," Learning About George Washington. Online at http://gwpapers.virginia.edu/lesson/k5/k5quest3.html. August 23, 2001.

Washington, Martha. Letter to Frances Washington. June 15, 1797. In *Martha Washington's Letter; Written from Philadelphia, June 15, 1794, to Mrs. Frances Washington,* unpag. St. Louis: privately printed, 1922. Online in database: North American Women's Letters and Diaries. February 25, 2002.

———. Letter to Mercy Otis Warren. December 26, 1789. In *"Worthy Partner": The Papers of Martha Washington,* ed. Joseph E. Fields, pp. 223–24. Westport, Conn.: Greenwood Press, 1994.

Waterman, Mary Anne. Letter to Lucretia Sibley. April 1844[?]. In "Mary Ann Water-man Writes about 'This thing of slavery,' Letter," Old Sturbridge Village, Online Resource Library. Online at http://www.osv.org/learning/DocumentViewer.php?DocID=5. February 22, 2005.

Waxham, Ethel and John Love. Ten letters. 1906–1909. In Barbara Love and Frances Love Froidevaux, *Lady's Choice: Ethel Waxham's Journals and Letters, 1905–1910*. Albuquerque: University of New Mexico Press, 1993. Also available in "P.S. I Like You Very Much," The West: Episode Eight. Online at http://www.pbs.org/weta/the west/program/episodes/eight/psilikeyou.htm. April 4, 2002. Reprinted by permission of Barbara Love and Frances Love Froidevaux.

Wells, Ida B. Letter to *The Westminster Gazette*. May 21, 1894. In "African-American Women in the Woman's Christian Temperance Union, 1880–1900," Women and Social Movements in the United States, 1830–1930, State University of New York at Binghamton. Online at http://womhist.Binghamton.edu/wctu2/doc30.htm. November 7, 2002.

Westbrook, Daisy. Letter to Louise Madella. July 19, 1917. In "Documents of the Race Riot at East St. Louis," *Journal of the Illinois State Historical Society*, vol. 65, no. 3, Autumn 1972, pp. 328–30. Lawrence Y. Sherman Papers, Box 133, Abraham Lincoln Presidential Library, Springfield, Illinois. Reprinted by permission of the library.

Wharton, Edith. Letter to W. Morton Fullerton. April, 1910. In *The Letters of Edith Wharton,* ed. Lewis R.W.B. Lewis and Nancy Lewis, pp. 206–8. New York: Charles Scribner's Sons, 1988. Reprinted by permission of the Estate of Edith Wharton and the Watkins/Loomis Agency.

————. Letter to William Roscoe Thayer. November 11, 1905. In *The Letters of Edith Wharton,* ed. Lewis R.W.B. Lewis and Nancy Lewis, pp. 96–97. New York: Charles Scribner's Sons, 1988. Reprinted by permission of the Estate of Edith Wharton and the Watkins/Loomis Agency.

Whitall, Hannah. Letter to Annie Whitall. April 25, 1847. In *Philadelphia Quaker: The Letters of Hannah Whitall Smith,* ed. Logan Pearsall Smith, p. 3. New York: Harcourt, Brace & Company, 1950.

————. Letter to Annie Whitall. February 17, 1850. In *Philadelphia Quaker: The Letters of Hannah Whitall Smith,* ed. Logan Pearsall Smith, pp. 3–4. New York: Harcourt, Brace & Company, 1950.

Whitman, Elizabeth. Note to her lover. July 1788. In "Miscellany," *The Massachusetts Centinel,* vol. 10, no. 2, September 20, 1788. "Newspaper articles reporting the death of Elizabeth Whitman," Course web pages, the University of Southern Mississippi. Online at http://www-org.usm.edu/~harvey/Whitman.htm. July 24, 2002.

————. Letter to the North Carolina legislature. November 29, 1800. In Cynthia A. Kierner, *Southern Women in Revolution, 1776–1800: Personal and Political Narratives,* p. 229. Columbia: University of South Carolina Press, 1998.

Wiebusch, Wilhelmine. Letter to Marie Kallmeyer. September 12, 1884. In *News From the Land of Freedom: German Immigrants Write Home,* ed. Walter D. Kamphoefner, Wolfgang Helbich, and Ulrike Sommer, trans. Susan Carter Vogel, pp. 595–97. Ithaca, N.Y.: Cornell University Press, 1991.

Wilkinson, Eliza. Letter to Mary Porcher. 1782. In Eliza Yonge Wilkinson, *Letters of Eliza Wilkinson,* pp. 39–43. New York: Samuel Colman, 1839. Reprint, New York: Arno Press, 1969.

Willard, Emma Hart. Letter to Almira Hart. July 30, 1815. In John Lord, *The Life of Emma Willard,* pp. 44–45. New York: D. Appleton, 1873.

Williams, Laura. Letter to Green Berry Williams, Jr. February 18, 1862. In "Tennessee Notes: 'Looking Every Minute for Them to Come,' " ed. Walter T. Durham. *Tennessee Historical Quarterly,* vol. 49, no. 2, August 2000, pp. 109–11.

Williams, Rose. Letter to Allettie Mosher. September 27, 1885. In *Read This Only to Yourself: The Private Writings of Midwestern Women, 1880–1910,* ed. Elizabeth Hampsten, p. 104. Bloomington: Indiana University Press, 1982.

Williams, Sarah. Letter to Sarah and Samuel Hicks. October 10, 1853. In "Plantation Experiences of a New York Woman," ed. James C. Bonner, *North Carolina Historical Review,* vol. 33, no. 3, July 1956, pp. 389–90.

Willis, Frances Gates. Letter to Andrew Willis. January 19, 1850. In *Hardship and Hope: Missouri Women Writing about Their Lives, 1820–1920,* ed. Carla Waal and Barbara Oliver Korner, pp. 54–55. Columbia: University of Missouri Press, 1997. Reprinted with permission of the University of Missouri Press. Copyright © 1997 by the Curators of the University of Missouri.

Winslow, Rose. Notes to her husband and to members of the National Women's Party. December 1917. In *Nonviolence in America: A Documentary History,* ed. Staughton Lynd and Alice Lynd, pp. 87–89. Maryknoll, N.Y.: Orbis Books, 1995.

Wister, Sally. Letter to Deborah Norris. June 3, 1778. In "Journal of Miss Sally Wister," *Pennsylvania Magazine of History and Biography,* vol. 10, no. 1, 1886, pp. 51–52.

————. Letter to Deborah Norris. October 19, 1777. In "Journal of Miss Sally Wister," *Pennsylvania Magazine of History and Biography,* vol. 9, no. 3, 1885, pp. 322–24.

Woman's Christian Temperance Union. Petition to Congress. May 1888. Online in database: Women and Social Movements in the United States, 1600–2000. October 10, 2004.

Women of Augusta County. Petition to the Virginia legislature. January 19, 1832. In *Root of Bitterness: Documents of the Social History of American Women,* ed. Nancy F. Cott et al., pp. 243–45. Boston: Northeastern University Press, 1996.

Wright, Margaret. Letter to Ethel Pape Wright. April 28, 1906. In " 'Yes, We Got It Safe': A 1906 Earthquake Letter," ed. Barrett Kennedy. *California History,* vol. 71, no. 4, Winter, 1992/93, pp. 511–14.

Wright, Martha Coffin. Letter to Lucretia Mott. November 19, 1841. In *Root of Bitterness: Documents of the Social History of American Women,* ed. Nancy F. Cott et al., pp. 162–65. Boston: Northeastern University Press, 1996.

Wylie, Elinor. Letter to Horace Wylie. May 20, 1927. In *The Oxford Book of Letters,* ed. Frank Kermode and Anita Kermode, pp. 49–50. New York: Oxford University Press, 1995.

Wyoming mother. Letter to Julia Lathrop. October 19, 1916. In *Raising a Baby the Government Way: Mothers' Letters to the Children's Bureau, 1915–1932,* ed. Molly Ladd-Taylor, p. 49. New Brunswick: Rutgers University Press, 1986.

Yarnell, Emma. Letter to L. R. April 18, 1865. In Catherine Hare, *Life and Letters of Elizabeth L. Comstock,* pp. 225–31. Philadelphia: John C. Winston & Company, 1895. Online in database: North American Women's Letters and Diaries. October 23, 2002.

Z.D.R. Letter to her daughter. May, 1824. In "Letter from a Lady to her Daughter," *The Ladies Magazine: Intended to Aid in the Cause of Piety, Religion and Morality,* vol. 1, no. 11, May 1824, pp. 332–35.

Every effort has been made to secure permission to reprint the letters in this book. If any copyright holders have been accidentally overlooked, we offer our sincere apologies.

## ADDITIONAL SOURCES

This list includes reference works that we consulted for the chapter openings and letter introductions, as well as books and websites in which we found partial versions of, or references to, some letters that we later found in more complete forms.

Angle, Paul M., ed. *The American Reader, from Columbus to Today.* New York: Rand McNally, 1958.

Archives of the West, 1856–1868. "New Perspectives on the West." Online at www.pbs.org/weta/thewest/resources/archives/four/.

Bayor, Ronald H., ed. *The Columbia Documentary History of Race and Ethnicity in America.* New York: Columbia University Press, 2004.

Bernikow, Louise. *The American Women's Almanac: An Inspiring and Irreverent Women's History.* New York: Berkley Books, 1997.

Bill Adler Books, comp. *Love Letters of a Lifetime: Romance in America.* New York: Hyperion, 2001.

Butturff, Dorothy Dow. *Eleanor Roosevelt, an Eager Spirit: The Letters of Dorothy Dow, 1933–45.* New York: Norton, 1984.

Collins, Gail. *America's Women: 400 Years of Dolls, Drudges, Helpmates, and Heroines.* New York: HarperCollins, 2003.

"Costumes and Textile Collection: 'Revolutionary' Clothing," The Connecticut Historical Society. Online at http://www.chs.org/textiles/rev_clo.htm.

Cott, Nancy F. ed., et al. *Root of Bitterness: Documents of the Social History of American Women.* Boston: Northeastern University Press, 1996.

Coulling, Mary P. *The Lee Girls.* Winston-Salem, N.C.: J. F. Blair, 1987.

Davis, David Brion and Steven Mintz, eds. *The Boisterous Sea of Liberty: A Documentary History of America from Discovery through the Civil War.* New York: Oxford University Press, 1998.

Desmond, Kevin. *A Timetable of Inventions and Discoveries: From Pre-History to the Present Day.* New York: M. Evans, 1986.

Duncan, William Cary. *The Amazing Madame Jumel.* New York: Frederick A. Stokes Company, 1935.

Encyclopædia Britannica Online.

Fairbanks, Carol and Bergine Haakenson, eds. *Writings of Farm Women, 1840–1940: An Anthology.* New York: Garland Publishing, 1990.

Ferrell, Robert H., ed. *The Twentieth Century: An Almanac.* New York: World Almanac Publications, 1985.

Frey, Sylvia R. *New World, New Roles: A Documentary History of Women in Pre-industrial America.* Westport, Conn.: Greenwood Press, 1986.

Goodfriend, Joyce D. *The Published Diaries and Letters of American Women: An Annotated Bibliography.* Boston: G. K. Hall, 1987.

Harris, Sharon M., ed. *American Women Writers to 1800.* New York: Oxford, 1996.

Harvey, Sheridan, et al. *American Women: A Library of Congress Guide for the Study of Women's History and Culture in the United States.* Washington, D.C.: Library of Congress, 2001.

Holt, Shan. "The Anatomy of a Marriage: Letters of Emma Spaulding Bryant, 1873," *Signs,* Autumn 1991.

Hymowitz, Carol and Michaele Weissman. *A History of Women in America.* New York: Bantam Books, 1978.

Jones, Constance. *1001 Things Everyone Should Know About Women's History.* New York: Broadway Books, 1998.

Kenyon, Olga. *800 Years of Women's Letters.* London: Alan Sutton, 1992.

Knappman, Edward W., ed. *Great American Trials: From Salem Witchcraft to Rodney King.* Detroit: Gale Research, Visible Ink Press, 1994.

Laas, Virginia Jeans. "Elizabeth Blair Lee: Union Counterpart of Mary Boykin Chestnut," *The Journal of Southern History,* vol. 50, no. 3, August 1984. Baton Rouge, La.: Southern Historical Association.

Lane, Mills, ed. *Georgia: History Written by Those Who Lived It.* Savannah, Ga.: Beehive Foundation, 1995.

Lerner, Gerda. *The Female Experience: An American Documentary.* Indianapolis: Bobs-Merrill, 1977. New York: Oxford University Press, 1992.

Litoff, Judy Barrett and David C. Smith, eds. *Since You Went Away: World War II Letters from American Women on the Home Front.* New York: Oxford University Press, 1991.

———. *We're in This War, Too: World War II Letters from American Women in Uniform.* New York: Oxford University Press, 1994.

Lunardini, Christine. *What Every American Should Know About Women's History: 200 Events That Shaped Our Destiny.* Holbrook, Mass.: Adams Media Corporation, 1997.

Mills, Kay. *From Pocahontas to Power Suits: Everything You Need to Know About Women's History in America.* New York: Plume, 1995.

Moynihan, Ruth Barnes, Cynthia Russett, and Laurie Crumpacker, eds. *Second to None: A Documentary History of American Women,* vol. 1, *From the 16th Century to 1865.* Lincoln: University of Nebraska Press, 1993.

New York Public Library. *American History Desk Reference.* New York: Macmillan, Stonesong Press, 1997.

Norton, Mary Beth. *Liberty's Daughters: The Revolutionary Experience of American Women, 1750–1800.* Ithaca: Cornell University Press, 1980.

Opdycke, Sandra. *The Routledge Historical Atlas of Women in America,* series ed. Mark C. Carnes. New York: Routledge, 2000.

Primary Source Documents, "John Brown's Holy War," The American Experience. Online at http://www.pbs.org/wgbh/amex/brown.

Reed, Amy L., ed. *Letters from Brook Farm, 1844–1847.* Poughkeepsie, N.Y.: Vassar College, 1928.

Shapiro, Larry. *A Book of Days in American History.* New York: Charles Scribner's Sons, 1987.

Stevenson, Louise L. *The Victorian Homefront: American Thought and Culture, 1860–1880.* Ithaca: Cornell University Press, 1991.

Urdang, Laurence, ed. *The Timetables of American History.* Reprint, New York: Simon & Schuster, Touchstone, 1996.

Waal, Carla and Barbara Oliver Korne, eds. *Hardship and Hope: Missouri Women Writing About Their Lives, 1820–1920.* Columbia: University of Missouri Press, 1997.

Woloch, Nancy, ed. *Early American Women: A Documentary History, 1600–1900.* Belmont, Calif.: Wadsworth, 1992.

# Photo Credits

Rosa Parks being fingerprinted on page 594 courtesy of AP/Wide World Photos

Senator Joseph McCarthy and the CBS logo on page 594 courtesy of AP/Wide World Photos

Jacqueline Kennedy at John F. Kennedy's Funeral on page 594 courtesy of Elliot Erwitt/Magnum Photos

Bill and Hillary Clinton on page 676 courtesy of Reuters/CORBIS

Microsoft Founders Bill Gates and Paul Allen on page 676 courtesy of Doug Wilson/CORBIS

Explosion of Space Shuttle on page 676 courtesy of www.corbis.com/CORBIS

Nicole Simpson on page 676 courtesy of Reuters/CORBIS

Oprah Winfrey on page 676 courtesy of Rufus F. Folkks/CORBIS

President George W. Bush on page 676 courtesy of Brooks Kraft/CORBIS

Twin Towers Behind Statue of Libery on page 676 courtesy of Joseph Sohm; Visions of America/CORBIS

All other images from the Library of Congress

# Acknowledgments

For their help in locating letters and/or providing important information about them, we would like to thank: Janet Bloom at the William L. Clements Library; Heidi Fetzer at Georgetown University Library; Peter Hardin of the *Richmond Times-Dispatch;* Charlotte Holliman at the Mary and John Gray Library Special Collections and Lamar University Archives; Ted Hutchinson at the Massachusetts Historical Society; Kristin Johnson; Thomas Knoles at the American Antiquarian Society; Tara Latsha at Harriton House; William Levebre at the Rosa L. Parks Collection, Wayne State University; Debra Levine at the University of Chicago Library; Lynn Novick; Steven Raab at The Raab Collection, Ardmore, Pennsylvania (www.raabcollection.com); Eric Rayman; Darryl Salk; Diane Windham Shaw at Skillman Library, Lafayette College; Margaret Sherry Rich and AnnaLee Pauls at Princeton University Library.

We are grateful to pretty much everyone we know for offering ideas, delivering letters, and tolerating a multi-year obsession.

At home, our children helped with copying and filing, and Donna Ash offered support of every kind.

Melissa Hankins located the rights-holders and secured the permissions for numerous letters in the book.

Dan Oppenheimer filled in many factual blanks, and Lydia Okrent gave us several months of a valuable summer to help with research.

We would also like to thank Lydia's father, Dan Okrent, the only person we know—or are ever likely to know—who can fact-check, without reference books, at 40,000 feet.

Sarah Lewis, in the home stretch, gave the manuscript her wise and wonderful eyes.

Michael Solomon, whose brilliance was finally matched, but only by his generosity, checked key sections for us with terrifying speed and accuracy.

Andrew Carroll, who heads the Legacy Project and has published the best-selling *Letters of a Nation, War Letters,* and *Behind the Lines: Powerful and Revealing American and Foreign War Letters and One Man's Search to Find Them,* shared his wealth of knowledge, contacts, and extraordinary unpublished letters, to support our project as if it were one of his own. We are indebted to him for his generosity, an inspiring quality in a competitive age.

We are lastingly grateful to Vincent Virga, whose knowledge, humor, and just plain delightful company are matched only by the greatness of his photo research.

Belina Huey designed our extraordinary jacket, and Judy Young made it possible by securing the permissions for all those stamps.

Chris Jerome, the best copy editor either of us has ever known, took on this book despite having done the first one and brought her customary brilliance to the job.

Once again, we would like to thank Liz Darhansoff and Kathy Robbins, whom we are still lucky enough to have as our friends and our agents.

Beth Rashbaum joined the team this time around as hands-on editor. Her patience, insight, enthusiasm, and skill will forever be appreciated.

And finally, we'd like to thank Susan Kamil, whose commitment to this book and to our previous volume has enhanced our lives on a daily basis for the last eight years. We will truly be forever grateful.

# Index

*Page numbers of illustrations appear in italics.*

A. V., letter from, 76–77

Abolitionists and anti-slavery movement, 80, 95, 146–49, 151, 171–72, 181, 220–21, 222, 223, 229, 247, 250, 252–53

   women of Augusta County, Virginia, letter from, 139–41

Abortion, 396–97, 466–67

   clinic bomber, letter from, 688–89

   letter exchange, mother-daughter, 667–70

   *Roe* v. *Wade,* 597, 667

Adams, Abigail, *10,* 11, 28, 47

   letters from, 28–34, 47–49

Adams, John, 11, 20, 47, 81–82, 94

   letters to, 28–34

Adams, John Quincy, 28, 47

   letter to, 47–49

Addams, Jane, 4, 402, 475

   letter from, 402–4

Adoption, 699–701

Advice

   columns, 413–14, 462–63, 498–500, 520–21

   deathbed, mother to son, 127–28

   on friendship, 62, 128

   health, 423–27, 520–21

   in Last Will and Testament, 70–71

   manners/morality, 40–41, 48–49, 95, 180–81

   on marriage, 12, 110–11, 315

   medical, 126–27, 414–15

   on sex, 655–57

   spiritual guidance, 5, 76–77, 128

   values and life principles, 4–5, 61, 652

   for wives, 128–30, 153–54

*Advocate of Moral Reform* magazine, 156

Afghanistan war, 747–48

African Americans

   baseball and color line broken, 595

   Black Power movement, 648

   Civil Rights Movement, *594,* 596–97, 625–26, 640–41

   Great Migration, 477

   Harlem Renaissance, 501–3

   lynching, 408–9

   Malcolm X assassinated, 596

   NAACP, 420, 625

   race riots, 1967, 646–47

   St. Louis race riots, 1917, 477–79

   Scottsboro trial, 508, 523–24

   segregation and prejudice, 541

   in World War II, 553–54

   *See also* Slaves and slavery

*Age of Innocence* (Wharton), 421, 434

AIDS, 676, 677–78, 714–15

Alamo, The, 95

Alaska, 337, 378–79

Alcoholics Anonymous, 508–9

Alcott, Louisa May, 337, 351–52
  letter from, 351–52
Allen, Paul, 676
Allen, Sarah, letter from, 111–22
Alston, Joseph, 106
Alston, Theodosia Burr, 106–7
Amazon.com, 678
American Colonization Society, 244
*American Cookery* (Simmons), 13
American frontier, 3, 149
  Alaska, 337, 378–79
  Donner Party, 3, 177, 185–86, 188–93,
    375, 376–77
  frontier widows, 124–25
  Gold Rush, 5, *178,* 179–80, 198–99,
    200–201
  Homestead Act, 262
  Kansas, 241–43, 247–49
  Kentucky, 82–85
  Lewis and Clark Expedition, 93
  life on, 457–60, 487–89
  life on ("Shirley Letters"), 211–20
  Los Angeles, 12
  pioneers, life of, 82–85
  Texas, trip to, 136–38
  tourism, 374–78
  Wyoming Territory, 337
*American Idol* viewer, letter from, 754
American Revolution, *10*
  British loyalists (Tories), 15–19, 36,
    57–58
  casualties, 64–65
  Constitution, *See* Constitution
  Declaration of Independence, 12, 33,
    40
  encounter with rebel soldier, 3, 18–19
  event summary, 1775–1799, 11–13
  flag, 11–12
  fundraising by women, 57–58
  government, early, 81–82, 89
  government, forming of a new, 29, 67,
    71–73
  letters between 1775 and 1799, 9–89
  looting or occupation of homes, 3,
    18–19, 62–64

Minute Men, 2
  Paris Peace Treaty, 12, 34
  ride of Deborah Champion, 24–28
  signal that the British are coming, 2
  Valley Forge, 12, 43–44
  war widows, 64–65
  wives to husbands in, 5, 6, 9, 15, 22,
    23–24, 34, 35, 38–39, 42–47
*American Tragedy, An* (Dreiser), 441
*American Woman's Journal,* letter to,
    405–6
Amundson, Amber, 748–49
Anderson, Marian, 541
Anderson, Mary, letter from, 543–44
Andrews, Sarah, letter from, 320–21
Annie (child), letter from, 314–15
Antarctica, 722–23
Anthony, Susan B., *336,* 337, 356,
    431–32
Antietam, Battle of, 262, 294
Art, *418,* 461, 507, 595. *See also* Cassatt,
    Mary
Arthur, Chester A., 397–98
Astrology, 701–2
Aurora, Lillian, letter from, 497
Austin, Stephen, 136

Baez, Joan, letter from, 638–39
Banister, Zilpah Grant, letter to,
    196–98
Barbie doll, 596, 678
Barnes, Christian, 3
  letter from, 18–19
Barrymore, Lionel, letter to, 406
Barton, Clara, *261,* 262
  letters from, 272–74, 292–93
Barnum, P. T., 338
Basset, William, letter to, 149–51
Bates, Ruby, letter from, 523–24
Beatles, letter to, 639–40
Beauregard, Pierre [P. G. T.], 270, 277,
    316
  letter to, 287
Beaver College, PA, 727
Bedell, Grace, letter from, 257–58

Beecher, Catharine, 196, 221
  letter from, 196–98
Bernstein, Aline, 5
  letter from, 522–23
*Bintel Brief,* letter to, 462–63
Bird, Isabella, letter from 374–78
Birth control, 4, 398–99, 409, 420,
  465–67, 472, 596, 623–24, 647,
  648–49
Blackwell, Antoinette
  letter from, 205–6
  letter to, 249–50
Blackwell, Elizabeth, 180
  letter from, 193–95
Blaine, Harriet, letter from, 385–86
Blaine, James, 394–96
Bloomer, Amelia, 206
Bly, Nellie, *336,* 339
Boon, Mary, letter from, 42
Bordon, Lizzie, 6–7
Bourke-White, Margaret, 509
Bow, Clara, *506*
  letter from, 517–19
Boyd, Belle, *261, 262*
Boyd, Virginia, letter from, 226–27
Brandywine, Battle of, 41
Brook Farm, 173–75
Brown, Addie, letter from, 250–51
Brown, Grace, letter from, 441–42
Brown, Helen Gurley, *594,* 596
  letter from, 662–63
Brown, John, *178,* 181, 251–53
  letter to, 254
Brown, Kay, letter exchange, 532–34
Brown, Rita Mae, 4, 666
  letter from, 666–67
Brown, Sargry, letter from, 164
Brown, Tabitha, letter from, 122–24
Brown, Tina, letter from, 715–18
Bryant, Emma Spaulding, letters from,
  368–74
Buell, Abel, 12
Bull, Mary Lucia, letter from, 52–54
Bullock, Mary, letter from, 289–91
Bull Run, First Battle of, 272–75, 277

Bull Run, Second Battle of, 298
Bunker Hill, Battle of, 5, 9, 22, 35, 42,
  43
Burn, Febb, 4
  letter from, 489
Burr, Aaron, 93, 104
  letter to, 106–7
Bush, George H. W., 678, 707
Bush, George W., *676,* 678–79
  letter to, 748–49
Butler, Frances, letters from, 335,
  341–44, 346–48
Butturff, Dorothy Dow, letter from,
  581–84

Cabot, Elizabeth, letter from, 428–29
California
  Bodie, town of, 384–85
  Gold Rush, 5, *178,* 179–80, 198–99,
    200–201
  life in early mining town ("Shirley
    Letters"), 211–20
  settlers, 198–200
  tourists, 374–78
California resident, letter from, 384–85
Carol (about sexual harassment), letter
  from, 512–14
Carrollton Viaduct, MD, 134, 135
Carson, Rachel, letter from, 631–33
Carter, Jimmy, 597
  letter to, 679
Cary, Sarah, letter from, 105–6
Cassatt, Mary, *418,* 460
  letter from, 460–61
Cather, Willa, 6, 445
  letter to, 445–47
Catt, Carrie Chapman, 4, 464, 489
*Century of Dishonor, A* (Jackson), 382
Chace, Elizabeth, letter from, 229–30
Chain letter, 529–30
*Challenger* space shuttle, *676,* 678
Champion, Deborah, 24
  letter from, 24–28
Chaplin, Charlie, *418,* 421
Charleston, SC, battle for, 52–54, 57

Cherokee people, 125
    Trail of Tears, 157–59
    woman, letter from, 125–26
Chicago, IL
    Great Fire, 338, 362–66
    Haymarket Riot, 392
    Hull House, 402, 475
    World's Columbian Exposition, 339
*Chicago Tribune,* 488, 489, 525
Child, Lydia Maria, 263
    letters from, 183–84, 252–53
China, adoption of girl babies from,
    699–701
Christian, Anne Henry, letter from, 37
*Christian's Secret of a Happy Life, The*
    (Smith), 202
Church, Angelica Schuyler, letter from,
    104–5
Civil War, 207, 261–334
    African Americans in, 299–300
    Appomattox Courthouse, surrender at,
        263–64, 320–21
    "Battle Hymn of the Republic," 262,
        280
    battles, 2, 262–63, 272–75, 292, 294,
        298–99, *see also specific battles*
    "Bleeding Kansas," 241–43, 254
    casualties, *261,* 262, 263, 265, 270,
        272–74, 287, 291, 292, 298–99
    Confederate States of America, 261,
        265
    draft riots, *261,* 263, 301
    events timeline, 1861–1865, 261–64
    Fort Sumter, 261, 265, 270
    Harper's Ferry, 251–52, 254
    prisoners of war, 299–300
    raising of an army, Confederacy, 272
    raising of an army, Union, 270–71,
        301
    Sherman's march to the sea, 263,
        316–20
    soldiers' letters, 259
    spies, *261,* 262, 277
    women's letters to husbands in, 295–96,
        310–11

    women nurses, 291–92, 298–99
    women soldiers, 297–98, 307
Clappe, Louise, letters from, 211–20
Clarke, Patsy, letter from, 714–15
Clemens, Olivia, letter from, 406–8
Clemens, Samuel (Mark Twain), 338,
    406–7
    letters to, 314–15, 406–8, 435–37
Cleveland, Grover, 394–96
Cline, Patsy, letter from, 627–28
Clinton, Bill (William Jefferson), *676,*
    678, 718
    letter to, 718–19
Clinton, Hillary, *676,* 679
Clothing and fashion, 13, 24, 40, 50, 82,
    83, 85–87, 88, 102, 109, 142, 159,
    185, 203–4, 206, 243, 263, 265, 272,
    339, 353–54, 405–6, 509, 628
Cocks, Judith, letter from, 79–80
Colburn, Charlotte, letter from, 576–78
Collins, Mary, letter from, 400–402
Columbia, SC, 316–20
Columbine School shooting, letter about,
    721–22
Communism
    Berlin Wall falls, 678
    McCarthyism, *594,* 595–96, 618–19
    Red Scare, 618
    Vietnam War and, 633–34
Conant, Charlotte Howard, letter from,
    383–84
*Confessions of Nat Turner, The* (Styron),
    139
Conney, Jane Ganz, letter from, 698–99
Conrad, R. E., letter from, 503–4
Constitution and Bill of Rights, 13, 29,
    32, 75, 94
    Eighteenth Amendment, 421
    Fifteenth Amendment, 338
    Fourteenth Amendment, 337
    Nineteenth Amendment, 421, 489
    Twelfth Amendment, 94
Conter, Monica, letter from, 547–48
Coogan, Jackie, *418*
Cook, Karin, letter from, 719–21

Conney, Joan Ganz, letter from, 657–59
*Coquette, The* (Foster), 69
Cosmetics, 503–4
*Cosmopolitan* magazine, 662–63
Craft, Ellen, letter from, 223–24
Crowther, Alice, letter from, 593, 620–23
Counterculture or youth revolution,
    1960s, *594,* 597, 650–51, 655
    letter exchange, Pat and her parents,
    659–62
Cribari, Shawn, letter exchange, 704–7
Crowther, Wendy, letter exchange, 704–7

Dana, Charles, 173, 339
Dance, 81–82, *92,* 94–95, 100, 262,
    612–14
Davis, Jefferson, 181, 261, 289, 329–31
Davis, Paulina Wright, 179
    letter to, 230–31
Davis, Varina, letter from, 329–31
"Dear John" letters, 486–87, 571–72
Death and grieving
    child, 106–7, 122, 123, 168–69,
        224–26, 247, 308–10, 386–87,
        459–60
    for Lincoln, 326–29
    parent, 78–79
    spouse, 122–24, 359–61, 411–12,
        629–30
De Hart, Abigail, letter from, 59–60
Deming, Sarah, letter from, 19–22
Detroit, MI, 646–47
Dickinson, Emily, 286, 288, *336,* 381
    letters from, 286–87, 288–89, 399
Dick-Read, Grantly, letter to, 603–4
Dickson, Annie, letter from, 256–57
Didrikson, Babe, letter from, 519–20
Disney, Walt, and Mickey Mouse, 421,
    *506*
Divorce, 698–99, 737–39
Dix, Dorothea, 298, 299
Dodd, Mary, letter from, 124–25
Dole, Robert, 663–64
Donner, Tamsen, letter from, 177,
    185–86

Donner Party, 3, 185, 188–93, 375,
    376–77
Douglass, Frederick, 250
Douglass, Sarah Mapps, letter from,
    149–51
Doyle, Mahala, letter from, 254
Drew, Louisa, letter from, 406
Drieser, Theodore, 441
Drinker, Elizabeth, 13
DuBerry, Helen, letter from, 321–24
DuBois, W. E. B., 420
Duchesne, Philippine, letter from,
    132–33
Duncan, Marijane Dill, letter from,
    647–48
Duncan, Robert, letter to, 540–41
Dunmore, Mrs. Charles, letter from,
    414–15
Duquette, Louise, letter from, 616–17
Dwight, Marianne, letter from, 173–75

Earhart, Amelia, *506, 509*
    letter from, 516–17
eBay, 678
Edison, Thomas A., *336,* 338, 420
    letter to, 490–91
Education
    of children, 103–4, 296–97
    colleges for women, 383–84
    of freed slaves, 345
    Freedom Schools, 640–41
    Spelman College for black women,
        338
    of women, 94, 103–4, 109, 132–33,
        196–97, 338, 383–84, 642–44
    Yale admits women, 338
Ehrlichman, John, letter to, 663–64
Einstein, Albert, 469
Eisenhower, Julie Nixon, letter from, 665
Elizabeth (train rider), letter from,
    134–36
Elizabethtown, NJ, 59
Ellin, Nancy, letter from, 640–41
Emerson, Ellen, letters from, 270–72,
    280–82

Emerson, Lidian Jackson
  letters from, 157–59, 168–71
  letter to, 270–72
Emerson, Ralph Waldo, *92,* 157, 158–59,
    173
  letters to, 168–71, 280–82
Emily (Civil War soldier), letter from, 307
England, Lynnde, 676
Environmentalism, 631
  Love Canal, 672–73
Expectant mother, letter from, 603–4

Factor, Max, 503–4
Fairfax, Beatrice, letter exchange, 413–14
Fannie (slave), letter from, 293–94
Farrar, Eliza, 95
Fassihi, Farnaz, letter from, 757–61
Felton, Rebecca Latimer, 421
Female Moral Reform Society of New
    York, 95
Feminism. *See* Women; Women's
    movement
Field, Sally, 677
Finn, Judy, letter from, 644
Fisher, Maude, letter from, 485–86
Fitch, Mrs. Edwin, letter from, 272
Fite, Katherine, letter from, 599–601
Fitzgerald, Emily, letters from, 378–79
Fitzgerald, Scott, letter to, 530–31
Fitzgerald, Zelda, letter from, 530–31
Fleet, Lillian Waite, letter from, 396–97
Florida, 387
Food and meals, 13, 55–57, 67–68, 82,
    83, 84, 143, 156, 166, 167, 170, 171,
    186, 243–44, 245, 262, 293, 342, 391,
    419, 420, 507, 596, 741–42
Forbes, Elizabeth, letter from, 64–65
Forbes, Rose, letter from, 315–16
Ford, Gerald, 597
Fort, Cornelia, letter from, 549–50
Fort Henry and Fort Donelson, fall of,
    282–84
Foster, Hannah, 69
Foster, Stephen, 180
Fox, Kate and Maggie, 206

Fredericksburg, Battle of, 292
Freedom of the press, 4, 663–64
Freedom of speech, 4, 618–19
Frémont, John, 275–76, 280, 281
Friedan, Betty, 7
  letter to, 666–67
Friedman, Mrs. Samuel, letter from,
    455–57
Frix, Matilda, letter from, 350–51
Fuller, Margaret, 162, 173, *178,* 179, 183,
    184
  letter from, 162–64
Fulton, Robert, *92,* 93

Gage, Gen. Thomas, 19, 20
Gallant, Hazel, 563–65
Galt, Edith, letter from, 467–68
Games and puzzles, 68, 69, 508, 595, 677
Garfield, James A., 338, 380–81, 385–86
  letter to, 355–56
Garfield, Lucretia, letters from, 355–56,
    380–81
Garland, Judy, *594,* 604
  letter from, 604–6
Gates, Betsey Shipman, letter from,
    394–96
Gates, Bill, *676*
Gay, Elizabeth, letter from, 301
Garrison, William Lloyd, letter to, 146–48
Gettysburg, Battle of, 2, 298–99
Gettysburg Address, 263
Gibson girl, *336,* 339
*Gilded Age, The* (Twain and Warner), 338,
    407
Gilman, Caroline, 95
Girl Scouts, letter to, 454–55
*Godey's Lady's Book,* 94, *178,* 180–81,
    209, 210, 303
Goldman, Emma, letter from, 464–66
Gomez, Angela, letter from, 702–4
*Gone with the Wind* (Mitchell), 509,
    532–34, 538
Goos, Margarette, letter from, 696–97
Gordon, Kate, letter from, 417, 476–77
Gordon, Ruth, letter from, 469–71

Gore, Al, 678–79

Gottlieb, Ruth, letter from, 625

Graham, Katherine, 4
    letter from, 663–64

Grant, Abigail, 5, 9, 34

Grant, Julia Dent, 352–53

Grant, Ulysses S., 264, 282, 320,
    352–53

Great Depression, 1929–1941, *506,*
    515–16, 508, 526–28, 538
    letters of, 511–44

Greeley, Horace, 173

Greenhow, Rose, letter from, 277–80

Greenleaf, Simon, letter to, 159–62

Grierson, Alice Kirk, letter from, 366–68

Grimké, Angelina, *92,* 149, 150, 151–52,
    162
    letters from, 146–48, 152–53
    letter to, 153–54

Grimké, Mary, letter from, 153–54

Grimké, Sarah, 149, 150, 151–52, 162

Guilford Courthouse, Battle of, 64–65

Gustafsson, Emma, letter from, 447–48


Haise, Mary, letter from, 654

Hale, Sarah Josepha, 94
    letter from 303–4

Hale, Susan, letters from, 429–30,
    448–49

Hall, Carrie, letter from, 348–50

Hamilton, Alexander, 77, 93, 104–5
    letter to, 77–78

Hampton, Sally Baxter, letter from,
    285–86

Hancock, Cornelia, 2, 6
    letters from, 298–99, 305–7

Hancock, John, 20, 30

Harper, Frances Ellen Watkins, letters
    from, 254–55, 361–62

Harper's Ferry, 251–52, 254

Harris, Jean, letter from, 681–88

Harrison, George, letter to, 639–40

Harte, Bret, 215

Haselton, Marjorie, letter from, 589–90

Hawthorne, Nathaniel, 173

Hayden, Maria Trenholm, letter from,
    206–8

Hellman, Lillian, 4, 618
    letter from, 618–19

Helms, Jesse, letter to, 714–15

Hemingway, Ernest, letter to, 486–87

Henderson, Caroline, letter from,
    526–28

Henderson, Grace, letter from, 404–5

Henry, Patrick, letter to, 37

Hersey, Heloise Edwina, letter from,
    423–27

Hershkowitz, Dora, letter from, 535–37

Higginson, Anna, letter from, 362–66

Hillhouse, James, 79–80
    letter to, 79–80

Hillyer, Mrs., letter from, 523

Hine, Mrs. James, letter from, 141–45

Hodgdon, Sarah, letter from, 133–34

Hodgkins, Sarah and Joseph, letter
    exchange, 42–47

Hoffman, Elizabeth, letter from, 646–47

Hohlwein, Kathryn, letter from, 636–37

Holley, Mary Austin, letter from, 136–38

Holloway, Priscilla, letter from, 586–89

Homosexuality, 4, 250–51, 520–21, 540,
    655–57, 666–67, 704–7

Hoover, J. Edgar, letter to, 650–51

Hoover, Lou Henry, letter to, 511–12

Houses and furnishings, 141–45, 390–91,
    678
    "double pen" log houses, 143

Housework and women's work, 40, 83,
    84, 165–68, 263–64

Howe, Elias, 179

Howe, Julia Ward, *261,* 280
    letter from, 280

Hughes, Langston, letter to, 501–3

Hulton, Anne, 2, 15–16
    letter from, 15–18

Hunt, Walter, 180

Huntington, Rachel, letter from, 85–87

Huntington, Susan Mansfield, letter from,
    127–28

Hurston, Zora Neale, letter from, 501–3

Hutin, Francisquy, 94
Hygiene and health
    bathing, 13, 95, 143
    flesh brush, 67, 68
    health food, 262, 420
    prenatal and infant care, 475–7
    soap-making, 84
    toothbrush, 61–62
    women's health, diet and exercise,
        423–27

Immigration, 202–5, 301, 389–92, 402–4,
    418, 447–48, 455–57, 462–63, 702–4
Incidents in the Life of a Slave Girl
    (Jacobs), 344
Inman, Elizabeth, letter from, 36
Internet, 727
    start-ups, 728–32
Iraq
    Gulf War, 678, 707–9
    War in, 679, 751–54, 757–61

Jackson, Andrew, 60–61, 94
    letter to, 60–61
Jackson, Charlotte Ann, letter from,
    307–8
Jackson, Elizabeth Hutchinson, 60–61
    letter from, 60–61
Jackson, Helen Hunt, 381–82, 400
    letter from, 381–83
Jackson, James Caleb, 262
Jackson, Lethe, 154–56
Jackson, Mary Anna, letter from, 295–96
Jackson, Thomas "Stonewall," 262, 272
    letter to, 295–96
Jacobi, Mary, 338
Jacobs, Harriet, letter from, 344–46
Jefferson, Thomas, 11, 93, 94, 102–3
    letter to, 102–4
Jewett, Helen, letter from, 145–46
Jewett, Sarah Orne, 6, 445
    letter from, 445–47
Jews, 455–57, 462–63, 535–37, 554, 555,
    575
    anti-Semitism, 542

Civil Rights movement and AJSS,
    625–26
concentration camps, liberation of,
    585–86
Johnson, Andrew, 330, 331
Johnson, Hannah, letter from, 299–300
Johnson, Lady Bird, letter from, 642
Johnson, Lyndon B., 638, 646
    letters to, 642, 644
Jones, Charlotte, letter from, 628–29
Jones, Constance, letter from, 591
Jones, Eva, letter from, 332–34
Jones, Martha Selden, letter from, 108–9
Jones, Mother [Mary Harris], letter from,
    430–31
Joplin, Janis, 4, 644
    letter from, 644–46
Joy of Cooking, The (Rombauer), 507

Kaczynski, Ted, letter to, 723–24
Kansas, 241–43, 247–49, 302, 509
Kathy, love letter from, 572–74
Keller, Helen, letters from, 399–400,
    435–37
Kendall, Keziah, letter from, 159–62
Kennedy, Edward "Ted," 561
Kennedy, Jacqueline, 594
    letter from, 634–35
Kennedy, Jean, 563
Kennedy, John F., 562, 634–35, 696
    assassination, 596, 635, 636–37
    letter to, 633–34
Kennedy, Joseph, Jr., 561–62
Kennedy, Kathleen, 562
Kennedy, Patricia, 562–63
Kennedy, Robert F., 561, 597
Kennedy, Rose, letter from, 561–63
Kentucky frontier, 82–85, 124–25
Kentucky Reporter, letter to, 124–25
Key, Francis Scott, 94
Key to Uncle Tom's Cabin, A (Stowe), 222
Khrushchev, Nikita, letter to, 634–35
Kidder, Isabel, letter from, 505, 560
Kincaid, Mary, 5
King, Billie Jean, 594, 597

King, Martin Luther, Jr., 596, 625
Kinkel, Kristin, letter from, 725–27
Knight, Leza and John, exchange, IM, 751–54
Knox, Henry, letter to, 38–39
Knox, Lucy, letter from, 38–39
Korean War, 606–11, 616–17
Kozlowski, L. Dennis, 741–42
Kroch, Gretchen, letter from, 574–75

Labor movement, 430–31, 524–26
   mill girls, 94, 133–34
   mining, 524–26
   strike in Lowell, MA, 95
   Triangle Shirtwaist factory fire, 2, 420, 462–63
   women working, 1890, 339
Ladies' Magazine, The, 128
Ladies Organization of Philadelphia, 57, 58
Lady's Life in the Rocky Mountains, A (Bird), 374–75
La Leche League, 596
Landman, Bette, letter from, 727
Lane, William Carr, letter to, 132–33
Lathrop, Julia, letter to, 475–76
Lathrop, Mrs. W. C., letter from, 490–91
Leary, Erin, letter from, 747–48
Lee, Elizabeth Blair, letter from, 274–75
Lee, Mary Custis, 289
   letters from, 268–70, 289, 359–61
Lee, Mrs. P., letter from, 405–6
Lee, Robert E., 263–64, 268, 270, 289, 295, 320, 342
   death of, 359–61
Lehmann, Jillian, letter from, 746–47
Lennon, John, 676, 735–37
   letter to, 639–70
Lesbianism. See Homosexuality
Lester, Vilet, letter from, 246–47
Leverett, Mary Maxcy, letter from, 316–20
Lewinsky, Monica, 678
   letter from, 718–19
Lewis and Clark Expedition, 93

Lexington, Battle of, 15, 20
Liberator, The, 146, 158, 159
Liberia, Africa, 244–45, 361
Lily, The, magazine, 206
Lincoln, Abraham, 178, 181, 220–21, 256, 257, 262, 265, 280, 311, 312–13, 316
   assassination, 2–3, 261, 264, 321–26, 352
   death threats, 268
   funeral train, 326–29
   Gettysburg Address, 263
   letters to, 257–58, 268, 275–76, 299–300, 303–4
Lincoln, Mary Todd, 5, 262, 352–53
   letter from, 352–55
   letters to, 256–57, 294–95
Lind, Jenny, 221
Lindbergh, Charles A., 421
   son kidnapped, 506, 508
Linn, Jeannette, letter from, 415–16
Liston, Henrietta, letters from, 81–82, 88–89
Literature and books, 95, 303, 419, 501–3, 597, 677. See also Alcott, Louisa May; Cather, Willa; Dickinson, Emily; Jewett, Sarah Orne; Mitchell, Margaret; Plath, Sylvia; Stowe, Harriet Beecher; Wharton, Edith
Little Women (Alcott), 337, 351–52
Logue, Sarah, letter from, 255–56
Loguen, J. W., letter to, 255–56
Louisiana Territory, 93
Love, John, exchange of letters, 443–45
Love Canal resident, letter from, 672–73
Lovejoy, Julia, letter from, 247–49
Love letters, 42–47, 152–53, 231–36, 250–51, 293–94, 355–56, 387, 443–45, 450–51, 467–68, 500–501, 505, 535–37, 566–68, 572–74, 584–85, 718
Low, Juliette Gordon, letter from, 454–55
Lowell, MA, 94, 95, 133
Ludington, Sybil, 12

MacArthur, Douglas A., 496–97

MacArthur, Mary, letter from, 496–97

Macaulay, Catharine, letter to, 71–72

MacLeod, Lila, letter from, 601–3

Madison, Dolley, 2, 92
  letter from, 107–8

Madison, James, 107–8

"Mademoiselle Miss," letter from, 468–69

Manning, Teresa, letter from, 664–65

Marconi, Guglielmo, 429–30

Marge, Dear John letter from, 571–72

Marriage, 12, 39, 516–17
  accusation of infidelity, 368–74
  advice on, 5, 110–11, 128–30, 153–54,
    315
    bigamy, 124–25
    education, 601–3
    frontier, 458–59
    sexual revolution and, 647–48
    women's rights and, 95, 97–98, 181

Mary, letter from on abstinence, 739–41

Matie, Julia, letter from, 265–67

Matsushita, Hanaye, letter from,
  550–52

Mauzy, Mary, letter from, 251–52

McAuliffe, Christa, 678

McCarthy, Jean, letter from, 629–30

McCarthy, Joseph, 594, 595–96, 618,
  629–30

McCarthy, Margaret, letter from, 202–5

McClellan, Gen. George, 280, 289

McClendon, Sarah, letter from, 82–85

McCord, Louisa, letter from, 222–23

McCormick, Katharine Dexter, letter
  from, 623–24

McDowell, Sally, exchange of letters,
  231–36

McDowell, Rebecca, letters from,
  296–97, 304–5, 308–10

McIntosh, Peggy and Susanna, letter
  from, 130–32

McKinley, William, 419, 428
  letter to, 413

McPherson, Aimee Semple, letter from,
  497–98

Medicine and disease
  abortion, *see* Abortion
  breast cancer, 631–33, 719–21,
    722–23
  cigarettes, health risks of smoking,
    696–97
  consumption (tuberculosis), 187–88,
    410–13, 432–34, 487
  first woman doctor, 180, 193–95
  forced sterilization, 514–15
  flux (dysentery), 525
  heart disease, 360
  home remedies, 126–27, 263
  influenza, 485–86
  in vitro fertilization, 689–94
  open heart surgery, 596
  parasites (worms), 87
  phthisis, 82
  polio, 596, 625
  "rest cure," 338–39
  smallpox, 4–5, 20, 23, 31, 35, 46,
    60–61, 76–77
  snakebite, 248–49
  surgery without anesthesia, 3, 236–41
  Sydenham's chorea (St. Vitus' dance),
    148, 149
  war, field hospitals, 571
  water cure, 196–98
  women's health, diet and exercise,
    423–27
  in woman's prison, 483
  yellow fever, 13, 61

Megquier, Mary Jane, letter from,
  198–200

Melville, David, 94

Melville, Herman, 252

Menninger, Karl, letter to, 520–21

Michie, Mary, letter from, 244–45

Millay, Edna St. Vincent, *418*, 491–92
  letter from, 491–95

Miller, Henry, 540

Miller, John, exchange of letters, 231–36

Mitchell, John, letter to, 430–31

Mitchell, Margaret, 509, 532–34
  letter from, 538

Mitscher, Audrey, letter from, 566–68

Mitten, Sandy, 707–9

Monmouth Courthouse, Battle of, 12

Monroe, James, 125

Monroe, Marilyn, 595
   letter from, 617

Moore, Annie, letter from, 670–72

Morrison, Gina, letter from, 742–45

Morse, Samuel F. B., 95

Moseley, Julia Daniels, letter from, 387

Mott, Lucretia, *92,* 180
   letter from, 195–96
   letter to, 165–68

Mount Vernon, VA, 87–88

Movies, *418,* 420, 421, 441, *506,* 509,
   517–19, 532–34, *594,* 595, 597,
   604–6, 677
   blacklist, 618
   first Academy Awards, 507

*Ms.* magazine, letter to, 664–65

Murders and famous cases, 51, 145, 421,
   441, *506,* 507, 508, 670–72, 678,
   681–82, 710
   school shootings, 721–22, 725–27

Murphrey, Elizabeth, letter from, 70–71

Murray, Judith Sergeant, 12

Music, *92,* 94, 180, *261,* 262, 285, 339,
   421, 429, 509, *594,* 589–90, 596, 597,
   627–28, 644–46, 677

Napier, Judy, letter from, 681

Nation, Carrie, letter to, 427–28

Native Americans, 6, 35, 143, 379
   Cherokee, Trail of Tears, 157–59
   Cherokee woman, letter from, 125–26
   Creek nation, 130–32
   Florida, 120–22
   Kentucky frontier and, 84–85
   missionary attempts to convert,
     400–402
   missionary schools, 132
   movement to stop injustice toward,
     382–83, 400
   Treaty of Indian Springs, 130
   war with, 379–80

New York City, 54, 85–87, 183–84, 337
   "Boss" Tweed, 338
   Brooklyn Bridge, *336,* 338
   capital of United States, 67–68
   Coney Island, Luna Park roller coaster,
     338
   Central Park, 282
   Crystal Palace, *178*
   draft riots, *261,* 263, 301
   Empire State Building, 508
   firefighters, letter to, 675, 745
   first skyscraper, 338
   police officer, letter to, 745–46
   population growth, 183
   September 11, 2001, 675, 679,
     742–47
   Triangle Shirtwaist factory fire, 2, 420,
     462–63
   World Trade Center, *676*

*New Yorker* magazine, 715–18

*New York Evening Journal,* 413

New York State Division of Parole, letter
   to, 735–37

*New York Sun,* letter to, 410

*New York Times,* letter to, 642–44

Niagara Falls, barrel over, 419

Nichols, Sarah, 5

Nielsen, Jerri, letter from, 722–23

Nin, Anaïs, letter from, 540–41

Nixon, Richard, *594,* 597
   letter to, 665

Noonan, Peggy, letter from, 694–96

"Nora," letter exchange, 413–14

Nuremberg Trials, 599–601

Oakley, Annie, *336*
   letter from, 413

O'Connor, Jessie Lloyd, letter from,
   524–26

O'Connor, Sandra Day, 677

O'Connor, Sharon, letter from, 733–35

Ogawa, Louise, letter from, 568–70

O'Hanlon, Virginia, letter from, 410

Oklahoma Dust Bowl, 526–28

*Old Farmers Almanac,* 13

Ono, Yoko, 676
  letter from, 735–37
Orlins, Susan Fishman, letter from,
  699–701
O'Rourke, Caroline, 6
  letter from, 388–89
Orphanages, 388–89
Oswald, Marina, letter from, 635–66
Otis, Elisha, 181
Ovington, Mary White, 420

Pacifism and peace movement, 4, 471–75,
  748–49
  antiwar movement, Vietnam, 597,
    638–39, 644, 655
Pacino, Al, letter to, 749–51
Pacitti, Beth, letter from, 741–42
Paine, Thomas, 11
Palfrey, Anna, letter from, 243–44
Parker, Bonnie (Bonnie and Clyde), 528
Parker, Dorothy, letter from, 1, 552–59
Parks, Rosa, 594, 596
  letter to, 625–27
Parsons, Lucy, letter from, 392–94
Patten, Ruth, letter from, 126–27
Paul, Alice, 482–84
Peabody, Elizabeth Palmer, 173, 175
Pendergrass, Bobbie Lou, letter from,
  633–34
*Pensacola News*, letter to, 688–89
Perkins, Frances, 508
  letter from, 579–81
Perkins, Priscilla, letter from, 712–13
Pershing, John J., letter to, 496–97
Peters, Lois, letter from, 22
*Photoplay* magazine, exchange of letters,
  498–500
Pierce, Franklin, 224
Pierce, Jane, letter from, 224–26
Pinkham, Lydia, letter to, 414–15
Pinzer, Maimie, letter from, 451–54
*Pioneer* magazine, 215
Pitcher, Molly, 10, 12
Planned Parenthood, 466
Plath, Sylvia, letter from, 611–16

Plimpton, James, 263
Poe, Edgar Allan, 179
Porter, E. E., letter from, 156–57
Powell, Michael, letter to, 754
Presley, Elvis, 594, 596, 628–29, 650
Prohibition, 418, 421, 507, 523
Prostitution, 95, 451–54, 503
Pulitzer, Courtney, letter from, 728–32
Putnam, George Palmer, letter to,
  516–17
Pyle, Ernie, 509

Quakers (Society of Friends), 41, 229
  abolitionists, 149, 229
  African American, 149–51, 244
Quigley, Joan, letter from, 701–2
Quincy, Eliza, letter from, 294–95
Quincy, Samuel, 30

R. J. Reynolds Tobacco Co., letter to,
  696–97
Railroads, 134–36, 374
Ramsey, Martha Laurens, letter from,
  78–79
Randolph, Martha Jefferson, letter from,
  102–4
Rankin, Jeannette, 418, 420
Rawe, Anna, letter from, 57–58
Reagan, Ronald, 677, 694–96
  assassination attempt, 677
  letter to, 701–2
Reed, Esther DeBerdt, 57, 58
  letter from, 58–59
Reed, Fannie, letters from, 410–13,
  432–34
Reed, Virginia, 3, 188–89
  letter from, 188–93
Reeve, Christopher, letter to, 718
Reeve, Dana, letter from, 718
Religion
  African American churches, 345
  church pew, fee for, 133
  evangelical Christians, 235, 497–98
  Jim Jones and the People's Temple,
    670–72

persecution, 147
Scopes Trial ("Monkey Trial"), 497–98
secularism vs., 597
spiritualism, 206–8
"True Love Waits" movement, 739–41
woman's aspiration to preach, 202
Revere, Paul, 6, *10*, 15
letter to, 15
Revere, Rachel, 6
letter from, 15
Reynolds, Maria, letter from, 77–78
Richmond, VA, defeat of, *261*
Ringler, Robyn DeSantis, letter from, 749–51
Robinson, Patricia et al, letter from, 648–49
Rombauer, Irma, 507
Roosevelt, Eleanor, *506*, 535, 581–84
letters from, 541–43
letters to, 529, 538–40
Roosevelt, Franklin Delano, 508, 509, 581–84
Roosevelt, Theodore, *418*, 419, 428–29
Ropes, Hannah Anderson, letters from, 241–43, 291–92
Rose, Hilda, letter from, 4, 487–89
Rosenberg, Ethel, letter from, 619–20
Ross, Betsy, 7, *10*, 11–12
Rush, Benjamin, 57
Russia (Soviet Union), 591, 619
Rutherford, Madge, letter from, 565–66

Sacagawea, 93
Sackville-West, Victoria, letter from, 397–98
Salk, Jonas, letter to, 625
Samuelson, Dora, letter from, 575–76
San Francisco, CA, 198–200, 509
earthquake of 1906, 420, 437–40
Sanger, Margaret, 4, *418*, 420, 465, 466
letter from, 466–67
letters to, 464–66, 623–24
Santa Claus, 410, 415
letter to, 415–16
Schuyler, Philip, letter to, 104–5

Science and technology
airplane, 419–20
Apollo 11 mission, 654
automobile, *418*, 420
Bakelite, 420
balloon, manned flight, 65, 69
bar codes, 597
bicycle, 339
computers, 597, 677
Cumberland Road, 94
electricity, 490–91
electric lightbulb, 338
elevator, 181
gaslight, *92*, 94
genetics, erroneous, 338
Golden Gate Bridge, 509
Kodak camera, 339
labor saving devices for the home, 490–91
machine gun, 262
moon walk, 597, 654
radio (wireless), 429
railroads, 134–36
roller skate, four wheel, 263
safety pin, 180
sewing machine, 179
solar eclipse, 105–6
sound barrier broken, 595
steamboat, 93
submarine, *92*
telegraph, 95
telephone, transatlantic, 421
transatlantic flight, 421
typewriter, *336*, 338
vitascope (movies), *336*
World Wide Web, 678
Scopes, John, letter to, 497
Secor, Lella, letter from, 471–75
Selznick, David, letter exchange, 532–34
September 11, 2001, attacks, 675, 679, 742–47
Seward, William H., 304
letter to, 277–80
Sex, 498–500, 574
assault or harassment, 400, 512–14

Sex (*cont.*)
  education, 601–3
  letter exchange, Pat and her parents, 659–62
  sexual revolution, 647–48, 655–57, 659–62
  "True Love Waits" movement, 739–41
  *See also* Birth control
*Sex and the Single Girl* (Brown), 596, 662
Sexton, Anne, 5, 652
  letter from, 652
Shapiro, Diana, letter from, 625–27
Shepherd, Julia, letter from, 2–3, 324–26
Sherman, Kathy Fitzgerald, 737–39
Sherman, William Tecumseh, 263, 316, 385
Shiloh, Battle of, 262, 287
Shippen, Alice Lee, letter from, 40–41
Shipwrecks, 111–22
Shrader, Martha, letter from, 514–15
Shulgold, Barbara, exchange of letters, 689–94
Silverman, Rachel, letter from, 697–98
Simmons, Amelia, 13
Simpson, Nicole, *676, 678*
  letter from, 710–12
Simpson, O. J., 678
  letter to, 710–12
Sipiora, Lynne, exchange of letters, 689–94
Slaves and slavery, 4, 6, *10,* 79–80, 83, 84, 148–49, 154–56, 164, 180, 220–21, 226–27, 228, 246–47, 254–56, 293–94
  abolitionism and anti-slavery societies, 80, 95, 139–41, 146–48, 149, 151, 171–72, 220–21, 222, 223, 247, 250
  abuse of slaves, 306, 307–8
  American Revolution and, 26–28, 64
  back to Africa movement, 244–45, 361
  "Bleeding Kansas," 241–43, 254
  contrabands, 305–8
  Dred Scott decision, 181
  education, 250, 280
  Emancipation Proclamation, *261,* 262, 294–95

Fifteenth Amendment, 338
Fourteenth Amendment, 337
Freedmen's Bureau, 337, 348–51
Frémont's emancipation of, 275–76
Fugitive Slave Law, 223–24
Harper's Ferry, 251–52, 254
Missouri Compromise, 94, 181
Nat Turner, 139
post-war situation and return, 343–48, 361–62
Underground Railroad, 254–55, 361
Smallwood, E. E., letter from, 528
Smallwood, William, 41, 42
Smith, Hannah Whitall, 3, 202
  letters from, 188, 202, 386–87
Smith, Juliana, letters from, 54–57, 61–62
Smith, Margaret Bayard, 91
  letter from, 98–99
Smith, Susan Mason, 11
Smythe, Mrs. A. M., letter from, 148–49
Social movements (socialism, anarchism, communism), 392–94, 403, 464–65
Sorenson, Ted, 696
South
  Civil Rights movement and, *594,* 596–97, 625–26, 640–41
  Civil War, 259–334
  Confederate States of America, 261
  defeat and destruction of, 332–34, 335, 341–48
  Jimmy Carter elected, 597
  Ku Klux Klan, *336,* 337
  life in, antebellum, 227–29
  lynching, 408
  miscegenation laws, 348
  Reconstruction, 344, 346–48, 361–62, 408
  secession of South Carolina, 181, *261*
  Twenty-Slave law, 290
  *See also* Civil War
Southgate, Eliza, letter from, 99–102
Spanish-American War, 1898, 339, 413
Spaulding, Mrs. A. E., letter from, 275–76
Spiritualism, 206–8
Spock, Benjamin, *594,* 595

Spooner, Bathsheba, letter from, 51

Sports and women sports figures, 519–20, *594, 595, 597,* 679

Stanton, Edwin, 298, 299, 337

Stanton, Elizabeth Cady, 4, 165, 180, 231, *336,* 339, 356
   letters from, 208–11, 423
   letters to, 195–96, 431–32

"Star Spangled Banner, The," *92, 94,* 508

Steinem, Gloria, 664

Stevenson, Helen, letter from, 606–11

Stewart, Alice, letter from, 511–12

Stewart, Martha, 679
   letter from, 755–57

Stock Market Crash, 1929, *506, 507*

Stone, Lucy, *178,* 181, 206, 231
   letter from, 249–50
   letter to, 205–6

Stone, Mrs. Peter, letter from, 515–16

Stowe, Harriet Beecher, *178,* 180, 196, 222, 223
   letter from, 220–21

Strong, Betsy, letter from, 187–88

Styron, William, 139

Summer camp, letter from, 697–98


Taft, Helen, letter from, 448

Taft, William Howard, 448

Tarnower, Herman, letter to, 681–88

Taylor, Anna Edson, 419

Taylor, Dorothea, letter from, 545–47

Teddy Bear, *418,* 419

Television, *594, 595, 596,* 651, 657–59, 677, 678, 698, 754

Temperance movement, *92, 95,* 202, 206, 338, 400, 427–28

Texas
   Alamo, 95
   secession of, 268
   trip to, 136–38

Thackery, William Makepeace, letter to, 285–86

Thanksgiving, 54–57, 303–4

Theater, 406, 469–71, 509, 597

Thomson, Charles, 67

Thomson, Hannah, letter from, 67–69

Thomson, Katie, letter form, 723–24

Thurston, Lucy, letter from, 3, 236–41

Tilghman, Molly, letter from, 65–67

*Time* magazine, letter to, 646–47

*Titanic,* 420

*To Girls, A Budget of Letters* (Hersey), 423

"Topsy Turvy," letter from, 356–59

Townsend, Jessie Easton, letter from, 464

Transcendental movement, 162, 173–75, 188

Travel and exploration, 134–36, 141–45, 374–78, 448–49, 492–95

*Treatise on Domestic Economy, A* (Beecher), 196

Troy Female Seminary, 94, 109

Truman, Bess, 583–84

Truman, Harry S., 509, 587, 591, 607

Truth, Sojourner, *178,* 180, 209, 311
   letter from, 311–14

Tuckerman, Joseph, 105

Tuffyas, Beryl, letter from, 655

Turner, Nat, 139

Twain, Mark. *See* Clemens, Samuel

Tyco Corp. scandal, 741–42


*Una, The,* magazine, 230–31

Unabomber, 723–24

*Uncle Tom's Cabin* (Stowe), *178,* 180, 220–21, 222, 223

Underhill, Julia, letter from, 310–11

United States
   assassination attempt of Reagan, 677
   assassination of Garfield, 228, 385–86
   assassination of Kennedy, 596, 635, 636–37
   assassination of Lincoln, 2–3, *261,* 264, 321–26
   assassination of McKinley, 419, 428
   assassination of a President, first attempt, 95
   Baby Boom era, letters, 1946–1979, 599–673
   change of administration (first), 91, 98–99

United States (*cont.*)

Capitol building, *92*

Civil War era, 1861–1865, letters,
265–334

Cold War, 591, 618–20, 634–35

currency, 261–62, 263, 337

death of President Franklin Roosevelt,
581–84

1854 Kansas–Nebraska Act, 241–43

expansion, 1845–1869, letters, 182–258

expansion of territory, 93, 95

events timeline, 1800–1844, 93–96

events timeline, 1845–1860, 179–81

events timeline, 1861–1865, 261–63

events timeline, 1866–1899, 337–39

events timeline, 1900–1928, 419–21

events timeline, 1929–1945, 507–9

events timeline, 1946–1979, 595–97

events timeline, 1980–2005, 677–79

first national park, 374

first postage stamp issued, 179

Great Depression, 1929–1941, letters
of, 511–44

Homestead Act, 262

immigration, *see* Immigration

Korean War, 606–11, 616–17

modern times, letters, 1900–1928,
423–504

national anthem, *92*, 94, 508

as a new nation, letters, 1800–1844,
91–175

1980s to 2005, letters, 681–761

political parties, 98

population, 180, 337, 419, 421

poverty in, 388, 392–94, 402–5

presidential election, 1884, debacle,
394–96

Reconstruction and the Gilded Age,
1866–1899, letters, 341–416

secession of South Carolina, 181

settlement houses, 402–4

Washington, DC becomes the capital,
93

World War II, 1941–1945, letters of,
545–91

*See also* Afghanistan; American
Revolution; Civil War; Iraq war;
Vietnam; War of 1812; World War I;
World War II

Utopian communities, 173–75, 187

Van Allen, Mary, letter from, 388

Van Buren, Martin, 157

Van Devanter, Lynda, letter from, 653–54

Van Wyck, Carolyn, letter exchange,
498–500

Vietnam War, 597, 633–34, 653–54

antiwar movement, 597, 638–39, 644,
655

Memorial, 633

Virginia Military Institute, 296–97,
304–5, 308

Von Kurowsky, Agnes, letter from,
486–87

Wakeman, Rosetta, letter from, 297–98

Wandry, June, letters from, 570–71,
585–86

War of 1812, 2, 93–94, 107–9

Ward, Samuel, letter to, 162–64

Warner, Charles Dudley, 338, 407

Warren, John, 29, 75

letters to, 23, 35

Warren, Mercy Otis, 23, 29

letters from, 23–24, 35, 71–73

letter to, 73–75

Washington, DC

burning of, War of 1812, 107, 108

as the capital, 93

cherry trees, 448

Civil War era, 265–67

design for the Capitol Building, *92*

September 11, 2001, attack, 748–49

social life, Gilded Age, 397–98

Washington Monument, 179

Washington, George, 11–12, 13, 24, 26,
28, 33, 34, 38, 40, 58, 65, 71–72,
73–75, 81–82, 87–89, 107, 179

letters to, 58–59, 75–76

Washington, Harriot, letter from, 75–76

Washington, Martha, 73, 75, 81, 87, 289
  letters from, 73–75, 87–88
*Washington Post,* 663–64
Watergate break-in, 597, 663, 665
Waterman, Mary Ann, letter from, 171–72
Waxham, Ethel, exchange of letters, 443–45
Weld, Theodore, letter to, 152–53
Wells-Barnett, Ida B., *336,* 408, 420
  letter from, 408–9
Westbrook, Daisy, letter from, 477–79
Wharton, Edith, 421, 449
  letters from, 434–35, 449–51
Wheatley, Phillis, *10*
Whitall, Hannah. *See* Smith, Hannah Whitall
Whitman, Elizabeth, letter from, 69
Whitworth, Elizabeth, letter from, 97–98
Wiebusch, Wilhelmine, letter from, 389–92
Wilkinson, Eliza, letter from, 62–64
Willard, Emma Hart, 94, 109–10
  letter from, 109–11
Willard, Frances, 405, 408
Williams, Laura, letter from, 282–84
Williams, Rose, letter from, 398–99
Williams, Sarah Hicks, letter from, 227–29
Willis, Frances Gates, letter from, 200–201
Will and testament, 70–71
Wilson, Woodrow, 476, 482
  letter to, 467–68
Winfrey, Oprah, *676*
Winslow, Rose, letter from, 482–85
Wister, Sally, letters from, 41–42, 49–51
Wolfe, Thomas, letter to, 5, 522–23
*Womankind* newspaper, 655
*Woman Rebel* magazine, 465
Woman's Christian Temperance Union (WCTU), 403, 408, 427–28
  letter from, 400

Women
  abuse by spouse, 710–12
  in Afghanistan war, 747–48
  beauty pageants, 421
  birth control, *see* Birth Control
  *Blondie* created, 507
  breastfeeding, 596
  childbirth, 69, 83, 396, 508, 593, 603–4, 620–23
  Civil War nurses, 291–92, 298–99
  Civil War soldiers, 297–98, 307
  "cult of true womanhood," 128
  education, *see* Education
  entertainment and amusement, 281–82, 293, 338, 406, 430, 508, 595, 611–15
  equality and civil rights, 30, 32, 95, 97–98, 99–102, 152, 159–62, 261, 337, 338, *see also* Women's movement
  fertility issues, 689–94
  first woman cabinet member, 508
  first woman doctor, 180, 193–95
  first woman Supreme Court Justice, 677
  forced sterilization, 514–15
  in government jobs, 419
  in Gulf War, 707–9
  gynecological exam, 368–74
  housework and women's work, 40, 83, 84, 165–68, 263–64, 390
  in Korean War, 606–11
  in labor force, 1890, 339
  literacy, 70
  magazines, 95
  menstruation, 338, 513
  miners, 215–16
  moral reform societies, 95, 156–57
  motherhood, 378–79, 617, 699–701, 712–13, 733–35
  19th century opinions about, 3
  parenting issues, 229–30, 249–50, 339, 385–86, *594,* 595, 733–35
  pregnancy, 5, 83, 366–68, 409–10, 584–85
  pregnancy out of wedlock, 69, 441–42
  prenatal and infant care, 475–76

Women (*cont.*)
  in public office, firsts, 420, 421
  rejection by husband or lover, 52, 69,
    77–78, 162–64, 441–42, 522–23,
    681–88
  repression of speaking by, 145
  sexual assault or harassment, 400,
    512–14
  social life, 99–102
  spinsterhood, 12
  substance abuse, 451
  temperance movement and, *92*, 95,
    202, 206, 338
  unmarried, 1920, 421
  in Vietnam, 653–54
  working, 310–11, 339, 404, 419, *506*,
    543–44, 579–60, 712–13
  in World War I, 421, 468–69, 479–82
  in World War II, 549–50, 565–68,
    570–71, 574–75, 576–78, 585–86
Women of Augusta County, Virginia, letter
  from, 139–41
*Women's Journal,* letter to, 356–59
Women's movement, 105–6, 230–31, 339
  Akron Falls, OH, convention, 208–11
  Equal Rights Amendment, 579–61
  dress reform, 206, 339, 405–6
  hunger strike, 482–85
  NOW, 657–59, 666–67
  opposition to, 218–19
  publications, 206, 231
  Seneca Falls, NY, convention, 165, 180,
    195–96, 205, 489
  voting rights (suffrage), 4, 12, 152, 165,
    337–38, 356–59, 421, 423, 431–32,
    464, 482–85, 489
  women's liberation, 1970s, 655–57,
    664–65
Woollcott, Alexander, letter to, 1, 552–59

World War I, *418*, 420–21, 469, 511–12
  gas and chemical weapons, 480–81
  influenza during, 485–86
  mother's letter to son in, 417, 476–77
  pacifism and, 471–75
  women in, 421, 468–69, 479–82
World War II
  casualties, *506*, 571, 585–86, 589
  enlistment, 553–55
  Germany surrenders (VE day), 509, 695
  Hiroshima and Nagasaki, *506*, 509,
    586–89
  internment of Japanese Americans,
    550–52, 568–70
  Japan surrenders, 509, 589, 591
  letters of, 545–91
  Nuremberg Trials, 599–601
  Pearl Harbor, *506*, 509, 545–50
  servicemen and women in, 509
  war effort and rationing at home, 509
  women in, 549–50, 565–68, 570–71,
    574–75, 576–78, 585–86
  women's letters to men at war, 505,
    560, 563–65, 566–68, 571–74,
    575–76, 584–85, 586–91
  women working during, *506*, 543–44
Wright, Margaret, letter from, 437–40
Wright, Martha Coffin, letter from,
  165–68
Wright, Orville and Wilbur, 419–20
Wyeth, Andrew, 595
Wylie, Elinor, letter from, 500–501
Wyoming Territory, 337, 443–45, 457–60,
  475–76

Yarnell, Emma, letter from, 326–29
*Young Lady's Friend, The* (Farrar), 95

Z. D. R., letter from, 128–30